CLASS 10

AF810059

CBSE QUESTION & CONCEPT BANK

CHAPTER-WISE & TOPIC-WISE

ENGLISH

LANGUAGE & LITERATURE

EDITION : Fourth

Published By: Physicswallah Limited

Physics Wallah Publication

ISBN : 978-93-7818-148-1

MRP : 549/-

Mobile App: Physics Wallah (Available on Play Store)

Website: www.pw.live

Youtube Channel: Physics Wallah - Alakh Pandey

Alakh Pandey - Class 10

Physics Wallah Foundation

NCERT Wallah

Email: publication@pw.live

SKU Code: BKP2603741359

PREFACE

In this era of cutthroat competition among Class 10th aspirants for great marks in Board Exams, only a few are prepared enough to achieve it. During the preparation, a student needs the most relevant study material to cover all topics, practice efficiently, and excel in Board exams and other 10th level competitive exams.

While there is an abundance of study materials available in the market, what we felt was missing was a self-driven and well-planned study material. We have addressed this issue by introducing the CBSE Class 10th Question Concept Bank.

CBSE Class 10th Question & Concept Bank is a book that covers all the important concepts and theories, along with a rich amount of practice questions. This book is designed to provide you with the perfect guidance you need. The study material is consistent with the syllabus offered in NCERT Books and has been curated by the **Physics Wallah Editorial Team** under the careful observation of Physics Wallah Faculties.

Their invaluable contributions have enriched the very essence of our books.

This book consists of the following features:

The content is made in such a way that you can invest your time to make a strong fundamental that will get compounded and will pay you the interest in every upcoming year of your competitive exam's preparation and board exam preparation.

This will help you stay ahead of your competitors.

Our content will help you secure excellent marks in CBSE Class 10th Board Exam.

Following are the different sections that we have provided to develop your skills:

In Theory:

- Narrative/Poetic Sketch
- Synopsis
- Memes
- Word Meanings
- Literary Devices
- Knowledge Hub
- Nailing the Right Answer
- Mistakes 101: What not to do!
- Reading Comprehension with Solved Examples
- Writing Section with Solved Examples
- Grammar Section

In Questions:

- Multiple Choice Questions
- Extract-Based Questions
- Subjective Questions (with Selected LAQs as per latest Board Exam)
- Integrated Grammar
- Answer Key & Explanations with Marking Scheme as per Latest CBSE Board Pattern

Includes Questions & Explanations from:

Sample Question Paper issued by CBSE – **(CBSE SQP)**

Additional Practice Questions issued by CBSE – **(CBSE APQ)**

Competency Focused Practice Questions issued by CBSE – **(CFPQ)**

Question Bank – **(CBSE QB)**

Previous Year Questions in CBSE Board Exams

A step to make our book even better for our students:

Provide your valuable feedback
or
Report the Error

View Errata
(Error Correction from our end)

SYLLABUS ISSUED BY CBSE

ENGLISH LANGUAGE AND LITERATURE

Code No. (184)

CLASS-X

2026-27

(80 marks)

Sections	Competencies	Total marks
Reading Comprehension	Conceptual understanding, decoding, analyzing, inferring, interpreting and vocabulary.	20
Writing Skills and Grammar	Creative expression of an opinion, reasoning, justifying, illustrating, of appropriacy of style and tone, using appropriate format and fluency. Applying conventions, using integrated structures with accuracy and fluency.	20
Language through Literature	Recalling, reasoning, appreciating, applying literary conventions illustrating and justifying etc. Extract relevant information, identifying the central theme understanding and sub-theme, understanding the writers' message and writing fluently.	40
Total		80

Section-A
Reading Skills

I. Reading Comprehension through Unseen Passage **(20 marks)**

1. Discursive passage of 400-450 words. **(10 marks)**
2. Case-based factual passage (with visual input- statistical data, chart etc.) of 200-250 words. **(10 marks)**

(Total length of two passages to be 600-700 words)

Multiple Choice Questions/Objective Type Questions, and Short Answer Questions (to be answered in 30-40 words) will be asked to assess comprehension, interpretation, analysis, inference, evaluation and vocabulary.

Section-B
Writing Skills and Grammar

II. Grammar **(10 marks)**

- ❐ Determiners
- ❐ Tenses
- ❐ Modals
- ❐ Subject-verb concord
- ❐ Reported speech

- Commands and requests
- Statements
- Questions

3. The courses at the secondary level seek to cement high professional grasp of grammatical items and levels of accuracy. Accurate use of spelling, punctuation and grammar in context will be assessed through Gap Filling/ Editing/Transformation exercises. Ten out of 12 questions will have to be attempted.

III. Writing Skills **(10 marks)**

4. Writing a Formal Letter based on a given situation, in 100-120 words. One out of two questions is to be answered. **(5 marks)**
5. Writing an Analytical Paragraph in 100-120 words on a given Map / Chart / Graph / Cue/s. One out of two questions is to be answered. **(5 marks)**

Section-C

Language through Literature **(40 marks)**

IV. Reference to the Context **(5 + 5 = 10 marks)**

6. One extract out of two from Drama/Prose.
7. One extract out of two from poetry.

Multiple Choice Questions/Objective Type Questions Very Short Answer Questions (one word/one sentence), Short Answer Questions (to be answered in 30-40 words) will be asked to assess inference, analysis, interpretation, evaluation and vocabulary.

V. Short & Very Long Answer Questions **(30 marks)**

8. Four out of Five Short Answer Type Questions to be answered in 40-50 words from the book FIRST FLIGHT to assess interpretation, analysis, inference and evaluation. **(4 × 3 = 12 marks)**
9. Two out of Three Short Answer Type Questions to be answered in 40-50 words each from FOOTPRINTS WITHOUT FEET to assess interpretation, analysis, inference and evaluation. **(2 × 3 = 6 marks)**
10. One out of two Long Answer Type Questions from FIRST FLIGHT to be answered in about 100-120 words each to assess creativity, imagination and extrapolation beyond the text and across the text. This can be a passage-based question taken from a situation/plot from the text. **(6 marks)**
11. One out of two Long Answer Type Questions from FOOTPRINTS WITHOUT FEET, on theme or plot involving interpretation, extrapolation beyond the text and inference or character sketch to be answered in about 100-120 words. **(6 marks)**

Chapter-wise Weightage and Trend Analysis of
CBSE Past 5 Years' Papers

ENGLISH										
CHAPTERS	**2022**		**2023**		**2024**		**2025**		**2026**	
	DL	**ODL**	**DL**	**ODL**	**DL**	**ODL**	**DL**	**ODL**	**DL**	**ODL**
Reading Comprehension	10	10	20	20	20	20	20	20	20	20
Grammar	5	5	10	10	10	10	10	10	10	10
Formal Letter	5	5	5	5	5	5	5	5	5	5
Analytical Paragraph	5	5	5	5	5	5	5	5	5	5
Article Writing (*Rationalised*)	–	–	–	–	–	–	–	–	–	–
Story Writing (*Rationalised*)	–	–	–	–	–	–	–	–	–	–
A Letter to God	–	–	3	3	3	3	6*, 3	6*	3	6*
Nelson Mandela - Long Walk to Freedom	–	–	6	–	6*, 5	6*	–	6*	5	5
Two Stories About Flying	–	–	8	6	–	3	6*	5, 3	–	6*
From the Diary of Anne Frank	–	–	–	5	6*, 5	–	5	–	–	3
The Hundred Dresses-I (*Rationalised*)	–	–	–	–	–	–	–	–	–	–
The Hundred Dresses-II (*Rationalised*)	–	–	–	–	–	–	–	–	–	–
Glimpses of India	2	2	3	3	6*	5, 3	3	3	–	3
Mijbil the Otter	–	–	–	–	–	–	–	–	3	3
Madam Rides the Bus	4	4	3	6	–	6*	–	3	3	3
The Sermon at Benares	4	2	6	3	3	6*	6*	–	6*	6*
The Proposal (Play)	2	4	5	3	–	–	3	6*	–	–
Dust of Snow	–	–	–	–	3	–	3	5	–	–
Fire and Ice	–	–	–	–	–	–	–	–	5	3
A Tiger in the Zoo	–	–	5	5	5	–	–	3	6*	–
How to Tell Wild Animals	–	–	–	5	–	5	3	–	5	5
The Ball Poem	–	–	–	–	5	6*	6*	–	3	–
Animals (*Rationalised*)	2	2	–	–	–	–	–	–	–	–
Amanda!	2	2	5	3	6*	3	–	5	–	5
The Trees	–	–	–	–	–	5	5	3	–	–
Fog	–	–	–	–	–	–	–	–	3	–
The Tale of Custard the Dragon	2	2	3	–	3	3	5	6*	6*	6*
For Anne Gregory	–	–	–	–	3	–	–	–	6*	–
A Triumph of Surgery	–	–	3	3	–	3	3	–	6	6
The Thief's Story	–	–	6	3	6	5	–	3, 6	–	3
The Midnight Visitor	–	–	3	–	–	–	3	5	3	–
A Question of Trust	–	–	–	–	6	–	–	3	–	–
Footprints Without Feet	–	–	–	5	3	6	6	–	–	–
The Making of a Scientist	2	2	3	3	–	3	–	–	3	5
The Necklace	4	2	6	6	3	6	5	–	6	3
The Hack Driver (*Rationalised*)	2	4	–	–	–	–	–	–	–	–
Bholi	–	–	–	6	3	–	3	6	3	3
The Book that Saved the Earth	–	–	–	–	–	3	6	3	5	6
The Diary of a Young Girl (*Rationalised*)	–	–	–	–	–	–	–	–	–	–
The Story of My Life (*Rationalised*)	–	–	–	–	–	–	–	–	–	–

**Some questions test students' knowledge of more than one literary text.*

**The marks allotment mentioned above is chapter-wise and includes internal choice questions as well. Therefore, the total might not match the Maximum Marks of the respective Previous Year Paper. Here, DL is Delhi, ODL is Outside Delhi.*

Question Typology

YEAR			Subjective Questions				
	RC	Writing	Grammar	Literature			
				MCQ	Extract Based	SAQ	LAQ
2026	2 (viii;ix)	2	1 (x)	-	2 (iv,iv)	2 (iv,ii)	2
2025	2 (viii;ix)	2	1 (x)	-	2 (iv,iv)	2 (iv,ii)	2
2024	2 (viii;viii)	2	1 (x)	-	2 (iv,iv)	2 (iv,ii)	2
2023	2 (x,x)	2	1 (x)	-	2 (v,v)	2 (iv,ii))	2
2022 (Term II)	2 (v,v)	1	2	-	-	1 (vi)	2 (ii)
2022 (Term I)	2 (MCQs 8,6)	1 (MCQs 5)	1 (MCQs 5)	10	4 (MCQs 5,5,5,5)	-	-

Evolving Trends in CBSE Exam Patterns

2022

- Term I(MCQ type of 40 m); Term II(40 m)
- Analytical Pragraph introduced in Writing Section
- Conversation-based question introduced in Grammar

2023

- Integrated Grammar section covers Error & Correction, Report the dialogue, MCQ, and Fill in the blanks.
- Literature involves analysis of two extracts and SAQs/ LAQs assessing content, organization, expression, and accuracy.

2024

- Reading section includes two passages each with 8 questions emphasizing analysis, inference, and justification to enhance critical text engagement.
- LAQs includes comparative analysis of two FIRST FLIGHT chapters and exploration of a Diary Entry & Character Arc from FOOTPRINTS WITHOUT FEET.

2025

- Assertion-Reason question has been added to the Reading Comprehension section, increasing the total number of questions to 9 (previously 8) in one of the two RCs.
- In the Literature section, extract-based questions have been introduced, focusing on poetry, with a particular emphasis on identifying the rhyme scheme.

2026

- Both passages fully case-based (real-world themes), Data + statistics integrated in Reading
- Writing shifts to strong analytical focus
- Literature stresses inference & interpretation over recall

HOW TO USE THIS BOOK

This book is structured to support your learning journey of preparing for your board exams through a variety of engaging and informative elements. Here's how to make the most of it:

CBSE Solved Paper of 2026: *Get yourself updated with the latest Board Question Papers. With handwritten style answers learn the practical application of concepts and effective answering techniques that can score high marks.*

CBSE Solved Paper

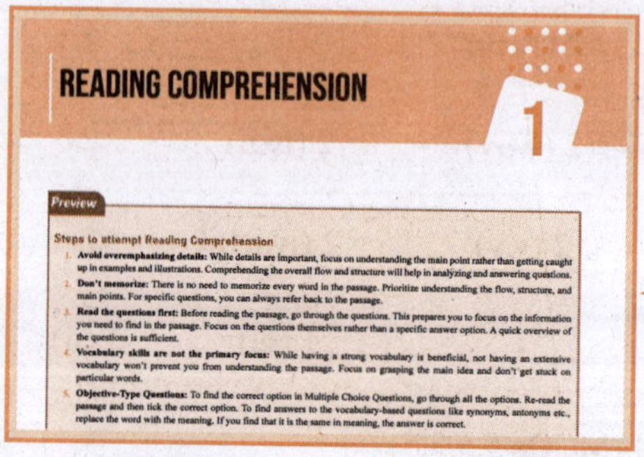

Preview

Reading Skills

Before you start each Reading Comprehension, the Preview will give you an overview of the highlights of this topic & steps to do an unseen passage.

Accompanying the preview are Exercise Questions which provide enough practice on doing the different types of Unseen Passages in exam.

Exercise with Explanations

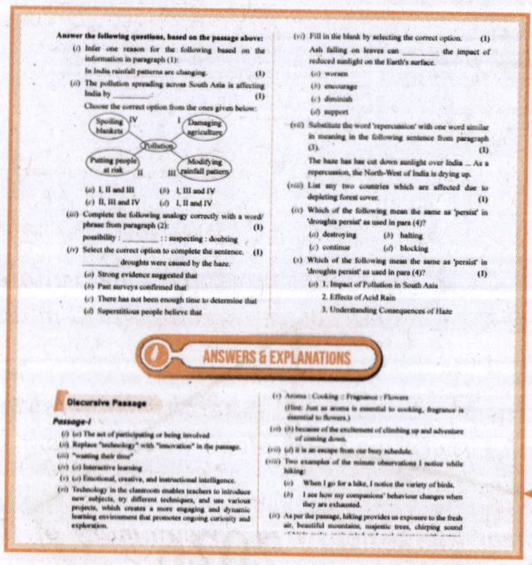

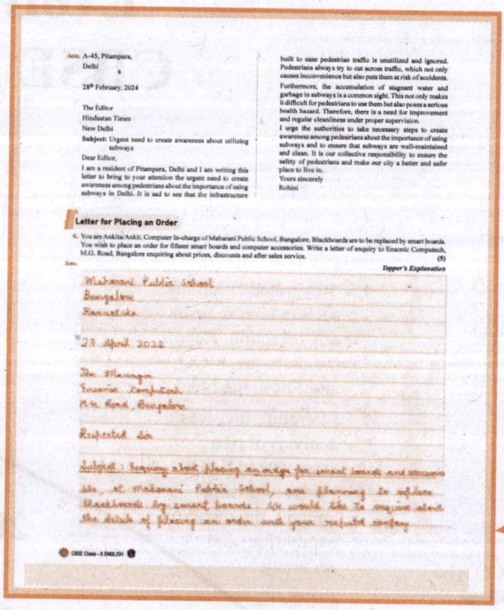

Topper's Explanations

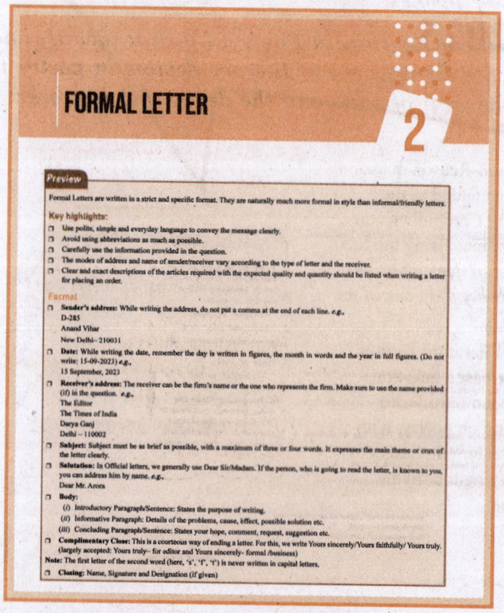

Writing Skills

A detailed Format guide for the writing tasks (Formal Letter and Analytical Paragraph) will provide the structure you need to craft your pieces effectively.

Practice your writing with ample questions, and learn from Topper's Explanations to understand the elements of high-scoring answers.

Grammar

All grammar topics are thoroughly explained to clear concepts before practicing integrated grammar exercise.

Ample Questions on each topic that is observed in the latest Board Exam is provided with Answer Key and Explanations.

Preview

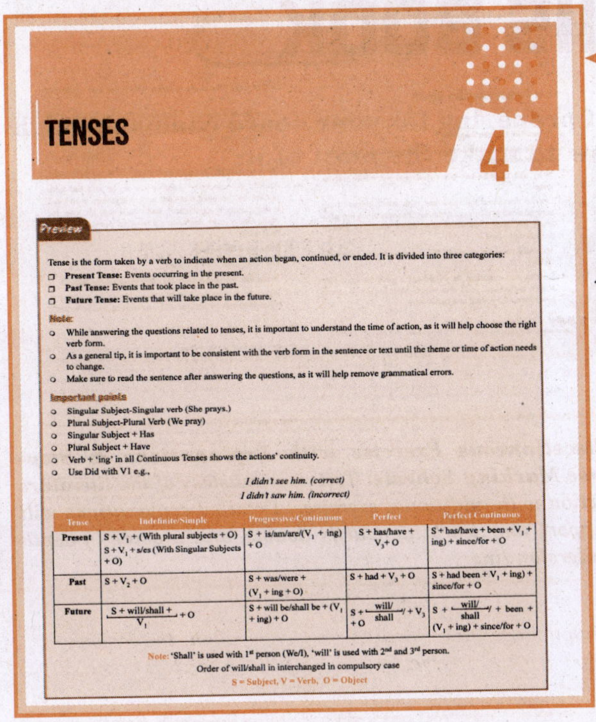

TENSES

4

Preview

Tense is the form taken by a verb to indicate when an action began, continued, or ended. It is divided into three categories:

- **Present Tense:** Events occurring in the present.
- **Past Tense:** Events that took place in the past.
- **Future Tense:** Events that will take place in the future.

Note:

- While answering the questions related to tenses, it is important to understand the time of action, as it will help choose the right verb form.
- As a general tip, it is important to be consistent with the verb form in the sentence or text until the theme or time of action needs to change.
- Make sure to read the sentence after answering the questions, as it will help remove grammatical errors.

Important points

- Singular Subject-Singular verb (She prays.)
- Plural Subject-Plural Verb (We pray)
- Singular Subject + Has
- Plural Subject + Have
- Verb + 'ing' in all Continuous Tenses shows the actions' continuity.
- Use Did with V1 e.g.,

I didn't see him. (correct)

I didn't saw him. (incorrect)

Tense	Indefinite/Simple	Progressive/Continuous	Perfect	Perfect Continuous
Present	$S + V_1$ + (With plural subjects + O) $S + V_1$ + s/es (With Singular Subjects + O)	S + is/am/are/(V_1 + ing) + O	S + has/have + V_3 + O	S + has/have + been + V_1 + ing) + since/for + O
Past	$S + V_2 + O$	S + was/were + (V_1 + ing + O)	S + had + V_3 + O	S + had been + V_1 + ing) + since/for + O
Future	$\frac{S + will/shall +}{V_1}$ + O	S + will be/shall be + (V_1 + ing) + O	S + $\frac{will/}{shall}$ + V_3 + O	S + $\frac{will/}{shall}$ + been + (V_1 + ing) + since/for + O

Note: 'Shall' is used with 1st person (We/I), 'will' is used with 2nd and 3rd person.

Order of will/shall in interchanged in compulsory case

S = Subject, V = Verb, O = Object

Integrated Grammar

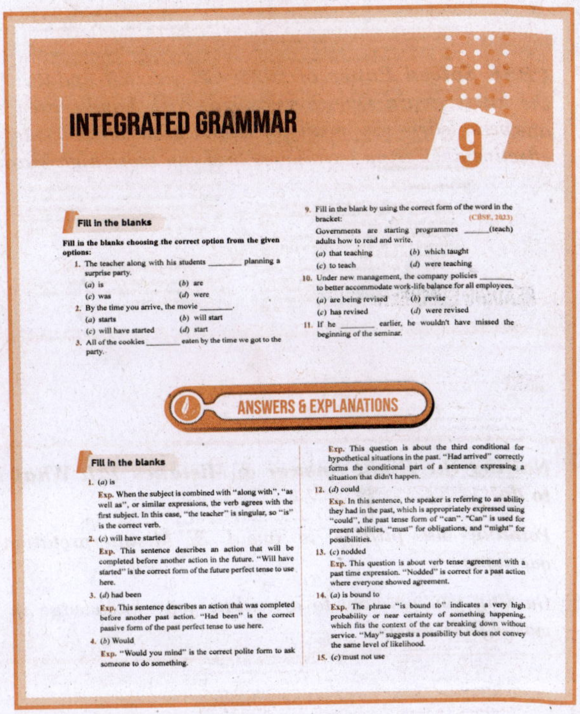

INTEGRATED GRAMMAR

9

Fill in the blanks

Fill in the blanks choosing the correct option from the given options:

1. The teacher along with his students _______ planning a surprise party.
   (a) is (b) are
   (c) was (d) were
2. By the time you arrive, the movie _______.
   (a) starts (b) will start
   (c) will have started (d) start
3. All of the cookies _______ eaten by the time we got to the party.

9. Fill in the blank by using the correct form of the word in the bracket: (CBSE, 2023)
   Governments are starting programmes _____(teach) adults how to read and write.
   (a) that teaching (b) which taught
   (c) to teach (d) were teaching
10. Under new management, the company policies _______ to better accommodate work-life balance for all employees.
   (a) are being revised (b) revise
   (c) has revised (d) were revised
11. If he _______ earlier, he wouldn't have missed the beginning of the seminar.

ANSWERS & EXPLANATIONS

Fill in the blanks

1. (a) is
   Exp. When the subject is combined with "along with", "as well as", or similar expressions, the verb agrees with the first subject. In this case, "the teacher" is singular, so "is" is the correct verb.
2. (c) will have started
   Exp. This sentence describes an action that will be completed before another action in the future. "Will have started" is the correct form of the future perfect tense to use here.
3. (d) had been
   Exp. This sentence describes an action that was completed before another past action. "Had been" is the correct passive form of the past perfect tense to use here.
4. (b) Would
   Exp. "Would you mind" is the correct polite form to ask someone to do something.

Exp. This question is about the third conditional for hypothetical situations in the past. "Had arrived" correctly forms the conditional part of a sentence expressing a situation that didn't happen.

12. (d) could
    Exp. In this sentence, the speaker is referring to an ability they had in the past, which is appropriately expressed using "could", the past tense form of "can". "Can" is used for present abilities, "must" for obligations, and "might" for possibilities.
13. (c) nodded
    Exp. This question is about verb tense agreement with a past time expression. "Nodded" is correct for a past action where everyone showed agreement.
14. (a) is bound to
    Exp. The phrase "is bound to" indicates a very high probability or near certainty of something happening, which fits the context of the car breaking down without service. "May" suggests a possibility but does not convey the same level of likelihood.
15. (c) must not use

Narrative Sketch/Poetic Sketch

Begin with the Concept Map that visually encapsulates the storyline, themes, and characters, serving as a quick reference to recall important highlights.

Theme & Important Characters' Sketch: *Understand the core message and the players involved in each story or poem with concise descriptions.*

After reading, review the Synopsis for a summary of the main events or themes.

Literary Devices Section in Poetry: *Learn to identify and understand the significance of literary devices in poetry to appreciate the craft of poets and the depth of their works.*

Synopsis

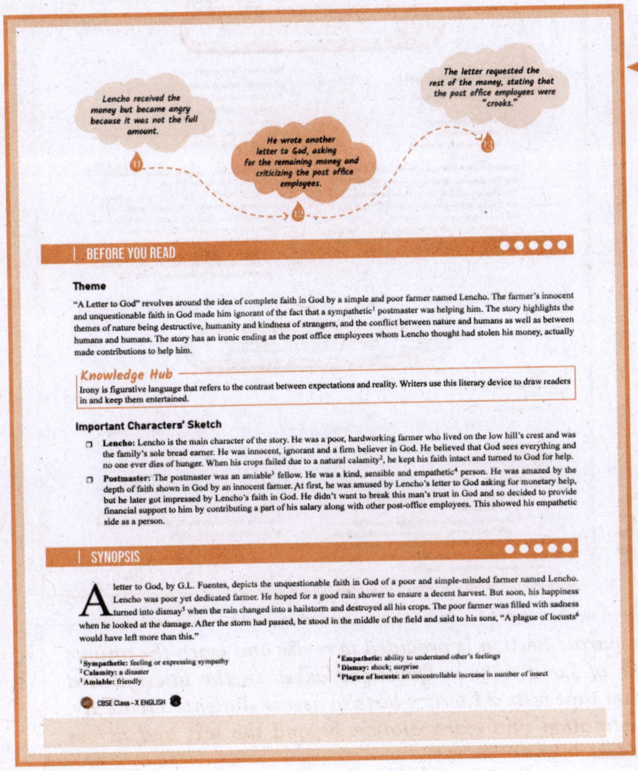

BEFORE YOU READ

Theme

"A Letter to God" revolves around the idea of complete faith in God by a simple and poor farmer named Lencho. The farmer's innocent and unquestionable faith in God made him ignorant of the fact that a sympathetic[1] postmaster was helping him. The story highlights the themes of nature being destructive, humanity and kindness of strangers, and the conflict between nature and humans as well as between humans and humans. The story has an ironic ending as the post office employees whom Lencho thought had stolen his money, actually made contributions to help him.

Knowledge Hub

Irony is figurative language that refers to the contrast between expectations and reality. Writers use this literary device to draw readers in and keep them entertained.

Important Characters' Sketch

- **Lencho:** Lencho is the main character of the story. He was a poor, hardworking farmer who lived on the low hill's crest and was the family's sole bread earner. He was innocent, ignorant and a firm believer in God. He believed that God sees everything and no one ever dies of hunger. When his crops failed due to a natural calamity[2], he kept his faith intact and turned to God for help.
- **Postmaster:** The postmaster was an amiable[3] fellow. He was a kind, sensible and empathetic[4] person. He was amazed by the depth of faith shown in God by an innocent farmer. At first, he was amused by Lencho's letter to God asking for monetary help, but he later got impressed by Lencho's faith in God. He didn't want to break this man's trust in God and so decided to provide financial support to him by contributing a part of his salary along with other post-office employees. This showed his empathetic side as a person.

SYNOPSIS

A letter to God, by G.L. Fuentes, depicts the unquestionable faith in God of a poor and simple-minded farmer named Lencho. Lencho was poor yet dedicated farmer. He hoped for a good rain shower to ensure a decent harvest. But soon, his happiness turned into dismay[5] when the rain changed into a hailstorm and destroyed all his crops. The poor farmer was filled with sadness when he looked at the damage. After the storm had passed, he stood in the middle of the field and said to his sons, "A plague of locusts[6] would have left more than this."

[1] **Sympathetic:** feeling or expressing sympathy
[2] **Calamity:** a disaster
[3] **Amiable:** friendly
[4] **Empathetic:** ability to understand other's feelings
[5] **Dismay:** shock; surprise
[6] **Plague of locusts:** an uncontrollable increase in number of insect

CBSE Class-X ENGLISH

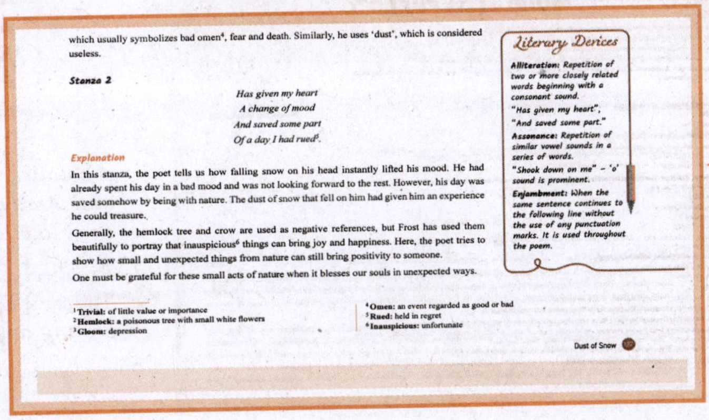

which usually symbolizes bad omen[4], fear and death. Similarly, he uses 'dust', which is considered useless.

Stanza 2

Has given my heart
A change of mood
And saved some part
Of a day I had rued[5].

Explanation

In this stanza, the poet tells us how falling snow on his head instantly lifted his mood. He had already spent his day in a bad mood and was not looking forward to the rest. However, his day was saved somehow by being with nature. The dust of snow that fell on him had given him an experience he could treasure.

Generally, the hemlock tree and crow are used as negative references, but Frost has used them beautifully to portray that inauspicious[6] things can bring joy and happiness. Here, the poet tries to show how small and unexpected things from nature can still bring positivity to someone.

One must be grateful for these small acts of nature when it blesses our souls in unexpected ways.

Literary Devices

Alliteration: *Repetition of two or more closely related words beginning with a consonant sound.*
"Has given my heart",
"And saved some part."
Assonance: *Repetition of similar vowel sounds in a series of words.*
"Shook down on me" – 'o' sound is prominent.
Enjambment: *When the same sentence continues to the following line without the use of any punctuation marks. It is used throughout the poem.*

[1] **Trivial:** of little value or importance
[2] **Hemlock:** a poisonous tree with small white flowers
[3] **Gloom:** depression
[4] **Omen:** an event regarded as good or bad
[5] **Rued:** held in regret
[6] **Inauspicious:** unfortunate

Dust of Snow

NCERT Exercise with Explanations: *NCERT Questions with Explanations will ensure you understand the reasoning behind each answer.*

NCERT EXERCISE

Oral Comprehension Check

(NCERT, Page 5)

1. **What did Lencho hope for?**

Ans. Lencho hoped for rain to come, which would get him a good harvest of his crops.

2. **Why did Lencho say the raindrops were like 'silver coins'?**

Ans. Lencho compared the raindrops with silver coins, which seemed to bring him a good harvest. The way coins (money) bring prosperity, the same way those raindrops looked promising to him.

3. **How did the rain change? What happened to Lencho's fields?**

Ans. Lencho was confident he would get a good harvest. The season welcomed good rain which soon became a storm accompanied by wind and hailstorms.

4. **What were Lencho's feelings when the hail stopped?** (CBSE, 2020)

Ans. When the hail stopped, Lencho was disheartened to see all his crops ruined. He had a sorrowful night as there would be no corn that year.

(NCERT, Page 6)

1. **Who or what did Lencho have faith in? What did he do?**

Ans. Amidst[7] the adversity[8] Lencho was in, he still had faith in God. He believed that God sees everything, even what is deep in one's conscience[9], and would ease his pain. He wrote God a letter demanding a hundred pesos to sow his field again.

2. **Who read the letter?**

Ans. The postmaster read the letter.

3. **What did the postmaster do after reading the letter?**

Ans. When the postmaster first saw the address, he laughed at it but soon turned serious and was moved by the writer's

[7]Amidst: in the middle of

[8]Adversity: a difficult situation

[9]Conscience: moral sense of right and wrong

---

the conversations of others on the bus and discreetly ask questions to gather more information about the journey. During the trip, Valli displayed confidence and maturity beyond her years, staying focused on fulfilling her dream and resisting the temptation to explore the town. On the return journey, she had a realization about death when she encountered[9] a dead cow, accepting it as a natural part of life. Overall, the bus journey taught Valli many valuable lessons.

4. Valli picked up various small details about the bus journey by listening carefully to conversations between her neighbours and people who regularly used the bus. She would ask a few detailed questions here and there to collect more information. She inquired secretly, seeking information about the bus schedule, travel time, and cost. Her curiosity led her to uncover every small detail related to the bus journey.

Long Answer Questions

CBSE Marking Scheme: Expression-2 M, Accuracy-1 M

5. Valli, the protagonist of 'Madam Rides the Bus', is an extraordinary girl who demonstrates self-confidence and courage in pursuing her ambition. **(1 M)**

Her determination to undertake the bus journey and her willingness to take risks in the process show how self-belief and courage can lead to success. **(1 M)**

Valli's journey also highlights the importance of seizing opportunities and learning from them, even if they come disguised as challenges. By stepping out of her comfort zone and believing in herself, Valli sets an inspiring example for others to follow. **(1 M)**

Nailing the Right Answer

Analyze the character traits of Valli to showcase her courage and determination.

Use specific examples from the text to support how Valli's risk-taking ability helped her achieve her dream.

7. Valli showed several admirable qualities, such as determination, confidence, and bravery. She was also a skilled planner and executor, as seen by her ability to sacrifice things like sweets and merry-go-round rides in order to save money for her bus journey. This level of sacrifice is impressive for a child of her age. **(1 M)**

Additionally, Valli showed confidence and maturity while on the bus, not allowing the presence of elders to intimidate[12] her. **(1 M)**

When the bus arrived at the town, Valli resisted the urge to explore or indulge in a drink, as she wanted to save her money for the return journey. She made wise decisions with her money and demonstrated[13] good manners by politely refusing the conductor's offer of a drink. **(1 M)**

Mistakes 101 : What not to do!

Students may describe Valli's actions without analyzing how they demonstrate qualities like determination, confidence, and bravery.

Miscellaneous Exercise with Explanations & Step-wise Marking Scheme: *Test your mastery of the literature section with additional exercises. Detailed explanations will support your learning, clarify doubts, and provide in-depth understanding.*

Nailing the Right Answer & Mistakes 101: What Not to do!

Pointing out pitfalls to avoid & Misinterpretation of questions

Guiding you on how to articulate your knowledge in the most effective way.

MISCELLANEOUS EXERCISE

Multiple Choice Questions

1. It was a celebration of South Africa's first ______ government.
   (a) Non-democratic, racial.
   (b) Democratic, non-racial.
   (c) Non-democratic, non-racial.
   (d) Monarch, racial.
2. Mandela refers to liberty as a "newborn" because-
   (a) The rule of the earlier government had ended.
   (b) It had recently been attained with lots of struggle.
   (c) It made people experience infant-like excitement.
   (d) He is talking about a newborn baby.
3. "We thank all of our distinguished international guests for having come to take possession with the people of our country of what is, after all, a common victory for ______."
9. Which party did Mandela join?
   (a) National African Congress.
   (b) African National Congress.
   (c) Indian National Congress.
   (d) He did not join any party.
10. Which of these lines from 'A Long Walk to Freedom' hints at the end of apartheid in South Africa? (CBSE SQP, 2023)
   (a) I was not born with a hunger to be free. I was born free — free in every way that I could know.
   (b) ...I yearned for the basic and honourable freedoms of achieving my potential, of earning my keep,...
   (c) Although that day, neither group knew the lyrics of the anthem they once despised, they would soon know the words by heart.
   (d) ...The white-skinned peoples of South Africa patched up their differences and erected a system of racial domination against the dark-skinned peoples...

ANSWERS & EXPLANATIONS

Answer Key

Multiple Choice Questions

1. (b) 2. (b) 3. (d) 4. (c) 5. (c) 6. (a) 7. (b) 8. (d) 9. (b) 10. (c)

Explanations

Extract-Based Questions

I. 1. (b) They will waste their lifetime opportunity.
2. (c) It is essential.
3. The extract suggests that in order to make full use of experiences in life, character development is essential.
• The author emphasizes that leaving the alma mater without a fully developed character would be a wasted opportunity of a lifetime. The extract highlights the importance of character over intelligence or talent, indicating that character development is a crucial aspect of education and personal growth.
4. 'Precincts of the alma mater'.

[24]Overwhelmed: have a strong emotional effect

SELECTED LAQs

As per the latest pattern observed in CBSE Board Exam 2024 for Q. 10 & Q.11

CBSE Marking Scheme: Content-3 M, Expression-2 M, Accuracy-1 M

1. **Evaluate the impact of friendship and companionship in both "Mijbil the Otter" and "From the Diary of Anne Frank." Compare and contrast the significance of friendship in the lives of the main characters, highlighting the role it plays in their emotional well-being, support system, and overall survival. Write this presentation draft, including your insights, in about 120 words.**

You may begin this way:

One acknowledges that both "Mijbil the Otter" and "From the Diary of Anne Frank" emphasize the importance of friendship and companionship in the lives of their main characters.

Ans. Good morning! Today, I want to discuss the importance of friendship in both the stories: "From the Diary of Anne Frank" and "Mijbil the Otter." In "Mijbil the Otter," a

elders who were ready to marry her to a man asking for dowry from her father. Additionally, her decision to reject the marriage proposal from the rich but greedy man-Bishamber showcases her self-worth and determination to prioritize her own happiness. Through these key moments, Bholi's growth highlights the power of self-acceptance in transforming one's life.

3. **You have been asked to present an evaluation of the theme of "faith" in both "A Letter to God" and "The Ball Poem." Write this presentation draft including your insights, in about 120 words, comparing the theme of faith in both.**

You may begin this way: ***One acknowledges that both "A Letter to God" and "The Ball Poem" portray characters who face challenging situations that test their faith; however, ...***

Selected LAQs

A separate Section is provided to revise and learn the unique style of Long Answer Questions asked in the latest Board Exam that tests 2 literary texts to assess students' creativity, imagination and extrapolation beyond the text and across the text.

MOCK TEST PAPER-2

Time allowed : 3 hours **Maximum Marks : 80**

GENERAL INSTRUCTIONS:

(i) *This question paper comprises 11 questions. All questions are compulsory.*

(ii) *The question paper contains THREE sections- Reading Skills, Writing Skills and Grammar, Literature Textbook.*

(iii) *Attempt questions based on specific instructions for each part.*

SECTION - A

READING SKILLS

(20 marks)

1. **Read the following text.** **(10 m)**

1. In the realm of Fantasy Adventure, heroes are often faced with daunting challenges that test their strength, courage, and determination. These challenges come in various forms, from treacherous quests to battles against formidable foes. Just like in our own lives, these challenges serve as opportunities for growth and self-discovery. They push the boundaries of what is possible and reveal the true potential within us.

2. Imagine a young hero, thrust into a world of magic and danger, tasked with a seemingly impossible mission. At first, they may feel overwhelmed, doubting their abilities and questioning whether they are capable of triumphing over the obstacles that lie ahead. But as they embark on their quest, they begin to realize that the greatest challenges often hide the greatest rewards. Through perseverance and unwavering determination, they learn to navigate treacherous terrains, outsmart cunning adversaries, and unlock their hidden strengths. It is through these challenges that they discover their true potential and become the heroes they were destined to be.

Mock Test Papers: *Test your preparedness with our Mock Test Papers designed to mirror the format and difficulty of real exams. Use the detailed explanations to identify areas of strength and opportunities for improvement.*

CONTENTS

Upcoming CBSE SQPs/APQs can be accessed through this QR

Section-C

CBSE SOLVED PAPER 2026

Time allowed : 3 hours | **Maximum Marks : 80**

GENERAL INSTRUCTIONS:

Read the following instructions carefully and follow them:

(i) *This question paper comprises 11 questions. All questions are compulsory*

(ii) *The question paper contains **THREE** section-*

***Section A** – Reading Skills*

***Section B** – Grammar and Creative Writing Skills*

***Section C** – Literature*

(iii) *Attempt question based on specific instructions for each part.*

SECTION - A

READING SKILLS

(20 marks)

1. Read the following passage carefully: **10**

(1) In the fast-evolving landscape of the present age, digital saturation and algorithmically curated lives, the phenomenon of FOMO — the Fear of Missing Out — has progressed from a fleeting psychological discomfort into a pervasive cultural condition. Initially, the term was coined to describe the anxiety provoked by the perception that others are participating in rewarding experiences from which one is absent. FOMO now pervades virtually in every dimension of contemporary existence, fuelled largely by the continuous updates of edited content on social media platforms. Significantly, it is the anxiety that others are experiencing something more fulfilling, exciting, or meaningful.

(2) The roots of FOMO lie in the interplay between the evolutionary instincts of an individual and modern technology. It may be traced as a fundamental human trait — the innate desire to belong. Man — being a social creature naturally, always tries to seek inclusion and belonging as a means of survival. Albeit, nowadays social media has escalated this instinct by bothering individuals with real-time updates of others' lives — carefully edited vacations, career milestones or even temporal joys framed as extraordinary. Each notification becomes a reminder of what we are not doing, a mirror reflecting our perceived inadequacies.

(3) FOMO is not solely a personal affliction; it is a cultural artifact also, shaped by the values of a society that equates busyness with worth and novelty with happiness. Moreover, consumerism fuels this fire with brands exploiting FOMO through limited time offers, exclusive events, and influencer-driven trends that promise belonging or status. The rise of the 'experience economy, where memories and moments are commodified, intensifies the pressure to participate in everything from music festivals to viral food craze.

(4) Furthermore, FOMO has created profound shifts in behaviour also. Due to this, the decision-making process has become increasingly worrisome, with people hesitating to commit to plans for fear of a better alternative emerging later. It often leads to impulsive choices, such as overspending on unnecessary products, overcommitting to events or making hasty life decisions to avoid feeling excluded. People, due to FOMO, struggle to focus on their priorities because they are distracted by what others are doing. Even highlighted reels of professional journeys shared online by others breed discontent and cause anxiety and dissatisfaction, where no experience feels complete.

(5) The gloomy side of FOMO manifests in lowered self-esteem, impaired concentration and in severe cases, depression. Ironically, the more one tries to engage with multiple activities to 'keep up', the greater it leads to emotional exhaustion. The illusion of missing out on something 'better' elsewhere robs individuals of their ability to engage themselves fully in their present experiences.

(6) To overcome the Fear of Missing Out we require intentional strategies. To avoid constant comparison, specific timings for checking the apps and social media should be set. One can also engage oneself in mindful breathing or meditation to stay grounded to the present. By prioritizing self-awareness and authentic experiences, one can take the edge off FOMO's grip and cultivate a richer, more satisfying life without chasing external validation. Finally, we need to recognize that carefully selected online portrayals, which are essentially selective, generate emotional resilience.

Answer the following questions based on the above passage:

(*i*) What is the primary psychological trigger behind FOMO in the context of social media usage? **Paragraph (1) 1**

(*a*) physical fatigue

(*b*) fear of rejection from loved ones

(*c*) need of privacy to keep oneself safe

(*d*) fear of being left out of rewarding experiences

Ans. (d) fear of being left out of rewarding experiences

(*ii*) Complete the following with the correct option from the two given below: **1**

FOMO has entered every dimension of a person's existence because ___________.

(*a*) more exciting events are taking place nowadays

(*b*) of constant edits and updates on the social media platforms **Paragraph (1)**

Ans. (b) of constant edits and updates on the social media platforms

(*iii*) What is the impact of the 'experience economy' on individuals? **Paragraph (3) 1**

Ans. The 'experience economy' increases pressure on individuals to participate in events and activities. As experiences and memories are treated as valuable and shareable, people feel compelled to constantly engage in trends, which strengthens their fear of missing out.

(*iv*) How does FOMO affect an individual's decision-making ability? **Paragraph (4) 2**

Ans. FOMO affects decision-making by creating anxiety about missing better opportunities. People make impulsive choices such as overspending on unnecessary products or committing to events without real interest. They also struggle to focus on their priorities due to constant comparison.

(*v*) Support the writer's viewpoint that FOMO leads to emotional consequences. **Paragraph (4) 1**

Ans. FOMO leads to emotional consequences such as low self-esteem, anxiety, and emotional exhaustion because people keep comparing their lives with others online.

(*vi*) List two effective ways to deal with Fear of Missing Out (FOMO). **Paragraph (6) 2**

Ans. Two effective ways to deal with FOMO are:

- Setting limits on social media use.
- Practising mindfulness and focusing on personal goals.

(*vii*) State whether the following statement is True or False: **1**

People need to make an effort to come out of their FOMO state of mind. **Paragraph (6)**

Ans. True

(*viii*) Complete the following with the correct option from the ones given below. 1

In the phrase 'generate emotional resilience', the word 'resilience' refers to the ability to Paragraph (6)

(*a*) support and create more social content.

(*b*) withstand emotional anxiety of FOMO.

(*c*) accelerate the notifications on social media.

(*d*) give in to digital social pressure.

Ans. (*b*) *withstand emotional anxiety of FOMO*

2. Read the following passage carefully: 10

(1) The craze for cosmetics has escalated globally, driven by evolving beauty standards and social media influence. The cosmetics industry thrives on innovation, offering various products catering to various skin types and preferences. In India, the cosmetics industry has witnessed a remarkable growth over the past decade, driven by rising 'disposable incomes', increased urbanization, and changing lifestyles. In contemporary times, people are more aware about their personal grooming.

(2) In the year 2024, the Indian cosmetics market generated revenue of approximately ₹1,34,000 crore and is projected to reach around ₹2,40,000 crore by 2028. This robust performance is driven as a result of strong e-commerce and growing demand for organic and premium product offerings due to increasing awareness of personal grooming, skin care routines among consumers, especially teenagers and young adults, who are the dominant demographic in cosmetics purchase, as they seek trendy and innovative solutions.

(3) The cosmetics industry is broadly divided into various segments such as skin care, hair care, colour cosmetics, fragrances, and personal hygiene products. Skincare leads the segments, accounting for nearly 35% of the market, followed by hair care at 25%. Colour cosmetics — including make-up products have seen significant growth, especially post-pandemic, due to the rise of e-commerce and social media. E-commerce platforms have played a crucial role in expanding access to cosmetics especially in Tier II and Tier III cities. In fact, online, sales contribute to around 25% of total cosmetics sales in India.

(4) Over and above that, men's grooming has emerged as a significant segment, valued at around ₹ 25,000 crore in the year 2024 with increasing demand for beard care, skin care and fragrances customized to men. This growth is fuelled by social media influencers, coupled with the increase of gender-neutral cosmetic formulations. This shows an aspirational pursuit of personal refinement, where appearance augments confidence, dismantling archaic stereotypes associated with male cosmetics consumption.

(5) Though the cosmetics industry plays a vital role in the Indian economy, it faces several challenges including managing intense competition, complying with regulations, ensuring product quality, and addressing ethical sourcing concerns. In addition, the industry struggles with copied products, adapting to changing consumer preferences and navigating the complexities of the supply chain.

Answer the following questions, based on the above passage:

(*i*) Complete the sentence with a reason:

The global demand for beauty products has intensified because of ____________. Paragraph (1) 1

Ans. evolving beauty standards and strong social media influence

(*ii*) What does the phrase 'thrives on innovation' tell us about the cosmetic industry? 1

(*a*) The industry is slow-growing.

(*b*) The industry is growing and evolving by the day.

(*c*) The industry is becoming popular in rural areas.

(*d*) The industry is gradually becoming more expensive. Paragraph (1)

Ans. (*b*) *The industry is growing and evolving by the day.*

(*iii*) Identify the word that indicates that the cosmetics industry is anticipated to grow. Paragraph (2) 1

Ans. The word is "projected."

(*iv*) Given that teenagers and young adults form the primary group for cosmetics purchases, what are the key factors that shape their buying decisions? Paragraph (2) 1

Ans. Teenagers and young adults prefer trendy and innovative products. Their buying decisions are influenced by social media, changing lifestyles, and rising awareness about personal grooming and skincare. They are attracted to modern trends, organic products, and premium cosmetic offerings.

(*v*) Select the option that is true for the Assertion and Reason given below. Paragraph (2) 1

Assertion: The Indian cosmetics market generated a profit of approximately ₹ 1,34,000 crore in 2024.

Reason: It became possible due to strong e-commerce and growing demand for organic and premium product offerings.

(*a*) Both the Assertion and the Reason are true, and the Reason is the correct explanation of the Assertion.

(*b*) Both the Assertion and the Reason are true, but the Reason is not the correct explanation of the Assertion.

(*c*) The Assertion is true, but the Reason is false.

(*d*) The Assertion is false, but the Reason is true.

Ans. (d) The Assertion is false, but the Reason is true.

(*vi*) How has the rise of e-commerce platforms impacted the revenue of the Indian cosmetics industry? Explain in 30 - 40 words. Paragraph (3) 1

Ans. The rise of e-commerce platforms has significantly increased the revenue of the Indian cosmetics industry. Online platforms have expanded sales, especially in Tier II and Tier III cities. In fact, online sales contribute about 25% of the total cosmetics market in India.

(*vii*) Based on your understanding of Paragraph (3), fill in the blank with suitable options: 1

The skincare segment currently dominates the Indian cosmetics industry. Currently its share is (20%, 25%, 35%) approximately.

Ans. 35%

(*viii*) Complete the sentence suitably. 1

That men's grooming has increased the demand for gender-neutral cosmetic formulations symbolizes. ______

Paragraph (4)

Ans. the breaking of traditional stereotypes about men using cosmetics

(*ix*) Mention any two major challenges faced by the cosmetics industry at present. Paragraph (5) 2

Ans. Two major challenges are intense competition and managing copied products.

SECTION – B

GRAMMAR AND CREATIVE WRITING SKILLS (20 marks)

GRAMMAR

3. Complete any ten of the following twelve tasks, as directed. **10 × 1 = 10**

(*i*) Fill in the blank by using the correct form of the word in the brackets, for the given portion of a report. 1

The group ________ (walk) for hours through forests and hills in Mexico before it reached the barbed wire fence, marking the boundary of the forest.

Ans. had walked

(*ii*) Fill in the blank by choosing the correct option given in the brackets: 1

________ (Several/Both/All) people attended the convention because the entry was open to all at a very nominal fee.

Ans. All

(*iii*) Read the given sentence from a story, identify, the error and supply the correction in the sentence. **1**

The farmer told his sons that he had hidden a treasure in the fields but he had forget the actual place.

Use the given format for your response.

Error	Correction

Ans.

Error	Correction
had forget	had forgotten

(*iv*) Report the dialogue between two friends by completing the sentence: **1**

Harry: Good morning Bobby, how do you do?

Bobby: Quite well, thank you; but these are hard times.

Harry wished Bobby good morning and enquired about his well-being. Bobby thanked him and said that he was quite well, but remarked ________.

Ans. that those were hard times

(*v*) Select the option that identifies the error and supplies the correction for the line given below:

I don't know what it is. It feel like an incredibly lucky day for me.

Option No.	Error	Correction
(A)	don't	doesn't
(B)	is	have
(C)	feel	feels
(D)	lucky	luckily

Ans. (c)

Error	Correction
feel	feels

(*vi*) Select the correct option to complete the reporting of the dialogue given below: **1**

Sahil said to Shekhar, "Which are your books?"

(*a*) Sahil asked Shekhar which his books were.

(*b*) Sahil asked Shekhar which books are yours.

(*c*) Sahil asked Shekhar which has been his books.

(*d*) Sahil asked Shekhar which are his books.

Ans. (b) Sahil asked Shekhar which books are yours.

(*vii*) Complete the given sentence with the correct form of the verb by selecting the correct option:

A case ______ against the unidentified truck driver for causing damage to the street poles due to negligence and rash driving.

(*a*) was registered

(*b*) is register

(*c*) have been registered

(*d*) may registered

Ans. (a) was registered

(viii) Fill in the blank by choosing the correct option from the brackets: 1

Anita ________ (ought to/would/have to) likely complete the project on time as her team is collaborating effectively.

Ans. would

(ix) Identify the error and supply the correction for the following note in a hair salon's instruction manual: 1

All tools and frequently touched surfaces must be disinfect after each client's treatment.

Use the given format for your response.

Error	Correction

Ans.

Error	Correction
disinfect	disinfected

(x) Suhani and Sneha decided to purchase books to focus on 'Reading Skills' in their summer vacations. 1

Report the question asked by Suhani to Sneha.

Which books are we going to purchase today from the Book Fest? Suhani asked Sneha ________.

Ans. which books they were going to purchase that day from the Book fest

(xi) Replace the underlined word used in the sentence with the best option given below: 1

Since Sheenam study diligently for months/she will clear the competitive exam.

(*a*) studying

(*b*) was studied

(*c*) has been studying

(*d*) have been studied

Ans. (c) has been studying

(xii) Identify the error and supply the correction for the following sentence. 1

True tradition is not in celebrations, but in the culture we carries forward.

Use the given format for your response.

Error	Correction

Ans.

Error	Correction
in	only

CREATIVE WRITING SKILLS 10 M

Note: *All details presented in the questions in the writing section are imaginary and created for assessment purpose.*

4. Attempt any one from (A) and (B) given below in about 120 words:

(A) You are Ishita/Ishit, Head Librarian of Happy Children's School, Adamshahr. You have observed that the students in your school have poor reading habits. Write a letter to the editor, highlighting the declining interest among children in reading. Emphasize on the importance of inculcating good reading habits. Draw attention to the benefits of reading, along with certain suggestive measures to encourage the culture of reading.

Ans. (A) Happy Children's School
Adamshahr

23 February 2026

The Editor
The Daily Times
Adamshahr

Subject: Declining Reading Habits Among Students

Respected Madam,

Through the columns of your newspaper, I would like to highlight the declining interest in reading among students. As the Head Librarian of Happy Children's School, I have noticed that many children prefer spending time on mobile phones and television instead of reading books.

Reading is very important for developing vocabulary, imagination, concentration, and knowledge. It also improves writing and communication skills. However, students today are losing the habit of regular reading.

Schools and parents should work together to encourage reading by organizing book fairs, reading competitions, and storytelling sessions. Creating attractive library spaces can also motivate students.

I hope necessary steps will be taken to promote a strong reading culture among children.

Yours sincerely,
Ishita

(B) You are Shivi/Shiva of Phase-II, Maya Vihar, Vayutown. Your Class X board exams are over and you want to join the Table Tennis Academy to pursue your interest in the game. Write a letter to the Director of Tinkering Table Tennis Academy to enquire about the procedure of admission, timings, duration, fees, and other relevant details.

Ans. (B) Phase-II, Maya Vihar
Vayutown

23 February 2026

The Director
Tinkering Table Tennis Academy
Vayutown

Subject: Enquiry About Admission to Table Tennis Academy

Respected Sir,

I have recently completed my Class X board examinations and I am keen to join your academy to pursue my interest in table tennis. I have been playing the game for the past three years and have represented my school in inter-school competitions. I now wish to receive professional coaching to improve my techniques and overall performance.

Kindly provide me with information about the admission procedure, required documents, and eligibility criteria. I would also like to know the batch timings, duration of the course, and fee structure. Please inform me about the training facilities, availability of equipment, and whether any trial session is conducted before admission. I am eager to begin training at the earliest.

Thanking you.

Yours sincerely,

Shivi

5. Attempt any one from (A) and (B) given below in about 120 words:

(A) Read the given details of the school activities that help children in their personality development.

- student councils, clubs
- activities in the Morning Assembly
- celebration of important days
- organization of various competitions
- sports and academic activities

Analyse the details and write an analytical paragraph about the impact of school activities on students. Focus on factors like fosters leadership, responsibility, communication skills, discipline, daily motivation, and team building.

Ans. School activities play an important role in the overall personality development of students. Student councils and clubs help students develop leadership qualities and a sense of responsibility. Activities in the morning assembly improve confidence and communication skills as students get opportunities to speak in front of others. Celebrating important days creates awareness and builds values such as respect and unity. Various competitions motivate students to perform better and discover their talents. Sports and academic activities teach discipline, teamwork, and time management. These activities also encourage healthy competition and cooperation among students. Overall, school activities not only support academic growth but also shape students into confident, responsible, and well-rounded individuals ready to face future challenges.

OR

(B) Read the following details about fashion trends.

In today's world, fashion is not just about clothes, it is driven by images and impressions. Fashion trends provide a powerful reflection of society's evolution, and creativity. Write an analytical paragraph about how the factors mentioned below have shaped the fashion trends in recent years with key causes, effects and future implications.

- creative expression
- social media influence
- celebrity endorsements
- blend of traditional and modern styles
- commercialization of festivals
- customized fashion choices
- rising e-commerce

Ans. In recent years, fashion trends have been shaped by many important factors. Creative expression allows people to show their personality and ideas through their clothing choices. Social media has a strong influence, as people follow trends shared by influencers and fashion bloggers. Celebrity endorsements also play a major role, as many individuals try to copy the styles of famous personalities. The blend of traditional and modern styles has made fashion more unique and meaningful. Festivals have become more commercialized, increasing the demand for special outfits. Customized fashion choices give people freedom to design clothes according to their taste. Rising e-commerce platforms have made fashion easily available to everyone. Overall, fashion trends reflect changing lifestyles and will continue to evolve with technology and creativity.

SECTION – C
LITERATURE
(40 marks)

6. Read the following extracts and answer the questions for any one of the given two, (A) or (B): 5

(A) Out of the experience of an extraordinary human disaster that lasted too long, must be born a society of which all humanity will be proud. We, who were outlaws not so long ago, have today been given the rare privilege to be host to the nations of the world on our own soil. We thank all of our distinguished international guests for having come to take possession with the people of our country of what is, after all, a common victory for justice, for peace, for human dignity.

(Nelson Mandela: Long Walk to Freedom)

(*i*) Which of the following options justifies the statement made by Mandela, "We, who were outlaws ..."? 1

(*a*) The international leaders who came to attend the ceremony

(*b*) Due to Apartheid, many countries broke diplomatic relations with South Africa

(*c*) The Commonwealth countries and their people

(*d*) The people who fought in the Anglo-Boer War

Ans. (b) Due to apartheid, many countries broke diplomatic relations with South Africa

(*ii*) Complete the sentence appropriately: 1

Mandela thanked all the distinguished international guests because ___________.

Ans. they had come to share and witness South Africa's victory for justice, peace, and human dignity

(*iii*) In the above lines, Mandela mentions 'extraordinary human disaster'. What is the significance of this phrase in his speech? 2

Ans. The phrase "extraordinary human disaster" refers to the long period of apartheid in South Africa. It highlights the suffering, racial discrimination, and injustice faced by the people. By using this phrase, Mandela emphasizes that the new democratic nation has risen from years of oppression and pain.

(*iv*) The tone of Mandela in the above excerpt is: 1

(I) unifying (II) determined (III) aggressive (IV) pessimistic (V) hopeless

Select the correct option:

(*a*) (I), (II) and (IV)

(*b*) (II) and (IV)

(*c*) (I) and (II)

(*d*) (IV) and (V)

Ans. (c) (I) and (II)

OR

(B) "Richard was competitive," Mr. Weiherer continued, "but not in a bad sense." He explained, "Richard wasn't interested in winning for winning's sake or winning to get a prize. Rather, he was winning because he wanted to do the best job he could. For the right reasons, he wants to be the best." And that is one of the ingredients in the making of a scientist. Start with a first-rate mind, add curiosity, and mix in the will to win for the right reasons. Ebright has these qualities. *(The Making of a Scientist)*

(*i*) In light of the excerpt, what can we infer about Richard from Mr. Weiherer's statement, "Richard was competitive, but not in a bad sense"? 1

Ans. Richard was competitive in a healthy way. He did not compete for prizes or recognition but to do his best work. He wanted to achieve excellence for the right reasons, which shows his sincerity and dedication.

(*ii*) Mention the 'ingredients' which are necessarily required in the making of a scientist. 2

Ans. The 'ingredients' required in the making of a scientist are a first-rate mind, strong curiosity, and the will to win for the right reasons.

(*iii*) Fill in the blank with the correct word from the brackets: 1

Mr. Weiherer suggests that Richard was ________. (lethargic/persistent)

Ans. persistent

(*iv*) As per the above excerpt, what is **not true** about Ebright? Select the correct option. 1

(*a*) strongly curious

(*b*) bright minded

(*c*) competitive spirit

(*d*) irrational

Ans. (d) irrational

7. **Read the following extracts and answer the questions for any one of the given two, (A) or (B):** **5**

(A) Though to distinguish beasts of prey
A novice might nonplus,
The Crocodile you always may
Tell from the Hyena thus:
Hyenas come with merry smiles;
But if they weep they're Crocodiles.
The true Chameleon is small,
A lizard sort of thing;
He hasn't any ears at all,
And not a single wing.
If there is nothing on the tree,
Tis the chameleon you see.

(How to Tell Wild Animals)

(*i*) How does the poet describe the crocodile's tears? Choose the correct option: **1**

(*a*) genuine and heartfelt
(*b*) joyful and sincere
(*c*) false and deceptive
(*d*) cold and indifferent

Ans. (c) false and deceptive

(*ii*) What confusion will a newcomer face while distinguishing between a hyena and a crocodile, as described humorously by the poet in the above extract? **1**

Ans. A newcomer may get confused because hyenas appear to smile pleasantly, while crocodiles seem to cry. Since both expressions are misleading, a novice might misunderstand their true nature and find it difficult to distinguish between them.

(*iii*) Mention any two characteristics of a chameleon on the basis of the given extract. **2**

Ans. Two characteristics of a chameleon are:

- It is small and looks like a lizard.
- It has no ears and no wings.

(*iv*) Fill in the blank with the correct option from those given in the brackets: **1**

The tone of the poet in the above lines is ________ (playful and humorous/serious and confused).

Ans. playful and humorous

OR

(B) Did you finish your homework, Amanda?
Did you tidy your room, Amanda?
I thought I told you to clean your shoes, Amanda!
(I am an orphan, roaming the street.
I pattern soft dust with my hushed, bare feet.
The silence is golden, the freedom is sweet.)

(Amanda!)

(*i*) Complete the sentence appropriately: **1**

Amanda wants to be an orphan because ________

Ans. she desires freedom from constant instructions and restrictions

(*ii*) What does the image of Amanda "roaming barefoot in the dusty street" signify? **2**

Ans. The image of Amanda roaming barefoot in the dusty street signifies her longing for freedom, simplicity, and independence. It reflects her desire to escape control and enjoy a peaceful life where "silence is golden" and "freedom is sweet."

(*iii*) Amanda's tone while imagining herself as an orphan is: 1

(*a*) excited

(*b*) fearful

(*c*) angry

(*d*) peaceful

Ans. (d) peaceful

(*iv*) What does the speaker do on the dust? 1

Ans. The speaker (Amanda) patterns the soft dust with her hushed, bare feet.

8. Answer any four of the following five questions in 40 – 50 words each: **4 × 3 = 12**

(*i*) In what ways do the symbols of 'Fire' and 'Ice' in the poem 'Fire and Ice' serve as metaphors for opposing human impulses? How do they contribute to the exploration of destructive capabilities of human beings?

Ans. In the poem, 'fire' symbolises intense desire and uncontrolled passion, while 'ice' represents hatred and cold indifference. Both emotions are destructive in nature. Frost suggests that whether through excessive desire or deep hatred, human impulses have the power to destroy the world.

(*ii*) What was the last task assigned to Anne Frank by Mr. Keesing due to her habit of talking and how does she show her ingenuity to answer it?

(From the Diary of Anne Frank)

Ans. Mr. Keesing punished Anne for talking in class by assigning her essays. Her final task was to write on "Quack, Quack, Quack, Said Mistress Chatterbox." Anne cleverly wrote a humorous poem, which amused her teacher. Impressed by her creativity, he stopped giving her extra work.

(*iii*) Mention the transition in the baker's costume from the Portuguese days to that of the author's childhood.

(Glimpses of India : A Baker from Goa)

Ans. During Portuguese rule, bakers wore a long frock called a kabai that reached their knees. By the author's childhood, this dress had changed to a shorter shirt and trousers. Though their attire changed over time, the baker's importance in Goan society remained the same.

(*iv*) In the statement, "When I returned, there was an appalling spectacle," which spectacle is the author referring to? Elucidate.

(Mijbil the Otter)

Ans. The "appalling spectacle" refers to the frightening scene inside the aircraft when Mijbil struggled violently inside his box and injured himself. When the author opened it, he found blood and chaos. The disturbing sight deeply shocked and upset him.

(*v*) What sacrifices did Valli have to make in order to save enough money for fulfilling her long-cherished desire and how do these sacrifices reflect her strong will power?

(Madam Rides the Bus)

Ans. To save money for her bus journey, Valli resisted spending on sweets, toys, and other small pleasures. She patiently collected coins over time. Her discipline, determination, and self-control clearly reflect her strong willpower and deep desire to fulfil her dream.

9. Answer any two of the following three questions in 40 - 50 words each: **2 × 3 = 6**

(*i*) Why does Hari Singh find it pleasant to work for Anil, though he was a thief?

(The Thief's Story)

Ans. Hari Singh found it pleasant to work for Anil because Anil treated him kindly and trusted him. Unlike others, Anil did not question his past or show suspicion. He also promised to teach Hari how to read and write, which gave him hope for a better future.

(*ii*) How does Matilda face 'the horrible life of necessity?

(The Necklace)

Ans. After losing the necklace, Matilda faced a life of poverty with courage and determination. She dismissed her maid, did household chores herself, bargained for food, and lived in a small room. For ten years, she and her husband worked hard to repay the debt.

(*iii*) The teacher built up Bholi's confidence on her first day at school. Discuss. *(Bholi)*

Ans. *On her first day at school, Bholi's teacher spoke to her gently and encouraged her to try speaking without fear. She assured Bholi that with practice she would improve. The teacher's kindness and patience gave Bholi confidence and removed her fear.*

10. Answer any one of the following two questions in 100 - 120 words: **6**

(A) How do Lencho in 'A Letter to God' and Kisa Gotami in 'The Sermon at Benares' respond to their experiences of suffering and loss? How did they overcome their respective losses?

Ans. *Lencho and Kisa Gotami both face deep loss but respond differently. Lencho's crops are destroyed by hail, yet he does not lose faith. He writes a letter to God asking for money and firmly believes that God will help him. His faith helps him emotionally overcome his loss, though he remains unaware of the postmaster's kindness. Kisa Gotami, on the other hand, is shattered by her son's death. She initially refuses to accept reality. However, after the Buddha asks her to find mustard seeds from a house untouched by death, she realises that death is universal. She overcomes her grief through acceptance and spiritual understanding.*

OR

(B) How does the contrast between the pilot's fear in 'The Black Aeroplane' and Custard's initial cowardice in 'The Tale of Custard the Dragon' highlight that courage can be found in the most unexpected characters when circumstances demand it? Discuss with reference to the two.

Ans. *In The Black Aeroplane, the pilot feels helpless and frightened when his plane enters a storm and the instruments fail. However, he continues flying bravely, trusting the mysterious black aeroplane that guides him to safety. His courage lies in not giving up despite fear.*

In The Tale of Custard the Dragon, Custard is mocked as a coward and always asks for a safe cage. Yet, when a pirate attacks, it is Custard who bravely fights and eats him, saving everyone.

Both texts show that true courage appears in moments of crisis. It is not the absence of fear but the ability to act despite it.

11. Answer any one of the following two questions in 100 - 120 words: **6**

(A) How does Dr. Herriot's approach to treat Tricki reflect his deep understanding of the animal's needs and bring to the fore the character traits of patience, observation and empathy in 'A Triumph of Surgery? Discuss.

Ans. *Dr. Herriot's treatment of Tricki reflects his deep understanding of the animal's real problem. He quickly realises that Tricki is not seriously ill but suffering from overfeeding and lack of exercise. Instead of prescribing medicines, he removes the dog from its luxurious but unhealthy environment and keeps him under strict supervision. Through careful observation, he puts Tricki on a controlled diet and allows him to regain strength naturally. Dr. Herriot shows patience by monitoring gradual improvement and empathy by handling Mrs. Pumphrey gently without humiliating her. His practical wisdom, kindness, and scientific approach highlight that true care involves understanding both the patient's physical needs and emotional circumstances.*

OR

(B) The Martians, despite their advanced technology, are outsmarted by their own ignorance and an old book of rhymes. Comment with reference to 'The Book that Saved the Earth'.

Ans. *In the play, the Martians consider themselves highly intelligent and technologically advanced, yet they misinterpret a simple book of nursery rhymes. Think-Tank wrongly concludes that Earthlings are aggressive and that the book is a coded message. His arrogance and ignorance prevent him from understanding its true nature. As a result, the Martians abandon their invasion plan out of fear. Ironically, an old, harmless book saves the Earth. The play humorously shows that overconfidence and lack of proper understanding can defeat even the most advanced beings. It highlights that wisdom and correct interpretation are more powerful than mere technology.*

CBSE SOLVED PAPER 2025

Time allowed : 3 hours **Maximum Marks : 80**

GENERAL INSTRUCTIONS:

Read the following instructions carefully and follow them:

(i) *This question paper comprises* ***11*** *questions. All questions are compulsory*

(ii) *The question paper contains* ***THREE*** *section-*

Section A *– Reading Skills*

Section B *– Grammar and Creative Writing Skills*

Section C *– Literature*

(iii) *Attempt question based on specific instructions for each part.*

SECTION - A

READING SKILLS

(20 marks)

1. Read the following passage carefully: **10 M**

(1) With the growing focus on sustainable living, the importance of kitchen gardens in urban regions has garnered greater acknowledgement. One significance of kitchen gardens in urban areas is their role in promoting food security. Rapid urbanization has led to increased distances between food production centres and urban settlements, resulting in longer food supply chains and a decrease in the freshness and nutritional value of food.

(2) By having a kitchen garden, urban dwellers can grow their own fresh produce at home, making good use of empty tins, old utensils, and clay flower pots, ensuring a constant supply of nutritious food for themselves and their families. This activity not only saves money and time but can also provide a healthy, practical, and environmentally friendly hobby for the whole family.

(3) Not only do kitchen gardens contribute to food security, but they also play a crucial role in environmental sustainability. Traditional agricultural practices often involve the use of synthetic fertilizers, pesticides, and intensive irrigation methods, which may have adverse effects on the environment. However, kitchen gardens promote organic farming, reducing the use of harmful chemicals and preserving soil health.

(4) In addition to fostering a sustainable environment, kitchen gardens provide numerous health benefits to urban dwellers. The availability of fresh and organic produce from the garden ensures a higher intake of essential nutrients, vitamins, and minerals, promoting better overall health and well-being.

(5) Furthermore, kitchen gardens have proven to be an effective tool for education and community development. They provide an opportunity for individuals to reconnect with nature and learn about the basics of agriculture. Besides providing fruits and vegetables, gardening provides an aesthetic and therapeutic exercise that helps relieve stress. The physical activity involved in tending to a garden helps individuals stay active, reducing the risk of obesity and related health issues.

(6) By involving children in gardening activities, they can develop an appreciation for the environment and learn essential life skills. Moreover, kitchen gardens can also serve as a platform for community engagement, fostering social interactions and promoting a sense of belonging among urban residents.

(7) Despite the numerous benefits of kitchen gardens, establishing and maintaining one in urban areas can be challenging. Limited space, lack of sunlight, and soil quality issues are common obstacles that urban gardeners face. However, innovative solutions such as vertical gardening, hydroponics, and rooftop gardens have emerged to overcome these challenges.

(8) It is imperative to provide support and resources to encourage urban gardening initiatives as this can transform urban areas into sustainable havens where residents not only live but thrive in harmony with nature.

Answer the following questions, based on the above passage:

(*i*) What does the writer's use of phrases like 'in urban regions kitchen gardens have garnered great acknowledgement' suggest about kitchen gardening today? **1**

(*a*) It has reduced inflation.

(*b*) It is an expensive hobby.

(*c*) It provides nutritious food.

(*d*) It does not minimize adverse effects on the environment. Paragraph (1)

Ans. (i) (C) It provides nutritious food.

(*ii*) Complete the following with a suitable explanation. **1**

Growing a kitchen garden is cost effective because ________. Paragraph (2)

Ans. (ii) Growing a kitchen garden is cost-effective because it allows urban dwellers to grow fresh produce at home, making use of empty tins, old utensils and Clay pots, reducing expenses on purchasing food while ensuring a Constant supply of nutritious food.

(*iii*) Identify two differences between the methods adopted in traditional farming and kitchen gardens. Paragraph (3) **2**

Ans. (iii) Traditional farming often involves the use of synthetic fertilizers, pesticides and intensive irrigation which may negatively impact the environment, whereas kitchen gardens promote organic farming, reducing the use of harmful chemicals and preserving soil health.

(*iv*) Substitute the underlined word with the correct word from Paragraph (4). **1**

The local residents' <u>nurturing</u> of their surrounding flora and fauna helps to create awareness about civic responsibilities.

Ans. (iv) The correct word is "fostering".

(v) Tending to a kitchen garden has many health benefits. Explain in about 40 words. Paragraphs (4) and (5) **2**

Ans. (v) Kitchen gardens provide fresh and organic produce, ensuring a higher intake of essential nutrients, vitamins and minerals. Gardening also serves as physical exercise, promoting better overall health and well-being while reducing the risk of Obesity and related health issues.

(vi) Select the option that best reflects the concept that kitchen gardening is an effective educational tool for children.

(a) It contributes to effective community development.

(b) It helps develop sensitivity and appreciation for nature. Paragraph (5) **1**

Ans. (vi) (b) It helps develop sensitivity and appreciation for nature.

(vii) What hurdles do kitchen gardeners face? Mention any two. **1**

Ans. (vii) Limited space in urban areas.
Lack of adequate sunlight and soil quality issues.

(viii) State whether the following statement is True or False: **1**

Kitchen gardening should be practised by everyone living in the cities.

Ans. (viii) True.

2. Read the following passage carefully: **10 M**

(1) Silk is a natural protein fibre, some forms of which can be woven into textiles. Silk has a long history in India. It is known as Resham in eastern and northern India, and Pattu in the southern parts of India. India is the second largest producer of silk in the world after China.

(2) Silk is renowned for its luxurious qualities with a natural soft and smooth texture that feels comfortable on the skin. One of its unique qualities is to absorb and release moisture, regulating the body temperature, and keeping the wearer cool and dry.

(3) Silk is one of the strongest natural fibres, but it loses up to 20% of its strength when wet. Its elasticity is moderate to poor: if elongated even a small amount, it remains stretched. It can be weakened if exposed to too much sunlight. It may also be attacked by insects, especially if left dirty.

(4) The process of silk production is known as sericulture. Silk is produced by several insects; but, generally, only the silk of moth caterpillars has been used for textile manufacturing. To produce 1 kg of silk, 104 kg of mulberry leaves must be eaten by 3000 silkworms.

(5) So what makes silk so costly? Firstly, cultivation of silk is a labour-intensive work. Secondly, the silk fabric is carefully derived from the larva of the silkworms which spin silk threads around themselves to make cocoons from natural sources. This makes the climate, availability of production limited due to factors like quality mulberry leaves and time required by silkworms to complete their lifecycle. Thirdly, the intensive work can only be carried out with specialized knowledge and expertise by skilled artisans and craftsmanship. Lastly, superior quality silk fabrics are made from long and uniform silk fibres giving them a smooth and lustrous appearance. Thus, production requires careful selection, adding to the cost.

In 2021, Karnataka was the highest producer of raw silk at 8483 metric tonnes followed by Andhra Pradesh at 5520 metric tonnes with Assam close behind at 5038 metric tonnes. At the other end of the spectrum there was Chhattisgarh (248 metric tonnes), Nagaland (230 metric tonnes) and UP trailed behind at 179 metric tonnes.

Answer the following questions, based on the above passage:

(*i*) Silk is a popular fabric in India.

Support the above statement in 40 words with evidence from the text. 2

Ans. (i) Silk is a popular fabric in India as it has a long history and is known as Resham in the north and Pattu in the south. India is also the second-largest producer of silk after China.

(*ii*) Select the option that is true for the assertion and reason given below. 1

Assertion: Silk feels comfortable to the skin.

Reason: It made of natural protein fibre.

(*a*) Both the assertion and the reason are true, and the reason is the correct explanation of the assertion.

(*b*) Both the assertion and the reason are true, but the reason is not the correct explanation of the assertion.

(*c*) The assertion is true, but the reason is false.

(*d*) The assertion is false, but the reason is true.

Ans. (ii) (a) Both the assertion and the reason are true and the reason is the correct explanation of the assertion.

(*iii*) Justify the following statement:

Though one of the strongest natural fibres, silk remains stretched. 1

Ans. (iii) Silk loses up to 20% of its strength when wet and its elasticity is moderate to poor. If elongated even slightly, it remains streched.

(*iv*) According to the passage, in what way is sunlight harmful to silk? 1

Ans. (iv) Silk can be weakened if exposed to too much sunlight and may also be attacked by insects, especially if left dirty.

(*v*) "To produce 1 kg of silk, 104 kg of mulberry leaves must be eaten by 3000 silkworms."
State any one inference that can be drawn from the above statement. 1

Ans. (v) Silk production is highly resource-intensive, requiring a large quantity of mulberry leaves and thousands of silkworms to produce a small amount of silk.

(*vi*) Complete the following with one suitable reason from the text:
Silk production work can be carried out by skilled artisans because ________. 1

Ans. (vi) It requires specialized knowledge and expertise in handling delicate silk fibres and maintaining craftsmanship.

(*vii*) Based on the given text, which state was the smallest producer of silk. 1

Ans. (vii) Uttar Pradesh (UP) was the smallest producer of silk, with 179 metric tonnes.

(*viii*) Complete the sentence suitably.
To carry out silk production requires careful selection because ________. 1

Ans. (viii) Superior quality silk fabrics require long and uniform silk fibres to give a smooth and lustrous appearence.

(*ix*) Give one reason to support why production of silk is limited. 1

Ans. (ix) Silk production is limited due to factors like Climate, the availability of quality mulberry leaves and the time required by silkworms to Complete their life-cycle.

SECTION – B

GRAMMAR AND CREATIVE WRITING SKILLS (20 marks)

GRAMMAR

3. Complete any **ten** of the following twelve tasks, as directed. **(10 × 1 = 10)**

(*i*) Fill in the blank by using the correct form of the word in the brackets, for the given portion of a letter. 1

Please do not hesitate to contact me if there are any further questions or if I can be of _________ (assist) in any way.

Ans. (i) assistance.

(*ii*) Read the given sentence from a travel blog. Identify the error and supply the correction in the sentence. 1

Spend a night under the stars in a traditional camp, where you can experience the warmth of our hospitable and savour the delicious local cuisine.

Use the given format for your response.

Error	Correction

Ans. (ii)

Error	Correction
hospitable	hospitality

(*iii*) Kriva and Manish had a conversation about the engagement of Kriva's brother. Report Manish's question. 1

How far is the engagement venue from your house?

Ans. (iii) Manish asked how far the engagement venue was from Kriva's house.

(*iv*) Read the dialogue between Ankita and her mentor, Sharwari, about the cultural exchange programme. 1

Ankita: Are we going to get some time off for sightseeing?

Sharwari: Oh yes! All the students will get two days for sightseeing.

Select the correct option to complete the reporting of the above dialogue.

Ankita asked Sharwari if they were going to get some time off for sightseeing, to which Sharwari replied in the affirmative __________ two days for sightseeing.

(*a*) that all the students should get

(*b*) that all the students would get

(*c*) that all the students ought to get

(*d*) that all students must be getting

Ans. (iv) that all the students would get.

(*v*) Fill in the blank by choosing the correct option, to complete a description of Notice Writing. 1

A notice is a type of social _________ (conversation/conveyance/communication) used to notify or present information to a specific set of people.

(*vi*) Identify the error and supply correction for the given sentence from an advertisement. 1

The board invite online applications from eligible candidates for the post of a senior English teacher.

Use the given format for your response.

Error	Correction

(*vii*) Identify and correct the error in the given line taken from a user manual of an ironing board. 1
Place the garment on the ironing board, smoothening out as many wrinkle as possible.

Options	Error	Correction
(*a*)	on	in
(*b*)	many	any
(*c*)	wrinkle	wrinkles
(*d*)	possible	impossible

Ans. (vii) (C)

Error	Correction
wrinkle	wrinkles

(*viii*) Complete the given sentence by filling in the blank with the correct option. 1
After she __________ her homework, Anaisha finally relaxed and watched a movie with her friends.

(*a*) finished
(*b*) had finished
(*c*) have finished
(*d*) will finish

Ans. (viii) (b) had finished

(*ix*) Report the dialogue between two friends by completing the sentence. 1

Ankita: Will you help me plan my itinerary?

Tanu: Yes, indeed! Where are you going?

Ankita asked Tanu if __________. Tanu enthusiastically replied in the affirmative and asked where she was going.

Ans. (ix) she would help her plan her itinerary

(*x*) Fill in the blank by choosing the correct option to complete the pop-up message appearing on a website. 1
Welcome to our website! You __________ enjoy 10 percent off on your first purchase with code WELCOME. Click here to start shopping!

(*a*) may
(*b*) will
(*c*) should
(*d*) might

Ans. (x) (b) will.

(*xi*) Complete the given sentence about the reaction of some students, by selecting the correct option.
Since morning the group of students ________ excited about the forthcoming cultural fest. 1

(*a*) are
(*b*) was
(*c*) has been
(*d*) were

Ans. (xi) (b) was

(*xii*) Identify the error and supply the correction for the following note on a food packet.
This product is manufacturing for infants and contains no additives. 1

Error	Correction

Ans. (xii)

Error	Correction
manufacturing	manufactured.

Note: *All details presented in the questions in the writing section are imaginary and created for assessment purpose.*

4. Attempt any one from (*a*) and (*b*) given below: **5**

(*a*) You are Neha/Nehal Panjwani, residing at 8576, Sarita Apartments, Hanger Street. As a responsible citizen, you believe in promoting environmentally responsible practices. Write a letter to the Director, Alternate Energy Commission, in about 120 words, sharing your views about 'Reducing the Carbon Footprint' by encouraging the use of renewable energy sources, such as solar and wind power and to provide subsidies to families who want to avail the facility.

OR

(*b*) As Shobita/Shobhit Das, a responsible citizen, residing in 14-A, GVR Colony, Hoshiyarbad, you have noticed that a road crossing in your area does not have a traffic signal which leads to chaos and traffic jams during peak hours. It is also an accident-prone area. Despite writing numerous letters to the Traffic Commissioner, no action has yet been taken. Write a letter to the editor of a national daily, in about 120 words, to draw the attention of concerned authorities to address the pressing issue affecting the commuters.

Ans. (b) Shobhit Das
14-A, GVR Colony
Hoshiyarpur

15th February 2025

The Editor
The Times of India
New Delhi, 110001

Subject: Lack of Traffic Signal causing Chaos at Road crossing in GVR Colony.

Dear Sir,
I am writing to bring attention to a serious issue that has been affecting the commuters in our area. I, Shobhit Das, a resident of GVR Colony, Hoshiyarpur, have noticed that a road crossing in our locality does not have a traffic signal. This has led to severe traffic jams, especially during peak hours, causing inconvenience to the Public

Moreover, the area has become an accident-prone zone. Despite writing numerous letters to the Traffic Commissioner, no action has been taken so far. It is urgent that this matter be addressed promptly to ensure the safety.

I kindly request the concerned authorities to take immediate action and install a traffic signal at the mentioned crossing.

Yours faithfully
Shobhit Das.

5. Attempt any one from (*a*) and (*b*) given below: **5**

(*a*) The effects of technology on education have been profound and multifaceted; influencing both teaching and learning in various ways. The data below shows the rising enrolment in online courses over the years. Analyze the data and write an analytical paragraph, in about 120 words, about how technology has transformed teaching and learning by shifting from classrooms to digital devices. Discuss benefits such as access to information and challenges like digital divide.

S.No.	Year	Total number of enrollments (in millions)
1.	2017	26
2.	2018	43
3.	2019	59
4.	2020	76
5.	2021	143
6.	2022	189

Ans. (a) The increasing enrollment in online courses over the past six years reflects the transformative role of technology in education, from 26 million in 2017 to 189 million in 2022. This shift from Traditional classroom-based learning to Digital platforms highlights the growing accessibility of education. Technology has made learning more flexible and available to students across various locations, offering access to information, resources and learning materials. The use of digital devices has removed geographical and time barriers, enabling people to pursue education at their convenience.

OR

(*b*) Read the given details about the pros and cons of artificial intelligence (AI). With the help of the given cues and your own ideas write an analytical paragraph in about 120 words on "AI - Benefits and Drawbacks".

- AI is possessed by machines
- Impacted our lives in many ways
- AI – Google maps
- Knowledge at our fingertips
- Cannot wholly replicate humans
- Increase in cyber crime

SECTION – C
LITERATURE

(40 marks)

6. Read the following extracts and answer the questions for any one of the given two, (*a*) or (*b*): 5

(*a*) The moon was coming up in the east, behind me, and stars were shining in the clear sky above me. There wasn't a cloud in the sky. I was happy to be alone high up above the sleeping countryside. I was flying my old Dakota aeroplane over France back to England. I was dreaming of my holiday and looking forward to being with my family. I looked at my watch: one thirty in the morning. (Two Stories About Flying)

(*i*) What time of the day is the above extract set in? 1

(*a*) dawn (*b*) afternoon

(*c*) night (*d*) dusk

Ans (i) (c) Night.

(*ii*) State any one inference about the writer from the given context. "I was looking forward to being with my family." 1

Ans. (ii) The phrase shows the writer's emotional attachment to their family and excitement about being with them.

(*iii*) Fill in the blank with the correct word from the brackets. 1

The use of the phrase 'clear sky' adds to a sense of __________ (favourable/flavourful) weather conditions.

Ans. (iii) Favourable.

(*iv*) How does the serene atmosphere described by the narrator contribute to the mood and anticipation of his journey back to England? Elaborate in about 40 words, with reference to the extract. 2

Ans. (iv) The peaceful setting, with the moon and clear sky, creates a calm feeling. This peaceful scene helps the writer feel relaxed and happy, making him look forward to his Journey and the reunion with his family in England.

OR

(*b*) "It's not my balcony," Ausable said with extreme irritation. "It belongs to the next apartment." He glanced explanatorily at Fowler. "You see," he said, "this room used to be part of a large unit, and the next room through that door there - used to be the living room. It had the balcony, which extends under my window now. You can get onto it from the empty room two doors down and somebody did, last month. The management promised to block it off. But they haven't."

(The Midnight Visitor)

(*i*) What was the management supposed to do regarding the balcony? 1

(*ii*) Which of the following was the reason that irritated Ausable about the balcony? 1

(*a*) its size and layout

(*b*) its location relative to his apartment

(*c*) its accessibility from the neighbouring unit

(*d*) its maintenance by the apartment management

(*iii*) How does Ausable's detailed explanation of the balcony's history and current accessibility contribute to the atmosphere of suspense or tension in the story? Answer in about 40 words. 2

(*iv*) Fill in the blank with the correct word from the brackets. 1

The reference to last month' and 'now' adds to a sense of ____________ (reconciliation/mystery).

7. Read the following extracts and answer the questions for any one of the given two, (*a*) or (*b*): 5

(*a*) The way a crow
Shook down on me
The dust of snow
From a hemlock tree
Has given my heart
A change of mood (Dust of Snow)

(*i*) Fill the blank to complete the sentence. 1

Shaking down of dust of snow gave the speaker a change of heart by __________.

Ans. (i) Lifting his spirits.

(*ii*) How does the interaction between the natural elements (crow, snow, hemlock tree) contribute to the speaker's emotional transformation in the poem ? Answer in about 40 words. 2

Ans. (ii) The crow, snow and hemlock tree bring an unexpected moment of joy and peace to the speaker. The falling snow from the hemlock tree and the crow's action unexpectedly uplift the speaker's mood turning his sorrow into a feeling of Contentment and hope.

(*iii*) 'Dust of Snow' is referred to as: 1

(*a*) mist

(*b*) dust of branches

(*c*) snow residue

(*d*) snowflakes

Ans. (iii) (c) Snow residue.

(iv) The crow and the hemlock tree represent _________. 1

1. sorrow
2. elation
3. hope
4. anxiety
5. enthusiasm

(a) 1 only (b) 2, 3 and 5

(c) 4 only (d) 1, 4 and 5

Ans. (iv) (d) 1, 4 and 5

OR

(b) Don't bite your nails, Amanda!
Don't hunch your shoulders, Amanda!
Stop that slouching and sit up straight,
Amanda!
(There is a languid, emerald sea,
where the sole inhabitant is me —
a mermaid, drifting blissfully.) (Amanda)

(i) How does the poet reinforce the contrast between what the narrator wants and what Amanda desires? 2

(ii) What tone is conveyed through the repetition of Amanda's name in the line? 1

(a) loving (b) instructive

(c) indifferent (d) playful

(iii) How does the imagery of the emerald sea with the mermaid contrast with Amanda's actions? 1

(iv) Select the option that applies the same rhyme scheme as the lines of the given extract. 1

(a) Sitting by the pond
Waving my wand
Awaiting my dearest
I looked above and beyond
Awaiting my love
A sudden sound, fluttered the dove
The crackle stopped, as so did my heart

(b) Sitting by the pond
Holding tight to my bond
I looked above and beyond Awaiting my love
I heard her come, a sudden sound
The crackle stopped, as so did my heart

(c) I sat beside the pond with her
Awaiting for her to come
I looked above and beyond
Awaiting my love
A sudden sound, I turned back
The crackle stopped, as so did my heart

(d) Sitting by the pond
Awaiting my love
I looked above and beyond
A sudden scream, I looked around
Then a shadow fell and there was no sound
The crackle stopped, as so did my heart

8. Answer any *four* of the following five questions in 40-50 words each: **(4 × 3 = 12)**

(*i*) The young seagull's fear of flying and reluctance to leave his ledge contribute to the development of the theme of independence and courage in the story. Justify. (Two Stories about Flying)

Ans. (i) The young seagull's fear of flying and his reluctance to leave his ledge highlight his dependence on comfort and safety, which contrasts with the theme of independence. However, when hunger forces him to fly, he overcomes his fear, showing the courage and self-reliance needed to grow and survive. This transformation emphasizes the importance of overcoming fear to achieve independence.

(*ii*) In what ways does the contrast between the tiger's natural habitat and its confinement in a concrete cell enhance the poem's exploration of captivity and its consequences for wild animals? (A Tiger in the Zoo)

Ans. (ii) The contrast between the tiger's natural habitat and its cage in the zoo highlights the pain of captivity. In the wild, the tiger is free and powerful but in the zoo, it is trapped and frustrated, symbolising the loss of its freedom.

(*iii*) The portrayal of the baker's attire and role in the village emphasize the cultural and social significance of bread-making within the community. Elaborate. (Glimpses of India - A Baker from Goa)

(*iv*) What happens to the house when the trees move out of it? Comment. (The Trees)

Ans (iv) When the trees move out of the house, the house is left empty and exposed. The absence of the trees symbolizes the loss of Nature and Shelter, leaving the house to face the harshness of the outside world without any protection or Comfort.

(*v*) How does Valli's desire to ride the bus reflect her aspirations and challenges in context of her daily life?

(Madam Rides the Bus)

Ans. (v) Valli's desire to ride the bus symbolizes her aspirations for independence and exploration beyond her village. She overcomes challenges like saving money and sneaking away, showing determination and courage. Her excitement after the journey reflects her longing to break free from routine and discover new experiences.

9. Answer any two of the following three questions in 40-50 words each: **(2 × 3 = 6)**

(*i*) How do Anil's initial reaction to Hari Singh's cooking and his subsequent actions reflect Anil's evolving relationship with Hari Singh ?

(The Thief's Story)

Ans. (i) Anil was initially disapointed with Hari Singh's cooking and gave the food to a stray dog. However, instead of scolding him, he patiently taught him to cook and helped him learn to read and write. This reflects Anil's evolving relationship with Hari, built on Trust, care and friendship.

(*ii*) The unexpected encounter with the voice in the doorway affects Horace's burglary attempt. Elaborate. (A Question of Trust)

Ans. (ii) Horace Danby's burglary attempt was affected when he unexpectedly encountered a woman in the doorway. She cleverly deceived him by pretending to be the owner's wife and tricked him into opening the safe for her. Trusting her, Horace removed his gloves, leaving fingerprints behind. This ultimately led to his arrest proving that he was outsmarted by other theif.

(*iii*) The play, "The Book that Saved the Earth', uses humour and misunderstandings between the Martians and Earthlings to explore the themes of perception and cultural differences. Comment.

10. Answer any *one* of the following two questions in 100 - 120 words: **6**

(*a*) Comment on the reactions and feelings of Lencho and Nelson Mandela when they faced challenges in their lives. (A Letter to God and Nelson Mandela: Long Walk to Freedom)

Ans. (a) Both Lencho and Nelson Mandela faced Challenges but reacted differently. Lencho, in a Letter to God, showed deep faith in God when a hailstorm destroyed his crops. He believed God would help him and wrote a letter asking for money. His trust was unshaken despite difficulties.

Nelson Mandela, in Long walk to freedom, faced years of oppression under apartheid. Instead of losing hope, he fought for justice and equality. His struggle led to the end of racial discrimination in South Africa. Unlike Lencho, who relied on divine help, Mandela believed in perseverance & Collective effort.

Both Men showed strong determination - Lencho through faith and Mandela through resilience and leadership. Their reactions highlight the power of belief in overcoming hardships.

OR

(*b*) Discuss how the writers use language to create humour in the poem "The Tale of Custard the Dragon' and the play "The Proposal'.

11. Answer any one of the following two questions in about 100 - 120 words: *6*

(*a*) Discuss how Bholi evolves through the story. What are the qualities that contribute to her transformation from a timid girl to a confident young woman? (Bholi)

Ans. (a) In the story Bholi, Bholi evolves from a timid, neglected girl into a confident and self-assured young woman, primarily through the support of her teacher and the power of education. Initially insecure due to her physical appearance and the mistreatment she faces at home, Bholi's self-esteem is fragile. However, as she begins to learn and grow, her teacher's encouragement gives her the courage to speak up. The turning point in her transformation comes when she stands up against the forced marriage, asserting her right to choose her own path.

This act of defiance demonstrates how her education and inner strength contributed to her newfound confidence and independence, ultimately enabling her to overcome her past and take charge of her future.

OR

(*b*) Hari's character evolves from being deceitful and opportunistic to remorseful and seeking redemption.

In the light of the above information, describe how his decision to return the money signifies a moral awakening in him and a newfound appreciation for Anil's kindness and mentorship. (The Thief's Story)

❑❑❑

READING SKILLS

READING COMPREHENSION

1

Preview

Steps to attempt Reading Comprehension

1. **Avoid overemphasizing details:** While details are important, focus on understanding the main point rather than getting caught up in examples and illustrations. Comprehending the overall flow and structure will help in analyzing and answering questions.
2. **Don't memorize:** There is no need to memorize every word in the passage. Prioritize understanding the flow, structure, and main points. For specific questions, you can always refer back to the passage.
3. **Read the questions first:** Before reading the passage, go through the questions. This prepares you to focus on the information you need to find in the passage. Focus on the questions themselves rather than a specific answer option. A quick overview of the questions is sufficient.
4. **Vocabulary skills are not the primary focus:** While having a strong vocabulary is beneficial, not having an extensive vocabulary won't prevent you from understanding the passage. Focus on grasping the main idea and don't get stuck on particular words.
5. **Objective-Type Questions:** To find the correct option in Multiple Choice Questions, go through all the options. Re-read the passage and then tick the correct option. To find answers to the vocabulary-based questions like synonyms, antonyms etc., replace the word with the meaning. If you find that it is the same in meaning, the answer is correct.
6. **Focus on the information within the passage:** The correct answer is always based on the information given in the passage. Avoid getting distracted by answer options that are out of scope.
7. **Be cautious of "trigger words":** Pay attention while reading and don't get trapped by "trigger words." These words may shift the focus of the passage or introduce contrasting information. Skimming or rushing through the passage may lead to confusion.
8. **Take notes:** When reading obscure or abstract texts, make quick notes for reference. Note down the general flow, structure, paragraph-wise flow, and important points. The notes don't have to be extensive, just highlight the essential markers/points in the passage.
9. **Anticipate questions:** Although challenging, try to identify possible questions while reading the passage. Predict which parts of the passage are likely to be the basis for questions.
10. **Pay extra attention to opening and closing paragraphs:** Questions like the main idea question often relate to the overall subject of the passage, and the answers are frequently found in the first and last paragraphs. Extract as much information as possible from these paragraphs.

Two types of Passages asked by CBSE

(*i*) Discursive Passage (400–450 words):

- Includes the opinion of a person, which is generally argumentative, persuasive and interpretative.
- Sometimes the author presents his views with great depth of reasoning to persuade the reader.

(*ii*) Case-Based Factual Passage (200–250 words):

- Composed of visual and verbal inputs such as graphs, pie charts, slope graphs etc.
- These passages focus completely on details or facts.

Passage-I

Read the passage given below. **(10 marks)**

1. The modern classroom has taken several steps forward in its evolution of the learning environment in the past 25 years. Many of the benefits that we have seen in this setting are due to the introduction of new technology options for students. Instead of having a single computer for a class to use or a laboratory environment for the entire school placed in one room, we can now help students learn at their table or desk with items issued to them directly. Thus, there are quite a lot of advantages of having technology in classrooms.
2. Technology helps children to stay motivated during the learning process. Most students don't like to go to school if they feel like they are wasting their time. When there is technology allowed in the classroom, then teachers have an opportunity to let children work at a pace which suits them the best without disturbing others. They can look up additional information about a subject they are learning about that day, play educational games that reinforce the lesson, or work on advanced material using a program.
3. Because many of today's technology options allow students to see how well they are doing compared to the average of all users, it gives them a chance to push harder for themselves and their education. Many of the programs that encourage learning also issue rewards or award certificates, which helps to make the lessons fun as well.
4. Technology encourages more communication between teachers and parents. When there is technology in the classroom, then there are more opportunities for parents and teachers to connect with each other. Using a blog for the classroom can help parents get to see what their children are learning each day. Apps and software options allow teachers to instantly report on a child's behaviour to let parents know in real-time what is happening throughout the day. There are options for chat boxes, instant messaging, and other forms of communication as well.
5. Let's not forget about email here either. Since the 1990s when this technology option came into the classroom, it created more reliability in messaging between teachers and parents should there be a need to talk.
6. Technology also creates new ways to learn for today's student. There are three critical forms of intelligence that we see in children today: emotional, creative, and instructional. The traditional classroom environment, which typically encourages lecture-based lessons, focuses more on the latter option. Standardized tests and similar ranking tools do the same. When children have access to technology then those who excel outside of the standard learning setup can still achieve their full potential.
7. Technology allows children to embrace their curiosity in multiple ways. They can try new things without embarrassment because their tech access gives them a level of anonymity. This process allows children to work, through trial-and error if they wish, to see if a different strategy helps them to learn more effectively.
8. It even encourages students to stay engaged with their learning environment. Children get bored very easily when they feel like they already know what is being taught in their classroom. Some children will transform into mentors or leaders in this situation to help their fellow students, but there are many more who disengage because they lack stimulation. By introducing technology to the classroom, there are fewer places where repetitive learning must take place. Teachers can introduce new subjects, try new techniques, or use different projects to encourage ongoing learning, which creates more overall engagement.

Answer the following questions, based on the passage above.

(*i*) What is the meaning of the word "engagement" as used in the passage? **(1)**

(*a*) The act of participating or being involved
(*b*) The feeling of excitement or interest
(*c*) The process of connecting or interacting
(*d*) The state of being occupied or busy

(*ii*) In the passage, replace the word "technology" with a suitable synonym. **(1)**

(*iii*) Complete the following line with a phrase from the passage: **(1)**

"Technology helps children to stay motivated during the learning process. Most students don't like to go to school if they feel like they are __________."

(*iv*) Complete the following analogy correctly based on the passage: **(1)**

Traditional Classroom : Lecture-based lessons :: Technology : ______

(*a*) Interactive learning (*b*) Virtual reality
(*c*) Communication tools (*d*) Online assessments

(*v*) According to the passage, what are the three critical forms of intelligence seen in children today? **(1)**

(*a*) Emotional, creative, and instructional intelligence.
(*b*) Analytical, logical, and problem-solving intelligence.
(*c*) Social, artistic, and verbal intelligence.
(*d*) Critical thinking, spatial, and mathematical intelligence.

(*vi*) Based on the reading of the passage, explain how technology in the classroom encourages ongoing learning and engagement, in about 40 words. **(2)**

(*vii*) Complete the sentence appropriately. **(1)**

Email in the classroom has improved communication between teachers and parents by __________.

(*viii*) Supply one point to justify the following statement: **(2)**

"Technology encourages more communication between teachers and parents."

Passage-II

Read the passage given below. **(10 marks)**

1. In addition to using libraries and visiting art museums, historic site visitation is another common form of public engagement with the humanities. According to the National Endowment for the Arts' Survey of Public Participation in the Arts (SPPA).

the percentage of people making at least one such visit fell steadily from 1982 to 2012, before rising somewhat in 2017. Visits to historic sites managed by the National Park Service (NPS) were substantially higher in 2018 than 1980, despite a decline in recent years.

In 2017, 28% of American adults reported visiting a historic site in the previous year. This represented an increase of 4.4 percentage points from 2012 but a decrease of 8.9 percentage points from 1982. The bulk of the decline in visitation occurred from 2002 to 2008.

The recent increases in visitation rates were statistically significant for the 35-44- and 45-54-year-old age groups 1. The larger change was found among 35-to-44-year-olds, whose visitation rate increased 8.7 percentage points. Despite the increase from 2012 to 2017 for these groups, there was a net decline in historic site visitation since 1982 for Americans of virtually all ages. Only among the oldest Americans (age 75 or older) was the rate of visitation higher in 2017 than 35 years earlier.

From 1982 to 2017, the differences among age groups with respect to rates of historic site visitation decreased. For example, in 1982, the rate of visitation among 25-to-34-year-olds (the group most likely to visit a historic site in that survey) was approximately 11 percentage points higher than that of the youngest age group (18-to-24-year-olds). and more than 17 points higher than that of people ages 65-74. By 2017, however, the visitation rate of 25-to-34-year-olds had dropped to within five percentage points of the younger cohort and was virtually identical of that for the older group.

2. While visitation rates are converging among the age cohorts, the differences by level of educational attainment are still pronounced. In 2017, as in earlier years, the visitation rate among college graduates was more than twice as high as the rate among those who finished their studies with a high school diploma (43% as compared to 17%). Among those who did not finish high school, visitation rates were below 10% throughout the 2008-2017 time period. Conversely, among Americans with a graduate or professional degree, visitation rates were in the vicinity of 50% during these years. Data from the National Park Service (NPS) indicate the types of historical sites visited most and also the demands made of these sites' physical infrastructure and staff. Visits to NPS historic sites rose from approximately 59.5 million in 1980 to almost 112 million in 2018. Throughout this time period, visits to historic sites constituted approximately a third of total NPS recreational visitation.

3. Since hitting a recent low in visits in 1995, total visits to historic sites of all types increased 58% to a high of 120.3 million in 2016, before falling 7%, to 111.9 million visits in 2018.

4. Much of the recent growth in visits to historic sites occurred among parks classified as national memorials and was driven by a particularly high level of visitation at sites that did not exist in 1995, such as the Franklin Delano Roosevelt Memorial (3.3 million visitors in 2018), the Martin Luther King, Jr. Memorial (3.6 million visitors), and the World War II Memorial (4.7 million visitors). As a result, visits to national memorials increased more than 300% from 1995 to 2016, even as the number of sites increased just 26% (from 23 to 29). In comparison, visits to national monuments increased only 3%, even as the number of sites in the category increased by 9% (from 64 to 70). From 2016 to 2018, the number of visits fell in every category, with the largest decline occurring at the memorial sites (down 10%), and the smallest drop at national monuments (3%).

Answer the following questions, based on the passage above.

(*i*) Complete the following line with a phrase from the passage:
"The recent increases in visitation rates were statistically significant for the 35-44- and 45-54-year-old age groups, indicating..." **(1)**

(*ii*) Supply one point to justify the following statement:
"Visitation rates to historic sites have shown a decline in recent years." **(2)**

(*iii*) In earlier years the visitation rate among college graduates was more than twice as high as the rate among those: **(1)**

(*a*) Who were employed individuals.
(*b*) Who had a graduate or professional degree.
(*c*) Who finished their studies with a high school diploma.
(*d*) Who did not finish high school.

(*iv*) Based on your reading of the text, list 2 historical memorials in America? **(1)**

1. ______ 2. ______

(*v*) Which age group had a higher rate of visitation to historic sites in 2017 than 35 years earlier in America? **(1)**

(*vi*) Inference-based question: Based on the passage, what can be inferred about the visitation rates to historic sites among different age groups? **(2)**

(*vii*) Which term from the passage refers to the act of visiting places of historical significance? **(1)**

(*a*) Memorabilia (*b*) Recreational
(*c*) Visitation (*d*) Converging

(*viii*) Substitute the word 'substantially' with one word similar in meaning in the following sentence from the passage:
"Visits to historic sites managed by the National Park Service (NPS) were substantially higher in 2018 than 1980, despite a decline in recent years." **(1)**

Passage-III

Read the passage given below. **(10 marks)**

1. Hiking is a great source of pleasure to us besides being beneficial for health. Once we leave the crowded streets of a city and go out for a walking tour away from the mad world, we really feel free. The open air has a bracing effect on the mind. The congestion of the city, the uproar and tumult, the intolerable noise of traffic, the hectic daily routine, all these are forgotten and the mind is at ease. We then feel like running, leaping, singing and laughing. We travel merrily mile after mile in the company of friends and associates.

2. Hiking takes us in the midst of nature. The sight of waterfalls, flowers, streams, trees and bushes is pleasing. A connect is established between us and nature. Various sounds of nature, like the murmur of a brook or the song of a bird, acquire a new meaning and significance to us.

3. You enjoy the beauty of nature. Minute observations like a snake casting its slough, a mouse peeping out of its hole, a squirrel leaping about on the branches of a tree, a bird flying past us, all these are noticed and they arouse our interest. We have no business worries, no fear of the examination, no anxiety about the home. We have leisure to stand, to walk and talk. It is more thrilling and pleasurable to hike in a mountainous region than in the plains. The excitement of climbing up to the top of a hill, the adventure of coming down a slope, the grandeur of sunset behind a mountain - All these sights lend a rare charm and interest to our journey.

4. We walk along a zig-zag motor road or cut across a mountain path in search of adventure. We may have bright sunny weather or might get caught in a shower of rain. We may look below us into the yawning chasm or up at the mountain peak. The feeling of unlimited freedom makes our hearts leap with joy.

5. Hiking is one of the healthiest sports. It ensures a complete escape from the urgent and busy activities of life and therefore gives solace to our brain. It regains its lost energy and is able to do twice as much work as before.

6. The fresh air, beautiful mountains, majestic trees, chirping sound of birds make one's mind and soul at peace with nature.

(CBSE, 2023)

Based on your understanding of the passage, answer the questions below: **(10 × 1 = 10)**

(*i*) To go out for a walking tour is
(*a*) to stroll (*b*) to ramble
(*c*) to hike (*d*) to saunter

(*ii*) Why does the writer say that the mind is at ease when you hike?
(*a*) because hiking is an inexpensive activity.
(*b*) because it brings families together.
(*c*) because of intolerable noise of traffic.
(*d*) because the depressing daily routine is forgotten.

(*iii*) Complete the following with a phrase:
The various sounds of nature acquire ....

(*iv*) Infer one reason for the following based on information in paragraph 2.
A contact is established between us and nature.

(*v*) Complete the following analogy correctly with a word from paragraph 2.
aroma :: cooking; fragrance: ....

(*vi*) Give one reason why it is a pleasure to hike in the mountains than in the plains.
(*a*) because observation is sharpened.
(*b*) because of the excitement of climbing up and adventure of coming down.
(*c*) because it is leisure to stand, to walk.
(*d*) because there are no worries.

(*vii*) Hiking gives the brain, the rest it needs because
(*a*) it is a short time activity.
(*b*) it is one of the healthiest sports.
(*c*) it makes us sleep peacefully.
(*d*) it is an escape from our busy schedule.

(*viii*) List any two examples of minute observations you make while on a hike.

(*ix*) Supply one point to justify the following:
Hiking gives us a feeling of unlimited joy.

(*x*) Substitute the word 'leap with joy' with one word similar in meaning in the following sentence from the passage.
The feeling of unlimited freedom makes our hearts leap with joy.

Passage-IV

Read the following text. **(10 marks)**

1. The invention of the safety bicycle in the late nineteenth century transformed the world of cycling. While early versions of bicycles had been used in Europe since the seventeenth century, it was the safety bicycle with its lightweight hollow steel frame and equal-sized wheels that revolutionised the cycling experience.

2. This resulted in enhanced mobility for both men and women, allowing them to explore the countryside freely and travel between towns. Bicycles symbolised freedom, particularly for women, granting them self-reliable transportation and the ability to participate in recreational activities, like bicycle racing. The rise of bicycles also brought a shift in fashion, with more functional and relaxed clothing tailored specifically for cycling.

3. Bicyclists also became a political force. They played a significant role in the development of road maps, guiding riders along the best routes. They campaigned for better infrastructure to enhance their riding experiences.

4. Today, advances in technology, ***wearables**** and complex data analysis have transformed sports science, particularly in endurance sports, like cycling. Cyclists can now gather vast amounts of data simply by using mobile apps to track their activities. This data not only encompasses exercise details, like its volume or intensity, but also external factorslike the impact of weather on the physiological response of the athlete. Furthermore, technology has made it very easy to monitor performance-influencing data outside of training, such as heart rate or sleep quality, through various wearables and cost-effective mobile apps.

5. However, just because we are able to monitor so much information does not mean that it is useful for improving the sports performance of our athletes. In this sense, we believe that we must be critical while adopting any new technologies or trends in training. The first thing we should know is whether there is scientific support for the use of that new gadget or wearable. For example, core temperature is of great importance in the mechanisms that produce fatigue and exhaustion in endurance sports. A few years ago, a device

came on the market that estimated this measurement in a non-invasive way and we saw many top cyclists and runners wearing it. However, a study later showed it is an invalid device for measuring one's temperature.

6. Innovation in cycling has evolved from the invention of safety bicycles to technological advancements in sports science. Maximizing the potential benefits of these developments requires critical thinking to enhance the training and performance of modern cyclists.

Glossary:

***wearables** - technological devices worn on the body for data collection

Sources (edited):

JSC Journal - 'https://www.jsc- journal.com/index.php/JSC/article/view/795/732,'

MNOPEDIA - 'https://www.mnopedia.org/event/bicycling-craze-1890s, (*404 words*) **(CBSE APQ, 2023)**

Answer the following questions based on the passage above.

(*i*) What is the passage mainly about? **(1)**

A. How did the advancement of sports science impact the fashion industry?

B. What were the primary societal changes brought about by the rise of bicycles?

C. How did the invention of the safety bicycle contribute to the development of wearable technology?

D. In what ways did early versions of bicycles differ from the safety bicycle in the late nineteenth century?

(*ii*) In which sentence does the author express uncertainty about the use of new technologies in training? **(1)**

A. "...advances in technology have transformed sports science." (paragraph 4)

B. "This data not only encompasses exercise details but also external factors like weather." (paragraph 4)

C. "...just because we can monitor so much information does not mean it is useful." (paragraph 5)

D. "Maximizing the potential benefits of these developments requires critical thinking." (paragraph 6)

(*iii*) Complete the sentence appropriately by providing two distinct reasons in the blank below. **(1)**

It can be said the world of cycling has seen massive changes because ____________________.

(*iv*) Which of these is opposite to 'invalid' as used in paragraph 5? **(1)**

A. ethical B. accurate

C. authentic D. trustworthy

(*v*) Using information solely from the passage, provide two distinct reasons to complete the sentence appropriately. **(1)**

Bicycles can be seen as a symbol of empowerment because ____________.

(*vi*) Imagine you are a sports scientist tasked with developing a new technological tool to aid cyclists in their training. Provide a brief description, within 40 words, of its specific features and why you chose to include them. **(2)**

(*vii*) Select the option that shows the correct relationship between (1) and (2). **(2)**

(1) Cyclists were able to improve the accuracy of maps.

(2) Cyclists became influential and campaigned for better infrastructure.

A. (2) is a contradiction of (1)

B. (2) is independent of (1)

C. (2) is an example of (1)

D. (2) is the cause of (1)

(*viii*) Below are statements from cyclists. Identify two statements that could be said by a cyclist in the late nineteenth century. **(2)**

1. "I like having a personal coach on my wrist. It just told me how many calories I have burned so far!"
2. "It's quite a struggle riding up these steep hills on my heavy steel- framed bicycle."
3. "I feel so liberated whenever I hop on my bicycle. I didn't have freedom like this before!"
4. "Ugh, there is so much traffic ahead. And I feel so pressured to meet my performance targets every time I hop on a bike."

Passage-V

Read the passage given below. (10 marks)

1. Keep your watch accurate. For some people, moving up the time on their watch will help them get up earlier. For others, they will remember that the time on the watch is wrong and will disregard it altogether. It may be helpful to set your watch just two minutes ahead instead of five or ten.
2. Keep a clock, phone, computer or anything that displays time in each room of your house. One of the easiest ways to run late is simply by not realising that the time is passing as quickly as it is.
3. Set all your clocks and watches to the same time. Don't be an optimist. Things usually take Longer than what you'd expect, even without major delays. If you have a dinner appointment at 7:30 p.m., don't think you can work till 7 p.m., then take a bath, dress and reach on time. Realistically, calculate the time you will take at each step and then add 10 minutes more to allow for unexpected delays, or you cannot get to your job done in time.
4. Wake up when you are supposed to wake up. Don't hit the snooze button, keep on lying in bed, and watch TV at the very start of your day. May be you can try even setting your clock 10 minutes earlier than you need. If you have difficulty with this, move your alarm clock to somewhere away from your

bed; that way, you will have to get up to turn it off. Commit yourself to being 15 minutes early for everything. If you have to reach your place of work at 8:00, don't even tell yourself this. Just tell yourself (and everyone else who listens—but don't annoy them or make them think that they are late or early!)

"I have to be at work at 7:45." If you do this, you will be on time even with little unforeseen delays. You will be on time even with a traffic jam.

Answer the following questions, based on the passage above.

(*i*) Substitute the word 'unforeseen' with ONE WORD similar in meaning, in the following, sentence from paragraph 4: **(1)**

Just tell yourself "I have to be at work at 7:45." If you do this, you will be on time even with little unforeseen delays.

(*ii*) Infer one reason for being delayed, based on information in paragraph 2. **(2)**

(*iii*) It is good to commit yourself _____ for everything. **(1)**

(*a*) to be late

(*b*) to delay

(*c*) to being 15 minutes early

(*d*) to search the last moment

(*iv*) What does the passage highlight? **(1)**

(*v*) To be punctual we should _____. **(1)**

(*a*) hit the snooze button of the alarm clock

(*b*) get up at the right time

(*c*) start watching TV in the morning

(*d*) keep on lying in bed

(*vi*) Complete the sentence appropriately: **(1)**

"It is important to set all your clocks and watches to the same time in order to _______."

(*vii*) Supply one point to justify the following: **(2)**

"Setting all clocks and watches to the same time help individuals in managing their time effectively."

(*viii*) Which strategy helps individuals manage their time effectively by reducing confusion and enabling accurate scheduling and coordination? **(1)**

(*a*) Keeping a clock, phone, or computer in each room

(*b*) Setting all clocks and watches to the same time

(*c*) Waking up on time without hitting the snooze button

(*d*) Being 15 minutes early for everything

Passage-VI

Read the passage given below. **(10 marks)**

1. Fossil fuels (oil, coal, and natural gas) are our most traditional sources for power generation. The energy that's produced from any source other than fossil fuels is termed as alternative energy. Between the two sources, using alternative energy has a lower environmental impact.
2. We now know that alternative energy sources are the sources we use to supplement or even replace traditional energy sources used for power generation. You could almost say the same thing about renewable energy sources. But there is one subtle difference between the two. All renewable energy sources fall under the category of alternative energy sources, but it doesn't work the other way around.
3. That's because renewable energy sources are derived from naturally replenished sources or processes of Earth, such as the sun, wind, and water. We refer to these resources as renewable or sustainable since, unlike fossil fuels, this naturally occurring continual renewal makes them inexhaustible. However, alternative energy sources are exhaustible, and therefore not renewable. That's the difference !
4. The equipment necessary to harness energy from alternative sources used to be so expensive that it wasn't practical for consumer use. However, thanks to increased demand, more experienced energy developers, competitive supply chains, improved renewable technologies, and enhanced energy efficiency capabilities, that's no longer the case.
5. When it comes to energy efficiency, the leader of the renewable energy pack is wind energy. Behind wind comes geothermal energy, hydropower, nuclear energy, and then solar power. Wind power serves both individuals and entire communities. It is versatile, and can be produced from small-scale windmills or wind turbines on residential properties. It can also be produced from large-scale offshore wind farms in the ocean.
6. We generate geothermal power by tapping into underground reservoirs of hot water and steam. Geothermal electricity can directly heat and cool buildings. Generated from the energy of moving water, hydroelectricity (also known as hydropower) is produced when water behind a dam causes turbine blades to move as it flows through an intake. The turbine blades then rotate a generator to produce electricity that is sent to power homes.
7. Nuclear energy is created in the form of heat through the fission process of atoms. The initial fission process creates energy and triggers a chain reaction that repeats the process and generates more energy. In nuclear power plants, the heat that fission produces creates steam. The steam then rotates a turbine, which leads to the production of electricity.
8. Solar power most commonly refers to the use of solar cells to create energy. On a small scale, you may see a few solar panels on a house roof used to produce energy for just that one home. On a larger scale, you may see a solar farm used as a power plant to produce electricity for its consumers. **(CBSE, 2024)**

Answer the following questions, based on the above passage:

(*i*) Which of the following statements best describes the difference between renewable energy sources and alternate energy sources? **(1)**

(*a*) Alternative energy sources are more expensive than renewable energy sources.

(*b*) Renewable energy sources are inexhaustible whereas alternate energy sources could be exhaustible.

(*c*) Alternative energy sources are as renewable as renewable energy sources.

(*d*) Renewable energy sources are exhaustible but alternative energy sources are inexhaustible.

(ii) What is the tone of the writer in the given lines from para (4)? Rationalise your response in about 40 words. **(2)**

"However, thanks to increased demand, more experienced energy developers, competitive supply chains, improved renewable technologies, and enhanced energy efficiency capabilities, that's no longer the case".

(iii) Complete the sentence appropriately: **(1)**

In the past, alternative energy sources were not used much by the consumers because ________.

(iv) The passage includes some words that are opposites of each other. From the sets (a) to (e) below, identify two sets of antonyms: **(1)**

(a) generate and produce

(b) exhaustible and inexhaustible

(c) subtle and versatile

(d) power and energy

(e) sustainable and exhaustible

(v) Who is the leader of renewable energy pack and why? **(1)**

(vi) Based on the reading of the passage, examine, in about 40 words, the difference between geothermal electricity and hydroelectricity. **(2)**

(vii) What is the message conveyed by the passage? **(1)**

(a) Only those energy sources should be used which are renewable.

(b) Wind energy is a renewable as well as inexhaustible source of energy.

(c) There are plenty of renewable energy sources that can be used to replace traditional energy sources.

(d) Alternative energy sources are the emerging energy trends and are still evolving.

(viii) State whether the following statement is **True** or **False** with reference to the given extract. **(1)**

Hydroelectricity as a renewable energy source is used for residential as well as commercial purposes.

Passage-VII

Read the passage given below. (10 marks)

1. The invention of the safety bicycle in the late nineteenth century transformed the world of cycling. While early versions of bicycles had been used in Europe since the seventeenth century, it was the safety bicycle with its lightweight hollow steel frame and equal-sized wheels that revolutionised the cycling experience.

2. This resulted in enhanced mobility for both men and women, allowing them to explore the countryside freely and travel between towns. Bicycles symbolised freedom, particularly for women, granting them self-reliable transportation and the ability to participate in recreational activities, like bicycle racing. The rise of bicycles also brought a shift in fashion, with more functional and relaxed clothing tailored specifically for cycling.

3. Bicyclists also became a political force. They played a significant role in the development of road maps, guiding riders along the best routes. They campaigned for better infrastructure to enhance their riding experiences.

4. Today, advances in technology, ***wearables**** and complex data analysis have transformed sports science, particularly in endurance sports, like cycling. Cyclists can now gather vast amounts of data simply by using mobile apps to track their activities. This data not only encompasses exercise details, like its volume or intensity, but also external factors like the impact of weather on the physiological response of the athlete. Furthermore, technology has made it very easy to monitor performance-influencing data outside of training, such as heart rate or sleep quality, through various wearables and cost-effective mobile apps.

5. However, just because we are able to monitor so much information does not mean that it is useful for improving the sports performance of our athletes. In this sense, we believe that we must be critical while adopting any new technologies or trends in training. The first thing we should know is whether there is scientific support for the use of that new gadget or wearable. For example, core temperature is of great importance in the mechanisms that produce fatigue and exhaustion in endurance sports. A few years ago, a device came on the market that estimated this measurement in a non-invasive way and we saw many top cyclists and runners wearing it. However, a study later showed it is an invalid device for measuring one's temperature.

6. Innovation in cycling has evolved from the invention of safety bicycles to technological advancements in sports science. Maximizing the potential benefits of these developments requires critical thinking to enhance the training and performance of modern cyclists.

Glossary:

***wearables** - technological devices worn on the body for data collection

Sources (edited):

JSC Journal - 'https://www.jsc- journal.com/index.php/JSC/article/view/795/732,'

MNOPEDIA - 'https://www.mnopedia.org/event/bicycling-craze-1890s, (*404 words*)

Answer the following questions, based on the above passage:

(i) What is the passage mainly about? **(1)**

(a) How did the advancement of sports science impact the fashion industry?

(b) What were the primary societal changes brought about by the rise of bicycles?

(c) How did the invention of the safety bicycle contribute to the development of wearable technology?

(d) In what ways did early versions of bicycles differ from the safety bicycle in the late nineteenth century?

(*ii*) In which sentence does the author express uncertainty about the use of new technologies in training? **(1)**

(*a*) "...advances in technology have transformed sports science." (paragraph 4)

(*b*) "This data not only encompasses exercise details but also external factors like weather." (paragraph 4)

(*c*) "...just because we can monitor so much information does not mean it is useful." (paragraph 5)

(*d*) "Maximizing the potential benefits of these developments requires critical thinking." (paragraph 6)

(*iii*) Complete the sentence appropriately by providing two distinct reasons in the blank below. **(1)**

It can be said the world of cycling has seen massive changes because ________.

(*iv*) Which of these is opposite to 'invalid' as used in paragraph 5? **(1)**

(*a*) ethical

(*b*) accurate

(*c*) authentic

(*d*) trustworthy

(*v*) Using information solely from the passage, provide two distinct reasons to complete the sentence appropriately. **(1)**

Bicycles can be seen as a symbol of empowerment because ____________.

(*vi*) Imagine you are a sports scientist tasked with developing a new technological tool to aid cyclists in their training. Provide a brief description, within 40 words, of its specific features and why you chose to include them. **(2)**

(*vii*) Select the option that shows the correct relationship between (1) and (2). **(1)**

(1) Cyclists were able to improve the accuracy of maps.

(2) Cyclists became influential and campaigned for better infrastructure.

(*a*) (2) is a contradiction of (1)

(*b*) (2) is independent of (1)

(*c*) (2) is an example of (1)

(*d*) (2) is the cause of (1)

(*viii*) Below are statements from cyclists. Identify two statements that could be said by a cyclist in the late nineteenth century. **(2)**

(*a*) "I like having a personal coach on my wrist. It just told me how many calories I have burned so far!"

(*b*) "It's quite a struggle riding up these steep hills on my heavy steel- framed bicycle."

(*c*) "I feel so liberated whenever I hop on my bicycle. I didn't have freedom like this before!"

(*d*) "Ugh, there is so much traffic ahead. And I feel so pressured to meet my performance targets every time I hop on a bike."

CASE BASED PASSAGE

Passage-I

Read the passage given below: **(10 × 1 = 10)**

(1) Starting Monday, the country's low-cost Mars mission with the red planet for an extended period will enter the "blackout" phase snapping communication with the satellite. From June 8 to 22 the Sun will block Mars from the Earth snapping communication with the satellite.

(2) A senior Indian Space Research Organisation official said. "This will be for the first time that there will be a communication break for such a long period of about 15 days. During this period, there will be no communication with the satellite", he added.

(3) Expressing confidence about regaining control over the satellite once the blackout phase is over, he said, "the scenario has been tested and the line of communication will be established." The spacecraft's life has been extended for another six months in March due to surplus fuel.

(4) Stating that the spacecraft has been "configured" for the blackout, the ISRO official said, "we are not sending any commands to the spacecraft now, till 8th June few hours of signals will be sent by the spacecraft that will be for about two to three hours per day". In May next year, the mission will have to go through a similar phase once again, if there is another extension of mission life when the Earth will come between the Sun and Mars.

(5) Scripting space history, India on September 24 last successfully placed its low-cost Mars spacecraft in orbit around the red planet in its very first attempt, breaking into an elite club of three countries. **(CBSE, 2023)**

Answer the following questions, based on the passage above.

(*i*) Infer one reason for the following based on information in paragraph 1.

The 'blackout' phase is significant__________.

(*ii*) Choose the appropriate option to fill in the blank.

From paragraph 1 & 2, we can infer that there will be __________.

1. no communication with the people.
2. blackout phase.
3. satellite will get no communication.
4. moon will block the earth.
5. the communication break will be for 15 days.

(*a*) 1, 2 & 3 (*b*) 1, 3 & 4

(*c*) 2, 3 & 5 (*d*) 3, 4 & 5

(*iii*) The communication with the satellite will break for approximately ________ days.

(*a*) 10 (*b*) 15

(*c*) 20 (*d*) 25

(*iv*) Complete the following analogy correctly with a word/ phrase from paragraph 2:

aroma: cooking::__________: space research

(Clue – just like aroma is integral to cooking, similarly______ is/are integral to Space Research.)

(*v*) According to ISRO official till 8th July, when Sun will block Mars, _____ signal/signals per day will be sent to the spacecraft.

(*a*) no

(*b*) considerable

(*c*) indefinite

(*d*) only for few

(*vi*) Select the correct option to complete the following sentence:

The ISRO officials are _____ about their control over the spacecraft after the blackout phase.

(*a*) doubtful (*b*) apprehensive

(*c*) confident (*d*) jittery

(*vii*) The spacecraft's life was extended by six months because of

(*a*) extra fuel

(*b*) incomplete work

(*c*) lack of communication amongst ISRO officials

(*d*) technical problems in its landing

(*viii*) Read the following sentences:

(A) The blackout was a sudden development.

(B) Because of this, the officials are very nervous about the success of the spacecraft.

(*a*) Both (A) & (B) are true.

(*b*) Both (A) & (B) are false.

(*c*) (A) is true and (B) is false.

(*d*) (A) is false and (B) is true.

(*ix*) Substitute the word 'nonpareil' with one word similar in meaning in the following sentence from paragraph 5.

India managed to get into the nonpareil club of Mars spacecraft in orbit.

(*x*) The word 'fascination' in the opening sentence means the same as

(*a*) enchantment (*b*) boredom

(*c*) disinterest (*d*) ugliness

Passage-II

Read the passage given below. (10 marks)

1. The Battle of Chancellorsville, one of the most famous battles of the Civil War, took place in Virginia in the spring of 1863. For months, the two armies had been staked out on opposite banks of a narrow river. The Confederate troops were led by perhaps the most revered military tactician in American history, General Robert E. Lee. The Union soldiers were led by "Fighting" Joe Hooker.

2. In appearance, personality, and lifestyle, these men were nearly perfect opposites. Lee, an older man in poor health with a gray beard, had a somber, measured demeanor. Hooker was a blond, strapping young man whose vanity over his appearance was but one aspect of his egotism. Whereas Lee was devout and principled, Hooker was known for his rollicking enjoyment.

3. Despite the fact that the Confederacy had won the last four major battles and the Union soldiers were famished, exhausted, and demoralized, Hooker proclaimed, "My plans are perfect. And when I start to carry them out, may God have mercy on Bobby Lee, for I shall have none." Why, aside from a propensity for narcissism, was Hooker so confident?

4. Hooker had used spies, analysts, and even hot air balloons to compile a vast amount of intelligence about Lee's army. He had discerned, for example, that Lee had only 61,000 men to Hooker's own 134,000. Buoyed by his superior numbers, Hooker covertly moved 70,000 of his men fifteen miles up and across the river, and then ordered them to sneak back down to position themselves behind Lee's army. In effect, Hooker had cut off the Confederate soldiers in front and behind. They were trapped. Satisfied with his advantage, Hooker became convinced that Lee's only option was to retreat to Richmond, thus assuring a Union victory.

5. Yet Lee, despite his disadvantages of both numbers and position, did not retreat. Instead, he moved his troops into position to attack. Union soldiers who tried to warn Hooker that Lee was on the offensive were dismissed as cowards. Having become convinced that Lee had no choice but to retreat, Hooker began to ignore reality. When Lee's army attacked the Union soldiers at 5:00 p.m., they were eating supper, completely unprepared for battle. They abandoned their rifles and fled as Lee's troops came shrieking out of the brush, bayonets drawn. Against all odds, Lee won the Battle of Chancellorsville, and Hooker's forces withdrew in defeat.

Casualties at the Battle of Chancellorsville

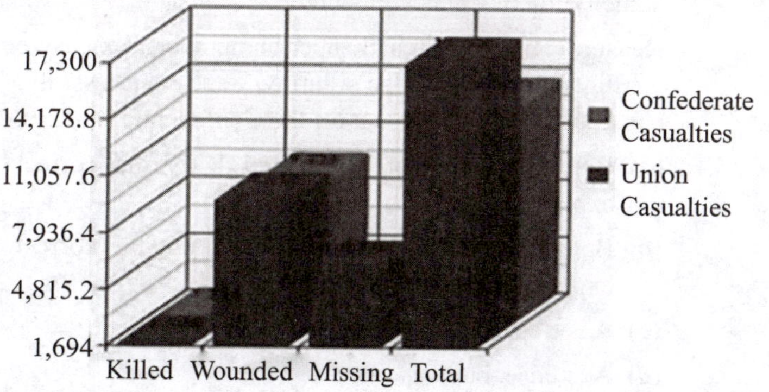

Answer the following questions, based on the passage above.

(*i*) What characterized the opposing commanders, General Robert E. Lee and "Fighting" Joe Hooker? **(1)**

(*a*) Lee was an older man in poor health, while Hooker was a young and vigorous individual.

(*b*) Lee was known for his vanity and appearance, while Hooker had a measured demeanor.

(*c*) Lee was a blond, strapping young man, while Hooker had a grey beard and somber personality.

(*d*) Lee was a devout and principled leader, while Hooker was known for his enjoyment and rollicking nature.

(*ii*) What were the key factors that contributed to General Hooker's defeat in the Battle of Chancellorsville? **(1)**

(*iii*) What factors contributed to General Hooker's confidence and his underestimation of General Lee's capabilities in the Battle of Chancellorsville? **(2)**

(*iv*) What was the outcome of the Battle of Chancellorsville? **(1)**

(*a*) Lee's forces retreated, securing a Union victory.

(*b*) Hooker's troops emerged victorious, inflicting a defeat on Lee.

(*c*) The battle ended in a stalemate with neither side achieving a clear victory.

(*d*) Against the odds, Lee won the battle, and Hooker's forces withdrew in defeat.

(*v*) Who was the Confederate general that General Hooker underestimated in the Battle of Chancellorsville? **(1)**

(*vi*) What does the term "rollicking" mean in this context? **(1)**

(*vii*) Supply one point to justify the following: **(1)**

"General Hooker's overconfidence in the Battle of Chancellorsville was fueled by his numerical advantage over General Lee."

(*viii*) Complete the line appropriately: **(1)**

"Hooker had used spies, analysts, and even hot air balloons__________."

(*ix*) Select the option that is true for the Assertion and Reason given below: **(1)**

Assertion (A): General Hooker was confident of victory at the Battle of Chancellorsville.

Reason (R): Hooker had superior numbers, extensive intelligence about Lee's army, and successfully positioned his troops to cut off the Confederate soldiers.

(*a*) Both A and R are true, and R is the correct explanation of A.

(*b*) Both A and R are true, but R is not the correct explanation of A.

(*c*) A is true, but R is false.

(*d*) A is false, but R is true.

Passage-III

Read the passage given below. (10 marks)

The UN's 2017 International Year tells that sustainable tourism is an important tool for development, most importantly in poor communities and countries. Today sustainability – environmental, social, and economic - is increasingly recognised as the benchmark for all tourism business. As noted by the UN World Tourism Organisation, 57% of international tourist arrivals will be in emerging economies, by 2030. The various "Tourism Terms" are defined as follows:

CATEGORY	DEFINITION
Ecotourism	Responsible travel to natural areas that conserves the environment, socially and economically sustains the well-being of local people, and creates knowledge and understanding through inter- pretation and education of all involved (including staff, travelers, and community residents)."
Ethical Tourism	Tourism in a destination where ethical issues are the key driver, e.g. social injustice, human rights, animal welfare, or the environment."
Geotourism	Tourism that sustains or enhances the geographical character of a place - its environment, heritage, aesthetics, culture, and well-being of its residents."
Pro-Poor Tourism	Tourism that results in increased net benefit for the poor people in a destination."
Responsible Tourism	Tourism that maximizes the benefits to local communities, minimizes negative social or environmental impacts, and helps local people conserve fragile cultures and habitats or species."
Sustainable Tourism	Tourism that leads to the management of all resources in such a way that economic, social, and aesthetic needs can be fulfilled while maintaining cultural integrity, essential ecological processes, biological diversity, and life-support systems.

Based on data collected by a survey by Travel Bureau, the following market profile of an ecotourist was constructed:

Age: 35-54 years old, although age varied with activity and other factors such as cost. Gender: 50% female and 50% male, although clear differences based on activity were found.

Education: 82% were college graduates, a shift in interest in ecotourism from those who have high levels of education to those with less education was also found, indicating an ex-pansion into mainstream markets.

Household composition: No major differences were found between general tourists and experienced ecotourists (Tourists that had been on at least one "ecotourism" oriented trip.)

Party composition: A majority (60%) of experienced ecotourism respondents stated they prefer to travel as a couple, with only 15% stating they preferred to travel with their families, and 13% preferring to travel alone.

Trip duration: The largest group of experienced ecotourists-(50%) preferred trips lasting 8-14 days.

Expenditure: Experienced ecotourists were willing to spend more than general tourists, the largest group (26%).

Important elements of trip: Experienced ecotourists top three responses were: (*a*) wilderness setting, (*b*) wildlife viewing, (*c*) hiking/trekking.

Motivations for taking next trip: Experienced ecotourists top two responses were (*a*) enjoy scenery/nature, (*b*) new experiences/places.

Answer the following questions, based on the passage above.

(*i*) Complete the line appropriately: **(1)**

"The survey clearly showed that the age range of ecotourists ________________."

(*ii*) Who isn't an experienced ecotourist? **(1)**

(*iii*) According to the survey conducted by the Travel Bureau, the total percentage of experienced ecotourists who DID NOT prefer to travel alone was __________. **(1)**

(*iv*) Write one of the elements that is important to ecotourists on trip. **(1)**

(*v*) In the line "......recognised as the benchmark", the word "benchmark" DOES NOT refer to **(1)**

(*a*) A basis for something.

(*b*) The criterion required.

(*c*) The ability to launch something new.

(*d*) A standard point of reference.

(*vi*) Based on your understanding from the passage, write of the inherent qualities geotourism. **(2)**

(*vii*) Choose the option that lists the correct answers for the following: **(1)**

(*i*) Asha Mathew, an NRI, loves animals and wishes to travel to places that safeguard their rights and inculcate awareness of their rights. What kind of tourist is she?

(*ii*) Gurdeep Singh from UK is an environmental scientist and has always chosen to travel to places that are examples of a symbiotic relationship between man and nature.

What kind of tourist is he?

(*a*) (*i*) is an ecotourist and (*ii*) is a geotourist

(*b*) (*i*) is an ethical tourist and (*ii*) is a geotourist

(*c*) (*i*) is a sustainable tourist and (*ii*) is a pro-poor tourist

(*d*) (*i*) is a geotourist and (*ii*) is a responsible tourist

(*viii*) Ideal duration preferred by experienced tourists for trips: **(1)**

(*a*) Less than 15 days

(*b*) More than 20 days

(*c*) 15 days

(*d*) None of the above

(*ix*) Select the option that is true for the Assertion and Reason given below: **(1)**

Assertion (A): Sustainable tourism is increasingly recognized as the benchmark for all tourism businesses.

Reason (R): Sustainable tourism leads to the management of all resources in a way that fulfills economic, social, and aesthetic needs while maintaining cultural integrity, essential ecological processes, biological diversity, and life-support systems.

(*a*) Both A and R are true, and R is the correct explanation of A.

(*b*) Both A and R are true, but R is not the correct explanation of A.

(*c*) A is true, but R is false.

(*d*) A is false, but R is true.

Passage-IV

Read the following text. (10 marks)

1. Reduction in green areas has caused various environmental problems. People squeezed between concrete structures are looking for various ways to meet their longing for green. One of the ways to do so, is vertical gardens and green walls. Vertical gardening is a unique method of gardening where plants are grown in a vertical position or upward, rather than in the traditional method of planting them on the ground.
2. The purpose of vertical gardens and green walls, which arises from the studies of different disciplines (landscape architects, architects, engineers, etc.), is to close the cold image of concrete and increase the visual value. In these systems, nature and structures are integrated, and thus, urban areas and the desired environment have become intertwined.
3. Vertical garden case studies often show that, though functionality should be in the foreground, when vertical gardens are planned, they are generally made as aesthetic elements in the city's underpasses and city squares, and decorative elements in residences, without seeking functionality.
4. Experts support that the visual quality and evaluation of landscape architecture is determined based on the satisfaction of the users. Hence, a survey questionnaire was prepared for residents of varied age groups from of a metropolitan city. The given **Table 1,** displays these responses:

Table 1 - Total number of participants : 400

No.	Survey statements	Strongly agree	Agree	Neutral	Disagree	Strongly disagree
Vertical gardens-						
1.	improve quality of life of people in urban areas	191	138	43	9	19
2.	reduce noise pollution	128	164	77	25	6
3.	increase air quality–indoors and outdoors	172	147	51	28	2
4.	reduce energy and water consumption	58	47	125	68	2
5.	positively impact global warming	114	144	106	30	6
6.	have a relaxing and calming effect	161	177	44	7	11
7.	cost too much	86	107	152	42	13
8.	make plants look beautiful	195	139	44	6	16
9.	add naturalness to the environs	135	173	55	25	12
10.	are among the determining factor to visiting a place	59	133	141	54	13
11.	are inconvenient indoors	9	84	123	126	48
12.	can be applied in every place	71	132	97	77	23
13.	have a functional feature	81	207	100	10	2
14.	distract drivers	34	101	106	131	28
15.	funds are best used for social issues	57	72	100	130	41

5. The study acknowledged that vertical gardening has the potential to transform urban spaces into green, sustainable areas, and further research should explore the impact of vertical gardening on the environment and human well-being.

Adapted for academic usage - 2019 case-study -Investigating the vertical garden applications in Turkey 225 words approx.

(CBSE SQP, 2023)

Answer the following questions, based on the passage above

(*i*) Complete the following analogy appropriately, based on your understanding of paragraphs 1 & 2. **(1)**

We can say that the situation of people living in concrete structures is comparable with a fish living in a fishbowl, and the need for vertical gardens to the need for decorations in the fishbowl because ______________.

(*ii*) Fill the blanks with the appropriate option from those given in brackets, based on your understanding of paragraph 2. **(1)**

The statement that , urban spaces have become more closely connected with the desired natural surroundings through the incorporation of nature and structures in vertical gardens and green walls, is a __________ (fact/opinion) because it is a ____________ (subjective judgement/objective detail).

(*iii*) Justify the following, in about 40 words. **(2)**

While the survey results suggest that vertical gardens may be effective in improving the quality of life in urban areas, further research and evaluation may be necessary to fully understand their effectiveness and potential drawbacks.

(*iv*) Based on the survey results, which two concerns should a city government, looking to install vertical gardens, address? **(1)**

(*v*) In Table 1, the statement 3, "*Vertical gardens increase air quality - indoors and outdoors,*" received the most neutral responses from participants, with 51 respondents indicating a neutral stance. State any one inference that can be drawn from this. **(1)**

(*vi*) Select the option that correctly displays what 'intertwined' signifies. (Reference-Paragraph 2) **(1)**

(*i*)

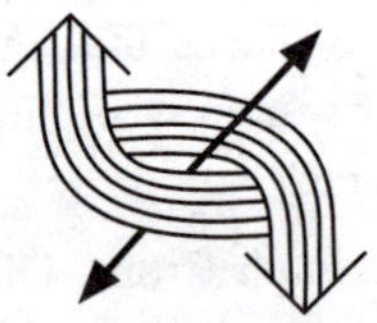
(*ii*)

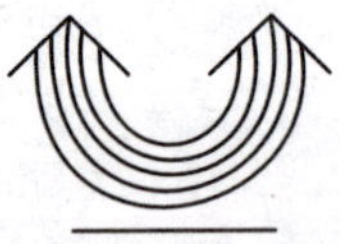
(*iii*)

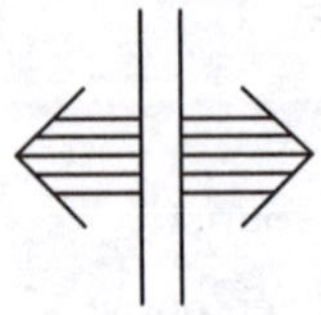
(*iv*)

(*v*)

A. (*i*), (*iv*) and (*v*)
B. Only (*ii*)
C. Only (*iii*)
D. (*ii*) and (*v*)

(*vii*) Infer one benefit and one drawback of vertical gardening, in comparison to other solutions, such as community gardens or parks. (Answer in about 40 words) **(2)** (*viii*) Which of the following is the main takeaway from the study mentioned in the passage? **(1)**

A. Vertical gardening has minimal impact on the environment or human well-being.

B. Vertical gardening is a sustainable practice that can transform urban spaces into green areas.

C. The impact of vertical gardening on the environment and human well-being has already been thoroughly explored.

D. The study needs to include experts from horticultural firms to offer any recommendations for further research.

Passage-V

Read the passage given below. **(10 marks)**

1. As the virus began to spread around the world, some Indians began to return home, to relative safety. When Kerala registered India's first COVID-19 case on 30th January, 2020 (IDFC Institute, 2020), the state was prepared. Four days before registering its first case, Government of Kerala (GoK) had already released novel corona virus-specific guidelines that established case definitions, screening and sampling protocol, hospital preparedness and surveillance.
2. The rapid screening and quarantining of patients and isolation of their contacts delayed the transmission from imported cases for up to 40 days, until Kerala witnessed its first cluster outbreak in the district of Pathanamthitta. A total of 14 confirmed cases were registered over the two days that followed.
3. Given the early spread of the virus in Kerala, it is commendable that the state had two consecutive days of zero new cases over the 100- day period from the day it registered the first case of COVID-19. Given its relatively efficient public health care systems, backed by strong socio-economic foundation and the experience of previously handling the Nipah virus in 2018, the State was able to act swiftly.
4. Kerala's public healthcare system is decentralized with facilities at the state, district, sub-district, panchayat, and ward level. The field-level staff including health inspectors, ASHA workers.
5. Coordination at the middle level was largely done by the District Collectors who worked in close coordination with the District Medical Officers and the district -level heads of the police. One of the flagship measures adopted by the State was the development of COVID First Line Treatment Centers and COVID-19 Care Centers.

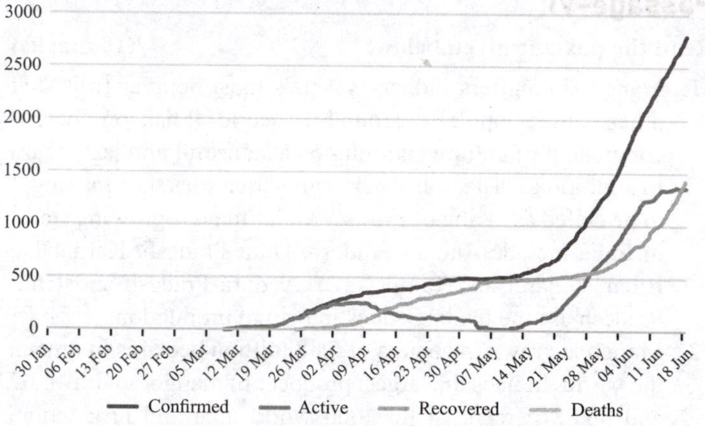

COVID-19 Kerala Graph, January-June 2020

Answer the following questions, based on the passage above.

(*i*) Select the option that gives the correct meaning of the following statement. **(1)**

"Kerala's public healthcare system is decentralised with facilities at the state, district, sub-district, panchayat and ward level'.

(*a*) It's not just the state that is responsible but every level.

(*b*) The state is solely responsible for the healthcare system.

(*c*) The Centre is solely responsible for the healthcare system.

(*d*) None of the above

(*ii*) Who did the District Collectors work with in coordination? **(1)**

(*iii*) List the steps taken by the Kerala Government to contain the spread of the virus. **(1)**

(*iv*) According to the passage, for how many days there was no case of corona virus in Kerala after the first case was registered? **(1)**

(*v*) Write two measures adopted by the state of Kerala. **(2)**

(*vi*) The passage suggests that ________ allowed Kerala to conduct mass screeni~gs and tests. **(1)**

(*a*) Local testing labs

(*b*) District-wise allocations

(*c*) Walk-in simple kiosks

(*d*) All of these

(*vii*) Kerala could act swiftly during Corona virus pandemic due to its previous experience of handling ________. **(1)**

(*viii*) Find the word from the passage which means the same as 'keeping separated from others'. **(1)**

(*ix*) **Assertion (A):** Kerala was able to delay the transmission of COVID-19 from imported cases for up to 40 days.

Reason (R): The state implemented rapid screening, quarantining of patients, and isolation of their contacts, which helped control the spread of the virus.

(*a*) Both A and R are true, and R is the correct explanation of A.

(*b*) Both A and R are true, but R is not the correct explanation of A.

(*c*) A is true, but R is false.

(*d*) A is false, but R is true.

Passage-VI

Read the passage given below. **(10 marks)**

1. India is a country of many languages. The constitution recognises 22 languages officially, but over 121 unique languages have been identified in the country.
2. To preserve and encourage the literary function of language, the government introduced 'classical languages' in 2004. According to the Ministry of Culture, a classical language is one that is at least 1,500 years old and has ancient, valuable literature recorded in it. Further, such a language is original and not derived from another language. Based on these guidelines, six languages have been classified as classical languages: Tamil, Sanskrit, Kannada, Telugu, Malayalam and Odia.

3. The following graph shows the percentage of Indian people whose mother tongue is a classical language. This is as per data collected by the ***census*** of 2011. The census was not conducted in 2021 due to the pandemic.

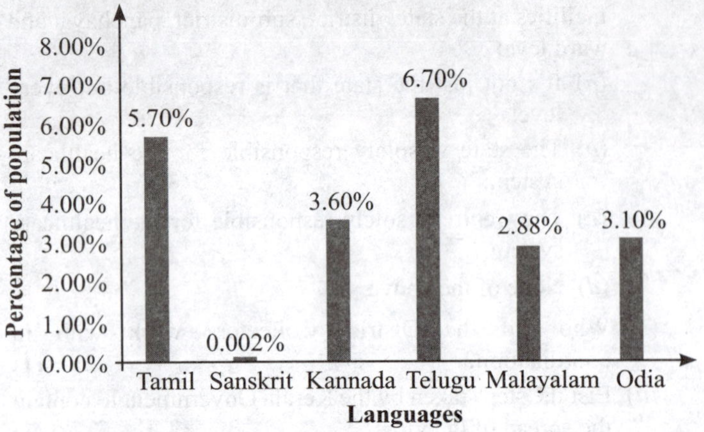

4. According to the graph, around 6.7% of the Indian population are native speakers of Telugu, whereas Sanskrit has been identified as a mother tongue by only 0.002% of the population, which is around 24,821 people. Malayalam has the second lowest number of native speakers, making up about 2.9% of Indians.

5. The 2011 census data also noted that a majority of the native speakers reside in the area that their mother tongue originated from. For example, 93% of Kannada speakers live in Karnataka. Similarly, 93% of Malayalam speakers live in Kerala.

6. Balancing preservation of culture and inclusivity is a delicate equation for a heterogeneous country like India. With growing awareness, concepts like 'classical languages' may help us achieve harmony.

Glossary:

census - a survey that is conducted every ten years to collect information about the population of the country

Source (Edited):

'Explainer: What are classical languages of India?' -https://factly.in/explainer-what- are-classical-languages-of-india/

(*258 words*)

Answer the following questions, based on the passage above.

(*i*) Which of these pieces of information can be confirmed by reading the passage? **(1)**

(I) the number of people in India who speak Tamil

(II) where the majority of native Sanskrit speakers live

(III) the reason Malayalam is considered a classical language

(IV) when the idea of classical languages was introduced in India

(*a*) Only I (*b*) Only IV

(*c*) Only I and II (*d*) Only III and IV

(*ii*) Fill in the blanks with the appropriate option from those given in brackets. **(1)**

Based on the passage, the ____________ (functional/historical) value of a language is of utmost importance while (preserving/categorising) it as a classical language.

(*iii*) Imagine that a committee was formed to ensure that classical languages have more native speakers by the time the next census is conducted. In 40 words, answer the following questions to help the committee achieve its objective. **(2)**

(1) Which classical language needs its attention most urgently and why?

(2) Which classical language would be THIRD on its priority?

(*iv*) State an example from the passage that shows that India is a *'heterogeneous country'*. Answer in one sentence. **(1)**

(*v*) Why has the writer stated the following line in the passage? Give a reason. **(1)**

The census was not conducted in 2021 due to the pandemic.

(*vi*) Complete the sentence based on information from the passage. **(1)**

If Tamil originated from Tamil Nadu, we can infer that ______ of the native Tamil speakers would be living in Tamil Nadu.

(*vii*) Which of these hypothetical situations would help India achieve harmony? Justify your answer in about 40 words. **(2)**

(*a*) if the majority of Indians who speak a classical language are settled abroad

(*b*) if more languages from remote and tribal areas of India are identified as classical languages

(*c*) if the percentage of Indians who are native Telugu speakers increases to more than 10 percent

(*viii*) Which of these sentences uses 'delicate' in the same way as paragraph (6) does? **(1)**

(*a*) She looked beautiful in the dress with the delicate floral pattern.

(*b*) He was frequently admitted to the hospital due to his delicate health.

(*c*) This discussion will require careful consideration as it is a delicate matter.

(*d*) Please handle these delicate items carefully during transportation as they break easily.

Passage-VI

Read the passage given below. (10 marks)

1. Mango (Mangifera indica) is Asia's most popular fruit, and it has gained popularity around the world. It has long been a component of culture and religion as a useful and tasty fruit. In addition to taste, it has many good qualities thus making it to be called as "King of Fruits". Major mango-growing states in India include Andhra Pradesh, Uttar Pradesh, Karnataka, Bihar, Gujarat and Tamil Nadu. Andhra Pradesh and Uttar Pradesh are the leading states in mango production.

2. Mango is grown in an area of 5.58 million hectares of area in the world. India is the largest producer of mangoes with 46.02 and 45.88 percent of the total world area and production, respectively. However, India being the major shareholder in

terms of mango production, exports only 0.52% of its total production indicating the huge gap in exporting of mangoes. Peru exports about 46%, Thailand 24%, Mexico 18% and Brazil 11% of their total mango production. These countries are the bigger challenges for Indian mango exports. Hence, efforts are needed to evolve cheap transportation mechanism, enhance the productivity.

3. The top importing country is United States of America, however India exports only two percent of its total exports to the USA. The USA, European countries, the UK, Malaysia and Russia can be the other hotspots where India can target to export the mangoes. The critical issue for exporting to the USA is transportation cost (due to sea route distance) and limited shelf life of mango, while for Europe transportation costs as well as competition by African countries are the major hurdles. The following chart shows the major export destinations of Indian mangoes in 2019-20: **(CBSE, 2024)**

Table:

Major Export Destination of Indian Mangoes in 2019-20:

S. No.	Country	Percentage
1.	U.S.A.	2
2.	Kuwait	2
3.	Saudi Arabia	3
4.	Qatar	6
5.	Bangladesh	6
6.	Oman	7
7.	U.K.	9
8.	Nepal	24
9.	United Arab Emirates	33
10.	Bahrain	2
11.	Others	6

(Adapted for academic usage.)

Answer the following questions, based on the passage above:

(*i*) Complete the following analogy appropriately, based on your understanding of Para (1): **(1)**

We can say that for becoming the king of jungle, Lion has to be the strongest, bravest and the fiercest. Similarly, Mango is known as the king of fruits because __________.

(*ii*) Fill in the blanks with the appropriate option from those given in brackets, based on your understanding of Para (2): **(1)**

The statement that, India is the largest producer of Mangoes with 45.88 percent of the total world production can be attributed to Indian orchardists, is (fact/opinion) because it is ________ a/an (subjective judgement/ objective detail)

(*iii*) Justify the following in about 40 words: **(1)**

India being the major shareholder in terms of mango production, exports only 0.52% of its total production.

(*iv*) Based on the table, which three countries were at par with each other in terms of mango import from India in 2019-20? **(1)**

(*v*) The top mango importing country is the U.S.A., however, India exports only two percent of its total exports to the U.S.A. State any one inference that can be drawn from this. **(1)**

(*vi*) In the given sentence taken from para-2, select the option that correctly replaces the underlined word, with its most likely antonym. **(1)**

These countries are the bigger challenges for Indian mango exports.

(*a*) enigmas (*b*) solutions

(*c*) provocations (*d*) disputes

(*vii*) Why is India described as the largest producer of mangoes in the world? (Answer in about 40 words.) **(2)**

(*viii*) Which of the following is the main takeaway from the study mentioned in the passage? **(1)**

(*a*) India needs to produce more mangoes so that more can be exported.

(*b*) The UAE imported most mangoes from India in 2019-20.

(*c*) India is the largest producer of mangoes and by putting in more efforts, has the potential to be the largest exporter too.

(*d*) More study is needed to find ways to increase the export of mangoes from India.

Passage-VIII

Read the passage given below. **(10 marks)**

1. According to a new study, a vast blanket of pollution stretching across South Asia is cutting down sunlight by 10 per cent over India, damaging agriculture, modifying rainfall patterns and putting hundreds of thousands of people at risk.

2. It is said, "Acids in the haze may, by falling as acid rain, have the potential to damage crops and trees. Ash falling on leaves can aggravate the impact of reduced sunlight on the Earth's surface. The pollution that is forming the haze could be leading to several hundreds of thousands of premature deaths as a result of higher levels of respiratory diseases."

3. "The haze has cut down sunlight over India by 10 per cent (so far) -a huge amount ! As a repercussion, the North-West of India is drying up," Prof. V. Ramanathan said when asked specifically about the impact of the haze over India. He said, "We are still in an early stage of understanding of the impact of the haze."

4. Prof. V. Ramanathan was asked whether the current droughts in most parts of India after over a decade of good monsoons was owing to the haze. He said, "It was too early to reach a conclusion. If the droughts persist for about four to five years, then we would start suspecting that it may be because of the haze." India, China and Indonesia are the worst affected owing to their population density, economic growth and depleting forest cover. **(CBSE, 2023)**

Answer the following questions, based on the passage above:

(*i*) Infer one reason for the following based on the information in paragraph (1):

In India rainfall patterns are changing. **(1)**

(*ii*) The pollution spreading across South Asia is affecting India by __________.: **(1)**

Choose the correct option from the ones given below:

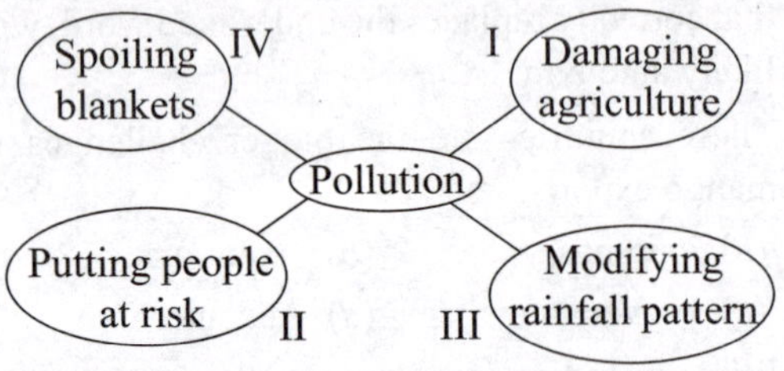

(*a*) I, II and III (*b*) I, III and IV

(*c*) II, III and IV (*d*) I, II and IV

(*iii*) Complete the following analogy correctly with a word/ phrase from paragraph (2): **(1)**

possibility : __________ : : suspecting : doubting

(*iv*) Select the correct option to complete the sentence. **(1)**

__________ droughts were caused by the haze.

(*a*) Strong evidence suggested that

(*b*) Past surveys confirmed that

(*c*) There has not been enough time to determine that

(*d*) Superstitious people believe that

(*v*) From the following pie chart, identify one reason each which does and does not contribute to weather disruption: **(1)**

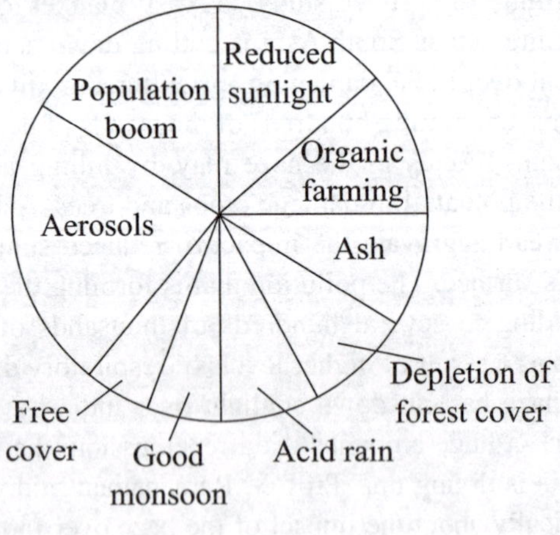

(*vi*) Fill in the blank by selecting the correct option. **(1)**

Ash falling on leaves can __________ the impact of reduced sunlight on the Earth's surface.

(*a*) worsen

(*b*) encourage

(*c*) diminish

(*d*) support

(*vii*) Substitute the word 'repercussion' with one word similar in meaning in the following sentence from paragraph (3). **(1)**

The haze has has cut down sunlight over India ... As a repercussion, the North-West of India is drying up.

(*viii*) List any two countries which are affected due to depleting forest cover. **(1)**

(*ix*) Which of the following mean the same as 'persist' in 'droughts persist' as used in para (4)?

(*a*) destroying (*b*) halting

(*c*) continue (*d*) blocking

(*x*) Which of the following mean the same as 'persist' in 'droughts persist' as used in para (4)? **(1)**

(*a*) 1. Impact of Pollution in South Asia
2. Effects of Acid Rain
3. Understanding Consequences of Haze
4. Debate over Droughts

(*b*) 1. Impact of Droughts
2. Understanding Acid Rain
3. Effect of Haze
4. Debate over Pollution

(*c*) 1. Impact of Pollution in South Asia
2. Effects of Acid Rain
3. Debate over Droughts
4. Understanding Haze

(*d*) 1. Impact of Haze
2. Understanding Acid Rain
3. Debate over Pollution
4. Effect of Haze

ANSWERS & EXPLANATIONS

Discursive Passage

Passage-I

(*i*) (*a*) The act of participating or being involved

(*ii*) Replace "technology" with "innovation" in the passage.

(*iii*) "wasting their time"

(*iv*) (*a*) Interactive learning

(*v*) (*a*) Emotional, creative, and instructional intelligence.

(*vi*) Technology in the classroom enables teachers to introduce new subjects, try different techniques, and use various projects, which creates a more engaging and dynamic learning environment that promotes ongoing curiosity and exploration.

(*vii*) Email in the classroom has improved communication between teachers and parents by providing a reliable and convenient messaging platform for immediate and efficient communication when needed.

(*viii*) Technology in the classroom facilitates seamless communication between teachers and parents, allowing for real-time updates on a child's progress and fostering greater parental involvement in their education.

Passage-II

(*i*) A promising trend in public engagement with historic sites.

(*ii*) The passage states that visitation rates to historic sites fell steadily from 1982 to 2012 and have shown a decline in recent years, indicating a decrease in overall visitation to these sites.

(*iii*) (*c*) Who finished their studies with a high school diploma.

(*iv*) 1. Franklin Delano Roosevelt Memorial

2. World War II Memorial

(*v*) Age group of 75 years or more.

(*vi*) The visitation rates to historic sites have declined overall since 1982 for Americans of virtually all ages, except for the oldest Americans (age 75 or older) who showed a higher rate of visitation in 2017 compared to 35 years earlier.

(*vii*) (*c*) Visitation

(*viii*) Significantly / markedly / considerably / notably

Passage-III

(*i*) (*c*) to hike.

(*ii*) (*d*) because the depressing daily routine is forgotten.

(*iii*) A new meaning and significance to us.

(*iv*) We experience great joy and a sense of connection when we are surrounded by the beauty of nature.

(*v*) Aroma : Cooking :: Fragnance : Flowers

(Hint: Just as aroma is essential to cooking, fragrance is essential to flowers.)

(*vi*) (*b*) because of the excitement of climbing up and adventure of coming down.

(*vii*) (*d*) it is an escape from our busy schedule.

(*viii*) Two examples of the minute observations I notice while hiking:

(*a*) When I go for a hike, I notice the variety of birds.

(*b*) I see how my companions' behaviour changes when they are exhausted.

(*ix*) As per the passage, hiking provides us exposure to the fresh air, beautiful mountains, majestic trees, chirping sound of birds make one's mind and soul at peace with nature. Therefore, it gives us a feeling of unlimitedjoy.

(*x*) cheerful/joyful/excited.

Passage-IV

(*i*) (*B*) What were the primary societal changes brought about by the rise of bicycles?

The passage primarily discusses the societal changes brought about by the rise of bicycles, such as enhanced mobility, greater freedom for women, and a shift in fashion for more functional clothing tailored for cycling.]

(*ii*) (*C*) "...just because we can monitor so much information does not mean it is useful." (paragraph 5)

[In this option, the author expresses uncertainty about the usefulness of the vast amount of data that can be monitored through new technologies. The phrase "does not mean it is useful" shows the author's hesitation and doubt regarding the practical benefits of collecting such extensive data.]

(*iii*) it transitioned from primarily using steel cycles to safety bicycles and saw technological advancements, like wearables in sports science.

(*iv*) (*B*) accurate

[In paragraph 5, the author discusses a device that was deemed 'invalid' for measuring core temperature. Here, 'invalid' means the device is not accurate in providing the intended measurement.

Therefore, the antonym for 'invalid' would be 'accurate', which means to correctly provide information.]

(v) they facilitated women's freedom to commute freely and easily between places and participate in recreational activities like bicycle racing.

(vi) The tool would offer customized training recommendations and plans, integrated GPS for improved navigation, analysis and feedback capabilities, and social features for connecting with fellow cyclists. This comprehensive approach would enhance cyclists' performance by providing tailored training opportunities and fostering a supportive community.

(vii) (D) (2) is the cause of (1)

[(2) indicates that the popularity of cycling provided cyclists with enhanced political influence, which they used to advocate for better infrastructure. With this influence, they were able to improve the accuracy of maps. Therefore, (2) is the cause of (1).]

(viii) 2, 3

Passage-V

(i) Unexpected

(ii) The major reason of delaying is not realizing that the time passes quickly.

(iii) (c) to being 15 minutes early

(iv) The importance of being ahead of time

(v) (b) get up at the right time

(vi) "It is important to set all your clocks and watches to the same time in order to synchronize your timekeeping and ensure consistency and accuracy in time management."

(vii) Setting all clocks and watches to the same time ensures consistency and helps individuals manage their time effectively by reducing confusion and enabling accurate scheduling and coordination.

(viii) (d) Being 15 minutes early for everything

Passage-VI

(i) (b) Renewable energy sources are inexhaustible whereas alternate energy sources could be exhaustible.

(ii) The tone of the writer in the given lines from paragraph (4) is optimistic. The writer is positive about the advancements in the field of alternative energy, reflecting on how the situation has improved over time due to several factors such as increased demand and technological advancements.

(iii) the equipment was too expensive and not practical for consumer use

(iv) (b) and (e)

(v) Wind energy is the leader of the renewable energy pack because it is highly efficient. Wind power can serve both individual homes and entire communities, and it is versatile enough to be generated from both small-scale residential windmills and large-scale offshore wind farms.

(vi) Geothermal electricity is generated by tapping into underground hot water and steam, providing direct heating and cooling to buildings. Hydroelectricity, on the other hand, is produced by the movement of water behind a dam that turns turbine blades, generating electricity for powering homes.

(vii) (c) There are plenty of renewable energy sources that can be used to replace traditional energy sources.

(viii) The statement is True. Hydroelectricity is described in the passage as being used to power homes, which includes residential and by extension, commercial purposes.

Passage-VII

(i) (b) What were the primary societal changes brought about by the rise of bicycles?

[The option aligns with the main idea of the passage. The passage primarily discusses the societal changes brought about by the rise of bicycles, such as enhanced mobility, greater freedom for women, and a shift in fashion for more functional clothing tailored for cycling.]

(ii) (c) "...just because we can monitor so much information does not mean it is useful." (paragraph 5)

[In this option, the author expresses uncertainty about the usefulness of the vast amount of data that can be monitored through new technologies. The phrase "does not mean it is useful" shows the author's hesitation and doubt regarding the practical benefits of collecting such extensive data.]

(iii) it transitioned from primarily using steel cycles to safety bicycles and saw technological advancements, like wearables in sports science.

(iv) (b) accurate

[In paragraph 5, the author discusses a device that was deemed 'invalid' for measuring core temperature. Here, 'invalid' means the device is not accurate in providing the intended measurement.

Therefore, the antonym for 'invalid' would be 'accurate', which means to correctly provide information.]

(v) they facilitated women's freedom to commute freely and easily between places and participate in recreational activities like bicycle racing.

(vi) The tool would offer customized training recommendations and plans, integrated GPS for improved navigation, analysis and feedback capabilities, and social features for connecting with fellow cyclists. This comprehensive approach would enhance cyclists' performance by providing tailored training opportunities and fostering a supportive community.

(vii) (d) (2) is the cause of (1)

[(2) indicates that the popularity of cycling provided cyclists with enhanced political influence, which they used to advocate for better infrastructure. With this influence, they were able to improve the accuracy of maps. Therefore, (2) is the cause of (1).]

(viii) (b) and (c)

Case Based Passage

Passage-I

(*i*) The 'blackout' phase is significant because the Sun will block Mars from Earth, resulting in a disruption of communication with the satellite.

(*ii*) (*c*) 2, 3 & 5

(*iii*) (*b*) 15

(*iv*) communication/signals/satellite

(*v*) (*d*) only for a few

(*vi*) (*c*) confident

(*vii*) (*a*) extra fuel

(*viii*) (*b*) Both (A) & (B) are false.

(*ix*) elite

(*x*) (*a*) enchantment

Passage-II

(*i*) (*a*) Lee was an older man in poor health, while Hooker was a young and vigorous individual.

(*ii*) General Hooker's defeat in the Battle of Chancellorsville can be attributed to his overconfidence, dismissal of contrary evidence, and underestimation of General Lee's capabilities.

(*iii*) General Hooker's confidence in the Battle of Chancellorsville stemmed from superior intelligence, numerical advantage, and strategic maneuvers, while his underestimation of General Lee's capabilities resulted from overconfidence and neglecting contrary evidence.

(*iv*) (*d*) Against the odds, Lee won the battle, and Hooker's forces withdrew in defeat.

(*v*) In the Battle of Chancellorsville, General Hooker underestimated the capabilities of General Robert E. Lee, the Confederate general.

(*vi*) The term "rollicking" in the context of General Hooker's personality signifies his lively and exuberant enjoyment of life.

(*vii*) General Hooker's numerical advantage over General Lee, with his force of 134,000 compared to Lee's 61,000, provided a basis for Hooker's overconfidence in the Battle of Chancellorsville.

(*viii*) To compile a vast amount of intelligence about Lee's army.

(*ix*) (*a*) Both A and R are true, and R is the correct explanation of A.

Passage-III

(*i*) Changed with the monetary requirements for the trip.

(*ii*) The person who is yet to travel even once as an ecotourist isn't an experienced ecotourist.

(*iii*) 75%

(*iv*) Wild and untouched surroundings

(*v*) (*c*)

(*vi*) Geotourism emphasizes sustainability, preservation and the well-being of residents. It values the environment, heritage, aesthetics and culture of a place, promoting responsible travel and appreciation for local communities.

(*vii*) (*b*) (i) is an ethical tourist and (ii) is a geotourist

(*viii*) (*a*) Less than 15 days.

(*ix*) (*a*) Both A and R are true, and R is the correct explanation of A.

Passage-IV

(*i*) ... a fish needs decorations such as plants or rocks, to simulate a natural environment and improve its quality of life, people living in urban areas need green spaces such as vertical gardens to improve their physical and mental wellbeing.

(*ii*) Opinion; subjective judgement

[This statement expresses a viewpoint or belief about the benefits of incorporating nature and structures through vertical gardens and green walls in urban spaces. While there may be evidence to support this opinion, such as research on the positive effects of greenery on well-being or the visual appeal of vertical gardens, it is still ultimately a subjective judgment rather than an objective fact that can be proven or disproven.]

(*iii*) True, because the majority of participants strongly agreed or agreed that vertical gardens can improve the quality of life, increase air quality, and have a relaxing and calming effect. However, the survey does not provide information on the long-term effectiveness of vertical gardens or their potential impact on other aspects of urban life, such as traffic or community engagement.

(*iv*) A city government looking to install vertical gardens should consider addressing these concerns:

- cost of installation and maintenance [should be reasonable]
- areas of installation should be where driver distraction is less of an issue.

(*v*) Participants may not be fully informed or aware of the effects of vertical gardens on air quality, which could contribute to the neutral response. [This suggests a need for more education and awareness campaigns around the benefits of vertical gardens.]

(*vi*) (*B*) Only (*ii*)

[Cambridge dictionary - to twist or be twisted together, or to be connected so as to be difficult to separate]. Hence, Option (*B*).

(*vii*) <u>Advantages of vertical gardens over other green spaces-</u>

- They can be installed in small spaces, making them ideal for urban areas with limited space.
- They also offer aesthetic and design benefits, as they can be customized to fit specific architectural styles or preferences.

Disadvantages of vertical gardens over other green spaces-

- May not provide as much space for outdoor recreation as community gardens or parks do.
- The cost of installation and maintenance may be higher than for other types of green spaces.

(*viii*) (*B*) Vertical gardening is a sustainable practice that can transform urban spaces into green areas.

Passage-V

(*i*) (*a*) The given statement means that not only the state or Central Governments but the districts, sub-districts, panchayats, etc., are also responsible.

(*ii*) The District Collectors worked with the District Medical Officers in coordination.

(*iii*) In order to contain the spread of virus, the Kerala Government began rapid screening of the patients, quarantining them and isolating them.

(*iv*) For two consecutive days, no corona case had been registered in Kerala after the first case was registered.

(*v*) The two measures adopted by Kerala include:

(i) the development of COVID First Line Treatment Centres.

(ii) COVID-19 Care Centres.

(*vi*) (*d*) 'Local testing labs', 'district-wise allocations' and 'walk-in simple kiosks' allowed Kerala to conduct mass screenings and tests.

(*vii*) Nipah virus

(*viii*) Isolation/Quarantine

(*ix*) (*a*) Both A and R are true, and R is the correct explanation of A.

Passage-VI

(i) (*d*) Only (III) and (IV)

[The passage mentions the basis on which a language can be categorised into a classical language, and it also mentions that the concept was introduced in 2004. Therefore, both these pieces of information can be confirmed by reading the passage.]

(ii) historical; categorising

[The passage states that a classical language is one which is at least 1,500 years old and original. Therefore, this historical value is important. The passage does not talk about how these languages are preserved; it only mentions how these languages are categorised.]

(iii). (1) Sanskrit, as it has the lowest percentage of people who identify it as their mother tongue

(2) Odia

(iv) India is considered a heterogeneous country because: (any one)

- a country of many languages
- over 121 unique languages identified in the country
- a variety of mother tongues that are different from each other

(v). Possible inferences (any one):

- to justify why data from a census as old as 2011 has been used
- to state that newer data is not available
- because readers would expect the next census to have been
- conducted in 2021 (10 years after the 2011 census) for more recent data
- to give a disclaimer to readers in case they find updated information in recent times that contradicts the stated data

(vi). most

- a majority
- any percentage that shows majority: 80% or above

[Paragraph 5 of the passage states that a majority of the native speakers were found to be living in the place that their mother tongue originated from. Therefore, most native Tamil speakers would have been living in Tamil Nadu.]

(vii) (*b*) if more languages from remote and tribal areas of India are identified as classical languages Justification (any one):

- The passage mentions that preservation and inclusivity are important. Therefore, including languages that are native to people who live in lesser-known areas of India would lead to more harmony.
- The recognition of lesser-known languages as 'classical languages' would make certain cultures and languages more nationally acceptable for citizens of the country.
- It would increase our awareness about our own country, which would lead us to understand unique cultures and languages with more curiosity than judgement.

(viii)(*c*) This discussion will require careful consideration as it is a delicate matter.

[In the passage, 'delicate' implies that the equation would require a lot of consideration since India is such a heterogeneous country. The given sentence correctly captures this meaning of 'delicate'.]

Passage-VII

(*i*) of its exceptional taste, cultural significance, and numerous positive qualities

(*ii*) fact, objective detail

(*iii*) India being the major shareholder in terms of mango production, exports only 0.52% of its total production. Despite India's large mango production, it exports a small percentage due to high domestic consumption, challenges in transport and preservation, and stiff competition from other exporting countries.

(*iv*) The three countries that were at par with each other in terms of mango import from India in 2019-20 are USA, Kuwait, and Bahrain each importing 2% of India's mango exports.

(v) One inference that can be drawn from this is that the critical issue for exporting to the USA is high transportation cost (due to sea route distance) and limited shelf life of mango.

(vi) (0) Solutions

(vii) India is described as the largest producer of mangoes in the world because it contributes 46.02% of the total mango area and 45.88% of the total world production. Additionally, India's favourable climate, diverse varieties, and agricultural expertise contribute to its dominance in mango production.

(viii) (c) India is the largest producer of mangoes and by putting in more efforts, has the potential to be the largest exporter too.

Passage-VIII

Topper's Explanation

2\. i. A vast blanket of pollution stretching across South Asia is cutting down sunlight by ten percent over India, leading to altered rainfall patterns.

ii. a. I, II and III (damaging agriculture, putting people at risk, modifying rainfall pattern).

iii. possibility : potential :: suspecting : doubting

iv. c. There has not been enough time to determine that

v. Depletion of forest cover contributes to weather disruption while organic farming does not.

vi. a. worsen

vii. The haze has cut down sunlight over India ... As a consequence/an impact, the North-West of India is drying up.

viii. Two countries which are affected due to depleting forest cover are India and China.

ix. c. continue

x. a. 1. Impact of Pollution in South Asia

2\. Effects of Acid Rain

3\. Understanding Consequences of Haze

4\. Debate over Droughts

WRITING SKILLS AND GRAMMAR

FORMAL LETTER

2

Preview

Formal Letters are written in a strict and specific format. They are naturally much more formal in style than informal/friendly letters.

Key highlights:

- Use polite, simple and everyday language to convey the message clearly.
- Avoid using abbreviations as much as possible.
- Carefully use the information provided in the question.
- The modes of address and name of sender/receiver vary according to the type of letter and the receiver.
- Clear and exact descriptions of the articles required with the expected quality and quantity should be listed when writing a letter for placing an order.

Format

- **Sender's address:** While writing the address, do not put a comma at the end of each line. ***e.g.,***
  D-285
  Anand Vihar
  New Delhi– 210031
- **Date:** While writing the date, remember the day is written in figures, the month in words and the year in full figures. (Do not write: 15-09-2023) ***e.g.,***
  15 September, 2023
- **Receiver's address:** The receiver can be the firm's name or the one who represents the firm. Make sure to use the name provided (if) in the question. ***e.g.,***
  The Editor
  The Times of India
  Darya Ganj
  Delhi – 110002
- **Subject:** Subject must be as brief as possible, with a maximum of three or four words. It expresses the main theme or crux of the letter clearly.
- **Salutation:** In Official letters, we generally use Dear Sir/Madam. If the person, who is going to read the letter, is known to you, you can address him by name. ***e.g.,***
  Dear Mr. Arora
- **Body:**
  (*i*) Introductory Paragraph/Sentence: States the purpose of writing.
  (*ii*) Informative Paragraph: Details of the problems, cause, effect, possible solution etc.
  (*iii*) Concluding Paragraph/Sentence: States your hope, comment, request, suggestion etc.
- **Complimentary Close:** This is a courteous way of ending a letter. For this, we write Yours sincerely/Yours faithfully/ Yours truly. (largely accepted: Yours truly– for editor and Yours sincerely- formal /business)

Note: The first letter of the second word (here, 's', 'f', 't') is never written in capital letters.

- **Closing:** Name, Signature and Designation (if given)

CBSE Marking Scheme:
Format-1 M, Content-2 M, Organisation of Ideas-1 M, Accuracy-1 M

Letter to Editor

1. You are Nehal Kumar, Head of the Computer Club in Sunshine School, Noida. Digital literacy refers to someone's ability to use digital technology to find, evaluate, create and communicate information. You believe that digital literacy and navigating the digital world responsibly is crucial in today's technology-dependent age. **(5)**

Write a letter to the Editor of a national daily, in about 120 words, stressing the need for promoting digital literacy among individuals of all age groups. Discuss the benefits and challenges of digital technology, and propose initiatives to empower people with digital skills. **(CBSE APQ, 2023)**

Ans. Suggested **Response:**

Sunshine School

Noida

31st March, 2024

The Editor

The Times

New Delhi

Subject: Digital Literacy is the Need of the Hour

Dear Ma'am

I am writing to highlight the crucial importance of digital literacy in today's technology-dependent age. As the Head of the Computer Club at my school, I firmly believe that digital literacy is a skill that can help every individual navigate a rapidly changing world.

Technology and the internet have made the world smaller than ever. Digital literacy is essential to enhancing communication, creating access to resources, and equipping everyone to participate in a digital society.

However, I am also aware of the challenges that come with technology. Issues such as cybersecurity, misinformation, and online privacy present dangers. Digital literacy programs can help people navigate the digital world safely and responsibly.

To promote digital literacy, initiatives such as community workshops for a variety of age groups, and collaborations between educational institutions and technology companies can be established.

By focusing on digital literacy, we can empower individuals to harness the full potential of technology.

Sincerely

Nehal Kumar

2. You are Shiv/Jui, a resident of 488, Sarita Vihar, New Delhi. You are worried to see your younger sister's frequent habit of using the Internet as a homework tool. Taking ideas from the hints given below and your own, write a letter to the Editor of a popular newspaper, expressing your opinion on the advantages and disadvantages of the dependence of youth on computers in the present times.

In the techno world–24-hour access to the Internet–no doubt school children use Internet as homework tool. has many advantages–quick way to find information update—more free time for other activities—provides a variety of sources. more drawbacks than advantages–students' reading, writing and thinking skills seem to be disappearing—just copy information—some websites may contain inaccurate information no interest in listening to teacher in school–concept of hard work disappearing in present generation–balanced, sensible use of Net required.

Ans. 488

Sarita Vihar

New Delhi.

7th March, 2024

The Editor

The Times of India

New Delhi

Subject: Expressing concern over students' habit of using Internet as homework tool

Dear Sir/Madam

Through the columns of your esteemed newspaper I wish to highlight the problem of growing dependence of the present generation on Internet as a homework tool.

In many ways, Internet is a boon for the students. It is one of the quickest ways to find information on any topic. Students have access to a variety of sources to gather information on any topic. This enriches their knowledge and may expose them to additional info. The time required to get answers to queries is very less.

However, it seems that internet has more disadvantage than advantage. There are chances that some websites may contain inaccurate and inappropriate information. Not only reading habits, but and thinking skills are deteriorating as students just copy information. They display lack of interest in listening to the teacher in school.

As we know an excess of anything is bad. A balanced, sensible and guided use of Internet is required so that our present generation enjoys the fruit of technology. I hope these views find a place in your newspaper and reach the expected audience.

Yours truly

Shiv

A concerned citizen

3. You are Rohan Mehra, a concerned citizen. Write a letter to the editor of a local newspaper, in about 120 words, expressing your views on the importance of arts education in schools. In your letter, highlight the benefits of arts education, the impact on students' creativity and critical thinking skills, and the need for continued support and funding.

Ans. D-354

Sector-9

Sonipat

19th March, 2024

The Editor

The Time of India

New Delhi

310031

Subject: Importance of arts education in schools

Dear Sir/Madam,

Through the columns of your esteemed newspaper, I would like to express my strong belief in the importance of arts education in schools. Arts education nurtures creativity and critical thinking skills, allowing students to explore their talents and develop a well-rounded personality. It encourages self-expression and fosters cultural appreciation.

With the integration of arts into the curriculum and the availability of qualified teachers, schools can provide a comprehensive education that prepares students for the future. Arts education enhances cognitive abilities, promotes teamwork, and boosts confidence. It also contributes to the preservation and promotion of our rich cultural heritage. Schools should organize art exhibitions, music concerts, and theater performances to showcase students' talents and create awareness about the importance of arts education.

In conclusion, investing in arts education is investing in the holistic development of our students. It is essential for a well-rounded education system.

Yours sincerely

Rohan Mehra

Mistakes 101 : What not to do!

Students tend to use a lot of abbreviations in Formal Letter Writing.

4. As Armaan Khan, the School Literary Captain of Ujjwal Academy, Old City, Kiladerabad, you believe that languages can help bridge regional divides and promote unity. **5**

Write a letter to the Editor of a national daily, in about 120 words, suggesting the introduction of an online regional language learning programme managed and run by student councils and language clubs in the city. The programme aims to help residents who have recently relocated to a new region in picking up the local language organically. Share the importance and credibility of such a programme and suggest a feasible way to execute it along with possible activities. **(CBSE SQP, 2023)**

Ans. Suggested response:

Ujjwal Academy

Old City, Kilandarabad

30th March, 2024

The Editor

India Samachar

Jamnagar, Kilandarabad

Subject: Introduction of Online Regional Language Learning Programmes

Dear Sir

As someone who believes that languages can help bridge regional divides and promote unity, I am writing to suggest the introduction of an online regional language learning programme in our city to help the recently relocated residents (of all ages) establish a healthy rapport with the local residents and promote mutual understanding.

This online programme, organised and run by student councils and language clubs, can help these residents pick up the local language organically. This initiative may be conducted only on weekends for three months, making it feasible for participants to attend without hindering their work or studies. Activities such as language exchange programmes, cultural events, and group discussions on the virtual platform can be undertaken to make this programme more engaging.

I hope that publishing of this letter in the columns of your Daily shall urge the community to support this programme for its potential, to bring people together, promote language proficiency, and foster a sense of brotherhood.

Yours truly

(Armaan Khan)

(Captain, Literary Club)

5. You are Rohit/Rohini of A-45, Pitampura, Delhi. You observed that the subways in Delhi are seldom used by pedestrians who are always trying to cut across traffic. You have decided to write a letter to the editor of 'Hindustan Times' highlighting the dire need of creating awareness about it. Based on the points given along with your own ideas write a letter in 100-120 words. **5**

- infrastructure unutilized
- pedestrians prone to accidents
- accumulation of stagnant water/garbage in subways
- need for improvement and regular cleanliness under proper supervision. **(CBSE, 2023)**

Ans. A-45, Pitampura,
Delhi

28th February, 2024

The Editor
Hindustan Times
New Delhi

Subject: Urgent need to create awareness about utilizing subways

Dear Editor,

I am a resident of Pitampura, Delhi and I am writing this letter to bring to your attention the urgent need to create awareness among pedestrians about the importance of using subways in Delhi. It is sad to see that the infrastructure built to ease pedestrian traffic is unutilized and ignored. Pedestrians always try to cut across traffic, which not only causes inconvenience but also puts them at risk of accidents.

Furthermore, the accumulation of stagnant water and garbage in subways is a common sight. This not only makes it difficult for pedestrians to use them but also poses a serious health hazard. Therefore, there is a need for improvement and regular cleanliness under proper supervision.

I urge the authorities to take necessary steps to create awareness among pedestrians about the importance of using subways and to ensure that subways are well-maintained and clean. It is our collective responsibility to ensure the safety of pedestrians and make our city a better and safer place to live in.

Yours sincerely
Rohini

Letter for Placing an Order

6. You are Ankita/Ankit, Computer In-charge of Maharani Public School, Bangalore. Blackboards are to be replaced by smart boards. You wish to place an order for fifteen smart boards and computer accessories. Write a letter of enquiry to Ensonic Computech, M.G. Road, Bangalore enquiring about prices, discounts and after sales service. **(5)**

Ans. ***Topper's Explanation***

Maharani Public School
Bangalore
Karnataka

27 April 2022

The Manager
Ensonic Computech
M.G. Road, Bangalore

Respected Sir

Subject : Enquiring about placing an order for smart boards and accessor

We, at Maharani Public School, are planning to replace blackboards by smart boards. We would like to enquire about the details of placing an order with your reputed company.

We wish to place an order for fifteen smart boards and the required computer accessories (Product code: SB002) with your company since you are the biggest wholesale supplier and offer the most competitive prices. Kindly let us know the prices offered by you. Since, we are your regular customers, we would like to ask for a good discount as well. Kindly also provide details about the after sales service that would be provided to us.

Looking forward to hearing from you as soon as possible.

Thanking you

Yours truly

Ankita

(Computer In-charge)

7. You are Neha/Nihal Singh, Computer In-charge of Army Public School. Your school wishes to buy 20 computers and computer accessories from Apple Inc., Nehru Place, New Delhi. Draft a letter placing an order for the same.

(100-150 words)

Ans. Army Public School

New Delhi

7th March, 2024

Apple Inc.

Nehru Place

New Delhi

Subject: Order for Computers and Computer Accessories.

Dear Sir/Madam,

I am writing on behalf of Army Public School to place an order for 20 computers and computer accessories from Apple Inc. We have carefully reviewed the products offered by your company and have decided to proceed with the purchase.

We would like to order the following items:

Computers: 20 units of the latest Apple desktop computers, with the specifications as mentioned in your product catalog.

Computer Accessories: We also require accompanying computer accessories such as keyboards, mice, cables, and monitors for each computer unit.

Please provide us with the necessary information regarding the pricing, discounts (if applicable), payment terms, and delivery schedule. We kindly request you to include any relevant warranties or after-sales services in your offer.

We would appreciate it if you could expedite the processing of our order, as we require the computers and accessories at the earliest to meet the educational needs of our students.

Thank you for your prompt attention to this matter. We look forward to a positive response and a successful business association.

Yours sincerely

Neha Singh

Computer In-charge

Army Public School

Complaint Letter

8. You are Aryan/Shobha, the Sports Secretary of Alpine International School, Faridabad. You have received the parcel of sports articles ordered by you, some of which are defective and old. Write a letter of complaint to Tiger Sports, Noida, the supplier of the sports articles.

Ans. Alpine International School

Sector-31

Faridabad

30th March, 2024

The Manager,

Tiger Sports

Noida

Subject: Complaint about the supply of defective sports articles

Dear Sir/Madam

I am writing to you in the capacity of the sports secretary of Alpine International School, Faridabad. I visited your store two weeks ago, along with one of my teachers. After checking the goods, I placed an order for some sports articles for our school.

I would like to bring it to your notice that the parcel of the sports articles was delivered yesterday. Though the delivery was prompt, some of the articles were defective and old.

I request you to kindly replace the faulty goods with good quality products. Please let us know when will you be getting the goods replaced.

Looking forward to a prompt reply from you.

Yours sincerely

Aryan

Sports Secretary

9. You are Sujal /Sujata of Pragya Public School, Nangal, Punjab who had arranged a trip for fifty students to Nanital in summer vacations for ten days with "Mount Travels and Tourism". The arrangements done by the travel agency were far below the standard.The accommodation and food facilities were inferior in quality .Write a letter of complaint to the director of the agency to stop duping tourists with false promises as it tarnishes the image of locals. (100-120 words) **(CBSE SQP, 2018)**

Ans. Pragya Public School

Nangal, Punjab

15th March, 2024

The Director

Mount Travels and Tourism

Nangal

Punjab, 310012

Subject: Complaint Regarding Poor Services on Trip to Nainital

Dear Sir/Madam,

I am writing to express my disappointment and concern regarding the recent trip organized by your agency, Mount Travels and Tourism, for fifty students from Pragya Public School, Nangal, Punjab. We had entrusted our students' safety, comfort, and enjoyment to your agency, but unfortunately, the arrangements made were far below the standard we expected.

During our ten-day trip to Nainital, we encountered numerous issues with the accommodation and food facilities provided by your agency. The quality of both was inferior, falling short of the promises made in your promotional materials. The students, who had eagerly anticipated a memorable experience, were left disappointed and dissatisfied.

Such substandard services not only affect the reputation of your agency but also tarnish the image of the local community. As responsible tour operators, it is imperative that you deliver on the promises made to your customers and provide services that meet or exceed the expected standards.

I urge you to take immediate action to rectify the situation and ensure that future trips organized by your agency maintain the promised standards. It is essential to stop duping tourists with false promises, as this not only damages your business but also negatively impacts the local community's reputation as a tourist destination.

I kindly request a prompt response addressing our concerns and outlining the measures you will take to prevent such incidents from occurring in the future. I hope that you will consider this matter seriously and take the necessary steps to improve your services.

Thank you for your attention to this matter.

Yours sincerely

Sujal

10. You are Armaan/Anjali of C-63, Panvel. You recently read a magazine article which highlighted the condition of underage children working in hazardous conditions. Instead of going to school, they are working in dimly lit factories, tea stalls, in garages, etc. to supplement family incomes. Write a letter to the editor of "The Times of India' in about 100- 120 words, drawing attention to this national problem and suggesting solutions. **(CBSE, 2023)**

Ans. ***Topper's Explanation***

C-63

Panvel

Mumbai - 400012

27 February 2023

The Editor

The Times Of India

24 Beach Road

Mumbai - 400005

Subject:- Pitiable condition of child labourers

Dear Sir/Madam

This is to bring to your notice, a pressing issue in today's society, about which I recently came across in a magazine article.

The article described the hazardous conditions that underage children are subjected to. Most of them belong to families living below the poverty line. Hence, school education is a distant dream for them. To supplement their family incomes, they are ~~coerced~~ coerced to work in dimly lit factories, tea stalls and in garages. To my absolute shock, the children in factories must work with sharp tools, capable of injuring them. Accompanying the article was a photograph of a young boy employed in a tea stall. The pain in his eyes was heart-wrenching. To make matters worse, most of them are ill-treated by their employers. The youth make up a large part of our nation's population. Children are our future, and if we do not protect them, who will?

As vigilant citizens, it is our responsibility to eradicate this menace. Boycott of enterprises ~~utilising~~ utilising child labour will force them to shut down. Providing low-cost education to these children will go a long way. Government agencies must take a more pro-active approach through surprise checks and hefty penalties. I fervently hope that this national problem is brought to the notice of the authorities concerned through the columns of your esteemed newspaper and the necessary measures are taken.

Yours truly

Anjali

(Anjali)

Letter of Enquiry

11. You are Shivam/Shivani of C-12, Janakpuri, Indore. You wish to make a pilgrimage to Badrinath, Kedarnath and Haridwar with your family of six. Write a letter to R.K. Travels, enquiring about the schedule of their conducted tour by Deluxe buses to these places. Ask about the charges, boarding and lodging arrangements and the total time needed for the tour. **(Word limit 100-120 words)** **(CBSE, 2023)**

Ans. C-12, Janakpuri,

Indore

15th March, 2024

The Manager,

R.K. Travels, Indore

Subject: Enquiry for Conducted Tour to Badrinath, Kedarnath, and Haridwar

Dear Sir/Madam,

I am writing to enquire about the tour conducted by Deluxe buses to Badrinath, Kedarnath, and Haridwar, as my family and I are planning a pilgrimage to these sacred destinations. We are a group of six individuals, including elderly members, and are seeking a comfortable and hassle-free travel experience.

Could you please provide us with the following information regarding the tour:

Schedule: Kindly share the dates and duration of the conducted tour.

Charges: Please provide details of the tour charges, including any additional expenses or optional activities.

Boarding and Lodging: We would appreciate information regarding the arrangements for accommodation during the tour. It would be helpful to know about the quality and facilities of the lodging provided.

Total Time Needed: Kindly specify the total duration of the tour, including travel time and the time allocated for visiting each destination.

We are keen to embark on this pilgrimage and would greatly appreciate your prompt response with the requested information. Thank you for your attention to this matter.

Yours sincerely

Shivam

12. You are Samina Zaveri, Class X, Vadodara, Gujarat. You come across the following information on a local library's notice board. **(CBSE, SQP 2022, Term II)**

> **Create Your Own Board Game Competition!**
>
> Create an educational board game, and send it to us at Teen-Toggle Games Pvt. Ltd, 307, Satija building, Colaba, Mumbai by July 2022. The top 10 winning board games will be featured on our international portal.
>
> Attractive scholarships for the winners

You wish to participate but require more information. Write a letter to Teen-Toggle Games Pvt. Ltd in about 120 words, enquiring about rules, scholarship details and deadlines. Also, enquire about specifications for solo or group entries.

Ans. D-45

Colaba, Mumbai

15th March, 2024

Teen-Toggle Games Pvt. Ltd.

307, Satija Building

Colaba, Mumbai

Subject: Enquiry regarding Create Your Own Board Game Competition

Dear Sir/Madam,

I am writing to enquire about the Create Your Own Board Game Competition, as advertised on the notice board of our local library. I am interested in participating in this competition and would appreciate it if you could provide me with further details.

Kindly share the complete set of rules and guidelines for the competition. This information will help me understand the requirements and criteria for creating an educational board game.

Could you please provide information about the attractive scholarships that will be awarded to the winners? It would be helpful to know the amount and any specific eligibility criteria for the scholarships.

I would also like to know about the deadline for submitting the board game entry. Knowing the specific date will enable me to plan and complete my submission accordingly.

Also, I would like to enquire if the competition allows for both solo and group entries. If there are any specifications or restrictions regarding the number of participants, please provide the necessary details.

I am excited about the opportunity to showcase my creativity and educational ideas through this competition. Thank you in advance for your assistance.

Yours sincerely

Samina Zaveri

Class X

Vadodara, Gujarat

13. You are Sonal/Samkit of Vidyanjali Public School, Lucknow. You have seen an advertisement in "The Times of India" related to new batches of "Astronomy Club" initiated by National Science Centre, Lucknow starting from the coming fortnight .You wish to join the Club. Write a letter to the Director, enquiring about the venue, duration, fee- structure, activities, transportation etc. Invent other necessary details **(100-120 words)** **(CBSE 2018)**

Ans. Vidyanjali Public School

Lucknow

05th March, 2024

The Director

National Science Centre

Lucknow

Subject: Enquiry regarding Astronomy Club

Dear Sir/Madam,

I am writing to enquire about the new batches of the Astronomy Club, as advertised in "The Times of India." I am a student of Vidyanjali Public School, Lucknow, and I am keenly interested in joining the club.

I would appreciate it if you could provide me with the following details:

- **Venue:** Kindly let me know where the club meetings will take place, as well as any other facilities associated with the club.
- **Duration:** Please inform me about the duration of the club sessions, including the frequency and timings of the meetings.
- **Fee-Structure:** I would like to know the fee structure for joining the Astronomy Club, including any additional costs that may be involved.
- **Activities:** Could you please provide information about the activities that will be conducted in the club? I am particularly interested in learning about any hands-on experiences or observations that we will be able to participate in.
- **Transportation:** If the club sessions are not held within the school premises, I would like to know if any transportation facilities are available or if I need to make my own arrangements.

I am eagerly looking forward to your response, as I am excited to be a part of the Astronomy Club and explore the fascinating world of astronomy.

Thank you for your attention to this matter.

Yours sincerely

Sonal

Class X

14. You are Aruna/Arjun C.C.A. incharge of St. Joseph's High School, Pune Cantt. You have read an advertisement by the National Tourist Corporation, offering excellent prices for group tours. **(CBSE, 2023)**

Write a letter to enquire about the following:

- Duration of tour
- Sight seeing itinerary
- Cost of package discount
- Mode of transport
- Destinations being offered

Ans. St. Joseph's High School

Pune Cantt.

20th March, 2024

National Tourist Corporation

Pune, 221001

Dear Sir/Madam,

I am writing to enquire about the group tours offered by the National Tourist Corporation. As the C.C.A. incharge of St. Jo School in Pune Cantt, I would like to gather information for our school's upcoming excursion.

Could you please provide the following details regarding the group tours:

1. Duration of the tour.
2. Sightseeing itinerary.
3. Cost of the tour package and any available discounts.
4. Mode of transport.
5. Destinations being offered.

Thank you for your attention to these inquiries. Your response will greatly assist us in making an informed decision about our participation in the group tours. We look forward to exploring the possibilities of collaboration between St. Joseph's High School and the National Tourist Corporation.

Yours sincerely

Aruna

CCA Incharge

15. You are Soumya/Soham, living at 43-B, Blue Apartments, Prashant Lok. You wish to take up a three-week summer course in baking after finishing your class X board exams. Write a letter in about 120 words, to the Principal of Excellent Cooking, Block-D, Mahesh Enclave, seeking information about the course structure, course duration, fees, class timings, on job trainings etc. **(CBSE, 2024)**

Ans. ***Topper's Explanation***

43-B

Blue Apartments

Prashant Lok

26 February 20XX

The Principal

Excellent Cooking

Block - D

Mahesh Enclave

Subject : Enquiry regarding baking course

Sir / Madam

I came across your advertisement in Hindustan Times dated 25 February 20XX. I was delighted to know that cooking school is providing cooking co courses. I am about to finish with my class X board exams and wish to learn cooking during my holidays. I love cakes and also bake them at my home. I want to open my own bakery and hence the need to learn baking. I want to opt the three week summer course in baking that was mentioned in your advertisement.

Please provide me with the details given below:-

- Course structure
- Course duration
- Fee structure
- Class timings
- Transport facilities
- On job trainings
- Internships available

It would be highly appreciated if you provide me with the details at the earliest so that I can join your classes soon after my exams end. Please inform about the things you think should be informed prior.

Thanking You

Yours Truly

Soumya

16. As Sharman Singh of 776, Hemkunt Apartments, Arampur, you believe that as a law abiding citizen who pays regular taxes you deserve regular supply of clean drinking water in your house. However, your locality is facing acute shortage as supply is often disrupted without notice causing problems to the residents. Write a letter to the Director of Jal Board of your city area, in about 120 words, apprising him of the situation; sharing the need for regular supply of clean water and requesting him to take necessary action to improve the situation. **(CBSE, 2024)**

Ans. 776

Hemkunt Apartments

Arampur

25th February, 2024

The Director

Jal Board

West Bengal

Subject: Request for regular supply of clean drinking water

Dear Sir/Madam,

I, Sharman Singh, am writing to inform you about the inconsistent supply of clean drinking water in our area. Despite being regular taxpayers, we face this crucial issue which affects our daily lives.

In recent times, the water supply has been unpredictable and often stops without any prior notice. This irregularity leads to severe inconvenience for all residents, making it difficult to manage daily chores and maintain hygiene. The absence of a reliable water source is a significant concern for our community.

We understand the importance of water and believe that access to clean water is a basic necessity. Therefore, we kindly request your immediate attention to address this problem. Ensuring a regular and uninterrupted water supply would greatly benefit the residents and help in maintaining the well-being of our community.

We trust that you will take prompt and effective action to resolve this issue.

Thank you for your understanding and support.

Yours sincerely

Sharman Singh

17. As Sonam Mehta, a resident of 14, Sunrise Apartment, Udaipur, you are distressed about the misuse and poor maintenance of the public park in your society. Write a letter to the editor of a local daily, in about 120 words, highlighting the condition, mentioning the inconvenience faced by the residents of the locality. Share the importance of public parks and suggest measures for its proper upkeep. **(CBSE, 2024)**

Ans. 14,

Sunrise Apartment

Udaipur

15th February, 2024

The Editor

The Daily

Udaipur

Subject: Restoration needed for our Community park

Dear Editor,

I am Sonam Mehta from Sunrise Apartment, and I wish to draw attention to the condition of our local park. It's in bad shape with garbage everywhere, and broken swings. The walking path is also not taken care of. This was a place where we all, especially children and elders, used to come for fresh air and peace.

Now, because the park is not looked after, many of us don't go there. It's not just about fun, but also health. We miss the clean air and the green space where we used to exercise and relax. A good park can bring us together and keep us healthy.

For making it better, we need regular cleaning and fixing the broken things. We could use signs to remind everyone to keep it clean. Maybe the park needs a guard or someone to look after it all the time.

Please help our community by sharing this in the newspaper. We hope the right people will see it and help fix our park.

Yours sincerely

Sonam Mehta

ANALYTICAL PARAGRAPH

3

Preview

Key highlights:

- Brief and comprehensive.
- Stick to the facts, use simple and accurate language.
- Choose the important information, organize it well.
- Look for the differences that are noticeable.
- Mention the aspect which is the smallest or the largest in the data given. Any aspect that is similar should be mentioned next.
- Further mention about the aspect that has remained unchanged or is constant throughout.

Format

Introduction: The first paragraph should describe in brief what the graph is about. It should be like an **opening paragraph** that introduces the reader to the context of the chart given. When writing the introductory paragraph, you need not go into the details.

Body: This part of the analytical paragraph should contain details of the graph/chart given in the question. It is extremely important to choose the significant details that should be included in the paragraph.

The body can be broken into two or three sub-paragraphs depending on the information extracted from the graph, if required. ***Breaking the body into* subparagraphs *makes it easy for the reader to understand.***

Conclusion: The last paragraph should conclude the paragraph giving the overall view or summary of the graph. It should be concluding in nature and act as the closing statement. One should keep in mind that one must not include any personal opinions, conclusions, or observations. You should simply stick to the facts.

Useful Tips for Writing an Analytical Paragraph

- For the introduction, use phrases such as The line graph shows.../The given table suggests.../The chart given above describes.../ The data given provides information about.../The pie chart illustrates..., etc.
- For describing trends, use phrases and words such as a pattern of growth.../rapidly doubled/skyrocketed/ striking increase/ peaked/declined/levelled off/stagnated/fluctuate/starting to rise/starting to fall/slightly etc.
- For describing quantities, use one-third of/nearly one- fourth of/30% of/almost 80%/majority of/on average/twice as much/ almost equal/the highest/the lowest/ roughly/approximately 5% of/just under three per cent etc.
- For establishing a relationship or contrast, use words and phrases like- relationship between/similarly/in contrast with/in comparison to/but in the opposite case/however/whereas/as opposed to/while/noticeable difference etc.
- For the conclusion and other connecting phrases, use-overall/subsequently/in a nutshell/for the chart given/in short/striking changes/therefore etc.

EXERCISE

1. The given bar graph shows the increasing use of skin care products by men and women over the period of three months. Write an analytical paragraph elaborating the given information in about **100** words: **(CBSE, 2023) (5)**

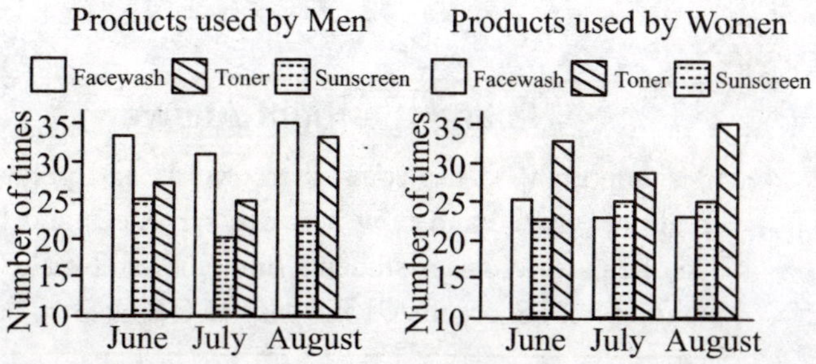

2. Tsering, of class X, is contesting for the post of the Junior School Captain, in the upcoming student council elections. Given below is her character traits' graphic, shared in the public domain, by the school counsellor, for the awareness of student voters, at school. **(CBSE SQP, 2023) (5)**

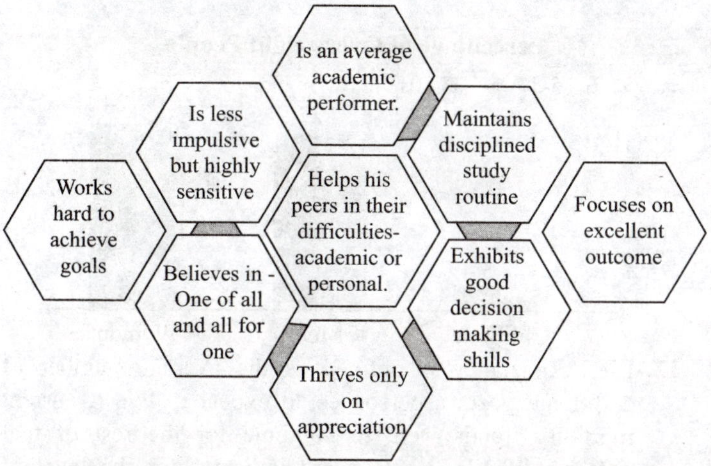

All Tsering's peers have been asked to write a paragraph in about 120 words, analysing these traits, to either support or oppose her candidature. As one of her peers, write this analytical paragraph, by selecting some of the traits that support your analysis.

You may begin like this:

As a responsible student voter, I believe Tesring possesses/does not possess the necessary traits to be a School Captain.

You may end like this:

For these reasons, I believe she has/does not have the potential to be a good School Captain and I support/oppose her candidature.

3. 'Mental health and mental health issues are as important to be taken care of as other diseases. People often look down upon the people who share their mental health issues which is why it has become a taboo. The given excerpt is from a health and wellness magazine.

Write a paragraph to analyse the given statement in 100-120 words. Think of alternative explanation to counter the given statement.

4. Given below are the pollution figures for some major towns and cities in India:: **(CBSE, 2023)**

	Suspended Particulate Matter	Sulphur Dioxide	Nitrogen Oxide
Permissible Limits	200	80	80
Ludhiana	453	20	64
Delhi	680	124	137
Mumbai	485	27	53
Chennai	262	45	**34**

Using the information given above along with your own ideas, write an analytical paragraph in 100-120 words.

Nailing the Right Answer

Remember, analytical paragraphs require you to analyze and interpret information, rather than simply summarizing it.

5. The pie-chart shows the expenditure of Mr. Sharma's family. Interpret the data in words.

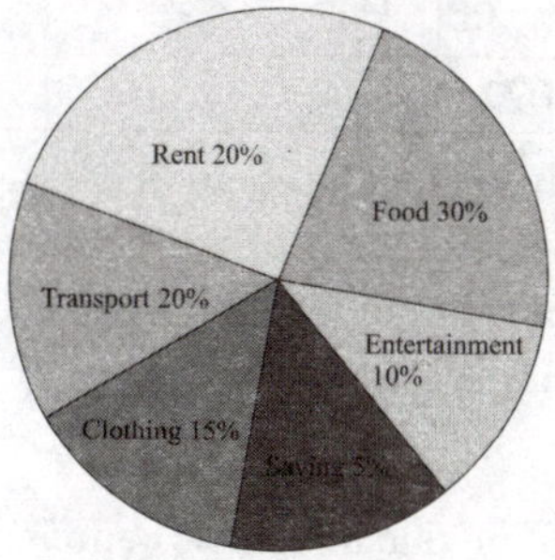

6. Read the given details about the advantages and disadvantages of social media. With the help of the given cues and your own ideas, write an analytical paragraph in about 120 words on "The Impact of Social Media – Boon or Bane?"

Cues:

- Connects people globally
- A great platform for learning and business
- Privacy concerns and cyberbullying
- Misinformation spreads quickly

- ❐ Addiction and reduced productivity
- ❐ Influences opinions and behavior

7. The rapid growth of technology has revolutionized shopping habits, shifting from traditional markets to online platforms. The data below shows the increasing number of online shoppers over the years. Analyze the data and write an analytical paragraph, in about 120 words, about how e-commerce has transformed consumer behavior. Discuss benefits such as convenience and variety, as well as challenges like cybersecurity risks and digital fraud.

S.No.	Year	Total Number of Online Shppers (in millions)
1.	2017	120
2.	2018	150
3.	2019	190
4.	2020	250
5.	2021	310
6.	2022	370

8. The demand for electric vehicles (EVs) has been rising due to concerns about pollution and fossil fuel depletion. The table below shows the increasing number of EVs sold globally over the years. Analyze the data and write an analytical paragraph, in about 120 words, about how electric vehicles are gaining popularity. Discuss benefits such as eco-friendliness and cost-effectiveness, along with challenges like charging infrastructure and battery disposal.

S.No.	Year	Number of EVs Sold (in millions)
1.	2017	2
2.	2018	3.5
3.	2019	5
4.	2020	7.5
5.	2021	12
6.	2022	18

9. Read the given details about the causes and effects of pollution. With the help of the given cues and your own ideas, write an analytical paragraph in about 120 words on **"The Growing Threat of Pollution."**

Cues:

- ❐ Air pollution due to vehicles and industries
- ❐ Water pollution due to plastic waste and chemicals
- ❐ Deforestation and climate change
- ❐ Health issues like respiratory problems
- ❐ Need for eco-friendly solutions and government policies
- ❐ Role of individuals in reducing pollution

10. The chart given below displays data about the number of gyms and the number of members in your city over the past decade. Write a paragraph analyzing the given data:

(CBSE 2024)

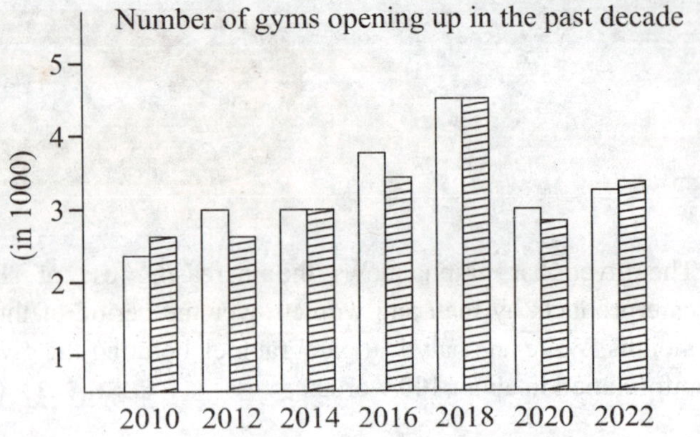

Nailing the Right Answer

It is important to use transitional words and phrases to create coherence and flow between sentences and ideas. This helps to coonect students' thoughts and make their paragraph more organized and easy to follow.

11. Cases of obesity, are on the rise. Experts fear a health emergency unless the growing obesity problem is tackled on a war footing. We can say that we are in an obesity epidemic in India. Based on the graph given below, write an analytical paragraph, in about 120 words, analyzing the percentage of overweight Indians and suggest possible solutions. **(CBSE 2024)**

Percentage of Overweight People

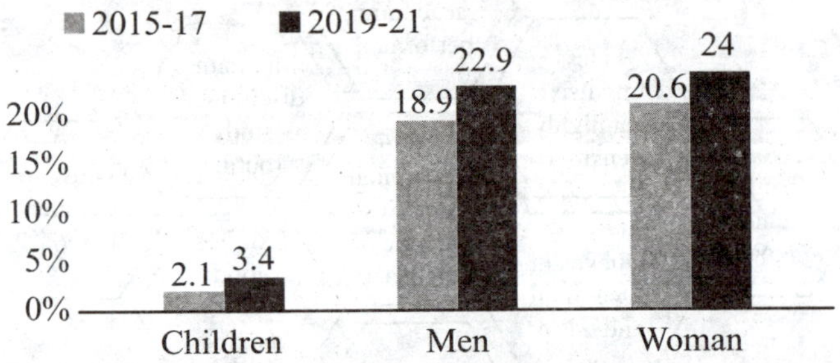

12. Life expectancy is defined as the average number of additional years a person could expect to live if current mortality trends were to continue for the rest of that person's life. It is a standard indicator for the level of socio-economic development. Based on the data given below, write an analytical paragraph, in about 120 words, analyzing the projected life expectancy of men and women over a period of time and assessing the possible causes. **(CBSE 2024)**

Projected Life Expectancy 2001-2025

Year	Age of Men	Age of Women
2001-2005	63.8	66.1
2006-2010	65.8	68.1
2011-2015	67.8	69.8
2016-2020	68.8	71.1
2021-2025	69.8	72.3

ANSWERS & EXPLANATIONS

CBSE Marking Scheme: Content-2 M, Organisation of Ideas-2 M, Accuracy-1 M

1. The provided graph depicts the usage of three skincare products - face wash, toner, and sunscreen - by both men and women over a period of three months. It is observed that both genders followed a similar skincare routine, with facewash being the most frequently used product among both men and women. However, the usage of toner and sunscreen varied between the genders, with women using toner more and men using sunscreen more. Over the period of three months, there was a significant increase in the usage of skincare products for both men and women. The highest rise in usage was observed for sunscreen in August. Overall, the data suggests that people are conscious of their skin's health and hygiene, with facewash being the most preferred skincare product.

2. Suggested response:

Supporting Tsering's candidature

As a responsible student voter, I believe Tsering possesses the necessary traits to be an excellent School Captain. Her disciplined study routine and hard work ethic indicate her ability to prioritize and manage her time effectively. Tsering is less impulsive but sensitive and focuses on the excellent outcome of tasks assigned to her demonstrating good decision-making skills. Additionally, her willingness to help peers in academic and personal difficulties highlights her empathetic and caring nature. Furthermore, Tsering believes in the "One for all and all for one" policy, which is pivotal in fostering a sense of community and promoting inclusivity in the school. While she may be an average academic performer, her positive attitude and desire for appreciation will motivate her in her pursuit of excellence. For these reasons, I believe she has the potential to be a good School Captain and I support her candidature.

Opposing Tsering's candidature

As a responsible student voter, I have reservations about Tsering's candidature for the School Captain's position. While she maintains a disciplined study routine, her average academic performance suggests a lack of academic discipline. Additionally, her quest for appreciation may cause her to prioritize recognition over the well-being of the school community. Moreover, Tsering's sensitivity, while admirable, may hinder her ability to make tough decisions and exercise effective leadership skills. While her willingness to help peers is commendable, it may also distract her from her responsibilities as the School Captain. Finally, Tsering's focus on the excellent outcome of tasks assigned to her may cause her to overlook the process and teamwork required to achieve those outcomes which are crucial for the school's smooth functioning. For these reasons, I believe she does not have the potential to be a good School Captain and I oppose her candidature.

3. Mental health issues are often unfairly treated as less important than physical health, which is why they have become a taboo in society. However, this is not correct. Mental health is just as important as physical health. Issues like stress, anxiety, and depression affect many people around the world, and it is essential to take them seriously. Instead of judging those who talk about their mental health problems, society should support them. Talking openly about mental health can help reduce the stigma. People should feel safe to share their feelings without being judged, and we must work towards creating a more understanding and accepting environment.

4. ***Topper's Explanation***

The Issue Of Air Pollution

The given table provides the pollution figures of some major Indian towns and cities. The data includes three major air pollutants namely, suspended particulate matter, sulphur dioxide and nitrogen oxides, their permissible levels and their levels in Ludhiana, Delhi, Mumbai and Chennai. The levels of suspended particulate matter in all four cities (453 in Ludhiana, 680 in Delhi, 485 in Mumbai and 262 in Chennai) far exceed the permissible level of 200. The abnormal levels of particulate matter may be attributed to the smoke and dust released by vehicles in these well-developed cities, apart from burning of agricultural produce in Delhi and Ludhiana. The permissible levels of both sulphur dioxide and nitrogen oxide are 80. The high proportions of sulphur dioxide and nitrogen oxide in Delhi (124 and 137 respectively) are alarming. However, in the other cities, these are fortunately well within the limit. The sulphur dioxide levels are lowest in Ludhiana at 20, followed by Mumbai at 27 and then Chennai at 45. The levels of nitrogen oxide follow the opposite trend with Chennai at 34 and then Mumbai at 53 and Ludhiana at 64. It is evident that air pollution is a major issue affecting big towns and cities in India. Unless we take steps to mitigate it, the quality of human life will only deteriorate in future. Let us work towards a cleaner and greener environment.

5. The pie chart provides a comprehensive breakdown of Mrs. Sharma's family's expenditures. The most significant portion of their spending is on food, which accounts for 30% of their total expenses. This indicates the importance they place on nutrition and sustenance. Rent, which often represents a significant fixed cost for many families, is also a major expense, constituting 20% of their budget. This is equal to their transport costs, which also stand at 20%, highlighting the importance of mobility and possibly the costs associated with commuting or travelling. Savings account for 5% and clothing at 15%. The allocation to savings suggests that the family is conscious about their future financial security. Entertainment, at 10%, is the least among the categories, suggesting discretionary spending on leisure and recreation. Overall, the data paints a picture of a family that prioritizes basic needs, while also ensuring future financial security and some leisure activities

6. Social media has become an integral part of our daily lives, offering both advantages and disadvantages. It connects people globally, making communication faster and more efficient. Platforms like Instagram, Facebook, and Twitter help businesses and individuals grow by providing learning and marketing opportunities. However, excessive use of social media can lead to privacy concerns, cyberbullying, and the spread of misinformation. Many users become addicted, leading to reduced productivity and mental health issues. Social media also influences opinions and behaviors, sometimes leading to unrealistic expectations. While it has revolutionized the way we interact, it is essential to use it responsibly to avoid its negative impacts.

7. The rapid advancement of technology has significantly influenced consumer behavior, leading to a rise in e-commerce. The data indicates a steady increase in online shoppers from 120 million in 2017 to 370 million in 2022. This growth is driven by the convenience of shopping from home, access to a wide variety of products, and attractive discounts. Platforms like Amazon and Flipkart have made purchasing easier with secure payment options. However, online shopping also presents challenges such as cybersecurity risks, digital fraud, and issues related to product quality. While e-commerce continues to expand, measures like secure transactions and better regulations are necessary to ensure a safe shopping experience.

8. The global shift towards sustainability has led to the increasing adoption of electric vehicles (EVs). According to the data, EV sales grew from 2 million in 2017 to 18 million in 2022, reflecting a growing preference for eco-friendly transportation. EVs help reduce dependence on fossil fuels and minimize air pollution. Companies like Tesla, Hyundai, and Tata Motors are expanding their EV models to cater to the rising demand. However, challenges such as inadequate charging infrastructure, limited battery life, and high costs still hinder widespread adoption. As technology advances and governments invest in charging stations and incentives, EVs are expected to dominate the automobile industry in the coming years.

9. Pollution is a major global concern, affecting both the environment and human health. Air pollution, caused by vehicle emissions and industrial waste, leads to respiratory diseases. Water pollution results from plastic waste and chemicals, making clean water scarce. Deforestation contributes to climate change and loss of biodiversity. Pollution also impacts agriculture and food quality. Governments and organizations are working towards eco-friendly solutions like renewable energy and waste management. However, individuals must also play their part by reducing waste, using public transport, and planting trees. Only a collective effort can help combat the growing threat of pollution and create a cleaner, healthier planet.

10. ***Topper's Explanation***

The presented bar graph illustrates the data about the number of gyms and the number of members in my city over the past decade. People are nowadays very concerned about their health and this is the reason of many people going to gyms.
The highest number of gyms were opened up in the year 2018. This year marks the upward trend regarding gymming. The same number of people joined the gyms in that particular year.
It is followed by the year 2016 when around 4000 ~~people joine~~ gyms were opened and around 3000 ~~pe~~ members joined. And then comes the third highest year 2022 where around the same number of gyms were opened and the members joined.
The given data shows that opening of gyms and joining of members followed an upward trend from year 2010 to 2016 and then took a jump in 2018 which was followed by a fall in 2020 due to the covid pandemic.
People are again getting cautious about their health and doing more physical activities in gyms which leads to the opening of more gyms and joining of more members in 2020.

11. The graph presents an alarming increase in obesity rates among the Indian population from 2015-17 to 2019-21. The percentage of overweight children went up from 2.1% to 3.4%, showing a growing trend in childhood obesity. Men and women have seen a significant rise in obesity rates too, with men's percentages going from 18.9% to 22.9% and women's from 20.6% to 24%. This data suggests that more individuals across different age groups are becoming overweight.

The rise in obesity rates could be linked to various factors, including dietary habits and physical activity levels. The higher figures in women might indicate lifestyle or cultural differences in diet or activity. The increase among children points to early lifestyle influences. Overall, the graph reflects a national increase in weight gain issues over the years.

12. The data indicates that from 2001 to 2025, life expectancy for both men and women has been projected to rise steadily. In 2001-2005, men had an average life expectancy of 63.8 years which is expected to increase to 69.8 years by 2021-2025, while women's life expectancy is projected to grow from 66.1 to 72.3 years in the same period. The consistent increase suggests an improvement in factors that influence mortality rates. This could be linked to advancements in healthcare services, better disease prevention, and improved living standards. The gap between the life expectancy of men and women remains throughout, with women living longer than men, which might be due to biological reasons or lifestyle differences. The data reflects a positive trend in societal health and longevity over the 24-year span.

TENSES

4

Preview

Tense is the form taken by a verb to indicate when an action began, continued, or ended. It is divided into three categories:

- **Present Tense:** Events occurring in the present.
- **Past Tense:** Events that took place in the past.
- **Future Tense:** Events that will take place in the future.

Note:

- While answering the questions related to tenses, it is important to understand the time of action, as it will help choose the right verb form.
- As a general tip, it is important to be consistent with the verb form in the sentence or text until the theme or time of action needs to change.
- Make sure to read the sentence after answering the questions, as it will help remove grammatical errors.

Important points

- Singular Subject-Singular verb (She prays.)
- Plural Subject-Plural Verb (We pray)
- Singular Subject + Has
- Plural Subject + Have
- Verb + 'ing' in all Continuous Tenses shows the actions' continuity.
- Use Did with V1 e.g.,

I didn't see him. (correct)

I didn't saw him. (incorrect)

Tense	Indefinite/Simple	Progressive/Continuous	Perfect	Perfect Continuous
Present	S + V_1 + (With plural subjects + O) S + V_1 + s/es (With Singular Subjects + O)	S + is/am/are/(V_1 + ing) + O	S + has/have + V_3 + O	S + has/have + been + V_1 + ing) + since/for + O
Past	S + V_2 + O	S + was/were + (V_1 + ing + O)	S + had + V_3 + O	S + had been + V_1 + ing) + since/for + O
Future	S + will/shall + V_1 + O	S + will be/shall be + (V_1 + ing) + O	S + will/shall / + V_3 + O	S + will/shall / + been + (V_1 + ing) + since/for + O

Note: 'Shall' is used with 1st person (We/I), 'will' is used with 2nd and 3rd person.

Order of will/shall in interchanged in compulsory case

S = Subject, V = Verb, O = Object

Tense is the form taken by a verb to indicate when an action began, continued, or ended. It is divided into three categories:

Present Tense: Events occurring in the present.

Past Tense: Event that took place in the past.

Future Tense: Events that will take place in the future.

These three categories are further divided into four sub-categories:

- Simple
- Continuous/Progressive
- Perfect
- Perfect Continuous

Let us understand each of these in detail.

Present Tense

1. Simple Present Tense is used

- To express a habitual action.

  e.g., She takes her dog for a walk.
- To express general or universal truth.

  e.g., Two and two make four.
- In quotations.

  e.g., Our teacher says, "Honesty is the best policy."
- In a future event that is part of a fixed programme or timetable.

  e.g., The train leaves at 4:20 pm.
- When two actions of the future are being talked about, one dependent on the other, the first action is represented by Present Simple, and the second by Future Simple.

  e.g., I shall go when my brother comes back.

Subject	Verb (s/es) (first form of the verb)	Object
Aryan	goes	to school.
Zoya	eats	green vegetables.
They	play	basket ball.

Knowledge Hub

1. Singular Subject - Singular Verb.
2. Plural Subject - Plural Verb.

noun subject — verb
The girl prays.
↑ Singular no 's' — ↑ Singular 's'

noun subject — verb
The girl prays.
↑ Plural 's' — ↑ Plural no 's'

2. Present Continuous Tense is used

- In actions going on at the time of speaking.

  e.g., It is raining heavily.
- In a temporary action that may not be happening at the time of speaking.

  e.g., He's working on a project.
- In actions arranged or planned to take part in the near future.

  e.g., He is travelling to Shimla tomorrow.

Subject	Am/Is/Are	Present Participle (verb + ing)	Object
I	am	reading	a newspaper.
Riya	is	studying	for her exam.
Students	are	learning	Tenses.

Knowledge Hub

1. Verb + 'ing' in all Continuous Tenses shows the actions' continuity.

3. Present Perfect Tense is used

- In activities that are completed in the immediate past.

  e.g., She has just arrived.
- In actions completed in the immediate past.

  e.g., I have solved the math sample paper.

  (Since no time frame is mentioned, we assume it to be 'by now'.)

  Note: Present Perfect is never used with adverbs of past time. In such cases, Past Simple tense should be used.

  e.g., India has won the match last week (Incorrect- as last week is not immediate past.)

  India won the match last week. (Correct)
- For long actions and situations started in the near past and continued until very recently.

  e.g., I have solved 25 test questions since this morning.

Subject	Have/Has	Past Participle (third form of the verb)	Object
Raghav	has	completed	the assignment.
Aruna	has	eaten	her lunch.
They	have	studied	for the test.

Knowledge Hub

1. Singular Subject + Has (He/She/It + Has).
2. Plural Subject + Have (I/You/We/They + Have).

4. Present Perfect Continuous Tense is used

- To express an action that began in the past and is still continuing.

  e.g., They have been building the road for a week now.

Past Tense

1. Simple Past Tense is Used

- To indicate the action took place in the past.

  e.g., I met her last week.
  [Adverbs of past time are used in this tense.]

- To indicate past habitual actions.

  e.g., I visited the museum every day in 2020.

- To express present imaginary situations or imaginary future events that may not happen.

  e.g., If I became a millionaire, I would travel the world.

Subject	Verb (second form of the verb)	Object
I	gave	my book to Ram.
He	ate	all the fruits.
They	went	to school at 7:00 am.

2. Past Continuous Tense is used

- To express an action happening sometime in the past.

  e.g., When I met him, he was studying with complete focus.

- When a new action takes place in the middle of a longer action, Past simple and Past Continuous are used together. Past simple will be used for the new action.

  e.g., The power went out while I was watching television.

Subject	Was/ Were	Present Participle (verb + ing form)	Object
She	was	dancing	in her room.
We	were	playing	with football.
You	were	studying	in the study room.

3. Past Perfect Tense is used

- To express an action completed before a certain period of time in the past.

  e.g., He had written a novel in his childhood.

  Note: When two actions happen in the past, the first is denoted in the Past Perfect, and the next is in the Simple Past tense.

  e.g., I had deposited the money in that bank when my friend came to meet me.

Subject	Had	Past Participle	Object
He	had	taken	a trial test.
I	had	completed	my work.
They	had	eaten	their breakfast.

4. Past Perfect Continuous Tense is used

- To express an action that began at a certain point in the past and continued till that time. Expressions like-for the last few days, since last month are generally used after perfect continuous tense.

  e.g., Kapil Dev had been playing for more than a decade when Tendulkar entered the Indian cricket team.

Subject	Had Been	Present Participle (verb + ing form)	Object
She	had been	teaching	English since 2015.
They	had been	praying	at the temple.
You	had been	disturbing	the guests.

Knowledge Hub

Use of DID

- Use Did with V1 (first form of the verb) in statements.
  e.g., I didn't eat today. (Correct)
  I didn't ate today. (Incorrect)
- Questions about the past
  e.g., What did you see? (The two verbs are did and see.)
  e.g., Did you see him? (did, eat)
- Negative statements about the past
  e.g., She didn't stay late. (didn't, stay)

Future Tense

1. Future Simple Tense is used

- To express an action that is yet to happen and will take place in the future.

  e.g., He will play football tomorrow.

Subject	Shall/Will	V1	Object
He	will	sing.	
We	shall	write.	
It	will	rain.	

2. Future Continuous Tense is used

- To express an action that will occur sometime in the future.

  e.g., He will be coming home this holiday.

Subject	Shall be/ Will be	Present Participle (verb + ing form)	Object
I	shall be	waiting	for the result.
We	shall be	visiting	our grandparents.
It	will be	raining	in the afternoon.

3. Future Perfect Tense is used

- To indicate the completion of an action at a specific time in the future.

  e.g., I shall have read 'Malgudi Days' when we meet next.

Subject	Shall have/ Will have	Past Participle	Object
I	shall have	completed	the assignment.
He	will have	built	the house by next year.
They	will have	studied	by Sunday.

4. Future Perfect Continuous Tense is used

- To express an action that is in progress and will end sometime in the future. Generally, the time period is mentioned.

  e.g., Mr. Hill will have been teaching for 25 years when he retires.

Subject	Shall have been/Will have been	Present Participle (verb + ing form)	Object
I	shall have been	singing	in the concert.
We	shall have been	eating	the dinner.
Jack	will have been	playing	with Kevin.

❑❑❑

MODALS

5

Preview

A *modal* is a type of verb indicating hypothetical conditions such as possibility, ability, necessity, likelihood, ability, permission, intent, request, capacity, suggestion, order, obligation, or advice.

Main Modals include:

Can, Could, Will, Would, Shall, Should, May, Might, Must, Ought to

Oftentimes the base form of a verb is accompanied by a modal verb so that its meaning changes slightly. They are never used alone. They are always followed by the base form (infinitive) of the main verb.

e.g., Soldiers **must obey** the orders of their officers.

(modal) (main verb)

Note:

- Modals do not change form based on the subject (***e.g.,*** He can, They can).
- Modals are followed by the base form of the verb (***e.g.,*** She must go).
- Questions with modals are formed without the auxiliary 'do' (***e.g.,*** Can you help?).

Might vs Could

'Might' and 'Could' are less definite and more hesitant than 'May', suggesting a smaller chance.

e.g., Joe might come with me. (perhaps a 30% chance)

I may go to London tomorrow. (perhaps a 50% chance)

Should vs Must

'Should' can be used as a weaker form of 'must'

e.g., That carpet should be cleaned. (It would be a good idea.)

That carpet must be cleaned. (It is absolutely necessary.)

Should vs Ought to

'Should' and 'ought to' are similar in meaning and can often replace each other. They are both used to talk about obligation and duty, to give and ask for advice, and to say what we think is right for people to do. Also, 'should' is more common than 'ought to' as it is less formal.

e.g., They ought to/should be more sensible.

Let us understand them in detail.

Can

It is used to express ability/inability (in negative sentences) or capacity.

e.g., I can pass the examination.

He can teach eight hours per day.

I cannot lift this object.

It is used to express permission.

e.g., Can I take a break?

If you have completed your homework, you can go to play.

It is used to express possibility or its absence in interrogative and negative sentences.

e.g., It cannot be possible.

Can you hear him?

Could

It is used as the past equivalent of *can*.

e.g., He could do fifty sit-ups at the age of eleven.

The Principal said that I could take one extra leave.

It is used as a less positive version of *can*.

e.g., Could you complete both the exercises today?

She could use her tablet once she is done with her homework.

It is used to make a polite request.

e.g., Could you do me a favour, please?

Could you drop me to his office?

May

It is used to express polite permission.

e.g., May I leave early tomorrow?

You may go on a trip.

It is used to express improbability (not likely).

e.g., He may fail in his next exam.

It is used to express a wish or prayer.

e.g., May you live long!

May God help you reach your goal!

Might

It is used as the past equivalent of *may*.

e.g., He might come today.

She might help you in Literature.

It is used as a less positive version of *may*.

e.g., I think it might rain.

It might be used.

It is used to show dissatisfaction or reproach.

e.g., You might not like it.

You might learn to face the difficulty.

Must

It is used to show necessity, fixed determination or obligation.

e.g., You must follow the routine. (obligation)

I must complete this exercise today. (determination)

You must apply for the leave or you won't get it on time. (necessity)

Need

It is used to show unacceptance or refusal in negative sentences.

e.g., You need not guide me any more.

She need not feel guilty.

Dare

Dare is a special kind of semi-modal which can also be used as a main verb.

As a modal verb, dare is used in negative and interrogative sentences, followed by a bare infinitive.

e.g., Dare not leave me here alone.

How dare she go there without permission?

Knowledge Hub

Bare Infinitive: The infinitive form of the verb without 'to' is called a bare infinitive. This is the verb's most basic form.

E.g., –	Think	–	play
–	eat	–	go

Ought To

It is used to express moral obligation, desirability or probability. Ought to can be used just like *should*.

e.g., We ought to respect our parents. (moral obligation)

It ought to rain. (probability)

You ought to be there on time. (desirability)

Ought is always followed by an infinitive (to).

e.g., You ought be among the seniors. (incorrect)

You ought to be among the seniors. (correct)

Shall/Will

They are used to express future; shall (first person) and will (second and third persons).

e.g., I shall visit the temple tomorrow.

He will come to the party tonight.

Will is used to express intention.

e.g., I will change the game.

Will is used to express characteristic or habit.

e.g., She will always sit in the corner.

He will wear jeans today.

Knowledge Hub

***Point of View/ Person Pronouns*:**

First person: The Speaker talks about themselves. (I, me, my, we, our, us, mine etc.)

Second person: The Speaker talks to the reader directly. (You, your, yourself)

Third person: The Speaker talks about other people. (He, she, it, they, them, herself, her, hers, his, themselves, their, theirs.)

Should/Would

They are used as past equivalents of *shall/will*.

e.g., I should complete my work.

He would get his salary on the first day of the month.

Should/Would is used to express probability.

e.g., You should be at home now.

He would be teaching now.

Should is used to express obligation or duty.

e.g., We should help the needy.

Would is used to express habitual action.

e.g., He would go to school daily.

Would is used to express condition.

e.g., He would be fired if he doesn't submit this assignment.

Would is used to make a polite request.

e.g., Would you lend me your pen?

Used To

It denotes the past situation or discontinued habit which no longer exists in the present.

e.g., They used to play daily in the park.

It expresses something existing in the past.

e.g., There used to be a cinema hall here.

❑❑❑

SUBJECT VERB AGREEMENT

6

Preview

Subject-verb agreement refers to the grammatical rule where the subject and verb in a sentence must agree in number (singular or plural). Some of the common points of Subject-Verb Agreement are:

- Singular subjects-Singular verbs.
- Plural subjects-Plural verbs.

Indefinite Pronouns: Pronouns such as everyone, someone, nobody, no one etc. take singular verbs.

e.g., Everyone is present.

Some vs Any: Some- used in positive sentences and questions when we offer or request, Any- used in negative sentences and questions

e.g., I don't have any pens. Do you have some pens?

Collective Nouns: Words like 'team', 'group', 'audience' are collective nouns and can take either singular or plural verbs, depending on whether the group is acting as one unit or as separate individuals.

e.g., The team is playing well. (as one unit)

The team are arguing among themselves. (as separate individuals)

Quantities: Expressions of quantity or amount (***e.g.***, 'a lot of', 'a few', 'some') take the verb form of the noun they refer to.

e.g., A lot of the cake is gone.

e.g., Some pages were lost.

Neither/Nor and Either/Or: When using 'neither/nor' or 'either/or', the verb agrees with the subject closer to it.

e.g., Neither the teacher nor the students are ready.

e.g., Either the students or the teacher is ready.

Titles and Names: Titles of books, movies, and other works, as well as names of countries or organizations that are plural in form, take a singular verb.

e.g., 'The United States is a country.'

e.g., 'The Chronicles of Narnia is a popular series.'

Amounts and Measurements: When considered as a single unit, amounts and measurements take a singular verb.

e.g., Five kilometres is a long distance to run.

e.g., Twenty pounds is a lot of money.

There is vs. There are: Use 'there is' for singular nouns and 'there are' for plural nouns.

e.g., There is a book on the table.

e.g., There are books on the table.

Subjects and verbs must agree in number (singular or plural). In other words, the verb of a sentence corresponds with the number and person of the subject of that sentence.

Note: The verb does not agree with the noun next to it. The verb agrees with the subject and NOT with the noun next to it.

e.g., **Each** of the students *writes* with a pen.

(Do not use the plural verb *write* just because the noun *students* next to it is plural. This is because the word *student* is not the subject. The subject in the sentence is **each**.)

Knowledge Hub

A common mistake in SVA is to assume that present tense verbs ending in "s" (e.g., plays, eats, swims) are plural.

Rules

1. The basic principle of the Subject Verb Agreement is that **singular subjects** take **singular verbs**. **Plural subjects** take **plural verbs:**

   Singular

   - The girl is singing.
   - My son has gone to school.
   - She runs fast.

   Plural

   - The girls are dancing.
   - The boys have gone to school.
   - They like sweets.

2. **Uncountable Noun:**

   When an uncountable noun is used as the subject of a verb, we use a singular verb:

   - Slow and steady wins the race.
   - Honesty is the best policy.

Exception

With the BE Verb, the first person singular is changed to 'am' (present) and 'was' (past), and the third person singular becomes 'is' (present) and 'was' (past).

I am here. (First person singular)

You are here. (Second person singular)

He is here/She is here/It is here. (Third person singular)

3. **Singular and Plural Nouns:**

   When a singular noun is used as the subject of a verb, a singular verb follows it. Likewise, a plural verb follows plural nouns:

   - The moon was shining in the sky.
   - The sun is about to set.
   - The children were swimming.

4. **One of + Plural Noun:**

   When the subject consists of 'one of + plural noun', the verb followed by it should be singular:

   - One of the boys was dancing.
   - One of the birds was chirping.
   - One of the students was reading.

5. **Long Subject:**

   When a clause or a long group of words is used as the subject, it is important to make the verb agree with the subject:

   - The chairs which I bought yesterday were a great bargain.
   - The man whom I met in the market was my nursery teacher.

6. (*a*) When sentences begin with "there" or "here," the subject is always placed after the verb; thus, it must be identified correctly.

   - Here is your book.
   - Here are your books.
   - There is a problem with my car.
   - There are problems in this text.

   (*b*) **Introductory 'there':**

   The verb has to agree with the real subject that follows the introductory 'there'. If the subject is singular, then a singular verb will follow 'there'. If the real subject is plural, then 'there' will be followed by a plural verb:

   - There is no fan in the room.
   - There are no fans in the room.

7. **Two or More Nouns:**

   When two or more nouns function as subjects, a plural verb is used:

   - Kate and her mother have gone to see a movie.
   - My friend and her sister are meeting us tomorrow.

8. **A collective noun** such as 'jury', 'committee', 'family', etc., take a singular verb when it is considered one unit. But when they are regarded as individuals, they take a plural verb:

   - The jury is about to give its decision.
   - The jury are divided in their opinion.
   - The committee is meeting tomorrow.
   - The committee have decided to raise the membership fee.

9. **Plural Names:**

   The title of a book, the name of a hotel in plural, takes a singular verb:

   - "Hotel Bahamas" is a five-star hotel.
   - "The Arabian Nights" has interesting stories.

10. **Plural Nouns with Singular meanings:**

    Nouns which are plural in form but singular in meaning usually take a singular verb:

    - Mathematics is not a boring subject.
    - Economics is an interesting subject.
    - Measles is an infectious disease.
    - The latest news is that the exam has been postponed.

11. **Singular Nouns with Plural Verb:**

    Some nouns which appear to be singular in form take a plural verb:

    - The police have arrested three terrorists.
    - The Indian cricket team won the match

12. Collective nouns

Nouns like group, crowd, flock, bunch, etc., are generally followed by a singular verb:

- ❒ A group of students was playing hockey.
- ❒ A crowd of people rushes into the mall.

13. 'Class' nouns such as food, furniture, clothing, etc., take a singular verb:

- ❒ This furniture is very old.
- ❒ This imported cutlery is very costly.
- ❒ His clothing consists of a bulletproof jacket.

14. Some nouns which appear to be plural in form when preceded by 'a pair of ' takes a singular verb, for example, shoes, scissors, trousers, etc.

- ❒ A pair of shoes was bought by her.
- ❒ A pair of trousers was washed by the helper.
- ❒ A pair of scissors was taken out of the box.

But when these nouns are used without a pair of, they take a plural verb:

- ❒ His shoes have worn out.
- ❒ My scissors do not cut well.

15. Some nouns are preceded by '*a lot of*', '*a great deal of*', '*plenty of*', etc. These nouns take a singular verb when they refer to *amount or quantity*; they take a plural verb when they refer to numbers:

- ❒ A lot of people visit the trade fair.
- ❒ Plenty of water was supplied to the farmers.

16. When a singular subject is joined by 'as well as ', 'in addition to' 'except', 'with', 'together with', 'along with', 'accompanied by', 'as well as', 'but', 'nothing but','besides', except','rather than', 'like','unlike','no less than', etc., with another noun or pronoun, we use a singular verb.

- ❒ Shikha, as well as her brother, has come.
- ❒ My father, in addition to our uncle, has gone out for a walk.
- ❒ Everyone except Ajay was present.

17. A singular verb is used with singular pronouns, e.g.,'each', 'either', 'neither', 'anyone', etc.

- ❒ Each of the athletes was given an award.
- ❒ Neither of the students was present.
- ❒ Everybody has helped her.

18. When the subjects joined by (Either-or) and (Neither-nor) are of different persons, the verb will agree in person and number with the noun closest to it.

- ❒ Neither she nor her cousins visit the concert.
- ❒ Either they or he is telling a lie.

19. Distances, Weight, etc.:

For distances, weight, height or amount of money, we use a singular verb even when the subject is plural:

- ❒ Fifteen thousand rupees is not a small sum.
- ❒ Two kilometres is a small distance,
- ❒ Two hundred feet above sea level is not a great height.

20. When some nouns are regarded as one unit, they take a singular verb:

- ❒ Bread and butter is my favourite snack.
- ❒ Brick and stone is scattered all over the place.
- ❒ The novelist and poet is dead.

21. Gerunds take the singular verb form of the verb when used as the subject of a sentence. However, when they are linked by **and**, they take the plural form.

- ❒ Dancing on ice was a bad idea.
- ❒ Swimming in the ocean and playing congo are my hobbies.

22. If connectives like *with*, *together with*, *accompanied by*, *as well as*, etc., are used to combine two subjects, the verb agrees with the subject mentioned first.

- ❒ The President of India, together with his secretaries, is invited to the award show.

23. When two singular nouns are joined by and refer to the same person or thing, the verb used with it should be singular.

- ❒ The poet and singer has been arrested. (When two singular nouns are joined by **and** refer to the same person or thing, the pronoun used for them should be singular.)

24. When two subjects are joined by 'AND', the verb is plural.

- ❒ My friend and his brother are in India.

25. The number/A number

- ❒ **The number is singular:** The number of forests destroyed by wildfires has increased drastically over the past decade.
- ❒ **A number is plural:** A number of students are standing outside the principal's office.

26. When two previously mentioned things are referred to, 'this' refers to the thing last mentioned and 'that' to the thing first mentioned.

- ❒ Fruits and vegetables are both rich in nutrients: this perhaps more than that.

27. None is used in the singular or plural as the sense may require.

- ❒ None of the chocolate was eaten.
- ❒ All the students entered the school premises, but none were present in the class.

❒❒❒

REPORTED SPEECH

7

Preview

Reported speech, also known as indirect speech, conveys what someone else has said, but without quoting their exact words. It is used to report the words of a speaker without quoting them directly.

Key Changes

1. Pronouns may change.
2. Tense often changes.
3. Time expressions might change.

e.g.,: Direct Speech: He said, "I am going to the market."
Reported Speech: He said that he was going to the market.

Tense Changes

Present Simple → Past Simple
Present Continuous → Past Continuous
Present Perfect → Past Perfect
Present Perfect Continuous → Past Perfect Continuous
Past Simple → Past Perfect (though can remain unchanged in some contexts)
Will → Would
Can → Could

Time Expression Changes

today → that day
tomorrow → the next day or the following day
yesterday – the day before or the previous day
here → there
now → then
last week/month/year → the previous week/month/year

Reporting Verb Changes

Commonly used verbs include: say, tell, ask, advise, suggest, order, etc.

Questions

Direct: "Where is the library?"
Reported: He asked where the library was.

Commands/Requests

Direct: "Close the door."
Reported: He asked me to close the door.

Statements

Direct: "I love chocolate."
Reported: She said that she loved chocolate.

Suggestions

Direct: "Let's go to the park."
Reported: He suggested going to the park.

Any speech that tells the audience or the readers what was said at a given point of time without using the direct words used by the speakers, is referred to as **Reported Speech or Indirect Speech**. In order to report what other people said, we use reported speech.

Reported speech is commonly used to write stories and can use the following types of sentences,

- Assertive/Declarative
- Exclamatory
- Imperative
- Interrogative

Direct Speech tells the reader or the audience the exact words that are said by the speaker using quotation marks.

For e.g.,: Parekh said "I like swimming in the river."

Here, the part within quotes, is the actual statement made by the speaker. The verb which establishes the speech is called the **Reporting verb**. In this case the verb is 'said'.

	Direct Speech	Indirect Speech
1.	He said, "I like my car."	He said that he liked his car.
2.	Jill said, "Jack came to school yesterday."	Jill said that Jack had come to school the previous day.
3.	Chris said, "I am walking here!"	Chris exclaimed that he was walking there.

NOTE:

If the reporting verb is in the past tense then we must change:

(i) The pronouns used within quotations

(ii) The tense and form of the verb

(iii) The adverbs of Place and Time.

If we refer to the table above, we will find these changes happening in sentence 2 and sentence 3.

Sentence 2:

Direct: Jill said, "Jack came to school yesterday."

Indirect: Jill said that Jack had come to school the previous day.

Verb changes: 'came' changes to 'had come'

Adverb changes: 'yesterday' changes to 'the previous day' **(Adverb of Time)**.

Sentence 3:

Direct: Chris said, "I am walking here!"

Indirect: Chris exclaimed that he was walking there.

Pronoun changes: 'I' changes to 'he'

Verb changes: 'am walking' changes to 'was walking'. The reporting verb changes from 'said' to 'exclaimed' due to '!'

Adverb changes: 'here' changes to 'there' (Adverb of Place).

All of these are part of the rules that become important while changing Direct Speech to Indirect Speech.

Pronoun Changes

When changing a sentence from direct to indirect speech, the following changes must be made to the pronouns.

Subject Pronouns		Object Pronouns	
Direct	**Indirect**	**Direct**	**Indirect**
I	he, she	me	him, her
we	they	us	them
you	he, she, they	you	him, her, them
my	his, her	mine	his, hers
our	their	ours	theirs
your	his, her, their	yours	his, hers, theirs

Place and Time Changes

The following changes are made to any words that denote the place or time, from Direct to Indirect Speech or vice-versa.

Direct Speech	Indirect Speech
today	that day
now	then/at that moment
yesterday	the day before
days ago	days before
last week	the week before
next year	the following year
tomorrow	the next day/the following day
here	there
this	that
these	those
ago	previously/before
tonight	that night

Tense Changes

While changing Direct to Indirect, the tenses must be changed as follows:

Tense	Direct Speech	Tense	Reported Speech
Present Simple	Hari said, "My mother **is** ill."	**Past Simple**	Hari said that his mother **was** ill.
Present Continuous	Hari said, "I **am working** very hard."	**Past Continuous**	Hari said that he **was working** very hard.
Past Simple	Hari said, "My mother **was** ill some days before."	**Past Perfect**	Hari said that his mother **had been** ill some days ago.
Past Continuous	Hari said, "I **was working** very hard."	**Past Perfect Continuous**	Hari said that he **had been working** very hard.
Present Perfect	Hari said, "I **have worked** hard."	**Past Perfect**	He said that he **had worked** very hard.
Present Perfect Continuous	Hari said, "I **have been working** very hard."	**Past Perfect Continuous**	Hari said that he **had been working** very hard.
Future Simple	Hari said, "I **will** do it soon." Darcy said, "I **shall** conquer this." Tommy said, "I **can** definitely do this."	**Conditional**	Hari said that he **would** do it soon. Darcy said that he **should** conquer that. Tommy said that he **could** definitely do that.

Points to Remember

The **verb form** will remain the same in Direct and Indirect Speech if:

1. The reporting verb uses Present Tense

Direct	Indirect
Rahul says, "I am feeling unwell."	Rahul says that he is feeling unwell.
Vineet says, "Mohini is not coming to the party."	Vineet says that Mohini is not coming to the party.

2. The reported fact is still true (universal truth)

Direct	Indirect
The educator said, "Honesty is the best policy."	The educator said that honesty is the best policy.
Soma said, "Asia is the largest continent."	Soma said that Asia is the largest continent.

3. If modals are used: would, could, should, might, ought to, used to, etc

Direct	Indirect
Ravi said, "I could fail without trying."	Ravi said that he could fail without trying.
Steve said, "You should stay in bed and rest."	Steve said that I should stay in bed and rest.

4. With the phrases, "would rather", "had better" , "it is time"

Direct	Indirect
The turtle said, "I would rather swim."	The turtle said that he would rather swim.
Rhea said, "We had better leave."	Rhea said that they had better leave.

5. Used with the conditional "if"/ Questions asked in Direct Speech become statements in Reported Speech

Direct	Indirect
"Where are you Michael?" said Kevin.	Kevin asked Michael where he (Michael) was.
"Should I do this now?" said Mary.	Mary wondered if she should do that then.

6. For request, command or advice we can use –

Verbs: ask, advise, beg, forbid, persuade, order, command, warn, demand

Direct	Indirect
"I want to see the manager!" said the woman.	The woman demanded to see the manager.
"Please have mercy on me" the young man said to the judge.	The young man begged the judge to have mercy on him.

DETERMINERS

8

Preview

A determiner is a word that is used before a noun or noun phrase to refer to the noun in the context.

e.g., I have lost my keys.

1. Articles

A and *An* are referred to as indefinite articles, whereas *the* is referred to as a definitive article. The distinction between *A* and *An* is made based on sound.

A: Before words that start with a consonant sound.
e.g., A one-rupee coin, a dog, a union, a European,etc.

An: Before words with a vowel sound.
e.g., An hour, an heir, an eye, an M.A., an S.D.O., an hour, etc.

The: Before unique nouns; when an entire class is referred to by a singular noun; before an adjective in the exemplary degree.
e.g., The sun, the dog, the tallest, etc.

2. Demonstratives

Demonstratives help us point to things, events, or people in relation to ourselves. They can show if something is close or far, both physically and in our minds. When we talk about things happening now, we usually use words like 'this' to point to them. When we talk about things from the past, we use words like 'that' to show they are farther away. Demonstratives include the words 'this,' 'these,' 'there,' 'those,' and 'that.'

3. Possessives

To indicate who owns or "possesses" something, we use possessive determiners. Possessive determiners, like all determiners, are placed in front of any adjective at the start of a noun phrase (s). Possessive determiners include pronouns such as 'my', 'your', 'our', 'his', 'her', 'their' and 'its'.

4. Quantifiers

Quantifiers are words which are placed before nouns to quantify a noun i.e., they indicate an amount or quantity.

e.g., some milk, most children, many pens, a few of them, a lot of fruits etc.

5. Cardinals or Numbers

Numbers such as on, three, hundred etc. are cardinal numbers. We most commonly use cardinal numbers as determiners (before nouns).

6. Ordinals

These determiners are used to tell the order of the nouns. These are to work out the class or present the position of the subject in the sentence.

e.g., first, last, next, eleventh, previous, subsequent etc.

7. Interrogatives

Interrogatives modifies a noun or pronoun in a direct or indirect question.

e.g., what, which, whose, who, how, when, why, etc.

8. Distributives

Distributives are used to refer to a group or to individual people or objects within a group.

e.g., all, each, every, both, half, either, neither, etc.

Types of Determiners

Types Of Determiners	Example	Noun
❑ ARTICLES	❑ A, An, The	❑ e.g., : The House
❑ DEMONSTRATIVES	❑ This, That, These, Those	❑ e.g., : These Houses
❑ POSSESSIVE ADJECTIVES	❑ My, your, her, his, our, its, their	❑ e.g., : Our house
❑ QUANTIFIERS	❑ A little, a few, many, much, a lot of, most, any, some, enough	❑ e.g., : A lot of houses
❑ DISTRIBUTIVES	❑ Both, all, half, neither, either, every, each	❑ e.g., : Both houses
❑ INTERROGATIVES	❑ What, which, whose	❑ e.g., : Which house?
❑ NUMBERS	❑ One, Five, Forty	❑ e.g., : Twenty houses

Articles

There are two types of articles:

Indefinite articles (A and An): They are used before a singular countable noun; and for something that is not specific or is mentioned for the first time.

- ❐ 'A' - it is used before consonant sounds.

  e.g., a University, a European etc.

- ❐ 'An' - it is used before vowel sounds.

  e.g., an hour, an apple etc.

  NOTE: We do not use a/an with uncountable nouns such as milk, water, sugar etc.

- ❐ They are used before a singular, countable noun which is an example of a class of things.

  e.g., A pet needs love and caring. (Here, class of things is pets.)

- ❐ They are used with certain exclamatory expressions (e.g., What a beautiful day!); with expression of frequency (e.g., once a week); units of price, speed, ratio, weight etc (e.g., 50 kms an hour)

Definite article (The) - It is used before a specific noun, when both the speaker and the listener know which noun is being referred to.

e.g., The dog that bit me ran away.

- ❐ Used before the names of invention, musical instruments, parts of the body, historical building, holy books, planets, rivers, oceans, gulf , group of islands, desert, hotels, names of direction, nationality.

  e.g., The Taj Mahal, The Sun, The Rajdhani Express, The Ramayana, The East, The English, The Radio etc.

- ❐ Used for superlative degree

  e.g., Lily is the most beautiful girl.

- ❐ In case of noun apposition

  e.g., Tagore, the poet was famous.

Knowledge Hub

If a ' language' word is used, 'The' article will be used.

Do you speak English language? (INCORRECT)

Do you speak the English language? (CORRECT)

Demonstratives

- ❐ They are used to identify or point to a particular person, event, or object.

  This and That - singular

  These and those - plural

  e.g., This chair is broken.

  These clothes are wet.

Possessive Adjectives

- ❐ They function as adjectives (it is a word that modifies nouns or pronouns) rather than pronouns.
- ❐ As they are adjectives, they appear before the noun that they are modifying.

  e.g., Do you like my new dress?

Subject pronoun	Possessive adjective	Examples
❑ I	❑ MY	❑ I like my dress.
❑ YOU	❑ YOUR	❑ Have you done your homework yet?
❑ HE	❑ HIS	❑ He took care of his grandparents.
❑ SHE	❑ HER	❑ She always eats her food.
❑ IT	❑ ITS	❑ The dog likes its food.
❑ WE	❑ OUR	❑ We began our work at noon.
❑ THEY	❑ THEIR	❑ Their house is near the town.

Quantifiers

A word or phrase that is used before a noun to show the amount or numbers.

Example of Quantifiers

Only with Uncountable Nouns	With both countable and Uncountable Nouns	Only with Countable Nouns
a little	no, none, not any	a few
a bit of	some, all	a number of
–	any	several
a great deal of	a lot of, lots of	a great number of
a large amount of	plenty of	a large number of

- Usually 'some' is used for affirmative sentences and 'any' is used for negative sentences.

  Example : I don't have any money with me.
- MUCH is used for uncountable nouns. eg : much milk etc.
- MANY is used for countable nouns. eg : many boys

Use of FEW and A FEW

- Few is used in a negative sense which emphasizes the lack of something.

  e.g., I have few friends in my new school. (means don't have many friends.)
- A few is used in the positive sense that something is there .

  e.g., I have a few friends in my previous organization. (means I have some friends)

Use of LITTLE and A LITTLE

- Little is used for uncountable nouns but in a negative sense which means hardly any.

  e.g., I drank little water this morning .
- A little is used for countable nouns. It is used in a positive sense that means something is there.

  e.g., I need a little sugar.

Distributive Determiner

- They are used to refer to a group or individual members of the group.
- It tells about people or things that are distributed and shared.

  e.g., Each student must attend the orientation program.

  Neither house is suitable for our needs.

  Both countries need to discuss the issues.
- EITHER and NEITHER are used for two things.
- ANY and NONE are used for more than two things.

Interrogative Determiner

- It is used to ask questions .
- 'Which' - is used to ask about a specific group of people or things.
- 'What' - is used when we are asking a general question.
- 'Whose' - is used to ask a question about possession.

  e.g., Which one do you like best?

  Whose pencil is this?

  What time will you come?

Numbers

It is of two types:

- CARDINAL - one, two, three etc. refers to counting .
- ORDINAL - first, second, fourth etc. refers to ranking or order .

  e.g., It is my sixteenth birthday.

  There are twenty students in the class .

INTEGRATED GRAMMAR

9

Fill in the blanks

Fill in the blanks choosing the correct option from the given options:

1. The teacher along with his students ________ planning a surprise party.
   (*a*) is (*b*) are
   (*c*) was (*d*) were
2. By the time you arrive, the movie ________.
   (*a*) starts (*b*) will start
   (*c*) will have started (*d*) start
3. All of the cookies ________ eaten by the time we got to the party.
   (*a*) was (*b*) were
   (*c*) have been (*d*) had been
4. ________ you mind turning down the music a little?
   (*a*) Will (*b*) Would
   (*c*) Can (*d*) Do
5. Select the correct option to fill in the blank for the given sentence: **(CBSE, 2023)**
   ______ you help me cross the road, young man?
   (*a*) Will (*b*) May
   (*c*) Shall (*d*) Might
6. Complete the given narrative, by filling in the blanks with the correct option: **(CBSE, 2023)**
   NO NEWS ________ GOOD NEWS.
   (*a*) HAS (*b*) HAD
   (*c*) IS (*d*) ARE
7. No sooner had the concert began than the lights ________ out.
   (*a*) went (*b*) go
   (*c*) goes (*d*) have gone
8. To enhance our understanding of ancient civilizations, the archaeologist suggested that we ________ the latest research on Egyptian hieroglyphics.
   (*a*) are reading (*b*) read
   (*c*) have read (*d*) reads
9. Fill in the blank by using the correct form of the word in the bracket: **(CBSE, 2023)**
   Governments are starting programmes ______(teach) adults how to read and write.
   (*a*) that teaching (*b*) which taught
   (*c*) to teach (*d*) were teaching
10. Under new management, the company policies ________ to better accommodate work-life balance for all employees.
    (*a*) are being revised (*b*) revise
    (*c*) has revised (*d*) were revised
11. If he ________ earlier, he wouldn't have missed the beginning of the seminar.
    (*a*) arrived (*b*) would arrive
    (*c*) had arrived (*d*) was arriving
12. When I was in college, I ________ study until late at night without feeling tired.
    (*a*) can (*b*) must
    (*c*) might (*d*) could
13. Everyone in the meeting ________ in agreement that a new strategy was essential for improving productivity.
    (*a*) nod (*b*) nods
    (*c*) nodded (*d*) nodding
14. This old car ________ break down if we don't service it soon. (is bound to/ may)
15. In an effort to maintain discipline, the school rules state that students ________ their mobile phones during class hours.
    (*a*) are using (*b*) used
    (*c*) must not use (*d*) have used
16. You should ________ your mother for your rude behaviour. **(CBSE, 2023)**
    (*a*) apologise for (*b*) apologise at
    (*c*) apologise with (*d*) apologise to
17. Every morning, the captain ________ the crew's tasks for the day.
    (*a*) lays out (*b*) lays in
    (*c*) lays on (*d*) lays off

18. The company encourages employees to ________ new ideas during brainstorming sessions.

(a) throw away (b) throw up

(c) throw out (d) throw down

19. After witnessing the event, the reporter aimed to capture the public's ________ (react) in her article.

20. Unexpectedly, the power outage ________ the conference, leading to an early adjournment.

(a) cut off (b) cut out

(c) cut down (d) cut short

21. To reach the scenic viewpoint, tourists must follow the clearly ________ (mark) path.

22. In preparation for the tournament, the athlete decided to ________ his speed and agility.

(a) focus off (b) focus out

(c) focus in (d) focus on

23. The marketing team was tasked with creating an ________ (engage) campaign for the new product launch.

24. Employees were encouraged to ________ issues affecting their work-life balance.

(a) speak up (b) speak out

(c) speak of (d) speak about

25. Mathematics ________ in many countries as a fundamental part of the curriculum.

(a) teaches (b) will be taught

(c) is taught (d) has been taught

26. Last summer, we ________ a fascinating journey across the Silk Road.

(a) undertake (b) undertook

(c) are undertaking (d) will undertake

27. The students ________ become quite restless towards the end of the school year. (usually/sometimes)

28. They had already left for the airport by the time I ________ them.

(a) call (b) called

(c) was calling (d) had called

29. ________ educated mind can teach many.

(CBSE, 2023)

(a) THE (b) A

(c) AN (d) THIS

30. The coach provided ________________ (detail) feedback after reviewing the game footage.

31. At the start of the class, the instructor ________ a brief meditation session.

(a) called off (b) called on

(c) called up (d) called out

32. After finishing their meals, diners are expected to ________ their trays in the cafeteria.

(a) put up (b) put in

(c) put away (d) put off

33. The researcher conducted interviews to gather ________ (inform) about the local community's traditions and customs.

34. ________ you please pass the salt?

(a) Could (b) Shall

(c) Will (d) Must

35. To navigate the dense forest, the explorer relied on the ________ (sign) paths provided by the local guides.

36. ________ of the answers provided in the quiz were correct.

(a) All (b) Some

(c) None (d) Any

37. She ________ be working late tonight to finish the report.

(a) has to (b) might

(c) will (d) have to

38. We ________ visit the new museum exhibit next weekend.

(a) could (b) must

(c) might (d) will

39. ________ of my friends has been to Africa.

(a) Each (b) Both

(c) Neither (d) Either

40. "Speak kindly, listen carefully, and ________ understanding in every conversation."

(a) foster (b) fosters

(c) fostering (d) to foster

Fill in the blanks choosing the correct option from the given options:

41. The FBI arrested two young men but neither of them ________ responsible for the robbery.

(a) was (b) were

(c) was being (d) have been

42. The child ________ be very naughty at times. (will/ can)

43. Mr Dhawan, accompanied by his wife Maya and his brother, ________ to the forest.

(a) has been banished (b) was banished

(c) were banished (d) none of these

44. If it rains today, we ________ cancel the extra class. (could/ will)

45. When I was young , I ________.

(a) can run ten miles (b) should run ten miles

(c) might run ten miles (d) could run ten miles

46. The number of people lined up at the ration shops ________ twenty three.

(a) was (b) were

(c) have been (d) none of the above

47. Dosa and sambar ________ my favourite breakfast.

(a) are (b) is

(c) has been (d) have been

48. ________ her soul rest in peace! (Would/May)

49. We ________ respect our parents.
(*a*) may (*b*) ought to
(*c*) will (*d*) can

50. A pair of socks ________ been missing from my drawer.
(*a*) have (*b*) is
(*c*) were (*d*) has

51. ________ you shut the door, please?
(*a*) Should (*b*) Might
(*c*) Could (*d*) May

52. The information provided to us ________ incorrect.
(*a*) were (*b*) are
(*c*) was (*d*) have been

53. Each and every student ________ to attend the event.
(*a*) has (*b*) have
(*c*) having (*d*) are

54. Half of the room ________ empty by 1:00 pm.
(*a*) were (*b*) was
(*c*) has (*d*) have

55. The French ________ known for their style and fashion.
(*a*) is (*b*) are
(*c*) will be (*d*) have been

56. I think I ________ have failed the test, but I'm not sure.
(*a*) ought to (*b*) might
(*c*) shall (*d*) will

57. I can stay at ________ hotel. Both are good .
(*a*) either (*b*) neither
(*c*) each (*d*) every

58. I ________ get there on time. (determination)
(*a*) may (*b*) can
(*c*) will (*d*) could

59. She ________ on her assignment since morning.
(*a*) is working (*b*) has been working
(*c*) was working (*d*) has worked

60. After reading the inspiring novel, she ________ a renewed sense of purpose in life.
(*a*) feels (*b*) feeling
(*c*) felt (*d*) to feel

61. The hospital board clearly mentioned that you ________ smoke in the hospital as it is a health hazard for all.
(CBSE SQP, 2021)
(*a*) cannot (*b*) must not
(*c*) need not (*d*) might not

62. English ________
(*a*) speaks all over the world.
(*b*) will be spoken all over the world.
(*c*) is spoken all over the world.
(*d*) has been spoken all over the world.

63. My family and I ________
(*a*) go to the cinema last night.
(*b*) went to the cinema last night.
(*c*) am going to the cinema last night.
(*d*) shall go to the cinema last night.

64. Alakh ________ this test recently.
(*a*) pass (*b*) passed
(*c*) have passed (*d*) has passed

65. Shikha had already begun eating her dinner by the time I ________ there.
(*a*) reached (*b*) had reached
(*c*) was reaching (*b*) had been reaching

66. He has ________ money.
(*a*) little (*b*) few
(*c*) many (*d*) a lot

67. Fill in the blank by using the correct form of the word in the bracket :
The teacher provided a clear ________ (instruct) on how to complete the assignment.

68. Complete the given narrative by filling in the blank with the correct option:
The teacher ________ the students' names during roll call.
(*a*) called off (*b*) called on
(*c*) called up (*d*) called out

69. Complete the given narrative by filling in the blank with the correct option:
The librarian reminded the students to ________ their books in the designated shelves after use.
(*a*) put up (*b*) put in
(*c*) put away (*d*) put off

70. Fill in the blank by using the correct form of the word in the bracket :
The journalist interviewed several witnesses to gather eyewitness ________ (account) of the incident.

71. Complete the given narrative by filling in the blank with the correct option:
The sudden rainstorm ________ our plans for a picnic in the park.
(*a*) called off (*b*) called on
(*c*) called up (*d*) called out

72. Fill in the blank by using the correct form of the word in the bracket :
The hiker followed the ________ (mark) trail to reach the mountain summit.

73. Complete the given narrative by filling in the blank with the correct option:
The coach advised the players to ________ their skills during the off-season.
(*a*) work off (*b*) work out
(*c*) work in (*d*) work on

74. Fill in the blank by using the correct form of the word in the bracket :

The manager emphasized the importance of effective ________ (communicate) within the team.

75. Complete the given narrative by filling in the blank with the correct option:

The supervisor requested the employees to ________ their grievances through the proper channels.

(*a*) bring off (*b*) bring up
(*c*) bring in (*d*) bring down

76. Fill in the blank by using the correct form of the word in the bracket :

The architect presented a detailed ________ (plan) for the construction of the new building.

77. The meeting has been rescheduled, and ________ (this/that/then) is reflected in the updated calendar.

78. Select the correct option to fill in the blank for the given line, from a health magazine. The advertisement read, 'If you smoke, statistically your story end 15% before it should'. **(CBSE SQP, 2023)**

(*a*) must (*b*) should
(*c*) will (*d*) ought to

79. There's never ________ petrol left after Mohan uses my bike.

(*a*) much (*b*) little
(*c*) many (*d*) a little

80. Do you ever learnt from a mistake you make? Which word in the sentence is grammatically wrong?

(*a*) Do (*b*) learnt
(*c*) from (*d*) make

81. Fill in the blank by using the correct form of the word in the bracket for the given portion of a letter: **(CBSE, 2024)**

We hope that you continue to work with the same zeal and keep ________ (surprise) us with such remarkable performances. We thank you and wish you good luck for your upcoming projects.

Regards.

82. Fill in the blank by choosing the correct option, to complete the line from the policy document of an insurance company: **(CBSE, 2024)**

It is our endeavour to settle your maturity claim on or before the due date. The Servicing Branch ________(likely/usually/occasionally) sends maturity claim intimations two months in advance.

83. Complete the given narrative by filling in the blank, with the correct option: **(CBSE, 2024)**

Finally, she went to the best doctor in town. The doctor spent months on ________ her until she was finally cured.

(*a*) treats (*b*) treated
(*c*) to treating (*d*) treating

84. Fill in the blank by choosing the correct option to complete the part of the "All Rights Reserved" note given in a textbook. **(CBSE, 2024)**

No part of this publication may be reproduced, transcribed, transmitted, stored or translated into any language. 'Any person ________' in relation to this publication may be liable to criminal prosecution and civil claims for damages.

(*a*) who will be doing any unauthorized act
(*b*) who is doing any unauthorized act
(*c*) who does any unauthorized act
(*d*) who may do any unauthorized act

85. Complete the slogan, by filling in the blank with the correct option: **(CBSE, 2024)**

There's No place Like Earth To Live and Work. So Let's ________ A Better Place.

(*a*) Making It (*b*) Creates It
(*c*) Make It (*d*) Create It

Reported Speech

86. Read the conversation given below and complete the paragraph that follows:

Coach: Have you finished your training schedule for the week?

Athlete: Not yet, but I plan to complete it by tomorrow.

Coach: It's important to stick to the schedule for optimal performance.

Athlete: I understand and will make sure to finish on time.

The coach inquired if the athlete (a) ____________ for the week. The athlete admitted that (b) ____________ but assured to complete it by tomorrow. The coach emphasized the importance of sticking to the schedule for optimal performance, to which the athlete agreed and promised to finish on time.

87. Read the conversations between a customer and a waiter. Complete the sentence by reporting the waiter's reply correctly: **(CBSE, 2023)**

Customer: Waiter, come here. The plate is dirty.

Waiter: I'll change it sir.

The customer asked the waiter to come there. He pointed out that the plate was dirty. The waiter politely offered ______________.

88. Read the conversation given below and complete the paragraph that follows:

Manager: Are we on track to meet the project deadline?

Team Leader: We're slightly behind schedule, but I'm confident we'll catch up.

Manager: What steps are you taking to ensure we meet the deadline?

Team Leader: We're allocating extra hours and prioritizing tasks more effectively.

The manager questioned if (*a*) ____________ to meet the project deadline. The team leader admitted that (*b*) ______________ behind schedule but expressed confidence in catching up by allocating extra hours and prioritizing tasks more effectively.

89. Read the conversation given below and complete the paragraph that follows:

Author: Can you provide feedback on my latest manuscript?

Editor: I've read through it and have some suggestions for improvement.

Author: I'm eager to hear your thoughts and make necessary revisions.

Editor: Great, let's schedule a meeting to discuss this in detail.

The author asked the editor if (*a*) ____________ on the latest manuscript. The editor confirmed that (*b*) ____________ and offered suggestions for improvement. The author expressed eagerness to hear the editor's thoughts and make necessary revisions, leading to scheduling a meeting to discuss details.

90. Read the conversation given below and complete the paragraph that follows:

Parent: Have you completed your homework for the day?

Child: I've finished most of it, but I'm stuck on a maths problem.

Parent: Do you need help with it?

Child: Yes, please. I can't seem to figure out the solution.

The parent asked the child if (*a*) ____________ for the day. The child replied (*b*) ____________ most of it but was stuck on a maths problem, seeking the parent's help for a solution. The parent then offered assistance, understanding the child's difficulty with the problem.

91. Select the correct option to complete the narration of a dialogue between a librarian and a patron.

Librarian: Do you need help finding a book?

Patron: Yes, I'm looking for books on ancient Greek history.

The patron asked the librarian if he needed help finding a book. The librarian replied that ____________.

(*a*) he were looking for books on ancient Greek history.

(*b*) he are looking for books on ancient Greek history.

(*c*) he was looking for books on ancient Greek history.

(*d*) he look for books on ancient Greek history.

92. Select the correct option to complete the narration of a dialogue between two colleagues.

Colleague 1: Will you be attending the webinar on digital marketing?

Colleague 2: Yes, I think it's a great opportunity to learn more about the field.

Colleague 1 asked Colleague 2 if they would be attending the webinar on digital marketing. Colleague 2 replied that ____________.

(*a*) he think it's a great opportunity to learn more about the field.

(*b*) he thought it's a great opportunity to learn more about the field.

(*c*) he thought it was a great opportunity to learn more about the field.

(*d*) he thinks it's a great opportunity to learn more about the field.

93. Select the correct option to complete the narration of a dialogue between a coach and an athlete.

Coach: Have you completed your training for today?

Athlete: Yes, I've just finished and feel ready for the competition.

The coach asked the athlete if the team had completed their training for today. The athlete replied that ________.

(*a*) Team have just finished and feel ready for the competition.

(*b*) Team just finished and felt ready for the competition.

(*c*) Team had just finished and felt ready for the competition.

(*d*) Team has just finished and feel ready for the competition.

94. Select the correct option to complete the narration of a dialogue between a writer and an editor.

Writer: Can you review my latest chapter by tomorrow?

Editor: Certainly, I'll have feedback for you by the end of the day.

The writer asked the editor if they could review their latest chapter by tomorrow. The editor replied that ____________.

(*a*) he'll have feedback for them by the end of the day.

(*b*) he would have feedback for them by the end of the day.

(*c*) he will have feedback for you by the end of the day.

(*d*) he would have feedback for you by the end of the day.

95. Select the correct option to complete the narration of a dialogue between a customer and a salesperson.

Customer: Do these shoes come in any other colors?

Salesperson: Yes, they're available in black, white, and red.

The customer asked the salesperson if the shoes came in any other colors. The salesperson replied that ____________.

(*a*) those are available in black, white, and red.

(*b*) they were available in black, white, and red.

(*c*) they are available in black, white, and red.

(*d*) they was available in black, white, and red.

96. Read the conversation between two colleagues. Complete the sentence by reporting the reply correctly.

Alice: Do you think you could help me with this project proposal?

Bob: Absolutely, I've got some free time this afternoon.

Alice asked Bob if he could help her with the project proposal to which Bob agreed and said that ________.

97. Read the conversation between two classmates. Complete the sentence by reporting the reply correctly.

Sam: Are you coming to the study group tonight?

Emma: Yes, I plan to. I really need to catch up on Physics.

Sam asked Emma if she was coming to the study group tonight. Emma replied that ____________ and added that ____________.

98. Report the dialogue between a patient and a doctor by completing the sentence.

Patient: Should I be worried about this persistent cough?

Doctor: It's good you came in. I should run some tests to be safe.

The patient asked the doctor ________, to which the doctor recommended ________.

99. Jake and Leah had a coversation regarding a meeting. Lisa inquired about a community event. Report her question.

Is there a meeting for the neighborhood this weekend?

100. Report the dialogue between two teammates by completing the sentence.

Mark: Will you be able to play in the match this Saturday?

Eric: Yes, my injury has healed completely.

Mark asked Eric (*a*) ________, and Eric confirmed, mentioning that (*b*) ________.

101. Read the conversation given below and complete the paragraph that follows: **(CBSE, 2022)**

Seema: Why haven't you brought my practical file ?

Rita: I had gone to my uncle's house with my parents, so I forgot to keep it.

Seema: Don't make an excuse. I want to know the truth.

Rita: I am sorry Seema. I was chatting with my friends till late. I forgot that you needed it urgently.

Seema asked Rita (*a*) ________. Rita said that she had gone to her uncle's house with her parents, so she had forgotten to keep it. Seema (*b*) ________. Rita said that she was sorry and further added she had been chatting with her friends till late and she had forgotten that Seema needed it urgently.

102. Read the conversation given below and complete the paragraph that follows:

Arun: I am surprised to see you here in London. When did you come ?

Varun: I came here yesterday. I have been offered a job here.

Arun told Varun that (*a*) ________ and asked when he had come. Varun replied that he had come the previous day and added that (*b*) ________.

103. Read the conversation given below and complete the paragraph that follows: **(CBSE, 2022)**

Doctor: You must exercise daily to keep your heart fit.

Patient: Is it enough if I go for a daily morning walk and do some breathing exercises ?

The doctor advised the patient that he (*a*) ________. The patient questioned whether it was enough if he (*b*) ________.

104. Read the conversation given below and complete the paragraph that follows: **(CBSE, 2022)**

Passenger: Please give me three tickets to India Gate.

Conductor: Ten rupees a ticket.

The passenger requested the conductor (*a*) ________. The conductor replied that (*b*) ________.

105. Read the conversation given below and complete the paragraph that follows: **(CBSE, 2022)**

Ritika: Can I borrow your Math book for a couple of days?

Mohit: Yes certainly, I have already studied for the test tomorrow.

Ritika asked Mohit (*a*) ________ for a couple of days. Mohit agreed and said that (*b*) ________.

106. Read the conversation between a policeman and a driver. Complete the sentence by reporting the driver's reply correctly. **(CBSE, 2023)**

Policeman: Why did you park your car here?

Don't you see a 'no parking area'.

Driver: Sorry Sir! The engine broke down.

The policeman asked the driver why he had parked the car there and if he didn't see it was a 'no parking area'.

The driver felt sorry and explained ________.

107. Read the conversation between two friends. Complete the sentence by reporting the reply correctly.

Supriya: I am surprised to see you here in Paris. When did you come?

Vijay: I have been offered a job here. I arrived yesterday.

Supriya told Vijay that she was surprised to see Vijay there in Paris and asked when he had come. Vijay replied that ________ and added that ________.

108. Report the dialogue between two business partners by completing the sentence.

Rina: Will you be attending the conference next week?

Sandeep: Yes, I have already registered and made travel arrangements.

Rina asked Sandeep ________, to which Sandeep confirmed and mentioned that ________.

109. Report Sarah's question and John's reply.

Sarah: Could you please proofread my essay?

John: Of course, I have experience in editing academic papers.

110. Alex shared some information about a nearby library. Report Emily's question.

Do you know when the library will close today?

111. Report the dialogue between two friends by completing the sentence.

Mia: Can you lend me your calculator for the math exam?

Daniel: Sure, I have already finished the exam and won't need it.

Mia asked Daniel ________, and Daniel agreed, mentioning that he had already finished the exam and wouldn't need it.

112. Kevin was talking about tonight's party. Report Sophia's question.

Will you be attending the party tonight?

113. Select the correct option to complete the narration of a dialogue between a student and a teacher.

Student: Could you please explain the concept of photosynthesis?

Teacher: Certainly, plants use sunlight to convert carbon dioxide into glucose.

The student asked the teacher if they could explain the concept of photosynthesis. The teacher replied that ______________________.

(*a*) plants used sunlight to convert carbon dioxide into glucose.

(*b*) plants use sunlight to convert carbon dioxide into glucose.

(*c*) plants use sunlight for converting carbon dioxide into glucose.

(*d*) plants use sunlight to convert carbon dioxide into sugar.

114. Select the correct option to complete the narration of a dialogue between a tourist and a local resident.

Tourist: Can you recommend a good restaurant nearby?

Local Resident: Yes, there's a popular Italian restaurant just around the corner.

The tourist asked the local resident if they could recommend a good restaurant nearby. The local resident replied that ______________________.

(*a*) there was a popular Italian restaurant just around the corner.

(*b*) there is a popular Italian restaurant just around the corner.

(*c*) there is a popular Italian restaurant just around the corner.

(*d*) there are a popular Italian restaurant just around the corner.

115. Select the correct option to complete the narration of a dialogue between an employee and a manager.

Employee: Is there a meeting scheduled for tomorrow?

Manager: Yes, the team will be discussing the project updates in the conference room at 10 AM.

The employee asked the manager if there was a meeting scheduled for tomorrow. The manager replied that ______________________.

(*a*) the team will discuss the project updates in the conference room at 10 AM.

(*b*) the team will be discussing the project updates in the conference room at 10 AM.

(*c*) the team would be discussing the project updates in the conference room at 10 AM.

(*d*) the team discussed the project updates in the conference room at 10 AM.

116. Tanu and Amit had a conversation about the execution of Tanu's travel plan.

Report Amit's question.

Will you be going with your family?

117. Read the dialogue between Karan and his friend, Parvaiz regarding Karan's winter vacation plans:

Karan: How is your winter vacation plan shaping up?

Parvaiz: Alas ! There are no plans. We have extra classes during our winter vacation.

Select the correct option to complete the reporting of the above dialogue.

Karan asked Parvaiz how his winter vacation plan was shaping up. Parvaiz sighed and said there were no plans. He further added that __________.

(*a*) they had extra classes during our winter vacation

(*b*) he has extra classes during their winter vacations

(*c*) they had extra classes during their winter vacation

(*d*) they have extra classes during their winter vacation

118. Report the dialogue between two friends, Madhur and Priyanka, by completing the sentence:

Madhur: Do you know the importance of water for our body?

Priyanka: Yes, indeed ! Water is essential for digestion and regulates body temperature.

Madhur asked Priyanka if she knew about the importance of water for their body. Priyanka answered in the affirmative and explained that __________.

Error Detection

Identify the error in the segment below and supply the correction. Use the given format for your response.

119. Every students in the class was given a chance to express their views.

ERROR	CORRECTION

120. She has been living in New York since three years.

ERROR	CORRECTION

121. The committee have decided to postpone the meeting to next month.

ERROR	CORRECTION

122. Many people believes that climate change is the most pressing issue of our time.

ERROR	CORRECTION

123. He gave me two advices that changed my life.

ERROR	CORRECTION

124. This is one of the best book I have ever read.

ERROR	CORRECTION

125. There is many reasons why I prefer to study at night.

ERROR	CORRECTION

126. She can speaks three languages fluently.

ERROR	CORRECTION

127. An university should be a place of light, of liberty, and of learning.

ERROR	CORRECTION

128. The team are working on the project day and night to meet the deadline.

ERROR	CORRECTION

129. He gave me some suggestion on how to improve my speaking skills.

ERROR	CORRECTION

130. A sun is necessary for plant growth and photosynthesis.

ERROR	CORRECTION

131. The professor gave a detailed explanation for the topic.

ERROR	CORRECTION

132. They went to the store to buy breads, milk, and eggs.

ERROR	CORRECTION

133. The educational infrastructure is still not developed in the way it might have been after so many years of Independence.

ERROR	CORRECTION

134. I has three years of experience as a receptionist in a company.

ERROR	CORRECTION

135. My current employer and coworkers feels that I am an asset to the team.

ERROR	CORRECTION

136. The word pollution is derive from the Latin word pollure, which means to make dirty.

ERROR	CORRECTION

137. Pollution was the process of polluting the environment by adding harmful substances.

ERROR	CORRECTION

138. I went to the temple with my parents, aunts and cousin sisters.

ERROR	CORRECTION

139. I like the poetries of Byron and Shelley.

ERROR	CORRECTION

140. Identify the error and supply correction for the following sentence taken from a copyright's document.
The information contained herein is subject to change without notice. Reproducing, adaptation or translation without prior written permission is prohibited. **(CBSE, 2024)**
Use the given format for your response.

ERROR	CORRECTION

141. Read the given sentence from a medical journal. Identify the error and supply the correction in the sentence:
A flu vaccine's most common side effects are soreness, redness and swelling at the injection site. These ought begin six to twelve hours after vaccination and can last upto two days. **(CBSE, 2024)**
Use the given format for your response.

ERROR	CORRECTION

142. Identify the error and supply correction for the given part of the note appearing on an educational website.
Please Note: An early and active communication is required as late notification may result in a delay redressal of your request. **(CBSE, 2024)**
Use the given format for your response.

ERROR	CORRECTION

Select the option that identifies the error and supplies the correction for the following line:

143. The information provided in the brochure are very useful for tourists.

	ERROR	CORRECTION
(*a*)	are	is
(*b*)	in	on
(*c*)	very	extremely
(*d*)	brochure	brochures

144. Each students in the class has to submit their project by the end of this week.

	ERROR	CORRECTION
(*a*)	students	student
(*b*)	has	have
(*c*)	their	his or her
(*d*)	by	unit

145. One of my friends are planning to start his own business next year.

	ERROR	CORRECTION
(*a*)	are	is
(*b*)	his	their
(*c*)	start	starting
(*d*)	business	businesses

146. Research show that regular exercise is beneficial for your health.

	ERROR	CORRECTION
(*a*)	research	researches
(*b*)	show	shows
(*c*)	is	are
(*d*)	your	our

147. The team is working hard to ensures they meet the deadline.

	ERROR	CORRECTION
(*a*)	ensures	ensure
(*b*)	is	are
(*c*)	meet	meets
(*d*)	the	a

148. He do not understand the significance of this ceremony.

	ERROR	CORRECTION
(*a*)	do	does
(*b*)	understand	understands
(*c*)	significances	significance
(*d*)	this	that

149. Identify the error in the segment below and supply the correction.

"The birds in the forest needs water to survive."

	ERROR	CORRECTION
(*a*)	needs	need
(*b*)	the forest	a forest
(*c*)	birds	bird
(*d*)	survive	survives

150. Identify the error in the segment below and supply the correction.

"He provided a comprehensive review for the book."

	ERROR	CORRECTION
(*a*)	for	of
(*b*)	provided	provides
(*c*)	the book	a book
(*d*)	review	reviews

151. Error Detection

Identify the error in the segment below and supply the correction.

"His understanding of the subjects are impressive."

	ERROR	CORRECTION
(*a*)	subjects	subject
(*b*)	are	is
(*c*)	His	He's
(*d*)	understanding	understand

152. You should not put your sign on any paper that you haven't read.

	ERROR	CORRECTION
(*a*)	should	can
(*b*)	paper	papers
(*c*)	sign	signature
(*d*)	haven't	doesn't

153. Satyajit Ray, who conceived, co-authored and directed a number of good films, was one of India's most talented filmmaker.

	ERROR	CORRECTION
(*a*)	filmmaker	filmmakers
(*b*)	a number of	the number of
(*c*)	was	had
(*d*)	most	the most

154. I shall not go to a party tonight since I have a lot of works to complete before I give the presentation tomorrow.

	ERROR	CORRECTION
(*a*)	give	gave
(*b*)	works	work
(*c*)	since	for
(*d*)	shall	am

155. The sceneries of Kashmir is very charming.

	ERROR	CORRECTION
(a)	sceneries	scenery
(b)	of	about
(c)	is	are
(d)	very	more

156. One of the firmest belief among the Hindus is that Karma affects their life and also the life after death.

	ERROR	CORRECTION
(a)	affects	affect
(b)	belief	beliefs
(c)	is	are
(d)	after	before

157. If you have a way with words, a good sense of design and administration ability you may enjoy working in the high pressure world of advertising.

	ERROR	CORRECTION
(a)	administration	administrative
(b)	with	of
(c)	ability	abilities
(d)	enjoy	enjoys

158. Select the option that identifies the error and supplies the correction for the following sentence: **(CBSE, 2023)**
More of the fun and excitement in our lives comes from using our imagination.

	ERROR	CORRECTION
(a)	More	Most
(b)	Our	The
(c)	From	Of
(d)	Using	Use

159. All his sister-in-laws are extremely co-operative and he doesn't miss his real sisters at all.

	ERROR	CORRECTION
(a)	he	they
(b)	are	is
(c)	sister-in-laws	sisters-in-laws
(d)	doesn't	didn't

160. She was wearing spectacle and so she was unable to see the gangster that attacked her.

	ERROR	CORRECTION
(a)	see	seeing
(b)	so	because
(c)	was wearing	wears
(d)	spectacle	spectacles

161. They left their luggages at home by mistake and went to the railway station.

	ERROR	CORRECTION
(a)	luggages	luggage
(b)	at	in
(c)	and	so
(d)	their	theirs

162. Select the option that identifies the error and supplies the correction for a line from a Research Report on Water Conservation.
Excess pumping of groundwater leads to decrease in groundwater levels but if continues, it can exhaust the resource.

	ERROR	CORRECTION
(a)	leads	lead
(b)	continues	continued
(c)	and	also
(d)	can	should

ANSWERS & EXPLANATIONS

Fill in the blanks

1. (*a*) is

   Exp. When the subject is combined with "along with", "as well as", or similar expressions, the verb agrees with the first subject. In this case, "the teacher" is singular, so "is" is the correct verb.

2. (*c*) will have started

   Exp. This sentence describes an action that will be completed before another action in the future. "Will have started" is the correct form of the future perfect tense to use here.

3. (*d*) had been

   Exp. This sentence describes an action that was completed before another past action. "Had been" is the correct passive form of the past perfect tense to use here.

4. (*b*) Would

   Exp. "Would you mind" is the correct polite form to ask someone to do something.

5. (*a*) "Will" is used to request someone to do something in the future. It is asking for the young man's assistance at that moment or in the immediate future.

6. The word "is" corresponds to the singular noun "news". The phrase is used to convey that the lack of new information might suggest that the situation remains stable and there are no problems to report.

7. (*a*) went

   Exp. "Went out" is the correct phrase to describe the action that occurred immediately after the concert began.

8. (*b*) read

   Exp. This question tests the subjunctive mood used for suggestions. "Suggested that we read" is the correct usage, indicating a recommendation rather than stating what is currently happening or has happened.

9. (*c*) to teach

   Exp. The infinitive form "to teach" is commonly used after a noun to explain why something is done.

10. (*a*) are being revised

    Exp. This question tests the passive voice in the present continuous tense, suitable for ongoing actions. "Are being revised" indicates that the process is currently happening.

11. (*c*) had arrived

    Exp. This question is about the third conditional for hypothetical situations in the past. "Had arrived" correctly forms the conditional part of a sentence expressing a situation that didn't happen.

12. (*d*) could

    Exp. In this sentence, the speaker is referring to an ability they had in the past, which is appropriately expressed using "could", the past tense form of "can". "Can" is used for present abilities, "must" for obligations, and "might" for possibilities.

13. (*c*) nodded

    Exp. This question is about verb tense agreement with a past time expression. "Nodded" is correct for a past action where everyone showed agreement.

14. (*a*) is bound to

    Exp. The phrase "is bound to" indicates a very high probability or near certainty of something happening, which fits the context of the car breaking down without service. "May" suggests a possibility but does not convey the same level of likelihood.

15. (*c*) must not use

    Exp. The correct answer is "must not use", which accurately conveys a prohibition within the context of school rules regarding the use of mobile phones during class hours. This choice reflects the necessity to adhere to a specific behavior as dictated by the rules.

16. (*d*) apologise to

    Exp. The preposition "to" is used to direct the apology at someone who has been wronged or offended. Other prepositions like 'for", "at", or "with" do not fit in this context.

17. (*a*) lays out

    Exp. "Lays out" means to explain something clearly or to arrange something in an orderly way, which fits the context of a captain assigning tasks.

18. (*c*) throw out

    Exp. "Throw out" is the correct phrase meaning to suggest or present an idea for consideration, suitable for a brainstorming context.

19. reaction

    Exp. The correct form of "react" in this context is "reaction," referring to how people responded to the event.

20. (*d*) cut short

    Exp. "Cut short" means to cause something to end before its planned conclusion, fitting the scenario of an interrupted conference.

21. marked

Exp. The correct form of "mark" in this context is "marked". Marked specifically refers to having a sign or other indicator on it.

22. (*d*) focus on

Exp. "Focus on" is the correct phrase meaning to concentrate on a particular task or aspect, applicable to an athlete's training regiment.

23. engaging

Exp. Engaging is an adjective that describes something that captures and holds people's attention and interest.

24. (*a*) speak up

Exp. "Speak up" means to express one's thoughts or concerns openly or publicly, fitting the encouragement for employees to discuss work-life balance issues.

25. (*c*) is taught

Exp. "Is taught" indicates that mathematics is currently taught across many countries, reflecting a general, ongoing action.

26. (*b*) undertook

Exp. "undertook" is the correct past tense form of "undertake," indicating a journey that happened in the past.

27. (*a*) usually

Exp. The word "usually" suggests that it is a common or regular occurrence, fitting the context of a recurring behaviour observed in students as the school year comes to an end. "Sometimes" implies that it happens less frequently or irregularly.

28. (*b*) called

Exp. In this sentence, "called" is the past tense form of the verb "call," which correctly indicates the action of making a phone call to "them" in the past.

29. (*c*) AN

Exp. In English, the article "an" is used before words that start with a vowel sound. Because "educated" starts with the vowel sound 'e', "an" is the appropriate choice.

30. detailed

Exp. Detailed emphasizes the comprehensiveness and thoroughness of the feedback the coach provided. It indicates that the coach went into specific points and aspects of the game footage.

31. (*b*) called on

Exp. "called on" is the right choice, implying the instructor initiated or began the session.

called off: to cancel or terminate something that was previously planned or scheduled.

called on: to visit or contact someone, typically for a specific purpose or reason.

called up: to summon or contact someone, often by telephone.

called out: to publicly challenge or criticize someone or something, often for their actions or behavior.

32. (*c*) put away

Exp. "Put away" correctly indicates the action of returning items to their proper storage place.

put up: to erect or assemble something, such as a structure or a poster.

put in: to insert or place something into a particular position or location.

put away: to store or stow something in its designated place, typically to tidy up or organize.

put off: to postpone or delay something to a later time or date.

33. information

Exp. "Inform" is a verb, while "information" is the correct noun form, indicating the data or details gathered by the researcher during the interviews.

34. (*a*)

Exp. The modal verb "could" is used to make polite requests. While "will" and "shall" can also be used to form requests, they are less polite in this context, and "must" is not appropriate as it implies obligation rather than request.

35. signed

Exp. "signed" means marked with signs, aiding navigation through potentially confusing or difficult terrain.

36. (*a*) All

Exp. The phrase "All of the answers provided in the quiz were correct" suggests that every single answer was right, making (a) All the correct choice.

37. (c) Will

Exp. Will be working indicates a future action that is planned or expected to happen.

"She might be working late tonight to finish the report" indicates a possibility or uncertainty about her working late. "Has to," "will," and "should" indicate necessity, certainty, and obligation/advisability respectively, which are not as suitable for expressing possibility.

38. (*d*) will

Exp. "We will visit the new museum exhibit next weekend" expresses a definite plan or decision to do something in the future, making (d) the correct choice.

39. (*c*) Neither

Exp. "Neither of my friends has been to Africa" is correct when referring to two friends, both of whom have not been to Africa.

40. (*a*) foster

Exp. In this slogan, the structure is a series of imperatives (commands or suggestions for action) linked by commas. The imperatives "Speak kindly" and "listen carefully" set the pattern, so the verb that follows should also be in the base form to maintain parallel structure and grammatical consistency. "Foster" in its base form fits perfectly, continuing the imperative mood.

41. (*a*) was
42. can
43. (*b*) was banished
44. will
45. (*d*) could run ten miles
46. (*a*) was
47. (*b*) is
48. May
49. (*b*) ought to
50. (*d*) has
51. (*c*) Could
52. (*c*) was
53. (*a*) has
54. (*b*) was
55. (*b*) are
56. (*b*) might
57. (*b*) either
58. (*c*) will
59. (*b*) has been working
60. (*c*) felt
61. (*b*) must not
62. (*c*) is spoken all over the world.
63. (*b*) went to the cinema last night.
64. (*d*) has passed
65. (*a*) reached
66. (*a*) little
67. instruction
68. called out
69. (*c*) put away
70. accounts
71. (*a*) called off
72. marked
73. (*d*) work on
74. communication
75. bring up
76. plan
77. this
78. (*c*) will
79. (*a*) much
80. (*a*) learnt
81. surprising
82. usually
83. (*b*) treating
84. (*c*) who does any unauthorized act
85. (*c*) Make It

Reported Speech

86. (*a*) had finished his/her/their training schedule
(*b*) he/she/they had not yet
87. to change it.
88. (*a*) they were on track
(*b*) they were slightly
89. (*a*) he could provide feedback
(*b*) he had read through it
90. (*a*) he had completed their homework
(*b*) he had finished
91. (*c*) he was looking for books on ancient Greek history.
92. (*c*) he thought it was a great opportunity to learn more about the field.
93. (*c*) Team had just finished and felt ready for the competition.
94. (*b*) he would have feedback for them by the end of the day.
95. (*b*) they were available in black, white, and red.
96. he had got some free time that afternoon.
97. she planned to, she really needed to catch up on Physics.
98. if he/she should be worried about his/her persistent cough, that he/she should run some tests to be safe.
99. Lisa inquired if there was a meeting for the neighbourhood that weekend.
100. (*a*) if he would be able to play in the match that Saturday,
(*b*) his injury had healed completely.
101. (*a*) why had she not brought her practical file.
(*b*) asked Rita not to make excuses and added that she wanted to know the truth.
102. (*a*) he was surprised to see him there in London
(*b*) he had been offered a job there
103. (*a*) had to exercise daily to keep his heart fit.
(*b*) went for a daily morning walk and did some breathing exercises.
104. (*a*) to give him three tickets to India Gate
(*b*) it cost ten rupees a ticket / a ticket cost ten rupees
105. (*a*) if she could borrow his Math book
(*b*) he had already studied for the test the next day
106. that the engine had broken down.
107. he had been offered a job there, he had come the previous day.
108. if he would be attending the conference next week , he had already registered and made travel arrangements.
109. Sarah requested John to proofread her essay, and John responded affirmatively, stating that he had experience in editing academic papers.
110. Emily inquired about the closing time of the library.
111. if he could lend her his calculator for the math exam.
112. Sophia asked Kevin if he would be attending the party tonight.

113. (*b*) plants use sunlight to convert carbon dioxide into glucose.

114. (*a*) there was a popular Italian restaurant just around the corner

115. (*c*) the team would be discussing the project updates in the conference room at 10 AM.

116. Amit asked Tanu if she would be going with her family.

117. (*c*) they had extra classes during their winter vacation

118. water is essential for digestion and regulates body temperature

Error Detection

119.

ERROR	CORRECTION
students	student

120.

ERROR	CORRECTION
since	for

121.

ERROR	CORRECTION
have	has

122.

ERROR	CORRECTION
believes	believe

123.

ERROR	CORRECTION
two advices	two pieces of advice

124.

ERROR	CORRECTION
book	books

125.

ERROR	CORRECTION
is	are

126.

ERROR	CORRECTION
speaks	speak

127.

ERROR	CORRECTION
An	A

128.

ERROR	CORRECTION
are	is

129.

ERROR	CORRECTION
suggestion	suggestions

130.

ERROR	CORRECTION
A	The

131.

ERROR	CORRECTION
For	About

132.

ERROR	CORRECTION
breads	bread

133.

ERROR	CORRECTION
might	should

134.

ERROR	CORRECTION
has	have

135.

ERROR	CORRECTION
feels	feel

136.

ERROR	CORRECTION
derive	derived

137.

ERROR	CORRECTION
was	is

138.

ERROR	CORRECTION
cousin sisters	cousins

139.

ERROR	CORRECTION
poetries	poetry

140.

ERROR	CORRECTION
Reproducing	Reproduction

141.

ERROR	CORRECTION
ought	ought to

142.

ERROR	CORRECTION
delay	delayed

143. (*a*)

ERROR	CORRECTION
are	is

144. (*a*)

ERROR	CORRECTION
students	student

145. (*a*)

ERROR	CORRECTION
are	is

146. (*b*)

ERROR	CORRECTION
show	shows

147. (*a*)

ERROR	CORRECTION
ensures	ensure

148. (*a*)

ERROR	CORRECTION
do	does

149. (*a*)

ERROR	CORRECTION
needs	need

150. (*a*)

ERROR	CORRECTION
for	of

151. (*b*)

ERROR	CORRECTION
are	is

152. (*c*)

ERROR	CORRECTION
sign	signature

153. (*a*)

ERROR	CORRECTION
filmmaker	filmmakers

154. (*b*)

ERROR	CORRECTION
works	work

155. (*a*)

ERROR	CORRECTION
sceneries	scenery

156. (*b*)

ERROR	CORRECTION
belief	beliefs

157. (*a*)

ERROR	CORRECTION
administration	administrative

158. (*a*)

ERROR	CORRECTION
more	most

159. (*c*)

ERROR	CORRECTION
sister-in-laws	sisters-in-law

160. (*d*)

ERROR	CORRECTION
spectacle	spectacles

161. (*a*)

ERROR	CORRECTION
luggages	luggage

162. (*a*)

ERROR	CORRECTION
continues	continued

❑❑❑

LITERATURE

- FIRST FLIGHT
- FOOTPRINTS WITHOUT FEET

A LETTER TO GOD

—G.L. Fuentes

1

Narrative Sketch

1. The story is about Lencho, a farmer, who lived in a solitary house in a valley, the only one in the area.
2. He eagerly awaited rain for his crops and observed the sky.
3. Lencho's family consisted of his wife, older boys working in the field, and smaller ones playing near the house.
4. Rain finally arrived, but it turned into a hailstorm that destroyed their cornfield.
5. Despite the loss, the family held onto hope for help from God.
6. Lencho, though a hardworking farmer, knew how to write and decided to write a letter to God.
7. In the letter, Lencho requested a hundred pesos to sow his field again and survive until the next crop.
8. He labeled the envelope "To God" and sent the letter to the post office.
9. The postmaster and employees were amused by the letter but wanted to support Lencho's faith.
10. They collected money and managed to send Lencho a little more than half of what he requested.

BEFORE YOU READ

Theme

"A Letter to God" revolves around the idea of complete faith in God by a simple and poor farmer named Lencho. The farmer's innocent and unquestionable faith in God made him ignorant of the fact that a sympathetic[1] postmaster was helping him. The story highlights the themes of nature being destructive, humanity and kindness of strangers, and the conflict between nature and humans as well as between humans and humans. The story has an ironic ending as the post office employees whom Lencho thought had stolen his money, actually made contributions to help him.

Knowledge Hub

Irony is figurative language that refers to the contrast between expectations and reality. Writers use this literary device to draw readers in and keep them entertained.

Important Characters' Sketch

- **Lencho:** Lencho is the main character of the story. He was a poor, hardworking farmer who lived on the low hill's crest and was the family's sole bread earner. He was innocent, ignorant and a firm believer in God. He believed that God sees everything and no one ever dies of hunger. When his crops failed due to a natural calamity[2], he kept his faith intact and turned to God for help.
- **Postmaster:** The postmaster was an amiable[3] fellow. He was a kind, sensible and empathetic[4] person. He was amazed by the depth of faith shown in God by an innocent farmer. At first, he was amused by Lencho's letter to God asking for monetary help, but he later got impressed by Lencho's faith in God. He didn't want to break this man's trust in God and so decided to provide financial support to him by contributing a part of his salary along with other post-office employees. This showed his empathetic side as a person.

SYNOPSIS

A letter to God, by G.L. Fuentes, depicts the unquestionable faith in God of a poor and simple-minded farmer named Lencho. Lencho was poor yet dedicated farmer. He hoped for a good rain shower to ensure a decent harvest. But soon, his happiness turned into dismay[5] when the rain changed into a hailstorm and destroyed all his crops. The poor farmer was filled with sadness when he looked at the damage. After the storm had passed, he stood in the middle of the field and said to his sons, "A plague of locusts[6] would have left more than this."

[1] **Sympathetic:** feeling or expressing sympathy
[2] **Calamity:** a disaster
[3] **Amiable:** friendly
[4] **Empathetic:** ability to understand other's feelings
[5] **Dismay:** shock; surprise
[6] **Plague of locusts:** an uncontrollable increase in number of insect

However, Lencho held onto one hope at this time. He firmly believed in God and was confident that God would help him. Thus, he decided to write God a letter. In the letter, he requested God to send him one hundred pesos to sow his fields again and support his family. Soon, he wrote a letter and went to the post office. He placed a stamp on the letter and dropped it into the mailbox.

When the postman took out the letter from the mailbox, he laughed heartily after reading it. He immediately rushed to the postmaster and showed him the strange letter. The postmaster read the letter, and he, too, laughed out loud when he noticed that the letter was addressed to God.

However, he was soon moved by the farmer's faith in which the letter was written to God. He felt that the poor man's faith in God should not be shaken and decided to help him. Soon, he asked the post office employees to contribute some money as an act of charity and also gave a part of his salary to help the man. The postmaster then put whatever money collected in an envelope and addressed it to Lencho with a single word as a signature from God.

Lessons to learn

- *Power of faith and belief in God.*
- *Compassion portrayed by the postmaster.*
- *Importance of gratitude.*

The following Sunday, Lencho went to the post office to check if there was a letter for him. The postmaster gently handed over the letter to him. Lencho was not surprised at all to see the letter with money inside the envelope. He confidently opened the envelope to count the money but got angry when he saw only seventy pesos in it. He was sure that God could have never made such a mistake. He instantly went to the window to ask for paper and ink, wrote another letter to God, and dropped it into the mailbox.

When Lencho had left the place, the postmaster opened and read his letter immediately. In it, Lencho had complained to God, saying he had requested one hundred pesos but was upset to find only seventy pesos in it. Furthermore, he criticized the post office employees for stealing the remaining thirty pesos from his envelope. He urged God to send him the rest of the money since he urgently needed it; however, he shouldn't do it through the mail because Lencho thought that the post office employees were a "bunch of crooks".

NCERT EXERCISE

Oral Comprehension Check

(NCERT, Page 5)

1. What did Lencho hope for?

Ans. Lencho hoped for rain to come, which would get him a good harvest of his crops.

2. Why did Lencho say the raindrops were like 'silver coins'?

Ans. Lencho compared the raindrops with silver coins, which seemed to bring him a good harvest. The way coins (money) bring prosperity, the same way those raindrops looked promising to him.

3. How did the rain change? What happened to Lencho's fields?

Ans. Lencho was confident he would get a good harvest. The season welcomed good rain which soon became a storm accompanied by wind and hailstorms.

4. What were Lencho's feelings when the hail stopped? (CBSE, 2020)

Ans. When the hail stopped, Lencho was disheartened to see all his crops ruined. He had a sorrowful night as there would be no corn that year.

(NCERT, Page 6)

1. Who or what did Lencho have faith in? What did he do?

Ans. Amidst[7] the adversity[8] Lencho was in, he still had faith in God. He believed that God sees everything, even what is deep in one's conscience[9], and would ease his pain. He wrote God a letter demanding a hundred pesos to sow his field again.

2. Who read the letter?

Ans. The postmaster read the letter.

3. What did the postmaster do after reading the letter?

Ans. When the postmaster first saw the address, he laughed at it but soon turned serious and was moved by the writer's

[7] **Amidst:** in the middle of
[8] **Adversity:** a difficult situation
[9] **Conscience:** moral sense of right and wrong

faith in God. He didn't want to shake Lencho's faith. So, he decided to collect money and send it to Lencho, signed with the name of God.

(NCERT, Page 7)

1. **Was Lencho surprised to find a letter for him with money in it?**

Ans. Lencho was not surprised to find a letter with money from God as he had complete faith in God and knew he would help him in his need.

2. **What made Lencho angry?**

Ans. After he received the letter, he started counting the money that God sent him. On counting, he found out that he had received only seventy pesos. Since he demanded a hundred pesos and did not receive the exact amount, he was furious. But he trusted God and knew God would not turn him down, so he concluded that the post office employees stole his money.

Thinking about the Text

(NCERT Page 7, 8)

1. **Who does Lencho have complete faith in? Which sentences in the story tell you this?**

Ans. Lencho has complete faith in God as he had been instructed that God knows everything and helps us with our problems. There are a few sentences that show this:

- But in the hearts of all who lived in that solitary house in the middle of the valley, there was a single hope of help from God.
- All through the night, Lencho thought only of his one hope: the help of God, whose eyes, as he had been instructed, see everything, even what is deep in one's conscience.
- "God", he wrote, "if you don't help me, my family and I will go hungry this year".
- He wrote 'To God' on the envelope, put the letter inside, and still troubled, went to town.
- God could not have made a mistake, nor could he have denied Lencho what he had requested.

2. **Why does the postmaster send money to Lencho? Why does he sign the letter God?**

Ans. Most people have faith in God, and they rely on him for their problems. But Lencho's faith was beyond anyone else's. He wrote a letter to God and demanded money from him as if asking a friend for financial assistance.

Since the postmaster was impressed by Lencho's letter to God, he didn't want Lencho to lose his faith. Hence, he sent him seventy pesos and signed the letter as God.

3. **Did Lencho try to find out who had sent the money to him? Why or why not?**

Ans. Lencho did not try to find out who had sent the money to him because he never doubted the existence of God and had complete faith in God.

He could not believe that it could be anybody else other than God who would send him the money. His faith in God was so strong that he thought he had sent him money for his help.

4. **Who does Lencho think has taken the rest of the money? What is the irony in the situation?**

(Remember that the irony of a situation is an unexpected aspect of it. An ironic situation is strange or amusing because it is the opposite of what is expected).

Ans. Lencho thinks that the post office employees have taken the remainder of the cash as he had demanded hundred pesos from God, and within the letter, there were only seventy pesos.

Lencho is certain that God couldn't have made an error and blames the post office employees of stealing the money.

The irony of this situation is that Lencho doubts the same people who helped him in his difficult time.

He thinks that the post office employees stole his money when it's they who collected the cash for him in the first place. He calls them a "bunch of crooks", though they are the ones who tried to keep his faith in God alive by giving him money.

5. **Are there people like Lencho in the real world? What kind of a person would you say he is? You may select appropriate words from the box to answer the question.**

greedy, naive, stupid, ungrateful, selfish, comical, unquestioning

Ans. It is difficult, but not impossible, to find a person like Lencho. Being literate[10], he doesn't even realise that his letter can't reach God. Thus, he can be considered a naïve[11] person with unquestioning faith in God.

6. **There are two kinds of conflict in the story between humans and nature and between humans themselves. How are these conflicts illustrated?**

Ans. There are two types of conflicts within the story:

1. The conflict between humans and nature: The conflict between humans and nature is illustrated by the destruction of Lencho's crop due to the hailstorm. Lencho was expecting good rainfall for his crops, which was the only hope he had for his earnings. He had worked hard to feed his family, but unfortunately, nature turned violent and destroyed everything.
2. The conflict between humans and humans: The story also illustrates another conflict between humans. When Lencho demanded money from God, the postmaster and other employees of the post office sent him some money, even though they didn't know Lencho. However, Lencho accused[12] them of stealing some cash, thinking God must have sent the total amount. He called them "a bunch of crooks". This shows that man doesn't have faith in another man, hence a conflict between humans.

[10] **Literate:** able to read and write
[11] **Naive:** innocent; inexperienced
[12] **Accused:** blame for

MISCELLANEOUS EXERCISE

Multiple Choice Questions

1. Lencho had a field of __________.
   (*a*) Rice (*b*) Cotton
   (*c*) Wheat (*d*) Corn

2. Lencho wrote the first letter to __________.
   (*a*) God (*b*) Postmaster
   (*c*) His best friend (*d*) A postman

3. Where was Lencho's house?
   (*a*) Behind the sea. (*b*) At the top of a hill.
   (*c*) At the bottom of a hill. (*d*) Along a valley.

4. Why did Lencho get angry when he counted the money?
   (*a*) Lencho received thirteen pesos less than what he had demanded from God.
   (*b*) Lencho received thirty pesos less than what he had demanded from God.
   (*c*) Lencho received no money.
   (*d*) Lencho received seventy pesos less than what he had demanded from God.

5. It made everything look so white that it seemed as if it was covered with salt". Why was snow compared to salt.
   (*a*) It was white in colour.
   (*b*) It was spread throughout the field.
   (*c*) It had damaged the crops.
   (*d*) All of the above.

6. Lencho is __________ when he says, "that's what they say: no one dies of hunger."
   (*a*) Dismissive (*b*) Hardworking
   (*c*) Worried (*d*) Happy

7. Complete the analogy by selecting the suitable word from the text- __________: fire: : snow: warm
   (*a*) frozen (*b*) ice
   (*c*) wood (*d*) hot

8. The word 'pass' in the following sentences has been used in the same sense as Lencho had said, "I hope it passes quickly"?
   (*a*) Last month, my friend's grandpa passed away due to a lung infection.
   (*b*) Shreya got free passes for the concert.
   (*c*) The passing score for the course is 40%.
   (*d*) The route was crowded, and the two cars could not pass.

9. Complete the line: "The field was white, as if covered with __________."
   (*a*) White pearls (*b*) Salt
   (*c*) Snow (*d*) Corn

10. 'Ox of a man' means –
    (*a*) Lethargic (*b*) Poor
    (*c*) Hardworking (*d*) Simple

Knowledge Hub

As strong as an ox (phrase): having great physical strength.

Extract-Based Questions

I. Read the extract given below and answer the questions/ complete the statements that follow: (5 M)

The moment the letter fell into the mailbox the postmaster went to open it. It said: "God: of the money that I asked for, only seventy pesos reached me. Send me the rest, since I need it very much. But don't send it to me through the mail because the post office employees are a bunch of crooks. Lencho." **(CBSE 2022 Term-1)**

1. Lencho wrote the second letter as he was: **(1)**
   (A) unhappy (B) curious
   (C) hopeful (D) thoughtful
   (E) confident
   (*a*) (A), (C) and (E)
   (*b*) (A), (B) and (C)
   (*c*) (B), (E) and (A)
   (*d*) (C), (D) and (E)

2. The postmaster opened the letter expecting it to: **(1)**
   (A) be full of thanks to God
   (B) show his happiness
   (C) be full of anguish for getting less money
   (D) be accusing God of being miserly
   (*a*) (C) and (D (*b*) (A) and (B)
   (*c*) (A) and (D) (*d*) (D) and (B)

3. On reading the letter the postmaster was **(1)**
   (*a*) surprised (*b*) dismayed
   (*c*) pleased (*d*) puzzled

4. 'the post office employees are a bunch of crooks'. The statement is: **(1)**
   (*a*) thoughtful (*b*) sad
   (*c*) dismissive (*d*) ironic

5. Find the suitable word from the extract to complete the following: **(1)**
   sanctioned: approved :: demanded:
   (*a*) fell (*b*) reached
   (*c*) went (*d*) asked

II. Read the following extract and answer the questions/ complete the sentences that follow. **(5 M)**

Lencho was a man of strong faith. For him, God was not an abstract belief but a concrete, physical presence. He went about his work and his life with the assurance of one who knows that God is always watching over him.

1. What is the main theme of this story? **(1)**
   (*a*) The power of faith and prayer.
   (*b*) The importance of hard work and perseverance.
   (*c*) The dangers of relying on others for help.
   (*d*) The consequences of greed and dishonesty.
2. What can be inferred about Lencho's perception of God based on the given extract? **(1)**
3. Which word from the extract means a feeling of confidence or certainty? **(1)**
4. What does the author imply about the nature of Lencho's relationship with God through the statement that God is a "concrete, physical presence"? **(2)**

III. Read the following extract and answer the questions/ complete the sentences that follow. **(5 M)**

When he finished, he went to the window to buy a stamp which he licked and then affixed to the envelope with a blow of his fist. The moment the letter fell into the mailbox, the postmaster went to open it. It said: "God: Of the money that I asked for, only seventy pesos reached me. Send me the rest, since I need it very much. But don't send it to me through the mail because the post office employees are a bunch of crooks. Lencho."

1. '...bunch of crooks.' Pick the option that DOES NOT collate with 'bunch of', correctly. **(1)**

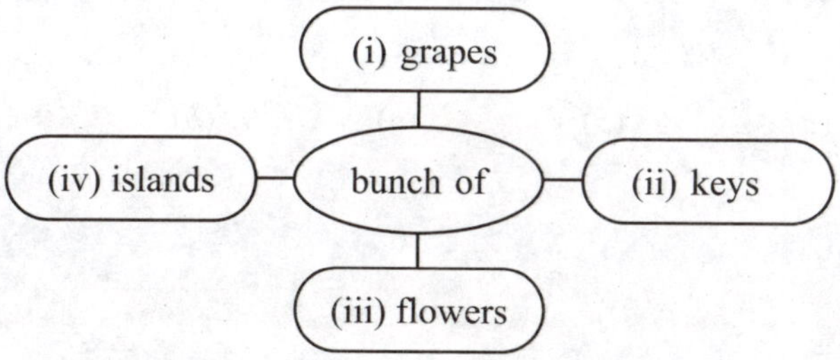

   (*a*) Option (i) (*b*) Option (ii)
   (*c*) Option (iii) (*d*) Option (iv)
2. What can be inferred about Lencho's perception of the post office employees based on the given extract? **(1)**
3. What does the word "affixed" mean in the context of the passage? **(1)**
4. How does Lencho's action of affixing the stamp with a blow of his fist reflect his frustration and distrust towards the post office employees? **(2)**

IV. Read the following extract and answer the questions/ complete the sentences that follow. **(5 M)**

The house- the only one in the entire valley -sat on the crest of a low hill. From this height one could see the river and the field of ripe corn dotted with the flowers that always promised a good harvest. The only thing the earth needed was a good downpour or at least a shower. Throughout the morning Lencho -who knew his fields intimately- had done nothing but see the sky towards the north-east.

(CBSE QB)

1. Based on the detail of the house's location, how can it best be described? **(1)**
   (*a*) majestic (*b*) imposing
   (*c*) solitary (*d*) unique
2. The field of corn dotted with flowers means that **(1)**
   (*a*) not a single flower was bigger than a dot
   (*b*) the flowers were scattered across.
   (*c*) the flowers were in shaped like dots.
   (*d*) the flowers had shrunk in size.
3. Lencho wished for a downpour or a heavy shower. Pick the option that correctly lists the correct match for kinds of rain. **(1)**

(1)	heavy rain	(i)	light rain that falls in very fine drops
(2)	thunderstorm	(ii)	very heavy rain, tropical rain
(3)	drizzle	(iii)	it's coming down quite strong and you get very wet very quickly
(4)	torrential rain	(iv)	really heavy rain that comes very suddenly
(5)	downpour	(v)	is a violent, short-lived weather disturbance associated with lightning, thunder and strong, gusty winds.

   (*a*) 1-(ii), 2-(iv), 3-(v), 4-(i), 5-(iii)
   (*b*) 1-(iv), 2-(i), 3-(iii), 4-(v), 5-(ii)
   (*c*) 1-(v), 2-(iii), 3-(iv), 4-(ii), 5-(i)
   (*d*) 1-(iii), 2-(v), 3-(i), 4-(ii), 5-(iv)
4. Based on the given extract, what is Lencho NOT likely to think while looking at his field?

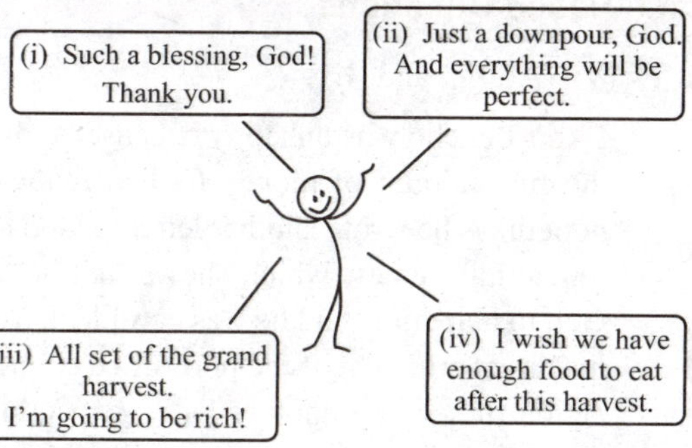

   (*a*) Option (i)
   (*b*) Option (ii)
   (*c*) Option (iii)
   (*d*) Option (iv)

5. Which quote supports the idea in the given extract?
   (*a*) "Farming is a profession of hope."
   (*b*) "I would rather be on my farm than be emperor of the world."
   (*c*) "Farming looks mighty easy when your plough is a pencil, you're a thousand miles from the corn field."
   (*d*) "Those too lazy to plough in the right season will have no food at the harvest."

Subjective Questions

Short Answer Questions (40-50 words) (3 M)

1. Lencho did not bother exploring any other means to resolve his situation but just turned to God. Do you feel that his approach was justified? Why/Why not? **(CBSE APQ, 2023)**
2. 'The field was white as if covered with salt.' This is how the field is described after the hailstorm. The pelting hailstones could have been easily seen as sugar cubes. Would comparing it with sugar be more appropriate? Why/Why not? **(CBSE, QB)**
3. 'Lencho was an ox of a man, working like an animal in the fields, but still, he knew how to write'. What does this line tell us about the norm amongst such farmers? **(CBSE, QB)**
4. Lencho addresses the post office employees as a 'bunch of crooks'; why? Give reasons to support your answer.
5. Did the letter reach God? Why did the postmaster send a reply to Lencho? **(CBSE, 2020)**
6. What are the raindrops compared to and why? **(CBSE, 2023)**
7. What idea does the Postmaster come up with ? What did he do to stick to his resolution? **(CBSE, 2024)**
8. In what way would writing a letter to God help Lencho tide over his crisis? **(CBSE, 2023)**

Long Answer Questions (100-120 words) (6 M)

9. "I wish I had the faith of the man." Describe Lencho's character in light of this statement.
10. "Humanity still exists"; this is what we get to know after reading 'A letter to God' in which the firm faith in God of a poor farmer and the helpfulness of the post office employees are aptly depicted. Write a paragraph on the values in it, in about 80-100 words. Give the paragraph a suitable title.
11. Why did Lencho say the raindrops were like 'new silver coins'? How did the same rain change the face of his cornfield?

ANSWERS & EXPLANATIONS

Answer Key

Multiple Choice Questions

1. (*d*) **2.** (*a*) **3.** (*b*) **4.** (*b*) **5.** (*d*) **6.** (*a*) **7.** (*a*) **8.** (*b*) **9.** (*b*) **10.** (*c*)

Explanations

Extract-Based Questions

I. 1. (*a*) (A), (C) and (E)

Exp.: Lencho was unhappy because he did not receive the full amount of money he had requested. He was hopeful as he wrote another letter to God asking for the remaining money, which shows that he still expected God to help him. And he was confident, as indicated by his direct criticism of the post office employees and his action of sending another letter, expecting a response from God.

2. (*b*) (A) and (B)

3. (*b*) dismayed

4. (*d*) ironic

5. (*d*) In the extract, Lencho "asked" for the remaining money, which is synonymous to "demanded" in the context provided, as "sanctioned" is to "approved".

II. 1. (*a*) The power of faith and prayer.

> **Mistakes 101 : What not to do!**
>
> Mistaking concrete details or actions (like Lencho working hard in his fields) as the main theme, thus choosing "The importance of hard work and perseverance" instead of understanding the overall theme of "The power of faith and prayer."

2. Lencho perceives God as a tangible and ever-present entity, not just an abstract belief.

3. "Assurance" in the context of the passage means a feeling of confidence or certainty.

4. The author implies that Lencho's faith is so strong that he perceives God as physically real and present in his life, indicating his deep faith and belief in God. This highlights the depth of Lencho's faith and his unwavering belief in God's presence.

III. 1. (*d*) Option (iv)

Key Takeaway

Understanding that the term 'bunch of crooks' does not correctly collate with 'bunch of islands' is the use of collocations in English. Collocations are words that are commonly used together. The term 'bunch' typically collocates with objects that can be grouped together naturally, such as keys, grapes, or flowers, but not with islands, which are not typically considered in a collective group.

2. Lencho perceives the post office employees as dishonest or corrupt, as indicated by his comment in the letter calling them a "bunch of crooks."

3. "Affixed" in the context of the passage means to attach or stick something firmly.

4. Lencho's forceful action of affixing the stamp with a blow of his fist suggests his anger and distrust towards the post office employees.

IV. 1. (*c*) Solitary

Exp.: The house is the only one in the valley, which suggests it is isolated or soliary.

2. (*b*) The flowers were scattered across.

3. (*d*) 1-(iii), 2-(v), 3-(i), 4-(ii), 5-(iv)

4. (*d*) Option (iv)

Exp.: This is unlikely because the extract suggests confidence in a good harvest due to the promising signs of the flowers among the corn.

5. This quote captures the essence of the farmer's hope for a good harvest, which is reflected in Lencho's lookout for rain to secure the prosperity of his crops.

Subjective Questions

Short Answer Questions

CBSE Marking Scheme: Content-1 M, Organisation of Ideas-1 M, Accuracy-1 M

1. Lencho's approach cannot be justified as we know that even God helps those who help themselves. Seeking help from someone is understood but not putting in any effort and depending on others or hoping for one's luck to work is something one cannot practically believe in.

2. A hailstorm can be compared to small balls of anything white in colour. But, here, the comparison to salt is much better than sugar cubes as sugar symbolises sweetness or happiness, whereas excess salt signifies spoiled taste or sadness.

   The hailstorm spoiled Lencho's fields totally. That's why it is said that the field was white as if covered with salt.

3. Ordinarily, farmers are expected to be illiterate and naive. Even though, Lencho was naive, he still knew how to write. Lencho's faith in God made him write a letter to God when a hailstorm destroyed his harvest.

   This tells us that, unlike many farmers, he was hardworking- like an ox, educated and was probably doing farming out of interest.

Nailing the Right Answer

The contrast in the sentence - physical labor versus literacy - should be addressed by students while answering.

4. The hailstones ruined Lencho's crop and left him helpless. So, he thought of writing a letter to God to help him save his family from hunger. Lencho requested God to send him hundred pesos. The postmaster, realising the farmer's faith, sent him 70 pesos. Lencho got disappointed when he counted the money. He blindly concluded that the post office employees took 30 pesos.

   Thus, he wrote another letter demanding God to send the remaining amount but not via mail as he felt those employees were a "bunch of crooks". The post office employees were kind and helpful and calling them 'crooks' was ironic.

5. No, the letter did not reach God and it was naive on Lencho's part to think of addressing a letter in the name of God.

   The postmaster, however, was a sympathetic man who was amazed by Lencho's faith in God. He didn't want Lencho's faith to be broken, hence he decided to send a reply to Lencho along with a partial amount to help him with his situation. He also signed the letter-God to keep Lencho's faith intact.

6. Raindrops are compared to coins by Lencho. The larger raindrops are compared to ten-cent coins, while the smaller ones to five-cent coins.

   He was aware that the rainfall would undoubtedly help him in reaping a bountiful harvest. Naturally, he would earn more money as a result. Hence the raindrops were like coins or money to him.

7. The postmaster, deeply moved by Lencho's faith, decides to help him by collecting money. He puts in some of his own money and asks his staff and friends to contribute. They couldn't meet Lencho's full request but managed to send a decent amount of money to him in an envelope, maintaining Lencho's faith.

8. ***Topper's Explanation***

Lencho was an ox of a man who worked like an animal on his field and was thus dependent on a good harvest for his living. Hence, when the hailstorm destroyed Lencho's crop, he was devastated. But, Lencho's faith was bigger than his fears as he had always been taught to believe that there was a single ray of hope - help from God. So unshakeable was Lencho's faith in the Almighty that it drove him to write a letter beseeching the Lord for a hundred pesos to sow his field again and live until the crop came. He was driven only by the faith that his devotion would not go unrewarded. In the end, it was Lencho's unalloyed devotion that impressed the postmaster who then decided to help the poor man, by urging his friends and employees to contribute their mite and also giving a part of his own salary, thus managing to collect seventy pesos to assist Lencho.

Long Answer Questions

CBSE Marking Scheme: Expression-2 M, Accuracy-1 M

8. Lencho was a poor but hardworking farmer who worked like an ox. He had immense faith in God and believed that God looks after everyone. **(1 M)**

When a hailstorm destroyed Lencho's crops, he turned to God for help. Displaying his faith and innocence, Lencho wrote a letter to God asking for monetary support to help him grow his crops again and save his family from starvation. **(1 M)**

This unshaken faith also impressed the postmaster, who looked at Lencho's letter for the first time. He was so amazed by Lencho's belief that he didn't want his faith to be broken. Thus, he made sure to provide monetary help to Lencho by collecting some money along with the post office employees, put it in an envelope and signed it God. **(1 M)**

9. After reading 'A letter to God', our faith in humanity gets stronger. We can see that people like the postmaster still exist who help others without any self-interest. The postmaster and the post office employees lay an example for all of us to be kind and sympathetic. **(1 M)**

Though they laughed at Lencho's letter at first, later got moved by the grip of faith he had in God. **(1 M)**

The way they all decided to help the stranger in his hard times restores our faith in the existence of humanity and motivates us to be noble and kind. **(1 M)**

Nailing the Right Answer

LAQ 8. should be answered beyond the text instead of simply writing the chapter's summary.

10. Lencho was a farmer who was waiting eagerly for rain as his crops needed a downpour. The rain did come and filled the people of the valley with hope and excitement. Lencho felt as if those raindrops were new coins. **(1 M)**

The big drops of rain, according to him, were ten-cent pieces, and the little ones were that of five. He was quite satisfied with the rainfall. Unfortunately, the strong wind began to blow, and very large hailstones began to fall with the rain. He hoped for it to pass quickly, which did not happen. The rain, which till then was a hope for a better future, changed. It shattered all his hopes and changed the face of his field. **(1 M)**

The whole harvest was ruined. Not a leaf remained on the trees, the corn was destroyed, and not a single flower was left on the plants. Thus the hailstorm left Lencho in need and his family on the brink of starvation. **(1 M)**

❑❑❑

NELSON MANDELA: LONG WALK TO FREEDOM

—Nelson Rolihlahla Mandela

2

Narrative Sketch

1. The inauguration of South Africa's first democratic, non-racial government took place on May 10.
2. The ceremonies were held at the Union Buildings in Pretoria, which had been the symbol of white supremacy.
3. International leaders and dignitaries attended the inauguration, making it the largest gathering of its kind in South Africa.
4. Thabo Mbeki and Mr de Klerk were sworn in as deputy presidents.
5. Nelson Mandela, accompanied by his daughter Zenani, pledged to uphold the Constitution and work for the well-being of the Republic and its people.
6. Mandela expressed gratitude to the international guests for their presence and acknowledged the victory for justice, peace, and human dignity.
7. The inauguration symbolized the end of apartheid and the birth of a democratic and non-racial society.
8. A display of South African military force during the event showcased their loyalty to the newly elected government.
9. Both the old and new national anthems were sung, symbolizing unity and reconciliation between different racial groups.
10. Mandela referred to the oppressive systems of government in the past, which created racial domination and inhumane societies.

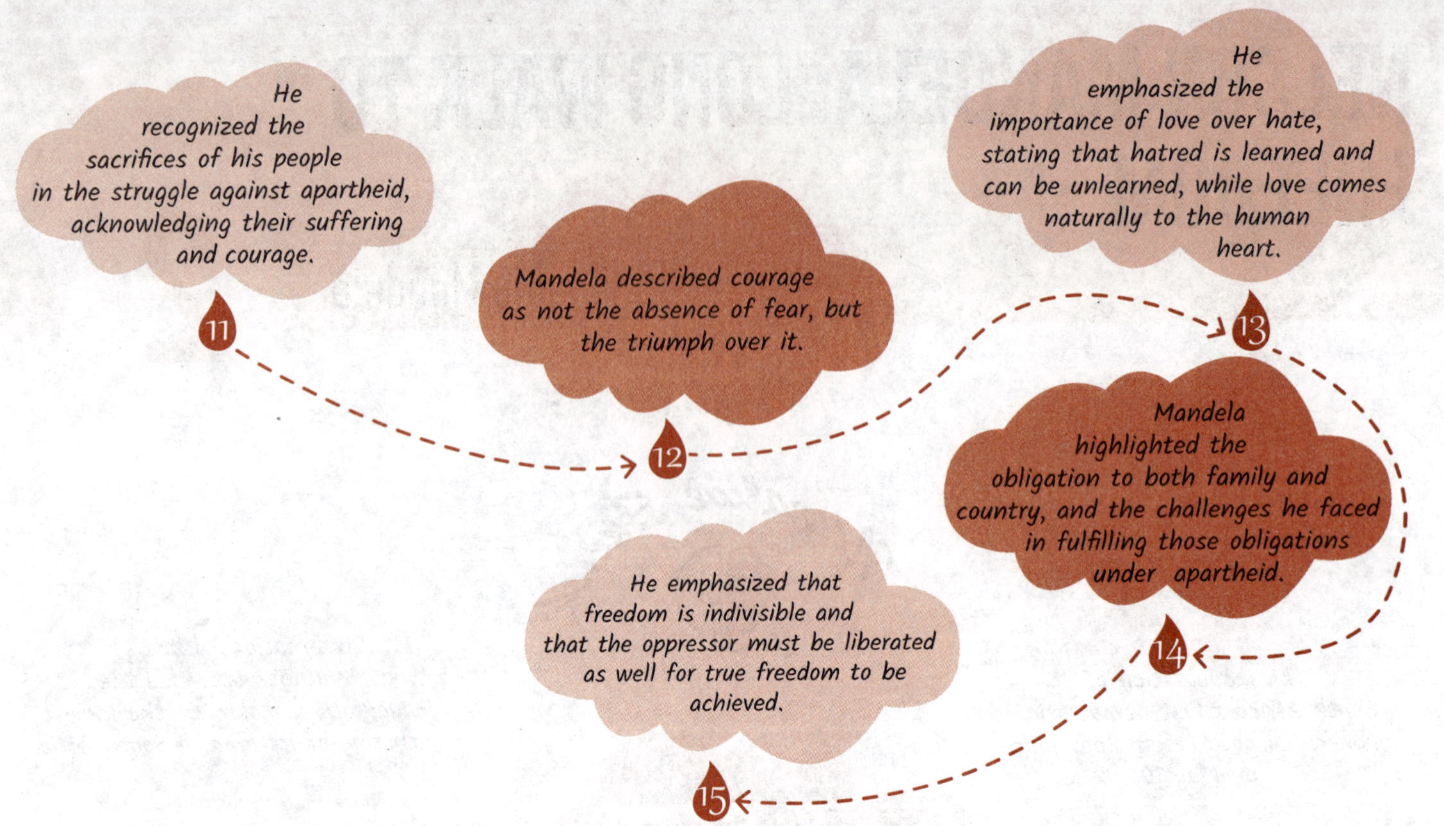

BEFORE YOU READ

Theme

The text highlights Nelson Mandela's struggle for freedom and equality in South Africa. It highlights the transformation of South Africa from a racially divided society under white supremacy to a democratic, non-racial government. Mandela expresses gratitude to international leaders for their support and emphasizes the ideals of justice, peace, human dignity, and the liberation of all people from poverty and discrimination. The text also explores Mandela's understanding of courage, the power of love over hate, and the interconnectedness of freedom for both the oppressed and the oppressor.

Important Characters' Sketch

- **Nelson Mandela:** Mandela was a South African revolutionary politician. He was a man of extraordinary bravery, intelligence and kindness. Mandela was a great patriot who fought against the apartheid[1] system and became the first black president of free South Africa. He possessed exceptional leadership qualities and had a commanding presence. After centuries of White rule, Mandela became the first black president of South Africa and led a democratic, non-racial government.

SYNOPSIS

"Nelson Mandela: Long Walk to Freedom" is an extract from the autobiography[2] of Nelson Rolihlahla Mandela that sheds light on the struggle for the freedom of black people in South Africa. On 10th May, 1994, Nelson Mandela took the oath as South Africa's first black president after more than three centuries of oppression by the Whites. His party, the African

[1] **Apartheid:** a system of racial discrimination that existed in South Africa where people of different racial origins could not live together in equality and harmony

[2] **Autobiography:** an autobiography allows the author to tell the true story of their own life

National Congress, had won 252 out of the 400 seats in the first democratic elections in the history of South Africa. Many political figures from several countries attended the inauguration ceremony in the amphitheatre in Pretoria. In his speech, Mandela addressed everyone respectfully and assured his fellow countrymen that his country would never experience similar suppression[3] again. While taking his vow as the first black president, he established democracy[4] in the country and said there would be no discrimination against people based on their caste, colour, creed or race. He assured that all the country's people would be treated equally.

10th May-the day of inauguration was symbolic for Mandela as the South African people sang two national anthems. A spectacular display of South African jets and helicopters roared in perfect formation over the Union Buildings. All these events reminded Mandela of the history of black-skinned people exploited[5] by Whites. He deeply felt the pain of his race. He said that this type of suppression and racial domination was an extraordinary human disaster which gave rise to one of the harshest and most inhumane[6] societies the world had ever seen. However, the decades of oppression and brutality[7] had another effect: it produced men of extraordinary courage, wisdom and generosity in his country who would never be known again. "Perhaps it requires such depths of oppression to create such heights of character." Mandela considered that the people of his country were the greatest wealth, finer than diamonds. He firmly believed that no person is born to hate another person based on skin colour, background or religion. He had learned the meaning of courage from the people of his country and believed that a person becomes brave not because he does not feel afraid but because he knows how to fight his fears. Furthermore, Mandela stated that every man has two major obligations[8] in his life. The first is an obligation towards his family, i.e., parents, wife and children, and the second is towards his country, people and community. Each person can fullfil those obligations according to their interests and nature. As a child, Mandela never felt he wasn't free in any way. Only when he became a young man did he realise that freedom was merely an illusion[9], and it was then that he got a hunger for it. At first, he only wanted freedom for himself, freedom to stay out at night, read what he liked and go where he liked. He saw that everyone who looked like him had no freedom. That is when he joined the African National Congress, and that is when the hunger for his freedom became the greater hunger for the freedom of his people. According to Mandela, a person who snatches another's freedom is also a prisoner of similar oppression, a prisoner of hatred. Thus, the oppressed and the oppressor alike are robbed of their humanity and should be set free like everyone else.

Lessons to learn

- ❒ The importance of inclusive leadership.
- ❒ The value of unity and solidarity.
- ❒ The significance of perseverance and resilience.
- ❒ The transformative potential of love and compassion.

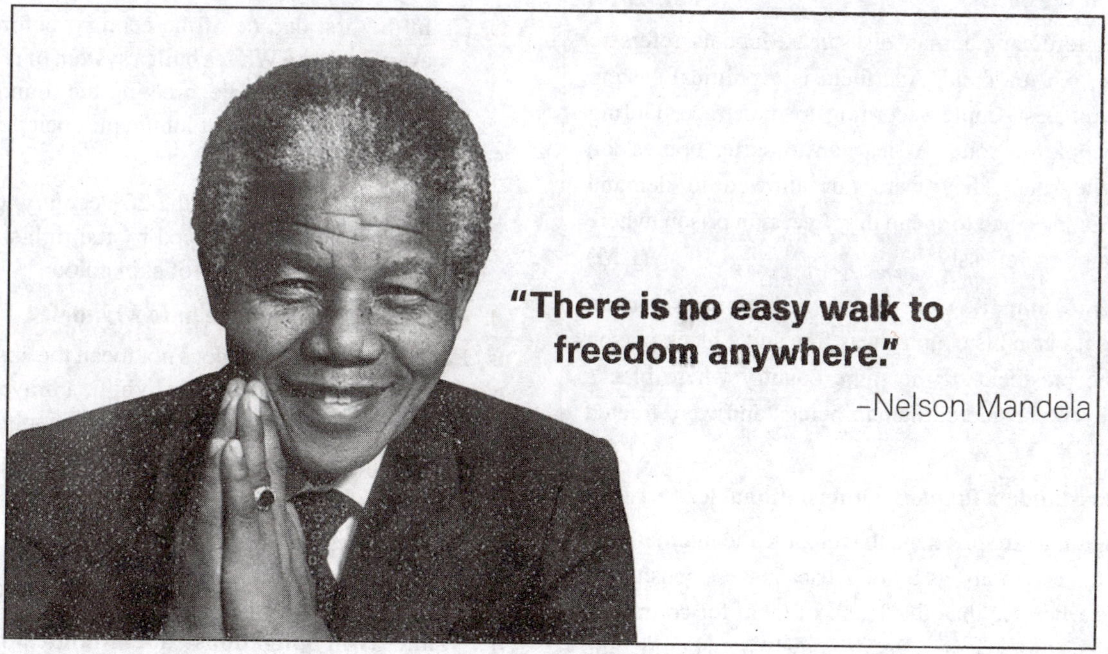

[3] **Suppression:** put down; the act of suppressing something or someone
[4] **Democracy:** a way of governing which depends on the will of the people
[5] **Exploited:** take advantage of
[6] **Inhumane:** cruel
[7] **Brutality:** cruelty
[8] **Obligation:** duty; commitment
[9] **Illusion:** a false idea or belief

NCERT EXERCISE

Oral Comprehension Check

(NCERT, Page 18,19)

1. Where did the ceremonies take place? Can you name any public buildings in India that are made of sandstones?

Ans. The ceremony took place in the amphitheatre of the Union Building of Pretoria, attended by political parties and leaders of many nations.

In India, the Parliament House and Red Fort are buildings made of red sandstone.

2. Can you say how 10th May is an 'autumn day' in South Africa?

Ans. Autumn is a season of shedding of dry leaves and the coming of green leaves. In the same way, Nelson Mandela saw the fall of White rule and a new Era of democratic rule on South African soil. Hence, 10th May can be considered an 'autumn day' in South Africa.

3. At the beginning of his speech, Mandela mentions "an extraordinary human disaster". What does he mean by this? What is the "glorious human achievement" he speaks of at the end? **(CBSE, 2020)**

Ans. By 'an extraordinary human disaster', Mandela refers to the practice of Apartheid. Apartheid is a political system that discriminates people according to their race. During this, the people of South Africa had to suffer oppression under White rule. They were not allowed to demand freedom. Mandela had to spend thirty years in prison, where he was beaten mercilessly. **(1 M)**

According to him, it was a great and glorious human achievement when his country was free and a black person became the president of the same country where blacks were not even considered human beings and were treated as slaves. **(1 M)**

4. What does Mandela thank the international leaders for?

Ans. Mandela felt it a rare privilege to welcome the international leaders at the ceremony, as South Africans were considered outlaws[10] earlier. He thus thanks all of them for coming to witness the historical ceremony in a newly born democratic nation.

5. What ideals does Nelson Mandela set for the future of South Africa?

Ans. Nelson Mandela set the ideals of releasing people from extreme poverty, suffering and all kinds of discrimination-race, caste, gender or colour.

(NCERT, Page 21)

1. What did the military generals do? How did their attitude change, and why?

Ans. The highest military generals of the South African defense force saluted Mandela and pledged their loyalty at the ceremony, which was of great significance. Mandela was aware of the fact that at the time when the apartheid system existed, these same officials would have arrested him.

The change in their attitude was because of the struggle and sacrifices of the various heroes of South Africa. That struggle brought a change in the mindsets of many.

2. Why were two national anthems sung?

Ans. On the day of the inauguration, two national anthems were sung: one by the Whites and the other by the Blacks, symbolising the equality and freedom of the two races.

3. How does Mandela describe the systems of government in his country

(i) in the first decade, and

(ii) in the final decade of the twentieth century?

Ans. (i) In the first decade of the century, before Mandela was even born, the Whites built a system of racial domination against black people, creating the foundation of one of the harshest and most inhumane societies the world had ever known.

(ii) In the last decade of the 20th century, that system was overturned and replaced by the rights and freedom of all people regardless of skin colour.

4. What does courage mean to Mandela?

Ans. For Mandela, courage does not mean the absence of fear but a victory over it. According to him, a brave man is not one who does not feel afraid but one who conquers[11] that fear.

5. What does Mandela think is natural, to love or to hate?

Ans. Mandela thought love comes naturally to the human heart more than hate.

(NCERT, Page 24)

1. What "twin obligations" does Mandela mention? **(CBSE SQP, 2020)**

Ans. Mandela mentions that every person has twin obligations. The first is to their family, parents, wife and children, and

---

[10] **Outlaws:** a person excluded from the benefit or protection of the law; a lawless person

[11] **Conquers:** overcomes; controls

the second obligation is towards their country, their people and their community.

2. **What did being free mean to Mandela as a boy and as a student? How does he contrast these "transitory[12] freedoms" with "the basic and honourable freedoms"?**

Ans. Mandela draws a contrast between the two kinds of freedom. He had a different understanding of freedom at different stages of his life. As a boy, he never felt he wasn't free during his childhood. As long as he obeyed his elders, he had the freedom to run in the fields, swim in the stream and so on.

Growing up as a student, he desired 'the basic and honourable freedoms' of staying out at night, reading what he liked and going where he chose.

Only when he became a young man did he realise that freedom was merely[13] an illusion, and it was then that he got a hunger for it and he decided to join the African National Congress.

3. **Does Mandela think the oppressor is free? Why/why not?**

Ans. Mandela thought that anyone who tried to oppress another person could never be free.

According to him, an oppressor is a victim of hatred who is behind bars of prejudice[14] and narrow-mindedness[15]. He believed both the oppressor and the oppressed are robbed of their humanity and peace.

Thinking about the Text

(NCERT, Page 24)

1. **Why did such a large number of international leaders attend the inauguration? What did it signify the triumph of?**

Ans. A large number of international leaders showed up at the inauguration, a sign of solidarity[16] and unity from the international community to the idea of the end of apartheid. It was the significance of the victory of good over evil and the triumph of a new society without any discrimination.

2. **What does Mandela mean when he says he is "simply the sum of all those African patriots" who had gone before him?**

Ans. Mandela wants to pay his tribute to all the people who have sacrificed their lives for the sake of freedom, by saying that he is "simply the sum of all those African patriots." He believed that all of them were standing there because of the unimaginable sacrifices of his people. He is sad as they would not be able to see the results of their sacrifices and how a new nation was born; however, he is grateful to them and everything they did for the nation and its people.

3. **Would you agree that the "depths of oppression" create "heights of character"? How does Mandela illustrate this? Can you add your own examples to this argument?**

Ans. It is true that depths of oppression can create heights of character. Nelson Mandela illustrated it by giving examples of the great heroes of South Africa who sacrificed their lives in the struggle for freedom.

There are numerous examples from our country as well. During our freedom struggle, great leaders like Mahatma Gandhi, JL Nehru, Chandra Shekhar Azad, Bhagat Singh and many more sacrificed so much to free our country from British rule. Because of the struggle, people learned about these noblemen and how courageous they were.

4. **How did Mandela's understanding of freedom change with age and experience?**

Ans. Mandela had a different understanding of freedom at different stages of his life. As a boy, he never felt he wasn't free during his childhood. As long as he obeyed his elders, he had the freedom to run in the fields, swim in the stream and so on.

At first, he only wanted freedom for himself- freedom to stay out at night, read what he liked and go where he liked. Only when he became a young man did he realise that freedom was merely an illusion, and it was then that he got a hunger for it. Slowly, he saw that everyone who looked like him didn't have any freedom at all.

That is when he joined the African National Congress, and that is when the hunger for his freedom became the greater hunger for the freedom of his people.

5. **How did Mandela's 'hunger for freedom' change his life?**

Ans. Mandela said he wasn't born with a hunger for freedom. Like any other kid, he felt he was born free. Later, he realised in his youth that it was an illusion, a temporary phase of freedom. He saw that it was not just his freedom that was being restricted, but the freedom of all blacks. This brought a change in him. It was then that he joined the African National Congress and changed into a person who fought against apartheid and built a new nation.

---

[12] **Transitory:** not permanent
[13] **Merely:** just; only
[14] **Prejudice:** pre-judgement; a preconceived opinion that is not based on reason
[15] **Narrow-minded:** not open-minded; not willing to accept opinions, beliefs or behaviours that are unusual or different from one's own
[16] **Solidarity:** unity or agreement of feeling or action, especially among individuals with a common interest

MISCELLANEOUS EXERCISE

Multiple Choice Questions

1. It was a celebration of South Africa's first __________ government.
   (a) Non-democratic, racial.
   (b) Democratic, non-racial.
   (c) Non-democratic, non-racial.
   (d) Monarch, racial.
2. Mandela refers to liberty as a "newborn" because-
   (a) The rule of the earlier government had ended.
   (b) It had recently been attained with lots of struggle.
   (c) It made people experience infant-like excitement.
   (d) He is talking about a newborn baby.
3. "We thank all of our distinguished international guests for having come to take possession with the people of our country of what is, after all, a common victory for __________."
   (a) Justice (b) Peace
   (c) Human dignity (d) All of the above.
4. Why does the speaker say it is a 'rare privilege'? He says this as they have:
   (a) Been deprived of this honour.
   (b) Rarely been given this honour.
   (c) Experienced it for the first time.
   (d) Been waiting for this privilege for years.
5. Whom did Mandela want to thank but couldn't?
   (a) His family.
   (b) Political leaders.
   (c) African patriots who no longer existed.
   (d) His countrymen.
6. According to Mandela, what is the greatest wealth of a nation?
   (a) People (b) Gold
   (c) Diamonds (d) Minerals
7. What did Mandela learn about courage?
   (a) It is the absence of fear. (b) It is the triumph over fear.
   (c) Both (a) and (b). (d) None of the above.
8. What are a man's obligations in life?
   (a) Obligation to countrymen.
   (b) Obligation to family.
   (c) Obligation to God.
   (d) Both (a) and (b).
9. Which party did Mandela join?
   (a) National African Congress.
   (b) African National Congress.
   (c) Indian National Congress.
   (d) He did not join any party.
10. Which of these lines from 'A Long Walk to Freedom' hints at the end of apartheid in South Africa?

    (CBSE SQP, 2023)

    (a) I was not born with a hunger to be free. I was born free — free in every way that I could know.
    (b) ...I yearned for the basic and honourable freedoms of achieving my potential, of earning my keep,...
    (c) Although that day, neither group knew the lyrics of the anthem they once despised, they would soon know the words by heart.
    (d) ...The white-skinned peoples of South Africa patched up their differences and erected a system of racial domination against the dark-skinned peoples...

Extract-Based Questions

I. Read the following extract and answer the questions/ complete the sentences that follow: (5 M)

The great university of life is full of experiences, but to make full use of those experiences, all of us students, teachers and professors—have to be cautious and on guard. The most essential requisite is character. If your character is lacking and you leave the precincts of the alma mater without your character fully developed, you will be wasting an opportunity of a lifetime.

1. What happens if someone quits their alma mater without fully developing their character, as indicated in the extract? **(1)**
   (a) They will miss out on valuable experiences.
   (b) They will waste their lifetime opportunity.
   (c) They will become successful regardless.
   (d) They will regret their decision.
2. Based on the given extract, what can we infer about the importance of character development in education? **(1)**
   (a) It is not important.
   (b) It is only important in some fields of study.
   (c) It is essential.
   (d) It is rarely important.

3. How does the given extract emphasize the importance of character development in education? **(2)**

4. The phrase '________' refers to the boundaries or confines of the educational institution from which one is leaving. **(1)**

II. Read the following extract and answer the questions/complete the sentences that follow: (5 M)

This is the occasion for mutual help and mutual cooperation. We must know what our duty is as true citizens. Your teacher has to impart that duty. Unless we learn to shoulder our responsibility in the true spirit of discipline and citizenship we cannot go ahead. We must strengthen our shoulders and our legs so that we can stand erect and bear the burden that has devolved on us. Then alone would we secure the real objective of freedom.

1. What is the objective of freedom according to the given extract? **(1)**

   (*a*) To stand erect. (*b*) To shoulder responsibility.
   (*c*) To bear burden. (*d*) To achieve independence.

2. What does the extract suggest about the relationship between discipline, citizenship, and achieving the objective of freedom? **(1)**

3. The phrase 'devolved on us' means ________. **(1)**

4. How does the given extract emphasize the importance of mutual cooperation and responsibility in achieving freedom? **(2)**

III. Read the following extract and answer the questions/complete the sentences that follow: (5 M)

"It was only when I began to learn that my boyhood freedom was an illusion, when I discovered as a young man that my freedom had already been taken from me, that I began to hunger for it. At first as a student I wanted freedom only for myself, the transitory freedoms of being able to stay out at night, read what I pleased and go where I chose. Later, as a young man in Johannesburg, I yearned for the basic and honourable freedoms..." **(CBSE, QB)**

1. The title that best suits this extract is **(1)**

   (*a*) Freedom for everything
   (*b*) Knowledge about Freedom
   (*c*) Significance of Freedom
   (*d*) Realisation of Freedom

2. Why do you think the speaker mentions some freedoms as 'transitory'? **(1)**

   (*a*) The freedoms are momentary and keep changing with time.
   (*b*) The definition of freedom is constant but perspectives differ.
   (*c*) Freedom means different things to different people.
   (*d*) Freedom is not that important after a certain age.

3. Choose the option that best fits the usage of the word 'illusion' as used in the extract. **(1)**

   (*a*) He was never able to get past the illusion.
   (*b*) The illusion I experienced was quite intriguing.
   (*c*) A large mirror in the room creates an illusion.
   (*d*) I was living under the illusion that this is possible.

4. The speaker says, 'at first as a student I wanted freedom only for myself.' **(1)**

   Why do you think he only thought about himself?

   (*a*) He didn't want to think about the freedom denied to others.
   (*b*) He was being selfish and was only bothered about himself.
   (*c*) He didn't think that freedom denied to him was important for others.
   (*d*) He was too young to realise that freedom was denied to others as well.

5. A part of the extract has been paraphrased. Choose the option that includes the most appropriate solution to the blanks in the given paraphrase of the extract. **(1)**

   The speaker's belief about freedom, since childhood proved false. It was not until the speaker grew up to be a young man when it (i) ________ on him that he was (ii) ________ of freedom. Then he began (iii) ________ it.

   (*a*) (i) desired (ii) dawned[17] (iii) depriving
   (*b*) (i) dawned (ii) deprived[18] (iii) desiring[19]
   (*c*) (i) dawned (ii) arrived (iii) desiring
   (*d*) (i) arrived (ii) deprived (iii) dawned

IV. Read the following extract and answer the questions/complete the sentences that follow: (5 M)

"To the assembled guests and the watching world, I said: Today, all of us do, by our presence here... confer glory and hope to newborn liberty. Out of the experience of an extraordinary human disaster that lasted too long, must be born a society of which all humanity will be proud. We, who were outlaws not so long ago, have today been given the rare privilege to be host to the nations of the world on our own soil."

1. The extract has been taken from Mandela's ________. **(1)**

   (*a*) Book (*b*) Autobiography
   (*c*) Biography (*d*) Speech

2. Pick the option that showcases the usage of 'host' as in the extract. **(1)**

   (*a*) Natalya was praised for her hospitality as the host of the party.
   (*b*) She was able to host the event without any hindrance.
   (*c*) He met the host and apologised for his friend's misbehaviour.
   (*d*) She is the best host that one can ever come across.

[17] **Dawned:** emergence of thought
[18] **Deprived:** denied
[19] **Desiring:** wanting to have

3. What does the phrase "extraordinary human disaster" refer to, and why does the speaker believe it lasted too long? **(2)**

4. How do you think the speaker feels? Choose the option that best fits his state of mind. **(1)**

(*a*) (i) honoured (ii) elated (iii) overwhelmed[20]

(*b*) (i) unmindful (ii)elated (iii) overwhelmed

(*c*) (i) unmindful (ii) elated (iii) emotional

(*d*) (i) elated (ii) honoured (iii) unmindful

Subjective Questions

Short Answer Questions (40-50 words) (3 M)

1. What did Nelson Mandela remember on the day of the inaugural ceremony? **(CBSE, 2020)**
2. Based on your reading of the lesson, what can you infer about Mandela as a father and as a leader? **(CBSE, QB)**
3. Mandela says that his country's greatest wealth is its people and not the purest diamonds. Justify his statement. **(CBSE, QB)**
4. Why does Mandela think that the generals saluting him would have arrested him a few years ago?
5. Why did Mandela feel that it is easier to love than to hate someone?

Long Answer Questions (100-120 words) (6 M)

6. Describe the value of freedom for human beings and how it is important for the growth of civilisation and humanism as described in the lesson 'Nelson Mandela: Long Walk to Freedom'.
7. Why does Mandela say that freedom is indivisible? How are the oppressed and the oppressor alike robbed of their humanity?
8. Describe the contribution of Nelson Mandela in the struggle for independence of the blacks of his country against the hated apartheid regime.

OR

Draw a character sketch of Nelson Mandela highlighting his struggle against the apartheid regime for the human rights of his people.

Nailing the Right Answer

- ❒ Students should correlate the answer with the content in the chapter rather than talk about Nelson Mandela in general.
- ❒ Learn and practice spelling words like apartheid, colleagues, inauguration etc.

ANSWERS & EXPLANATIONS

Answer Key

Multiple Choice Questions

1. (*b*) 2. (*b*) 3. (*d*) 4. (*c*) 5. (*c*) 6. (*a*) 7. (*b*) 8. (*d*) 9. (*b*) 10. (*c*)

Explanations

Extract-Based Questions

I. 1. (*b*) They will waste their lifetime opportunity.

2. (*c*) It is essential.

3. The extract suggests that in order to make full use of experiences in life, character development is essential. The author emphasizes that leaving the alma mater without a fully developed character would be a wasted opportunity of a lifetime. The extract highlights the importance of character over intelligence or talent, indicating that character development is a crucial aspect of education and personal growth.

4. 'Precincts of the alma mater'.

[20] **Overwhelmed:** have a strong emotional effect

II. 1. (*b*) To shoulder responsibility.

2. The extract suggests that the true spirit of discipline and citizenship is essential to shoulder responsibility and achieve the objective of freedom.

3. The phrase 'devolved on us' means to pass on or transfer responsibility to someone.

4. The extract suggests that mutual help and cooperation are crucial in achieving freedom, and individuals must learn to shoulder their responsibility in the true spirit of discipline and citizenship. The extract highlights the importance of strengthening one's shoulders and legs to bear the burden of responsibility, which is essential for achieving the objective of freedom.

III. 1. (*c*) Significance of Freedom

2. (*a*) The freedoms are momentary and keep changing with time.

3. (*d*) I was living under the illusion that this is possible.

4. (*d*) He was too young to realise that freedom was denied to others as well.

5. (*b*) (i) dawned (ii) deprived (iii) desiring

IV. 1. (*b*) Autobiography

2. (*b*) She was able to host the event without any hindrance.

3. (*d*) The phrase "extraordinary human disaster" refers to the apartheid regime in South Africa, which was marked by severe racial discrimination and oppression.

The speaker believes it lasted too long because it caused immense suffering and injustice for many years, delaying the country's progress toward equality and freedom.

4. (*a*) (i) honoured (ii) elated (iii) overwhelmed

Subjective Questions

Short Answer Questions

CBSE Marking Scheme: Content-1 M, Organisation of Ideas-1 M, Accuracy-1 M

1. On the day of the inaugural ceremony, Mandela remembered the history of his nation, the birth of apartheid, its effect on his people and the long fight for freedom.

He remembered the first decade when the whites ruled over South Africa and how they discriminated against the blacks. They behaved cruelly and inhumanly. They treated blacks like slaves. He also remembered the freedom fighters who sacrificed their lives for freedom.

2. Mandela was a loving father as well as a great leader. However, to free his country from apartheid, he had to prioritise his role as a leader and stay away from his family.

Nonetheless, he sacrificed his life of comfort, his home and his family for the struggle for freedom against racial discrimination in South Africa.

3. Mandela believed that the people of his nation were the greatest wealth compared to any other form of wealth. He laid emphasis on people and their power to change the system and bring a new change in society.

Even though his country was known to be rich in minerals and diamonds, he particularly believed its greatest wealth to be its people.

4. During Mandela's lifetime, the apartheid policy existed in South Africa. Using this policy, the white population would oppress the black population of the country. People who fought against apartheid were killed or imprisoned and Mandela himself was arrested several times for wanting equal rights for all people.

The policy was discarded with the establishment of the new racially equal government with Mandela as the President. As this change was very new, Mandela remembered how only a few years ago he would have been arrested by the same white generals who were saluting him.

5. Mandela believes that hate as a quality is taught to us by society. Unless differences are pointed out to us, we are happy to live in harmony with all. When Apartheid was imposed by the South African government, no one had a choice but to obey.

When Mandela and his fellow comrades were arrested for opposing oppression, Mandela could see that even the prison guards whose job it was to torture them and break them down, seemed hesitant to beat them up. He could see a glimpse of kindness in their eyes. This made him feel that some love and kindness was always present in humans.

Long Answer Questions

CBSE Marking Scheme: Expression-2 M, Accuracy-1 M

6. Everyone wants to live with complete freedom, as freedom is natural to all living beings. The value of freedom is better known to that human being who has never tasted it. **(1 M)**

A person who is chained or whose rights are restricted values freedom more than anyone else. For instance, Mandela valued freedom as he had to remain behind bars for most of his life. **(1 M)**

In the same way, a bird or animal that is meant to be free, should not be caged. Similarly, life becomes hell if we are deprived of freedom. A civilisation can only grow when one has freedom; without freedom, there is nothing to live for. **(1 M)**

7. Nelson Mandela believed that freedom is indivisible. His hunger for his own freedom became the greater hunger for the freedom of his people. He couldn't live with dignity and self-respect if his people were bound in chains. **(1 M)**

The chains on any one of his people were the chains on all of them. The chains on all of his people were the chains on him. **(1 M)**

Mandela realised that the oppressor must be set free as surely as the oppressed. A man who takes another's freedom is a prisoner of hatred and narrow-mindedness. He is not truly free if he takes away someone else's freedom. Thus, the oppressed and the oppressor alike are robbed of their humanity. **(1 M)**

8. Mandela contributed immensely to the struggle for independence and the fight against apartheid in South Africa. He had to go through extreme suffering and torture in prison, which ultimately led the country to have its first democratic, non-racial government. **(1 M)**

Mandela, as he said, was not born with a hunger to be free. He had a different understanding of freedom at different stages of his life. As he grew, he realised that his boyhood freedom was an illusion. Only when he joined the African National Congress, his own freedom became the greater hunger for the freedom of his people. **(1 M)**

Mandela was grateful for the unimaginable sacrifices of thousands of black heroes for the freedom of their people. Modestly, he realises that freedom is indivisible. **(1 M))**

❑❑❑

TWO STORIES ABOUT FLYING

3

I. HIS FIRST FLIGHT

—Liam O' Flaherty

Narrative Sketch

1. The young seagull was afraid to fly and remained on the ledge while his siblings flew away.
2. His parents tried to motivate and threaten him to fly.
3. He watched his family flying and catching fish while he stayed behind.
4. The seagull was hungry and begged his mother for food.
5. When his mother flew towards him with food, he dived to catch it but ended up flying instead.
6. Initially terrified, he gained confidence and joined his family in flying.
7. He flew over the ocean and enjoyed the experience.
8. His family praised him and offered him food as he successfully completed his first flight.
9. Other birds watch in amazement as he soars through the air.
10. The story explores themes of overcoming fear, gaining independence, and trying new things.

BEFORE YOU READ

Theme

The story highlights the point that our fear blocks our progress. Once we overcome that fear, it is easy to take the first step towards success. The young seagull in the story was afraid to fly as he did not trust his wings. Despite several attempts by his parents, he could not gather the courage to fly. However, in the moment of sheer hunger because of the temptation[1] by the seagull's mother, the young seagull couldn't resist flying fearlessly.

Important Characters' Sketch

- **Young Seagull:** He was a timid sea-bird, afraid of flying. In the story, he comes across as a scared bird who refuses to learn to fly. The young seagull is stubborn, as he does not listen to repeated requests from his parents. He is also comfort-loving because he relies on his parents to get him food. When his mother tempts him with food (fish), the young seagull forgets his fear of flying and makes his first flight.
- **Mother Seagull:** In the story, 'His First Flight', the seagull's mother is portrayed as a tough but motivating character. She understood that her child needed a little motivation to achieve his goal of flying. Initially, she tried threatening the young seagull in many ways, but that did not work. Finally, a little temptation with food and clever thinking helped her child take his first flight.

SYNOPSIS

His First Flight, by Liam O' Flaherty, is about a young seagull afraid to take his first flight because he couldn't trust his wings. His siblings bravely took the plunge[2] to fly even with relatively shorter wings. One day, the young seagull was alone on his ledge. His two brothers and his sister had already flown away the day before. When he attempted to fly, he could not gather the courage to do so. His father and mother tried all they could; they called him shrilly, scolded him and threatened to let him die of hunger. But the young seagull could not move.

Twenty-four hours went by, and no one had come near him. He watched his parents flying about with his brothers and sister, perfecting their art of flight, teaching them how to dive for fish.

The whole family taunted him for his cowardice.[3] The day was getting hotter, and the seagull had not eaten since the previous night. The seagull stood on the brink of the ledge, trying to get his family's attention, closed his eyes, standing on one leg. He had the other leg hidden under his wing.

He pretended to fall asleep. However, the mother was looking at him. He saw her tearing at a piece of fish that lay at her feet. The sight of the food maddened him. He gave out a sound begging his mother to give him some food. His mother screamed back at him. She picked a piece of the fish and flew across to him. He leaned out, trying to get nearer to her as she flew across.

The seagull had the food within reach of his beak. But he could not get it. The seagull waited for a moment in surprise, wondering why his mother did not come closer. He was mad with hunger that he dived at the fish. With a scream, he fell outwards and downwards into space. His heart stood still, and he could hear nothing. But that terror only lasted a minute. The next moment he felt his wings spread outwards. He was soaring gradually downwards and outwards. He was no longer afraid, just a little dizzy. He soared high upwards when his mother swooped[4] past him. Both of them were screaming with joy. Then his father flew over him screaming. The young seagull saw his two brothers and his sister flying around him, roaring and diving.

Lessons to learn

- *Courage and Determination.*
- *Self-Discovery and Individuality.*
- *Patience and Perseverance.*
- *Acceptance of Differences.*

The once-afraid seagull had forgotten that he had not always been able to fly. He was proud of himself. He saw a vast green sea beneath him. When his parents, brothers, and sister landed on the green surface of the water ahead of him, they called him to do the same thing. He dropped his leg to stand on the green sea. But his legs sank into it. He cried with fear and tried to rise again, flapping his wings. But he was weak with hunger and could not rise, tired by the strange exercise. His belly touched the green sea, but he sank no further. He was floating on it. His family screamed around him, praised him, and their beaks offered him scraps of dogfish as he had made his first flight.

[1] **Temptation:** the desire to do something
[2] **Plunge:** jump or dive quickly and energetically
[3] **Cowardice** (noun): lack of bravery
[4] **Swooped:** move rapidly downwards

When your seagull mom suggests therapy for your flightless sibling.

NCERT EXERCISE

Thinking about the Text

(NCERT, Page 36)

1. **Why was the young seagull afraid to fly? Do you think all young birds are afraid to make their first flight or are some birds more timid than others? Do you think a human baby also finds it a challenge to take its first steps?**

Ans. The young seagull was afraid to fly because he couldn't trust his wings for his first flight. It is natural to be scared to do something for the first time. Surely all young birds must be afraid to make their first flights. Similarly, a human baby also finds it challenging to take the first step.

2. **"The sight of the food maddened him." What does this suggest? What compelled5 the young seagull to finally fly?** **(CBSE, 2020)**

Ans. When the young seagull couldn't take his first flight, his family tried everything to get him to do so. They even threatened[6] to let him starve.[7] Twenty-four hours went by, and the young seagull was getting hungry. His hunger only intensified[8] when he saw his mother tearing at a piece of fish that lay at her feet. It cried to her, begging her to give him some food.

When his mother came towards him with food in her beak, he screamed joyfully. However, she stopped midway, which made the seagull wonder in surprise. Unable to control his

[5]**Compelled:** forge; oblige
[6]**Threatened:** make threats against
[7]**Starve:** suffer or die from hunger
[8]**Intensified:** increase; rise

hunger any longer, he dived at the food in his mother's beak. At that moment, his hunger made him overpower his fear. Finally, he was able to take his first flight.

3. "They were beckoning[9] to him, calling shrilly. "Why did the seagull's father and mother threaten him and cajole[10] him to fly?

Ans. The young seagull was afraid to fly and take his first flight. Even when he saw his brothers and sister flying, he could not gather enough courage to make that flight.

Then, his father and mother started calling him shrilly and scolding him. They threatened to let him starve on the ledge if he did not fly. They did so because they wanted him to overcome his fear and learn to fly.

4. Have you ever had a similar experience where your parents encouraged you to do something that you were too scared to try? Discuss this in pairs or groups.

Ans. (Suggested Answer) Yes, I had a similar childhood experience while learning to ride a bicycle. In my initial attempts, I fell too many times and developed a fear of cycling, which was challenging to overcome. No amount of provoking and cajoling could let me try it again, but my father encouraged me to overcome the fear and helped me. He took me around on a spacious ground and made me ride the bicycle for a couple of hours. After a few days, I started enjoying it without fear which developed my confidence.

5. In the case of a bird flying, it seems a natural act and a foregone conclusion that it should succeed. In the examples you have given in answer to the previous question, was your success guaranteed, or was it important for you to try, regardless of the possibility of failure?

Ans. We face some problems in the initial stage while learning a new skill. Due to the fear of failure, we hesitate to perform a task or do something new.

In the case of the seagull, his parents persuaded him to fly. In the previous answer, I shared my experience of how my father persuaded me to learn to ride a bicycle.

It was important for my father to make me overcome my fear. He motivated me to do something. As the saying goes, "Practice makes a man perfect", which was applicable in my case correctly.

MISCELLANEOUS EXERCISE

Multiple Choice Questions

1. The theme of the lesson is:
   (*a*) Courage and fearlessness.
   (*b*) Dependability.
   (*c*) Pride and prejudice.
   (*d*) None of the above.

2. Why did his family taunt him about his cowardice?
   (*a*) He went with his sister and brothers.
   (*b*) He was not listening to them.
   (*c*) He was not liked by them at all.
   (*d*) He was not accepting their request to fly with them.

3. How did the young seagull start flying?
   (*a*) His brothers and sister helped him.
   (*b*) He was hungry and started to fly in search of food.
   (*c*) He did not learn to fly at all.
   (*d*) His mother tempted him with food and moved away from him to make him fly.

4. Which of the following statements is not true of the young seagull?
   (*a*) His family helped him fly.
   (*b*) He wanted to fly but was afraid to do so.
   (*c*) He was lazy and did not want to fly.
   (*d*) His hunger made him fly.

5. Out of excitement, his family members offer him
   (*a*) Worms (*b*) Dogfish
   (*c*) Herring fish (*d*) seagull

6. What food did the seagull's mother get for it?
   (*a*) Worms (*b*) Fish
   (*c*) Insects (*d*) Rodents

7. Why did his mother stop midway while giving him the fish?
   (*a*) She was mad at him.
   (*b*) She didn't want to give him the fish.
   (*c*) To push him to fly out of hunger.
   (*d*) She saw something midway.

8. The lesson "His First Flight" is about a ____________
   (*a*) Pilot (*b*) Seagull
   (*c*) Seabird (*d*) Pigeon

[9] **Beckoning:** make a gesture
[10] **Cajole:** persuade (someone) to do something

9. The young seagull lacked __________
(*a*) Fear (*b*) Courage
(*c*) Hunger (*d*) Motivation

10. Select the correct option to fill in the blanks below:
Risk: risky: __________ : __________
(*a*) Danger: dangerously
(*b*) Hazard: hazardous
(*c*) Fear: fearless
(*d*) Caution: precaution

Extract-Based Questions

I. Read the following extract and answer the questions/ complete the sentences that follow: (5 M)

The day before, all day long, he had watched his parents flying about with his brothers and sister, perfecting them in the art of flight, teaching them how to skim the waves and how to dive for fish. He had, in fact, seen his older brother catch his first herring and devour it, standing on a rock, while his parents circled around raising a proud cackle. And all morning the whole family had walked about on the big plateau midway down the opposite cliff taunting him with his cowardice.

1. How did the family taunt the protagonist? (1)
(*a*) By flying high above him.
(*b*) By teaching him to dive for fish.
(*c*) By taunting him with his cowardice.
(*d*) By catching more fish than him.

2. What does the term "plateau" mean in the given context? (1)

3. What can be inferred about the bird's feelings and experience? (2)

4. The word __________ in the extract means to 'move lightly just above the surface of the sea'. (1)

II. Read the following extract and answer the questions/ complete the sentences that follow: (5 M)

The day before, all day long, he had watched his parents flying about with his brothers and sister, perfecting them in the art of flight, teaching them how to skim the waves and how to dive for fish. He had, in fact, seen his older brother catch his first herring and devour it, standing on a rock, while his parents circled around raising a proud cackle. And all morning the whole family had walked about on the big plateau midway down the opposite cliff taunting him with his cowardice. **(CBSE, QB)**

1. Based on the given sentence, pick the option that corresponds to what human parents would say. 'While his parents circled around raising a proud cackle.' (1)
(*a*) Well done! (*b*) Oh no!
(*c*) Ready? (*d*) Really!

2. Which option lists the image nearest to 'skim the waves'? (1)

(i)  (ii) 

(iii)  (iv) 

(*a*) image (i) (*b*) image (ii)
(*c*) image (iii) (*d*) image (iv)

3. Imagine that the young gull attended a workshop on inspiration and confidence building and received a couple of pieces of advice. Choose the option that reflects these pieces of advice, most relevant to his situation. (1)

(i) 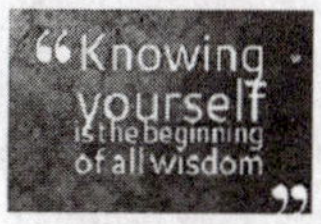

(ii) 

(iii) 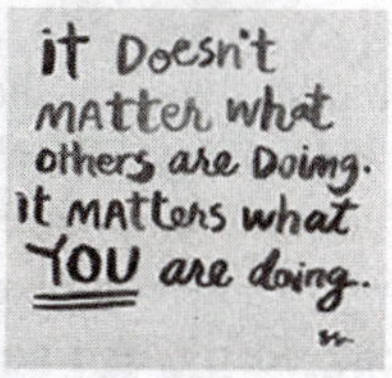

(iv) 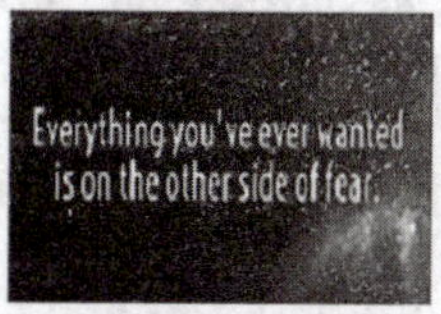

(*a*) (i) and (ii) (*b*) (ii) and (iii)
(*c*) (iii) and (iv) (*d*) (i) and (iv)

4. Which of the following feelings did the young gull, NOT feel according to the given context? "...all day long, he had watched his parents flying about with his brothers and sister..." (1)
(i) sad (ii) incompetent
(iii) excluded (iv) ungrateful
(v) inspired (vi) jealous
(vii) anxious
(*a*) (i), (iii), (vi) (*b*) (ii), (v), (vii)
(*c*) (ii), (iii), (vii) (*d*) (iv), (v), (vi)

5. Select the most appropriate option for the following: devour: guzzle:: nibble: __________ (1)
(*a*) chew (*b*) savour
(*c*) peck (*d*) gulp

III. Read the following extract and answer the questions/ complete the sentences that follow: (5 M)

He waited a moment in surprise, wondering why she did not come nearer, and then, maddened by hunger, he dived at the fish. With a loud scream, he fell outwards and downwards into space. Then a monstrous terror seized him and his heart stood still. He could hear nothing. But it only lasted a minute. The next moment he felt his wings spread outwards. The wind rushed against his breast feathers, then under his stomach, and against his wings. He could feel the tips of his wings cutting through the air. He was not falling headlong now. He was soaring gradually downwards and outwards. He was no longer afraid.

1. How did the birds feelings change after the initial terror? **(1)**

   (*a*) They intensified.

   (*b*) They disappeared.

   (*c*) They turned into hunger.

   (*d*) They transformed into courage.

2. What does the term "soaring" mean in the given context? **(1)**

3. What can be inferred about the protagonist's experience? **(2)**

4. The phrase ____________ means 'he became very frightened'. **(1)**

IV. Read the following extract and answer the questions/ complete the sentences that follow: (5 M)

He was soaring gradually downwards and outwards. He was no longer afraid. He just felt a bit dizzy. Then he flapped his wings once and he soared upwards. "Ga, ga, ga, Ga, ga, ga, Gaw-col-ah," his mother swooped past him, her wings making a loud noise. He answered her with another scream. Then his father flew over him screaming. He saw his two brothers and his sister flying around him curveting and banking and soaring and diving. Then he completely forgot that he had not always been able to fly, and commended himself to dive and soar and curve, shrieking shrilly.

1. How did the seagull respond to his family members flying around him? **(1)**

   (*a*) He ignored them.

   (*b*) He joined them in flying and making noises.

   (*c*) He felt scared and tried to hide.

   (*d*) He watched them from a distance.

2. The term "curveting" in the given context means ____________. **(1)**

3. What can be inferred about the seagull's transformation and integration into his family's flying activities? **(2)**

4. Which literary device is used in the phrase 'shrieking shrilly'? **(1)**

Subjective Questions

Short Answer Questions (40-50 words) (3 M)

1. What did the young seagull experience when he dived at the fish in his mother's beak? **(CBSE, 2021/2019)**
2. How did the young seagull overcome his fear and make his first flight? **(CBSE, 2020)**
3. Describe the young seagull's emotions when he flew over the sea. **(CBSE, QB)**
4. How did the young seagull's family celrebrate his first flight?
5. Briefly bring out the contrast between the young seagull's initial attempts to fly and his first successful flight. **(CBSE, 2024)**

Long Answer Questions (100-120 words) (6 M)

6. Was the young seagull same at the beginning and at the end of the lesson? Compare and contrast the two kinds of the same seagull in the lesson.
7. Look at the image of different parenting styles and what they signify. Which parenting styles would you attribute to the young seagull's parents? **(CBSE, QB)**

	Sensitive & Responsive	Stern & Punitive
Demanding	Authoritative	Authoritarian
Doesn't Enforce Limits	Permissive	Uninvolved

Fig. 1: The Four Parenting Styles

Do you think there was a difference between the mother's and father's attitudes? Support your answer with reference to the text. **(CBSE, QB)**

8. What message does the story 'His First Flight' convey?

ANSWERS & EXPLANATIONS

Answer Key

Multiple Choice Questions

1. (*a*) 2. (*d*) 3. (*d*) 4. (*c*) 5. (*b*) 6. (*b*) 7. (*c*) 8. (*b*) 9. (*b*) 10. (*b*)

Explanations

Extract-Based Questions

I. 1. (*c*) By taunting him with his cowardice.

2. A plateau refers to a relatively flat elevated area or landform on a cliff or mountain, characterized by a leveled surface.

3. Based on the passage, it can be inferred that the protagonist, the youngest of his siblings, feels left out and neglected. He witnesses his family engaging in activities that he is unable to participate in, such as flying and catching fish, which creates a sense of isolation and inadequacy.

4. 'Skim' is the correct word.

II. 1. (*a*) Well done!

2. (*c*) image (iii)

3. (*c*) (iii) and (iv)

4. (*d*) The young bird was full of feelings of sadness (for not being able to enjoy flying from one place to another), incompetence (as he thought that he cannot fly), excluded (as others enjoyed in water and he used to sit alone outside) and anxious (as he also wanted to fly). However, he never felt ungrateful, inspired or jealous of his parents or siblings.

5. (*b*) savour

Exp.: Devour and Guzzle refer to eating in big bites and quick swallowing. Nibble and Peck refer to eating in small titbits and lazily eating. Chew refers to biting and grinding with teeth the bite taken. Savour refers to enjoying food. Gulp also refers to eating big bites and quick swallowing, so does not match with nibble.

III. 1. (*d*) They transformed into courage

2. Soaring refers to flying or gliding in the air with graceful and effortless movements.

3. Based on the passage, it can be inferred that the bird, initially surprised by his mother's behaviour, becomes desperate due to hunger and attempts to catch the fish. Despite the initial fear, he experiences a transformation and a sense of freedom and fearlessness as he learns to fly.

4. The phrase 'monstrous terror seized him' means 'he became very frightened'.

IV 1. (*b*) He joined them in flying and making noises.

2. "Curveting" refers to making quick and agile turns or movements while flying.

3. Based on the passage, it can be inferred that the seagull quickly adapts to his new found ability to fly and immerses himself in the flying activities with his family. His eagerness to join them, mimic their sounds, and engage in flying activities indicates a sense of belonging.

4. Onomatopoeia and alliteration are used in the given phrase.

Key Takeaway

Alliteration is a literary device where consecutive words in a phrase begin with the same consonant sound, in this case, the 'sh' sound in "shrieking" and "shrilly." "Onomatopoeia" is a literary device where the word's pronunciation imitates the sound it represents. "Shrieking" is an onomatopoeic word as it mimics the actual sound of a high-pitched scream or yell, making the description more vivid and impactful for the reader.

Subjective Questions

Short Answer Questions

CBSE Marking Scheme: Content-1 M, Organisation of Ideas-1 M, Accuracy-1 M

1. The young seagull screamed as he fell outward and downward while diving for the fish. His heart stopped as a tremendous terror seized him.

   He quickly spread out his wings and could feel the tips of them cutting through the air. He then landed safely in the sea and started to float on it fearlessly.

2. The young seagull was terrified of flight, but he overcame it and discovered how to fly. His mother intentionally tore a chunk of fish and flew around him. She approached him but did not get any closer. He dived at the fish as he was enraged by hunger.

This incident made him spread his wings and master the skill of flying. He momentarily felt terror as he fell downward and outward into space, but it only lasted a short while. The next second, he was flying through the air. He had finished his first flight.

3. When the young seagull flew over the sea, he no longer felt afraid. He fell off as he leaned forward, and a monstrous terror seized him, and his heart stood still. He could hear nothing. But it only lasted a minute. The next moment he felt his wings spread outwards.

   He was soaring gradually downwards and outwards, flapped his wings once and soared upwards. Then he completely forgot that he had not always been able to fly and commended himself for taking his first flight.

4. When the young seagull finally took a plunge and had his first flight, the family celebrated by screaming, praising him and offering him scraps of dogfish.

   As he started to fly, all his family members flew towards him, soaring and diving around him. He and his family were happy, relieved and proud of him to have completed his first flight.

5. The young seagull was initially afraid to fly; he didn't think his wings could support him. When hunger overcame his fear, he leaped towards his mother for food and began to fly. His fear turned into excitement as he realized he was flying.

Long Answer Questions

CBSE Marking Scheme: Expression-2 M, Accuracy-1 M

6. No, the young seagull was not the same at the beginning and at the end of the lesson. In the beginning, the young seagull used to be all alone on his ledge. His two brothers and his sister had flown away the day before. **(1 M)**

   He had been afraid of flying with them. Whenever he tried to flap his wings, he was certain that his wings would never support him. His father and mother flew around calling him shrilly. They were constantly scolding and taunting him. They were threatening to let him starve on his ledge unless he flew away. **(1 M)**

   Maddened by hunger, he dived at the fish. After trials and errors, he was soaring gradually downwards forgetting all his hesitations and fears. His success was welcomed by his family. **(1 M)**

Nailing the Right Answer

Focus on character growth and family influence to showcase the young seagull's journey effectively.

7. The seagull's parents can be considered stern and demanding. The young seagull, unlike his other siblings, could not fly.

   Both his mother and father didn't pay attention to him on purpose. They called him shrilly, scolded him and threatened to let him die of hunger. But the young seagull could not move. **(1 M)**

   However, the seagull's mother can be termed as authoritative. She was stern about making his child learn the art of flying and removing his fear of flying. **(1 M)**

   When the young seagull was looking for food, the mother knew it was the right time to teach him, so instead of spoon-feeding, she played a trick with him.

   She halted just a few steps away from the seagull. The sight of food maddened the hungry seagull, and he jumped towards her, which worked like magic, and he could take up his first step towards flying. **(1 M)**

8. The story conveys the message that we learn by taking courage and not by sitting idle. A young seagull is fed lovingly by his parents. But when the time comes for him to fly, he feels afraid. **(1 M)**

   His parents try many tricks to teach him to fly. But he is so afraid that he refuses to fly. At last, his mother tempts him with food in her beak. But she only flies near his ledge and does not land there. In order to get food, the hungry seagull comes to the edge of the rock and falls from it. **(1 M)**

   At first, he is terrified but then he opens his wings and starts flying. He is happy to note that he did not fall in the sea. In this way, the young seagull makes the first flight of his life when he takes courage. **(1 M)**

II. BLACK AEROPLANE

—Frederick Forsyth

Narrative Sketch

1. The narrator is flying an old Dakota aeroplane from France to England, looking forward to being with his family.
2. As the flight progresses, the narrator encounters storm clouds ahead, but decides to continue rather than turning back.
3. Inside the storm clouds, visibility becomes zero, and the compass, radio, and other instruments malfunction.
4. In the midst of the storm, the narrator spots another aeroplane flying nearby without lights.
5. The pilot of the mysterious black aeroplane waves and signals the narrator to follow.
6. Grateful for the assistance, the narrator obediently follows the black aeroplane, which turns northward.
7. The black aeroplane continues leading the narrator through the storm for half an hour.
8. Suddenly, the narrator emerges from the clouds and sees a runway with lights ahead, indicating an airport.
9. However, when the narrator looks for the black aeroplane, it has disappeared.
10. The narrator lands safely, feeling relieved and walks away from his old Dakota.
11. Upon questioning airport staff about the other pilot, she informs the narrator that no other planes were flying that night.
12. The narrator is left puzzled, as they wonder who guided them through the storm and helped them reach the airport safely without the use of instruments or communication.

BEFORE YOU READ

Theme

The story shifts between mystery and miracle. It talks about mysteries of life which often remain unsolved. A mysterious aeroplane appeared in the sky to help the narrator escape dark stormy clouds. On landing safely, when the narrator inquired[1] about the black aeroplane, he found that he was the only person flying that night. If the experience resulted from the narrator's subconscious[2] or was a supernatural element remains a mystery.

Important Characters' Sketch

- **Young Pilot:** The narrator, Frederick Forsyth himself, was the pilot. He was flying from Paris to London, eagerly waiting to be with his family. He was excited to have a good English breakfast when he reached London. In that eagerness, he decided to fly through the dark clouds even though he had less fuel. His adventurous spirit is reflected in his willingness to take risks and fly straight into the storm. His idea of being led by another aeroplane could be the subconscious mind that guides him in the right direction.

SYNOPSIS

The story's narrator is a young pilot flying alone from France to London in his aeroplane 'Old Dakota' at one thirty in the morning. He was dreaming of his holiday and looking forward to being with his family. He expected to be on time for a good, big English Breakfast.

When Paris was about 150 kilometres behind him, he saw huge, stormy clouds approaching[3] his plane. It was a fierce storm, and the clouds were like black mountains. He didn't have enough fuel to fly around them to the north or south. He thought of going back to Paris, but he also wanted to have breakfast with his family.

The pilot gathered the courage to take the risk and flew his plane straight through the stormy clouds. As he flew into dark clouds, everything turned black. He wasn't able to see anything outside.

The plane jumped and twisted in the air. He tried to contact the control centre through the radio, but there was no answer. He was lost in the storm, and his compass, radio and other equipment were all dead.

Then, out of nowhere, in the black clouds, he saw another aeroplane. He was glad to see another person. The other pilot signalled the narrator to follow him and moved north. He was like an obedient child following the strange aeroplane.

There was only enough fuel in the old Dakota's last tank to fly for five or ten more minutes. The narrator was feeling frightened again. Suddenly he came out of the clouds and saw the airport runway. He was elated[4] to be out of danger. He turned to look for his friend in the black aeroplane, but it was gone. The sky was empty!

Lessons to learn

- *Trust your instincts.*
- *Perseverance in challenging circumstances.*
- *Assistance can come from unexpected sources.*
- *Courage and risk-taking.*

He landed safely at the airport and gladly walked away from his Old Dakota. He asked the lady at the control centre who the other pilot was as he wanted to thank him. The lady looked at the narrator strangely and replied that no other aeroplanes were flying that night; his was the only plane flying in the storm.

---

[1] **Inquired:** asked for information
[2] **Subconscious:** unconscious human mind
[3] **Approaching:** coming near
[4] **Elated:** happy

NCERT EXERCISE

Thinking about the Text

(NCERT, Page 40)

1. "I'll take the risk." What is the risk? Why does the narrator take it?

Ans. The narrator talks about the risk of flying his old Dakota through the black storm clouds.

The narrator took the risk because he wanted to reach England to celebrate Christmas with his family and have a big English breakfast.

2. Describe the narrator's experience as he flew the aeroplane into the storm.

Ans. As the narrator entered the storm, his plane started jumping and twisting. He tried to contact the control centre through the radio, but there was no answer. He was lost in the storm, and his compass, radio and other equipment were all dead. It was a terrible and fearsome experience for him. The fuel tank was almost empty, and he could not fly for more than ten minutes. Suddenly, he saw another aeroplane. Its pilot waved at him, asking him to follow.

He was glad to find a helper. He was using his last fuel tank, and there was only enough fuel to fly for five or ten minutes. Then, the other pilot started to go down, and he followed. He followed him without any choice and landed safely on the runway.

3. Why does the narrator say, "I landed and was not sorry to walk away from the old Dakota…"?

Ans. The narrator, a young pilot, was happy to land safely out of dark stormy clouds.

He wasn't sorry to walk away from the old Dakota as he had a horrific experience flying that plane. However, he felt bad when he could not thank the mysterious[5] pilot who saved him from the dark storm.

4. What made the woman in the control centre look at the narrator strangely?

Ans. The woman in the control room gave a puzzled look when the narrator asked about the other aeroplane and its pilot. The lady looked at the narrator strangely and replied that no other aeroplanes were flying that night; his was the only plane flying in the storm.

5. Who do you think helped the narrator to reach safely? Discuss this among yourselves and give reasons for your answer.

Ans. The narrator's experience in the story "Black Aeroplane" could result from his subconscious. There was no other plane in the storm, as the woman at the control centre could see only his plane on the radar. Also, no other plane was flying that night. He was a good pilot, and his faith in himself gave him the courage to get out safely from the horrific situation.

[5] **Mysterious:** strange; puzzling

MISCELLANEOUS EXERCISE

Multiple Choice Questions

1. The pilot was flying from _____ to _____.
   (a) England, France (b) France, India
   (c) France, England (d) England, India
2. How would you describe the "risk" the narrator took?
   (a) Calculated (b) Impetuous[6]
   (c) Unavoidable (d) Navigable
3. Read the statements below, and then select the option that best describes the given statements.
   Statement-I: The narrator's desire to reach home and see his family made him complacent.[7]
   Statement-II: The narrator was unaware of the threat that the adversarial[8] storm clouds presented
   Statement-III: The narrator's decision-making was quick but irresponsible as well as dangerous.
   (a) Statement-I is False, Statement-II is True, Statement III cannot be inferred.
   (b) Statements-I and III are True; statement-II cannot be inferred.
   (c) Statement-I cannot be inferred, Statement-II is False, and Statement-III is True.
   (d) Statements-I and II are False, and Statement-III is True.
4. In what way might the reference to the Dakota as "old" be relevant?
   (a) Its antique value made it precious to the narrator.
   (b) It shows the narrator's love and affection.
   (c) It did not have enough fuel to fly around the storm clouds.
   (d) Its ability to negotiate the storm clouds might have been suspected.
5. What instruments had stopped working during the storm?
   (a) Radio (b) Compass
   (c) Both of them (d) None of them
6. How far was the narrator from Paris when he saw dark clouds in the sky?
   (a) 50 km (b) 100 km
   (c) 150 km (d) 200 km
7. Why could the narrator not fly over or around the storm clouds?
   (a) Due to lack of fuel.
   (b) Due to a broken compass.
   (c) Due to a broken radio.
   (d) Due to the darkness.
8. How could the narrator have flown around the storm?
   (a) By flying to the north.
   (b) By flying to the south.
   (c) By flying either to the north or south.
   (d) None of these.
9. Give the noun form of 'believe'.
   (a) Believed (b) Believing
   (c) Belief (d) Believes
10. Why did he try the radio?
    (a) The other instruments were working.
    (b) The other instruments weren't functioning.
    (c) The compass was dead.
    (d) He was high up in the sky.

Extract-Based Questions

I. Read the following extract and answer the questions/ complete the sentences that follow: (5 M)

I was safe! I turned to look for my friend in the black aeroplane, but the sky was empty. There was nothing there. The black aeroplane was gone. I could not see it anywhere. I landed and was not sorry to walk away from the old Dakota near the control tower. I went and asked a woman in the control centre where I was and who the other pilot was. I wanted to say 'Thank you'. She looked at me very strangely and then laughed. "Another aeroplane? Up there in this storm? No other aeroplanes were flying tonight. Yours was the only one I could see on the radar." So, who helped me…

1. What was the protagonist's reaction upon realizing the black aeroplane was gone? **(1)**
   (a) Relief (b) Disappointment
   (c) Confusion (d) Fear

---

[6] **Impetuous:** impulsive or hasty
[7] **Complacent:** satisfaction with oneself or one's achievements
[8] **Adversarial:** involving conflict or opposition

2. How did the woman at the control center react when the protagonist asked about the other pilot? **(1)**

(*a*) She provided information about the pilot.

(*b*) She looked surprised and worried.

(*c*) She laughed and found it amusing.

(*d*) She denied the existence of another aeroplane.

3. The term "control tower" in the given context refers to ____________. **(1)**

4. What was the mysterious fate of the black aeroplane and its significance for the protagonist's experience? **(2)**

II. Read the following extract and answer the questions/ complete the sentences that follow: (5 M)

"Paris Control? Paris Control? Can you hear me?" There was no answer. The radio was dead too. I had no radio, no compass, and I could not see where I was. I was lost in the storm. Then, in the black clouds quite near me, I saw another aeroplane. It had no lights on its wings, but I could see it flying next to me through the storm. I could see the pilot's face — turned towards me. I was very glad to see another person. He lifted one hand and waved. "Follow me," he was saying. "Follow me." 'He knows that I am lost,' I thought. 'He's trying to help me.'

1. Why did the protagonist need to contact Paris Control? **(1)**

(*a*) To request landing clearance.

(*b*) To inform them about the lights of a big city.

(*c*) To report an emergency situation.

(*d*) To check the time.

2. Based on the passage, what can be inferred about the protagonist's emotions and intentions during the flight? **(2)**

3. The phrase "nose of the aeroplane" in the given context refers to ____________. **(1)**

4. Why did the other pilot say 'Follow me'? **(1)**

III. Read the following extract and answer the questions/ complete the sentences that follow: (5 M)

Suddenly I came out of the clouds and saw two long straight lines of lights in front of me. It was a runway! An airport! I was safe! I turned to look for my friend in the black aeroplane, but the sky was empty. There was nothing there. The black aeroplane was gone. I could not see it anywhere.

1. What was the protagonist's initial reaction upon seeing the runway and airport? **(1)**

(*a*) Panic and fear.

(*b*) Relief and a sense of safety.

(*c*) Confusion and disbelief.

(*d*) Excitement and curiosity.

2. What does the term "runway" refer to in the given context? **(1)**

3. Based on the protagonist's inability to find the black aeroplane, what can be inferred about its disappearance? **(2)**

4. What does 'sky was empty' mean in this extract? **(1)**

Subjective Questions

Short Answer Questions (40-50 words) (3 M)

1. Why was the pilot of the Dakota airplane frightened again? **(CBSE, 2020)**

2. What was crossing the narrator's mind when he was flying over Paris?

3. The pilot was lost in the storm. Who rescued him, and how?

4. James Lane Allen says, "Adversity reveals character". What do you learn about the narrator from experience? Mention any two traits supported by the textual evidence. **(CBSE, QB)**

Long Answer Questions (100-120 words) (6 M)

5. In the lesson, the black airplane is a mystery. How?

6. Why did the writer want to thank another pilot after his safe landing? What values of the writer can be reflected in his actions?

7. Why and when did the narrator say that 'everything' was going well, it was an easy flight? **(CBSE, 2020)**

ANSWERS & EXPLANATIONS

Answer Key

Multiple Choice Questions

1. (*c*) **2.** (*b*) **3.** (*c*) **4.** (*d*) **5.** (*c*) **6.** (*c*) **7.** (*a*) **8.** (*c*) **9.** (*c*) **10.** (*b*)

Explanations

Extract-Based Questions

I. 1. (*a*) Relief

2. (*c*) She laughed and found it amusing.

3. The term "control tower" refers to a tall structure at an airport from where air traffic controllers monitor and manage the movements of aircraft.

4. The mysterious fate of the black aeroplane and its significance for the protagonist's experience remain unknown and open to interpretation.

II. 1. (*a*) To request landing clearance.

2. Based on the passage, it can be inferred that the protagonist was experiencing a sense of contentment and anticipation during the flight, with a focus on their upcoming holiday and the joy of being alone high above the countryside.

3. The phrase "nose of the aeroplane" refers to the front or forward section of the aircraft.

4. The other pilot said 'Follow me' as he knew that the narrator was lost.

III. 1. (*b*) Relief and a sense of safety.

2. The term "runway" refers to a long strip of prepared ground at an airport, used for the takeoff and landing of aircraft.

3. The disappearance of the black aeroplane suggests that it may have departed suddenly or vanished altogether. The protagonist's inability to locate it anywhere in the sky implies that the black aeroplane has left the protagonist's vicinity, leaving them alone and without its presence.

4. In this extract, 'sky was empty' means there was no other aeroplane in the sky.

Subjective Questions

Short Answer Questions

CBSE Marking Scheme: Content-1 M, Organisation of Ideas-1 M, Accuracy-1 M

1. The narrator felt terrified and helpless due to bad weather conditions. Then he saw an anonymous plane and the pilot of that plane asked the narrator to follow him. He started to lead the way through the clouds.

But after some time, the narrator noticed that the Dakota's tank was nearly empty, and this is the moment when the narrator was once again frightened.

2. At one thirty in the morning, the narrator was flying his old Dakota aeroplane over Paris. Everything seemed in perfect order, especially the weather and the thought of a big English breakfast waiting back home, then meeting his family.

He decided to call the Paris Control room and switched on the radio. However, the author's excitement was short-lived as soon as the aeroplane entered into black clouds, all the equipment stopped working, and everything turned black.

3. The narrator, a young pilot, was lost in the storm. Suddenly, a mysterious black aeroplane appeared, which guided him. The other pilot asked the lost pilot to follow him. The black aeroplane flew before him, cutting the clouds and showing him the way.

Then he flew down, and the narrator followed through the storm. He came out of the storm and saw the airport realising he was safe. He was grateful for 'his friend', who saved him from the horrific experience.

> **Mistakes 101 : What not to do!**
>
> One might fail to provide detailed textual evidence to support the traits mentioned, leading to a lack of depth in the analysis.

4. The narrator seemed to lack professional ethics and responsibility. He was about 150 km away from Paris when the dark clouds appeared. He didn't have enough fuel to go around them. Still, he took the risk to go through them as he wanted to reach England soon.

The narrator was a grateful man. After reaching safely at the runway, he went to the Paris control to ask about the other pilot who saved his life.

While the narrator had many traits, these two were evident in the text.

Long Answer Questions

CBSE Marking Scheme: Expression-2 M, Accuracy-1 M

5. With vintage Dakota 088, the author set out on his journey. The sky was clear at that moment. But all of a sudden he found himself completely lost in the storm of black cloud. **(1 M)**

   There was no visibility; everything was pitch black. He was unable to flee and was also unable to fly above the clouds due to the plane's lack of fuel. The narrator suddenly noticed a dark plane with no lights on its wings. **(1 M)**

   He could make out the pilot's features as it turned to face him. He was overjoyed to see another human in that storm. The pilot of the aeroplane assisted him. He arrived at the airport safely, but nobody noticed the mysterious black plane, which is still a mystery. **(1 M)**

6. The pilot (writer) of the old Dakota was stuck in the storm. He lost his contact with the control room and eventually, his compass stopped working. In this situation, his fuel tank was also empty. He lost all his hopes but suddenly a black unknown plane appeared in that storm. **(1 M)**

   The pilot of the black plane asked the writer to follow him. The writer followed him blindly through the storm and went out of the clouds and landed safely. After his landing, he wanted to thank the pilot of that strange black plane. **(1 M)**

   This action of the writer shows gratitude towards the pilot of the Black Plane. He was thankful to him for saving him when he had lost all his hopes of being alive. This shows that the writer had the quality of being grateful towards others. **(1 M)**

7. The story 'Black Aeroplane' is about a pilot who feels happy and content to fly over a city at night. He is flying from Paris to London. He is looking forward to enjoying his holiday with his family. As soon as he crosses Paris, he gets a look at dark clouds indicating an upcoming storm. **(1 M)**

   But still, his desire to reach his family and have a delicious breakfast with them made him risk his and his passenger's life. Then the pilot thought of informing the Paris Control Personnel about its presence and for instructions. **(1 M)**

   After receiving the instructions, the pilot geared up and followed them while putting the last fuel tank into operation. He was calm as everything was going as planned. So, he says that 'Everything' was going well; it was an easy flight. However, things took a sharp turn soon. **(1 M)**

❑❑❑

FROM THE DIARY OF ANNE FRANK

—Anne Frank

4

Narrative Sketch

1. A thirteen year old girl, Anne, finds writing in a diary to be a strange experience as a thirteen-year-old schoolgirl.
2. She decides to keep a diary as a way to confide in someone, as paper has more patience than people.
3. Anne reveals that she lacks a true friend despite having a loving family and several acquaintances.
4. She introduces the diary as her friend, whom she names "Kitty," and plans to share her thoughts and experiences with.
5. She provides a brief sketch of her life, including her family background and past experiences.
6. She mentions the forthcoming meeting in school where the teachers will decide the students' progression to the next form, creating anxiety and excitement among her classmates.
7. Discusses her relationship with her teachers and recalls an amusing incident involving a punishment for talking in class.
8. She cleverly writes an essay on the topic of "Quack, Quack, Quack, Said Mistress Chatterbox" to turn the joke on her teacher.
9. The essay gains attention and appreciation from her teacher and classmates, leading to a change in her classroom dynamics.

The chapter ends with the protagonist signing off her diary entry, expressing her contentment with the current situation.

BEFORE YOU READ

Theme

The lesson is an excerpt from the autobiography of a young girl, Anne Frank. Anne tells about her experience keeping a diary as she doesn't have a friend. She expressed her thoughts in that diary she named-Kitty.

She wrote while in hiding with her family and four friends in Amsterdam during the German occupation of the Netherlands during World War II. She spent her adolescent years hidden from the outside world, and her diary kept all her secrets. This diary was eventually translated from its original Dutch into many languages and became one of the world's most widely read books.

Important Characters' Sketch

- **Anne Frank:** Anne Frank is the writer and the main character of 'From the Diary of Anne Frank'. Her diary entries give an insight[1] into her character and personality. Anne considers her diary-Kitty-to be her true friend. She shares everything in her diary. She was thirteen years old and still thought very deeply. She knew the difference between friendship and true friendship. She had loving parents and a good home. Yet there was no one in whom she could confide.[2] So, she decided to keep a diary as a friend.
- **Mr Keesing:** Mr Keesing was an old-fashioned teacher. He was not rigidly strict but expected discipline and silence in his class while teaching. When Anne used to talk in class, he punished her and gave her extra homework to write. He cannot be entirely labelled as a strict teacher. At the end of the lesson, he can be seen as a fun-loving person who cracks jokes in class.

SYNOPSIS

In the lesson, Anne Frank, the writer, talks about not having a true friend in her life. While writing in a diary, she finds the experience quite strange and unusual. She feels that no one, including herself, would read about a thirteen-year-old schoolgirl's musings[3] in the future. However, she puts these thoughts away and decides to get all kinds of things off her chest. One day, when she was depressed, she came up with a saying, 'Paper has more patience than people,' which she believes is true. She also mentions that she doesn't have a friend. She explains it is not that she is entirely alone in the world. She has loving parents and an elder sister who is sixteen. There are about thirty people she can call friends. She has a family, loving aunts and a good home. On the surface, she seems to have everything except a true friend. For this reason, she has decided to write in her diary and wants it to be her friend. She decides to name her diary "Kitty", and unlike other people, she will not mention just facts. She starts by giving a brief sketch of her life before starting with her musings.

She refers to her father as the most adorable father she has known. Her father was thirty-six when he married Anne's mother, who was twenty-five then. Anne was born on 12th June, 1929. She had a three year older sister. She lived in Frankfurt until she was four. When her father immigrated[4] to Holland in 1933, her mother followed him, and she, along with her sister Margot was sent to Aachen to stay with their grandmother. Anne Frank was sent to the Montessori school until she was six. When Anne was in sixth form, her teacher was Mrs Kuperus, the headmistress. Both had a great love for each other.

Lessons to learn

- *Self-discovery*
- *Resilience*
- *Creativity*
- *Friendship*
- *The transformative power of writing.*

In 1941, her grandmother fell ill and had an operation. She passed away in January 1942. Anne deeply missed her grandma and lit a candle for her on that year's birthday.

On Saturday, 20th June, 1942, Anne Frank made her first entry in her diary. It was in the form of a letter addressed to her diary, 'Kitty'. She mentions how her class is nervous about their results, while the only subject she is unsure about is mathematics. According to Anne, about a quarter of the class should not pass as they did not participate in any activities.

Then, Anne describes her experiences with her Mathematics teacher, Mr Keesing and recalls him punishing her for talking in his class. He gave her extra homework as punishment. The first punishment is to write an essay on

---

[1] **Insight:** perception; intuition
[2] **Confide:** tell someone about a secret and trusting them not to repeat it to others
[3] **Musings:** a period of reflection or thought
[4] **Immigrated:** come to live permanently in a foreign country

"Chatterbox". She presents concrete arguments on how talking is a student's trait. She writes that she will try to better herself, but she is almost sure she wouldn't be able to cure herself of the habit since her mother talked a lot, and there's not much you can do about inherited traits.[5]

Mr Keesing finds her arguments amusing but gives another essay to write when Anne did not change her nature. This time the essay was on the topic 'An Incorrigible Chatterbox.' Again, Mr Keesing had nothing to complain about the second essay. However, during the third lesson, he had finally had enough and gave the third essay entitled — 'Quack, Quack, Quack, Said Mistress Chatterbox'.

While Anne had exhausted herself of her creativity on these topics, she came up with a funny poem. It was about a mother duck and a father swan with three baby ducklings who were bitten to death by the father because they quacked too much.

Mr Keesing took it in a good and light spirit. He read the poem in many of his classes, adding his own comments. From that day onwards, Anne was allowed to talk in class.

NCERT EXERCISE

Oral Comprehension Check

(NCERT, Page 51)

1. What makes writing in a diary a strange experience for Anne Frank?

Ans. Anne felt that writing in a diary was a strange and unusual experience for her as she had never written anything personal like that before. Moreover, she thought nobody would be interested in reading her diary entries.

2. Why does Anne want to keep a diary?

Ans. Anne wants to keep a diary as she doesn't have a true friend. Therefore she decides to keep a diary and consider it her companion. She calls her diary-'Kitty' and shares her feelings with it instead of merely stating facts in it.

3. Why did Anne think she could confide more in her diary than in people?

Ans. Anne believes that paper has more patience than people. She also mentions that she doesn't have a true friend in whom she can confide. She liked to talk about ordinary everyday

[5] **Inherited traits:** derived genetically from one's parents or ancestors

things, and she seemed not to get closer to any of the friends she had around her. So, she decided to write and confide in a diary.

(NCERT, Page 51)

1. Why does Anne provide a brief sketch of her life?

Ans. Anne provides a brief sketch of her life since no one would understand a word of her musings if she were to jump right in with her day-to-day thoughts and experiences.

2. What tells you that Anne loved her grandmother?

Ans. Anne loved and missed her grandmother deeply. When her grandmother passed away in January 1942, no one understood Anne's love for her. Moreover, the touching gesture of lighting up one candle for her grandmother during Anne's birthday also tells us of her love for her grandmother.

(NCERT, Page 54)

1. Why was Mr Keesing annoyed with Anne? What did he ask her to do?

Ans. Mr Keesing was annoyed with Anne as she used to talk frequently in class. He gave her extra homework, asking her to write an essay on the topic, 'A Chatterbox'.

2. How did Anne justify her being a chatterbox in her essay?

Ans. She gave strong arguments to justify her being a 'Chatterbox'. She argues that talking is a student's trait.

He writes that she will try to better herself, but she is almost sure she wouldn't be able to cure herself of the habit since her mother talked a lot, and there's not much you can do about inherited traits.

3. Do you think Mr Keesing was a strict teacher?

Ans. Mr Keesing was an old-fashioned teacher. He was not rigidly strict but expected discipline and silence in his class while teaching. When Anne used to talk in class, he punished her and gave her extra homework to write an essay on 'A Chatterbox'. When Anne wrote a convincing essay on it, he accepted it with a good laugh. However, when Anne continued talking, he punished her again by asking her to write another essay on 'An Incorrigible Chatterbox'. However, during the third lesson, he'd finally had enough and gave the third essay entitled — 'Quack, Quack, Quack, Said Mistress Chatterbox'. He was trying to play a joke on her. However, she came up with a brilliant poem, and he read her poem in class, adding his own comments. Therefore, in regard to these events, Mr Keesing cannot be entirely labelled as a strict teacher. At the end of the lesson, he can be seen as a fun-loving, amiable person.

4. What made Mr Keesing allow Anne to talk in class?

Ans. Mr Keesing, Anne's maths teacher, used to get annoyed as Anne talked too much. Every time he gave extra homework to her in the form of essays, she could justify her talkative nature. However, on each occasion, he was impressed by her arguments. He took her final poem in a light spirit as a joke and had a good laugh about it. Finally, Mr Keesing accepted that Anne would always be that way. Hence, she was allowed to talk in class.

Thinking about the Text

(NCERT, Page 54)

1. Was Anne right when she said that the world would not be interested in the musings of a thirteen-year-old girl?

Ans. Anne Frank felt that no one would be interested in the musings of a 13-year-old schoolgirl. No, she wasn't right in saying so. In fact, her diary was published after her death under the name, 'The Diary of a Young Girl, and got a lot of recognition.

2. There are some examples of diary or journal entries in the 'Before You Read' section. Compare these with what Anne writes in her diary. What language was the diary originally written in? In what way is Anne's diary different?

Ans. Anne's diary was originally written in Dutch and was later translated into different languages. Her diary is different from the others in many aspects. Firstly, she named her diary 'Kitty' and considered it her only true friend in whom she could confide. She treated it as another person listening to her daily accounts instead of only stating facts. She wrote all her stories in it. She started by writing 'Dearest kitty' and ended the account by writing, 'Yours, Anne'. Her diary was a lot more personal than other diaries.

3. Why does Anne need to give a brief sketch of her family? Does she treat 'Kitty' as an insider or an outsider?

Ans. Anne Frank came up with a saying, 'Paper has more patience than people'. She usually sat depressed and all alone. Even though on the surface she has everything, she doesn't have a true friend with whom she can confide her feeling.

Therefore, she decides to write in a diary and gives a brief sketch of her background. She talks about her adorable father, compassionate mother, grandmother, and loving sister, Margot.

She treated her diary, Kitty, as an insider as she used to share her thoughts and feelings with her. She wanted her diary to be her best friend.

4. How does Anne feel about her father, her grandmother, Mrs Kuperus and Mr Keesing? What do these tell you about her?

Ans. Anne has fond memories of her father, grandmother, Mrs Kuperus and Mr Keesing. How she represents them in her diary reveals that Anne had good relations with them.

The first person she mentions in her diary is her father. Anne felt her father was the most adorable father she had ever seen.

Anne had moved to her grandmother's house when her father emigrated to Holland. In 1942, when her grandmother died, Anne missed her deeply. She wrote in her diary that no one knew how often she thought of her grandmother and still loved her.

In the sixth form at the Montessori nursery school, her teacher was Mrs Kuperus, the headmistress. They were both in tears at the end of the year as they said a heartbreaking farewell.

Mr Keesing was Anne's maths teacher. He used to expect discipline from his students and didn't like when students talked in class. He used to give extra homework to Anne when she was found talking in class. However, Anne could justify her talkative nature whenever Mr Keesing punishes her. On each occasion, he was impressed by how she presented her arguments.

All these incidents show Anne's deep bond with people. Everybody was attached to her, and even Mr Keesing could not help but laugh at her essays and acknowledge her smartness.

5. What does Anne write in her first essay?

Ans. In her first essay, titled 'A Chatterbox', Anne wanted to come up with convincing arguments to prove the necessity of talking.

She thought about the topic and wrote three pages on it. She argued that talking was a student's trait and that she would do her best to keep it under control. However, she was almost sure she would never be able to cure herself of the habit since her mother talked as much as she did.

There was not much that one could do about inherited traits. She submitted her essay to Mr Keesing, and he had a good laugh reading her arguments.

6. Anne says teachers are most unpredictable. Is Mr Keesing unpredictable? How?

Ans. Anne felt that a quarter of her class should be kept back and not promoted to the next class. However, she also felt teachers were the most unpredictable creatures on earth.

Mr. Keesing, Anne's old-fashioned maths teacher, could be termed as unpredictable. He used to be annoyed with Anne for talking too much in class. However, after giving several warnings to her, all Mr Keesing did was assign her extra homework.

She had to write an essay on 'A Chatterbox'. In this way, he tried to play a joke on her. Each time that he asked her to write such essays, she wrote very well. She kept giving impressive arguments in her essays. One could not have predicted that he would take all the jokes in the right spirit. Finally, when she wrote a funny poem, he accepted her talkative nature and had a good laugh at her writing. From that day onwards, Anne was never stopped from talking, and Mr. Keesing started making many jokes in his classes. Thus, Mr. Keesing can be considered unpredictable.

7. What do these statements tell you about Anne Frank as a person?

(i) We don't seem to be able to get any closer, and that's the problem. Maybe it's my fault that we don't confide in each other.

(ii) I don't want to jot down the facts in this diary the way most people would, but I want the diary to be my friend.

(iii) Margot went to Holland in December, and I followed in February when I was plunked down on the table as a birthday present for Margot.

(iv) If you ask me, there are so many dummies that about a quarter of the class should be kept back, but teachers are the most unpredictable creatures on earth.

(v) Anyone could ramble on and leave big spaces between the words, but the trick was to come up with convincing arguments to prove the necessity of taking.

Ans. (i) These lines show that Anne was an innocent girl with no close friends. She understood herself quite well.

She liked to talk about ordinary everyday things but seemed not to get closer to any of her friends.

For that, she took the blame on herself, thinking it must be her fault that she couldn't confide in her friends or get closer to them.

(ii) The line shows that Anne considered her diary as a friend, an alive person who could listen to her thoughts. She shared her feelings and day-to-day musings in her diary. She did not want just a diary in which she could write down the facts as others did. She considered it her friend and named her Kitty.

(iii) This statement shows Anne's humorous side. She was witty and knew how to present things in a funny way. The use of 'plunked down' indicates her sense of humour.

(iv) This statement shows that Anne had an opinion on everything. She thought that a quarter of her class should not get promoted, signifying that she was intelligent enough to make it to the next class.

She thought of teachers as the most unpredictable creatures on earth because nobody could say which students they would fail and which would be passed on to the next class.

(v) This statement shows that Anne was a creative girl. She was good at creative writing. She took it in good spirits when she was given the task of writing an essay by her maths teacher.

She did not want to write it like others who merely left big spaces between the words to make the essay big.

She knew the trick was to come up with a convincing argument to prove the necessity of talking.

She was different in her approach from everybody else and convinced her old-fashioned maths teacher with her arguments.

MISCELLANEOUS EXERCISE

Multiple Choice Questions

1. Who would Anne allow to read her diary?

(*a*) Her sister (*b*) Her grandma
(*c*) A real friend (*d*) Everyone

2. On which date did Anne record the incident in Mr Keesing's class in her diary?

(*a*) 20 June, 1942 (*b*) 21 June, 1942
(*c*) 12 June, 1942 (*d*) 22 June, 1942

3. In which language was the diary originally written?

(*a*) Spanish (*b*) English
(*c*) Dutch (*d*) French

4. What does 'had a good laugh' imply in the context of Mr Keesing? It means that he

(*a*) Celebrated his ability to make Anne write the essay.
(*b*) Made Anne feel embarrassed in front of the whole class.
(*c*) Pulled up Anne for her arguments in the essay.
(*d*) Realised the humour in it and was amused.

5. Why do you think Mr Keesing chose the title-'An Incorrigible Chatterbox'-for Anne to write on? This was because he expected-

(*a*) Anne to express her inability to elaborate on that topic.
(*b*) That this would embarrass Anne and would check her indiscipline.
(*c*) Her to apologise and not repeat her talkative behaviour.
(*d*) Anne to explore her creative writing skills.

6. How did Anne feel when she was punished the third time by Mr Keesing?

(*a*) Was happy as she had to write three essays on the same topic.
(*b*) Enjoyed making fun of Mr Keesing in her way.
(*c*) Was worried as she had run out of original ideas for her essay.
(*d*) Was thrilled at another opportunity to showcase her writing abilities.

7. What did she write in her last essay?

(*a*) A sensitive poem (*b*) A joke
(*c*) A paragraph (*d*) A funny poem

8. What does the phrase "Get all things off my chest" mean?

(*a*) It means to get rid of things around.
(*b*) To get rid of people who are weighing you down.
(*c*) To get rid of people who are competing with you.
(*d*) To get rid of feelings which depress you.

9. How many siblings did Anne have?

(*a*) 1 (*b*) 2
(*c*) 3 (*d*) 4

10. In which city were Anne and Margot sent to live with their grandmother?

(*a*) Berlin (*b*) Aachen
(*c*) Munich (*d*) Bonn

Extract-Based Questions

I. Read the following extract and answer the questions/ complete the sentences that follow: (5 M)

To enhance the image of this long-awaited friend in my imagination, I don't want to jot down the facts in this diary the way most people would do, but I want the diary to be my friend, and I'm going to call this friend 'Kitty'. Since no one would understand a word of my stories to Kitty if I were to plunge right in, I'd better provide a brief sketch of my life, much as I dislike doing so.

1. Why does the protagonist provide a brief sketch of their life? **(1)**

(*a*) To entertain Kitty.
(*b*) To fulfill a writing requirement.
(*c*) To enhance the image of their friend.
(*d*) To explain the purpose of the diary.

2. "Jot down" in the context means __________. **(1)**

3. Based on the passage, why does the protagonist want to enhance the image of their friend in their imagination? **(2)**

4. Which of the following is TRUE about the characteristics of Anne Frank? **(1)**

(*a*) She was a careless person.
(*b*) She shares everything with her friends.
(*c*) She was an outspoken and extrovert person.
(*d*) She was a reserved and introvert person.

II. Read the following extract and answer the questions/ complete the sentences that follow: (5 M)

"Paper has more patience than people" I thought of this saying on one of those days when I was feeling a little depressed and was sitting at home with my chin in my hands, bored and listless, wondering whether to stay in or go out. I finally stayed where I was, brooding: Yes, paper does have more patience, and since I'm not planning to let anyone else read this stiff-backed notebook grandly referred to as a 'diary' unless I should ever find a real friend, it probably won't make a bit of difference."

1. Why does the protagonist refer to their notebook as a 'diary'? **(1)**
   (*a*) To make it sound more important.
   (*b*) To keep their thoughts organized.
   (*c*) To maintain a sense of tradition.
   (*d*) To reflect its purpose as a personal record.
2. "Brooding" means _________. **(1)**
3. What can be inferred about the protagonist's social interactions based on their statement about finding a real friend? **(2)**
4. Which of the following statement is true? **(1)**
   (*a*) The protagonist plans to share their diary with anyone who finds it.
   (*b*) The protagonist refers to their notebook as a 'diary' to sound more important.
   (*c*) The protagonist feels bored and listless while sitting at home with their chin in their hands.
   (*d*) The protagonist believes that their diary will make a significant difference in their life.

III. Read the following extract and answer the questions/ complete the sentences that follow: (5 M)

"Mr. Keesing had a good laugh at my arguments, but when I proceeded to talk my way through the next lesson, he assigned me a second essay. This time it was supposed to be on 'An Incorrigible Chatterbox'. I handed it in, and Mr Keesing had nothing to complain about for two whole lessons.

However, during the third lesson, he'd finally had enough. "Anne Frank, as a punishment for talking in class, write an essay entitled—'Quack, Quack, Quack, said Mistress Chatterbox'." **(CBSE, QB)**

1. What convincing argument was made by Anne?
   (*a*) She was talkative just like any other student in the class.
   (*b*) She had the right to be talkative, as it was a classroom and not a prison.
   (*c*) She had inherited the trait from her mother, so couldn't stop being talkative.
   (*d*) She found it impossible to be quiet like the others as she couldn't change herself.
2. What does 'had a good laugh' imply, in the context of Mr. Keesing? It means that he
   (*a*) celebrated his ability to make Anne write the essay.
   (*b*) ridiculed Anne in front of the whole class.
   (*c*) pulled up Anne for her arguments in the essay.
   (*d*) realised the humour in it and was amused.
3. Based on this extract, pick the option with the list of words that best describe Mr. Keesing.
   (*a*) jovial and creative (*b*) strict and innovative
   (*c*) tolerant and strict (*d*) innovative and jovial
4. Why do you think Mr Keesing chose the title - 'An Incorrigible Chatterbox' - for Anne, to write on?
   This was so because he expected
   (*a*) Anne to express her inability to elaborate on such a topic.
   (*b*) that this would embarrass Anne and would check her indiscipline.
   (*c*) her to apologise and not repeat her talkative behaviour.
   (*d*) Anne to explore her creative writing skills.
5. How did Anne feel when she was punished the third time by Mr Keesing? She –
   (*a*) was happy as she had to write three essays on the same topic.
   (*b*) enjoyed making fun of Mr. Keesing in her own way.
   (*c*) was worried as she had run out of original ideas for her essay.
   (*d*) was thrilled at another opportunity to showcase her writing abilities.

IV. Read the following extract and answer the questions/ complete the sentences that follow: (5 M)

I started right away at the Montessori nursery school. I stayed there until I was six, at which time I started in the first form. In the sixth form my teacher was Mrs. Kuperus, the headmistress. At the end of the year we were both in tears as we said a heartbreaking farewell. In the summer of 1941 Grandma fell ill and had to have an operation, so my birthday passed with little celebration. **(CBSE, 2023)**

1. The narrator 'I' refers to
   (*a*) Mr. Keesing (*b*) Mrs. Kuperus
   (*c*) Anne Frank (*d*) Miss Margot
2. The phrase 'right away' in this extract most nearly means
   (*a*) with delay (*b*) the correct way
   (*c*) immediately (*d*) overtaking from right
3. What does the narrator mean by saying 'we were both in tears'?
4. Complete the analogy by selecting a word from the text: dawn : dusk : mourning: _______.
5. Select the option that correctly captures the application of the word 'form' as used in the extract.
   (*a*) Raghav was in good form while playing the match.
   (*b*) Saheb was promoted to the next form after the annual exam.
   (*c*) My brother did not know how to form a circle.
   (*d*) Anne saw the form on the headmaster's desk.

V. Read the following extract and answer the questions for ANY ONE of the given two: (5 M)

I started right away at the Montessori Nursery School. I stayed there until I was six, at which time I started in the first form. In the sixth form, my teacher was Mrs. Kuperus, the headmistress. At the end of the year we were both in tears as we said a heartbreaking farewell. In the summer of 1941, Grandma fell ill and had to have an operation, so my birthday passed with little celebration. **(CBSE, 2024)**

1. "In the summer of 1941, Grandma fell ill and had to have an operation, so my birthday passed with little celebration." State any one inference about Anne from the above context. **(1)**

2. The first education of Anne started at __________. (1)
   (*a*) some Kindergarten School
   (*b*) a Nursery School
   (*c*) Montessori Nursery School
   (*d*) Elementary School
3. Who was Mrs. Kuperus? What kind of relationship did Anne share with her? (2)
4. Substitute the word 'heartbreaking' with a word similar in meaning in the following sentence:
   "At the end of the year we were both in tears as we said a heartbreaking farewell." (1)

Subjective Questions

Short Answer Questions (40-50 words) (3 M)

1. Mr. Keesing reacted to Anne's third essay on verse. What was his response? Do you notice any difference in him?
2. Comment on the teacher-student relationship shared between Anne and Mr. Keesing. **(CBSE, QB)**
3. Anne says that there were so many dummies in the class that about a quarter of them shouldn't be promoted. Is she being rude or brutally honest? Evaluate. **(CBSE, SQP)**
4. The classmates of Anne Frank were shaking with fear and nervousness. Why?

Long Answer Questions (100-120 words) (6 M)

5. Justify the title, 'The Diary of A Young Girl'. **(CBSE, 2019)**
6. How did Anne respond to the punishment by Mr Keesing? What light does it throw on her nature?
7. Why did Anne Frank think that she could confide more in her diary than in the people?
8. Why did Mr. Keesing call Anne an 'Incorrigible Chatterbox'? **(CBSE SQP, 2020)**

Nailing the Right Answer

- ❒ Thorough reading of the chapter can prevent students from getting mixed up with the different punishments given by Mr. Keesing.
- ❒ Writing practice can help remember the facts.

ANSWERS & EXPLANATIONS

Answer Key

Multiple Choice Questions

1. (*c*) **2.** (*a*) **3.** (*c*) **4.** (*d*) **5.** (*b*) **6.** (*c*) **7.** (*d*) **8.** (*d*) **9.** (*a*) **10.** (*b*)

Explanations

Extract-Based Questions

I. 1. (*d*) To explain the purpose of the diary.

2. "Jot down" means to quickly write or record something in a brief and informal manner.

3. The protagonist wants to enhance the image of their friend in their imagination because they view the diary as a companion and confidant. By creating a vivid and lively image of their friend, Anne seeks to establish a deep connection and make the diary a source of comfort and understanding.

4. (*d*) She was a reserved and introvert person.

II. 1. (*d*) To reflect its purpose as a personal record

2. The term "brooding" means to think deeply and anxiously about something, often with a sense of sadness or discontent.

3. Based on the protagonist's statement, it can be inferred that Anne currently lacks a close and trustworthy friend. Their reference to finding a real friend suggests a desire for genuine companionship and someone they can share their thoughts and feelings with.

4. (*c*) The protagonist feels bored and listless while sitting at home with their chin in their hands.

III. 1. (*c*) She had inherited the trait from her mother, so couldn't stop being talkative.

2. (*d*) realised how funny it was and was amused.

3. (*b*) strict and innovative

4. (*b*) that this would embarrass Anne and would check her indiscipline.

5. (*c*) was worried as she had run out of original ideas for her essay.

IV. 1. (*c*) Anne Frank.

2. The phrase 'right away' in this extract most nearly means (*c*) immediately.

3. The narrator means that both the narrator and Mrs. Kuperus (the headmistress) were crying as they said their farewell, suggesting a strong emotional connection and sadness.

4. dawn : dusk : mourning: celebration.

5. (*b*) Saheb was promoted to the next form after the annual exam. The word 'form' in the extract refers to a grade or class level in the school context.

V. ***Topper's Explanation***

Ans 6-(B)) (i) From the above context, one inference that can be stated about Anne is that she loved her grandmother and shared a deep bond with her. Thus Anne was a loving granddaughter.

(ii) (C) Montessori Nursery School

(iii) Mrs. Kuperus was the headmistress of the Montessori Nursery school. She was Anne's class teacher in her sixth form. Anne shared a deep bond with Mrs. Kuperus. Their tears at the time of departure is a testament to this statement.

(iv) At the end of the year we were both in tears as we said a melancholic farewell.

Subjective Questions

Short Answer Questions

CBSE Marking Scheme: **Content-1 M, Organisation of Ideas-1 M, Accuracy-1 M**

1. Mr. Keesing understood Anne's humour correctly. He understood Anne's message by relating the deaths of three ducklings.

He recited the poetry to the students, intermingled with his own comments. She had been allowed to speak since then, and she had not been assigned any additional schoolwork because he was now a transformed man.

2. "From the diary of Anne Frank" sheds light on the teacher-student relationship. Anne, who talks a lot in class, gets punished by Mr Keesing, her Maths teacher. He asked her to write essays on weird topics, which was a form of learning as he wanted her to focus on her studies. He cannot be blamed for that as he did that for the development of Anne.

Their relationship is neither completely amiable nor very serious. Both of them try to play jokes on each other but in a humorous and healthy manner.

3. According to me, Anne was trying to be honest when she made the statement.

It was the day of the meeting in which the teachers decided who'll move up to the next form and who'll be kept back.

Everyone in Anne's class made bets regarding who would go to the next class and who would not; most of the students in her class were not confident about making it to the next class.

Most of them feared they might fail. On the basis of this observation, Anne must have made the statement.

Nailing the Right Answer

Use textual evidence and critical thinking to support your evaluation effectively.

4. The classmates of Anne Frank were shaking with fear and nervousness because it was the day of the meeting when the teachers were to decide the fate of the students. **(1 M)**

The teachers were deciding as to which students would be promoted to the next class and which one should stay back in the same class. Anne, however, was confident about herself and her girlfriends of passing; except for one subject Maths. **(1 M)**

Long Answer Questions

CBSE Marking Scheme: **Expression-2 M, Accuracy-1 M**

5. Anne Frank was a thirteen-year-old Jewish girl who wrote 'The Diary of a Young Girl.' She began writing her journal because she lacked a friend with whom she could discuss her thoughts and feelings. **(1 M)**

The red and white checkered diary came to her rescue, and she confided in it throughout her life, giving it the name "Kitty." She handled it like a close friend. She expressed herself in her diary. Some of the entries are personal, while others are critical of her parents and friends. **(1 M)**

She wrote her emotions during the war, including her fear, disappointments, and anger at the Germans' treatment of Jews. The entire book is written in the form of a journal and focuses on the life of a young girl named Anne Frank. As a result, the title is appropriate. **(1 M)**

6. When Mr Keesing punished Anne for her talkativeness again and again by asking her to write essays, one after the other, Anne made sure that the joke was on him. **(1 M)**

The third time when Mr Keesing gave her a topic to write, she composed a humorous poem on 'The incorrigible Chatterbox' and gave a message through it to the teacher. Mr Keesing took the joke in the right way and read it in front of the class, adding his own comments. **(1 M)**

This shows that Anne was capable of writing good essays and poems and winning the heart of her old-fashioned teacher. It also reflects her fearlessness as well as her creativity and humorous approach to dealing with her annoyed teacher. **(1 M)**

7. Anne, a young 13 year old schoolgirl, felt alone and depressed. Even though she had loving parents, a sister and thirty other people who she could call friends, she felt a true friend was missing in her life. She had a happy family but somehow, she felt she could not confide in them. **(1 M)**

   She wanted someone with whom she could share her secrets. Moreover, she felt that 'Paper has more patience than people'. Hence, she decided to keep a diary and consider it her true friend. **(1 M)**

   She found a real friend in her diary, 'Kitty'. She could confide more ideas in her diary than in people because people are not always interested in listening to what you are telling them. **(1 M)**

Mistakes 101 : What not to do!

Students might overlook the significance of Anne Frank's statement "Paper has more patience than people" and its impact on her decision to confide in her diary.

8. Anne used to talk a lot in her class. Mr Keesing, her maths teacher, was annoyed by the fact as he didn't like this habit of hers. One day, he punished her by giving her an essay to write on the topic 'A Chatter Box.' **(1 M)**

   She wrote her first essay justifying that talking is a student's trait and that she would do her best to control it. Though she was sure that she won't be able to cure this habit since her mother is also talkative. So, moving away from the inherited trait wouldn't be possible. **(1 M)**

   On reading her arguments, Mr. Keesing had a good laugh, but when Anne continued to talk in the next lesson too, he assigned her a second essay on 'An Incorrigible Chatterbox'. By giving this topic, he was highlighting the fact that Anne truly cannot be improved. **(1 M)**

Knowledge Hub

Chatterbox: This term means someone who talks a lot. It's usually a friendly way to say that someone enjoys chatting and is very talkative.

Incorrigible Chatterbox: When you add "incorrigible" in front of chatterbox, it means that the person talks a lot and can't or won't change this habit. "Incorrigible" suggests that this trait is very strong in them and not likely to go away.

❑❑❑

GLIMPSES OF INDIA

5

I. A BAKER FROM GOA

—Lucio Rodrigues

Narrative Sketch

1. The traditional Goan village baker is an important figure in Goan society.
2. The Portuguese influence on Goan culture is still evident in the bread-making traditions.
3. The bakers use age-old, time-tested furnaces to bake their loaves of bread.
4. The thud and jingle of the traditional baker's bamboo can still be heard in some places, heralding his arrival in the morning.
5. Cakes and bolinhas are a must for Christmas as well as other festivals.
6. Bread is an important part of Goan life and culture, with many people reminiscing nostalgically about the good old Portuguese days and their famous loaves of bread.
7. Despite changes over time, including modernization and competition from commercial bakeries, some traditional bakers continue to carry on their family profession.

BEFORE YOU READ

Theme

The author has created a pen-portrait of a traditional Goan village baker who continues to play an essential role in society. The Portuguese may have left, but the bread-makers continue to exist. The famous Portuguese loaves of bread are still remembered by the elderly. The author hopes to preserve the tradition of Goan history by highlighting the importance of the bread-making business.

Important Characters' Sketch

- **The Author:** The author and narrator of the story is nostalgic[1] and describes the traditions of the Goan community. During his childhood, the author considered the baker a friend and guide. He can recall the fragrance of the loaves of bread sold by the bread-sellers.
- **The Baker:** The baker or bread-seller of those days used to wear a peculiar[2] dress known as the "kabai". He used to visit the houses at least twice a day and made his musical entry with the traditional baker's bamboo. The baker usually collected his bills at the end of the month, which used to be recorded on some wall in pencil. The baker and his family never starved in the old days and looked happy and prosperous. These bakers are, even today, known as "pader" in Goa.

SYNOPSIS

'A Baker from Goa' relates to the time when the Portuguese ruled Goa. The story is of a baker living in a Goan village. During those times, people ate loaves of bread made in big furnaces. The bakers, known as paders, would come to sell this bread in the street. Their traditional bamboo's 'thud and jingle' can still be heard in places. Maybe the father of the family is not there, but the son continues the family profession of bread-making.

The author remembers his childhood when the baker came at least twice a day to sell freshly baked bread. The baker was a friend, companion and guide to the author. The author recalls their excitement about seeing the baker. The bread used to be bought by the maid-servant of the house, whereas the author longed for the bread- bangles. Loaves were for the elders, and bangles for the children. The author mentions how enthusiastic they used to be that nobody cared to brush their teeth or wash their mouths properly.

Lessons to learn

- Cultural Significance.
- Family Professions.
- Community Connection.
- Appreciation for simple pleasures.

Bakery products had great importance in the culture and traditions of Goa, Bol or sweet bread, was an essential part of marriage gifts. The lady of the house must prepare sandwiches for her daughter's engagement. Cakes and bolinhas were a must for Christmas as well as other festivals. Thus, the baker's furnace in the village was essential.

Also, the baker had a peculiar dress known as the 'Kabai'. It was a single-piece frock that would reach up to the knees. During the author's childhood, bakers wore a shirt and trousers slightly shorter than usual and longer than half pants.

The bakers usually collect their bills at the end of every month. Monthly accounts used to be recorded on some wall in pencil. Baking was indeed a profitable business in the old days. The bakers led a happy and prosperous life.

[1] **Nostalgic:** feeling of nostalgia; sentimental
[2] **Peculiar:** unusual; strange

What did the baker say when someone asked him about his secret to success?

NCERT EXERCISE

Oral Comprehension Check

(*NCERT, Page 86*)

1. **What are the elders in Goa nostalgic about?**

Ans. The elders in Goa are nostalgic about the good old Portuguese days and their famous loaves of bread.

2. **Is bread making still popular in Goa? How do you know?**

Ans. Bread making is still popular in Goa, as the author mentions that the eaters of the loaves might have vanished, but the makers are still there. The presence of mixers, moulders and those who bake the loaves still exist along with the old furnaces.

3. **What is the baker called?**

Ans. The bakers in Goa are called paders.

4. **When would the baker come every day? Why did the children run to meet him?**

Ans. In the old times, the baker used to come at least twice a day to sell loaves of bread for the adults and bread bangles for the children. Once, he set out in the morning on his selling round and again when he returned after emptying his bread basket. The children ran to meet him because they wanted to eat the bread bangles they had chosen carefully.

(*NCERT, Page 87*)

1. **Match the following. What is a must**

	Column-I		Column-II
(i)	**As marriage gifts**	1.	**Cakes and bolinhas**
(ii)	**For a party or a feast?**	2.	**Sweet bread called bol**
(iii)	**For a daughter's engagement?**	3.	**Bread**
(iv)	**For Christmas?**	4.	**Sandwiches**

Ans.

	Column-I		Column-II
(i)	As marriage gifts	2.	Sweet bread called bol
(ii)	For a party or a feast?	3.	Bread
(iii)	For a daughter's engagement?	4.	Sandwiches
(iv)	For Christmas?	1.	Cakes and bolinhas

2. **What did the bakers wear:**
   (i) **in the Portuguese days?**
   (ii) **when was the author young?**

Ans. (i) The bakers used to wear a single-piece long dress reaching down to the knees called-Kabai.
(ii) When the author was young, the bakers used to wear a shirt and trousers. The trousers were shorter than full-length ones and longer than half pants.

3. **Who invites the comment- 'he is dressed like a padder'? Why?**

Ans. The author mentions that even today, anyone who wears a half-pant which reaches just below the knees invites the comment that he is dressed like a padder. It was so because, during the author's childhood days, bakers wore trousers shorter than full-length ones and longer than half pants.

4. **Where were the monthly accounts of the baker recorded?**

Ans. The monthly accounts of the baker were recorded on a wall in pencil.

5. **What does a 'jackfruit-like appearance' mean?**

Ans. It means a plump person with a pleasantly fat body.

Thinking about the Text

(NCERT, Page 88)

1. **Which of these statements are correct?**
   (i) **The pader was an important person in the village in old times.**
   (ii) **Paders still exist in Goan villages.**
   (iii) **The paders went away with the Portuguese.**
   (iv) **The paders continue to wear a single-piece long frock.**
   (v) **Bread and cakes were an integral part of Goan life in the old days.**
   (vi) **Traditional bread-baking is still a very profitable business.**
   (vii) **Paders and their families starve in the present times.**

Ans. (i) Correct (ii) Correct
(iii) Incorrect (iv) Incorrect
(v) Correct (vi) Correct
(vii) Incorrect

2. **Is bread an important part of Goan life? How do you know this?**

Ans. Yes, bakery products had great importance in the culture and traditions of Goa Bol, or sweet bread, was an important part of marriage gifts. The lady of the house used to prepare sandwiches for her daughter's engagement. Cakes and bolinhas were a must for Christmas as well as other festivals.

3. **Tick the right answer. What is the tone of the author when he says the following?**
   (i) **The thud and the jingle of the traditional baker's bamboo can still be heard in some places.** **(nostalgic, hopeful, sad)**
   (ii) **May be the father is not alive, but the son still carries on the family profession.** **(nostalgic, hopeful, sad)**
   (iii) **I still recall the typical fragrance of those loaves.** **(nostalgic, hopeful, naughty)**
   (iv) **The tiger never brushed his teeth. Hot tea could wash and clean up everything so nicely, after all.** **(naughty, angry, funny)**
   (v) **Cakes and bolin has are a must for Christmas as well as other festivals.** **(Sad, hopeful, matter of fact)**
   (vi) **The baker and his family never starved. They always looked happy and prosperous.** **(matter-of-fact, hopeful, sad)**

Ans. (i) Nostalgic (ii) Hopeful
(iii) Nostalgic (iv) Funny
(v) Matter-of-fact (vi) Matter-of-fact

MISCELLANEOUS EXERCISE

Multiple Choice Questions

1. Who ruled over Goa?
   (*a*) British (*b*) Portuguese
   (*c*) French (*d*) Dutch
2. The baker was also their ______.
   (*a*) Friend (*b*) Companion
   (*c*) Guide (*d*) All of the above
3. Which word in the following means the same as 'sweet smell'?
   (*a*) Bol (*b*) Loaves
   (*c*) Fragrance (*d*) Kabai

4. Which name is used for the sweet bread?
(a) Bol (b) Kabai
(c) Pedar (d) Cake

5. When were the bills collected?
(a) Daily
(b) Weekly
(c) Fortnightly
(d) At the end of the month

6. What type of people are bakers?
(a) Poor (b) Prosperous
(c) Both (a) and (b) (d) Starving

7. The elders in Goa are nostalgic about:
(a) The Portuguese people.
(b) The good old Portuguese days.
(c) Their famous loaves of bread.
(d) All of the above.

8. How are bakers in their physique?
(a) Weak (b) Plump
(c) Sick looking (d) All of the above

9. Choose the answer that lists the correct option about the recording of the baker's monthly accounts.

(a) 
(b) 
(c) 
(d) 

10. The extract uses the phrase, 'invites (the) comments'. Which of the following expressions is INCORRECT with respect to the word 'invites'?

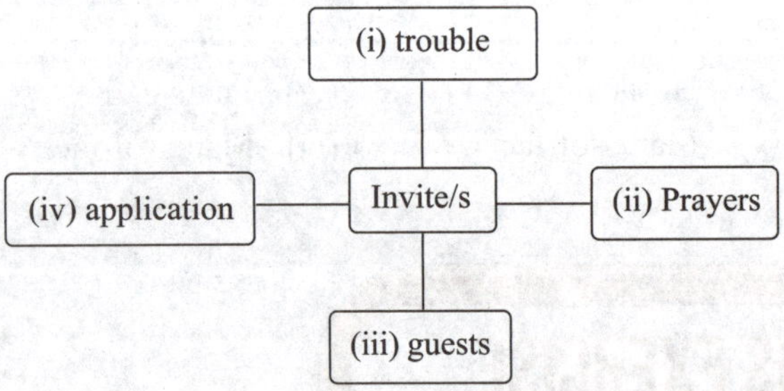

(a) (i) (b) (ii)
(c) (iii) (d) (iv)

Extract-Based Questions

I. Read the following extract and answer the questions/ complete the sentences that follow: (5 M)

"Our elders are often heard reminiscing nostalgically about those good old Portuguese days, the Portuguese and their famous loaves of bread. Those eaters might have vanished, but the makers are still there. We still have the mixers, the moulders and those who bake the loaves. Those age-old, time-tested furnaces still exist. The fire in these furnaces has not yet been extinguished. The thud and jingle of traditional baker's bamboo, heralding his arrival in the morning, can still be heard in some places."

1. What is the main focus of the passage? (1)
(a) The disappearance of traditional bakers.
(b) The nostalgia for Portuguese bread.
(c) The preservation of traditional baking methods.
(d) The modernization of baking equipment.

2. What does "nostalgically" mean in the context of the passage? (1)

3. What can be inferred about the traditional bakers mentioned in the passage? (1)

4. What is the significance of the mention of "age-old, time-tested furnaces" in the passage? Discuss how the preservation of traditional furnaces contributes to the authenticity and quality of the baked goods, and how it reflects the cultural heritage of the bakers. (2)

II. Read the following extract and answer the questions/ complete the sentences that follow: (5 M)

He would greet the lady of the house with 'Good Morning' and then place his basket on the vertical bamboo. We kids would be pushed aside with a mild rebuke, and the loaves would be delivered to the servant. But we would not give up. We would climb a bench or the parapet and peep into the basket somehow. I can still recall the typical fragrance of those loaves. Loaves for the elders and bangles for the children.

1. Why does 'he' rebuke the kids? (1)
(a) He didn't like the kids.
(b) He wanted to deliver the bread to the servants.
(c) He wanted to meet the servants only.
(d) He didn't want to sell his bread.

2. The phrase which would mean the same as "the female family member who has the most responsibility for taking care of and making decisions about the household"__________. (1)

3. What can be inferred about the children's fascination with the baker's loaves and their willingness to go to great lengths to catch a glimpse of them? (1)

4. Discuss the cultural significance of the interaction between the baker and the lady of the house. How does the act of greeting the lady and delivering the loaves symbolize a sense of respect and tradition within the community? (2)

Subjective Questions

Short Answer Questions (40-50 words) (3 M)

1. What did the baker mean to the narrator during his childhood, how many times did he pay a visit?
2. Even today, any person with a jackfruit-like physical appearance is easily compared to a baker. Explain.
3. 'During our childhood in Goa, the baker used to be our friend, companion and guide.' What does this statement imply in relation to the character of the baker?
4. Bread and cakes were essential to Goan life in the older days. Describe the memories that the author recollects about the good old Portuguese days and their loaves of bread.
5. Who are paders and why are they friends of children? **(CBSE, 2023)**
6. How did the baker become synonymous with celebrations and occasions in Goa? **(CBSE, 2022)**

Long Answer Questions (100-120 words) (6 M)

7. The narrator shares, "Baking was indeed a profitable profession in the old days."?
   (*a*) What do you feel has changed now? Why?
   (*b*) State any one way you feel the paders can regain their lost glory. **(CBSE, QB)**
8. After reading the story 'A Baker from Goa", do you think our traditions, heritage, values and practices are the roots that nourish us? Why/why not?

ANSWERS & EXPLANATIONS

Answer Key

Multiple Choice Questions

1. (*b*) 2. (*d*) 3. (*c*) 4. (*a*) 5. (*d*) 6. (*b*) 7. (*d*) 8. (*b*) 9. (*c*) 10. (*b*)

Explanations

Extract-Based Questions

I. 1. (*c*) The preservation of traditional baking methods.

2. "Nostalgically" in the context means "with a sense of longing for the past".
3. It can be inferred about the traditional bakers from the passage that they have maintained their baking practices despite changing times.
4. The mention of "age-old, time-tested furnaces" highlights the importance of preserving traditional baking methods. These furnaces play a crucial role in imparting unique flavours and textures to the bread. By using them, bakers not only maintain the authenticity of their products but also showcase their cultural heritage, keeping alive the traditions of their ancestors.

II. 1. (*b*) He wanted to deliver the bread to the servants.

2. The lady of the house.
3. The children's fascination and eagerness to see the baker's loaves suggest that the bread holds a strong allure and is highly desirable to them.
4. The interaction between the baker and the lady of the house holds cultural significance as it embodies respect and tradition. The act of greeting the lady and delivering the loaves establishes a sense of hierarchy and acknowledges the lady's authority. It symbolizes the community's values of interpersonal relationships, social cohesion, and upholding age-old customs in their interactions and daily routines.

Subjective Questions

Short Answer Questions

CBSE Marking Scheme: Content-1 M, Organisation of Ideas-1 M, Accuracy-1 M

1. The baker was an important person in the author's life. He was treated like a friend. He used to come twice a day, once in the morning to sell bread and then while returning after emptying his basket.

The author used to run to meet him in order to take the bread-bangles. He chattered and gossiped with him.

2. In the lesson, 'A Baker from Goa', we learn that the bakers are, even today, known as paders. A 'jack fruit-like appearance' means a plump physique. A baker used to resemble such a physique and it was believed that he and his family never starved.

   Baking was a profitable profession, and the baker, his family and his servants always looked happy and prosperous. Therefore, even today, anyone with a pleasantly fat body and jack fruit-like physical appearance is easily compared to a baker.

3. This statement tells us that the bakers in Goa were respected people in Goan society. The author of the lesson, Lucio Rodrigues, mentions how the baker used to be a friend, companion and guide to him.

   This could be the result of him teaching the children about good behavior—for example, when he mildly rebuked them for peeping into his basket—and showing respect for the elderly—for example, when he greeted the lady of the house "Good morning."

   The author considered him a friend and companion. He was not simply a vendor interested in selling what he made. Thus, he was an important character in the Goan society of those days.

4. In the older days, when the Portuguese ruled Goa, baking was considered an essential and profitable profession in Goan society. The Portuguese were famous for preparing loaves of bread. Baking was the traditional family profession.

   Bakery products had great importance in the culture and traditions of Goa. Bol, or sweet bread, was an important part of marriage gifts. Any event or celebration was incomplete without these bakery products. Baking was a profitable profession in the older days. Thus, the author, as well as his elders, nostalgically remembers those good old days.

5. Pader is another name for baker in Goa. He used to be a friend, companion and guide for the kids. The bread bangles he bought for them were popular with the kids. This was a very special sweet bread.

6. An occasion in Goa loses its charm without the bread made by the baker i.e. pader. Marriage gifts are incomplete without the pader's sweet bread called bol. Christmas and feasts also consist of the baker's bread. A mother is expected to make sandwiches on the occasion of her daughter's engagement. Hence, the baker has become synonymous with celebrations in Goa.

Long Answer Questions

CBSE Marking Scheme: Expression-2 M, Accuracy-1 M

7. (*a*) The narrator has correctly said that baking was a profitable profession in the old days. However, many things have changed that have probably reduced the profitability of the local bakers. Big brands have replaced small bakers with their competitive prices. The new generation usually gets attracted to fancy advertisements and prefers to buy highly advertised products. Local Bakers, on the other hand, find it difficult to sell their high-quality but less-known or less-advertised products. **(2 M)**

   (*b*) One way to help the paders regain their lost glory could be through people's support for local products. With the growing Internet and Social Media age, people can voluntarily use it to help local bakers advertise their bakery products. Anything true to its quality will automatically gain people's attention. **(1 M)**

8. 'A Baker from Goa' shows the importance of the traditional practice of making bread for every occasion and festival of the Goan people. The tradition is followed till today. This shows how our traditional practices can keep our past and heritage near to us. **(1 M)**

   Yes, our traditions, heritage, values, and practices can be the roots that nourish us. They provide a sense of identity, continuity, and belonging. Our cultural heritage connects us to our ancestors, preserving their wisdom and experiences. Values passed down through generations shape our moral compass and guide our actions. **(1 M)**

   Traditions and practices strengthen family and community bonds, fostering a sense of unity. They can instil pride in our roots and cultural identity. However, it is important to evaluate and adapt them to changing times to ensure they align with our values and progress in a rapidly evolving world. **(1 M)**

II. COORG

—Lokesh Abrol

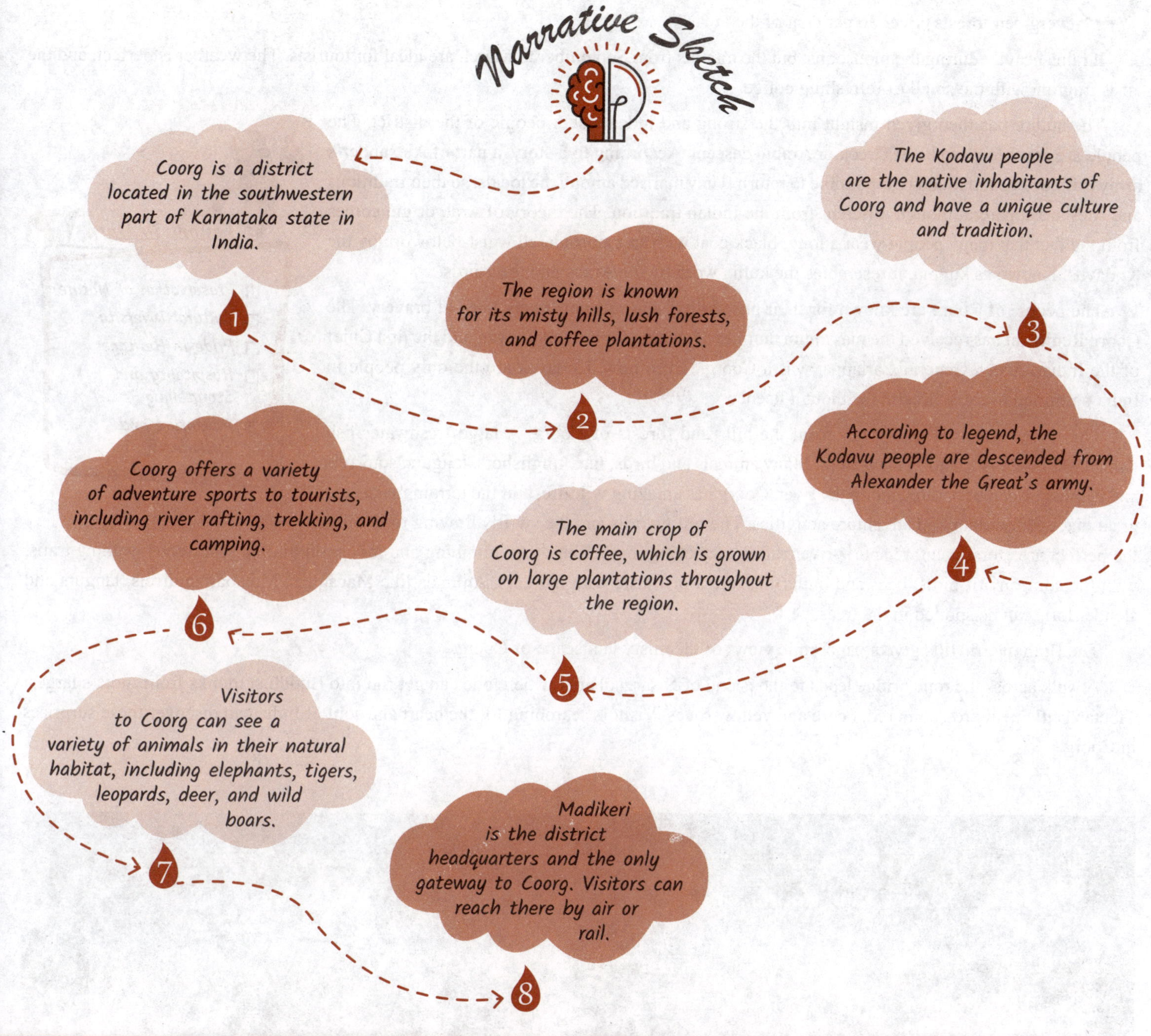

BEFORE YOU READ

Theme

The lesson, 'Coorg', gives us an insight into the smallest district of Karnataka and its people. The author calls the place a 'piece of heaven', inhabited by a proud race of martial[1] men, beautiful women and wild creatures. The people of Coorg are known to be one of the bravest. The place has amazing weather throughout the year, with enough rain during the monsoon season.

[1] **Martial:** having to do with war

SYNOPSIS

Coorg is a beautiful place located in the western ghats of Karnataka, located midway between Mysore and Mangalore.

Coorg, or Kodagu, is the smallest district of Karnataka and is home to evergreen forests, spices and coffee plantations. The evergreen forests cover 30 per cent of the area.

It rains heavily during the monsoons, but the months from September to March are ideal for tourists. The weather is perfect, and the air is fragrant with the smell of refreshing coffee.

The author has then given insight into the strong and independent people of the district. The people are considered to be of Greek or Arabic descent. According to a story, a part of Alexander's army drifted here and found it impossible to return. They married among the locals, so their traditions and rites are apparent, though different from the Indian tradition. The theory of Arab origin comes from the fact that many people wear a long, black coat with an embroidered waist-belt worn by the Kodavus. Known as kuppia, it resembles the kuffia worn by the Arabs and the Kurds.

Lessons to learn

- Preservation of Nature
- Cultural Diversity
- Pride in Heritage
- Hospitality and Storytelling
- Adventure and Exploration

The people of Coorg are known for their hospitality[2] and recount[3] many tales of bravery. The Coorg Regiment has received the maximum number of awards for bravery in war, and the first Chief of the Indian Army, General Cariappa, was a Coorgi. Even now, Kodavus are the only people in India permitted to carry firearms without a licence.

The river Kaveri obtains water from the hills and forests of Coorg. A large freshwater fish named Mahaseer is found in the waters. Many animals and birds, like kingfishers, langurs, squirrels and elephants, can be spotted along the river. Coorg has amazing wildlife, and the terrain makes it a great place for outdoor and adventure activities. The rolling hills and the swiftly flowing river offer the perfect area for adventure sports-river rafting, canoeing, rappelling, rock climbing and mountain biking. Numerous walking trails, with the company of birds, bees and butterflies, are a favourite with trekkers. Animals like Macaques, Malabar squirrels, langurs and slender loris can be spotted in the trees.

The Brahmagiri Hills give a panoramic view[4] of the misty landscape of Coorg.

A walk across the rope bridge leads to the island of Nisargadhama, where one can get run into Buddhist monks from India's largest Tibetan settlement dressed in red, ochre and yellow robes. Visitors searching for the heart and soul of India can discover these surprises in Coorg.

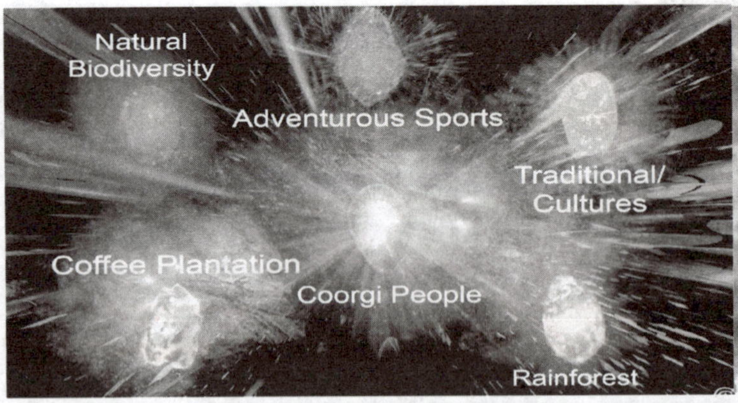

[2] **Hospitality:** warm and friendly reception and entertainment of guests, and visitors
[3] **Recount:** tell someone about something
[4] **Panoramic view:** a view of a wide area of land

NCERT EXERCISE

Thinking about the Text

(NCERT, Page 92)

1. Where is Coorg?

Ans. Coorg is midway between Mysore and the coastal town of Mangalore.

2. What is the story about the Kodavu people's descent?

Ans. According to a story, a part of Alexander's Army drifted here and found it impossible to return. They married among the locals, so their traditions and rites are apparent, though different from the Indian tradition.

The theory of Arab origin comes from the fact that many people wear a long, black coat with an embroidered waist-belt worn by the Kodavus. Known as kuppia, it resembles the kuffia worn by the Arabs and the Kurds.

3. What are some of the things you now know about

(i) the people of Coorg?

(ii) the main crop of Coorg?

(iii) the sports it offers to tourists?

(iv) the animals you are likely to see in Coorg?

(v) its distance from Bangalore, and how to get there?

Ans. (i) The people of Coorg are independent and hospitable. They are possibly of Greek or Arabic descent.

(ii) The main crop of Coorg is Coffee.

(iii) Coorg offers its tourists the perfect area for adventure sports-river rafting, canoeing, rappelling, rock climbing and mountain biking.

(iv) The animals you will likely see in Coorg are birds, bees, butterflies, macaques, Malabar squirrels, langurs, slender loris and wild elephants.

(v) Coorg is 260 km away from Bangalore. One can reach there by air, rail or road.

4. Here are six sentences with some words in italics. Find phrases from the text that have the same meaning.

(Look in the paragraphs indicated)

(i) During monsoons, it rains so heavily *that tourists do not visit* Coorg. (para 2)

(ii) *Some people say that* Alexander's Army moved south along the coast and settled there. (para 3)

(iii) The Coorg people *are always ready to tell* stories of their sons' and fathers' valour. (para 4)

(iv) *Even people who normally lead an easy and slow life get smitten by* the high-energy adventure sports of Coorg. (para 6)

(v) The theory of the Arab origin *is supported by* the long coat with embroidered waist-belt they wear. (para 3)

(vi) Macaques, Malabar squirrels *observe you carefully* from the tree canopy. (para 7)

Ans. (i) Keep many visitors away

(ii) As one story goes

(iii) Are more than willing to recount

(iv) The most laid back individuals become converts to

(v) Draws support from

(vi) Keep a watchful eye

MISCELLANEOUS EXERCISE

Multiple Choice Questions

1. Another name for the Coorg district is:

(*a*) Kodagu (*b*) Kuppia
(*c*) Kuffia (*d*) None of the above

2. Coorg is famous for ____________.

(*a*) Cotton (*b*) Tea
(*c*) Coffee (*d*) Jute

3. How much of Coorg is covered with rain forest?

(*a*) Thirty percent (*b*) Forty percent
(*c*) Seventy percent (*d*) Hundred percent

4. Which is the best season in Coorg?

(*a*) January to March
(*b*) April to September
(*c*) September to March
(*d*) November to January

5. The first chief of the Indian Army is from _____.

(*a*) Coorg (*b*) Madhya Pradesh
(*c*) Mysore (*d*) Kerala

6. _____ river obtains its water from Coorg.

(*a*) Ganga (*b*) Narmada
(*c*) Kaveri (*d*) Yamuna

7. "The climb to the _____ hills brings you into a panoramic view of the entire misty landscape of Coorg."

(*a*) Brahmagiri (*b*) Nilgiri

(*c*) Himalayan (*d*) Parvati

8. What are the activities available in Coorg?

(*a*) River-rafting (*b*) Rock Climbing

(*c*) Mountain biking (*d*) All of the above

9. Mahaseer is a large:

(*a*) Langur (*b*) Wild elephant

(*c*) Kingfisher (*d*) Freshwater fish

10. Who can you run into on a walk across the rope bridge?

(*a*) Animals (*b*) People

(*c*) Indian Army (*d*) Buddist Monks

Extract-Based Questions

I. Read the following extract and answer the questions/ complete the sentences that follow: (5 M)

Coorgi homes have a tradition of hospitality and they are more than willing to recount numerous tales of valour related to their sons and fathers. The Coorg Regiment is one of the most decorated in the Indian Army and the first Chief of the Indian Army, General Cariappa, was a Coorgi. Even now, Kodavus are the only people in India permitted to carry firearms without a licence.

1. What kind of stories are the Coorg people always ready to tell? (1)

(*a*) Tales of the valour of their fathers.

(*b*) Tales of bravery and courage of their sons.

(*c*) Tales of their own bravery.

(*d*) Both (*a*) and (*b*) are correct.

2. Which word in the passage means the same as 'friendliness'? (1)

3. Based on the passage, what can be inferred about the cultural significance of valour and military service among the Coorgi community? (1)

4. How does the privilege of carrying firearms without a license contribute to the cultural identity of the Kodavus and what impact might it have on their community? (2)

II. Read the following extract and answer the questions/ complete the sentences that follow: (5 M)

Birds, bees and butterflies are there to give you company. Macaques, Malabar squirrels, langurs and slender loris keep a watchful eye from the tree canopy. I do, however, prefer to step aside for wild elephants. The climb to the Brahmagiri hills brings you a panoramic view of the entire misty landscape of Coorg. A walk across the rope bridge leads to the sixty-four-acre island of Nisargadhama. Running into Buddhist monks from India's largest Tibetan settlement, nearby Bylakuppe, is a bonus. The monks, in red, ochre and yellow robes, are amongst the many surprises that wait to be discovered by visitors searching for the heart and soul of India, right here in Coorg.

1. Who are the surprises waiting to be discovered by visitors in Coorg? (1)

(*a*) Birds and bees

(*b*) Macaques and langurs

(*c*) Buddhist monks in red, ochre, and yellow robes

(*d*) Wild elephants and slender loris

2. Which word in the passage means the same as 'Providing a wide and comprehensive view.'? (1)

3. What can be inferred about Coorg based on the passage? (2)

4. Choose the option that lists the set of statements that are NOT TRUE according to the given extract. (1)

(i) A large bird called Mahseer is found in the river Kaveri.

(ii) Squirrels and langurs enjoy the waterfalls by throwing half-eaten fruits in these waters.

(iii) The government has made various paths to the hills for visitors.

(iv) While taking a walk in Coorg, one may find a variety of animals.

(v) Due to the presence of monks wearing red,orange and yellow coloured garments, visitors keep themselves away from this city.

(*a*) (i), (iii) and (v) (*b*) (i), (ii) and (iv)

(c) (ii), (iv) and (v) (*d*) (ii), (iii) and (iv)

Subjective Questions

Short Answer Questions (40-50 words) (3 M)

1. Why does the author in 'Coorg' say that the visitors' search for the heart and soul of India would be found in Coorg? **(CBSE QB)**

2. Why is Coorg called the land of rolling hills? **(CBSE, 2022)**

3. The people of Coorg have a tradition of courage and bravery. How has it been recognised in modern India?

OR

How is the Coorgi tradition of courage and bravery?

4. The most laid back individuals become converts to the life of high-energy adventure. Elaborate with reference to Coorg. **(CBSE, 2024)**

5. Valour and hospitality are inherent in the people of Coorg. Explain. **(CBSE, 2023)**

Long Answer Questions (100-120 words) (6 M)

6. What do the people of Coorg teach us? **(CBSE QB)**

7. 'Coorg' seems to share a lot of historical perspectives. Do you think knowledge of such historical facts is important for us? **(CBSE QB)**

8. Describe the cultural significance of the Coorgi community in India as depicted in the chapter "Glimpses of India".

ANSWERS & EXPLANATIONS

Answer Key

Multiple Choice Questions

1. (*a*) **2.** (*c*) **3.** (*a*) **4.** (*c*) **5.** (*a*) **6.** (*c*) **7.** (*a*) **8.** (*d*) **9.** (*d*) **10.** (*d*)

Explanations

Extract-Based Questions

I. 1. (*d*) Both (*a*) and (*b*) are correct.

2. Hospitality

3. Valour and military service are culturally significant among the Coorgi community, as demonstrated by their hospitality, tales of valour, and the renowned Coorg Regiment.

4. The privilege of carrying firearms without a license contributes to the cultural identity of the Kodavus by emphasizing their unique status in India. It may instill a sense of self-reliance, security, and pride, while also potentially influencing their traditional practices and social dynamics.

II. 1. (*c*) Buddhist monks in red, ochre, and yellow robes.

2. Panoramic

3. Coorg is a biodiverse region with abundant wildlife, scenic landscapes, cultural diversity (Tibetan settlement), and a potential destination for tourists seeking an authentic Indian experience.

4. (*a*) 1, 3 and 5

Subjective Questions

Short Answer Questions

CBSE Marking Scheme: Content-1 M, Organisation of Ideas-1 M, Accuracy-1 M

1. The author says that the heart and soul of India would be found in Coorg because different Indian cultures can be seen there. Coorg represents different cultures, traditions and ethnicities of India.

This beautiful city comprises beautiful sightseeing and landscapes, Buddhist monks and monasteries. Coorgis are famous for hospitality and valour, which is India's heart and soul.

2. Coorg is called the land of rolling hills because it has a lot of hills; the city is situated on sloping hills. Brahmagiri hills have a panoramic view. Coorg is a coffee-growing region in Karnataka. It is midway between Mysore and Mangalore.

This country's jungles and spices are well-known. Coorg is nicknamed the "Land of Rolling Hills" because the city is constructed on gradually sloping hills.

3. The Coorgi tradition of courage and bravery has been recognised by awarding the Coorg Regiment of the army with the most number of awards for bravery in war.

Besides, the Coorgis are the only Indian citizens allowed to carry firearms without a license. Thus, the valour of the Coorgis is apparent in Modern India.

4. Coorg's natural beauty and adventurous activities change even the most relaxed people into lovers of exciting adventures. This place has fast river rafting, quiet canoeing, thrilling rock climbing, and the excitement of moving down ropes on steep cliffs. Coorg's fresh, lively air makes everyone feel like trying these adventures.

5. ***Topper's Explanation***

Coorgi homes have a tradition of hospitality. While sipping a cup of steaming hot, aromatic coffee, one will be regaled by the tales of valour narrated by the Kodavus about their sons, brothers and fathers. Unsurprisingly, the first Chief of the Indian Army, General Cariappa was a Coorgi. To this day, the courageous Kodavus are the only people in India, permitted to carry fire-arms without a licence.

Long Answer Questions

CBSE Marking Scheme: Expression-2 M, Accuracy-1 M

6. Coorg people are famous for their hospitality and valour which is the heart and soul of India. There are many things that one can learn from the people of Coorg.

(1 M)

Adventurous sports like river rafting, canoeing, rappelling, rock climbing and mountain biking are great motivators for all tourists. **(1 M)**

The Coorg Regiment is famous for receiving the maximum number of awards for its bravery. The first Chief of the Indian Army, General Cariappa, was a Coorgi, a fact that made the citizens of India proud. The Coorgis are more than willing to recount numerous tales of valour related to their sons and fathers. Even now, Kodavus are the only people in India permitted to carry firearms without a license. **(1 M)**

7. The author of the lesson "Coorg" informs us that the fiercely independent Coorg people are possibly of Greek or Arabic origin.

According to a story, a part of Alexander's army drifted here and found it impossible to return. They married among the locals, so their traditions and rites are apparent, though different from the Indian tradition. **(1 M)**

The theory of Arab origin draws support from the dresses they wore. The author also tells us that the first General of the Indian Army, General Cariappa was a Coorgi. **(1 M)**

It is important for us to know about the cultural background of our country and heritage so that we become aware of the fact that our culture has always welcomed people from other cultures and absorbed them into its own. Anyone in search of the heart and soul of India can discover it in Coorg. **(1 M)**

8. The Coorgi community in India, as depicted in the chapter, showcases their tradition of hospitality, tales of valour, and their contribution to the Indian Army. **(1 M)**

The Coorg Regiment is highlighted as one of the most decorated regiments in the Indian Army. General Cariappa, a Coorgi, being the first Chief of the Indian Army, adds to their cultural significance. **(1 M)**

Additionally, the mention of Kodavus being allowed to carry firearms without a license showcases their unique cultural privilege. Overall, these glimpses depict the pride, bravery, and distinctive cultural identity of the Coorgi community. **(1 M)**

III. TEA FROM ASSAM

—Arup Kumar Datta

Narrative Sketch

1. The characters, Pranjol and Rajvir, are travelling on a train and enjoying cups of tea along with other passengers.

2. The train journey takes them through picturesque landscapes filled with greenery and tea plantations.

3. Pranjol, being familiar with tea plantations due to his upbringing, is less enthused by the sight, while Rajvir finds it exciting.

4. Rajvir shares legends about the discovery of tea, including the Chinese emperor's story and the Indian legend of Bodhidharma.

5. Tea has a long history, originating in China around 2700 B.C., and it reached Europe in the sixteenth century.

6. The boys reach Dhekiabari Tea Estate, managed by Pranjol's father, and witness tea pluckers at work during the sprouting period.

7. Rajvir demonstrates his knowledge of the tea industry, mentioning the second-flush or sprouting period that yields the best tea, which occurs from May to July.

8. Rajvir's enthusiasm and eagerness to learn about tea impresses Pranjol's father.

9. The chapter highlights the cultural significance of tea, its popularity worldwide, and its historical and medicinal associations.

10. The setting of the tea plantation and the introduction of characters with different perspectives create a sense of anticipation for further exploration and learning.

BEFORE YOU READ

Theme

'Tea from Assam' is an informative story written by Arup Kumar Datta. The central theme of the story is the tea gardens of Assam. The author has insight into how popular tea has become a beverage[1] worldwide. Over 80 crore cups of tea are drunk every day throughout the world. It shows the increasing popularity of tea.

Important Characters' Sketch

- **Pranjol:** He had been born and brought up on a tea plantation. He studied with Rajvir in Delhi. His father was the manager of a tea garden in Upper Assam. He invited Rajvir, his classmate, to visit his home and the Dhekiabari Tea Estate during summer vacation. He was a fan of detective stories and was busy with those stories during the train ride home.
- **Rajvir:** He was a youngster and a classmate of Pranjol. Both of them study in a school in Delhi. Pranjol invited him to spend summer vacation at his home in Assam. He was excited to visit the tea estate in Assam. He was a fan of detective stories but preferred looking at the beautiful scenery from the train window. He had done a lot of reading about tea, and his in-depth knowledge of the subject surprised Pranjol's father.

SYNOPSIS

The story revolves around the history and discovery of tea. It begins with the scene where two friends, Pranjol and Rajvir, are set to go to Assam, Pranjol's hometown when a tea vendor asks them if they want to have some tea. Almost everyone in their compartment was drinking tea too. At that time, Rajvir mentions that over eighty crore cups of tea are consumed daily worldwide. Pranjol was surprised to hear how popular tea is. Their train journey begins, and Pranjol starts reading his detective book while Rajvir prefers to enjoy the scenic beauty from the window. The view was magnificent, and Rajvir had never seen so much greenery before.

Tea bushes followed soft green paddy fields. Rajvir gets excited about seeing a tea garden, but Pranjol is unable to match the same level because he was born and brought up in Assam; hence it was a usual thing for him.

Lessons to learn

- Cultural Significance
- Historical Awareness
- Curiosity and Learning
- Environmental Appreciation
- Cultural Exchange

Before coming for the trip, Rajvir had done a lot of reading and had learned different legends[2] about tea. There's the one about the Chinese emperor who always boiled water before drinking it. One day a few leaves of the twigs burning under the pot fell into the water, giving it a delicious flavour. It is said they were tea leaves. He told another Indian legend about Bodhidharma, an ancient Buddhist who cut off his eyelids because he felt sleepy during meditations. Ten tea plants grew out of the eyelids. The leaves of these plants, when put in hot water and drunk, banished[3] sleep. Rajvir added that tea was first consumed in China as far back as 2700 B.C. and reached Europe in the 16th century, where it was most popular for its medicinal properties. As they discussed, the train stopped at Mariani Junction, where Pranjol's parents had come to receive them. They were going to visit Dhekiabari, the tea garden managed by Pranjol's father. They passed a cattle bridge and entered the Tea Estate on their way. There were acres of tea bushes around them, and groups of tea-pluckers, with bamboo baskets on their backs, wearing plastic aprons,[4] were plucking the newly sprouted leaves.

A tractor filled with tea leaves passed by when Rajvir mentioned that it was the second sprouting season, which lasted from May to July and yielded the best tea.

Pranjol's father was surprised to hear all that and impressed that Rajvir had read a lot before coming on this vacation. Rajvir agreed and intended to learn a lot more on his trip there.

---

[1] **Beverage:** a drink (other than water)
[2] **Legends:** a famous story or person
[3] **Banished:** send away
[4] **Aprons:** a protective garment worn over the front of one's clothes and tied at the back

Rajvir researching about Tea, it's origin and legends

MISCELLANEOUS EXERCISE

Multiple Choice Questions

1. Which of the statements is NOT TRUE?

(*a*) Pranjol was a youngster from Assam.

(*b*) Rajvir was going to Assam for the first time.

(*c*) Rajvir liked reading detective stories.

(*d*) Pranjol was interested in the tea gardens outside.

2. Bodhidharma was a ____________ ascetic.

(*a*) Buddhist (*b*) Jain

(*c*) Chinese (*d*) None of these

3. According to the Indian legend, what did the Buddhist monk cut to prevent feeling sleepy?

(*a*) Tongue (*b*) Eyelids

(*c*) Ears (*d*) Hair

4. Where was tea first consumed?

(*a*) India (*b*) Europe

(*c*) China (*d*) Japan

5. Which word means a 'drink'?

(*a*) Meal (*b*) Estate

(*c*) Legend (*d*) Beverage

6. When did tea come to Europe?

(*a*) Seventeenth century (*b*) Sixteenth century

(*c*) Fifth century (*d*) Eighteenth-century

7. Pranjol was busy reading ____________.

(*a*) Poem (*b*) Love story

(*c*) Science Fiction (*d*) Detective book

8. The train reached:

(*a*) Malgudi Station (*b*) Mariani junction

(*c*) Maligaon (*d*) Madari junction

9. Dhekiabari Tea Estate was managed by:

(*a*) Rajvir's father (*b*) Pranjol's brother

(*c*) Pranjol's father (*d*) Pranjol

10. The second sprouting period of the year lasts from:

(*a*) March to May (*b*) May to august

(*c*) February to April (*d*) May to July

Extract-Based Questions

I. Read the following extract and answer the questions/ complete the sentences that follow: (5 M)

"Tell me another!" scoffed Pranjol. "We have an Indian legend too. Bodhidharma, an ancient Buddhist ascetic, cut off his eyelids because he felt sleepy during meditations. Ten tea plants grew out of the eyelids. The leaves of these plants, when put in hot water and drunk, banished sleep." "Tea was first drunk in China," Rajvir added, "as far back as 2700 B.C.! In fact, words such as tea, chai and chini are from the Chinese. Tea came to Europe only in the sixteenth century and was drunk more as medicine than as Beverage."

1. Why do you think Pranjol 'scoffed'? **(1)**
   (*a*) He was upset with the legend Rajvir shared.
   (*b*) He was mocking Rajvir for his lack of knowledge.
   (*c*) He was amused and tickled at what Rajvir shared.
   (*d*) He was impressed with what Rajvir had shared.
2. What does the term "ascetic" mean in the context of the passage? **(1)**
3. Based on the passage, what can be inferred about the cultural significance of tea in both China and Europe? **(1)**
4. Discuss the historical and cultural implications of tea being introduced to Europe as medicine rather than as a beverage. How did this perception of tea evolve over time? **(2)**

II. Read the following extract and answer the questions/ complete the sentences that follow: (5 M)

"Chai-garam... garam-chai," a vendor called out in a high-pitched voice. He came up to their window and asked, "Chai, sa'ab?" "Give us two cups," Pranjol said. They sipped the steaming hot liquid. Almost everyone in their compartment was drinking tea too. "Do you know that over eighty crore cups of tea are drunk every day throughout the world?" Rajvir said. "Whew!" exclaimed Pranjol. 'Tea really is very popular.'

1. What was Pranjol's reaction upon hearing about the global tea consumption? **(1)**
   (*a*) Surprise
   (*b*) Disbelief
   (*c*) Excitement
   (*d*) Indifference
2. Write a word from the passage for "emitting steam". **(1)**
3. Based on the passage, what can be inferred about the popularity of tea among the passengers in the compartment? **(1)**
4. Explore the global consumption of tea and its impact on the economy and trade. How does the high demand for tea affect tea-producing regions and international tea markets? **(2)**

III. Read the following extract and answer the questions/ complete the sentences that follow: (5 M)

The train pulled out of the station - Pranjol buried his nose in his detective book again. Rajvir too was an ardent fan of detective stories but, at the moment he was keener on looking at the beautiful scenery. It was green, green everywhere. Rajvir had never seen so much greenery before. Then the soft green paddy fields gave way to tea bushes. It was a magnificent view. Against the backdrop of densely wooded hills a sea of tea bushes stretched as far as the eye could see. Dwarfing the tiny tea plants were tall, sturdy, shade-trees and amidst the orderly rows of bushes busily moved doll-like figures.

(Glimpses of India - Tea from Assam)

1. State any one inference about Rajvir from the given context: **1**
   "Rajvir too was an ardent fan of detective stories, but at the moment he was keen on looking at the beautiful scenery."
2. State True or False: **1**
   The reason Rajvir was interested in looking at the beautiful scenery was that the detective book he was reading, was not interesting.
3. People who live in big cities are always fascinated by the natural beauty and abundant greenery. Elaborate in about 40 words, with reference to the extract. **2**
4. Which phrase would correctly substitute 'doll-like figures', in the given sentence from the extract? **1**
   Dwarfing the tiny tea plants were tall sturdy shade-trees and amidst the orderly rows of bushes busily moved doll-like figures.

Subjective Questions

Short Answer Questions (40-50 words) (3 M)

1. Pranjol buried his head in his detective book while Rajvir was eager to look at the beautiful scenery during the train journey. Why was there a difference in their attitude? **(CBSE, QB)**
2. What are the two Legends about Tea?
3. When did tea come to Europe? Which language are the words 'Chai' and 'Chini' derived from?
4. Rajvir did his study before his visit to the tea plantation. Is it good to do one's research before the start of a new venture, or does it take away from the thrill of discovery? Elucidate your stance. **(CBSE, QB)**

Long Answer Questions (100-120 words) (6 M)

5. "You seem to have done your homework before coming." Answer the given question in light of this statement. Rajvir seemed to have a lot of information about tea. What did he tell? What character trait of his is revealed? Is it essential for children?
6. Discuss the significance of tea and its production in Assam, as depicted in the chapter "Glimpses of India".

ANSWERS & EXPLANATIONS

Answer Key

Multiple Choice Questions

1. (*d*) **2.** (*a*) **3.** (*b*) **4.** (*c*) **5.** (*d*) **6.** (*b*) **7.** (*d*) **8.** (*b*) **9.** (*c*) **10.** (*d*)

Explanations

Extract-Based Questions

I. 1. (*c*) He was amused and tickled at what Rajvir shared.

2. A person who practises self-discipline and abstinence.

3. Tea was deeply rooted in Chinese culture since ancient times, while in Europe, it gained popularity later as a medicinal drink.

4. The medicinal perception of tea in Europe initially limited its consumption. However, as its taste and social value became appreciated, it gradually transformed into a widely consumed and socially significant beverage. This transition brought forth changes in tea's cultural and social roles in European society.

II. 1. (*a*) Surprise

2. Steaming

3. Most people in the compartment prefer tea as their beverage of choice.

4. The global consumption of tea, as mentioned in the passage, indicates the significant economic impact of the tea industry. High demand for tea leads to increased production and export, benefiting tea-producing regions economically and contributing to international trade dynamics and market trends in the tea industry.

III. 1. One inference about Rajvir from the given context is that he has a great appreciation for natural beauty. Despite being an ardent fan of detective stories, he is drawn away by the fascinating scenery outside.

2. False

3. People living in cities love seeing nature and lots of greenery because their usual surroundings are full of buildings and roads. Being around big open spaces, fresh air, and lots of plants and trees feels relaxing and offers a nice change from their busy city lives. Nature is very different from the city, which feels like a breath of fresh air compared to the usual city scenes of concrete and structured buildings.

4. small and motionless figures/ miniature models

Subjective Questions

Short Answer Questions

CBSE Marking Scheme: Content-1 M, Organisation of Ideas-1 M, Accuracy-1 M

1. Pranjol was born and brought up in Assam. He must have been used to Assam's scenic beauty since childhood, whereas Rajvir was visiting Assam and experiencing the greenery for the first time. Hence, Pranjol was busy reading a detective book while Rajvir looked out of the window and was amazed to see huge fields full of green plantations.

Even though Rajvir was a fan of detective stories, but at the moment he was keener on looking at the beautiful scenery.

2. The different legends that we get to know in the lesson, 'Tea from Assam,' are:

Chinese legend: A Chinese emperor who always boiled water before drinking it. One day a few leaves of the twigs burning under the pot fell into the water, giving it a delicious flavour. It is said they were tea leaves.

Indian legend: Bodhidharma, an ancient Buddhist monk, cut off his eyelids because he felt sleepy during meditations. Ten tea plants grew out of the eyelids. The leaves of these plants, when put in hot water and drunk, banished sleep.

Knowledge Hub

To avoid mixing the two legends associated with the origin of tea, students should write and practice.

3. Tea was first consumed in China as far back as 2700 B.C. and reached Europe in the 16th century, where it was most popular for its medicinal properties.

The words 'Chai' and 'Chini' were derived from the Chinese language.

4. Rajvir was an enthusiastic person who read the history of tea before coming on his vacation to Pranjol's home in Assam. His research and study amazed both Pranjol and his father.

Knowing about the destination and learning about things before the start of a journey can help a person explore the place in a better way. Some people like the thrill of discovery and do not prefer knowing about things beforehand.

Long Answer Questions

CBSE Marking Scheme: Expression-2 M, Accuracy-1 M

5. Rajvir had been invited to Assam by his classmate Pranjol He was quite excited about the trip and had gathered a lot of information about the history of tea. He had learned a lot of facts and legends related to it; facts about where tea originated and how it became a popular beverage. He informed that about 80 crore cups of tea are consumed daily and that the words tea, chai, and chini originated from the Chinese language. He narrated two popular legends about the origin of tea. He knew that the sprouting season of tea leaves lasted from May to July. **(1 M)**

Rajvir exhibits an important character trait-curiosity and eagerness to know. Moreover, he is enthusiastic about exploring new places and collecting relatable information. He likes to have some prior knowledge about the destination before visiting it. **(1 M)**

This is very appreciable, and children should develop this habit of finding out about the place they are visiting. These are desirable traits for all learners. **(1 M)**

Mistakes 101 : What not to do!

Students may mention character traits without linking them back to the evidence provided in the chapter, resulting in a disconnected analysis.

6. The chapter "Glimpses of India" delves into the significance of tea and its production in Assam. Assam's tea gardens hold immense importance in India's tea industry, benefiting from the region's favourable climate and fertile soil. **(1 M)**

The chapter explores the labour-intensive process of tea production, highlighting the meticulous hand-plucking of tender tea leaves by workers, often belonging to marginalised communities. It also sheds light on the social and economic dynamics within the tea estates, with the owners exerting significant influence. **(1 M)**

Moreover, the chapter emphasizes the cultural significance of tea in Indian society, from its daily rituals to its role in social gatherings. Overall, it provides a comprehensive understanding of the significance of tea production in Assam. **(1 M)**

❑❑❑

MIJBIL THE OTTER

—Gavin Maxwell

6

Narrative Sketch

1. The chapter introduces the author, Gavin Maxwell, who lives in Iraq and decides to adopt an otter named Mijbil.
2. Mijbil arrives at Maxwell's house and becomes a mischievous yet endearing companion.
3. Maxwell describes Mijbil's playful nature and how he creates havoc by flooding the house.
4. The author describes Mijbil's mischievous behavior, such as rolling in water and nuzzling his face.
5. The author also discusses the challenges of caring for an otter, including feeding him live fish and dealing with his strong odor.
6. The chapter explores themes of companionship, responsibility, and the relationship between humans and animals.
7. The author reflects on his own emotional attachment to Mijbil and how it changed his perspective on animals as pets.

BEFORE YOU READ

Theme

The story, 'Mijbil the Otter', clearly reflects the love that the author had for animals. The author talks about how his life changed when he kept an otter as his pet after losing his dog. He shares all his experiences with his pet, which he named Mijbil. He takes us through his journey of playing, adjusting, and travelling with Mijbil (or Mij), the otter. The readers also observe a bond that develops between the two on their journey from Iraq to London.

Important Characters' Sketch

- **Gavin Maxwell:** Gavin Maxwell is the author and narrator of the lesson, Mijbil the otter. He shares his experience of keeping a pet otter when his pet dog Jonnie died. He is a sensitive person who understands the commitment of keeping a pet and tries his best to keep his pet otter, Mijbil, in the best way possible. His life changed when Mijbil came into his life, and he was happy to enjoy his time with his pet.
- **Mijbil:** Mij, short for Mijbil, is the otter gifted by the author's friend when he expressed his desire to have a pet otter on their trip to Southern Iraq. Mij was a fun-loving, intelligent otter who loved to play with water and different kinds of toys. Initially, the otter was aloof and indifferent to the author but later, it became friendly and attached to the author.

SYNOPSIS

In 1956, the author Gavin Maxwell and his friend, travelled to Basra to the Consulate-General to collect and answer their mail from Europe. It crossed his mind that he would like to keep an otter instead of a dog.

During their journey, when Maxwell expressed his desire to keep an otter as a pet, his friend suggested getting an otter from the Tigris marshes in Iraq. When they reached their destination, his friend received the mail immediately, while Maxwell had to wait a few more days to receive it. Once he received the mail, he took the sack that was brought by two Arabs carrying a message from his friend and discovered an otter inside it. The creature resembled[1] a small dragon, which the author named 'Mijbil' and was often called Mij.

For the first twenty-four hours, he was neither hostile[2] nor friendly; he was aloof[3] and indifferent,[4] choosing to sleep on the floor far away from the writer. It took a while for the little creature to adapt to its surroundings. In due course, Maxwell observed that Mij enjoyed playing with water and even learnt to turn the tap on. Soon Mij had learnt to follow the writer without a lead and came to him when his name was called. He spent most of his time playing, marbles being his favourite toy for pastime.

Lessons to learn

- *The importance of companionship*
- *The responsibilities of pet ownership*
- *The value of empathy*

The days passed peacefully at Basra, and it was time for Maxwell to return to England with his pet otter. However, the British airline to London do not fly animals, so the author booked a flight to Paris with another airline and from there to London. The airline insisted that Mij should be packed into a box not more than eighteen inches square.

Therefore, Maxwell arranged for a box, put Mijbil inside one hour before the flight to make him accustomed[5] to the box, and left to grab a quick meal.

When he returned, he found holes in the box, and the edges were stained with blood. Mij had torn the lining of the box to shreds. The author cleaned the box properly and rushed to the airport a few minutes before the flight took off. When he boarded the flight, he explained the entire incident to an air hostess who suggested he should keep his pet on his lap rather than locking his pet inside the container. Maxwell was filled with gratitude for her kind words. Mij was out of the box in a flash. He escaped the box and caused chaos on the flight. The author tried to catch him, but couldn't. The air hostess, then, offered to get Mij back to the author. After an eventful journey, Mij and Maxwell reached London and stayed there for nearly a month.

---

[1] **Resemble:** look or seem alike
[2] **Hostile:** unfriendly
[3] **Aloof:** unfriendly; distant
[4] **Indifferent:** unconcerned
[5] **Accustomed:** adapt; adjust

In London, Mij would play for hours with toys– ping-pong balls, marbles, rubber fruit, and a terrapin shell. The game Mij had created with a broken bag amazed the author. He was exercised like a dog on a leash by the author. During these strolls across the streets of London, Mij developed some habits.

Maxwell often took Mij for a walk, and the people of London would make strange guesses about his pet. People made different assumptions about Mij, comparing him to a baby seal, walrus, leopard, bear cub, squirrel, or hippo, and a few more would refer to the otter as a 'brontosaur'. Mij was anything but an otter to these people.

However, the most surprising response came from a labourer digging a hole in the street when he asked the author, "Here, Mister– what is that supposed to be?"

NCERT EXERCISE

Oral Comprehension Check

(NCERT Page 104)

1. What 'experiment' did Maxwell think Camusfearna would be suitable for?

Ans. Maxwell had travelled to Southern Iraq in early 1956 when he came up with a desire to keep an otter instead of a dog. He thought that Camusfearna, which is surrounded by water, is close to its entrance and would make a good location for the trial of keeping an otter as a pet.

2. Why does he go to Basra? How long does he wait there, and why?

Ans. Gavin Maxwell, the author, travelled to Basra with a friend to the Consulate-General to collect and respond to their mail from Europe. But they found that while the author's mail had not arrived, his friend's had. Maxwell cabled to England, and when, three days later, nothing had happened, he tried to telephone. On the first day, the line wasn't in order. On the second day, the exchange was closed due to a religious holiday. Another breakdown occurred on the third day. Finally, after five days, the author's mail arrived.

3. How does he get the otter? Does he like it? Pick out the words that tell you this.

Ans. When the author received his mail, he carried it to his bedroom to read. There, he saw two Arabs with a sack that twisted from time to time. They handed him a note from his friend saying he had sent him an otter.

Yes, we can say that he liked it. He felt a new phase had begun in his life, which he wished would never end. He had developed an 'otter fixation', a strong attachment towards otters, shared by most people who owned one.

(NCERT Page 105)

1. **Why was the otter named 'Maxwell's otter'?**

Ans. The zoologists named the otter Lutrogale Perspicillata Maxwelli. In short, it was called Maxwell's otter.

2. **Tick the right answer. In the beginning, the otter was**

❐ aloof and indifferent

❐ friendly

❐ hostile

Ans. In the beginning, the otter was aloof and indifferent. He was neither hostile nor friendly.

3. **What happened when Maxwell took Mijbil to the bathroom? What did it do two days after that?**

Ans. When Maxwell took Mijbil to the bathroom, the otter went wild with joy in the water for half an hour. It was plunging and rolling in it, shooting up and down the length of the bathtub underwater and making enough slosh and splash for a hippo.

Two days after that, it escaped from his bedroom to the bathroom. By the time Maxwell had reached, Mijbil was up on the end of the bathtub and fumbling at the chromium taps with its paws. In less than a minute, it had turned the tap far enough to produce some water and, after a moment, achieved the full flow.

(NCERT Page 108 & 109)

1. **How was Mij to be transported to England?**

Ans. The British airline to London did not fly animals, so Maxwell booked a flight to Paris with another airline, and from there, flew to London. The airline insisted that Mij be packed into a box not more than eighteen inches square and carried on the floor at the author's feet.

2. **What did Mij do to the box?**

Ans. Maxwell arranged for the box in which Mij was to be carried on the flight to London. He put Mij inside the box one hour before the flight to make him accustomed to the box and left to grab a quick meal. When he returned, there was complete silence from the box. Blood was coming down from the airholes and lid. He had torn the lining of the box to shreds to escape from it.

3. **Why did Maxwell put the otter back in the box? How do you think he felt when he did this?**

Ans. Mij hurt himself in the author's attempt to accustom the otter to the box in which he would be transported to London. Miz tore the box's lining to pieces as he struggled to get out, harming himself in the process. It was ten minutes before their flight when the author discovered Mij in this state. Mij had to be packed into the box as he hurried to the airport. He must have felt sorry for the otter because of how he had hurt himself. Moreover, he must be worried as well.

4. **Why does Maxwell say the air hostess was "the very queen of her kind"?** **(CBSE, 2019)**

Ans. Maxwell said that the air hostess was "the very queen of her kind" because she was kind and helpful. He took the air hostess into confidence about the incident with the box.

She understood the situation and suggested that he might prefer to have his pet on his knee. Hearing this, the author developed a profound admiration for the air hostess. She understood the pain of both the otter and its owner.

5. **What happened when the box was opened?**

Ans. Mij escaped the box as soon as it was opened. He disappeared at high speed down the aircraft. There were cries and chaos all around. A woman stood up in her seat, screaming. Maxwell saw Mij's tail disappearing beneath the legs of a White- turbaned Indian; he tried to catch it but missed. The air hostess, with a charming smile, suggested that the author should sit and that she would find the otter for him. After a while, Mij returned to him. He climbed on the author's knee and began to rub his nose on his face and neck.

(NCERT Page 110)

1. **What game had Mij invented?**

Ans. Mij invented a game with the ping-pong ball, which could keep him busy for up to half an hour. A suitcase had been damaged on the journey home, so the lid when closed, remained at a slope from one end to the other. Mij discovered that if he placed the ball on the high end and dashed around to the other end to ambush[6] its arrival, hide from it, crouching, spring up and take it by surprise, grab it and trot off with it to the high end, again.

2. **What are 'compulsive habits'? What does Maxwell say are the compulsive habits of**
   (i) school children (ii) Mij?

Ans. Compulsive habits are habits without clear reason or control.

In the story, Maxwell mentions the rituals of children who, on their way to and from school, must place their feet squarely on the centre of each paving block, must touch every seventh upright of the iron railings or pass to the outside of every second lamp post.

Similarly, Mij had made it a habit to jump onto the school wall and gallop along its thirty yards length.

3. **What group of animals do otters belong to?**

Ans. Otters belong to a comparatively small group of animals called Mustellines, shared by the badger, mongoose, weasel, stoat, mink and others.

4. **What guesses did the Londoners make about what Mij was?**

[6] **Ambush:** make a surprise attack

Ans. The author did not find it strange that the average Londoner does not recognise an otter. However, the author received some random guesses about who Mij was. They guessed it was a baby seal, a squirrel, a walrus, a hippo, a beaver, a bear cub, a leopard and a brontosaur. The most surprising of all was when a labourer asked the author what it was supposed to be.

Thinking about the Text

(NCERT Page 110-111)

1. What things does Mij do which tell you that he is an intelligent, friendly and fun-loving animal who needs love? (CBSE, 2015)

Ans. Mij was an intelligent animal. He invented his own game out of ping-pong balls and a broken suitcase of the author. Another instance of his intelligence was when he opened the tap in the bathroom. He screwed the tap till water began to flow, and then he would play and splash in the water.

Though Mij was aloof and indifferent initially, he soon became friendly. He formed a special attachment with Maxwell and responded when Maxwell called out his name. He grew desperate when Maxwell left him in a box, and he got hurt while trying to escape it. When let out, he clung to the author's feet. He was a fun-loving animal who enjoyed playing games with various toys, ping-pong balls, marbles, rubber fruit, and a terrapin shell.

2. What are some of the things we come to know about otters from this text?

Ans. We learn a lot of things about otters through this text. Otters belong to a comparatively small group of animals called Mustellines, shared by the badger, mongoose, weasel, stoat, mink and others. They are found in large numbers in marshes, often tamed by the Arabs. It is characteristic of otters that every drop of water must be extended and spread about the place; a bowl must be overturned, or, if it would not be overturned, be sat in and splashed in until it overflowed. For them, water must be kept on the move. Otters are intelligent, fun-loving animals who love playing various games, especially with a ball.

3. Why is Mij's species now known to the world as Maxwell's otter?

Ans. Maxwell's otter was of a race previously unknown to science and was at length named by zoologists Lutrogale perspicillata maxwelli or Maxwell's otter.

4. Maxwell, in the story, speaks for the otter, Mij. He tells us what the otter feels and thinks on different occasions. Given below are some things the otter does. Complete the column on the right to say what Maxwell says about what Mij feels and thinks.

What Mij does	How Mij feels or thinks
Plunges, rolls in the water and makes the water splosh and splash	*(a)* ________
Screws the tap in the wrong way	*(b)* ________
Nuzzles Maxwell's face and neck in the aeroplane	*(c)* ________

Ans. *(a)* He thinks it is happy and having fun.

(b) He chitters with irritation and disappointment.

(c) He feels much comfort and content after his distressed chitter.

5. Read the story and find the sentences where Maxwell describes his pet otter. Then choose and arrange your sentences to illustrate those statements below that you think are True.

Maxwell's description

(i) makes Mij seem almost human, like a small boy.

Ans. True – He spent the majority of his time playing.

(ii) shows that he is often irritated with what Mij does.

Ans. False

(iii) Shows that he is often surprised by what Mij does.

Ans. True – I stood there in awe as he cranked the tap far enough to generate a trickle of water in far less than a minute, then increased the flow to full flow after a few moments.

(iv) of Mij's antics is comical.

Ans. False

(v) shows that he observes the antics of Mij very carefully.

Ans. True – On his way home, a bag I had brought to Iraq had been broken, and the top, when closed, stayed at a slope from one end to the other. Mij realised that if he put the ball on top of the luggage, it would roll down the length of it. He'd dash around to the opposite end to ambush its arrival, hide from it while crouched, then jump up and catch it off guard, grab it, and trot away with it.

(vi) shows that he thinks Mij is a very ordinary otter.

Ans. False

(vii) shows that he thinks the otter is very unusual.

Ans. True - It's not surprising that the typical Londoner doesn't recognise an otter, but the wide range of answers as to what kind of animal this is surprised me. Mij was far from an otter.

MISCELLANEOUS EXERCISE

Multiple Choice Questions

1. Where does the author live?

(*a*) Southern Iraq (*b*) Scotland
(*c*) Basra (*d*) None of the above

2. When the author saw the otter for the first time, it resembled a ______.

(*a*) Dog (*b*) Dragon
(*c*) Cat (*d*) Seal

3. How would Mij follow the author?

(*a*) Like a pet (*b*) With a lead
(*c*) Without a lead (*d*) None of these

4. Why was Camusfearna a suitable spot for the author's experiment?

(*a*) It was marshy.
(*b*) It was ringed by water.
(*c*) He was a stranger there.
(*d*) He loved that spot.

5. The otter was brought to the author by ______.

(*a*) His friend (*b*) Two Arabs
(*c*) Air hostess (*d*) A stranger

6. According to the otter, what must be kept on the move and made to do things?

(*a*) Sand (*b*) Water
(*c*) Blood (*d*) Marbles

7. In the Tigris, marshes otters were as common as ______.

(*a*) Bees (*b*) Lizards
(*c*) Rats (*d*) Mosquitoes

8. What were Mijbil's favourite toys?

(*a*) Stones (*b*) Marbles
(*c*) Soft toys (*d*) Water

9. Where did the Arabs keep the otter?

(*a*) In a sack (*b*) In a bag
(*c*) In a box (*d*) In the water

10. What did the author find at the Constable General?

(*a*) His mail hadn't arrived.
(*b*) His friend's mail had arrived.
(*c*) His pet had arrived.
(*d*) Both (*a*) and (*b*).

Extract-Based Questions

I. Read the following extract and answer the questions/ complete the sentences that follow: (5 M)

When I returned, there was an appalling spectacle. There was complete silence from the box, but from its airholes and chinks around the lid, blood had trickled and dried. I whipped off the lock and tore open the lid, and Mij, exhausted and blood-spattered, whimpered and caught at my leg. He had torn the lining of the box to shreds; when I removed the last of it so that there were no cutting edges left, it was just ten minutes until the time of the flight, and the airport was five miles distant. I put the miserable Mij back into the box, holding down the lid with my hand. I sat in the back of the car with the box beside me as the driver tore through the streets of Basra like a ricocheting bullet.

1. Choose the speaker that uses the phrase 'appalling spectacle' correctly.

Speaker 1 – We got back home to see that our pet dog had eaten *kheer* my mother had kept out of the fridge. Indded, an appalling spectacle.

Speaker 2 – We got back home and witnessed that our cousin and dressed our pet dog in his t-shirt. Have to admit that it was an appalling spectacle.

Speaker 3 – We got back home to see that our pet dog sitting with a mangled rat. It was an appalling spectacle.

Speaker 4 – We got back home from the airport and observed our pet dog sound asleep on the rug. What an appalling spectacle!

(*a*) Speaker 1 (*b*) Speaker 2
(*c*) Speaker 3 (*d*) Speaker 4

2. "whipped off", is an example of a phrasal verb i.e. a combination of a verb and a preposition. Choose the option that DOES NOT fit the given definition.

(1) take: down, after, out, off

(2) look: up, out, along, down

(3) give: up, in, away, back

(4) get: in, up, out, back

(*a*) Option (1) (*b*) Option (2)
(*c*) Option (3) (*d*) Option (4)

3. Choose the option that is closest in resemblance to the box's condition in which Mij was kept.

(1) (2) (3) (4)

(*a*) Option (1) (*b*) Option (2)

(*c*) Option (3) (*d*) Option (4)

4. Select the option that DOES NOT state the possible reason for Maxwell's cutting the box edges off.

(*a*) Mij could have injured himself further

(*b*) It could have made the place untidy

(*c*) Mij could have accidently swallowed the torn pieces

(*d*) It could have obstructed the shutting of the lid

5. Choose the option that correctly states Maxwell's likely feelings, in the situation below.

"__________ I put the miserable Mij back into the box, holding down the lid with my hand."

(1) anxious (2) disappointed (3) terrified

(4) guilty (5) insulted

(*a*) (1) and (5) (*b*) (2) and (3)

(*c*) (1) and (4) (*d*) (3) and (5)

II. Read the following extract and answer the questions/ complete the sentences that follow: (5 M)

For the first twenty-four hours, Mijbil was neither hostile nor friendly; he was simply aloof and indifferent, choosing to sleep on the floor as far from my bed as possible. The second night, Mijbil came onto my bed in the small hours and remained asleep in the crook of my knees until the servant brought tea in the morning, and during the day, he began to lose his apathy and take a keen, much too keen, interest in his surroundings. I made a body belt for him and took him on a lead to the bathroom, where for half an hour, he went wild with joy in the water, plunging and rolling in it, shooting up and down the length of the bathtub underwater and making enough slosh and splash for a hippo.

1. Based on the passage, what can be inferred about Mijbil's behavior towards water? **(1)**

2. Write a word for 'Move or splash around with force' from the passage. **(1)**

3. "Mij was neither hostile nor friendly; he was simply aloof and indifferent... "From the actions of the given set of people, choose the person whose behaviour is likely to resemble Mijbil's. **(1)**

(*a*) Raman was distant for a while after losing his grandmother.

(*b*) Ayush was amicable since the day he walked into his new classroom.

(*c*) Aryan became nasty as soon as he started earning money.

(*d*) Zaid rudely tells his brother to stop calling.

4. Discuss the change in Mijbil's behaviour from being aloof and indifferent to showing interest in his surroundings. What factors might have contributed to this change? **(2)**

III. Read the following extract and answer the questions/ complete the sentences that follow: (5 M)

Two days later, Mijbil escaped from my bedroom as I entered it, and I turned to see his tail disappearing round the bend of the corridor that led to the bathroom. By the time I got there he was up on the end of the bathtub and fumbling at the chromium taps with his paws. I watched, amazed; in less than a minute he had turned the tap far enough to produce a trickle of water, and after a moment or two achieved the full flow.

1. Discuss the impact of Mijbil's escape and his actions in the bathroom on the narrator's perception of the otter. How does this incident contribute to the development of their relationship? **(2)**

2. Based on the passage, what can be inferred about Mijbil's intelligence and adaptability? **(1)**

3. What does the term "chromium" refer to in the passage? **(1)**

4. A. Mij loves water.

B. Mij was intelligent enough to open the water taps. **(1)**

(*a*) (A) is true (B) is false.

(*b*) (A) is false (B) is true.

(*c*) Both are true.

(*d*) Both are false.

Subjective Questions

Short Answer Questions (40-50 words) (3 M)

1. "...every drop of water must be, so to speak, extended and spread about the place...". Describe Maxwell's observation regarding Mij with reference to the given quote. **(CBSE, QB)**

2. Mijbil caused a sensation in London. Expound with reference to the chapter "Mijbil the Otter". **(CBSE, QB)**

3. Maxwell's fear of sending Mijbil to England was legitimate. Give a reason.

4. Comment on the childish habit of Mij.

Long Answer Questions (100-120 words) (6 M)

5. What is the main theme of "Mijbil the Otter" by Gavin Maxwell? How does the author explore this theme?

6. How does the author use descriptive language and imagery to create a sense of place in "Mijbil the Otter"?

ANSWERS & EXPLANATIONS

Answer Key

Multiple Choice Questions

1. (*b*) **2.** (*b*) **3.** (*c*) **4.** (*b*) **5.** (*b*) **6.** (*b*) **7.** (*d*) **8.** (*b*) **9.** (*a*) **10.** (*d*)

Explanations

Extract-Based Questions

I. 1. (*c*) Speaker 3

2. (*b*) Option (2)

3. (*d*) Option (4)

4. (*b*) It could have made the place untidy

5. (*c*) (1) and (4)

II. 1. He is fascinated by water.

2. Slosh

3. (*a*) Raman was distant for a while after losing his grandmother.

4. The change in Mijbil's behavior can be attributed to spending time with the narrator, gaining familiarity and comfort in the new environment, and experiencing the joy of water during his time in the bathroom. These factors likely helped him overcome his initial aloofness and indifference.

III. 1. Mijbil's escape and his actions in the bathroom likely amazed and intrigued the narrator, leading to a deeper sense of fascination and connection with the otter. This incident showcases Mijbil's curiosity, cleverness, and ability to interact with his environment, which would have strengthened the bond between the narrator and Mijbil.

2. Mijbil is skilled at manipulating objects.

3. A type of metal used for the taps.

4. (*c*) Both are true.

Subjective Questions

Short Answer Questions

CBSE Marking Scheme: Content-1 M, Organisation of Ideas-1 M, Accuracy-1 M

1. Mij, the fun-loving otter, loved to play in the water. When the author took Mijbil to the bathroom, he witnessed Mijbil being almost mad with excitement, plunging and rolling in water, splashing water all around.

The author learnt this characteristic of otters; every drop of water must spread about the place; a bowl must be overturned or be sat in and sploshed in until it overflows. Water must be kept on the move and made to do things; when static, it is wasted and provoking.

2. The average Londoner was amazed to see a unique animal like Mijbil. However, the author was not surprised to hear some wild guesses about the otter.

On seeing Mijbil, some people called him a baby seal, a squirrel, or a walrus. Others called him a beaver, a bear cub and a leopard. The best response came from a labourer digging a hole in the street. On seeing Mijbil, he asked the author, "Here, Mister — what is that supposed to be?"

3. Maxwell's fear of transporting Mij to England was legitimate. The British airline to London would not fly animals, so he had to book a flight to Paris on another airline and from there to London. The airline insisted that Mij should be packed into a box not more than eighteen inches square.

It must be a dreadful feeling to keep your pet locked in a box, so we can assume that Maxwell must have felt afraid to take the otter this way.

4. Mij was an Otter. He was full of intelligence and diligence. His activities are like the child. He invented a game ping-pong Ball. He enjoyed playing games.

He had compulsive habits. He played with ball. He was fun loving and friendly. He played splashed and thoroughly enjoyed like a hippo in water.

Long Answer Questions

CBSE Marking Scheme: Expression-2 M, Accuracy-1 M

5. The main theme of "Mijbil the Otter" by Gavin Maxwell is the deep and complex relationship between humans and animals, specifically focusing on the bond formed between the author and Mijbil, an otter. **(1 M)**

Maxwell explores this theme by sharing his personal experiences with an otter he decides to keep as a pet after the death of his dog. Through the narrative, he highlights the responsibilities and challenges of caring for a pet, especially an otter. **(1 M)**

Maxwell's detailed account of Mijbil's behavior, playfulness, and interactions not only reflects on the otter's intelligence and adaptability but also on the mutual affection that develops between them. The story illustrates how animals can enrich human lives, bringing joy and companionship, but also underscores the commitment and empathy required to meet their needs and ensure their well-being. **(1 M)**

6. In "Mijbil the Otter," the author uses descriptive language and imagery to create a vivid sense of place, particularly in his descriptions of the Scottish countryside and the natural environment where Mijbil the otter lives. **(1 M)**

For example, the author describes the Scottish landscape in great detail, painting a picture of the rugged hills, misty valleys, and rocky shores that make up the region. He uses sensory language to convey the sights, sounds, and smells of the natural world, such as the "dank, mossy smell" of the forest floor or the "soft, cushioned silence" of the snow-covered hills. **(1 M)**

The author also uses descriptive language to convey the specific environment where Mijbil lives. He describes the river where Mijbil is caught as a "turbulent, boiling torrent," and he provides detailed descriptions of the various pools, waterfalls, and rapids that make up the river's landscape. Through his descriptions, the author creates a vivid sense of the natural environment that Mijbil inhabits, and he shows how this environment shapes the otter's behaviour and instincts. **(1 M)**

Nailing the Right Answer

(*a*) Use specific examples from the text to support your points.

(*b*) Analyze the impact of descriptive language on creating the sense of place.

7

MADAM RIDES THE BUS

—Vallikkannan

Narrative Sketch

1. Valli is a curious girl who likes to observe the street from her front door.
2. Developed a desire to ride the bus that passed every half an hour from her village to the nearest town.
3. She listened to the conversations between her neighbours and regular bus users to get the details of the bus journey.
4. Made a wise plan for her first bus ride and saved sixty paise for the fare.
5. Stopped the bus, got on it all by herself, the conductor was amused by Valli's behaviour and started calling her MADAM as a joke.
6. Was annoyed by the concern of some people but enjoyed the views outside the window.
7. Reached the town, all the passengers got off the bus except Valli.
8. Did not go to the stall and have a drink because she had no money and even declined the offer of a cold drink by the conductor.
9. On the return journey, saw the same cow from earlier lying dead by the roadside, and the sight made her very sad.
10. Got off the bus and reached her home where her mother was talking to her aunt, not knowing about Valli's ride alone.

BEFORE YOU READ

Theme

In the story 'Madam Rides the Bus', the readers see life from an eight-year-old girl's perspective. Through Valli, the story's central character, the author depicts the curious nature of the children. The story shows how children are easily attracted to new things, and their curiosity doesn't end without experiencing them. Valli's desire to ride a bus and her courage to fulfill that desire, takes her on a journey of unforgettable experiences.

Important Characters' Sketch

- **Valli:** Valli is the story's central character, an eight-year-old girl. She doesn't have any friends to play with; hence she enjoys standing at the front door of her house, watching the street outside. She built up the desire to ride the bus that travelled between her village and a nearby town and courageously fulfilled this desire. The journey showed how mature Valli was for her age and capable of taking care of herself, though she was easily affected by the things around her.
- **Conductor:** The bus conductor in the story was a cheerful man. Seeing an eight-year-old girl travelling alone, he was surprised and helped her board the bus. He was a jolly man who liked to make jokes on the journey to keep his passengers entertained. He took great care of Valli, addressed her 'Madam' and invited her for another ride on the bus in the future.

SYNOPSIS

Valliammai, Valli for short, is an eight-year-old, curious girl. She did not have any playmates of her age and would pass her time standing at the front doorway of her house, watching the street outside. It was as enjoyable to her as the elaborate[1] games played by other children. Observing the street gave her many new, unusual experiences. Her favourite part was seeing the hourly bus pass through her village. Every time the bus passed, she would be filled with joy as she looked at the new passengers.

Gradually, she developed a desire to ride the bus, even if only once. She continued to pick up little details about the bus trip over the following days and months by paying close attention to conversations between her neighbours and regular bus users. Just like this, she knew the town was six miles away from her village, and it took the bus forty-five minutes to get there. The one-sided fare was thirty paise, which seemed a fortune for Valli to collect. She started planning and re-planning so that she could sneak out during her mother's afternoon nap and come back without her knowing anything. On reaching the town, if she stayed in her seat and paid another thirty paise, she could return home on the same bus. This meant she could take the afternoon bus, reach the town at one forty-five, and be back home by about two forty-five. She kept calculating the whole scenario.

One spring day, when the afternoon bus was about to leave the village, a tiny hand was raised, stopping the bus with a command. The conductor was surprised to hear that Valli was travelling alone. She explained how she intended to go to town and showed the coins to make the conductor believe her. The conductor stretched out a hand to help her get up, but the brave girl wanted to do it all by herself. The conductor was jolly and liked to make jokes. Looking at the young girl's maturity and attitude, he amusingly[2] started calling her 'madam'. Valli caught everyone's attention, and they all began to laugh with the conductor. It was a new bus, and Valli was enjoying everything in front of her eyes. There was a beautiful clock in front of Valli above the windshield. The seats were soft and luxurious. She tried to look out the window, but a canvas blind blocked her view, so she stood on the seat to peep outside. Valli was enjoying the beautiful view when an elderly man called her a child and advised her not to stand on the seat, but she was annoyed[3] by his attention. In his own funny way, the conductor asked her to sit on the seat since she had paid for the ticket. Valli still wanted to stand and would get irritated when somebody would call her a child. An elderly woman sat beside her, asking if she was travelling alone. Valli found the woman repulsive[4]; she was irritated by the smallest details about the woman, from her ugly earrings to the smell of the betel nut[5] from her mouth. She answered her rudely and didn't want to be bothered[6]. However, the woman kept asking more questions. Valli asked the woman not to worry about her and started looking outside the window.

[1] **Elaborate:** fancy
[2] **Amusingly:** causes laughter and provides entertainment
[3] **Annoyed:** irritated
[4] **Repulsive:** arousing disgust; repellent
[5] **Betel nut:** a fruit of a south Asian plant that people chew
[6] **Bothered:** disturbed

Lessons to learn

- ❐ Be curious like Valli
- ❐ Plan ahead
- ❐ Be independent and gracious
- ❐ Enjoy along the way

Then, we discover the elaborate plans she had to undertake for her first ride. She resisted the desire to buy peppermints, toys, balloons, and her desire to ride the merry-go-round at the village fair in order to save the sixty paise necessary for this bus ride. The next challenge was leaving the house without her mother noticing, which, surprisingly, Valli handled without much difficulty. Valli knew that every day after lunch, when her mother took a nap from one to four, she could sneak out to take her first bus ride. She liked to look out the window, and the sight of a running cow in the middle of the road suddenly made her laugh. She laughed until there were tears in her eyes. The bus passed a train station and came to a shopping street with a glittering display of clothes and other things for sale. The conductor asked Valli to get down, but she politely refused and said she was returning on the same bus. The idea of getting off the bus and looking at the sights all by herself scared her.

The conductor was amused by her reply and asked how she wasn't scared to come on this bus ride alone. Valli said there was nothing to be afraid of that. The conductor offered to get a cold drink for her, which she refused as she didn't have enough money.

It was time for the return journey and the wonderful sights Valli would enjoy looking out. She was not bored and had the same excitement this time as well. But suddenly, she saw the same cow lying dead by the roadside, just where it had been struck by some fast-moving vehicle. She was shocked to see how a lovable, beautiful creature now looked horrible lying on the road, lifeless. The memory of the dead cow haunted[7] her and took away her enthusiasm. The bus reached the village at three forty. Valli bid goodbye to the conductor.

When she got home, her mother was up and chatting with an aunt from South Street. When her aunt asked her where she had gone, Valli simply smiled. She enthusiastically agreed as she listened to her mother and aunt discussing things that take place without our knowledge. The women didn't comprehend[8] or suspect anything as Valli smiled to herself.

[7] **Haunted:** disturb; worry
[8] **Comprehend:** understand

NCERT EXERCISE

Oral Comprehension Check

(NCERT Page 119)

1. What was Valli's favourite pastime?

Ans. Valli's favourite pastime was standing in the front doorway of her house, watching what was happening outside the street.

2. What was a source of unending joy for Valli? What was her strongest desire?

Ans. The sight of the bus, filled each time with a new set of passengers, was a source of unending joy for Valli. Her strongest desire was to travel on the bus and ride to the nearby town and back.

3. What did Valli find out about the bus journey? How did she find out these details?

Ans. Valli picked up various small details about the bus journey by listening carefully to conversations between her neighbours and people who regularly used the bus. She would ask a few detailed questions here and there to collect more information. Just like this, she knew the town was six miles away from her village, and one-side travel was 45 minutes. The one-sided fare was thirty paise.

4. What do you think Valli was planning to do?

Ans. Valli was planning to fulfill her desire to travel by bus outside the village.

(NCERT Page 122)

1. Why does the conductor call Valli 'madam'?

Ans. She did not want anyone to treat her like a child. So, the conductor amusingly started calling her 'madam'.

2. Why does Valli stand up on the seat? What does she see now?

Ans. Valli stood on the seat to enjoy the outside scenery from the moving bus. Her view was blocked by a canvas blind covering the window's lower part. To watch the scenery outside, she stood up on the seat and peered over the blind. The bus was moving on a very narrow road. It had a canal on one side, beyond which there were palm trees, grasslands, distant mountains and a blue sky. On the other side, there was a deep ditch followed by greenery as far as one could see.

3. What does Valli tell the elderly man when he calls her a child?

Ans. Valli was enjoying the beautiful view standing in her seat when an elderly man called her a child and advised her not to stand on the seat. The man was genuinely concerned for her, but Valli was annoyed by his attention. Valli told him she was not a child and could take care of herself. She had paid the fare of thirty paise for the ticket like everyone else.

4. Why didn't Valli want to make friends with the elderly woman?

Ans. Valli was already annoyed with everyone treating her like a child. When the elderly woman came and started asking questions from Valli, she found her repulsive. The woman had big holes in her ear lobes. And she was wearing ugly earrings. Moreover, Valli could smell the betel nut the woman was chewing and see the betel juice about to come out of her mouth. Thus, the elderly woman was not a socially desirable person, according to Valli.

(NCERT Page 125)

1. How did Valli save up money for her first journey? Was it easy for her?

Ans. Valli made elaborate plans for her first bus journey alone. She made painstaking efforts to save the money she needed to take the bus ride from her village to the town. She saved sixty paise for this bus ride, resisting every temptation to buy peppermints, toys, balloons, and her desire to ride the merry-go-round at the village fair.

No, it was not easy for her.

2. What did Valli see on her way that made her laugh?

Ans. Valli clapped her hands with glee when she saw a young cow running along the road and came in front of the bus. As the driver honked, it started running in front of the bus. The more the driver blew the horn, the frightened the animal became, but it did not get out of the way. Somehow this was funny for Valli, and she kept on laughing till she had tears in her eyes.

3. Why didn't she get off the bus at the bus station?

Ans. Valli didn't get off the bus on reaching the town as she had only planned for the bus ride. She had no plan to get out on the shopping street or had any money to buy a cold drink. All she had desired was a bus ride from her village to the town. On being asked by the conductor, she replied that she was too afraid to look at the sights all by herself. The bus ride, however, was nothing to be afraid of.

4. Why didn't Valli want to go to the stall and have a drink? What does this tell you about her?

Ans. Valli was too afraid to get off the bus alone. Moreover, she had saved only sixty paise for the trip and didn't have enough money to buy herself a drink. So, when the conductor suggested she get down and have a drink, she refused. She also denied the treat offered by the conductor, which showed that she was a mature child with pride.

Thinking about the Text

(NCERT Page 127)

1. **What was Valli's deepest desire? Find the words and phrases in the story that tell you this.**

Ans. Valli's deepest desire was to go on a bus ride. The words and phrases in the story that tell this are 'overwhelming desire', 'dreams', 'hopes', 'wish became stronger and stronger', 'the most fascinating thing of all', and 'source of unending joy'.

2. **How did Valli plan her bus ride? What did she find out about the bus, and how did she save up the fare?**

Ans. When Valli developed a desire to take a bus ride outside her village, she planned and calculated everything to fulfill this desire. Valli picked up various small details about the bus journey by listening carefully to conversations between her neighbours and people who regularly used the bus. She would ask a few detailed questions here and there to collect more information.

She collected the money by resisting every temptation ranging from peppermints, toys, balloons and merry-go-round at the village fair. After much effort, she finally saved sixty paise for her two-side bus ride.

3. **What kind of person is Valli? To answer this question, pick out the following sentences from the text and fill in the blanks. The words you fill in are the clues to your answer.**

Ans. (i) "Stop the bus! Stop the bus!" And a tiny hand was raised commandingly.

(ii) "Yes, I simply have to go to town," said Valli, still standing outside the bus.

(iii) "There's nobody here who's a child," she said haughtily. "I've paid my thirty paise like everyone else."

(iv) "Never mind," she said, "I can get on by myself. You don't have to help me. I'm not a child, I tell you," she said irritably.

(v) "You needn't bother about me. I can take care of myself," Valli said, turning her face toward the window and staring out.

(vi) Then she turned to the conductor and said, "Well, sir, I hope to see you again."

For Valli, the bus journey probably symbolised the adult world. She felt great pride and satisfaction in buying her own ticket. Though a child, Valli wanted to be treated as a grown-up on the bus. She had a great sense of self-respect, preventing her from taking anyone's help. She felt she could take care of herself very well and was easily irritated when anyone treated her as a child.

4. **Why does the conductor refer to Valli as 'Madam'?**

Ans. (Refer to Oral Comprehension Check Question 1 above.)

5. **Find the lines in the text which tell you that Valli was enjoying her ride on the bus.**

Ans. The following lines in the text show that Valli was enjoying her ride on the bus:

(i) "Valli devoured everything with her eyes."

(ii) "On the one side, there was the canal and, beyond it, palm trees, grassland, distant mountains, and the blue, blue sky. On the other side was a deep ditch and then acres and acres of green fields– green, green, green, as far as the eye could see. Oh, it was all so wonderful!"

(iii) "Everyone laughed, and gradually Valli too joined in the laughter. Suddenly, Valli clapped her hands with glee."

(iv) "Somehow, this was very funny to Valli. She laughed and laughed until there were tears in her eyes."

(v) "Valli wasn't bored to the slightest and greeted everything with the same excitement she'd felt the first time."

6. **Why does Valli refuse to look out of the window on her way back?**

Ans. On her way back to the village, Valli saw a lifeless cow lying on the roadside. It was the same cow that was so joyful on their journey to the town. She was shocked to see how a lovable, beautiful creature now looked horrible lying on the road, lifeless. The memory of the dead cow haunted her and took away her enthusiasm. Thus, she sat on her seat silently after this and refused to look out of the window.

7. **What does Valli mean when she says, "I was just agreeing with what you said about things happening without our knowledge."**

Ans. When she got home, her mother was up and chatting with an aunt from South Street. When her aunt asked her where she had gone, Valli simply smiled.

Listening to their conversation, Valli agreed that things happen without our knowledge. She smiled to herself as her mother had no knowledge about Valli's ride alone and would possibly never know about it. Hence, she agreed with what her mother said.

8. **The author describes the things that Valli sees from an eight-year-old's point of view. Can you find evidence from the text for this statement?**

Ans. The author has described the things Valli saw from an eight-year-old's point of view.

Her favourite pastime was standing in the front doorway of her house, watching what was happening outside the street. Watching the bus filled with a new set of people each time was a source of unending joy for her, and she built a desire to take a bus ride.

We learn that, like any other child, she had the temptation of peppermints, toys, balloons, and a merry-go-round ride at the fair. However, she resisted the temptation so that she could save the money to have her desire fulfilled.

The description of the view outside the window was also from an eight-year-old's eyes. The 'blue, blue sky' and the 'acres and acres of green fields – green, green, green' show the enthusiasm of a kid looking at different colours. Valli clapped her hands in glee on watching a cow run in front of the bus. She found it so funny that tears came to her eyes. On the other hand, she was overcome with sadness on her way back when she saw the same cow lying dead. These sudden emotions are usually expressed by a little child.

MISCELLANEOUS EXERCISE

Multiple Choice Questions

1. What was Valli's full name?

(*a*) Valliammai (*b*) Vallikkannan
(*c*) Valliannai (*d*) Vallikannam

2. What was her favourite pastime?

(*a*) Watching the street outside.
(*b*) Playing outside.
(*c*) Riding the bus.
(*d*) Talking to her friends.

3. How did Valli feel when the elderly man expressed concern that she was standing?

(*a*) Shocked (*b*) Happy
(*c*) Displeased (*d*) Embarrassed

4. Choose the option that lists the set of statements that are NOT TRUE according to the given extract.

(i) Valli was travelling without a guardian.
(ii) The conductor was bullying Valli.
(iii) Valli was nervous in her interactions.
(iv) Valli was a child passenger.
(v) Valli followed the elderly man's advice.
(vi) Valli's response to the elderly man was respectful.
(vii) It took Valli some time to participate in the playful conversations.

(*a*) ii, iii, iv (*b*) v, vi, vii
(*c*) iii, v, vii (*d*) ii, iii, vi

5. "Valli would stare wistfully at the people who got on or off the bus." What is the meaning of wistfully?

(*a*) Happily (*b*) Carefully
(*c*) Willingly (*d*) Longingly

6. Pick the option that correctly classifies the fact/s (F) and opinion/s (O) of the students below.

(*a*) F - 1,2 and O - 3,4 (*b*) F - 2,3,4 and O - 1
(*c*) F - 2,4 and O - 1,3 (*d*) F - 3 and O - 1,2,4

7. Choose the characteristic displayed by the conductor when he addressed Valli and declared that she couldn't be ' a mere girl'.

(*a*) Encouragement (*b*) Indulgence
(*c*) Embarrassment (*d*) Authority

8. What was the next challenge once she had saved enough money for the bus ride?

(*a*) Tell her mom about it.
(*b*) Ask for her mother's permission.
(*c*) Buy the ticket.
(*d*) To sneak out of the house.

9. What character trait of Valli is visible when she refuses to accept the conductor's treat?

(*a*) Responsible (*b*) Stubborn
(*c*) Arrogant (*d*) Disrespectful

10. Who was a "real chatterbox"?

(*a*) Valli (*b*) Bus conductor
(*c*) Valli's mother (*d*) Valli's aunt

Extract-Based Questions

I. Read the following extract and answer the questions/ complete the sentences that follow: **(5 M)**

The most fascinating thing of all was the bus that travelled between her village and the nearest town. It passed through her street each hour, once going to the town and once coming back. The sight of the bus, filled each time with a new set of passengers, was a source of unending joy for Valli.

1. Which of the following is NOT a reason why Valli finds joy in the sight of the bus? **(1)**

(*a*) The bus travels between her village and the nearest town.
(*b*) The bus passes through her street each hour.
(*c*) The bus is always filled with a new set of passengers.
(*d*) Valli gets to ride the bus for free.

2. In about 40 words, analyze Valli's emotions when she sees the bus filled with a new set of passengers each time. **(2)**

3. Which of the following best describes the extract? **(1)**

(*a*) A description of Valli's fascination with the bus.
(*b*) A dialogue between Valli and the bus driver.
(*c*) A narrative of Valli's journey on the bus.

4. If this extract were to be performed on stage, how should the actor emphasize the word "joy" to convey Valli's excitement? **(1)**

II. Read the following extract and answer the questions/ complete the sentences that follow: (5 M)

"Day after day she watched the bus and gradually a tiny wish crept into her head and grew there: she wanted to ride on that bus, even if it was just once. This wish became stronger until it was an overwhelming desire. Valli would stare wistfully at the people who got on and off the bus when it stood at the street corner. Their faces would kindle in her longings, dreams, and hopes. If one of her friends happened to ride the bus and tried to describe the sights of the town to her, Valli would be jealous to listen and would shout, in English: "Proud! Proud!" **(CBSE, QB)**

1. Valli would stare wistfully at the people as she: **(1)**
   (*a*) Had been watching the bus for a long time.
   (*b*) Was inspired by the people travelling on the bus.
   (*c*) Had a strong desire to take a ride on the bus.
   (*d*) Envied the people who could travel on the bus.
2. Pick the option that shows the list of words that collocate with 'overwhelming'. (e.g., overwhelming desire) **(1)**
   (i) Response (ii) Lies
   (iii) Support (iv) Majority
   (v) Pets (vi) Places
   (*a*) (i), (v) and (vi) (*b*) (i), (iii) and (iv)
   (*c*) (ii) and (v) (*d*) (iii), (v) and (vi)
3. 'Valli would be jealous to listen...' This indicates Valli's: **(1)**
   (*a*) Longing to ride the bus.
   (*b*) Nature as an envious person.
   (*c*) Denial to accept her situation.
   (*d*) Inclination to trouble travellers.
4. A part of the extract has been paraphrased. Choose the option that includes the most appropriate solution to the blanks. **(1)**
   The desire became so (i) _______ that it transformed into an (ii) _______ one. Valli would look (iii) _______ at people who boarded the bus and got off.
   (*a*) (i) active (ii) overt (iii) longingly
   (*b*) (i) vigorous (ii) overpowering (iii) cheerfully
   (*c*) (i) staunch (ii) overt (iii) joyfully
   (*d*) (i) vigorous (ii) overpowering (iii) longingly
5. What does the line 'gradually a tiny wish crept into her head and grew there', mean? **(1)**
   (*a*) The wish developed in her head over a period of time.
   (*b*) The wish was a feeling of wanting to prove her strength.
   (*c*) The wish was planted in her head by someone's suggestion.
   (*d*) The wish was small and was overpowered by a sense of doubt.

III. Read the following extract and answer the questions/ complete the sentences that follow: (5 M)

Valli found the woman absolutely repulsive — such big holes she had in her ear lobes, and such ugly earrings in them! And she could smell the betel nut the woman was chewing and see the betel juice that was threatening to spill over her lips at any moment. Ugh! — who could be sociable with such a person? "Yes, I'm travelling alone," she answered curtly. "And I've got a ticket too." "Yes, she's on her way to town," said the conductor. "With a thirty-paise ticket." But the old woman went on with her drivel. "Is it proper for such a young person to travel alone? Do you know exactly where you're going in town? What's the street? What's the house number?" "You needn't bother about me.

1. "Valli found the woman absolutely repulsive". What do you mean by "repulsive"? **(1)**
   (*a*) Causing strong dislike (*b*) Showing displeasure
   (*c*) Attractive (*d*) Admirable
2. Valli told the conductor to mind his own business and laughed as well. This shows that Valli... **(1)**
   (*a*) Was not bothered about what the conductor said.
   (*b*) Didn't like the conductor speaking about her.
   (*c*) Disliked what the conductor said but was amused.
   (*d*) Was impressed with what the conductor said.
3. The old woman went on with her drivel. Why is the word 'drivel' used here? It is used to show that the old woman: **(1)**
   (*a*) Was talking non-stop.
   (*b*) Kept muttering a lot of nonsense.
   (*c*) Was giving advice on request.
   (*d*) Spoke non-stop about herself.
4. Describe Valli's reaction to the elderly woman's questions and appearance in about 40 words. **(2)**

Subjective Questions

Short Answer Questions (40-50 words) (3 M)

1. How does "Madam Rides the Bus" challenge the societal norms and expectations regarding gender roles and independence?
2. Valli was sensitive, but at the same time she was fearless and quite determined. Explain with reference to the text. **(CBSE, 2022)**
3. Observing people and the environment can provide a wealth of knowledge, as demonstrated in the story "Madam Rides the Bus", where Valli learns many lessons during her bus ride. Mention the traits of her character which help her to learn from her surroundings.
4. How did Valli gather the details of the bus journey? **(CBSE, 2023)**

Long Answer Questions (100-120 words) (6 M)

5. Valli was an extra-ordinary girl who had self-confidence and courage to realise her ambition by planning and drawing on her spirit of adventure. Discuss in reference to the chapter 'Madam Rides the Bus'. **(CBSE, 2023)**
6. "Never mind", she said, "I can get on by myself." "You don't have to help me," said Valli to the conductor. She shows extraordinary courage in taking the bus journey all alone. Taking inspiration from Valli's character, write how the ability and courage to take risks are essential to fulfill one's dream.

OR

Valli shows extraordinary courage in taking a bus journey all alone. Explain how ability and courage are essential to fulfill one's dream. **(CBSE SQP, 2020)**

7. What kind of person is Valli? Illustrate your answer from the text that you have read.
8. The people and surroundings are a great book to learn from. Valli in the lesson 'Madam Rides the Bus' learns a lot from others. Mention the traits of her character which help her to learn from people and her surroundings. **(CBSE, 2023)**

ANSWERS & EXPLANATIONS

Answer Key

Multiple Choice Questions

1. (*a*) **2.** (*a*) **3.** (*c*) **4.** (*d*) **5.** (*d*) **6.** (*d*) **7.** (*b*) **8.** (*d*) **9.** (*a*) **10.** (*d*)

Explanations

Extract-Based Questions

I. 1. (*d*) Valli gets to ride the bus for free.

2. Valli's emotions when she sees the bus filled with a new set of passengers each time are likely characterized by excitement and wonder. The continuous arrival of new passengers may evoke curiosity and a sense of adventure in her, making her feel delighted as she observes the ever-changing faces and stories of the people who board the bus.

3. (*a*) A description of Valli's fascination with the bus.

4. In performing the extract, the actor should emphasize the word "joy" with an enthusiastic tone and animated expression to convey Valli's excitement.

II. 1. (*c*) Had a strong desire to take a ride on the bus.

2. (*b*) (i), (iii) and (iv)

3. (*a*) Drivel means nonsense. Here, the old lady was continuously muttering something to herself that no one else could make any meaning of.

4. (*d*) (i) vigorous (ii) overpowering (iii) longingly.

5. (*a*) The wish developed in her head over a period of time.

III. 1. (*a*) Causing strong dislike.

2. (*c*) Disliked what the conductor said but was amused.

3. (*b*) Kept muttering a lot of nonsense.

4. Valli really didn't like the woman sitting next to her on the bus because of the woman's large earrings and the way she chewed betel nut. She thought the woman looked and smelled unpleasant. Even when the woman tried to talk to her, Valli was very brief and a bit rude in her response. She just wanted to be left alone and enjoy her ride. She made it clear that she was independent, showing she didn't need help or company, especially not from someone she didn't find pleasant.

Subjective Questions

Short Answer Questions

CBSE Marking Scheme: Content-1 M, Organisation of Ideas-1 M, Accuracy-1 M

1. "Madam Rides the Bus" tells the story of Valliammai, a young girl who bravely takes a bus ride alone, showcasing her independence and courage. In a society where girls are often expected to be protected and sheltered, Valli's adventure challenges these norms. Her confidence in navigating the journey without adult supervision defies traditional gender roles. The story highlights that age

and gender shouldn't limit one's curiosity and desire for independence. Valli's journey symbolizes breaking free from societal expectations and taking charge of one's own experiences.

2. Valli was an eight years old confident and bold young girl. In order to fulfill her overwhelming desire of going on a bus journey to the nearby town, she with her determination planned and re-planned her journey smartly. She did not feel afraid to travel alone in the bus and confidently executed her journey. She enjoyed watching the young cow galloping with her tail up in front of the bus while on her journey to the town.

   She resisted all her temptation before the bus journey and also when she reached the town due to her determination. Her sensitive nature could be seen when she sees the same cow dead on the roadside on her way back home and became extremely sad. Hence, Valli was a confident, determined, sensitive and fearless young girl.

3. Valli had a dream of riding on a bus and was very eager to make it happen. This curiosity drove her to listen to the conversations of others on the bus and discreetly ask questions to gather more information about the journey.

   During the trip, Valli displayed confidence and maturity beyond her years, staying focused on fulfilling her dream and resisting the temptation to explore the town. On the return journey, she had a realization about death when she encountered[9] a dead cow, accepting it as a natural part of life. Overall, the bus journey taught Valli many valuable lessons.

4. Valli picked up various small details about the bus journey by listening carefully to conversations between her neighbours and people who regularly used the bus. She would ask a few detailed questions here and there to collect more information. She inquired secretly, seeking information about the bus schedule, travel time, and cost. Her curiosity led her to uncover every small detail related to the bus journey.

Long Answer Questions

CBSE Marking Scheme: Expression-2 M, Accuracy-1 M

5. Valli, the protagonist of 'Madam Rides the Bus', is an extraordinary girl who demonstrates self-confidence and courage in pursuing her ambition. **(1 M)**

   Her determination to undertake the bus journey and her willingness to take risks in the process show how self-belief and courage can lead to success. **(1 M)**

   Valli's journey also highlights the importance of seizing opportunities and learning from them, even if they come disguised as challenges. By stepping out of her comfort zone and believing in herself, Valli sets an inspiring example for others to follow. **(1 M)**

6. To achieve one's goals, one must have the ability and courage to take calculated risks. Valli, an eight-year-old girl, mustered[11] the courage to take a bus journey by herself. Valli had set the target to take a bus ride outside her village even if just once. She was aware that she might face various challenges, but her strong will didn't let anything come in the way. She carefully considered her options and began saving money for the ride. She resisted every temptation that came her way. **(1 M)**

   With firm determination and strong will, she was able to fulfil her desire all on her own.

   Her confidence and dignity made the conductor call her 'Madam'. She fulfilled her desire with extraordinary courage and self-respect. **(1 M)**

   Nevertheless, we can say that the task that seems to be difficult is not so challenging, we can easily accomplish it if we have the ability and courage to take the risk. If we do not dare to take risks, we lose opportunities to get better. **(1 M)**

Nailing the Right Answer

Analyze the character traits of Valli to showcase her courage and determination.

Use specific examples from the text to support how Valli's risk-taking ability helped her achieve her dream.

7. Valli showed several admirable qualities, such as determination, confidence, and bravery. She was also a skilled planner and executor, as seen by her ability to sacrifice things like sweets and merry-go-round rides in order to save money for her bus journey. This level of sacrifice is impressive for a child of her age. **(1 M)**

   Additionally, Valli showed confidence and maturity while on the bus, not allowing the presence of elders to intimidate[12] her. **(1 M)**

   When the bus arrived at the town, Valli resisted the urge to explore or indulge in a drink, as she wanted to save her money for the return journey. She made wise decisions with her money and demonstrated[13] good manners by politely refusing the conductor's offer of a drink. **(1 M)**

Mistakes 101 : What not to do!

Students may describe Valli's actions without analyzing how they demonstrate qualities like determination, confidence, and bravery.

[9] **Encountered:** unexpected meeting
[10] **Perseverance:** determination
[11] **Mustered:** gathered; collected
[12] **Intimidate:** scare
[13] **Demonstrated:** showed

Valli, an eight-year old girl, drew pleasure from the simplest of things. The most fascinating thing of all, to her, was the bus that plied between her village and the nearby town. So enthralled was she by it that she decided to ride on the bus. But, this was not bravado of the foolhardy kind for her decision was accompanied by meticulous planning.

Over a period of several days and months, Valli listened carefully to the conversations between her neighbours and those who travelled by the bus and herself asked discreet questions here and there. In this manner, she picked up numerous small details about the journey- the distance (six miles), the duration (forty five minutes), the fare (thirty paise one way) and the bus schedule. That she saw her plans executed to perfection was apparent from the way she thriftily saved whatever stray coins came her way, resisting every temptation to purchase toys, peppermints, balloons and a ride on the merry-go-round at the village fair and finally slipping out of the house without her mother's knowledge (while her mother took her afternoon nap).

Her pride at being able to afford the fare was evident from how she repeatedly stressed on her having bought a ticket on her own. Her childlike fascination for the scenery, the shops and the crowds was contagious. She was observant enough to have recognised the young cow lying dead by the roadside and spared a moment to grieve for it - a proof of her sensitive nature. Letting nothing spoil her fun, she took every precaution for a safe journey - refusing to divulge information to strangers, disembarking from the bus and wandering alone on the crowded streets. But, what stood out was her self-respect and maturity when she declined the conductor's offer of a drink as she was unable to pay for it. In this world of civilised, apathetic adults, Valli's innocence was refreshing.

THE SERMON AT BENARES

[Source: Betty Renshaw Values and Voices: A College Reader (1975)]

8

Narrative Sketch

1. Gautama Buddha, born as Siddhartha Gautama, was a prince in northern India who lived from 563 B.C. to 483 B.C.
2. At the age of twenty-five, he encountered the sufferings of the world for the first time and was deeply moved.
3. Seeking enlightenment, he wandered for seven years and eventually sat under a peepal tree, vowing not to move until he attained enlightenment.
4. After seven days, he achieved enlightenment and became known as the Buddha or the Enlightened One.
5. The Buddha began teaching and sharing his newfound wisdom.
6. He encountered Kisa Gotami, a grieving mother, and used her experience to convey the universal nature of suffering and death.
7. Kisa Gotami was a woman who experienced profound grief when her only son died.
8. Desperate to find a cure for her son, she sought help from her neighbours, but they told her that her child was dead.
9. Eventually, she learned about the Buddha and went to him, pleading for medicine that could bring her son back to life.
10. The Buddha asked her to bring him a handful of mustard seeds from a house where no one had experienced the death of a loved one, teaching her a valuable lesson about the universality of suffering and death.

11 The Buddha emphasized that death is inevitable and affects all living beings.

12 He advised against excessive grief and lamentation, stating that they do not bring peace or save the dead.

13 Instead, he encouraged seeking peace of mind and overcoming sorrow through inner composure.

BEFORE YOU READ

Theme

The Sermon at Benares highlights the early life of Gautam Buddha and his preachings[1] that ended the suffering of a grieving mother, Kisa Gautami. The Buddha says that everything in this world is subject to death. He further states that the world is deeply affected by suffering, disease, or pain. The one who overcomes that sorrow will be free from it and be blessed.

Important Characters' Sketch

- **Kisa Gautami:** Kisa Gautami was a grieving mother who had lost her son. With Buddha's preachings, Kisa realised she was selfish in her grief. She understood the bitter truth that sorrows are part and parcel of life, and one can attain peace only by acceptance.
- **Gautam Buddha:** Siddhartha Gautama, born into a royal family in North India and raised as a prince, embarked on his educational journey with the Hindu sacred texts at the age of twelve. At twenty-five, during a hunting expedition, a transformative encounter with a sick individual, an elderly person, a funeral, and a monk seeking alms profoundly altered his perspective. Motivated by these revelations, he chose to forsake his royal privileges in search of deeper spiritual insights. Following his enlightenment, he began to share his teachings, earning the title "Buddha," signifying the Awakened or Enlightened One.

SYNOPSIS

Gautama Buddha, was born a prince in Northern India, as Siddhartha Gautama. At the age of twelve, he was sent away to study sacred Hindu scriptures. At sixteen, he returned home to marry a princess. Soon, both were blessed with a son, and they continued to live a royal life for about ten years. Until about the age of twenty-five, the Prince did not know of suffering for himself and the world.

One day, on his way to hunt, the Prince crossed paths with a sick man, an aged man, a funeral procession and a monk who was begging. The experience acted as an eye-opener for him, and he left the royal life behind to seek a higher sense of spiritual knowledge concerning those sufferings.

After wandering for seven years, he sat under a peepal tree to wait for enlightenment.[2]

Enlightened after seven days, he renamed the tree the Bodhi Tree (Tree of Wisdom) and began preaching. Now known as the Buddha (the Awakened or the Enlightened), he gave his first sermon in the city of Benares. It reflects Buddha's wisdom on one of the most sorrowful incidence. A lady named Kisa Gotami had lost her only son. Suffering from unending pain, she went from house to house, asking for medicine to bring her son back to life. People thought that the lady had lost her senses. One day, she met a man who directed her towards Buddha, who could have a solution to her problem. When Kisa reached him and asked for the cure for his boy, Buddha asked her to get mustard seeds from a house where no one had lost a child, husband, parent, or friend. The poor woman now went on a search from house to house. While people offered her a mustard seed, they asked her not to remind them of their greatest grief as every household had more deaths than the living. There was no house where a beloved had not died.

[1] **Preaching:** religious teaching
[2] **Enlightenment:** wisdom; awakening

Kisa was disheartened and hopeless. She sat at the edge of the road watching the lights of the city flickering[3] and extinguishing[4] again, leading to darkness all around. At that moment, Kisa realised how selfish she had been. She recognised that the lives of men are like those flickering lights which flicker and extinguish at the end. She realised that death is common to all and no one can escape it.

Buddha said that mortals are affected by grief and pain, and there is no way in which a living being can avoid death. As a ripe fruit is in danger of falling, a living being is always in danger of dying. As an earthen vessel ends up being broken, such is the life of mortals irrespective of wisdom, power or wealth. A father cannot save his son, nor can kinsmen[5] save their relations. The world is affected by suffering, disease or pain; therefore, the wise do not grieve, knowing the reality of life.

Nobody receives peace of mind by weeping or grieving; the suffering increases, and the body suffers in pain. The dead do not come alive. One who wants peace should draw out sorrow, complaints and grief. It is the only way to attain peace of mind and be blessed.

Lessons to learn

- Highlights the universality of suffering and death.
- External remedies may be unhelpful.
- True healing must come from within.
- True wisdom and enlightenment come from letting go of your pain.

NCERT EXERCISE

Thinking about the Text

(NCERT, Page 135)

1. When her son dies, Kisa Gotami goes from house to house. What does she ask for? Does she get it? Why not?

Ans. When Kisa Gotami lost her only son, she was filled with grief. She carried her son and went from house to house, asking for medicine to cure her child. No, she did not receive it, and people felt she had lost her senses. There is no medicine in the world that could bring a dead person to life.

2. Kisa Gotami again goes from house to house after she speaks with the Buddha. What does she ask for the second time around? Does she get it? Why not?

Ans. When Kisa Gotami cried and asked Buddha for medicine to revive her son, he told her to get mustard seeds from a house where no one had lost a child, husband, parent, or friend. She went from house to house trying to get the condition fulfilled, but she couldn't find any house where no loved

[3] **Flickering:** wavering; shining unsteadily
[4] **Extinguish:** put out; cease to burn
[5] **Kinsmen:** (formal use)- blood relative/family

one had died. People said that the living are fewer and the dead are many. They didn't want to be reminded of their grief.

3. **What does Kisa Gotami understand the second time that she failed to understand the first time? Was this what the Buddha wanted her to understand?**

Ans. Kisa Gotami understood that death is inevitable[6]. Nobody can escape death, and she was being selfish in her mourning. In her search to get mustard seeds, there was no home where a loved one had not died. Yes, the Buddha wanted her to understand this, and she had the realisation while watching the city lights flickering and extinguishing.

4. **Why do you think Kisa Gotami understood this only the second time? In what way did the Buddha change her understanding?**

Ans. When Kisa Gotami lost her only son, she was just thinking about her grief and looking for a cure to bring her dead son to life. The second time Kisa met Buddha, he asked her to get a handful of mustard seeds from a house where no one had died. When she found no house like that, she got hopeless and sat on the wayside, watching the city lights flickering and extinguishing. During this experience, Kisa realised that the lives of mortals flicker up and are extinguished. Death affects everyone, and it was selfish of her to be grieving.

This was the message the Buddha wanted her to receive. He said that mortals are affected by grief and pain, and there is no way in which a living being can avoid death. This is the lesson that Kisa Gotami learned because of Gautam Buddha's preachings.

5. **How do you usually understand the idea of 'selfishness'? Do you agree with Kisa Gotami that she was being 'selfish in her grief'?**

Ans. Selfishness is when a person only thinks about themselves. They are concerned about their own happiness and suffering. When Kisa Gotami lost her only son, she couldn't bear the pain of it. She carried the dead child from house to house, searching for medicine to revive her son. She didn't realise that she was not the only one facing the harsh reality of life. Every house has seen death and suffered the pain of losing their loved ones.

It is natural to be saddened by the death of someone close to you. However, Kisa Gotami was so consumed by her grief that she forgot to see the truth of life.

MISCELLANEOUS EXERCISE

Multiple Choice Questions

1. Till what age was Gautam Buddha shielded from the sufferings of the world?
   (*a*) Twenty-two (*b*) Twenty-four
   (*c*) Twenty-nine (*d*) Twenty-five
2. Under which tree Buddha vowed to say until enlightenment came?
   (*a*) Banyan (*b*) Bodhi
   (*c*) Ashoka (*d*) Peepal
3. What does the ripe fruit fear?
   (*a*) Someone eating it (*b*) Rotting
   (*c*) Falling down (*d*) None of these
4. Which of the following represents the correct understanding of the word "poor" in the phrase "Poor Kisa Gautami"?
   (*a*) Inferior (*b*) Unfortunate
   (*c*) Weak (*d*) In need of money
5. "Do not remind us of our deepest grief." The tone of the speaker is ______________.
   (*a*) Disillusioned (*b*) Sceptical
   (*c*) Ironic (*d*) Solemn
6. Pick the option that explains — '...the living are few, but the dead many.'
   (*a*) It shows the high death rate and low birth rate in the city of Benares.
   (*b*) It highlights the holy status of Benares, where many Hindus go to die.
   (*c*) It throws light on the numerous loved ones the villagers had lost over time.
   (*d*) It reflects that many children had died in the village for various reasons.
7. How can one become free from sorrow?
   (*a*) By overcoming it.
   (*b*) By feeling it.
   (*c*) By forgetting it.
   (*d*) We cannot get rid of it.
8. What is the world afflicted with?
   (*a*) Love (*b*) Diseases
   (*c*) Death and Decay (*d*) All of these

[6] **Inevitable:** unavoidable

9. In his childhood, what was Gautam Buddha shielded from?

(a) Pleasures (b) Death

(c) Wisdom (d) Sorrows of the world

10. What did Gautam Buddha name the tree under which he got enlightenment ________ tree.

(a) Peepal (b) Banyan

(c) Ashoka (d) Bodhi

Extract-Based Questions

I. Read the following extract and answer the questions / complete the sentences that follow: (5 M)

The Buddha answered, "I want a handful of mustard seed." And when the girl in her joy promised to procure it, the Buddha added, "The mustard seed must be taken from a house where no one has lost a child, husband, parent or friend." Poor Kisa Gotami now went from house to house, and the people pitied her and said, "Here is mustard seed; take it!" But when she asked, "Did a son or daughter, a father or mother, die in your family?" they answered her, "Alas! the living are few, but the dead are many. Do not remind us of our deepest grief." And there was no house but some beloved one had died in it.

1. Why did Buddha ask Gotami to take mustard seed? (1)

(a) To see her the growing nature of mustard seeds

(b) To show her how nature work

(c) To see her the truth of life and death

(d) To see her how many house give her the seeds

2. Before taking mustard seeds, why did Gotami ask in every house whether anyone had ever died in that house? (1)

(a) Because Buddha made her realize that death is the ultimate reality.

(b) Because Buddha told her that she could use the mustard seeds for her son.

(c) Because she wanted to grow in her field.

(d) She wanted to check that any house wouldn't have.

3. Based on the passage, what can be inferred about the common human experience of loss and grief? (1)

4. How do the responses of the people Kisa Gotami visited contribute to the overall theme of the passage? (2)

II. Read the following extract and answer the questions/ complete the sentences that follow: (5 M)

Buddha said, "The life of mortals in this world is troubled and brief and combined with pain. For there is not any means by which those that have been born can avoid dying; after reaching old age there is death; of such a nature are living beings. As ripe fruits are early in danger of falling, so mortals, when born, are always in danger of death. As all earthen vessels made by the Potter end in being broken, so is the life of mortals. Both young and adult, both those who are fools and those who are wise, all fall. into the power of death, all are subject to death."

1. 'As all earthen vessels made by the Potter end in being broken', what is the meaning of this line by Buddha? (1)

(a) Life of the mortal ultimately fall in happiness.

(b) Life of the mortal ultimately fall in death.

(c) Life of the immortal ultimately fall in death.

(d) There is no life in the mortal world.

2. According to the passage, could both young and adults who are wise be saved from death? (1)

(a) Yes they could be saved because they are wise.

(b) No they couldn't be saved.

(c) Only young could be saved.

(d) Only adults could be saved.

3. Based on the passage, what can be inferred about the inevitability of death in the life of mortals? (1)

4. Why does the Buddha compare the life of mortals to ripe fruits and earthen vessels made by a Potter? (2)

III. Read the following extract and answer the questions / complete the sentences that follow: (5 M)

Not from weeping nor from grieving will anyone obtain peace of mind; on the contrary, his pain will be greater and his body will suffer... He who seeks peace should draw out the arrow of lamentation and complaint and grief. He who has drawn out the arrow and has become composed will obtain peace of mind. **(CBSE QB)**

1. If the Buddha were a counsellor, which of the following options would you find in a brochure of his service? (1)

(i) (ii) (iii) (iv)

(a) Image (i) (b) Image (ii)

(c) Image (iii) (d) Image (iv)

2. Which of the following statements cannot be attributed to the Buddha based on the given extract? (1)

(i) Pain and grief are unavoidable and necessary.

(ii) The inevitability of death makes grieving futile.

(iii) Universality of grief and pain makes us sad.

(iv) Understanding that life is finite leads to wisdom.

(a) (i) and (ii) (b) (i) and (iii)

(c) (iii) and (iv) (d) (i) and (iv)

3. Chose the option that appropriately completes the following: (1)

lamentation : grief : ________ : ________

(a) laughter : joke

(b) discomfort : fear

(c) celebration : joy

(d) resignation: loss

4. According to the Buddha, peace of mind is attainable by those who **(1)**

(*a*) renounce worldly life like the Buddha
(*b*) take out the arrow and become strong
(*c*) grieve, suffer and then move on
(*d*) recognise terms of life and let go of complaint

5. The given extract is paraphrased below. Choose the option that includes the most appropriate solutions for the blanks. **(1)**

The act of (i) _______ is not only pointless but rather (ii) ______, causing pain and suffering. It only serves to (iii) __________ peace of mind. (iv) __________ without complaint is crucial to well-being and peace.

(*a*) grief, harmful, destroy, accepting
(*b*) grieving, counterproductive, take away, acceptance
(*c*) weeping, productive, take away, lamentation
(*d*) grieving, harmful, destroying, lamenting

IV. Read the following extract and answer the questions / complete the sentences that follow: **(5 M)**

At about the age of twenty-five, the Prince, heretofore shielded from the sufferings of the world while out hunting, chanced upon a sick man, then an aged man, then a funeral procession, and finally a monk begging for alms. These sights so moved him that he at once went out into the world to seek enlightenment concerning the sorrows he had witnessed.

1. Who was the Prince? **(1)**

(*a*) Siddhartha Gautama (*b*) Son of Siddhartha Gautama
(*c*) Kisa Gotami's son (*d*) None of the above

2. What is enlightenment in the given passage? **(1)**

(*a*) Honesty (*b*) Strong will
(*c*) Deep understanding (*d*) Spiritual knowledge

3. Based on the passage, what can be inferred about the impact of witnessing suffering on the Prince? **(1)**

4. How did the Prince's sheltered life prior to witnessing suffering contribute to his decision to seek enlightenment? **(2)**

Subjective Questions

Short Answer Questions (40-50 words) (3 M)

1. What is the significance of the Buddha's request for a handful of mustard seeds and the addition of a condition to it? **(CBSE SQP, 2021)**
2. Do you think being enlightened placed a far greater responsibility on the Buddha than being king would have? Justify your stance. **(CBSE, QB)**
3. Why did Buddha choose Benares to preach his first sermon?
4. Why did Prince Siddhartha decide to renounce the world?
5. What did Kisa Gotami do after the death of her only son? **(CBSE, 2023)**

Long Answer Questions (100-120 words) (6 M)

6. Describe the journey of Siddhartha Gautama becoming the Buddha. **(CBSE, 2020)**
7. 'As ripe fruits are in danger of falling early, so mortals when born are always in danger of death'. With this statement of the Buddha find out the moral values that Kisa Gotami learnt after the death of her child. **(CBSE, 2023)**
8. What lesson on death and suffering did the Buddha teach Kisa Gotami in the chapter, 'The Sermon at Benares'?
9. How does Buddha bring about a different perspective in Kisa Gotami's understanding of life? **(CBSE, 2022)**
10. What message might the Buddha's story hold for those who are in positions of power and privilege? **(CBSE, 2024)**
11. What did Siddhartha Gautama come across by chance when he was about twenty-five years old? **(CBSE, 2023)**

ANSWERS & EXPLANATIONS

Answer Key

Multiple Choice Questions

1. (*d*) **2.** (*d*) **3.** (*c*) **4.** (*b*) **5.** (*d*) **6.** (*c*) **7.** (*a*) **8.** (*c*) **9.** (*d*) **10.** (*d*)

Explanations

Extract-Based Questions

I. 1. (*c*) To see her the truth of life and death

2. (*a*) Because Buddha made her realize that death is the ultimate reality.

3. The passage suggests that the experience of loss and grief is a universal and shared aspect of the human condition.

4. The responses of the people emphasize the universality of loss and grief. Each household acknowledges that death has touched them and that the living are few while the dead are many. This reinforces the idea that suffering is a shared human experience and highlights the futility of seeking a mustard seed from a house untouched by loss.

II. 1. (*b*) Life of the mortal ultimately fall in death.

2. (*b*) No they couldn't be saved.

3. The passage implies that death is an unavoidable reality for all living beings, regardless of their age, wisdom, or circumstances.

4. The Buddha uses these metaphors to illustrate the vulnerability and fragility of human life. Just as ripe fruits are prone to falling and earthen vessels are destined to break, mortals are always at risk of death. This comparison highlights the universal nature of mortality and the temporary nature of existence.

Key Takeaway

Simile and metaphor are both figures of speech used to make comparisons, but they do so in slightly different ways:

Simile: A simile explicitly compares two different things by using connecting words such as "like" or "as." It helps to make a description more vivid and understandable by linking an unfamiliar or complex idea with a familiar one.

Metaphor: A metaphor makes a comparison too, but it does so directly, without using connecting words. It states that one thing is another, creating a symbolic relationship between them.

It can provide a strong image or idea by asserting that one thing embodies another's qualities or characteristics.

III. 1. (*c*) Image (iii)

2. (*b*) (i) and (iii)

3. (*c*) celebration : joy

4. (*d*) recognise terms of life and let go of complaint

5. (*b*) grieving, counterproductive, take away, acceptance

IV. 1. (*a*) Siddhartha Gautama

2. (*d*) Spiritual knowledge

3. Witnessing suffering prompted the Prince to seek enlightenment.

4. The Prince's sheltered life shielded him from the harsh realities of the world, but witnessing the sufferings of others shattered his illusion of a carefree existence. The stark contrast between the Prince's sheltered life and the sufferings he witnessed shattered his illusions, compelling him to seek enlightenment and gain a deeper understanding of the human experience.

Subjective Questions

Short Answer Questions

CBSE Marking Scheme: Content-1 M, Organisation of Ideas-1 M, Accuracy-1 M

1. Mustard seeds were readily available in every household. When Kisa Gotami heard Buddha asking for a handful of mustard seeds, she happily promised to get them. The Buddha added that the seeds must be procured from a house where no one has lost a loved one. The Buddha's request for a handful of mustard seeds was significant.

The same mustard seeds were common in every household, and death and suffering were common too.

2. Yes, being enlightened placed a far greater responsibility on the Buddha than being king would have.

If he had stayed in the royal family, he would have had to serve his kingdom and people. However, by being enlightened and gaining wisdom, he had to serve the whole of humanity which is a greater responsibility than being a king.

Nailing the Right Answer

Justify your stance with a comparison between serving the kingdom as a king and serving humanity as an enlightened being.

3. Benares is the holiest of the dipping places along the river Ganges.

When Prince Siddharth Gautama went out to seek enlightenment, he sat under a peepal tree. After seven days, he gained enlightenment and became known as the Buddha. He preached his first sermon in the city of Benares, which has been preserved till now.

4. One day when Siddhartha set out for a city tour he encountered people in different states of their being. He came across an old man, a sick man, a funeral procession and a monk begging for alms.

Looking at their conditions, he was filled with pity and curiosity to find the reason behind all that. He decided to look for the truth of life, eventually, he renounced the world and set out searching for the truth.

5. After the death of her only son, Kisa Gotami went from house to house, asking if anyone had a medicine to cure her son. When someone suggested she visited the Buddha, she went to him and asked if he could bring her son back to life. He asked her to bring him mustard seeds from a house where no one had died, and in doing so, she realized the universality of death and the need to accept it.

Long Answer Questions

CBSE Marking Scheme: Expression-2 M, Accuracy-1 M

6. Gautam Buddha was born as Prince Siddhartha Gautam in northern India. Till the age of about twenty-five, he had been shielded from the sufferings of the world. **(1 M)**

   One day, while hunting, he saw a sick man, an aged man, a funeral and a monk asking for help. These sights moved him so much that he went out into the world to seek enlightenment concerning the sorrows he had witnessed. **(1 M)**

   He wandered for seven years, finally sat down under a peepal tree, and received enlightenment after seven days. He renamed the tree the Bodhi Tree (Tree of Wisdom). He then came to be known as the Buddha. The Buddha preached his first sermon in the city of Benares, which is still preserved. **(1 M)**

Mistakes 101 : What not to do!

Students may fail to explain the significance of Siddhartha's Enlightenment.

Key Takeaway

The "tree of wisdom" is a metaphorical concept that represents growth in knowledge and understanding, similar to how a tree grows and expands.

7. The statement of Lord Buddha carries profound moral values that Kisa Gotami learned after the death of her child. Firstly, she realized the universal nature of death, understanding that every mortal being is inevitably bound to face death. This taught her the value of acceptance and the futility of resisting the natural order of life. **(1 M)**

   Secondly, Kisa Gotami learned the impermanence of life, comparing it to ripe fruits that are prone to decay. This understanding led her to appreciate the transient nature of existence and the importance of cherishing each moment. **(1 M)**

   Overall, the moral values Kisa Gotami acquired included acceptance, appreciation of the present, recognition of life's impermanence, and the importance of finding inner tranquility by acknowledging the universal reality of death. **(1 M)**

8. Buddha taught that death is an inevitable part of life that all mortals experience. Just as ripe fruits fall off trees and come to an end, so do the lives of individuals. **(1 M)**

   It is a natural law that cannot be avoided. Weeping and lamenting over death cannot bring the deceased back to life. Wise individuals understand this and do not grieve excessively. **(1 M)**

   Weeping and lamenting only harm one's health and increase suffering. By letting go of sorrow and finding composure, one can attain peace of mind and overcome sorrow. **(1 M)**

9. In the story "The Sermon at Benaras," Buddha brings about a different perspective in Kisa Gotami's understanding of life by teaching her about the impermanence and universality of suffering. **(1 M)**

   When Kisa Gotami approaches Buddha in deep grief over the death of her child and asks him to bring the child back to life, Buddha instructs her to bring mustard seeds from a house where no one has experienced the loss of a loved one. As she goes from house to house, she realizes that every family has experienced the pain of death. **(1 M)**

   Through this exercise, Buddha helps Kisa Gotami understand that suffering is a natural part of life, and no one is exempt from it. This realization allows her to accept the loss of her child and find solace in the universal truth of impermanence. **(1 M)**

10. *Topper's Explanation*

(V) Gautama Buddha's story stands true for each and every person on this earth regardless of their social and political status. The people in positions and power think themselves as the rulers of the world. But they forget that whoever has taken ~~b~~ birth on this earth has to die one day. Humans are mortal. All their power, position as well as wealth will be left behind once they die. Buddha believes that only good deeds of a person remains with him always. According to Buddha, we should not be self-centered in our life because ~~this~~ it is the truth of life that 'no one can escape the cycle of life'. Wise people are those who do not grieve.

11. *Topper's Explanation*

Prince Siddhartha Gautama had hitherto been sheltered from the sufferings of the world. Once, while out hunting, he chanced upon an aged man, a sick man, a funeral procession and at last, a monk begging for alms. He was so moved by these sights, that he, at once, left his life of luxury and set out into the world, seeking ~~enlightenment~~ enlightenment which he attained under a peepal tree (the Bodhi Tree).

THE PROPOSAL

—Anton Chekhov

9

Narrative Sketch

1. "The Proposal" is a comedic one-act play by Anton Chekhov about marriage and property disputes.
2. Lomov arrives at Chubukov's home to ask for his daughter, Natalya's hand in marriage, dressed formally for the occasion.
3. Initial excitement from Chubukov about the marriage proposal quickly turns into a quarrel over property boundaries.
4. The dispute centers around the ownership of Oxen Meadows, claimed by both families.
5. The argument escalates with both of them repeatedly asserting their ownership of the land.
6. Chubukov intervenes and sides with his daughter, declaring that the meadows belong to their family.
7. The tension and disagreement between the characters heighten, setting the stage for further conflict and resolution.
8. The play satirizes the social conventions of the Russian landed gentry and their absurd concerns over status.
9. Eventually, Lomov and Natalya awkwardly and chaotically become engaged, hinting at a future filled with disputes.
10. Chekhov humorously portrays the irony of human nature, where material disputes overshadow personal connections.
11. "The Proposal" remains a classic for its comedic examination of marriage negotiations and human relationships.

BEFORE YOU READ

Theme

The play by Anton Chekhov is a farce[1] drama dealing with three quarrelsome[2] characters. The characters frequently quarrel over trivial matters. However, amidst the quarrelling, they forget the main issue: the marriage proposal. Lomov, a wealthy bachelor, came with a marriage proposal for Chubukov's daughter, Natalya. Although both fought throughout the play, economic sense wins in the end. In order to maintain their social status, wealthy families have a tendency to seek out relationships with other wealthy families.

Important Characters' Sketch

- **Stepan Stepanovitch Chubukov:** Chubukov is a greedy, short-tempered but practical landowner and a neighbour of Lomov, another wealthy landowner. Chubukov wishes to get his daughter married to Lomov. As soon as he hears that the latter has come with a marriage proposal, he joins in the fights immaturely. However, in the end, he hurriedly gets his daughter married to Lomov before another argument pops up.
- **Natalya Stepanovna:** Natalya, twenty-five, is the daughter of Chubukov. Her father calls her 'love-sick' as she is desperate to get married and would accept any man who proposes to her. She has a bad temper and fights on various occasions with her neighbour, who has brought a marriage proposal for her. Lomov considers Natalya an educated, average-looking, excellent housekeeper who might be a suitable match for him. She ends up marrying him even though they quarrel a lot until the end.
- **Ivan Vassilevitch Lomov:** Lomov is a thirty-five-year-old wealthy man who suffers from palpitations and has trouble sleeping peacefully. He wants to get married. He is a neighbour of Chubukov and wishes to marry Chubukov's daughter, Natalya. Even though he is not entirely in love with her, he finds no harm in marrying her as she is a suitable match. The two tend to fight over minor issues and call mean things to each others' families, but they end up getting married.

SYNOPSIS

The play begins with Lomov, a wealthy landowner, entering his neighbour Chubukov's house dressed formally. Chubukov asked if he was going somewhere. Lomov revealed that he specifically came to meet Chubukov. Chubukov assumed Lomov must have arrived to borrow money which Chubukov would not give.

Lomov stated that he had come to seek Natalya Chubukov's hand in marriage. Chubukov was overjoyed to hear this, as he had been hoping for this for a long time.

Lomov wondered if Natalya would agree to it. Chubukov added that he couldn't see why Natalya would not and exited to call her. Lomov wondered whether choosing to marry Natalya was the correct decision. He believed that she was a good housekeeper, well-educated and average looking. However, he is at a critical age of 35, suffers from palpitations and gets upset quickly. The worst of his problems is sleeping and getting up because of a pull he feels almost twenty times.

Natalya Stepanovna enters and asks Lomov for lunch, and both of them sit down. She then offers him to smoke and begins chatting with him about the weather and her field. When questioned about his coming, Lomov starts to talk about the friendly ties between their families. He mentions his Oxen Meadows touching Stepanovna's birchwoods while talking about his land.

Natalya interrupts him saying that Oxen Meadows are theirs, not his. Both argue for a while when Lomov thinks he can show the documents to clarify the confusion. However, Natalya is surprised and angry as she believes it is unfair to be told so suddenly that the land does not belong to them when they have had it for nearly three hundred years.

Both of them continued to argue that Oxen Meadows is theirs, and the argument turned heated. Chubukov then entered and the discussion continued. Lomov continued to yell because he had

Lessons to learn

- *Communication is crucial.*
- *Assumptions can lead to misunderstandings.*
- *Emotional reactions can cloud judgment.*
- *Property disputes can strain relationships.*
- *Pride can hinder resolution.*

[1] **Farce:** a comic, dramatic work
[2] **Quarrelsome:** (adjective) Ready for a fight; Argumentative

severe heart palpitations.[3] Then, infuriated[4], he called Chubukov a grabber and said he would take the matter to court. Finally, Natalya jumped into the discussion and asked her father to send the mowers[5] out to the Meadows[6] as she would not give up her Oxen Meadows.

They continued fighting and began defaming[7] each other's families.

In between the argument, Lomov's left foot went numb, and he started feeling sick and went out of the door. Talking ill about him, Chubukov then mentions to Natalya that Lomov had come up with a proposal for her. Natalya was surprised and wanted to bring him back immediately. Chubukov called Lomov back and exited in disappointment.

Natalya politely apologised and told Lomov that the Oxen Meadows belonged to him only. She pressed on moving past this topic so that Lomov could start with the proposal. However, he continued about his dog, named Guess. He was upset that his best dog, for whom he had paid 125 roubles, had gone lame. At this point, Natalya commented that it was too much as the dog was very cheap compared to his father's Squeezer, who they got at 85 roubles. They enter into a debate on their dogs and continue to do so till Lomov says his heart is palpitating and he can not continue to debate on this. Chubukov enters the scene only to make things worse again.

Everyone gets hyper, and Lomov faints because of palpitations. Chubukov, too, is feeling sick; Natalya notices Lomov has fallen and panics thinking he is dead.

They give him some water to drink, and Chubukov pushes Lomov to get married to his daughter as she is ready. Finally, they agree to get married and kiss each other. However, the quarrelling continues as Natalya keeps persisting that Squeezer is better than Guess, but Lomov refuses to accept this, and the quarrelling continues between the characters.

NCERT EXERCISE

Thinking about the Text

(NCERT, Page 157)

1. **What does Chubukov at first suspect that Lomov has come for? Is he sincere when he later says 'And I've always loved you, my angel, as if you were my own son'? Find reasons for your answer from the play.**

Ans. When Lomov came to visit Chubukov's house dressed formally, Chubukov suspected that Lomov had come to borrow money. Therefore, he was not sincere when he told Lomov that he had always loved him and that he was like his own son because he had decided not to give any money to Lomov. Only when Lomov asked for his daughter's hand in marriage did his attitude change, and he rushed out to call his daughter, Natalya.

2. **Chubukov says of Natalya: "....... as if she won't consent! She's in love; egad, she's like a lovesick cat......" Would you agree? Find reasons for your answer.**

Ans. Yes, it was true that Natalya would give her consent easily. It was clear by how she behaves when she learns that Lomov came to propose to her. She started weeping and asked her father to bring Lomov back at once. However, she didn't

[3] **Palpitations:** noticeably rapid or irregular heartbeat
[4] **Infuriated:** extremely angry
[5] **Mowers:** a person who cuts grass; a machine which cuts grass
[6] **Meadows:** a piece of grassland
[7] **Defaming:** damage the good reputation of (someone)

seem to be in love with Lomov. It seemed that both of them were more concerned about their land and their dogs.

3. (i) Find all the words and expressions in the play that the characters use to speak about each other, and the accusations and insults they hurl at each other. (For example, Lomov in the end calls Chubukov an intriguer; but earlier, Chubukov has himself called Lomov a "malicious, double-faced intriguer." Again, Lomov begins by describing Natalya as "an excellent housekeeper, not bad-looking, well-educated.")

(ii) Then think of five adjectives or adjectival expressions of your own to describe each character in the play.

(iii) Can you now imagine what these characters will quarrel about next?

Ans. (i) The words and expressions that have been used to describe each other by various characters of the play are:

Chubukov: intriguer, grabber, old rat

Natalya: a lovesick cat, an excellent housekeeper, not bad-looking, well-educated.

Lomov: a good neighbour, impudent, pettifogger, malicious, double-faced intriguer, rascal, blind hen, turnip ghost, villain, scarecrow, stuffed sausage, etc.

(ii) Lomov: assertive, weak-hearted, pretentious, proud, self-serving, argumentative.

Natalya: quarrelsome, foolish, idiotic, unwise, immature, mean

Chubukov: mean, assertive, low-minded, abusive, quarrelsome, insensible

(iii) All three characters are short-tempered and would probably fight over any minor issue. Moreover, they would fight sooner rather than later.

MISCELLANEOUS EXERCISE

Multiple Choice Questions

1. What is the play about?
   (*a*) Tendency of wealthy families to seek ties with other wealthy families.
   (*b*) Tendency of wealthy families to increase their estates.
   (*c*) Encouragement of marriages that make good economic sense.
   (*d*) All of the above.
2. The word 'proposal' has several meanings can you guess what sort of proposal the play is about?
   (*a*) A suggestion, plan or scheme for doing something.
   (*b*) An offer for a possible plan or action.
   (*c*) The act of asking someone's hand in marriage.
   (*d*) None of the above.
3. CHUBUKOV: [aside] He's come to borrow money. Shan't give him any!
   The given line reflects that Chubukov is
   (*a*) Selfish (*b*) Pretentious[8]
   (*c*) Greedy (*d*) Hypocrite[9]
4. What is their first dispute over?
   (*a*) Over the ownership of oxen meadows.
   (*b*) Over their dogs.
   (*c*) Over their marriage.
   (*d*) Over Lomov's health.
5. How much are the meadows worth approximately?
   (*a*) 200 roubles (*b*) 300 roubles
   (*c*) 400 roubles (*d*) 450 roubles
6. If, according to Chubukov and Natalya, Lomovs are not "honourable people", why do they still consider Lomov's proposal?
   (*a*) Natalya wanted to marry close by so she could take care of her father.
   (*b*) They were saying it for the sake of argument.
   (*c*) Lomov's honour and status were overrated.
   (*d*) Lomov's status is attractive to them.
7. "Are you going to a ball or what? Though I must say you look better...."
   Who is speaking and to whom?
   (*a*) Natalya to Lomov (*b*) Lomov to Natalya
   (*c*) Chubukov to Lomov (*d*) Natalya to Chubukov
8. "And it's impossible for me not to marry". Who says this?
   (*a*) Lomov (*b*) Chubukov
   (*c*) Lomov's grandmother (*d*) Natalya
9. Why was Natalya arguing about the land?
   (*a*) She liked to argue about anything.
   (*b*) It was worth a lot.
   (*c*) She can't stand unfairness.
   (*d*) All of the above.
10. Who threatened to take the matter to court?
    (*a*) Chubukov (*b*) Lomov
    (*c*) Natalya (*d*) Anton Chekhov

[8] **Pretentious:** attempting to impress artificial

[9] **Hypocrite:** fraud; imposter; cheater

Extract-Based Questions

I. Read the following extract and answer the questions/ complete the sentences that follow: (5 M)

LOMOV: It's cold... I'm trembling all over, just as if I'd got an examination before me. The great thing is , I must have my mind made up. If I give myself time to think, to hesitate, to talk a lot, to look for an ideal, or for real love, then I'll never get married. Brr...It's cold! Natalya Stepanovna is an excellent housekeeper, not bad-looking, well-educated. What more do I want? But I'm getting a noise in my ears from excitement. (Drinks) And it's impossible for me not to marry.

In the first place, I'm already 35_ a critical age, so to speak. In the second place, I ought to lead a quiet and regular life. I suffer from palpitations, I'm excitable and always getting awfully upset; at this very moment my lips are trembling, and there's a twitch in my right eyebrow. **(CBSE SQP, 2023)**

1. Which of the following is NOT a reason why Lomov thinks he must marry? **(1)**

   A. He is already 35 years old.

   B. He suffers from palpitations.

   C. He is excitable and easily upset.

   D. He is in love with Natalya.

2. Why is it fair to say that Lomov's tone, when he says "What more do I want?", is uncertain and questioning? Answer in about 40 words. **(2)**

3. Read the following descriptions (A)-(C) and identify which one correctly corresponds to the extract. **(1)**

   A. A debate is a formal discussion on a particular topic, usually with two or more people presenting different viewpoints and arguments.

   B. A soliloquy is a speech given by a character alone on stage, which reveals their innermost thoughts and feelings to the audience.

   C. An aside is a brief comment or remark made by a character directly to the audience, which is not intended to be heard by other characters on stage.

4. If an actor were to enact this extract, what would he be required to focus on, while modulating his voice? **(1)**

II. Read the following extract and answer the questions/ complete the sentences that follow: (5 M)

I can make you a present of them myself because they're mine! Your behaviour, Ivan Vassilevitch, is strange, to say the least! Up to this, we have always thought of you as a good neighbour, a friend; last year we lent you our threshing machine, although on that account we had to put off our own threshing till November, you behave to us as if we were gypsies. Giving me my own land, indeed! No, really, that's not at all neighbourly! In my opinion, it's even impudent, if you want to know.

1. The word "impudent" in the passage most closely means: **(1)**

   (*a*) Friendly (*b*) Polite

   (*c*) Arrogant (*d*) Generous

2. Which of the following statements represents the speaker's opinion? **(1)**

   (*a*) "Your behavior is strange, to say the least!"

   (*b*) "We have always thought of you as a good neighbor, a friend."

   (*c*) "You behaved to us as if we were gypsies."

   (*d*) "Last year we lent you our threshing machine, although on that account we had to put off our own threshing till November."

3. Based on the passage, what can be inferred about the speaker's relationship with Ivan Vassilevitch? **(1)**

4. How does the speaker feel about Ivan Vassilevitch giving them their own land? **(2)**

III. Read the following extract and answer the questions/ complete the sentences that follow: (5 M)

Natalya Stepanovna is an excellent housekeeper, not bad-looking, well-educated. What more do I want? But I'm getting a noise in my ears from excitement. [Drinks] And it's impossible for me not to marry. In the first place, I'm already 35 — a critical age, so to speak. In the second place, I ought to lead a quiet and regular life. I suffer from palpitations, I'm excitable and always getting awfully upset; at this very moment my lips are trembling, and there's a twitch in my right eyebrow. But the very worst of all is the way I sleep.

1. What is the main reason for Natalya Stepanovna's desire to get married? **(1)**

   (*a*) She wants to have children.

   (*b*) She wants to lead a quiet life.

   (*c*) She is in love with someone.

   (*d*) She wants financial stability.

2. Based on the passage, what can be inferred about Natalya Stepanovna's current emotional state? **(1)**

3. What does "palpitations" mean in the context of the passage? **(1)**

4. What are the two main reasons Natalya Stepanovna gives for feeling compelled to get married? **(2)**

IV. Read the following extract and answer the questions/ complete the sentences that follow: (5 M)

Lomov: But you can see from the documents, honoured Natalya Stepanovna. Oxen Meadows, its true were once the subject of dispute, but now everybody knows they are mine. There's nothing to argue about. You see my aunts grandmother gave the free use of these Meadows in perpetuity to the peasants of your father's grandfather, in return for which they were to make bricks for her. The peasants belonging to your father's grandfather had the free use of Meadows for forty years, and had got into the habit of regarding them as their own, when it happened that..................

Natalya: No, it isn't at all like that! Both grandfather and great grandfather reckoned that their land extended to Burnt Marsh -which means Oxen Meadows were ours. I don't see what there is to argue about, its simply silly. **(CBSE, 2023)**

1. The subject of dispute was regarding **(1)**
   (*a*) free use of Meadows
   (*b*) making of bricks
   (*c*) peasants using Meadows
   (*d*) ownership of Meadows
2. Find the word from the extract which means 'continuance': **(1)**
   (*a*) dispute (*b*) perpetuity
   (*c*) belonging (*d*) reckoned
3. Lomov's aunt's grandmother gave Oxen Meadows to Natalya's father's grandfather in lieu of .... **(1)**
4. According to Natalya why did Oxen Meadows belong to them? **(1)**
5. Fill in the blank with ONE WORD only: **(1)**
   The peasants had free use of Meadows for .... years.

Subjective Questions

Short Answer Questions (40-50 words) (3 M)

1. Which two issues about himself convinced Lomov of his decision to get married? **(CBSE SQP, 2021)**
2. Natalya was not Lomov's real love. But still, he wanted to marry her. Give reasons for his decision.
3. How did Chubukov react when Lomov asked for the hand of his daughter in marriage? **(CBSE, 2023)**
4. Why does Natalya have an argument with Lomov? What is the end result?
5. Describe how Chubukov married Natalya to Lomov.

Long Answer Questions (100-120 words) (6 M)

6. Farce is a kind of comedy which includes situations and dialogues that are ridiculous, exaggerated and even absurd. Evaluate the play, The Proposal, as a farce. **(CBSE SQP, 2021)**
7. The proposal of the marriage was forgotten amidst the arguments over petty things. Which right approach should have been followed by Lomov and Natalya? **(CBSE, 2020)**
8. The characters Natalya and Lomov lose their temper on unimportant issues. What does it show and which skill they both are required to have? Suggest some ways that help you in maintaining good and healthy relationships with people around you.

ANSWERS & EXPLANATIONS

Answer Key

Multiple Choice Questions

1. (*d*) **2.** (*c*) **3.** (*a*) **4.** (*a*) **5.** (*b*) **6.** (*d*) **7.** (*a*) **8.** (*a*) **9.** (*c*) **10.** (*b*)

Explanations

Extract-Based Questions

I. 1. (*d*) He is in love with Natalya.

2. Lomov's tone when he says "What more do I want?" is uncertain and questioning because he is trying to convince himself that Natalya Stepanovna is a suitable match for him, but at the same time, he seems to be struggling with doubts and fears. His tone suggests that he is trying to reassure himself that he has made the right decision, but he is not entirely convinced.

3. (*b*) A soliloquy is a speech given by a character alone on stage, which reveals their innermost thoughts and feelings to the audience. [cannot be (*a*) as it is not a formal discussion and cannot be (*c*) because what he speaks is certainly not brief]

4. The actor would be required to convey Lomov's nervousness and excitement through his voice modulation. [For example, he could raise his voice when Lomov is getting excited or lower it when he is feeling anxious.]

II. 1. (*c*) Arrogant

2. (*a*) "Your behavior is strange, to say the least!"

3. The speaker's relationship with Ivan Vassilevitch was previously positive and friendly.

4. The speaker is clearly displeased and finds Ivan Vassilevitch's act of giving them their own land impudent and lacking in neighbourly behaviour. They express their opinion, stating, "No, really, that's not at all neighbourly! In my opinion, it's even impudent, if you want to know."

III. 1. (*b*) She wants to lead a quiet life.

2. Natalya Stepanovna is anxious and restless, experiencing emotional turmoil and seeking stability in her life.

3. Rapid or irregular heartbeat.

4. Natalya Stepanovna provides two main reasons for feeling compelled to get married. Firstly, she mentions being 35 years old, which she considers a critical age. Secondly, she desires to lead a quiet and regular life due to her excitable nature, health issues, and the way she sleeps.

IV. 1. (*d*) ownership of Meadows

2. (*b*) perpetuity

3. the services provided by his peasants who built bricks for her.

4. Natalya said that her grandfather and great grandfather believed their land extended all the way to Burnt Marsh. As a result, she believed Oxen Meadows to be her family's property.

5. forty

Subjective Questions

Short Answer Questions

CBSE Marking Scheme: Content-1 M, Organisation of Ideas-1 M, Accuracy-1 M

1. Lomov was convinced that it was time to settle and lead a quiet and regular life. He was at the critical age of thirty-five and still unmarried. Moreover, he needed a partner as he suffered from palpitations and was always getting upset. The worst of his problems is sleeping and getting up because of a pull he feels almost twenty times. As a result, he decided to get married to his neighbour Chubukov's daughter, Natalya.

> **Nailing the Right Answer**
>
> Here, students need an answer to the points Lomov thought about himself. Those favouring Natalya are not relevant here.

2. Even though Lomov was not in love with Natalya, he decided to marry her because he badly wanted a companion. He was a thirty-five-year-old bachelor who was sick with heart ailments. The worst of his problems was sleeping and getting up because of a pull he felt almost twenty times. He needed a companion who could take care of him.

   He believed that he must have his mind made up. If he gave himself time to think or fall in love with someone, he would never get married! Thus, he convinced himself that Natalya was a suitable match for him as she was average looking, well-educated and a good housekeeper.

3. Chubukov felt extremely happy and told Lomov that he had been 'hoping for it for a long time'.

   In fact, extreme joy threw him a little off his balance, and in his excitement, he hurriedly called for his daughter to meet Lomov. He was certain that his daughter was going to grab the opportunity without any hesitation.

4. Lomov and Natalya argued over a plot of property. They were both passionate about claiming the same piece of land, Oxen Meadows. They then fought over their dogs to show one's superiority over the other.

   Lomov and Natalya cannot agree on which dog is superior because Natalya is proud of her dog, Squeezer, who is young and has a pedigree, whereas Lomov considers it uppershot and boasts of his pet 'Guess,' which he considers to be a first-rate dog. Natalya, on the other hand, thinks 'Guess' is as old and ugly as an old taxi horse. After Chubukov's entrance, the situation becomes worse, and Lomov leaves Chubukov's house.

5. Chubukov assumed Lomov had come to borrow money from him, but when he learned that he had come to propose to his daughter, he burst into tears. He kissed and hugged Lomov. He told Lomov that he had been wishing for this for a long time.

   He also informed Lomov that he adored him as if he were his own kid. Actually Chubukov secretly desired Lomov would marry his daughter since he knew Lomov was a wealthy farmer and his only daughter, Natalya could live comfortably with him. He was pleased to learn that Lomov was there to propose to his daughter.

Long Answer Questions

CBSE Marking Scheme: Expression-2 M, Accuracy-1 M

6. Farce is a comedy which amuses the audience with situations which are highly exaggerated,[10] extravagant[11], and thus improbable[12].

   'The proposal' is a humorous play by the Russian playwright Anton Chekhov. The three characters in the play act comically, argumentatively, and ludicrously[13]. The play is a satire, filled with arguments over trivial matters, but economic sense prevails in the end. The pair fights irrationally over little issues, which serves as the satire's main plot. **(1 M)**

   The elements of the farce are seen in several scenes. Both Lomov's attire and his actions are amusing. We observe situations when Chubukov and Natalya argue with him badly. At the same point, Natalya can be considered a dominating woman who wishes to marry any man that comes her way. Chubukov, who should have been a mature man, joins in the fight with Natalya and Lomov. **(1 M)**

   One moment, they are arguing and insulting each other, and the next moment they solve the issue and start fighting over another matter. How the final proposal is made amidst all the chaos makes the play a farce. **(1 M)**

7. Lomov came to seek the hand of Chubukov's daughter, Natalya in marriage. However, all three were quarrelsome people and they began to quarrel over petty issues such as their land and their dogs. **(1 M)**

   Amidst this quarrelling they completely forget the real issue about the marriage proposal. This was not the right approach. Lomov and Natalya should have kept their trivial issues aside and focused on the more important issue of marriage. **(1 M)**

   They should have shown patience and compassion towards each other. They could have avoided the argument if they had emphasized the positive aspects in each other. **(1 M)**

8. The characters Natalya and Lomov lose their temper easily on unimportant issues, it shows that this type of short tempered behaviour can affect any good relationship. They both are required to have anger management skills and learn to have respect for each other. **(1 M)**

   Writer of this play wants to convey the message that being silly and angry on any such unimportant issues may result in loss of relationships and others suffer too. **(1 M)**

   There are many ways in which we can make good relationship with people around us:

   - Be a good listener first and then speak
   - Do not argue without full knowledge of the topic
   - Be courteous to everyone
   - Avoid the habit of complaining all the time
   - Follow the rule of forgiving and forgetting
   - Don't be self centered and always help others
   - Respect others points of view as well **(1 M)**

Nailing the Right Answer

It is important to revise the characteristics of all three characters properly. For better clarity, students should write and revise the different arguments that take place in the play.

[10] **Exaggerated:** overemphasised, dramatic
[11] **Extravagant:** excessive; reckless
[12] **Improbable:** unlikely; doubtful
[13] **Ludicrously:** in a way that is foolish, unreasonable, or out of place as to be amusing

DUST OF SNOW

—Robert Frost

1

Poetic Sketch

1. The poem starts with a crow shaking snow off itself, creating a picture where the dark crow and the clean, changing snow stand out against each other.

2. The snowflakes from the hemlock tree represent a brief, surprising moment of beauty that changes things.

3. Just the simple action of snowflakes landing on the speaker makes them feel better, showing how nature can heal and change us.

4. This snowflake moment helps the speaker feel better, pulling them out of a bad mood.

5. The poem tells us it's important to notice and enjoy the little things.

6. Using the hemlock tree, which is usually linked to poison and death, adds to the poem by showing beauty and change can come from where you least expect it.

7. The main idea is about how nature has the power to make us feel better, change us, and bring us joy.

BEFORE YOU READ

Central Idea

'Dust of Snow' is a short poem by Robert Frost with a deeper meaning. This poem talks about how a simple moment with nature can have a healing impact.

This poem conveys the message that nothing in life is small. Every trivial[1] thing can bring a positive change in our life. Likewise, the poem teaches a lesson that every small act in life can liven our souls and make our sad days turn better.

STANZA-WISE ANALYSIS

Stanza 1

The way a crow
Shook down on me
The dust of snow
From a hemlock[2] tree

Explanation

In this stanza, we learn that the poet was in a bad mood and was sitting under a hemlock tree. A crow sitting on the branch of the tree shook the branch of the tree, and tiny particles of snowflakes fell on the poet.

The two agents of nature, the hemlock tree and the crow, signify sadness and gloom[3], just like the poet's mood in the beginning. The poet did not prefer using other trees like oak, maple or pine. Instead, he chose the hemlock tree, typically related to poison and toxicity, and the black crow, which usually symbolizes bad omen[4], fear and death. Similarly, he uses 'dust', which is considered useless.

Rhyme Scheme

The rhyme scheme of the poem by Robert Frost is ABAB CDCD. The first and third lines of each stanza rhyme, and the second and fourth lines of each stanza rhyme, creating an alternating pattern.

Stanza 2

Has given my heart
A change of mood
And saved some part
Of a day I had rued[5].

Explanation

In this stanza, the poet tells us how falling snow on his head instantly lifted his mood. He had already spent his day in a bad mood and was not looking forward to the rest. However, his day was saved somehow by being with nature. The dust of snow that fell on him had given him an experience he could treasure.

Generally, the hemlock tree and crow are used as negative references, but Frost has used them beautifully to portray that inauspicious[6] things can bring joy and happiness. Here, the poet tries to show how small and unexpected things from nature can still bring positivity to someone.

One must be grateful for these small acts of nature when it blesses our souls in unexpected ways.

Literary Devices

Alliteration: *Repetition of two or more closely related words beginning with a consonant sound.*
"Has given my heart", "And saved some part."

Assonance: *Repetition of similar vowel sounds in a series of words.*
"Shook down on me" – 'o' sound is prominent.

Enjambment: *When the same sentence continues to the following line without the use of any punctuation marks. It is used throughout the poem.*

---

[1] **Trivial:** of little value or importance
[2] **Hemlock:** a poisonous tree with small white flowers
[3] **Gloom:** depression
[4] **Omen:** an event regarded as good or bad
[5] **Rued:** held in regret
[6] **Inauspicious:** unfortunate

Poet's brain before the crow shook down

His brain after dust of snow

NCERT EXERCISE

Thinking about the Poem

(NCERT, Page 14)

1. What is a "dust of snow"? What does the poet say has changed his mood? How has the poet's mood changed?

Ans. "Dust of snow" means the tiny particles of snow. The particles mentioned by the poet are so small that they are called "dust". The poet was in a bad mood when suddenly, snow particles fell on him from a tree. This instantly changed the poet's state of mind, and made his day.

2. How does Frost present nature in this poem? The following questions may help you to think of an answer.

(i) What are the birds that are usually named in poems? Do you think a crow is often mentioned in poems? What images come to your mind when you think of a crow?

(ii) Again, what is "a hemlock tree"? Why doesn't the poet write about a more 'beautiful' tree such as maple, an oak, or a pine?

(iii) What do the 'crow' and 'hemlock' represent — joy or sorrow? What does the dust of snow that the crow shakes off a hemlock tree stand for?

Ans. (i) Birds like sparrows, peacocks or nightingales are usually mentioned in poems. Unlike these birds, crows are hardly mentioned in poetry and are often seen as indicators of fear and death. They are often used as negative references.

(ii) Hemlock tree is a poisonous tree with white flowers. The poet has probably used such a negative indicator to present his sad mood.

(iii) Both the crow and the hemlock tree are considered inauspicious and represents sorrow. Frost has used such negative indicators (crow and the hemlock tree) to bring positivity and transform his day for the better. He has tried to make us understand that we should see the world not as it is but as we want to see it. Thus, the crow and the hemlock tree made his day better. The dust of snow that fell on the poet brought joy to him and changed his mood.

3. Have there been times when you felt depressed or hopeless? Have you experienced a similar moment that changed your mood that day?

Ans. Everyone feels depressed or hopeless at some point. No human being is an exception. Dull and gloomy days do depress me. I feel sad and hopeless. However, being in nature or sitting under the shade of a tree can uplift my spirits and make my mood cheerful.

MISCELLANEOUS EXERCISE

Multiple Choice Questions

1. The use of the word "crow" in the first line of the poem suggests:
   (*a*) A sense of foreboding[7] or darkness.
   (*b*) The presence of a bird in the scene.
   (*c*) A contrast between nature and urban settings.
   (*d*) The speaker's love for birds.
2. The dust of snow falling from the hemlock tree can be seen as a symbol of:
   (*a*) Winter's harshness and coldness.
   (*b*) Nature's ability to cleanse and transform.
   (*c*) The fragility of life.
   (*d*) The speaker's connection to the natural world.
3. Has given my heart a change of mood (Dust of Snow). What is the poet's mood now?
   (*a*) Appreciative of nature
   (*b*) Thoughtful
   (*c*) Happy
   (*d*) Cool **(CBSE 2022, Term 1)**
4. The phrase "saved some part of a day I had rued" suggests that:
   (*a*) The speaker had a deeply regrettable day.
   (*b*) The speaker was able to salvage a portion of a bad day.
   (*c*) The speaker's entire day was ruined.
   (*d*) The speaker's previous mood was irreparable.
5. The use of the word "rued" indicates that the speaker:
   (*a*) Felt a sense of contentment.
   (*b*) Experienced remorse or regret.
   (*c*) Was surrounded by sadness.
   (*d*) Was relieved from a burden.
6. The juxtaposition of "dust" and "snow" highlights:
   (*a*) The speaker's indifference towards nature.
   (*b*) The fragility of the natural world.
   (*c*) The speaker's awareness of the changing seasons.
   (*d*) The beauty of small, unexpected moments.
7. The poem's overall tone shifted to:
   (*a*) Hopeful and optimistic.
   (*b*) Somber and introspective.
   (*c*) Lighthearted and whimsical.
   (*d*) Apathetic and detached.
8. The theme of the poem can be best described as:
   (*a*) The transformative power of nature's beauty.
   (*b*) The insignificance of human emotions.
   (*c*) The importance of embracing everyday moments.
   (*d*) The destructive force of regret.
9. The use of personification in the poem is evident in:
   (*a*) "A crow shook down on me".
   (*b*) "The dust of snow from a hemlock tree".
   (*c*) "Given my heart a change of mood".
   (*d*) "Saved some part of a day I had rued".
10. The poem can be interpreted as a reflection on:
   (*a*) The fleeting nature of happiness.
   (*b*) The interconnectedness of all living things.
   (*c*) The harshness of winter landscapes.
   (*d*) The healing power of natural experiences.

Extract-Based Questions

I. Read the following extract and answer the questions that follow: (5 M)

The way a crow
Shook down on me
The dust of snow
From a hemlock tree

1. What is the rhyme scheme of first stanza of Dust and Snow? **(1)**
   (*a*) ABBA (*b*) ABAB
   (*c*) ABCA (*d*) ABCB
2. Which literary device has been used in 'Shook down on me'? **(1)**
   (*a*) Assonance (*b*) Personification
   (*c*) Alliteration (*d*) Enjambment
3. What do the words 'Crow' and 'Hemlock' represent in Dust of Snow? **(1)**
   (*a*) Pessimism[8] (*b*) Optimism[9]
   (*c*) Mannerism (*d*) All of these

[7] **Foreboding:** a feeling that something bad will happen
[8] **Pessimism:** hopelessness
[9] **Optimism:** hope

4. Which literary device has been used throughout the poem? **(1)**

(*a*) Simile (*b*) Personification

(*c*) Alliteration (*d*) Enjambment

5. Select the option that applies the same rhyme scheme as the first four lines of the given extract. **(1)**

(*a*) The river flows
Under the skies
The cool wind blows
As birds flew

(*b*) The sun shines bright
The trees stand tall
The stars at night
Make shadows small

(*c*) The soft wind blows
Over the hills
The flowers grew
Near tiny rills

(*d*) The rain did pour
On lands so dull
It touched the shore
And clouds passed by

II. Read the following extract and answer the questions that follow: (5 M)

The way a crow
Shook down on me
The dust of snow
From a hemlock tree
Has given my heart
A change of mood
And saved some part
Of a day I had rued.

(CBSE QB, 2021)

1. Of the many symbols the hemlock tree represents, choose the one that Frost drew upon in all likelihood, for this poem. **(1)**

Symbol of

(*a*) Longevity (*b*) Togetherness

(*c*) Healing (*d*) Protection

2. Choose the option that lists the possible feelings of the poet prior to the experience shared in the poem. **(1)**

(1) Reassured (2) Disappointed
(3) Curious (4) Demotivated
(5) Thankful (6) Disheartened
(7) Impulsive

(*a*) (1), (3) and (7) (*b*) (2), (4) and (6)

(*c*) (5) and (7) (*d*) (1) and (3)

3. Identify the option that DOES NOT use the word 'rue' correctly. **(1)**

(*a*) The film was a disaster and he rued his decision to act in it.

(*b*) I am sure she rued the day she listened to a fortune-teller.

(*c*) It wasn't long before I rued my disobedience and my deceit.

(*d*) Others finally rue the one who is dishonest and heartless.

4. Synecdoche is a poetic device that uses a part to represent the whole.

E.g. That's a great set of wheels! (Set of wheels has been used for the car.) Pick an example of synecdoche from the poem. **(1)**

(*a*) Has given my heart/ A change of mood.

(*b*) The way a crow/ Shook down on me.

(*c*) The dust of snow/ From a hemlock tree.

(*d*) And saved some part/ Of a day I had rued.

5. Choose the option showing the reason NOT corresponding with "... a crow/ Shook down on me/ The dust of snow". **(1)**

(*a*) The crow's landing on the branch of the tree.

(*b*) The shivering of the crow, due to the cold.

(*c*) The readjustment of the position of the crow on the branch.

(*d*) The cawing of the crow hidden in the foliage.

III. Read the following extract and answer the questions that follow: (5 M)

Has given my heart
A change of mood
And saved some part
Of a day I had rued.

1. The phrase "Has given my heart" suggests that: **(1)**

(*a*) The speaker experienced a physical sensation in their heart.

(*b*) The speaker's emotions have been altered.

(*c*) The speaker received a gift.

(*d*) The speaker's heart has been physically changed.

2. The phrase "A change of mood" implies that: **(1)**

(*a*) The speaker was previously in a positive mood.

(*b*) The speaker's mood shifted dramatically.

(*c*) The speaker's mood became more stable.

(*d*) The speaker's mood remained unchanged.

3. Select the option that applies the same rhyme scheme as the first four lines of the given extract. **(1)**

(*a*) The sky so blue
Brings joy to me
The morning dew
Shines on the tree

(*b*) The sun shines
Upon the land
The birds take flight
In skies so bright

(*c*) The waves rise above
And touch the sand
The seagulls fly
Above the land

(*d*) The cold wind blows
And chills my face
The soft white snows
Cover the place all over.

4. The phrase "Of a day I had rued" indicates that: **(1)**

(*a*) The speaker had a deeply regrettable day.

(*b*) The speaker was able to salvage (rescue; save) a portion of a bad day.

(*c*) The speaker's entire day was ruined.

(*d*) The speaker's previous mood was irreparable.

5. What is the overall tone of the extract? **(1)**

Subjective Questions

Short Answer Questions (40-50 words) (3 M)

1. What is the underlying message for us in our hectic life with reference to the poem, 'Dust of Snow'?
2. 'Dust of Snow' is one of Frost's most loved poems. Elaborate why you think this is so.
3. How does the dust of snow save a part of the speaker's day?
4. What mood of the poet is reflected in the poem 'Dust of Snow' initially? What images are used by the poet to bring about the effect? Comment. **(CBSE, 2024)**

Long Answer Questions (100-120 words) (6 M)

5. A simple moment proves to be very significant and saves the rest of the day of the poet from being wasted. Explain on the basis of the poem 'Dust of Snow'.
6. Discuss the impact of nature and its transformative power as depicted in the poem extract. Explore how the crow and the dust of snow symbolize nature's influence on the speaker's emotions and their perception of the world around them.
7. In the poem, Dust of Snow, the crow symbolically transforms the narrator's mood, while in the story, His First Flight, the baby seagull undergoes a literal transformation as it learns to fly. Analyse how these avian characters play similar or different thematic roles in their respective poem and story. **(CBSE, APQ)**

Nailing the Right Answer

When answering questions about Robert Frost's poem, highlight how the poet emphasizes the transformative power of seemingly insignificant events. Emphasize the idea that even small gestures or experiences can have a significant impact on our lives. Use examples and quotes from the poem to support your answer.

ANSWERS & EXPLANATIONS

Answer Key

Multiple Choice Questions

1. (*a*) **2.** (*b*) **3.** (*c*) **4.** (*b*) **5.** (*b*) **6.** (*d*) **7.** (*a*) **8.** (*a*) **9.** (*a*) **10.** (*d*)

Explanations

Extract-Based Questions

I. 1. (*b*) ABAB

2. (*a*) Assonance

3. (*a*) Pessimism

4. (*d*) Enjambment

5. (*b*) The correct answer is (*b*).

II. 1. (*c*) Healing

Exp.: Frost had tried to bring his aching heart to peace. In other words, he has used it as a symbol of healing his aching heart.

2. (*b*) (2), (4) and (6)

Exp.: The poet was upset or saddened (disappointed), discouraged (demotivated) and dismayed and dejected (disheartened).

3. (*d*) Others finally rue the one who is dishonest and heartless.

Exp.: The meaning of 'rue' is sorrow or regret. The ones who are dishonest or heartless are not sorrowed or regretted. They are rather hated.

4. (*a*) Has given my heart / A change of mood

Exp.: The poet has mentioned that his heart was given a change of mood, not only his heart but his entire self, who has been given a change of mood by the dust of snow.

5. (*d*) The cawing of the crow hidden in the foliage.

Exp.: The dust of snow fell upon the poet when the crow makes some movement, like landing on the branch of the tree, shivers due to cold, or readjusts its position on the branch. The mere cawing of the crow does not make any movement and will not correspond with "...a crow/ Shook down on me/ The dust of snow".

III. 1. (*b*) The speaker's emotions have been altered.

2. (*b*) The speaker's mood shifted dramatically.

3. (*a*) The correct answer is (*a*).

4. (*b*) The speaker was able to salvage a portion of a bad day.

5. The tone of the extract is reflective and suggests a moment of positive transformation or relief for the speaker.

Subjective Questions

Short Answer Questions

CBSE Marking Scheme: Content-1 M, Organisation of Ideas-1 M, Accuracy-1 M

1. The underlying message in the poem, 'Dust of Snow', is that we should spend time in nature and have a positive outlook towards simple acts.

These small and simple acts can lead to learning more significant lessons about enjoying life. Nature has healing power, and things which are negative too have the ability to carry positive experiences with them.

2. The poem 'Dust of Snow,' expresses the poet's feelings very well. He says that nature has great healing power and helped save his day from getting ruined.

The poem has a rhyme scheme and various poetic devices like synecdoche, alliteration, enjambment and imagery. All these make the poem one of Frost's most loved poems.

3. The dust of snow falling from the hemlock tree saves a part of the speaker's day by altering their mood.

It serves as a transformative moment that helps the speaker salvage and find some positivity in a day that they had previously regretted.

4. *Topper's Explanation*

'Dust of Snow' is a beautiful poem written by 'Robert Frost' illustrating the beauty of nature. Initially in the poem, the poet was feeling melancholic and highly despondent. He was wasting his time in grief.

The images of crow, hemlock tree and snow has been used by the poet for positive effect. Though these images are seen as harbingers of doom and bad omen, the poet uses them as a ~~catylyst~~ catalyst for positive change. The falling of snow from a hemlock tree that too by action of a crow, makes the poet happy for the rest of the day. This shows that whatever the event may be, our response to it matters.

Long Answer Questions

CBSE Marking Scheme: Expression-2 M, Accuracy-1 M

5. Robert Frost, in his poem, has conveyed that simple and ordinary moments can significantly impact our lives. He has tried to make us understand that we should see the world not as it is but as we want to see it. **(1 M)**

Sometimes unimportant things can change the meaning of life unexpectedly. The simple gesture of a crow sitting on top of a tree shaking off the dust of snow on the poet changed his entire mood. He realized he had just wasted his day repenting (regretting) and mourning. **(1 M)**

However, the improvement in his mood persuaded him to spend the rest of the day doing something productive and happy.

The light dusting of snow dust washed away his sadness. His spirits were restored, and he was prepared to make the most of the remaining day. This is how the simple movement of the falling snow dust proves significant as it drastically changes the poet's mood. **(1 M)**

6. In the poem nature is depicted as having a transformative power on the speaker's emotions and their perception of the world. The crow and the dust of snow symbolize this influence. **(1 M)**

The crow's presence and the act of it shaking down the dust of snow from the hemlock tree create a moment of unexpected beauty and contrast in the speaker's life. This encounter with nature changes the speaker's mood, suggesting that even the smallest natural occurrences can have a profound impact on one's emotional state and outlook. **(1 M)**

It highlights the ability of nature to uplift, inspire, and provide solace, reminding us of the powerful connection between humans and the natural world. **(1 M)**

7. In Dust of Snow, the crow and the baby seagull in His First Flight, both serve as pivotal symbols of transformation and redemption, in their distinct ways. The crow's sudden interaction with the speaker in the poem brings about an unexpected change in the narrator's mood. The simple act of the crow shaking off snow onto the speaker becomes a metaphor for a transformative moment, shifting the narrator from a state of sadness to a renewed appreciation for the beauty of nature. On the other hand, the baby seagull's literal transformation through flight in the story signifies a rite of passage and growth. Through this literal transformation, the seagull not only learns to navigate the physical world but also gains a newfound sense of confidence and independence, contributing to the overall theme of self-discovery and growth in the narrative. The avian characters, while differing in their modes of impact, share the thematic role of catalyzing positive change, whether through a change in perspective or the achievement of a significant milestone.

FIRE AND ICE

—Robert Frost

2

Poetic Sketch

1. The poem explores different theories about how the world will end, either in fire or in ice.

2. The speaker aligns with those who believe in the end by fire, based on the speaker's experience of desire.

3. The speaker also thinks about hate, suggesting that intense dislike or hate, represented by ice, could also destroy the world.

4. The poem suggests that both fiery desire and icy hate are powerful enough to cause destruction, showing they are both dangerous.

5. In the end, the speaker believes that whether through the heat of desire or the coldness of hate, both forces are capable of ending the world, highlighting the impact of strong emotions.

BEFORE YOU READ

Rhyme Scheme

The rhyme scheme of Robert Frost's poem 'Fire and Ice' is ABAABCBCCB.

Central Idea

Robert Frost's poem "Fire and Ice" is a symbolic poem where he uses two contrasting components metaphorically[1] and compares them with self-destructing human emotions. Fire symbolises the emotion of desire or greed, and ice represents hatred. The poet has given possible explanations for each of the ideas which support why they can destroy the world. The poem sends a definite message to the readers, warning them that nothing in the world is eternal. If we let our emotions rule us, they will surely bring us all to the verge of chaos[2] and destruction.

---

[1] **Metaphorically:** in a way that uses or relates to a metaphor; figuratively
[2] **Chaos:** disorder

Literary Devices

Assonance: Repetition of similar vowel sounds in a series of words.

The long "o" sound in "I hold with those who favour fire."

Alliteration: Repetition of two or more closely connected words beginning with a consonant sound.

The sound of "f" in "favour fire" and "w" in "world will"

Imagery: It makes readers perceive things involving their five senses.

"Some say the world will end in fire"

"To say that for destruction ice Is also great"

Anaphora: The repetition of a word or expression at the start of two or more consecutive lines.

Example-"Some say" is repeated at the start of lines 1 and 2.

Personification: Personification is to give human qualities to inanimate objects.

In the poem, fire and ice have been personified as they are given the mind and power to destroy anything.

Enjambment: When the same sentence continues to the next line without the use of any punctuation marks, it is called enjambment.

Examples from the poem- "From what I've tasted of desire.
I hold with those who favour fire."

Stanza 1

Some say the world will end in fire
Some say in ice.
From what I've tasted of desire
I hold with those who favour fire.

Explanation

In the stanza, the poet is analysing the end of the world. Some people are of the opinion that the Earth will get heated up and destroyed by fire. While others think that the world will be destroyed by ice as the temperatures go down. Here, the poet has metaphorically compared fire with the emotion of desire or greed. He conveys that if humanity lets its desires rule, the world will be destroyed soon.

Stanza 2

But if it had to perish[3] twice,
I think I know enough of hate
To say that for destruction ice
Is also great
And would suffice[4]

Explanation

The poet is analyzing the end of the world in detail. Fire, in his opinion, would be the likely cause. He does, however, add that if the world were to end twice, it would be because of the hatred he represented by the word "ice." The poet believes that there is already enough hatred present in the world. One day, this hatred might bring the world to an end.

Hatred has the same destructive potential for humanity as desire. Frost mentions that he has seen enough hate himself and is pretty sure it carries enough destruction.

[3] **Perish:** die
[4] **Suffice:** be sufficient

NCERT EXERCISE

Thinking about the Poem

(NCERT, Page 15)

1. There are many ideas about how the world will 'end'. Do you think the world will end someday? Have you ever thought about what would happen if the sun got so hot that it 'burst' or grew colder and colder?

Ans. Unfortunately, the world is going to end one day, and there is nothing we can do about it. There are many ideas about how it will end, but one can't be sure. If the sun gets so hot one day that it is on the verge of bursting, it will lead to rapid destruction as there will be fire everywhere. On the other hand, if it grows colder, there will be ice everywhere on Earth and life in any form will not sustain itself at such low temperatures.

2. For Frost, what do 'fire' and 'ice' stand for? Here are some ideas: greed, conflict, insensitivity, avarice, fury, cruelty, intolerance, coldness, indifference, lust, rigidity, hatred

Ans. According to Frost, 'fire' stands for greed, conflict, fury, cruelty, lust and avarice[5], whereas 'Ice' stands for insensitivity, coldness, intolerance, indifference, rigidity and hatred.

3. What is the rhyme scheme of the poem? How does it help in bringing out the contrasting ideas in the poem?

Ans. The rhyme scheme of the poem is "abaa bcbcb". The poet uses rhyming beautifully to bring about contrasting ideas in the poem. He has used the views of two groups who believe that the world would come to a catastrophic[6] end due to fire or ice.

Simultaneously, he portrays these two contrasting components as features of destructive human emotions: desire and hatred. Just like these negative emotions can cause damage to an individual in an irreparable manner, fire and ice can lead the world to the verge of chaos and destruction.

MISCELLANEOUS EXERCISE

Multiple Choice Questions

1. The speaker in the poem suggests that the world will end:
   (*a*) In fire
   (*b*) In ice
   (*c*) In desire
   (*d*) In destruction
2. The phrase "From what I've tasted of desire" implies that the speaker:
   (*a*) Has experienced both fire and ice.
   (*b*) Has a strong preference for desire.
   (*c*) Has had some exposure to desire but may not have a deep understanding of it.
   (*d*) Has a personal connection to desire.
3. The speaker holds with those who favour fire because:
   (*a*) Fire is more destructive than ice.
   (*b*) Fire is associated with desire.
   (*c*) Fire is a natural element.
   (*d*) Fire is more powerful than ice.
4. If the world had to perish twice, the speaker believes that:
   (*a*) Fire would be the cause of the first destruction.
   (*b*) Fire and ice would both be equally destructive.
   (*c*) Ice would be the cause of the second destruction.
   (*d*) The world cannot perish twice.
5. The speaker's view on hate suggests that they:
   (*a*) Have experienced intense hatred.
   (*b*) Believe that hate is more destructive than fire or ice.
   (*c*) Have a deep understanding of hate.
   (*d*) Hold a negative opinion about hate.
6. The phrase "for destruction ice is also great" implies that:
   (*a*) Ice has the power to destroy desire.
   (*b*) Ice is as destructive as fire.
   (*c*) Ice is more destructive than fire.
   (*d*) Ice is a natural element associated with destruction.

[5] **Avarice:** extreme greed for wealth or material gain.

[6] **Catastrophic:** causing sudden damage or suffering.

7. The poem suggests that the world's end will be determined by:

(*a*) Desire and hate.

(*b*) Fire and ice.

(*c*) The speaker's preference.

(*d*) Natural forces beyond human control.

8. The speaker's choice to favour fire over ice reflects their belief in:

(*a*) The destructive power of desire.

(*b*) The intensity of fire as an element.

(*c*) The inevitability of the world's destruction.

(*d*) The significance of personal experiences.

9. The speaker's perspective on the world's end can be described as:

(*a*) Pessimistic[7] (*b*) Optimistic

(*c*) Indifferent (*d*) Contradictory

10. The overall theme of the poem can be best described as:

(*a*) The destructive nature of desire and hate.

(*b*) The unpredictability of the world's end.

(*c*) The power and potential of fire and ice.

(*d*) The complexity of human preferences and beliefs.

Extract-Based Questions

I. Read the following extract and answer the questions that follow: (5 M)

Some say the world will end in fire
Some say in ice.
From what I've tasted of desire
I hold with those who favour fire.

1. Select the option that applies the same rhyme scheme as the first four lines of the given extract. (1)

(*a*)	(*b*)
The stars shine bright	The night is cold
The night is long	The stars shine high
They give us light	The moon looks old
Like a sweet song.	And lights so bold

(*c*)	(*d*)
The river flows	The rain will fall
The flowers bloom	The wind will blow
The cold wind blows	We hear the call
Through silent gloom.	As storms will grow.

2. What is the significance of the word "desire" in the poem, and how does it shape the poem's overall mood and tone? Answer in about 40 words. (2)

3. Based on the content of the poem, what do the contrasting elements of fire and ice symbolise? (1)

(*a*) Passion and destruction (*b*) Desire and hatred

(*c*) Urban and rural (*d*) Warmth and coldness

4. Which literary device is predominantly used in the poem to convey its central theme? (1)

II. Read the following extract and answer the questions that follow: (5 M)

Some say the world will end in fire,
Some say in ice.
From what I've tasted of desire
I hold with those who favour fire.
But if it had to perish twice,
I think I know enough of hate
To say that for destruction ice
Is also great
And would suffice.

(CBSE, QB)

1. Choose the CORRECT statement about the given poem. (1)

(*a*) Fire and ice are images—they help the readers visualise the power of nature over man.

(*b*) Fire and ice are symbols—not of natural disasters but of humanity's ability to create disasters of its own.

(*c*) Fire and ice are elements—not of nature but man-made and possess the ability to create havoc for mankind.

(*d*) Fire and ice are agents—they change the thinking of mankind from negative to positive and bring harmony.

2. Select the option that correctly classifies the connotations of fire and ice, as suggested in the poem. (1)

(i) Rage (ii) Violence

(iii) Indifference (iv) Hate

(v) greed

(*a*) Fire – (iii), (iv); Ice – (i), (ii), (v)

(*b*) Fire – (ii), (v); Ice – (i), (iii), (iv)

(*c*) Fire – (i), (iii), (v); Ice – (ii), (iv)

(*d*) Fire – (i), (ii), (iv); Ice – (iii), (v)

3. The poem is a ________, put across by the poet. (1)

(*a*) Powerful warning (*b*) Heartfelt apology

(*c*) Earnest appeal (*d*) Vengeful threat

4. The poet uses the phrasal verb-hold with. Choose the option that DOES NOT indicate a valid phrasal verb. (1)

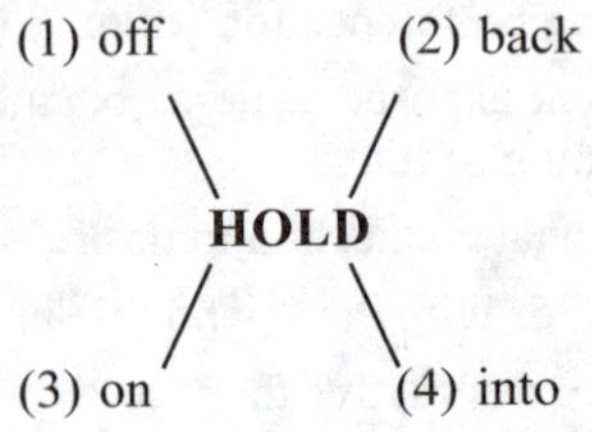

(*a*) Option 1 (*b*) Option 2

(*c*) Option 3 (*d*) Option 4

[7] **Pessimistic:** tending to see the worst aspect of things.

5. Pick the option that is NOT TRUE about the poet according to the extract. **(1)**

The poet

(*a*) Is inclined to believe that the world would most likely end with fire.

(*b*) Has heard divided opinions about the way the world would end in all likelihood.

(*c*) Preaches love and kindness to combat the spread of hate among all.

(*d*) Declares the power of ice to be as destructive as that of fire.

III. Read the following extract and answer the questions that follow: (5 M)

But if it had to perish twice
I think I know enough of hate
To say that for destruction ice
Is also great
And would suffice **(CBSE, SQP, 2023)**

1. Fill the blank with one word. **(1)**
When the speaker says that ice could also bring about the end of the world he refers to _____, as the means for destruction.
2. What does the speaker's alignment with those who favour ice, suggest? **(1)**
3. Which of the following best describes the speaker's attitude towards destruction caused by ice? **(1)**
A. Indifferent B. Fearful C. Dismissive D. Respectful
4. Comment on the poet's use of language in these lines. **(2)**

Subjective Questions

Short Answer Questions (40-50 words) (3 M)

1. The tone of the speaker contrasts with the seriousness of the subject matter. Justify. **(CBSE, QB)**
2. Fire and Ice projects a pessimistic outlook. Comment. **(CBSE, QB)**
3. What do people think about the end of the world? Who does the poet side with, and why?
4. What does the speaker mean by saying, "But if it had to perish twice"? How does the speaker perceive the destructive power of ice?

Long Answer Questions (100-120 words) (6 M)

5. The author presents two reasons which will lead to the destruction of human quality. What values do you garner from the 2 possible reasons provided by him?
6. The use of symbolism in the poem 'Fire and Ice' conveys the poet's message effectively. Expand with reference to the poem.
7. How does Robert Frost use figurative language in "Fire and Ice" to convey the theme of destructive passion?

Nailing the Right Answer

When analyzing a poem, pay attention to the figurative language used by the poet. Look for metaphors, personification, and paradoxes to understand how the poet conveys their message or theme.

ANSWERS & EXPLANATIONS

Answer Key

Multiple Choice Questions

1. (*a*) **2.** (*c*) **3.** (*b*) **4.** (*c*) **5.** (*c*) **6.** (*b*) **7.** (*b*) **8.** (*b*) **9.** (*a*) **10.** (*c*)

Explanations

Extract-Based Questions

I. 1. (*b*) The correct answer is (*b*)

2. The word "desire" in the poem suggests strong wants or cravings, contributing to the theme that intense emotions can lead to the world's end. It sets a serious and thoughtful tone.

3. The contrasting elements of fire and ice symbolise:
(*b*) Desire and hatred

4. The literary device predominantly used in the poem is symbolism, with 'fire' symbolising passion and 'ice' symbolising hate.

II. 1. (*b*) Fire and ice are symbols—not of natural disasters but of humanity's ability to create disasters of its own.

2. (*d*) Fire – (i), (ii), (iv); Ice – (iii), (v)
3. (*a*) Powerful warning
4. (*d*) Option 4
5. (*c*) Preaches love and kindness to combat the spread of hate among all.

III. 1. hatred/indifference/bitterness/apathy/detachment/rigidity

2. The speaker's alignment with those who favour ice suggests that they have seen the destructive consequences of a lack of empathy and emotional connection.
3. (*d*) Respectful

Exp.: The use of the word "great" implies a sense of awe or respect for the power of ice to cause destruction.

4. The language used in these lines is simple and straightforward. The words and phrases are easy to understand and the poem is written in a conversational tone. Despite its simplicity, however, the poem carries a profound message about the destructive power of both fire and ice, and the inevitability of destruction. The use of simple language in this context makes the message more accessible to a wider audience and adds to the poem's overall impact.

Subjective Questions

Short Answer Questions

CBSE Marking Scheme: Content-1 M, Organisation of Ideas-1 M, Accuracy-1 M

1. The speaker is presenting his personal opinion on a serious topic: the possibility of the world ending. However, the tone of the speaker is casual and conversational.

No one would want the world to end.

However, the poet uses words like "I hold with those who favour fire", which might seem like he wants the world to end. Furthermore, the line "To say that for destruction ice is also great" is sarcastic[8]. Surely, he does not want this to happen and warns humans to control their emotions to save the world from destruction.

2. The poem talks about the end of the world. The poem's theme is negative as it talks about destruction. The poet says fire represents desire or greed, and ice represents hatred and coldness. He links the two emotions to be the reason for the possible extinction of the world.

Moreover, Frost warns people in a sarcastic way to control their emotions and not let them rule over humanity. These emotions, if not controlled, carry the ability to ruin the world. Thus, it makes the reader sad because no one wants the world to be destroyed.

Mistakes 101 : What not to do!

A common error is misinterpreting the tone of the poem. Students may overlook the underlying sarcasm or misread the seriousness of the themes. It's important to recognize and convey the tone Frost uses to discuss the end of the world.

3. People are divided in their opinion over the cause of the end of this world. Some think that 'fire' symbolised by desires, fury and violence will destroy this world.

Others believe that 'ice' is symbolised by cold reasoning, indifference and hatred will cause destruction.

The poet sides with those who believe that 'fire' will result in the destruction of the world. However, soon he mentions that if the world were to end twice, then the ice (coldness and hatred) would also suffice.

4. The speaker suggests that if the world had to come to an end on two separate occasions, they have enough knowledge and understanding of hate to believe that ice would also be a sufficient agent of destruction.

The speaker acknowledges that ice is also capable of great destruction and believes it would be enough to cause the end of the world.

Long Answer Questions

CBSE Marking Scheme: Expression-2 M, Accuracy-1 M

5. The poet provides and deals with two possible causes for the end of the world. He points more towards the sentimental and emotional side of the issue. **(1 M)**

As for him, fire denotes deep burning desire and passion, while ice is highlighted for its icy cold and hatred side of the emotions. He favours both the arguments and says that either the deep burning passion or the jealousy factor and cold hatred will push people to walk on the path of destruction.

The poet is sure of this destruction of human quality. First, he talks about the destruction caused by fire and in case this fails, then ice will end the world. **(1 M)**

The love that people have for one another will turn into hatred. In the race to climb up and outdo one another, people will tend to hate each other. These negative emotions will become so strong that it will surpass all the love and lead to the destruction of humanity. **(1 M)**

6. The poem 'Fire and Ice' by Robert Frost discusses how the world can end.

Two natural images were employed by the poet, and both are quite hazardous[9].

They are the elements of 'fire' and 'ice'. These elements represent aggression[10] as well as coldness in human interactions, respectively. **(1 M)**

However, the fire here symbolises desire and greed, and ice symbolises the hate and coldness of relations. According to the poet, both of these emotions would destroy humanity as greed leads a person to commit blunders, and so does hate. **(1 M)**

He is trying to warn people about these negative emotions and sarcastically sends a message to stop letting these emotions

[8] **Sarcastic:** ironic; ridiculing

rule over them. With a sarcastic and conversational tone, he has sent his message very clearly through symbolism.

(1 M)

7. In "Fire and Ice," Robert Frost employs figurative language by using fire to represent burning passion and desire, while ice depicts cold hatred. These metaphors show how extreme emotions can lead to destruction. **(1 M)**

Frost's choice of fire and ice as symbols illustrates the potential for self-destruction in human feelings, suggesting that whether it's the hot flames of passion or the coldness of hate, both have the power to end the world. **(1 M)**

Overall, frost's use of figurative language in "Fire and Ice" helps to create vivid and memorable imagery that conveys, the poems theme of destructive passion. **(1 M)**

Nailing the Right Answer

It's important for students to understand the complete meaning of the poem and not just the literal sense of it. The vocabulary and imagery used in the poem add meaning to it.

[9] **Hazardous:** risky; dangerous
[10] **Aggression:** force; violence

A TIGER IN THE ZOO

—Leslie Norris

3

Poetic Sketch

1. The poem starts with a tiger which is confined in a cage and moves within a limited space.
2. The poet describes the tiger's movements as silent and graceful, despite its anger.
3. The poem paints a picture of where the tiger should be living—in the wild, hunting, and hiding near water.
4. The poet highlights how different the tiger's life is now, stuck in a cage, away from the jungle.
5. The tiger is trapped in a cell, separated from it's natural habitat.
6. The tiger's strength and power are limited by the bars of the cage.
7. The tiger ignores the visitors and remains focused on its surroundings.
8. The sound of the patrolling cars contrast with the natural life of the tiger, away from the civilization.
9. The poem concludes with the tiger gazing at the stars, symbolizing its longing for freedom.

BEFORE YOU READ

Central Idea

The central idea of "A Tiger in the Zoo" by Leslie Norris is about a tiger that lives a restricted life in a zoo, far from its natural habitat. In the jungle, the tiger would be free to roam, hunt, and be wild. But in the zoo, it can only walk a few steps and is trapped in a concrete cell. The poem highlights how the tiger has lost its freedom and the sadness of living in captivity, far from the wild where it belongs.

STANZA-WISE ANALYSIS

Stanza 1

He stalks[1] in his vivid stripes[2]
The few steps of his cage,
On pads of velvet quiet,
In his quiet rage.

Explanation

The poet describes the appearance and movement of the tiger that is confined[3] in a cage. The tiger moves up and down, and his dark stripes can be seen from afar. He can take only a few steps because moving inside that small cage is difficult. His footsteps can not be heard because he has very soft feet, like velvet, due to which there is no sound of his footsteps. The tiger suppresses his anger by quietly walking into the small area of his cage. He has suppressed his rage as he is not free and helpless here.

Rhyme Scheme

The rhyme scheme of the poem by Leslie Norris is ABCB.

Stanza 2

He should be lurking[4] in the shadow,
Sliding through long grass
Near the water hole
Where plump[5] deer pass.

Explanation

The poet is filled with pity in this stanza. He was thinking that this tiger should have been in the forest. If he was free, he would have hidden behind the long grass near the water bodies so that he could easily catch a deer to have it as its food. The poet highlights that the actual life of a tiger is to live in a jungle where he can wander, catch his prey and eat it but the tiger in the cage is not free to do so.

Stanza 3

He should be snarling[6] around houses
At the jungle's edge,
Baring[7] his white fangs[8], his claws,
Terrorizing[9] the village

---

[1] **Stalks:** follow
[2] **Vivid stripes:** bright narrow bands
[3] **Confined:** small, limited
[4] **Lurking:** to wait or move in a secret way
[5] **Plump:** healthy
[6] **Snarling:** to make deep, rough sound (usually in anger)
[7] **Baring:** showing; displaying
[8] **Fangs:** teeth
[9] **Terrorizing:** frightening; creating a state of extreme fear

Literary Devices

Personification: It is a poetic device which gives human qualities to non living things or animals.

The tiger is personified because the poet refers him as 'he'.

Metaphor: Comparison of two different things without using words 'like' and 'as'.

"On pads of velvet"

(Tiger's paws are compared to velvet)

Oxymoron: Two consecutive words which have opposite meanings. (quiet rage)

Alliteration: Repetition of two or more closely related words beginning with a consonant sound.

"Where plump deer pass"

"His strength behind bars."

Enjambment: Line continues to the next line without punctuation marks.

"He should be snarling around houses At the jungle's edge"

"Sliding through long grass
Near the water hole
Where plump deer pass."

Explanation

The poet says that if the tiger would have been free or failed to find any prey in the jungle, he would have snarled and growled[10] around the houses located on the outskirts of the forest. He would scare all the people with his white fangs, sharp tooth, and claws. This would create terror among the people living in the villages.

Stanza 4

But he's locked in a concrete[11] cell,
His strength behind bars,
Stalking[12] the length of his cage,
Ignoring visitors.

Explanation

Now the poet comes to the reality of a tiger being confined in a cage. He says that the cage is made of strong building material. The poet further mentions that as the tiger is in the cage, his ferociousness[13] is also confined in the cage. He slowly and silently moves to and fro in the cage. He neither pays attention to visitors nor terrorizes them as his power is restricted by the cage.

Stanza 5

He hears the last voice at night,
The patrolling cars,
And stares with his brilliant eyes
At the brilliant stars.

Explanation

The tiger stays awake at night and hears the sound of the patrolling cars (vehicles of police which are used to guard at night). He also remains disturbed due to the sound of these cars. He stares at the stars with his shining eyes. The poem highlights how the tiger has lost its freedom and the sadness of living in captivity.

[10] **Growled:** to make a low, rough sound
[11] **Concrete:** solid
[12] **Stalking:** moving to and fro
[13] **Ferociousness:** wild, fierce

NCERT EXERCISE

Thinking about the Poem

(NCERT, Page 14)

1. Thinking about the poem

(i) Find the words that describe the movements and actions of the tiger in the cage and in the wild.

Arrange them in two columns.

(ii) Find the words that describe the two places, and arrange them in two columns.

Now try to share ideas about how the poet uses words and images to contrast the two situations.

Ans. (i)

In the Cage	In the Wild
Stalks	Lurking in shadow
Few steps of his cage	In the Wild
Quiet rage	Lurking in shadow
Locked in concrete cell	Sliding through long grass
Stalking the length of his cage	Snarling around houses Baring his white fangs, his claws
Stares with his brilliant eyes at the brilliant stars	Terrorizing the village

(ii)

Places in the Cage	Places in the wild
Pads of velvet quiet	shadow
Concrete cell	grass
Behind bars	Water hole jungle's edge

2. Notice the use of a word repeated in lines such as these

(i) On pads of velvet quiet,

In his quiet rage.

(ii) And stares with his brilliant eyes

At the brilliant stars.

What do you think is the effect of this repetition?

Ans. (i) The repetition of 'Quiet' expresses the intensity of the tiger's anger and agony.

'Velvet quiet' refers to the slow movements of the tiger as it is confined in a cage. 'Quiet rage' refers to his anger and ferociousness which is suppressed due to his confinement in a cage.

(ii) The repetition of 'brilliant' expresses both the despair and brightness in the eyes of the tiger. 'Brilliant' word used for stars as well as a tiger's eyes as he stares at stars with his shining eyes, longing for his freedom and thinking about how beautiful life could be if it is in its natural habitat.

MISCELLANEOUS EXERCISE

Multiple Choice Questions

1. What is the main theme of the poem?
   (*a*) The beauty of nature. (*b*) The cruelty of captivity.
   (*c*) The power of predators. (*d*) The danger of wildlife.
2. What is the tiger's physical appearance?
   (*a*) Vivid stripes (*b*) Padded paws
   (*c*) Velvet fur (*d*) Brilliant eyes
3. Why should the tiger be lurking in the shadow?
   (*a*) To find food. (*b*) To rest and hide.
   (*c*) To escape capture. (*d*) To stalk its prey.
4. 'A tiger in the zoo ignoring visitors' is an example of **(CBSE 2022-Term 1)**
   (*a*) Metaphor (*b*) Simile
   (*c*) Irony (*d*) Personification
5. How does the tiger feel about being locked in a concrete cell?
   (*a*) Angry and vengeful.
   (*b*) Content and peaceful.
   (*c*) Indifferent and unaffected.
   (*d*) Fearful and anxious.

6. What does the tiger do to terrorize the village?
   (*a*) Roams through the jungle.
   (*b*) Shows its white fangs.
   (*c*) Attacks houses at the edge of the jungle.
   (*d*) Hunts and kills deer.
7. What does the tiger hear at night?
   (*a*) Visitors in the zoo. (*b*) The patrolling cars.
   (*c*) The village commotion. (*d*) Other wild animals.
8. Study the following statements:
   (A) The villagers don't feel happy that the tiger is caged.
   (B) We feel sad that the tiger is caged.
   (C) The tiger is happy that he doesn't have to hunt for his food. **(CBSE 2022-Term 1)**
   (*a*) (A) is right and (B) is wrong.
   (*b*) (B) is right and (A) is wrong.
   (*c*) (C) is right and (A) is wrong.
   (*d*) (A) is wrong and (C) is right
9. What is the overall mood of the poem?
   (*a*) Joyful and playful. (*b*) Calm and serene.
   (*c*) Frustrated and trapped. (*d*) Dangerous and menacing.
10. What does the poem suggest about the impact of captivity on the tiger?
   (*a*) It brings out its true nature.
   (*b*) It makes the tiger more docile.
   (*c*) It fosters a sense of security.
   (*d*) It leads to frustration and confinement.

Extract-Based Questions

I. Read the following extract and answer the questions that follow: (5 M)

He hears the last voice at night,
The patrolling cars,
And stares with his brilliant eyes
At the brilliant stars.

1. What is the contrast between the "last voice" and the "brilliant stars" in the poem? **(1)**
   (*a*) The last voice represents captivity, while the stars represent freedom.
   (*b*) The last voice symbolizes danger, while the stars symbolize tranquility.
   (*c*) The last voice signifies human presence, while the stars signify the natural world.
   (*d*) The last voice signifies confinement, while the stars signify vastness and wonder.
2. Select the option that applies the same rhyme scheme as the first four lines of the given extract. **(1)**

(*a*)	(*b*)
The sun sets in the west The sky turns red The birds return to their nest As the daylight spreads	The river flows so deep Under the sky so blue The fishes take a plunge And dance in waters new.
(*c*)	(*d*)
The trees stand tall The wind blows strong The birds give a call And sing a song.	The stars shine bright The moon is white The sky glows at night A truly beautiful sight.

3. How does the poet's use of the phrase "brilliant eyes" contribute to the theme of the poem? Elaborate. **(2)**
4. Which word can substitute 'brilliant' in the following phrase: And stares with his ________ (natural/glistening/amazing) eyes. **(1)**

II. Read the following extract and answer the questions that follow: (5 M)

He should be lurking in the shadow,
Sliding through long grass
Near the water hole
Where plump deer pass.

1. According to the extract, the poet wishes for the tiger to be 'sliding' through the foliage as this would **(1)**
   (*a*) Assist in keeping the prey unsuspecting of the predator's[14] sound.
   (*b*) Aid in camouflaging[15] the presence of the predator before it rushes in.
   (*c*) Help the predator pounce[16] on the prey comfortably without getting tired.
   (*d*) Support the predator's vision as it eyes its prey.
2. Which fact does not connect with the significance of the water hole for the tiger? **(1)**
   (*a*) Many tigers chase prey into the water and hold the victim's head underwater until it drowns.
   (*b*) Prey feed in the water on water-lilies, and often wander into the middle of the water hole, where they are vulnerable and easy for the tiger to kill.
   (*c*) Prey which has quenched its thirst ensures the consumption of hydrated meat for the tiger.
   (*d*) Chasing the panicked prey from shallow to deep water where the tiger grabs it.
3. Pick the option that does not use 'lurking' correctly to fill in the blank. **(1)**
   (*a*) The thug was ________ in the alley late evening, for unsuspecting passers-by.
   (*b*) The hyena was ________ in its den after a good meal.
   (*c*) The detective cautioned her team about the ________ dangers likely to impact the case.
   (*d*) The prejudices ________ beneath the surface create misunderstandings.

[14] **Predator:** animal of prey
[15] **Camouflaging:** hide; disguise
[16] **Pounce:** jump; leap

4. Select the option that applies the same rhyme scheme as the first four lines of the given extract. **(1)**

(*a*) The sun sets behind the trees,
The birds chirp in the air,
The cool breeze flows with ease,
As leaves fall everywhere.

(*b*) The river flows beyond the sand,
Its waves rise up so high,
The view so vast and grand,
As clouds drift in the sky.

(*c*) The stars shine bright in the night,
The moonlight glows so fair,
The sky is filled with silver light,
As the wind sways through the air.

(*d*) The cat creeps under the table,
Waiting for the mice,
It hides behind the wooden chair,
With sharp and watchful eyes.

5. Pick the phrase that does not suggest that the forest in the extract is lush. **(1)**

(*a*) Long grass (*b*) The water hole
(*c*) Plump deer (*d*) Lurking in the shadow

III. Read the following extract and answer the questions that follow: (5 M)

He stalks in his vivid stripes
The few steps of his cage,
On pads of velvet quiet,
In his quiet rage.
He should be lurking in shadow,
Sliding through long grass
Near the water hole
Where plump deer pass.

(CBSE, 2023)

1. 'Quiet rage' refers to the tigers ....

(*a*) helplessness
(*b*) he has not been able to hunt
(*c*) his prey has not come to the water hole
(*d*) he is not free

2. He is lurking in shadows because ....

3. Complete the sentence appropriately:

It is clear that metaphor is the poetic device used for 'pads of velvet' because .... (clue-explain how metaphor applies here).

4. Find a word from the extract which means- to walk with measured, stiff or haughty strides:

(*a*) steps (*b*) lurking
(*c*) pads (*d*) stalk

5. State whether the following statement is TRUE or FALSE:

The tiger is stealthily waiting for the deer to come to the water hole

Subjective Questions

Short Answer Questions (40-50 words) (3 M)

1. How does Leslie Norris use vivid imagery and metaphorical language in A Tiger in the Zoo, to effectively depict the confinement and oppression, experienced by the captive tiger. **(CBSE SQP, 2023)**
2. Why should the tiger snarl around houses at the edge of the forest?'.
3. Where should the tiger have been according to the poet?
4. Mention some of the activities of the tiger as stated in the poem.

Long Answer Questions (100-120 words) (6 M)

5. Love for freedom is the natural instinct of every living being. Comment.
6. The poet celebrates the strength of the tiger in this poem. Draw a contrast to the statement.
7. Is it right to confine wild animals into cages and take their freedom? Why or why not?

ANSWERS & EXPLANATIONS

Answer Key

Multiple Choice Questions

1. (*b*) **2.** (*a*) **3.** (*d*) **4.** (*c*) **5.** (*a*) **6.** (*c*) **7.** (*b*) **8.** (*b*) **9.** (*c*) **10.** (*d*)

Explanations

Extract-Based Questions

I. 1. (*a*) The last voice represents captivity, while the stars represent freedom.

2. (*b*) The correct answer is (*b*)

3. The mention of the tiger's brilliant eyes highlights its inherent beauty and magnificence, contrasting with the confinement it experiences. It emphasizes the loss of freedom and the potential for greatness that is restrained within the concrete cell.

4. Glistening

II. 1. (*a*) Assist in keeping the prey unsuspecting of the predator's sound.

2. (*c*) Prey which has quenched its thirst ensures the consumption of hydrated meat for the tiger.

3. (*b*) The hyena was __________ in its den after a good meal.

4. (*d*) The correct answer is (*d*).

5. (*d*) Lurking in the shadow

III. 1. (*a*) helplessness

2. he is watching for the deer, his prey, to approach the river.

3. it compares the softness of the tiger's paws to velvet.

4. (*d*) stalk

5. True

Subjective Questions

Short Answer Questions

CBSE Marking Scheme: Content-1 M, Organisation of Ideas-1 M, Accuracy-1 M

1. Leslie Norris uses vivid imagery and metaphorical language in "A Tiger in the Zoo" to effectively depict the confinement and oppression experienced by the captive tiger.

- The use of the words "vivid stripes" and "pads of velvet quiet" creates a powerful image of the tiger's physical beauty and grace that is restricted within the confines of the cage.
- The contrast between the tiger's natural habitat and its captivity is highlighted through the description of its expected behaviour in the wild such as "sliding through long grass" and "snarling around houses" and its actual behaviour within the cage.
- The metaphorical language used in "quiet rage" and "ignoring visitors" conveys the tiger's frustration and anger at being confined.
- The last two lines, "He hears the last voice at night, the patrolling cars, and stares with his brilliant eyes at the brilliant stars," depicts the tiger's longing for freedom and its natural habitat.
- Finally, the poem explores the psychological impact of captivity on the tiger through the use of vivid imagery and metaphorical language.

2. The tiger should snarl around houses at the edge of the forest as the villagers will not disturb the peace of the forest , they will not kill the animals for money or just for entertainment.

He wanted to show his ferociousness and create terror in villagers.

3. The poet thinks that the tiger should have been in its natural habitat , hiding in the shadow of long grass to catch his prey such as deer which is near the water hole.

He should have been on the outskirts of the jungle snarling and growling around houses and terrifying villagers.

4. Some of the activities of the tiger as mentioned in the poem are stalking within the confines of his cage, displaying his vivid stripes; moving quietly on soft and silent velvet paws, revealing his suppressed anger; being locked in a concrete cell, with his strength restrained behind bars.

Other activities like pacing the length of his cage, disregarding the presence of visitors; hearing the last voice at night and gazing with his brilliant eyes at the brilliant stars, representing a longing for freedom and connection with the wild.

Nailing the Right Answer

When answering, it is important to identify and discuss the specific activities or actions mentioned in the poem. By addressing these key actions and their significance, students can provide a comprehensive response to the question.

Long Answer Questions

CBSE Marking Scheme: Expression-2 M, Accuracy-1 M

5. It is true that love for freedom is the instinct of every living being. Everybody loves freedom and no one wants to live in confinement. **(1 M)**

Similarly, the tiger also longed for freedom. He was so annoyed at being in a cage that he even ignored the visitors. He moves to and fro in the cage to pass time. **(1 M)**

The tiger wanted to escape this captivity. All living beings are equal which implies that the animals too have the right to freedom.

His shining eyes towards brilliant stars show how much he longs for freedom. They should not be confined. It is their right to run freely in the forest, and catch their prey. Mankind should respect their freedom and should not capture them. **(1 M)**

6. The poet mentions the strength and fury of the tiger but also counters by showing that it is caged and unfree. His strength is taken away from him, and the tiger is frustrated as the mighty animal feels helpless in confinement. **(1 M)**

The tiger, unlike his forest life, has no freedom to move around and hunt in the small zoo. **(1 M)**

On the other hand, the real natural life of the majestic tigers involves walking in the tall grass and hunting the deer that pass near the pond. This proves that there was a time when they used to roam proudly and freely in the jungles. **(1 M)**

Nailing the Right Answer

When asked to draw a contrast, students should look for opposing views or situations presented in the text. They should identify the difference between the tiger's potential strength and its actual powerless state due to confinement.

7. Wild animals are made to live in the wilderness. They are not made to be caged or displayed in zoos. We all know that tigers are on the verge of extinction. **(1 M)**

There was a time when they used to roam proudly and freely in the jungles. They are not meant to live a life in cages. They have the right to freedom like all other human beings. **(1 M)**

To take someone's freedom leads to depression and misery. Moreover, their children lose their hunting capabilities as they are never trained to hunt in the wild. As a result, they do not know how to hunt their prey and feed themselves. Also, confining wild animals disturbs the whole ecological balance and natural cycles. We should, thus, let the animals be free in the wild. They are made for the forest and not for the cage. **(1 M)**

❑❑❑

HOW TO TELL WILD ANIMALS

—Carolyn Wells

4

Poetic Sketch

1. The poem is a funny take on how to recognize dangerous wild animals when they approach you.

2. If you're in the eastern jungle and a large, golden-brown animal roars at you, that's how you know it's the Asian Lion.

3. When a grand animal with yellow skin and black stripes comes up to you and decides to eat you, that's your clue it's the Bengal Tiger.

4. Should a creature with a coat full of spots leap at you, you can be sure that you've encountered a Leopard.

5. If you're in your yard and run into an animal that hugs you very tightly, you're dealing with a Bear.

6. Differentiating predators can be tough, but you can recognize a Crocodile if it cries, while a smiling one is a Hyena.

7. A Chameleon is a tiny lizard that blends in well with the trees because it has no ears or wings to make it stand out.

8. The whole poem uses humor to teach you about these animals' distinct and sometimes dangerous traits.

BEFORE YOU READ

Central Idea

The poem's central idea is to provide a humorous and light-hearted guide to identifying various dangerous animals that one may encounter while travelling through the jungles in the east. The poem gives simple and amusing rules for distinguishing between different creatures, such as the Asian lion, Bengal tiger, leopard, bear, crocodile, hyena, and chameleon. It portrays the wild animals as fierce, graceful, powerful, clever, and majestic creatures, emphasising their beauty and strength. It also conveys a message of respect for wildlife and the importance of observing them from a safe distance in their natural environment. The author employs humour to make the poem engaging and memorable, while also imparting practical advice for those who may find themselves in such situations.

STANZA-WISE ANALYSIS

Stanza 1

If ever you should go by chance
To jungle in the East
And if there should to you advance
A large and tawny[1] beast[2]
If he roars at you as you're dyin'.
You will know it is the Asian lion.

Explanation

In this stanza, the poet describes the characteristics of Asiatic lions. She claimed that if you ever get the chance to visit the eastern forest and happen to witness a yellowish-brown beast approaching you with a terrifying roar, you would believe you are about to die. If so, you are definitely in Asiatic lion territory[3]. She describes the Asiatic lion's roar as an important characteristic.

Stanza 2

Or if sometime when roaming round,
A noble wild beast greets you,
With black stripes on a yellow ground,
Just notice if he eats you.
This simple rule may help you learn
The Bengal Tiger to discern[4].

Explanation

She describes a royal creature that lives in the forest with yellow skin and black stripes. She claims that if he tries to kill and eat then it is undoubtedly a Bengal Tiger. She has once again used dark humour to describe how a tiger appears.

Stanza 3

If strolling[5] forth, a beast you view,
Whose hide with spots is peppered,[6]
As soon as he has lept on you,
You'll know it is the Leopard.
'T will do no good to roar with pain,
He'll only lep[7] and lep again.

[1] **Tawny:** yellowish-brown
[2] **Beast:** an animal; especially a large one
[3] **Territory:** area; region
[4] **Discern:** notice; observe
[5] **Strolling:** walking in a relaxed way
[6] **Peppered:** spotted
[7] **Lep:** jump

Rhyme Scheme

The rhyme scheme of the poem by Carolyn Wells is ABABCC.

Literary Devices

Alliteration: Repetition of two or more closely related words beginning with a consonant sound.

'Roaming round',

'Novice might nonplus'

Irony: It is used to express something other than and especially the opposite of the literal meaning.

e.g., A noble wild beast greets you.

He'll give you just one more caress.

Personification: It is a poetic device which gives human qualities to non living things or animals.

e.g., Animals are personified because the poet refers to them as 'he'.

Hyena's smile and crocodile's tears are personified here.

Assonance: Prominent sound of vowel

e.g., Or if sometime when roaming round. ('o' vowel sound)

'Strolling forth, a beast you view. ('o' vowel sound)

Whose hide with spots.

Do no good to roar.'

You meet a creature there. ('e' vowel sound)

Explanation

According to the poet, if you are casually strolling in a jungle, you will run into an animal whose skin is covered with spots. This animal is so swift[8] that it will instantly jump on you. This will be an indication that it is a Leopard. Furthermore, she continues, crying out in pain will not be helpful because the animal will continue to jump on you. The poet has described a leopard's characteristics throughout this stanza.

Stanza 4

If when you're walking round your yard,
You meet a creature there,
Who hugs you very, very hard,
Be sure it is the Bear.
If you have any doubt, I guess
He'll give you just one more caress.[9]

Explanation

If you are strolling through your lawn at home, a creature who might hug you tightly will be a bear. She further adds that if you are still in doubt regarding the animal, the easiest way is that he will keep hugging and touching you very gently. This act of his will make you sure about its identity. This is again said in a humoristic and ironic tone.

Stanza 5

Though to distinguish beasts of prey
A novice[10] might nonplus,[11]
The Crocodiles you always may
Tell from Hyenas thus:
Hyenas come with merry smiles;
But if they weep, they're Crocodiles.

Explanation

According to the poet, it will be difficult for someone just learning how to identify animals to identify creatures that hunt other animals for survival. By describing the differences between the two creatures, the poet attempts to assist the readers in this instance. While hyenas will be seen smiling, crocodiles are the animals that are always in tears.

Stanza 6

The true Chameleon is small,
A lizard sort of thing;
He hasn't any ears at all,
And not a single wing.
If there is nothing on the tree,
'T is the Chameleon you see.

Explanation

The poet says that the chameleon is the next creature in line. Although it has a lizard-like appearance, chameleons are different from lizards in that they lack ears and wings. She also claims that chameleons may alter their colour to match the surface they are resting on. As a result, if there is nothing else on a tree when you look at it, a chameleon must be there. It has changed its colour to match the colour of the tree.

[8] **Swift:** rapid; fast
[9] **Caress:** touch; stroke
[10] **Novice:** beginner; learner
[11] **Nonplus:** confused

What did the crocodile say when it shed a tear while hunting?

NCERT EXERCISE

Thinking about the Poem

(NCERT, Page 45)

1. **Does 'dyin' really rhyme with 'lion'? Can you say it in such a way that it does?**

Ans. The word 'dyin' is a poetic shortening of 'dying,' used here to force a rhyme with 'lion.' However, by dropping the 'g' in 'dying,' the poet intends for the ending to mimic the 'ion' sound in 'lion,' thus creating a slant rhyme.

Knowledge Hub

A slant rhyme is a type of rhyme with words that have similar, but not identical sounds.

2. **How does the poet suggest that you identify the lion and the tiger? When can you do so according to him?**

Ans. The poet differentiates between the two in the following manner:

He says that if the beast is yellowish-brown and roars out so fiercely that you may die out of fear, then this is an Asian lion.

Whereas, if the animal has black stripes on the yellow skin and he attacks to kill you, then it is a Bengal tiger.

3. **Do you think the words 'lept' and 'lep' in the third stanza are spelt correctly? Why does the poet spell them like this?**

Ans. The words 'lept' and 'lep' have not been spelled correctly. The correct spelling is leap and leapt . It is used by the poet to lay emphasis and maintain the rhythm of the poem.

4. **Do you know what a 'bearhug' is? It's a friendly and strong hug-such as bears are thought to give, as they attack you! Again, hyenas are thought to laugh and crocodiles to weep ('crocodile tears') as they swallow their victims. Are there similar expressions and popular ideas about wild animals in your own languages?**

Ans. Yes, in various languages and cultures, there are similar expressions and ideas about wild animals. For example, a "wolf in sheep's clothing" describes someone with a deceptive (to make somebody believe something that is not true) appearance. "Eagle-eyed" refers to someone with sharp vision. These phrases, like in the poem, use animal behaviors to describe human traits or actions, reflecting how people across cultures draw parallels between animal behavior and human characteristics.

5. **Look at the line 'A novice might nonplus." How would you write this 'correctly'? Why is the poet's 'incorrect' line better in the poem?**

Ans. The line "A novice might nonplus" can be correctly written as"A novice might be nonplussed". The incorrect line by the poet works better in the poem since it keeps the rhyme pattern. Nonplus, when written that way rhymes with 'thus'.

6. **Much of the humour in the poem arises from the way language is used, although the ideas are funny as well. If there are particular lines in the poem that you especially like, share these lines with the class, speaking briefly about what it is about the ideas or the language that you like or find funny.**

Ans. Yes, it is true that the poet has used the language in a way that it brings humour. The poet has used many lines that are funny such as:

'If he roars at you as you're dyin'. You'll know it is the Asian Lion...'

'A noble wild beast greets you'. The poet's description of the characteristics of the wild animals is quite funny.

MISCELLANEOUS EXERCISE

Multiple Choice Questions

1. Which of the following best describes the author's purpose in writing the poem. How to tell wild animals?
   (a) To provide a humorous guide to identifying dangerous animals in the eastern jungles.
   (b) To give a serious warning about the dangers of encountering wild animals.
   (c) To encourage readers to explore the natural beauty of the eastern jungles.
   (d) To describe the unique characteristics of various animals found in the eastern jungles.
2. What is the significance of the rule "If he roars at you as you're dyin', You'll know it is the Asian Lion"?
   (a) It shows how difficult it is to distinguish between different types of lions.
   (b) It emphasizes the danger of encountering an Asian Lion in the wild.
   (c) It suggests that the Asian Lion is more aggressive than other lion species.
   (d) It highlights the importance of being able to recognize the roar of different animals.
3. What can be inferred about the author's attitude towards the Chameleon in the poem?
   (a) The author is fascinated by the Chameleon's ability to blend in with its surroundings.
   (b) The author views the Chameleon as a dangerous predator to be avoided.
   (c) The author considers the Chameleon to be a harmless and unremarkable creature.
   (d) The author admires the Chameleon's unique physical features, such as its lack of ears and wings.
4. What is the effect of the author's use of rhyme and rhythm in the poem?
   (a) It creates a lighthearted and playful tone.
   (b) It emphasizes the seriousness of the message about animal safety.
   (c) It makes the poem more difficult to understand.
   (d) It detracts from the overall meaning of the poem.
5. Choose the option that matches with the rhyme scheme of the extract.

(1)	(2)	(3)	(4)
proud	wild	wild	loud
loud	jungle	proud	jungle
child	child	child	wild
wild	mingle	loud	child
jungle	loud	jungle	mingle
mingle	proud	mingle	proud

   (a) Option (1) (b) Option (2)
   (c) Option (3) (d) Option (4)
6. Whose roar is strong enough to die?
   (a) Lion (b) Leopard
   (c) Tiger (d) Dog
7. Choose the option that DOES NOT describe a 'novice'.
   (a) Lucky has cooked for the first time today.
   (b) Seema has been singing for the last ten years.
   (c) Riya went for her first Spanish class yesterday.
   (d) Aarav baked a cupcake to improve his baking skills.
8. Which animals are the beasts of prey?
   (a) Hyena (b) Crocodile
   (c) Both of them (d) None of them
9. 'A novice might nonplus', write this correctly.
   (a) A novice may nonplus.
   (b) A novice might nonplussed.
   (c) A novice nonplus might be.
   (d) A novice might be nonplussed.
10. "Noble wild beast", which literary device is represented here?
    (a) Alliteration (b) Metaphor
    (c) Oxymoron (d) Personification

Extract-Based Questions

I. Read the following extract and answer the questions that follow: **(5 M)**

If strolling forth, a beast you view,
Whose hide with spots is peppered,
As soon as he has lept on you,
You'll know it is the Leopard.
'Twill do no good to roar with pain,
He'll only lep and lep again.

(CBSE, 2023)

1. One can find out that it is a leopard by the way it __________.

(*a*) leaps (*b*) eats

(*c*) looks (*d*) roars

2. State whether the following statement is true or false:
When an animal repeatedly leaps at a person, it is a leopard.

3. Complete the sentence appropriately:
It is clear that repetition is a poetic device used for 'lep and lep again' because ________.
(Clue: explain how repetition is applied here.)

4. The Royal Bengal Tiger has black stripes on yellow skin whereas a leopard has ________.

5. Complete the analogy with a word from the extract:
claws : nails ________ : skin

II. Read the following extract and answer the questions that follow: (5 M)

"If when you're walking round your yard
You meet a creature there,
Who hugs you very, very hard,
Be sure it is a Bear,
If you have any doubts, I guess
He'll give you just one more caress."

1. What should you be sure of if a creature in your yard hugs you very hard? **(1)**

(*a*) It is a bear. (*b*) It is a rabbit.

(*c*) It is a squirrel. (*d*) It is a bird.

2. Select the option that applies the same rhyme scheme as the first six lines of the given extract. **(1)**

(*a*) The stars shine bright in the night,
The moon is glowing high,
The sky is filled with silver light,
As the cold winds pass by.
The trees sway left and right,
As clouds float in the sky.

(*b*) The wind is strong, the trees bend low,
The birds take flight with grace,
The river flows with steady flow,
And finds a resting place.
The night is cold, the stars shine bright,
The moon glows in the silver light.

(*c*) The sun will rise, the sky turns blue,
The birds will fly so high
The morning brings a golden hue,
As light fills up the sky.
The rivers flow, the flowers bloom,
The soft winds gently blow.

(*d*) The cat walks slow in the dark,
It leaves behind a tiny mark,
Its eyes shine in the night,
Before it slips out of sight.
The moon is bright, the air is still,
As it moves past the window sill.

3. What is the antonym of 'Disregard' (Choose from the above given extract)? **(1)**

4. The text is meant to be taken as a metaphor. Elaborate in about 30-40 words. **(2)**

III. Read the following extract and answer the questions that follow: (5 M)

Or if some time when roaming round,
A noble wild beast greets you,
With black stripes on a yellow ground,
Just notice if he eats you.
This simple rule may help you learn
The Bengal Tiger to discern.

1. How can you recognise a Tiger? **(1)**

(*a*) By black stripes on its yellow body.

(*b*) By its changing colour.

(*c*) By the way it hugs you.

(*d*) None of the above.

2. Why does the poet call him a noble animal? **(1)**

(*a*) He does not roar loudly.

(*b*) He helps others.

(*c*) Because he greets everyone.

(*d*) None of the above.

3. How is the Bengal Tiger different from the other animals? **(1)**

(*a*) As he roams quietly.

(*b*) His black stripes on yellow body.

(*c*) Both (*a*) and (*b*).

(*d*) None of the above.

4. What does the word 'ground' mean here? **(1)**

(*a*) It means the background of the skin.

(*b*) It means yellow land.

(*c*) It means yellow trees.

(*d*) None of the above.

5. Who has written these lines? **(1)**

(*a*) Lesslie norris (*b*) Carolyn wells

(*c*) Robert frost (*d*) William Wordsworth

IV. Read the following extract and answer the questions that follow: (5 M)

Though to distinguish beasts of prey
A novice might nonplus,
The Crocodile you always may Tell
from the Hyena thus:
Hyenas come with merry smiles;
But if they weep they're Crocodiles.

1. Choose the option that DOES NOT describe a 'novice'. **(1)**

(*a*) Lakshman has played cricket for the first time today.

(*b*) Samiksha has been teaching for the last ten years.

(*c*) Srishti went for her first French class yesterday.

(*d*) Gautam baked a second cake to improve his skills.

2. Where does a novice may get confused? (1)

(*a*) In differentiating between a hyena and crocodile.

(*b*) In differentiating leopard and tiger.

(*c*) Both (*a*) and (*b*).

(*d*) None of the above.

3. What, according to the extract, would cause bewilderment (confused)? (1)

(*a*) Discovering the similarity between different preys of beasts.

(*b*) Analysing habits of beasts that prey on hyenas.

(*c*) Knowing the difference between several beasts of prey.

(*d*) Drawing the similarities between crocodiles and hyenas.

4. Choose the line from the given stanza that the poet takes liberty with, to fit to the rhyme scheme. (1)

(*a*) Though to distinguish beasts of prey.

(*b*) A novice might nonplus.

(*c*) The Crocodile you always may.

(*d*) Hyenas come with merry smiles.

5. Complete the analogy here:

Hyena: Smile :: Crocodile: ________

(*a*) Laugh (*b*) Cry

(*c*) Swim (*d*) Bask

V. Read the following extract and answer the questions that follow: (5 M)

Or if some time when roaming round,
A noble wild beast greets you,
With black stripes on a yellow ground,
Just notice if he eats you.
This simple rule may help you learn
The Bengal Tiger to discern.

(CBSE, 2023)

1. Who is the 'noble wild beast' in the above lines? (1)

(*a*) zebra

(*b*) Asian Tiger

(*c*) Asian Lion

(*d*) Bengal Tiger

2. Complete the sentence appropriately.

It is clear that 'Alliteration' is the poetic device used for 'roaming round' because ________. (Clue : example how alliteration applies here) (1)

3. State whether the following statement is True or False: (1)

The extract helps to identify a Royal Bengal Tiger.

4. In the given lines, what effect does the poet create? (1)

'Just notice if he eats you,
This simple rule may help you learn
The Bengal Tiger to discern.'

(*a*) irony (*b*) terror

(*c*) sympathy (*d*) criticism

5. Which word in the extract tells you that you have recognised the 'noble beast'? (1)

(*a*) rule (*b*) discern

(*c*) roaming (*d*) notice

Subjective Questions

Short Answer Questions (40-50 words) (3 M)

1. How does a leopard behave when he sees someone?
2. What is so weird about the Hyena and the crocodile?
3. How can knowledge of an animal's typical behaviour and characteristics help in identifying wild animals?
4. Explore the use of imagery and descriptive language in the poem. How does it enhance the reader's experience?

Nailing the Right Answer

When answering questions about the use of imagery and descriptive language in a poem, it is helpful to provide specific examples from the poem to support your points.

Long Answer Questions (100-120 words) (6 M)

5. The poet has successfully used humour to be able to 'tell' or identify 'wild animals'. How do you think we need lots of it in our daily life?
6. How does the poem "How to tell wild Animals" by Carolyn Wells use humorous exaggeration and absurdity to not only entertain but also convey a deeper message about human perception and the inherent wildness within all of us?

Nailing the Right Answer

When analyzing a humorous poem like Carolyn Wells' "How to tell wild Animals," it's important to highlight the use of exaggeration and absurdity as literary devices. Students can explain how these techniques contribute to the overall entertainment value of the poem and how they create a sense of surprise and delight for us as readers.

ANSWERS & EXPLANATIONS

Answer Key

Multiple Choice Questions

1. (*a*) **2.** (*b*) **3.** (*a*) **4.** (*a*) **5.** (*c*) **6.** (*a*) **7.** (*b*) **8.** (*c*) **9.** (*d*) **10.** (*c*)

Explanations

Extract-Based Questions

I. 1. (*a*) leaps

2. True

3. it creates a rhyming effect and emphasizes the agility and quick movements of the leopard.

4. dark spots on its skin.

5. claws : nails : hide : skin

II. 1. (*a*) It is a bear.

2. (*b*) The correct answer is (*b*).

3. The antonym of 'disregard' is 'caress'.

4. This text uses a bear hug as a metaphor to describe a situation that is very intense or overwhelming, just like a strong hug from a bear. It's not about an actual bear but compares a powerful, hard-to-escape feeling or situation to a bear's big, tight hug. It adds fun to the idea of facing something very strong or big.

III. 1. (*a*) By black stripes on its yellow body.

2. (*a*) He does not roar loudly.

3. (*c*) Both (*a*) and (*b*).

4. (*a*) It means the background of the skin.

5. (*b*) Carolyn wells

IV. 1. (*b*) Samiksha has been teaching for the last ten years.

2. (*a*) In differentiating between a hyena and crocodile.

3. (*c*) Knowing the difference between several beasts of prey.

4. (*b*) A novice might nonplus.

5. (*b*) Cry

V. ***Topper's Explanation***

i. a. Bengal Tiger

ii. It is clear that 'alliteration' is the poetic device used for 'roaming round' because the same consonant sound - 'r' sound has been used at the start of two consecutive or closely-placed words.

iii. The given statement is true.

iv. a. irony

v. b. discern

Subjective Questions

Short Answer Questions

CBSE Marking Scheme: Content-1 M, Organisation of Ideas-1 M, Accuracy-1 M

1. When a leopard sees someone , it jumps over him at once and there is no use of crying.

It keeps on pouncing continuously on its victim, attacks and starts eating him.

2. According to the poet, the crocodile may be recognised by its tears, whereas the hyena can be recognised by its laugh. Here, the poet refers to an expression, "crocodile tears," which signifies fake tears, as well as the call of hyenas, which is known as the "hyena's laugh" since it sounds like a laugh of a human.

3. Knowledge of an animal's typical behaviour and characteristics help in identifying wild animals by providing insights into their natural tendencies and habits.

By understanding how certain animals behave, individuals can look for specific cues or actions, as highlighted in the poem, to differentiate them from other species. This knowledge serves as a valuable tool for accurately identifying wild animals in real-life situations.

4. The poem employs vivid imagery and descriptive language to enhance the reader's experience. Through colourful and imaginative descriptions of animals engaging in absurd behaviours, the reader is transported into a whimsical and fantastical world.

   This rich imagery not only adds to the humour and entertainment value of the poem but also allows readers to visualize and connect with the outrageous scenarios, making the reading experience more engaging and memorable.

Long Answer Questions

CBSE Marking Scheme: Expression-2 M, Accuracy-1 M

5. The poet uses humorous ways to describe various wild animals. Humour plays an essential role in our stressful lives. It would become difficult to continue life without humour. Today, the life of an ordinary man is typically filled with stress, tension, problems and sadness. **(1 M)**

   It relieves us from our monotonous routine and helps us face life with optimism. **(1 M)**

   Thus, the poet's successful use of humour helps enliven our minds and brings smiles to our faces. **(1 M)**

6. The poem "How to Tell Wild Animals" by Carolyn Wells uses funny and silly ideas to make people laugh and think. **(1 M)**

   It talks about dangerous animals in a joking way, like saying you'll know a tiger because it might eat you. This makes us smile, but it also makes us think about how we see animals and the wild parts inside us. **(1 M)**

   The poem shows that sometimes we don't understand nature well and use our imagination to fill in the gaps. It's a fun way to look at our mistakes and learn more about our connection with nature. **(1 M)**

❑❑❑

THE BALL POEM

—John Berryman

5

Poetic Sketch

1. The poem is about a boy who has lost his ball and is left with a feeling of grief.
2. The speaker observes the boy's reaction to the loss and notes that there is no consolation that can be offered.
3. The idea that "other balls" exist or that he can buy another does not comfort the boy.
4. Through this experience, the boy learns an important lesson about the nature of possessions and the transient nature of material things.
5. The poem expands the boy's loss to a universal level, suggesting that everyone will, at some point, experience loss.
6. The poem hints at the resilience of the human spirit—how individuals learn to cope with loss and eventually continue with their lives.

BEFORE YOU READ

Central Idea

The poem "The Ball Poem" tells the story of a young boy who experiences great distress after losing his ball. Although losing a toy may seem of little value, the ball represents the boy's childhood and his reluctance[1] to let go of it. Through the boy's experience, the poet emphasizes the importance of cherishing every moment in life because time passes quickly. The poem suggests that accepting change and learning to let go of the past are essential for personal growth.

STANZA-WISE ANALYSIS

Lines 1 to 4

What is the boy now, who has lost his ball,
What, what is he to do? I saw it go
Merrily bouncing, down the street, and then
Merrily over — there it is in the water!

Explanation

In the first four lines we see that a young boy has already lost his ball and he doesn't know what to do. The poet says that he himself has seen the ball bounce down the street and then fall into the water. Now the ball is lost, and the boy is left wondering what to do next. The situation captures a moment of childhood innocence and the unexpected, sudden experiences of loss and confusion that can come with it.

Lines 5 to 9

No use to say 'O there are other balls':
An ultimate shaking grief fixes the boy
As he stands rigid, trembling, staring down
All his young days into the harbour where
His ball went. I would not intrude on him;

Explanation

The poet says that it is useless to comfort the young boy by saying there are other balls, because to the young boy that particular ball is irreplaceable[2]. Due to this fact, the boy is extremely upset and cannot be consoled. His body is stiff ,but he is trembling as he stares at the water in the harbour where the ball fell and got lost. The poet understands that he will not be able to help the young boy in any way. He doesn't want to disturb the boy while the young boy is processing the emotion of loss in regards to the ball. In Line 4 the poet does equate the ball with the childhood or "young days" of the boy.

Lines 10 to 13

A dime, another ball, is worthless. Now
He senses first responsibility
In a world of possessions. People will take
Balls, balls will be lost always, little boy.

Explanation

The poet says that money or any other ball is useless because nothing can take the place of the lost ball. After the ball is gone, the young boy understands the idea of loss for the first time. He senses responsibility for losing something that belongs to him. This is a new feeling for the boy. The poet then says that society will always take away things, which are important to us.

---

[1] **Reluctance:** state of being hesitant
[2] **Irreplaceable:** cannot be replaced

Since the ball represents the young boy's childhood, the loss of innocence and the journey of the young boy into a world of experience is being talked about in these lines. Losing balls or having them taken away is like a symbol for how we leave our childhood behind and grow up, influenced by the world around us.

Rhyme Scheme

The ball poem does not follow a specific rhyme scheme. It is written in blank verse.

Lines 14 to 18

And no one buys a ball back. Money is external.
He is learning, well behind his desperate eyes,
The epistemology of loss, how to stand up
Knowing what every man must one day know
And most know many days, how to stand up.

Explanation

According to the poet, the lost ball cannot be bought back with money as it is external. The young man is learning about the epistemology (the theory of knowledge) of loss in a desperate way. The poet talks to the reader directly, (as he has done many times in the poem) and informs them that every man must one day know how to stand up and many men know how to do so already.

The poet is saying that money can only buy material objects, it can never buy back someone's childhood or innocence (as symbolized by the ball). Every human being has to accept that their childhood is over and grow up, which is represented by the last two lines of the poem.

Literary Devices

Alliteration: the 'b' sound in "buys a ball back"; consecutive words with the same starting sound.

Anaphora: repeated words in two or more consecutive lines.

Line 1 What is the boy...
Line 2 What, what is he...
Line 3 Merrily bouncing
Line 4 Merrily over.

Personification: The poet applies the adverb 'merrily' to the ball as it bounces down the street. The ball is given a human quality.
Line 3 'Merrily bouncing, down the street...'

That moment when your ball takes an unexpected dive into the water...

NCERT EXERCISE

Thinking about the Poem

(NCERT, Page 47)

1. **Why does the poet say, "I would not intrude[3] on him"? Why doesn't he offer him money to buy another ball?**

Ans. The poet says that he would not intrude on the boy because the poet cannot do anything to help him. The boy will learn from his grief about the loss of the ball; the boy will process his own grief in his own way and grow up in the process.

The poet doesn't offer money to replace the ball because the ball is a metaphor for the loss of innocence. It doesn't exist as something physical and cannot be replaced.

2. **"… staring down/All his young days into the harbour where/His ball went …" Do you think the boy has had the ball for a long time? Is it linked to the memories of days when he played with it?**

Ans. It is possible that the boy has had the ball for a very long time. He may have grown up playing with it and those memories of his childhood are very important to him. Just as the ball has now sunk in the harbour, the childhood memories associated are also at the bottom of the sea. In other words, the poet has lost his childhood memories.

3. **What does "in the world of possessions" mean?**

Ans. 'The world of possessions' represents the adult world filled with capitalism and consumerism where a person's worth is determined by what they have.

It is the world that we all live in, and in this poem this world represents adulthood.

4. **Do you think the boy has lost anything earlier? Pick out the words that suggest the answer.**

Ans. This is the first loss that the boy has experienced. There are many words in the poem which suggest the loss of the ball has upset the boy greatly. The boy feels 'ultimate shaking grief' when he loses the ball, and he stands rigidly, looking down at the harbour where the ball has disappeared.

He also feels responsible for an object for the first time, as shown by the words 'first responsibility'. The fact that the boy's grief is uncontrollable lets the reader know that the boy has indeed experienced a first time loss. This is why it is so hard for him to get over it.

5. **What does the poet say the boy is learning from the loss of the ball? Try to explain this in your own words.**

Ans. The poet believes that through the loss of the ball, the child will understand the concept of loss. Losing things that are important to us as we get older, is a vital[4] part of growing up. This loss of childhood and innocence is something that is faced by every person as they grow up. Society takes away the child's metaphorical ball and facing these hardships, the child becomes an adult. This is a cycle that happens over and over, which every human must go through.

6. **Have you ever lost something you liked very much? Write a paragraph describing how you felt then, and saying whether — and how — you got over your loss.**

Ans. When I was young, there was a beautiful mango tree in my grandfather's garden. As a child, I would climb the tree, and when the midday[5] sun became too strong, I would rest under its shade and watch the clouds in the sky. The tree was so strong. It survived the hot summers and the rainy season when hail would fall from the sky. In the autumn when the leaves of the tree would shed and the fruits would fall, I would play in the leaves, and then pick up the fallen mangoes from the ground and enjoy them.

As our neighbourhood grew, the fallen leaves from the tree started to anger the people around us. The people who had enjoyed the fruits of the tree started to curse the tree and they would constantly complain to my grandfather. When the whole neighbourhood got involved in this affair, my grandfather cut down the tree. The tree had been planted by my grandfather's mother and it had a history with my family. When it was cut down all of us felt the loss.

I felt that I had lost my childhood friend. I still feel sad when I think about the tree. I hope that I can plant trees in the future to keep the memory of the mango tree alive.

[3] **Intrude:** invade
[4] **Vital:** important
[5] **Midday:** 12 noon

MISCELLANEOUS EXERCISE

Multiple Choice Questions

1. In "The Ball Poem," what is the ball a symbol of?

(*a*) The boy's childhood.

(*b*) The boy's favourite toy.

(*c*) The boy's happiness.

(*d*) The boy's future.

2. How does the boy feel when he first loses the ball?

(*a*) Happy (*b*) Indifferent

(*c*) Upset (*d*) Excited

3. The loss of a possession should make one feel ______.

(The Ball Poem)

(*a*) angry (*b*) responsible

(*c*) sad (*d*) careless

(CBSE 2022- Term I)

4. According to the poet, every man should know how to overcome the ______.

(*a*) loss (*b*) difficulties

(*c*) problems (*d*) failures

5. What is the boy's attitude towards the ball at the end of the poem?

(*a*) He is still upset about losing it.

(*b*) He has completely forgotten about it.

(*c*) He is resigned to the fact that it is gone.

(*d*) He has learned to let it go and move on.

6. According to the poet, what is the child learning?

(*a*) To bear loss. (*b*) To take care of things.

(*c*) To be responsible. (*d*) To be careful.

7. Does the poet console the boy?

(*a*) Can't say (*b*) Yes

(*c*) No (*d*) All of them

8. Why does the poet decide not to console the boy?

(*a*) He is busy. (*b*) He is indifferent.

(*c*) It will be of no use. (*d*) He is happy.

9. Name the literary device used in "Merrily bouncing, down the street, and then Merrily over — there it is in the water!"

(*a*) Metaphor (*b*) Simile

(*c*) Alliteration (*d*) Anaphora

10. Name the literary device used in "And no one buys a ball back."

(*a*) Metaphor (*b*) Simile

(*c*) Alliteration (*d*) Anaphora

Extract-Based Questions

I. Read the following extract and answer the questions that follow: (5 M)

A dime, another ball, is worthless. Now
He senses first responsibility
In a world of possessions. People will take balls,
Balls will be lost always, little boy,

1. What is a dime? **(1)**

(*a*) An ancient artefact. (*b*) A coin of small value.

(*c*) A sloping dome. (*d*) A massive coin.

2. Why is another ball 'worthless'? **(1)**

(*a*) The boy doesn't like balls.

(*b*) The new ball is not as attractive.

(*c*) The original ball is irretrievable.

(*d*) The original ball is irreplaceable.

3. What is meant by 'world of possessions'? **(1)**

(*a*) A world full of suffering.

(*b*) We belong to the world.

(*c*) We can possess the world.

(*d*) A world of material objects.

4. Select the option that applies the same rhyme scheme as the lines of the given extract: **(1)**

(*a*) The moon shines bright in the sky
I hear the soft winds blow
The stars twinkle, flying by
While the clouds move slow

(*b*) A car drives fast down the street
The engine roars, a thunderous sound
The wheels spin, moving with heat
The road stretches far, unbound

(*c*) A bird flies high in the sky
The sun is setting low
I watch as it soars up high
With the wind gently blowing slow

(*d*) The clock ticks slowly on the wall
I listen as it counts the time
The minutes pass, the hours too
Life moves forward, as we do it .

5. Pick the sentence which explains '...balls will be lost always' **(1)**

(*a*) Children will always lose their toys.

(*b*) Toys are often lost while playing.

(*c*) We must get used to the feeling of loss.

(*d*) We will feel a lot of pain when we lose something.

II. Read the following extract and answer the questions that follow: **(5 M)**

What is the boy now, who has lost his ball,
What, what is he to do? I saw it go
Merrily bouncing, down the street, and then
Merrily over- there it is in the water!

(CBSE, QB)

1. The extract suggests that the poet is _____.
   (*a*) an onlooker observing
   (*b*) a parent recounting the incident
   (*c*) the boy talking about himself
   (*d*) imagining the incident
2. The poet seems to have indicated the merry bouncing of the ball to ____________.
   (*a*) create a sense of rhythm in these lines.
   (*b*) support the happiness of the experience of playing.
   (*c*) contrast with the dejected feeling of the boy.
   (*d*) indicate the cheerful mood of the boy.
3. Choose the situation that corresponds to the emotion behind the exclamation mark in the poem.

(1)	(2)
Hey! Hey! That's no way to dispose off the garbage. Have you no community sense? Please but it in the bin.	I knew it! I knew he'll fare well in his auditions for 'Young Chef'. Now, we prepare for the semi-finals.

(3)	(4)
I dont know where I've placed my ID-card. Let me check the bag once more. Ah, finally!	I've been trying to call mom for the past 20 minutes and can't get through. I don't know how... Aarrgh! Again!

   (*a*) Option (1) (*b*) Option (2)
   (*c*) Option (3) (*d*) Option (4)
4. The poem begins with a question. Based on your reading of the poem, the speaker ____________.
   (*a*) wants the boy to answer the question.
   (*b*) expects the passers-by to respond.
   (*c*) is looking for answers in a self-help book.
   (*d*) is thinking to himself.
5. Alliteration is a literary device that occurs with the same letter or sound at the beginning of adjacent or closely connected words.
   Pick the option that showcases an example of alliteration from the extract.
   (*a*) What is the boy now (*b*) who has lost his ball
   (*c*) I saw it go (*d*) and then/ Merrily over

III. Read the following extract and answer the questions that follow: **(5 M)**

What is the boy now, who has lost his ball,
What, what is he to do? I saw it go
Merrily bouncing, down the street, and then
Merrily over — there it is in the water!
No use to say 'O there are other balls':
An ultimate shaking grief fixes the boy

1. The boy has lost his ball. What does he have to do now? **(1)**
   (*a*) Buy a new ball.
   (*b*) Replace the ball with another toy.
   (*c*) Think about the ball.
   (*d*) Deal with the loss of the ball.
2. The ball bounces down the street __________. This is an example of __________. **(1)**
   (*a*) Merrily, Simile
   (*b*) Merrily, Imagery
   (*c*) Merrily, Personification
   (*d*) Merrily, Metaphor
3. Why is it useless to say 'there are other balls'? **(1)**
   (*a*) The ball will be found.
   (*b*) The ball will never be found.
   (*c*) The ball is irreplaceable.
   (*d*) Other balls are better than this ball.
4. How does the boy react to the loss of the ball? **(1)**
   (*a*) He cries a lot.
   (*b*) He doesn't care.
   (*c*) He cannot move with sadness and shock.
   (*d*) He laughs at losing the ball.
5. In the context of the poem, a synonym for 'ultimate' is **(1)**
   (*a*) Best (*b*) Conclusive
   (*c*) Fundamental (*d*) Ideal

IV. Read the following extract and answer the questions that follow: **(5 M)**

And no one buys a ball back. Money is external.
He is learning, well behind his desperate eyes,
The epistemology of loss, how to stand up
Knowing what every man must one day know
And most know many days, how to stand up.

1. What is the meaning of 'epistemology'? **(1)**
   (*a*) Theory of knowledge.
   (*b*) The origin of a word.
   (*c*) The theory of words.
   (*d*) The knowledge of words.

2. Select the option that applies the same rhyme scheme as the first four lines of the given extract: **(1)**

(*a*) The clock ticks on, so slow and loud,
I hear the whispers in the night,
I search for answers, but there's no end,
I know the future is shining bright,

(*b*) The storm rages on, the winds will blow,
I stand my ground, I will not fall,
The world is vast, the future unknown,
I'll keep my faith, and stand up tall,

(*c*) The stars above, they flicker bright,
I feel the warmth of the fire's glow,
I search for truth, I search for lie
But the darkness will always fall behind,

(*d*) A road stretches out, so wide and long,
I walk with courage in my heart,
The journey is tough, but I stay strong,
The world keeps changing, falling apart,

3. Why is money external? **(1)**

(*a*) It can only buy possessions.

(*b*) It can make you happy on the outside.

(*c*) Money can be touched and seen.

(*d*) Money is not inside us.

4. Complete the analogy:

Loss : Understanding :: ________ : ________

(*a*) Reading : Knowledge (*b*) Exercise : Health

(*c*) Money : Happiness (*d*) Growth : Pain

5. 'Desperate eyes' is an example of **(1)**

(*a*) Assonance (*b*) Metaphor

(*c*) Imagery (*d*) Personification

V. Read the following extract and answer the questions that follow: **(5 M)**

No use to say 'O there are other balls
An ultimate shaking grief fixes the boy
As he stands rigid, trembling, staring down
All his young days into the harbour where his ball went.
I would not intrude on him,
A dime, another ball, is worthless. Now
He senses first responsibility
In a world of possessions. People will take
Balls, balls will be lost always, little boy
And no one buys a ball back. Money is external
He is learning.....

(CBSE, 2024)

1. Which of the following best describes the speaker's attitude towards the boy's reaction to losing his ball **(1)**

(*a*) Indifferent as the ball is inexpensive

(*b*) Sympathetic, understanding the depth of the boy's loss

(*c*) Mocking, finding the boy's reaction exaggerated and unnecessary.

(*d*) Panicked, sharing the boy's distress over the lost ball.

2. Comment on the use of metaphor in the above extract. **(1)**

3. Explain the phrase 'all his young days into the harbour' with reference to the extract. **(1)**

4. Briefly state in about 45 words the boy's journey from 'shaking grief' to 'he is learning' in the above extract. **(2)**

Subjective Questions

Short Answer Questions (40-50 words) (3 M)

1. How does the boy feel when he loses the ball? What must he do now that the ball is lost?
2. Why is it useless to say 'O there are other balls'?
3. Why does the poet say that 'Money is external'?
4. 'He senses first responsibility' - What responsibility is referred to here? **(CBSE, 2018)**

Long Answer Questions (100-120 words) (6 M)

5. 'Loss is an important part of life'. How is this idea explored in 'The Ball Poem'?
6. "After death or separation from our loved ones, we feel unbearable pain." Comment on this statement.
7. "Losses after losses be lifted and losses after losses be left behind. Losses are a part of our inseparable life. We cannot isolate them." Comment on this statement.

ANSWERS & EXPLANATIONS

Answer Key

Multiple Choice Questions

1. (*a*) **2.** (*c*) **3.** (*b*) **4.** (*a*) **5.** (*d*) **6.** (*a*) **7.** (*c*) **8.** (*c*) **9.** (*d*) **10.** (*c*)

Explanations

Extract-Based Questions

I. 1. (*b*) A coin of small value.

2. (*d*) The original ball is irreplaceable.

3. (*d*) A world of material objects.

4. (*d*) The correct answer is (*d*).

5. (*c*) We must get used to the feeling of loss.

II. 1. (*a*) an onlooker observing.

2. (*c*) contrast with the dejected feeling of the boy.

3. (*d*) Option (4)

4. (*d*) is thinking to himself.

5. (*b*) who has lost his ball.

III. 1. (*d*) Deal with the loss of the ball.

2. (*c*) Merrily, Personification

3. (*c*) The ball is irreplaceable.

4. (*c*) He cannot move with sadness and shock.

5. (*b*) Conclusive

IV. 1. (*a*) Theory of knowledge.

2. (*c*) The correct answer is (*c*).

3. (*a*) It can only buy possessions.

4. (*d*) Growth : Pain

5. (*d*) Personification

V. ***Topper's Explanation***

(i) (B) Sympathetic, understanding the depth of the boy's loss

(ii) 'Ball' is used as a metaphor in the above extract. Ball, here, symbolises the child's innocence and his childhood memories which he had lost and is now gaining maturity while sensing his responsibilities.

(iii) 'All his young days into the harbour' refers to the boy's memories. The harbour reminds the boy of his young days when he used to play with his ball which was now lost into the harbour. The harbour is triggering the memories of his young

(iv) The boy's journey from 'shaking grief' to 'he is learning' represents his journey from his ~~young~~ young innocent days towards his maturity along with his responsibilities. The boy first feels despondent and ultimate grief on losing the ball which leaves him stationery and rigid. Soon, he realizes his responsibility of losing things in this materialistic world. He is learning that money cannot buy back his memories but could only buy materialistic things.

Subjective Questions

Short Answer Questions

CBSE Marking Scheme: Content-1 M, Organisation of Ideas-1 M, Accuracy-1 M

1. When the boy loses the ball he feels devastated. From a young boy's point of view, the ball cannot be replaced. The poet also feels the same way.

Once the ball is lost, the young boy must understand that losing things is a part of growing up. Everyone faces loss, and they have to deal with it and move on.

2. The ball that the young boy had was special to him. No other ball can ever be the same as that particular lost ball.

The lost ball held special significance for the young boy as it was tied to his childhood memories, a new ball would not hold the same significance for him.

3. In the poem, 'money is external' means that money can only buy worldly or materialistic things.

The poet aims to convey the idea that money cannot buy emotions, connections, love, childhood, etc. Once lost, these things are lost forever and will never be found again.

4. The responsibility referred to here is that of accepting the loss of something very dear to us. One should learn to get ones used the fact of losing something and move on. This is the first taste of all adversities waiting for your in this world. Thus, we should keep in mind that if we don't take proper care of things which are very dear to us, while its under our possession, we will regret when we lose it.

Long Answer Questions

CBSE Marking Scheme: Expression-2 M, Accuracy-1 M

5. 'The Ball Poem' centres around the idea of loss. The young boy loses a ball, and it affects him deeply. He is in shock and unable to move. **(1 M)**

   From his reaction to the loss of the ball, the readers can understand that it is his first loss. **(1 M)**

   When we lose something or someone important for the first time, it is difficult to deal with that deep sadness. We can recover from that grief slowly, over time. **(1 M)**

6. Losing a loved one is a devastating experience that can cause immense pain and suffering. According to John Berryman, the loss of anything can be painful and miserable, and losing a loved one is no exception. **(1 M)**

   For example, Losing a loved one in childhood or at any age can be incredibly difficult, and the feelings of grief and loss can be hard to put into words. **(1 M)**

   As A.L. Tennyson observed, change is an inevitable part of life, and we must learn to accept it. Death, separation, and loss are natural and unavoidable aspects of life, and they can be painful, troublesome, and unpleasant. While we may be unable to escape the pain of these losses, we can work to accept their inevitability and find ways to cope with the grief and sorrow they bring. **(1 M)**

7. Loss is an inevitable part of life, and we must learn to cope with it. Whether it is losing a beloved object like a ball, or losing a loved one to death or separation, loss can bring feelings of sadness and grief. **(1 M)**

   As we grow older, we come to understand that losses are a natural part of the human experience and cannot be avoided. While we may feel a deep attachment to the things and people we have lost, it is important to remember that nothing in this world is permanent. **(1 M)**

   As the saying goes, "losses after losses be lifted and losses after losses be left behind." While it may be difficult to let go of the past, we must learn to accept the reality of our losses and find ways to move forward. Ultimately, loss is an integral part of life that we cannot isolate or escape, but with patience and perseverance, we can learn to live with it and find ways to heal and grow. **(1 M)**

Nailing the Right Answer

When discussing the theme of loss, it's important to acknowledge the universal nature of this experience and its various forms, such as losing objects or losing loved ones through death or separation. Connect loss to the broader concept of impermanence, emphasizing that nothing in life is permanent and that accepting this reality is crucial for coping with loss.

AMANDA!

—Robin Klein

6

Poetic Sketch

1. The poem talks about a girl named Amanda who is often told what to do and is criticized.
2. Amanda dreams of being a mermaid, an orphan, and Rapunzel, because she wants to be free and away from real life.
3. Her dreams show she wishes for a different and happier life.
4. The poem is about how people are expected to act a certain way and how Amanda finds happiness in her dreams.
5. She ignores the criticism and stays in her dream world, which is her way of not following what everyone expects her to do.
6. The poem shows there is a struggle between what Amanda is being told to do and what she wishes for in her imagination.

BEFORE YOU READ

Central Idea

The poem 'Amanda' reflects the feelings of a girl child about her parents. This poem is about the upbringing of a child and setting a code of conduct for the same. It indicates that parents are concerned about their children and they want them to learn all the good habits and good behaviour but at the same time people forget that children also have sentiments and feelings. Scolding kids all the time and setting rules for them snatches their freedom.

Stanza 1

Don't bite your nails, Amanda!
Don't hunch[1] your shoulders, Amanda!
Stop that slouching[2] and sit up straight,
Amanda!

Explanation

The poet here focuses on aspects related to the upbringing of a child (especially a girl).In this stanza, Amanda is being criticised, for biting her nails and her sitting posture. The tone of instruction here is an authoritative one. Hence, it can be assumed that Amanda's parents are talking to her here. Parents often want their kids to represent brilliance. They feel a need for them to be appreciated and recognised for "appropriate behaviour". The word 'Amanda!' with an exclamation mark expresses her parents' annoyance and frustration.

Stanza 2

(There is a languid[3], emerald[4] sea,
where the sole inhabitant[5] is me-
a mermaid, drifting[6] blissfully.)

Explanation

In this stanza, lines are given in brackets as Amanda's views. She uses her imagination as an escape from the day-to-day instruction of her parents. She finds peace in her imaginative world, where there are no restrictions. She imagines herself to be a mermaid, sailing joyfully without any restraint[7] alongside the soft waves of the green sea. This world of Amanda is free from social rules and her happiness does not require the presence of another human being. The mermaid is a symbol of freedom.

Stanza 3

Did you finish your homework, Amanda?
Did you tidy your room, Amanda?
I thought I told you to clean your shoes,
Amanda!

Explanation

Amanda is questioned if she has finished her homework, cleaned up her room and cleaned her shoes. It highlights how she is always being questioned and overlaid with directions, which robs her of freedom and independence. Her name being called again with an exclamation mark shows her parents seem to be losing their cool over her behaviour.

Stanza 4

(I am an orphan, roaming the street.
I pattern soft dust with hushed[8], bare feet.
The silence is golden, the freedom is sweet.)

Explanation

In this stanza, we can observe how her parents' continuous questions make her annoyed and frustrated. Amanda escapes into her imaginary world. She imagines herself to be an orphan suggesting how annoyed she is with the continuous questioning of her parents. She has no shoes on her feet instead she is getting her feet even dirtier by making designs on the dusty ground with them. She cherishes the silence as well as the freedom to do as she likes in that world of her imagination. Her love for silence is the consequence of continuous nagging[9] and yelling she receives by her parents.

Stanza 5

Don't eat the chocolate Amanda!
Remember your acne,[10] Amanda!
Will you please look at me when I'm speaking to you,
Amanda!

[1] **Hunch:** to lean forward with your shoulders raised
[2] **Slouching:** sitting in a lazy manner
[3] **Languid:** relaxed
[4] **Emerald:** a bright green precious stone
[5] **Inhabitant:** a person or animal that lives in a particular area
[6] **Drifting:** moving slowly and freely
[7] **Restraint:** to prevent from doing or expressing something
[8] **Hushed:** quiet and still
[9] **Nagging:** complaining, annoying
[10] **Acne:** pimple

Rhyme Scheme

The rhyme scheme of Robin Klein's poem is AABA CCC.

Literary Devices

Alliteration: It is the occurrence of the same letter or sound at the beginning.

e.g., 'Stop that slouching and sit up straight.'

'Stop that sulking.'

Anaphora: Repeated use of certain word at start of two or more lines.

e.g., (don't bite... don't hunch,)

(Did you finish......did you tidy)

Assonance: use of vowel sound 'o'.

e.g., (don't hunch your shoulders)

Metaphor: It is a comparison between two different things.

e.g., 'silence is golden' – silence is said to be as precious as gold.

'freedom is sweet' – freedom is said to be like a sweet taste.

Allusion: Indirect reference to a person, event, or thing to a part of another text.

e.g., Mermaid: (taken from fairy tales) it is a sea creature with the head and upper body of a woman and the tail of a fish.

Rapunzel: (character of German fairy tale)

Refrain: Repetition of a sentence. ('Amanda!')

Explanation

The poet describes how the role of appearance is given more importance than values and creativity in our society. Amanda's parents want her to understand the value of external beauty, and take steps to preserve it. She is stopped by her parents from eating chocolate as it has caused her acne in the past. Here, it implies how a child is made conscious of her looks. Still, Amanda is lost in her thoughts and not even looking at her parents. This behaviour annoys her parents.

Stanza 6

(I am Rapunzel, I have not a care;
life in a tower is tranquil and rare;
I'll certainly never let down my bright hair!)

Explanation

Amanda is still lost in her imaginative world. She imagines herself to be the fabled, golden-haired Rapunzel who lived in a castle and had nothing to worry about. She feels Rapunzel's life must have been very peaceful in the tower. Amanda doesn't want her peace to be disturbed. She wants to lead a life where there is no intervention[11] by any other human being. Hence she observes that she will never let down her hair like the character so that she can achieve uninterrupted peace. We can observe here how the continuous instructions and commands of her parents had made her resistance to any human connection.

Stanza 7

Stop that sulking[12] at once, Amanda!
You're always so moody, Amanda!
Anyone would think that I nagged at
you, Amanda!

Explanation

The parents keep instructing Amanda on the dos and don'ts, but Amanda remains lost in her dreams. Her parents assume that Amanda is not responding because she is annoyed. Amanda's behaviour concerns her parents as they wanted to look responsible. They are concerned how society will perceive them if their child does not conform[13] to the rules of society.

[11] **Intervention:** interfere, involve
[12] **Sulking:** bad tempered
[13] **Conform:** obey

NCERT EXERCISE

Thinking about the Poem

(NCERT, Page 62)

1. How old do you think Amanda is? How do you know this?

Ans. Amanda's age might be between 10-12 years as references to a mermaid or Rapunzel is given which are from children tales. Her parents are constantly scolding her for usual teenager behaviour.

2. Who do you think is speaking to her?

Ans. Amanda is being spoken to by one of her parents. Most likely, it is her mother. We can say this as, traditionally, mothers are considered a child's first teacher. This is evident here as Amanda is being asked to do things a certain way.

3. Why are Stanzas 2, 4 and 6 given in parenthesis?

Ans. Parenthesis is added to a sentence, to provide an explanation.

So, in stanzas 2, 4 and 6 parentheses are used to describe Amanda's thoughts between the instruction and continuous nagging she is being given by her mother. In alternate stanzas the child's thought and the mother's nagging is described.

Knowledge Hub

Parentheses are a pair of curved marks that you put around words or numbers to indicate that they are additional or separate.

4. Who is the speaker in Stanzas 2, 4 and 6? Do you think this speaker is listening to the speaker in Stanzas 1, 3, 5, and 7?

Ans. The speaker in Stanzas 2, 4 and 6 is Amanda. No, she is not paying any attention to what her mother says.

She is lost in her own imaginative world where she imagines herself as a mermaid, an orphan and Rapunzel.

5. What could Amanda do if she were a mermaid?

Ans. Amanda wants to be a mermaid so that she can sail freely in the beautiful green sea. She thinks that her life will be peaceful and relaxing in the sea and she will be the only inhabitant of that emerald sea and able to enjoy her freedom without any intervention.

6. Is Amanda an orphan? Why does she say so?

Ans. No, Amanda is not an orphan. She is constantly being scolded and pointed out by her parents so she was upset.

She wants to be free from the restraints of her parents and wants to roam freely. Therefore, she feels that it would have been much better and peaceful if she had been an orphan.

7. Do you know the story of Rapunzel? Why does she want to be Rapunzel?

Ans. The story of Rapunzel is of a girl who is captured by an old witch in a tower. To make the old witch climb up the tower, she let down her long hair through a window. One day, a Prince visits her by climbing the tower with the help of her long hair. Amanda wants to be Rapunzel because she knows that there is no intervention of any human form if she will not let her hair down the window to help others to climb.

Amanda feels that life in the tower will be very peaceful and calm. She decided to never let her hair down for anyone as she doesn't want any restriction and disturbance.

8. What does the girl yearn for? What does this poem tell you about Amanda?

Ans. The girl Amanda yearns for peace and freedom in her life. She is constantly reminded of her mistakes.

Her parents want her to conform to the rules of society and behave accordingly. The poet has drawn the reader's attention to the condition of children who are constantly oppressed due to social rules.

9. Read the last stanza. Do you think Amanda is sulking and is moody?

Ans. No, Amanda is not moody. She feels oppressed because of her parent's constant chiding.

She doesn't want to be pointed out for such small things like cleaning the room, sitting straight, cleaning her room, etc. She longs for her freedom but she is under the constant pressure of trying to be the society's and her parents' definition of ideal.

MISCELLANEOUS EXERCISE

Multiple Choice Questions

1. Amanda wants to be all alone in the sea.

(*a*) Can definitely say.

(*b*) Can not say it definitely.

(*c*) Can somewhat say.

(*d*) None of the above.

2. What is the meaning of "slouching"?

(*a*) Bend (*b*) Sit in a lazy way

(*c*) Lie down (*d*) Bend backwards

3. Name the literary device used in the line
"Don't bite your nails, Amanda!
Don't hunch your shoulders, Amanda!"

(*a*) Anaphora (*b*) Enjambment

(*c*) Metaphor (*d*) Alliteration

4. What does Amanda imagine being when she pictures herself in a tower?

(*a*) Mermaid (*b*) Orphan

(*c*) Rapunzel (*d*) None of the above

5. What will Amanda's behaviour make people think?

(*a*) Her mother loves her.

(*b*) Her mother harasses her.

(*c*) Her mother is understanding.

(*d*) Both (*a*) and (*c*).

6. What does the speaker forbid Amanda to eat?

(*a*) Food (*b*) Fruit

(*c*) Chocolate (*d*) All of the above

7. Who was Rapunzel?

(*a*) A fairy (*b*) A witch

(*c*) A prince (*d*) All of the above

8. Amanda would rather indulge in fantasies than ________.

(*a*) Clean her room or her shoes.

(*b*) Listen to her parents.

(*c*) Wasting time studying.

(*d*) Going to school.

9. What tasks were given to Amanda by her mother (parent)?

(*a*) Cleaning her shoes. (*b*) Cleaning her room.

(*c*) Doing her homework. (*d*) All of the above.

10. What does a child never like, as mentioned in the poem?

(*a*) Nagging parents. (*b*) Unwanted instructions.

(*c*) Overprotective parents. (*d*) All of the above.

Extract-Based Questions

I. Read the following extract and answer the questions that follow: (5 M)

Don't bite your nails, Amanda!
Don't hunch your shoulders,
Amanda! Stop that slouching
and sit up straight, Amanda!

1. Select the option that applies the same rhyme scheme as the lines of the given extract: **(1)**

(*a*) Don't touch your face, Emily!
Don't wear that dress, Emily!
Put your shoes on,
hurry now, Emily!

(*b*) Please sit up, little boy!
Hold your pen, don't make noise,
Listen well, it's time to learn,
Don't let distractions be your toy.

(*c*) Don't lose your keys, Michael!
Don't be so quiet, Michael!
Put the papers in the file, Michael!
Behave yourself , Michael !

(*d*) Close the door, please, Karen!
Take your coat off, Karen!
The rain will stop soon, Karen!
We can step out karen !

2. What kind of tone is being used here in the stanza? **(1)**

(*a*) Requesting (*b*) Suggestive

(*c*) Commanding (*d*) All of the above

3. Which figure of speech is used in the expression 'stop that slouching'? **(1)**

(*a*) Metaphor (*b*) Alliteration

(*c*) Repetition (*d*) Personification

4. Which word is similar to the word 'hunch'? **(1)**

(*a*) Curve

(*b*) Bend

(*c*) Bow

(*d*) All of the above

5. How does the use of repetitive commands in the poem contribute to the understanding of Amanda's behaviour and the speaker's tone towards her? **(1)**

II. Read the following extract and answer the questions that follow: **(5 M)**

Don't eat that chocolate Amanda!
Remember your acne, Amanda!
Will you please look at me when I'm speaking to you Amanda!
(I am Rapunzel, I have not a care; life in tower is tranquil and rare, I'll certainly never let down my bright hair)

(CBSE, 2023)

1. The Speaker's tone is **(1)**
   (*a*) loving (*b*) hopeful
   (*c*) instructive (*d*) indifferent
2. Complete the analogy with a word from the extract:
   rare : uncommon :: peace : __________. **(1)**
3. State whether the following statement is TRUE or FALSE: **(1)**
   Amanda did not want anyone to invade her privacy and silence.
4. Select the appropriate option: **(1)**
   Amanda's mother is continuously ________ Amanda.
   (*a*) encouraging (*b*) reprimanding
   (*c*) motivating (*d*) disappointing
5. Which word in the extract is opposite in meaning to the word 'dull'? **(1)**
   (*a*) dreary (*b*) shady
   (*c*) bright (*d*) angry

III. Read the following extract and answer the questions that follow: **(5 M)**

(I am an orphan, roaming the street.
I pattern soft dust with my hushed, bare feet.
The silence is golden, the freedom is sweet.)

1. The tone of the given lines is **(1)**
   (*a*) Analytical (*b*) Despairing
   (*c*) Peaceful (*d*) Nervous
2. Read the statements A and B given below, and choose the option that correctly evaluates these statements. **(1)**
   Statement A: The figure 'I' imagines a less than realistic view of being an orphan.
   Statement B: The figure 'I' does not like the speaker.
   (*a*) A is true, B is false, according to the extract.
   (*b*) A is true, B cannot be clearly inferred from the extract.
   (*c*) A cannot be clearly inferred from the extract, B is false.
   (*d*) A is true and can be inferred from the poem, B is true too.
3. The golden silence is contrasted with the __________. **(1)**
   (*a*) Chaos of the street.
   (*b*) Constant instructions received.
   (*c*) Sweetness of freedom.
   (*d*) Hushed, bare feet.
4. The rhyme scheme 'aaa' in the above extract is followed in all other stanzas of the poem that are written in parenthesis, i.e., (). Why? **(1)**
   Read the reasons given below, and choose the option that lists the most accurate reasoning:
   (i) It shows the simplicity of the child's thoughts.
   (ii) It reflects the harmony and rhythm of the child's inner world.
   (iii) It mirrors a child's expression.
   (iv) It highlights the poet's aesthetic sensibility.
   (*a*) (i) and (iv) (*b*) (i) and (ii)
   (*c*) (ii) and (iii) (*d*) (iii) and (iv)
5. Pick the option that lists the usage of the word 'pattern', as in the extract above. **(1)**
   (*a*) That is a lovely pattern for a wallpaper.
   (*b*) He decided to wear a patterned shirt to the party.
   (*c*) Poetry is a form of pattern making.
   (*d*) She patterned her hair after her favourite celebrity.

Subjective Questions

Short Answer Questions (40-50 words) (3 M)

1. Amanda was blamed for a number of things. Mention any two. **(CBSE, 2022- Term II)**
2. Why does Amanda seem moody most of the times?
3. Why does Amanda wish to be a mermaid? **(CBSE, 2023)**
4. Is the purpose of someone constantly instructing Amanda being fulfilled? Comment.
5. Who is Amanda? What idea do you form of her by the poem?
6. 'Amanda is alone but not lonely in the world she envisions.' Give instances from the poem to justify. **(CBSE, 2022- Term II)**
7. How does the repeated use of the name 'Amanda' influence the overall tone of the poem? **(CBSE APQ, 2023)**
8. Explain why Amanda wants to be an orphan. Refer to the given lines, from the text - I am an orphan, roaming the street. I pattern soft dust with my hushed, bare feet. The silence is golden, the freedom is sweet. **(CBSE, 2024)**
9. What impression do you form about Amanda in the poem? **(CBSE, 2023)**

Long Answer Questions (100-120 words) (6 M)

10. State the key points in the poem Amanda. What do you learn from it?
11. Is Amanda's attitude typical teenage behaviour? What is the lesson for parents from this poem?
12. "Don't bite your nails, Amanda!
    Don't hunch your shoulders, Amanda!"
    Amanda's parents were over-anxious about her. She often found their instructions very stifling. Reading the poem and based on Amanda's experience, write a paragraph on the topic "Should parents be allowed to control children?"

ANSWERS & EXPLANATIONS

Answer Key

Multiple Choice Questions

1. (*a*) **2.** (*b*) **3.** (*a*) **4.** (*c*) **5.** (*b*) **6.** (*c*) **7.** (*a*) **8.** (*a*) **9.** (*d*) **10.** (*d*)

Explanations

Extract-Based Questions

I. 1. (*b*) The correct answer is (*b*).

2. (*b*) Suggestive

3. (*b*) Alliteration

4. (*d*) All of the above

5. The repetitive commands in the poem highlight the speaker's constant dissatisfaction with Amanda's behaviour and their desire for her to conform to certain standards of posture and behaviour.

II. 1. (*c*) instructive

2. solitude/quiet [Hint - Synonym]

3. True

4. (*b*) reprimanding

5. (*c*) bright

III. 1. (*a*) Analytical

2. (*c*) A cannot be clearly inferred from the extract, B is false.

3. (*a*) Chaos of the street.

4. (*a*) (i) and (iv)

5. (*c*) Poetry is a form of pattern making.

Subjective Questions

Short Answer Questions

CBSE Marking Scheme: Content-1 M, Organisation of Ideas-1 M, Accuracy-1 M

1. Amanda's mother consistently reminded her about essential manners for a young girl to be graceful and elegant. She was constantly advised to sit straight without slouching and to keep her room and shoes clean.

2. Amanda seems moody as she wants to escape her harsh reality where she is nagged by her parents. She is getting instructed continuously which annoys her. It is indeed a difficult situation for a young child like Amanda to bear. Here the only escape is her imagination where she often imagines herself free from conformity to social rules and nagging by her parents. Hence, she seems moody and uninterested.

3. Amanda wishes to be a mermaid who lives a carefree, unrestricted existence on the languid emerald sea.

Mermaids represent a kind of escape from the mundane and ordinary world, and Amanda longs for a life where she is not stopped by her parents for being lazy, sitting as she likes or eating chocolates.

4. No, Amanda hates and becomes moody whenever someone gives her too many instructions. She does not listen to her mother and doesn't want to follow the instructions but she also can't dare to ignore them.

Parents face challenges to make their children well-behaved that's why they keep ordering them.

5. Amanda is a very young school-going girl. She loves fairy tales like Rapunzel and stories of Mermaids.

She doesn't like getting too many instructions or nagging from her parents, making her sulk and moody at times. Then she does not want to listen to her mother's instructions attentively and always starts daydreaming in her head.

Nailing the Right Answer

When answering questions based on the provided question, students can focus on the themes of parental expectations, the desire for freedom, and the impact of upbringing on a child's sense of self. Students should support their answers with specific examples from the poem to demonstrate their understanding of the themes and messages conveyed.

6. Amanda wants to live alone and away from her parent's do's and don'ts. She imagines herself as a mermaid who is drifting happily in the sea. She envisions herself enjoying her solitude, whereas a lonely person feels sad and upset in almost every facet of their life. That's why it is said that Amanda is alone and not lonely in the world she envisions.

7. The given detailed reference points can be drawn upon to structure the desired response:

- The repeated use of the name 'Amanda' throughout the poem creates a sense of authority and control.
- As the name 'Amanda' is repeated throughout the poem, it conveys a commanding tone, as if someone in a position of authority, such as a parent, is speaking directly to Amanda.
- Since the name 'Amanda' is repeated numerous times, followed by instructions or directions, it also creates a tone of frustration or annoyance. The repetition of the name also adds a sense of familiarity and intimacy to the tone. It suggests a close relationship between the speaker and Amanda, indicating that the instructions and restrictions come from a place of care and concern.

8. Amanda wishes to be an orphan to experience a life of freedom and quiet. In the poem, her fantasy is about being alone, roaming the streets without anyone to tell her what to do. She dreams for a life where she can be carefree and doesn't have to follow orders, where the silence is comforting, and her freedom is not restricted.

9. ***Topper's Explanation***

Amanda was a young girl who was constantly nagged by her mother, in a bid to fit Amanda into the mold dictated by society. In the process, Amanda felt that her individuality was curtailed. That Amanda felt restricted by the numerous instructions clamped down on her by her mother is evident from how Amanda escaped into a world of fantasy. In this world, she was, at times, a mermaid drifting blissfully in the sea and at others, an orphan rambling down the street, drawing patterns in the sand with her bare feet or Rapunzel, secluded from the bustle of human existence, in her tall tower. All Amanda yearned for was freedom - a freedom that gave wings to her fantasies, that just let her be herself and live in a world not bound by any restrictions.

Long Answer Questions

CBSE Marking Scheme: Expression-2 M, Accuracy-1 M

10. Every child is unique in themselves, and it requires a great deal of patience and love to make them understand this. This poem deals with the upbringing of children and the struggles faced by them. It is natural for a child like Amanda to seek freedom and peace at her place. Often parents tend to impose the ideal definition of a kid on them. They see adherence to those norms as a representation of. **(1 M)**

This poem shows how a child feels trapped and yearns for freedom and peace due to the continuous nagging and instruction of her parents. **(1 M)**

We see that her parents are miserable when Amanda wishes to be an orphan in order to be free. Parents are accountable for their child's upbringing, so they should keep this in mind so it doesn't feel like imprisonment to them. **(1 M)**

11. Amanda's attitude is typical of a teenager. Teenagers can be rebellious and apparently hot-headed with a highly independent perspective. **(1 M)**

In such circumstances, yelling at them and nagging them, as done in the poem with Amanda, will only make matters worse. **(1 M)**

Forcing decisions on them only makes them more detached as we see in Amanda's case, where she wishes to be a love mermaid, an orphan or the lonely Rapunzel. She doesn't want to listen to anyone. **(1 M)**

12. It goes without saying that no child can survive the early years of their lives without the care and protection of their parents. But some parents are so overprotective and over-anxious about their children that they don't let their children live in peace. **(1 M)**

They don't allow them to explore and find things on their own. Such parents kill the child's initiative in learning. These parents always boss around and irritate their children. They don't trust their child's capability to do things independently. **(1 M)**

However, the parents may control the children and guide them as long as it is necessary. Equipped with knowledge and confidence they will be able to face the world boldly. Gradually the child should be allowed to grow on its own and be responsible for its actions. When parents give freedom to their children they gain confidence and learn to do things in a better way. **(1 M)**

❑❑❑

THE TREES

7

—Adrienne Rich

BEFORE YOU READ

Central Idea

Adrienne Rich's poem "The Trees" has a profound meaning. Nature has a strong and natural drive to take back its place from areas built by humans. The poem describes trees that were trapped inside as breaking free and returning to the wild. As they move, a place that was once empty and quiet becomes lively and full of trees again. This change shows nature's power to come back to life and grow, even after being held back by people and their buildings.

The poet is known to be a feminist and is probably comparing the confinement of nature to women's position in a patriarchal society. Society has oppressed women, limiting their development and binding them with so-called societal norms.

STANZA-WISE ANALYSIS

Stanza 1

The trees inside are moving out into the forest,
the forest that was empty all these days
where no bird could sit
no insect hide
no sun bury[1] its feet in shadow
the forest that was empty all these nights
will be full of trees by morning.

Explanation

According to the poet, trees are leaving houses. They are emerging from the artificial "glasshouses" in which humans have imprisoned them. This is unreal because trees cannot be moved. The poem has a symbolic meaning in this context. It translates trees as females who are confined within four walls. They have healed and are now free to roam the world and fulfil their several purposes, out their in the real world. She emphasises that the forest has been empty for many days, so no birds can be seen because there are no branches for them to sit on, no insects can hide, and the Sun cannot disappear under the shadow of trees. As trees move outside, forests will become more dense.

Stanza 2

All night the roots work
to disengage[2] themselves from the cracks
in the veranda floor.
The leaves strain toward the glass
small twigs[3] stiff with exertion
long-cramped boughs[4] shuffling under the roof
like newly discharged patients
half-dazed[5], moving
to the clinic doors.

Explanation

The poet describes the plants' struggle to break free from the confines of the house. She emphasises that the roots worked hard all night to separate themselves from the veranda floor. The leaves worked hard to reach the glass window and get outside. Every part of the tree, including the small stems, worked hard to break free from their confinement. The large branches were also attempting to leave the room. The poet describes the long and continuous struggle of women for liberation and freedom, implying that women are working hard to break down the walls that confine them, and their effort is compared to that of a child.

[1] **Bury:** hide underground
[2] **Disengage:** detach
[3] **Twigs:** stem
[4] **Long crumpled boughs:** branches that are confined or restricted
[5] **Dazed:** unable to act and think properly; amazed

Rhyme Scheme

Adrienne Rich's poem does not follow a consistent rhyme scheme. It is written in free verse, which means it lacks a regular pattern of end rhymes.

Literary Devices

Personification: It is a poetic device that gives human qualities to non living things or animals.

e.g., "The trees inside are moving out into the forest."

"No sun bury it's feet in shadow."

"Winds rush them to meet them."

"Roots working for the whole night."

Alliteration: It is the occurrence of the same letter or sound.

e.g., Long Letters,

Sky Still

Leaves and Lichen

Metaphor: It is a comparison between two different things.

e.g., The 'house' is a metaphor for a society that confines a woman inside and 'the trees' are women who have to move outside breaking the glass.

Simile: Comparing two unlike things that is often introduced by like or as.

e.g., The moon is compared to a mirror. (Moon is broken like a mirror).

Trees compared to patients. (like newly discharged patients).

Stanza 3

I sit inside, doors open to the veranda
writing long letters
in which I scarcely mention the departure
of the forest from the house.
The night is fresh, the whole moon shines
in a sky still open
the smell of leaves and lichen[6]
still reaches like a voice into the rooms.

Explanation

The poet claims to be sitting on her veranda, writing long letters in which she does not mention the trees that are leaving her house. In this context, "house" refers to a patriarchal society-created a prison that led women to believe that they should always be confined within four walls. She also claims that the night is crystal clear. She can see the full moon, which is shining brightly. The smell of leaves and lichens is referred to as a woman's voice, which is yelling and expressing a desire for freedom from the confines of the house.

Stanza 4

My head is full of whispers
which tomorrow will be silent
Listen. The glass is breaking
The trees are stumbling[7] *forward*
into the night. Winds rush to meet them.
The moon is broken like a mirror,
its pieces flash now in the crown
of the tallest oak.

Explanation

The poet's mind is filled with the whispers and murmurs of the trees, who are desperate to leave. These noises will not be heard in the morning because they will have already left the house. Here are the whispers of women who wish to break free from the patriarchal mindset. As she hears the breaking of a glass window and the stumbling of trees in the night, the poet describes how change is about to occur. Outside, the wind is blowing. These occurrences represent societal change. The norms have now been altered. The moon is like a mirror, and it appears to be broken into pieces as the oak tree's shadow divides it into many fragments. Here, the oak tree is described as the tallest, which means women have defeated the patriarchy.[8]

[6] **Lichen:** small group of plants
[7] **Stumbling:** moving with difficulty

[8] **Patriarchy:** system in which men have all the power

NCERT EXERCISE

Thinking about the Poem

(NCERT, Pages 100 & 101)

1. (i) Find, in the first stanza, three things that cannot happen in a treeless forest.

(ii) What picture do these words create in your mind: "... sun bury its feet in the shadow..."? What could the poet mean by the sun's 'feet'?

Ans. (i) The three things that cannot happen in a treeless forest:

(a) Sitting of a bird on branches,

(b) Insects will not find any place to hide.

(c) The sun cannot bury its feet in the shadow of the forest, which means the sun cannot find any shade in a treeless forest.

(ii) The poet uses personification, as the sun is personified as having manly feet. The given words create an image of a blazing sun unable to cool its feet because there are no trees in the forest. If the forest is dense, the sun will appear to be burying its feet in the shadows cast by the trees.

2. (i) Where are the trees in the poem? What do their roots, leaves, and their twigs do?

(ii) What does the poet compare their branches to?

Ans. (i) The trees can be found in the poet's home. Their roots try to escape the cracks in the veranda floor. They had been working all night to get away from the house.

The leaves work hard to move towards the glass; even the small twigs help the leaves by stiffening up to move outside.

(ii) The poet compares the "long-cramped" branches to newly discharged patients who appear half-conscious as they rush towards the clinic doors after long illnesses and being out of the hospital. Similarly, the branches are cramped under the roof to escape the confinement of four walls. They desired to spread out in the fresh air.

3. (i) How does the poet describe the moon:

(a) at the beginning of the third stanza, and

(b) at its end? What causes this change?

(ii) What happens to the house when the trees move out of it?

(iii) Why do you think the poet does not mention "the departure of the forest from the house" in her letters? (Could it be that we are often silent about important happenings that are so unexpected that they embarrass us? Think about this again when you answer the next set of questions.)

Ans. (i) The full moon is shining on a clear night at the start of the third stanza. At the end of the stanza, she compares the moon to a broken mirror that has been shattered into many pieces. Because there were no trees, the poet could see the full moon.

They'd made their way from her house to the street. Their branches have risen into the sky, obstructing the poet's view of the moon; as a result, the moon appears to be broken into many pieces.

(ii) When the trees leave the house, there is complete silence, glasses are shattered, and the smell of the leaves and lichens reaches the rooms like a voice.

(iii) The poet does not mention the trees' departure from the house in her letters because it was marked by struggle and hard-won freedom. She emphasises that if humans were concerned about the trees, they would never have consider confining them in the house. Their departure was unexpected and significant, which could have embarrassed the poet.

4. Now that you have read the poem in detail, we can begin to ask what the poem might mean. Here are two suggestions. Can you think of others?

(i) Does the poem present a conflict between man and nature? Compare it with "A Tiger in the Zoo." Is the poet suggesting that plants and trees, used for 'interior decoration' in cities while forests are cut down, are 'imprisoned', and need to 'break out'?

(ii) On the other hand, Adrienne Rich has been known to use trees as a metaphor for human beings: this is a recurrent image in her poetry. What new meanings emerge from the poem if you take its trees to be symbolic of this particular meaning?

Ans. (i) Yes, the poem depicts a clash between man and nature. Nature is more free and unbounded; man has cut down forests and replaced them with colonies and buildings. They use plants to decorate houses, kill animals for food or other purposes, and confine them in zoos. In all of these ways, man limits nature and animals, making them appear to be imprisoned.

The poem depicts plants being confined within four walls and rebelling against men because they cannot fully develop.

In 'A Tiger in the Zoo,' the same conflict is highlighted. The poet illustrates how animals feel confined by cages because they cannot leap inside them, despite their desire to run and leap.

(ii) If trees represent humans, then houses represent human society as a whole, which is dominated by patriarchy.

Trees could represent women who, like men, want to break free from patriarchal society. They, like men, want to explore and enjoy their freedom.

They continue to work hard in their routines despite being confined within four walls. They are fighting for freedom by speaking out against male dominance.

MISCELLANEOUS EXERCISE

Multiple Choice Questions

1. What is the main subject of the poem?
   (a) Trees (b) Patriarchy
   (c) Veranda (d) Glass
2. What is the condition of the forest before the events in the poem?
   (a) Empty (b) Overgrown
   (c) Colorful (d) Noisy
3. What are the trees doing in the poem?
   (a) Moving into the forest.
   (b) Growing taller.
   (c) Swaying in the wind.
   (d) Losing their leaves.
4. What is happening to the moon in the poem?
   (a) It is shining brightly.
   (b) It is hidden by clouds.
   (c) It is broken like a mirror.
   (d) It is disappearing.
5. What is the poet doing inside the house?
   (a) Writing letters (b) Sleeping
   (c) Watching the trees (d) Painting
6. What are the roots of the trees doing?
   (a) Growing deeper.
   (b) Breaking through the floor.
   (c) Entangling with each other.
   (d) Absorbing sunlight.
7. What does the poet compare the long-cramped boughs to?
   (a) Patients (b) Shadows
   (c) Doors (d) Mirrors
8. What is the overall mood of the poem?
   (a) Joyful (b) Sad
   (c) Mysterious (d) Angry
9. What senses are evoked in the poem?
   (a) Sight and sound (b) Taste and touch
   (c) Smell and taste (d) Sound and touch
10. What does the poet imply about the future in the poem?
    (a) It will be uncertain.
    (b) It will be dark.
    (c) It will be full of surprises.
    (d) It will be peaceful.

Extract-Based Questions

I. Read the following extract and answer the questions that follow: (5 M)

My head is full of whispers
which tomorrow will be silent
Listen. The glass is breaking
The trees are stumbling forward
into the night. Winds rush to meet them.
The moon is broken like a mirror,
its pieces flash now in the crown
of the tallest oak.

1. Why would the whispers be silent tomorrow? (1)
   (a) As trees will move outside the house.
   (b) As trees don't know how to move.
   (c) As trees don't how to speak.
   (d) None of the above.
2. Select the option that applies the same rhyme scheme as the first four lines of the given extract: (1)
   (a) The moon is high in the sky
   Its light is glowing bright
   The stars are shining, so far away
   I feel their warmth, it's such a delight.
   (b) The breeze is soft and slow
   Whispers travel through the trees
   They hum a tune, a quiet glow
   And shake the branches with such ease.
   (c) The rain falls gently on the ground
   The world is silent, calm, and still
   The leaves are dancing all around
   While night embraces all with a chill.
   (d) The clouds are drifting apart,
   The sky is dark, the stars are few.
   The winds are whispering a prayer
   While shadows grow, so does their silence.
3. Which poetic device has been used in the sixth line of the stanza? (1)
   (a) Simile (b) Oxymoron
   (c) Antithesis (d) None of the above
4. What is the significance of the breaking glass and the trees stumbling forward into the night in the given extract? How do these images contribute to the overall theme or message of the poem? (2)

II. Read the following extract and answer the questions that follow: **(5 M)**

All night the roots work
to disengage themselves from the cracks
in the veranda floor.
The leaves strain toward the glass
small twigs with exertion
long-cramped boughs shuffling under the roof
like newly discharged patients
half-dazed, moving
to the clinic doors.

(CBSE QB, 2021)

1. Choose the option that lists the examples of exertion. **(1)**
   (i) Neha had been up all-night keeping accounts and now she's resting.
   (ii) Swati was running for five miles non-stop last evening.
   (iii) Hemant is watching his favourite show and having snacks.
   (iv) Sachin helped a senior citizen board a flight in the morning.
   (*a*) (i), (ii) (*b*) (ii), (iii)
   (*c*) (iii), (iv) (*d*) (i), (iv)
2. Choose the image that represents the main object of the extract literally. **(1)**

(i)  (ii) 

(iii)  (iv) 

(*a*) (i) (*b*) (ii)
(*c*) (iii) (*d*) (iv)

3. Choose the correct option that mentions the correct poetic device against the correct example. **(1)**

(i)	simile	long cramped boughs
	metaphor	like newly discharged patients
(ii)	personification	small twigs stiff with exertion
	simile	like newly discharged patients
(iii)	refrain	under the roof
	simile	leaves strain toward the glass
(iv)	personification	like newly discharged patients
	refrain	half-dazed, moving

(*a*) (i) (*b*) (ii)
(*c*) (iii) (*d*) (iv)

4. The poet of the poem is **(1)**
   (*a*) Robin Klein (*b*) Walt Whitnan
   (*c*) Anrienne Rich (*d*) Robert Frost
5. Choose the option listing the image that the poem metaphorically represents. **(1)**

(i)  (ii) 

(iii)  (iv) 

(*a*) Option (i) (*b*) Option (ii)
(*c*) Option (iii) (*d*) Option (iv)

III. Read the following extract and answer the questions that follow: **(5 M)**

My head is full of whispers
Which tomorrow will be silent.
Listen. The glass is breaking.
The trees are stumbling forward
into the night. Winds rush to meet them.
The moon is broken like a mirror,
its pieces flash now in the crown
of the tallest Oak.

(CBSE, 2024)

1. Identify the figure of speech used in the line: "The Trees are stumbling forward into the night". **(1)**
2. Explain the significance of the line: **(2)**
   "The moon is broken like a mirror, its pieces flash now in the crown of the tallest Oak." Answer in about 40 words.
3. Complete the sentence with the appropriate option. In the third line, the word 'Listen' is used to ________. **(1)**
   (*a*) serve no purpose but to complete the sentence.
   (*b*) emphasize listening carefully to the sound of glass breaking.
   (*c*) emphasize listening carefully as a change is about to take place.
   (*d*) make the reader more attentive.
4. What does the line: "My head is full of whispers which tomorrow will be silent" tell us about the poet's state of mind? **(1)**

Subjective Questions

Short Answer Questions (40-50 words) (3 M)

1. Justify the revolt of the trees and state two values which the man should possess to stop the revolt.
2. How does the poet describe the night? How does she feel?
3. In the poem 'Trees', where are the trees ? What are their roots, twigs, etc. trying to do?

Long Answer Questions (100-120 words) (6 M)

4. What is the central idea of the poem 'The Trees'.

ANSWERS & EXPLANATIONS

Answer Key

Multiple Choice Questions

1. (*a*) **2.** (*a*) **3.** (*a*) **4.** (*c*) **5.** (*a*) **6.** (*b*) **7.** (*a*) **8.** (*c*) **9.** (*a*) **10.** (*c*)

Explanations

Extract-Based Questions

I. 1. (*a*) As trees will move outside the house.

2. (*a*) As they hurry in to move outside.

3. (*a*) Simile

4. The breaking glass and the trees stumbling forward into the night symbolize breaking of barriers and a movement towards transformation. These images suggest a sense of liberation and the embrace of change, reflecting the poem's theme of embracing new experiences and letting go of the familiar.

II. 1. (*a*) (i), (ii)

2. (*d*) The correct answer is (*d*).

3. (*b*) (ii)

4. (c) Anrienne Rich

5. (*d*) Option (iv)

III. 1. The figure of speech used here is personification because the trees are given the human action of stumbling, which trees cannot literally do.

2. The line means that the moon looks like it has shattered into pieces, and these pieces seem to shine in the top branches of the tallest oak tree. It creates a picture of something beautiful turning into chaos but still having moments of beauty, as the broken pieces light up the tree.

3. (*c*) emphasize listening carefully as a change is about to take place.

4. The line indicates that the poet is having a lot of thoughts or concerns ("whispers") that are supposed to stop ("will be silent"), implying a desire for a calmer or more resolved state of mind.

Subjective Questions

Short Answer Questions

CBSE Marking Scheme: Content-1 M, Organisation of Ideas-1 M, Accuracy-1 M

1. Because of the limited space, the plants or trees brought in for interior decoration feel suffocated. As they grow older, they feel trapped in the house. They try to break free from the cracks in the veranda floor. They make an effort to get some fresh air.

They have every right to revolt. Men should recognise the negative consequences of their actions.

2. The poet describes the full moon shining brightly in the open sky. It was a peaceful night, concealing the silent struggle. Her mind is filled with whispers in the form of their voices, in which plants are longing for freedom. The aroma of leaves and lichens filled the space.

However, she believes that the next day, the trees will leave the forest and be free.

3. Trees are located in the poet's home in the poem. To free themselves from the gaps in the veranda floor, their roots struggle all night.

While the tiny twigs become stiff from the effort, the leaves make an effort to move towards the glass.

Long Answer Questions

CBSE Marking Scheme: Expression-2 M, Accuracy-1 M

4. According to the poem 'The Trees,' it is the conflict between humans and nature in the rebellion of trees against human oppression.

The natural habitat of trees and animals is a forest. Humans have harmed them greatly by confining them in houses. Trees have been uprooted and placed in artificial glasses by man. **(1 M)**

The value of nature and large forests has declined; trees have been felled, animals have been killed, and water bodies have been destroyed for their benefit.

They can grow naturally and freely in the forest rather than in an artificial glass house. The poet is attempting to convey that trees, too, require freedom. **(1 M)**

They break free from all bonds and return to their natural state. The destructive forms of nature, e.g., flood, earthquake, etc., teach man that the real power lies with nature, and it can do anything. **(1 M)**

Nailing the Right Answer

When answering questions related to the poem "The Trees," it is important to focus on the conflict between humans and nature. Students should support their answers with evidence from the poem and to consider the broader implications of human-nature relationships.

FOG

—Carl Sandburg

8

BEFORE YOU READ

Central Idea

The poem "Fog" by Carl Sandburg is about how fog can change the way we see the world. The fog is described as a living thing that moves like a cat, and it makes everything look different and mysterious. The poem suggests that fog is a natural phenomenon that we can't fully understand, but it has the power to transform the way we see things. The poet's unique take on nature makes the poem an interesting read.

Rhyme Scheme

The poem does not follow any specific rhyme scheme. It is a short poem also known as a 'haiku'.

Literary Devices

Metaphor: The entire poem is a metaphor for the fog as a cat that moves stealthily and silently, covering everything in its path.

Alliteration: The phrase 'little cat feet' uses alliteration, which repeats the 't' sound.

Assonance: The words 'fog', 'comes' and 'on' utilize the same 'o' sound, which repeats in the poem and makes it sound musical.

Transferred Epithet: When any quality (adjective) is transferred from its original object to another, it is called a transferred epithet. The adjective 'silent' in Line 5, "on silent haunches", has been transferred from the cat-like fog to the haunches or the backside, which makes it a transferred epithet.

Lines 1-2

The fog comes
on little cat feet.

Explanation:

In the poem, the poet Carl Sandburg uses a metaphor to compare the fog to a cat, or rather a cat-like creature. The comparison is drawn because both the fog and the cat approach[1] their respective targets silently and unnoticed. The use of "little" implies a sense of cuteness and innocence, while "cat feet" suggests gracefulness and fluidity[2]. Like a cat's soft and padded[3] feet, the fog also moves noiselessly and covers its surroundings. The poet believes that the fog operates in a similar way to a cat in this regard.

Lines 3-4

It sits looking
over harbour and city

Explanation:

These lines further develop the metaphor of the fog as a cat, describing it as observing the world around it. Like a predator[4], the fog is waiting patiently, perhaps in an effort to catch some prey[5]. In nature, we can see that when fog descends[6], it lingers[7] for a long time before it disappears. The poet highlights the similarity between the cat's hunting behaviour and the fog's lingering presence, both lasting for a long time before disappearing.

Lines 5-6

on silent haunches[8]
and then moves on.

Explanation:

The image of the fog sitting on "silent haunches" suggests that it is ready to pounce[9] or take action, further emphasizing its power and unpredictability. The poet says that fog waits quietly for some time in a silent manner, and then it finally vanishes. These lines concludes[10] the fog's journey. The word 'silent' emphasizes how the fog is quiet, just like the quiet and peaceful cat.

Knowledge Hub

What is a haiku?

A haiku is a specific type of short Japanese poetry which uses a particular syllabic structure, the most common being five syllables followed by seven and then followed again by five syllables. 'The Fog' uses a similar structure but changes all the lines to seven syllables.

[1] **Approach:** come near in distance or time
[2] **Fluidity:** the ability to flow easily
[3] **Padded:** filled or covered with soft material for the purpose of protection, comfort, or to add shape
[4] **Predator:** an animal that naturally preys on others
[5] **Prey:** an animal that is caught and killed by another for food
[6] **Descends:** move or fall downward
[7] **Lingers:** wait around
[8] **Haunches:** the back end of an animal
[9] **Pounce:** spring or swoop suddenly
[10] **Conclude:** bring (something) to an end

NCERT EXERCISE

Thinking about the Poem

(*NCERT, Pg. 115*)

1. (i) What does Sandburg think the fog is like?

(ii) How does the fog come?

(iii) What does 'it' in the third line refer to?

(iv) Does the poet actually say that the fog is like a cat? Find three things that tell us that the fog is like a cat.

Ans. (i) The poet Carl Sandburg thinks that the fog is like a cat-like creature.

(ii) The fog comes and surrounds everything very quietly, like a cat with its small padded feet which makes no noise.

(iii) In the third line, 'It' refers to the titular fog which the poet describes as a natural phenomenon.

(iv) Yes, the poet actually says that the fog is like a cat. He says this because

(*a*) It arrives on its 'little cat feet', as stated in the first line of the poem.

(*b*) The fog looks at the city like a cat watching its surroundings.

(*c*) The fog disappears very quietly with cat-like haunches, as used in Line 5.

2. You know that a metaphor compares two things by transferring a feature of one thing to the other.

(i) Find metaphors for the following words and complete the table below. Also, try to say how they are alike. The first is done for you.

Storm	tiger	Pounces over fields, growls
Train	snake	Rope-like body, fast-moving
Fire	sun	Gives lights, burns, removes darkness
School	factory	Factory produces average products; school makes average students
Home	shelter	Safe place to grow and thrive

(ii) Think about a storm. Try to visualize the force of the storm, hear the sound of the storm, feel the power of the storm and the sudden calm that happens afterwards. Write a poem about the storm, comparing it with an animal.

Ans (ii) *The students have to write the poem on their own.*

Answering Tip

The storm is like a tiger about to pounce
Once the prey is captured,
The tiger sits silently, eating.

3. Does this poem have a rhyme scheme? Poetry that does not have an obvious rhythm or rhyme is called 'free verse'.

Ans. The poem does not have a rhyme scheme, and it is written in free verse. There are no sentences which start or end with similar-sounding words.

MISCELLANEOUS EXERCISE

Multiple Choice Questions

1. What is the central idea of the poem "Fog" by Carl Sandburg?

(*a*) The dangers of fog.

(*b*) The beauty of fog.

(*c*) The transformative[11] power of fog.

(*d*) The science behind fog.

2. How does the speaker characterize the movement of the fog?

(*a*) As slow and deliberate[12].

(*b*) As fast and chaotic[13].

(*c*) As graceful and fluid.

(*d*) As rough and jagged[14].

3. What does the speaker mean when he says that the fog "comes on little cat feet"?

(*a*) The fog is quiet and stealthy[15], like a cat.

(*b*) The fog is small and cute, like a cat.

(*c*) The fog moves quickly and unpredictably, like a cat.

(*d*) The fog is mysterious and magical, like a cat.

4. What does the speaker mean when he says that the fog "sits looking over harbour and city"?

(*a*) The fog is observing the city and harbour.

(*b*) The fog is resting on top of the city and harbour.

(*c*) The fog is controlling the city and harbour.

(*d*) The fog is hiding the city and harbour.

5. What does the speaker suggest about the nature of fog?

(*a*) That it is a living creature.

(*b*) That it is a scientific phenomenon.

(*c*) That it is a supernatural force.

(*d*) That it is a metaphor for something else.

6. The poem which uses the cat as an extended metaphor is:

(*a*) Animals (*b*) Amanda

(*c*) Fog (*d*) The Trees

7. Which scenic beauty is captured in the poem 'Fog'?

(*a*) A waterfall.

(*b*) A winter day.

(*c*) The moment when the fog comes over the harbour.

(*d*) Snow-covered mountains.

8. How does the poem 'Fog' represent nature?

(*a*) In its natural side.

(*b*) In its artificial surroundings.

(*c*) As animal-like.

(*d*) None of the above.

9. What does the fog do in the end?

(*a*) Comes rapidly. (*b*) Continues being there.

(*c*) Moves on. (*d*) All of the above.

10. What is the tone of the poem "Fog" by Carl Sandburg?

(*a*) Frightening (*b*) Matter-of-fact

(*c*) Scientific (*d*) Mysterious

Extract-Based Questions

I. Read the following extract and answer the questions that follow: **(5 M)**

The fog comes
on little cat feet.
It sits looking
over harbour and city
on silent haunches
and then moves on. **(CBSE SQP, 2023)**

1. In what way does the language used in this poem challenge traditional ideas of what poetry should be? **(1)**

2. What is the significance of the use of the word "little" to describe the fog in the poem and how does this word choice contribute to the overall mood and tone of the poem? Answer in about 40 words. **(2)**

3. Complete the sentence with the appropriate option.

The lines from the poem tell us that the city is _____. **(1)**

A. hilly B. coastal C. industrial D. under-developed

4. Identify the type of imagery used in the lines of the poem. **(1)**

II. Read the following extract and answer the questions that follow: **(5 M)**

'The fog comes
on little cat feet.
It sits looking
over harbour and city
on silent haunches
and then moves on'

(CBSE, QB)

[11] **Transformative:** causing a change in someone or something
[12] **Deliberate:** done on purpose
[13] **Chaotic:** in a state of confusion and disorder
[14] **Jagged:** spiky; rough
[15] **Stealthy:** secretive; hidden

1. Choose the option with the qualities of the cat that Carl Sandburg applies to the fog. **(1)**

1. Cats are independent animals, they don't follow the rules, and they slip and slide in and out of our lives as they like.
2. Cats are distrustful of strangers and can be jealous and moody.
3. Cats are stealthy, moving in slow motion at times, and they appear to be moving in a mysterious fashion.
4. Cats often communicate with a combination of distinctive sounds and body language.
5. Cats like to move on at their own pace, and before you know it, they've disappeared.

(*a*) Only 1 (*b*) Only 4
(*c*) 1, 3 and 5 (*d*) 2, 3 and 4

2. Which one/s of the following applies to the given lines? **(1)**

1. Personification is a literary device where you give an animal, object or natural phenomenon, qualities or abilities that only a human can have.
2. Transferred epithet a literary device when an adjective usually used to describe one thing is transferred to another.
3. Imagery is the language used by poets, and writers to create visual representation of ideas in the minds of the readers.
4. Oxymoron is a figure of speech in which contradictory terms appear side by side.

(*a*) 1 and 4 (*b*) 2 and 3
(*c*) Only 1 (*d*) Only 3

3. Choose the option that DOES NOT list the movement of the fog. **(1)**

1. It stole in on us like a foot-pad Somewhere out of the sea and air... *-EJ. Pratt*
2. A fog drifts in, the haevy-laden Cold white ghost of the sea- *-Sara Teasdale*
3. The fog it tricks the eye The wonder of the veil of white Under the clear blue sky. *-K.C. Cox*
4. ...comes gliding, rolling in at ground level, pressing its white featureless face against... *-R.H. Grenville*

(*a*) Option 1 (*b*) Option 2
(*c*) Option 3 (*d*) Option 4

4. Pick the option that includes an image of the cat on its haunches. **(1)**

(1) (2) (3) (4)

(*a*) Option 1 (*b*) Option 2
(*c*) Option 3 (*d*) Option 4

5. Which figure of speech is prominent in the poem, 'Fog'? **(1)**

(*a*) Simile (*b*) Personification
(*c*) Alliteration (*d*) Metaphor

III. Read the following extract and answer the questions that follow: (5 M)

'It sits looking
over harbour and city
on silent haunches
and then moves on'

1. Select the option that applies the same rhyme scheme as the lines of the given extract: **(1)**

(*a*) The wind is blowing
through the empty streets
as the trees sway gently
while the shadow enlightens

(*b*) The stars are shining
high above the sea
the waves are rolling
and then they set me free.

(*c*) The moon is rising
across the vast sky
the birds are calling
as the clouds float by.

(*d*) The rain is falling
on the quiet town
it whispers softly
and then it comes down.

2. Haunches refer to **(1)**

(*a*) Legs (*b*) Backside
(*c*) Stomach (*d*) Thighs

3. The words 'harbour and city' tell us that **(1)**

(*a*) The city has a sea beach.
(*b*) The city has a shipyard.
(*c*) The city overlooks the sea.
(*d*) The city gets foggy due to the sea.

4. The literary device used in "on silent haunches" is **(1)**

(*a*) Personification
(*b*) Metaphor
(*c*) Transferred epithet
(*d*) Assonance

5. 'It sits looking/over harbour and city'. This means that the fog **(1)**

(*a*) Covers everything and makes it hard to see.
(*b*) Stays for some time.
(*c*) Gazes at the landscape.
(*d*) Makes it hard to breathe.

Subjective Questions

Short Answer Questions (40-50 words) (3 M)

1. Describe the similarities that have been mentioned in the poem between the fog and a cat.
2. How does Carl Sandburg describe the arrival, stay and departure of the fog through the image of a metaphorical cat?
3. What effect does the short structure of the poem Fog have on its meaning?

Long Answer Questions (100-120 words) (6 M)

4. The poet has a unique point of view on a natural phenomenon. Discuss with reference to 'The Fog'.
5. What metaphor has the poet used in the poem 'Fog'? Do you think it is appropriate?

ANSWERS & EXPLANATIONS

Answer Key

Multiple Choice Questions

1. (*c*) **2.** (*a*) **3.** (*a*) **4.** (*a*) **5.** (*d*) **6.** (*c*) **7.** (*c*) **8.** (*a*) **9.** (*c*) **10.** (*d*)

Explanations

Extract-Based Questions

I. 1. Unlike traditional poetry that often relies on complex rhyme schemes and metaphors, this poem uses simple, everyday language to create a vivid picture in the reader's mind to create a powerful and evocative mood.

2. The word "little" used to describe the fog in the poem suggests the subtle and quiet nature of the fog. The word "little" also evokes a sense of innocence and vulnerability, as if the fog is a harmless creature moving through the city. This contributes to the overall mood and tone of the poem, which is calm and peaceful, with a touch of mystery.

3. (*b*) coastal [the evidence lies in the use of the word 'harbour']

4. visual/animal imagery

II. 1. (*c*) 1, 3 and 5

2. (*d*) Only 3

3. (*c*) Option 3

4. (*b*) Option 2

5. (*d*) Metaphor

III. 1. (*a*) The correct answer is (*a*).

2. (*b*) Backside

3. (*c*) The city overlooks the sea.

4. (*c*) Transferred epithet

5. (*b*) Stays for some time.

Subjective Questions

Short Answer Questions

CBSE Marking Scheme: Content-1 M, Organisation of Ideas-1 M, Accuracy-1 M

1. The poem "Fog" by Carl Sandburg draws similarities between the fog and a cat in several ways.

   The fog is compared to a cat in its ability to move silently and stealthily. The first line of the poem describes the fog as coming "on little cat feet." This creates an image of the fog moving quietly and smoothly, just like a cat.

   Both the fog and the cat have an air of mystery around them. The fog is described as "looking over harbour and city on silent haunches", which creates an image of the fog observing everything quietly.

   Overall, the poem "Fog" uses the image of a cat to convey the quiet and mysterious nature of the fog.

2. In the poem "Fog," Carl Sandburg uses the image of a metaphorical cat to describe the arrival, stay, and departure of the fog. Sandburg begins the poem by comparing the fog to a cat, saying that it "comes on little cat feet." This creates an image of the fog creeping in silently and smoothly, just like a cat.

   Sandburg goes on to describe how the fog settles over the city, saying that it "sits looking over the harbour and city on silent haunches."

   Finally, Sandburg describes the fog lifting and moving away, saying that it "moves on". This creates an image of the fog departing just as quietly and smoothly as it arrived, like a cat slipping away unnoticed.

3. The poem Fog is short and concise which helps contribute to the overall meaning of the poem.

- The short and precise nature of the poem creates a clear and focused message. It conveys the simplicity of the fog's presence.
- The short lines and quick pacing create a sense of swiftness and movement, mirroring the nature of the fog itself. This also mirrors the agile nature of a cat as mentioned in the poem.
- The concise structure allows for vivid and impactful visual imagery. Each line presents a distinct image, such as the fog sitting "looking over harbour and city" or "on silent haunches." Each visual image depicted contributes to the overall mood and atmosphere of the poem.

Long Answer Questions

CBSE Marking Scheme: Expression-2 M, Accuracy-1 M

4. In the poem "Fog," Carl Sandburg offers a unique perspective on a natural phenomenon that is often considered ordinary and unremarkable. Through his use of metaphor, Sandburg gives the fog a personality and presence that is both mysterious and interesting. **(1 M)**

By describing the fog as moving "on little cat feet," Sandburg suggests that it is stealthy and almost magical presence, one that can sneak up on us and then disappear just as quickly. **(1 M)**

Moreover, Sandburg's description of the fog as "sitting" and "looking over harbour and city on silent haunches" creates an image of the fog as an observer, watching everything with a quiet and patient presence. This contrasts with the more common perspective on fog, which is often seen as simply a thick, obstructive cloud that can cause inconvenience and discomfort. **(1 M)**

Nailing the Right Answer

In the case of LAQs, students should use the points from the knowledge hub to elaborate on the type of poem which is otherwise not mentioned. They must use their own observation skills and see how the cat compares to the fog.

5. In the poem "Fog," Carl Sandburg uses a metaphorical comparison between the fog and a cat to emphasize the silent and mysterious nature of the fog. The poet draws a parallel between the fog's quiet movement and a cat's silent footsteps. **(1 M)**

The comparison between the fog and a cat highlights how both leave an impression and make their presence felt. **(1 M)**

The comparison also emphasizes the fog's stealthy approach, which is similar to a cat's. Overall, Sandburg's comparison of the fog to a cat is an effective way of conveying the elusive[16] and unpredictable nature of the phenomenon. **(1 M)**

❑❑❑

[16] **Elusive:** difficult to find

9

THE TALE OF CUSTARD THE DRAGON

—Ogden Nash

Poetic Sketch

1. Belinda lives in a little white house with a variety of animals: a black kitten (Ink), a grey mouse (Blink), a yellow dog (Mustard), and a pet dragon (Custard).
2. Custard, the dragon, is described as cowardly, with sharp teeth, spikes, scales, and daggers on his toes.
3. Belinda is brave, while Custard is afraid and cries for a safe cage.
4. Ink, Blink, and Mustard tease Custard and laugh at him in a red wagon.
5. Belinda tickles Custard mercilessly while the others mockingly call him Percival.
6. Suddenly, a pirate climbs into the house, wielding pistols and a cutlass.
7. Belinda calls for help, Mustard flees, Ink hides, and Blink strategically escapes through a mousehole.
8. Custard, however, confronts the pirate bravely, attacking him with a clattering tail.
9. The dragon devours the pirate, and Belinda and the others embrace Custard.
10. Mustard regrets being flustered, while Ink and Blink believe they could have been braver.

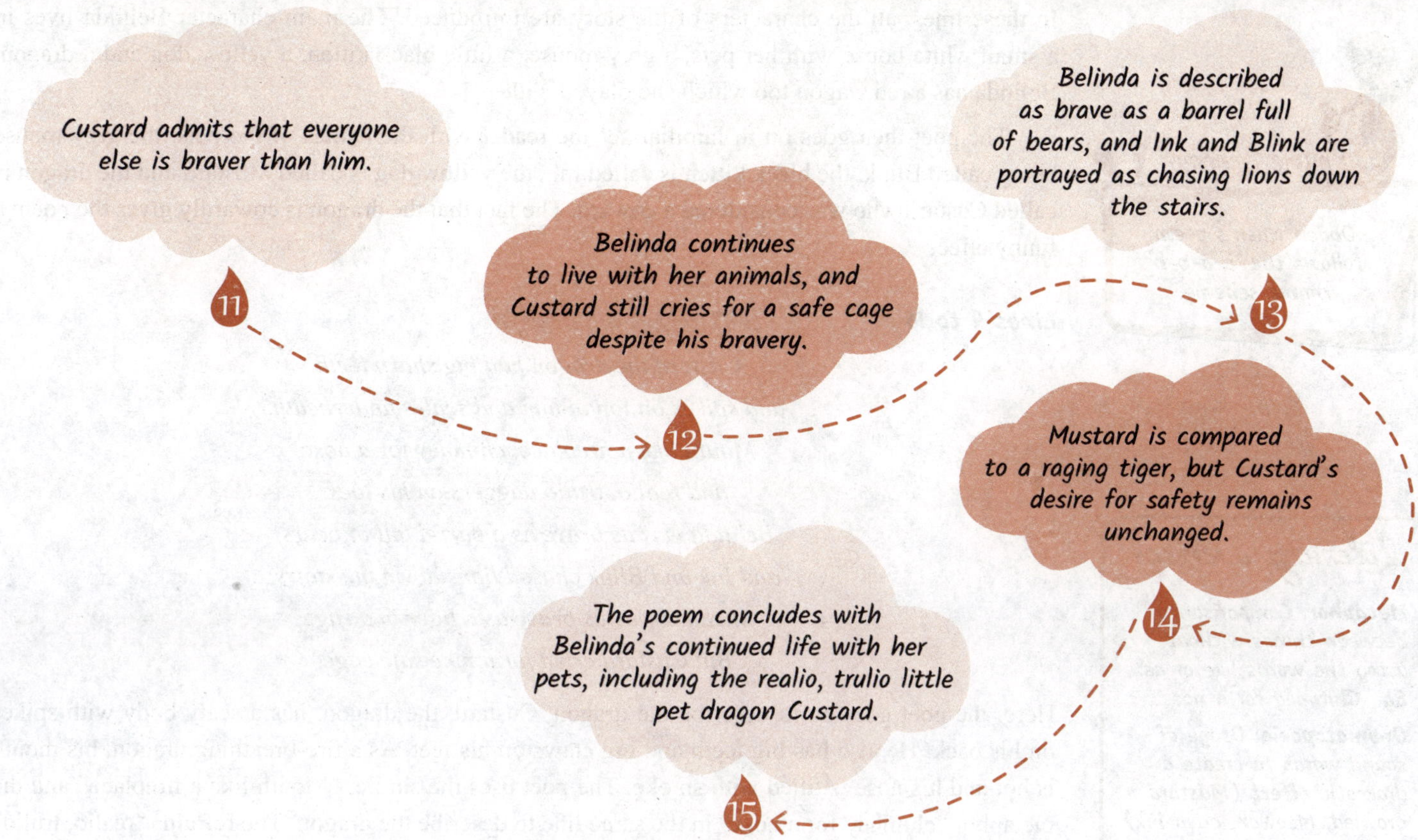

BEFORE YOU READ

Central Idea

The central idea of the poem is the exploration of bravery and cowardice through the characters of Belinda, her pets, and her pet dragon, Custard. While Belinda, Ink, Blink, and Mustard display courage and fearlessness in the face of danger, Custard is portrayed as a timid and fearful character who longs for safety and confinement. The poem conveys the message that bravery can come from unexpected sources and that true courage is not always determined by outward appearances. Despite Custard's initial reluctance, the poem concludes with the understanding that bravery takes various forms, and Belinda and her pets continue to live happily together in their little white house.

STANZA-WISE ANALYSIS

Each stanza is four lines long except one stanza (Lines 49 to 54) which contains six lines.

Lines 1 to 8

Belinda lived in a little white house,
With a little black kitten and a little grey mouse,
and a little yellow dog and a little red wagon,
and a realio, trulio, little pet dragon.
Now the name of the little black kitten was Ink,
and the little grey mouse, she called him Blink,
and the little yellow dog was sharp as Mustard,
But the dragon was a coward, and she called him Custard.

In these lines, all the characters of the story are introduced. The main character Belinda lives in a small white house with her pets, a grey mouse, a little black kitten, a yellow dog and a dragon. Belinda has a red wagon too which she played with.

The poet then goes on to familiarize[1] the reader with the names of the pets, the grey mouse being called Blink, the black kitten is called Ink, the yellow dog is called Mustard and the dragon is called Custard who was considered a coward. The fact that the dragon is cowardly gives the poem a funny effect.

Rhyme Scheme

Ogden Nash's poem follows the 'a-a-b-b' rhyme scheme.

Lines 9 to 16

Custard the dragon had big sharp teeth,
and spikes on top of him and scales underneath,
Mouth like a fireplace, chimney for a nose,
and realio, trulio daggers on his toes.
Belinda was as brave as a barrel full of bears,
and Ink and Blink chased lions down the stairs,
Mustard was as brave as a tiger in a rage,
But Custard cried for a nice safe cage.

Here, the poet goes on to describe the dragon. Custard, the dragon, has a scaly body with spikes on his back. He also has big teeth and big claws on his feet. As a fire-breathing dragon, his mouth is hot and his nose is filled with smoke. The poet uses the simile, "Mouth like a fireplace" and the metaphor "chimney for a nose" in the same line to describe the dragon. The refrain[2] "realio, trulio" is also repeated from the previous stanza to continue the comic effect by twisting the real words.

The irony of the situation is intensified[3] when the poet goes on to describe the bravery of Belinda and her little pets, and then the cowardice of the pet dragon. This also adds a fun twist for the reader because they would expect a dragon to be ferocious but the dragon here 'cried for a nice, safe cage."

Literary Devices

Metaphor: Comparison between things without using the words like or as. Eg., Chimney for a nose.

Onomatopoeia: Usage of sound words to create a dramatic effect (Mustard growled, Meowch, cried ink). 'With a clatter and a clank and a jangling squirm' in Line 39; the words 'clatter', 'clank' and 'jangling' refers to the sounds made by Custard as he attacks.

Anaphora: Lines 6-7 start with 'and the little'; this repetition is called anaphora.

Alliteration: In Line 13 "Belinda was as brave as a barrel full of bears", the repeated 'b' sound is an example of alliteration.

Refrain: Repetition of a sentence. (and a realio, trulio)

Lines 17 to 24

Belinda tickled him, she tickled him unmerciful,
Ink, Blink and Mustard, they rudely called him Percival,
They all sat laughing in the little red wagon
At the realio, trulio, cowardly dragon.
Belinda giggled till she shook the house,
and Blink said Weeck! which is giggling for a mouse,
Ink and Mustard rudely asked his age,
When Custard cried for a nice safe cage.

The poet says that Custard the dragon was favoured by Belinda above her other pets. They used to tickle each other playfully, but Custard's sharp claws would hurt her accidentally. The word 'unmerciful' applies to the dangerous claws. The other pets are envious[4] of Custard's popularity with Belinda. They call him 'Percival' in reference to the knight of the same name at King Arthur's court. Percival was King Arthur's favourite knight because of his kindness and courage. When Custard cries, they ask him how old he is, to tease him. Belinda would also laugh with enjoyment joined by her pets. The poet uses onomatopoeia with the word 'weeck' which denotes the grey mouse's laughter.

[1] **Familiarize:** known
[2] **Refrain:** repeated phrase
[3] **Intensify:** to become or to make something greater or stronger
[4] **Envious:** wanting something that is someone else's.

Lines 25 to 32

Suddenly, suddenly they heard a nasty sound,
and Mustard growled, and they all looked around.
Meowch! cried Ink, and ooh! cried Belinda,
For there was a pirate, climbing in the winda.
Pistol in his left hand, pistol in his right,
and he held in his teeth a cutlass bright,
His beard was black, one leg was wood;
It was clear that the pirate meant no good.

The poet opens these lines with the word 'suddenly', which provides the poem a tense turn. When a disturbance happened, Mustard the dog growled. Belinda and her pets turned around after hearing the growl. The blank kitten Ink cried and so did Belinda because a pirate was entering through the window in Belinda's house. The poet uses onomatopoeia and pun here with the word 'meowch' combining 'meow' and 'ouch'.

The pirate was dangerous because he was carrying two pistols in his hands and a cutlass (a short sword) in his mouth. He had come to harm Belinda and her pets. He had a black beard and a wooden leg, which made him scary.

Lines 33 to 40

Belinda paled, and she cried Help! Help!
But Mustard fled with a terrified yelp,
Ink trickled down to the bottom of the household,
and little mouse Blink strategically mouseholed.
But up jumped Custard, snorting like an engine,
Clashed his tail like irons in a dungeon,
With a clatter and a clank and a jangling squirm,
He went at the pirate like a robin at a worm.

In the face of danger, Belinda and her other pets, who had bragged about their bravery, acted timidly. Belinda, who was as courageous as 'a barrel full of bears' cried for help, becoming pale with fear. Mustard, the dog who was compared to a 'tiger in rage' ran away terrified. The black kitten Ink hid in the lowest part of the house, while the grey mouse Blink hid in his hole. This section of the poem pokes fun at the irony of the situation showing how neither Belinda nor her pets turn out to be as they claimed to be.

Custard, the dragon who had been called a coward, showed his true colours by protecting Belinda and the other pets. He charged at the pirate with full force, attacking him as a bird attacks a worm. The poet describes the full strength of the dragon's power in Lines 37 to 40. Fire came out of his nostrils like steam coming out of an engine, and Custard thrashed his powerful tail like the iron chains in a dungeon and made a jangling sound. This showed how brave Custard was when faced with danger.

Lines 41 to 48

The pirate gaped at Belinda's dragon,
and gulped some grog from his pocket flagon,
He fired two bullets, but they didn't hit,
and Custard gobbled him, every bit.
Belinda embraced him, Mustard licked him,
No one mourned for his pirate victim.
Ink and Blink in glee did gyrate
Around the dragon that ate the pirate.

The pirate was surprised to see a big dragon, and drank an alcoholic drink to steady himself. He then shot two bullets at the dragon, but he missed. Custard ran at the pirate and ate the pirate up, saving Belinda and her other pets from danger. After Custard saved everyone, Belinda hugged him and Mustard, the dog, licked him happily. Ink the black kitten, and Blink the grey mouse danced around Custard with joy because he had eaten the pirate. Everyone celebrated the dragon's victory.

Lines 49 to 54

But presently up spoke little dog Mustard,
I'd have been twice as brave if I hadn't been flustered.
and up spoke Ink and up spoke Blink,
We'd have been three times as brave, we think,
and Custard said, I quite agree
That everybody is braver than me.

After the danger passes and the pirate is no more, Mustard claims that if he had not been nervous, he could have been twice as brave as the dragon. Ink and Blink echo his feelings by saying they could have been three times as brave as the dragon. The poet uses the phrase "we think" which implies that the cat, the mouse and the dog were only brave in their own imagination, but not in the real life situation.

The whole situation exemplifies[5] the irony of their words. Custard, however, agrees with their statements and says that all of the other pets are braver than him.

Lines 55 to 62

Belinda still lives in her little white house,
With her little black kitten and her little grey mouse,
and her little yellow dog and her little red wagon,
and her realio, trulio little pet dragon.
Belinda is as brave as a barrel full of bears,
and Ink and Blink chase lions down the stairs,
Mustard is as brave as a tiger in a rage,
But Custard keeps crying for a nice safe cage.

The last eight lines are a refrain, repeating the same lines (Lines 1-4, 13-16) from the beginning of the poem. They bring the poem to a conclusion by implying that things have returned to the way they were. All the pets claim to be brave, while Custard keeps crying for his cage. Perhaps Custard did all this in the heat of the moment, and he is still a coward. The poet keeps the fun tone till the end.

[5] **Exemplifies:** illustrate; be a typical example

NCERT EXERCISE

Thinking about the Poem

(NCERT Page 132)

1. Who are the characters in this poem? List them with their pet names.

Ans. The characters in the poem are as follows,

(*a*) Belinda, the only human in the poem.

(*b*) A black kitten named Ink.

(*c*) A yellow dog named Mustard.

(*d*) A grey mouse named Blink.

(*e*) A pet dragon named Custard.

2. Why did Custard cry for a nice safe cage? Why is the dragon called a "cowardly dragon"?

Ans. Custard cried for a nice, safe cage because he was a coward, unlike Belinda and her other pets who were brave.

Belinda had the bravery of many bears, a cat and the mouse were courageous enough to chase lions out of the house and the yellow dog was as brave as a furious tiger. Custard on the other hand was afraid of everything and looked for a safe place where he could hide. This is why Custard is called a "cowardly dragon".

3. "Belinda tickled him, she tickled him unmerciful..." Why?

Ans. Custard, being a cowardly dragon was vulnerable. Belinda made fun of Custard by tickling him unmercifully. As Custard was not brave like the other pets, he used to cry for a safe cage. This also suggests Custard's friendly nature towards Belinda as his sharp claws could have accidentally hurt her, but never did.

4. The poet has employed many poetic devices in the poem. For example: "Clashed his tail like iron in a dungeon" — the poetic device here is a simile. Can you, with your partner, list some more such poetic devices used in the poem?

Ans. There are quite a few poetic devices which the poet has used in the poem.

Apart from the simile we can also find,

Anaphora: repetition of words or phrases

Line 3-4: 'And a little yellow dog and a little red wagon, And a realio, trulio, little pet dragon.'

Line 6-7: 'And the little grey mouse, she called him Blink, And the little yellow dog was sharp as Mustard,'

Onomatopoeia: a word or combination of words whose sound closely resembles the denoted sound. For e.g., 'clatter', 'clank',' jangling'

Line 39: With a clatter and a clank and a jangling squirm…

5. Read stanza three again to know how the poet describes the appearance of the dragon.

Ans. The poet creates a fierce imagery of the dragon. Custard had big sharp teeth. He had scaly skin and spikes on his back. He would breathe fire, so his mouth was as hot as a fireplace. Smoke would come out of his nostrils. Custard also had huge claws on his feet.

6. Can you find out the rhyme scheme of two or three stanzas of the poem?

Ans. The rhyme scheme throughout the poem is 'a a b b', where in a stanza of four lines, the first two and the last two rhyme with each other. For example

From Lines 1-4, 'house','mouse','wagon' and 'dragon'.

From Lines 5-8, 'Ink','Blink','Mustard' and 'Custard'.

From Lines 9-12,'teeth','underneath','nose' and 'toes'.

7. Writers use words to give us a picture or image without actually saying what they mean. Can you trace some images used in the poem?

Ans. In many stories and poems, we see writers using words to describe images without telling the reader what the meaning is.

The poet, Ogden Nash, has used such words to create images such as 'Belinda was as brave as a barrel full of bears', which means Belinda is a very brave person; 'Mustard was as brave as a tiger in a rage', which means the yellow dog Mustard was also really courageous; while describing the dragon he uses the phrase 'chimney for a nose', which means that the big dragon had a gigantic nose which fumed with smoke.

8. Do you find The Tale of Custard the Dragon to be a serious or a light-hearted poem? Give reasons to support your answer.

Ans. The poem has a comical tone, but a serious moral lesson. The comedy in the poem comes from the fact that Belinda and her pet cat, mouse and dog are all brave, while the dragon is cowardly even though, traditionally dragons are associated with strength and power. The irony of the situation makes it funny.

The poem does teach us not to make fun of someone who may be weak but has the strength to fight when real danger happens.

When faced with the threat of the pirate, Custard forgets his cowardice and jumps into action to save Belinda and the other pets. Thus, the poem teaches us an important lesson.

The rhyme of the poem gives it a sing-song quality which the poet maintains by playfully misspelling the word 'window' as 'winda' adding to the poem's fun appeal.

9. This poem, in ballad form, tells a story. Have you come across any such modern song or lyric that tells a story? If you know one, tell it to the class. Collect such songs as a project.

Ans. To be done by the students.

Answering Tip

Some other poems in ballad form are:

La Belle Dame sans Merci by John Keats

Lochinvar by Sir Walter Scott

The Rime of the Ancient Mariner by S.T Coleridge

The Ballad of Reading Gaol by Oscar Wilde

MISCELLANEOUS EXERCISE

Multiple Choice Questions

1. Who was called cowardly?
(*a*) Blink (*b*) Custard
(*c*) Ink (*d*) Rither

2. Where did Belinda live?
(*a*) In a white house. (*b*) In a yellow house.
(*c*) In a small hut. (*d*) In a castle.

3. What did Custard do to the pirate?
(*a*) To beat him.
(*b*) To annoyed him.
(*c*) To see him he hid himself.
(*d*) Ate him.

4. What does the dragon possess?
(*a*) Big sharp teeth. (*b*) Spike on top of him.
(*c*) Sharp toes. (*d*) All of them.

5. What does taunting by all the pets show?
(*a*) They are all braver than Custard.
(*b*) They are not as brave as Custard.
(*c*) They make fun of Custard's cowardice.
(*d*) None of the above.

6. Name the poetic device used in the line "mouth like a fireplace"
(*a*) Oxymoron (*b*) Metaphor
(*c*) Assonance (*d*) Simile

7. Belinda also had yellow coloured __________.
(*a*) Wagon (*b*) Cat
(*c*) Dragon (*d*) Dog

8. The dragon's feet were like __________.
(*a*) Knife (*b*) Sword
(*c*) Fireplace (*d*) Chimney

9. Belinda was as brave as a group of –
(*a*) Lion (*b*) Tiger
(*c*) Bear (*d*) Elephant

10. __________ compared with a coward knight Percival.
(*a*) Custard (*b*) Ink
(*c*) Mustard (*d*) Belinda

11. The pirate had a wooden __________.
(*a*) Leg (*b*) Teeth
(*c*) Hand (*d*) Pistol

12. Belinda's dog was 'sharp' meaning-
(*a*) Foolish (*b*) Intelligent
(*c*) Sloth (*d*) None of the above

Extract-Based Questions

I. Read the following extract and answer the questions that follow: **(5 M)**

Belinda lived in a little white house,
With a little black kitten and a little grey mouse,
And a little yellow dog and a little red wagon,
And a realio, trulio, little pet dragon.
Now the name of the little black kitten was Ink,
And the little grey mouse, she called him Blink,
And the little yellow dog was sharp as Mustard,
But the dragon was a coward, and she called him Custard.

1. Who was Belinda? **(1)**
(*a*) She was a young girl. (*b*) She was an old lady.
(*c*) She lived with her pets. (*d*) Both (*a*) and (*c*).

2. Who all lived with Belinda? **(1)**
(*a*) Kitten & Mouse (*b*) Dog
(*c*) Dragon (*d*) All of the above

3. The expression realio, trulio is an example of: **(1)**

(*a*) Simile (*b*) Internal rhyme

(*c*) Free verse (*d*) Both (*b*) and (*c*)

4. Use of the word 'And' in the last two lines of the stanza is an example of: **(1)**

(*a*) Alliteration (*b*) Repetition

(*c*) Anaphora (*d*) All of the above

5. Identify the figure of speech used in the following line

With a little black kitten and a little grey mouse, **(1)**

(*a*) Alliteration (*b*) Repetition

(*c*) Anaphora (*d*) All of the above

II. Read the following extract and answer the questions that follow: (5 M)

Custard the dragon had big sharp teeth,
And spikes on top of him and scales underneath,
Mouth like a fireplace, chimney for a nose,
And realio, trulio daggers on his toes.
Belinda was as brave as a barrel full of bears,
And Ink and Blink chased lions down the stairs,
Mustard was as brave as a tiger in a rage,
But Custard cried for a nice safe cage.

1. Fill in the Blank:

In the poem, it is mentioned that "Custard cried for a ________." **(1)**

2. Select the option that applies the same rhyme scheme as the first four lines of the given extract: **(1)**

(*a*) The sky was dark, the moon so bright,
The stars were twinkling, soft in sight,
The breeze was calm, the air so still,
While shadows danced on the hill.

(*b*) The ocean roared, the waves did crash,
The sea was wild, the shore so deep,
The wind was fierce, the clouds did flash,
While all the creatures went to sleep.

(*c*) The fire blazed, the warmth did glow,
As the night around me slowly flew.
The smoke was thick, the embers low,
The flames did flicker, the shadows grew,

(*d*) The leaves did fall, the air was crisp,
The birds took flight with a gentle wisp,
The forest whispered with a zist;
As the day drifted along.

3. Which of the following best describes Custard's character in the poem? **(1)**

(*a*) Brave and Fearless

(*b*) Cowardly and Timid

(*c*) Aggressive and Threatening

(*d*) Calm and Peaceful

4. Comment on the use of similes in the poem to describe the characters. **(2)**

III. Read the following extract and answer the questions that follow: (5 M)

Suddenly, suddenly they heard a nasty sound,
and Mustard growled, and they all looked around.
Meowch! cried Ink, and ooh! cried Belinda,
For there was a pirate, climbing in the winda.
Pistol in his left hand, pistol in his right,
and he held in his teeth a cutlass bright,
His beard was black, one leg was wood;
It was clear that the pirate meant no good.

1. Select the option that follows the same rhyme scheme as the given extract. **(1)**

(*a*) Under the sky so blue,
I watched the birds that flew.
The flowers swayed, the trees stood tall,
A gentle breeze touched them all.

(*b*) The world was filled with joy for me.
The evening air was warm and sweet.
The grass felt soft beneath my feet,
I smiled as I ran so free,

(*c*) I stared at the waves
I sat by the lake
With a thought to forsake
And the birds in their caves

(*d*) The thunder roared, the lightning flashed,
As raindrops fell and branches crashed.
The storm was wild, the night was cold,
A fearful sight for young and courageous

2. What is the significance of the word "nasty" in the poem, and how does it shape the poem's overall mood and tone? Answer in about 40 words. **(2)**

3. The poem suggests that the setting is ______. **(1)**

(*a*) a peaceful village (*b*) a house

(*c*) a pirate ship (*d*) a haunted cast

4. Which literary device is predominantly used in the poem to convey its central theme? **(1)**

IV. Read the following extract and answer the questions that follow: (5 M)

The pirate gaped at Belinda's dragon,
And gulped some grog from his pocket flagon,
He fired two bullets, but they didn't hit,
And Custard gobbled him, every bit.

1. The pirate gaped at Belinda's dragon, because __________ **(1)**

(*a*) He was happy. (*b*) He was angry.

(*c*) He was shocked. (*d*) He wanted to slay it.

2. Here the word 'gape' means, **(1)**

(*a*) Glare (*b*) Look

(*c*) Stare (*d*) Gaze

3. The literary device used in 'And gulped some grog' is **(1)**

(*a*) Resonance (*b*) Assonance

(*c*) Consonance (*d*) Imagery

4. State whether True or False. (1)
The pirate was able to shoot Custard

5. A synonym for 'flagon' would be (1)
(a) Cup (b) Bowl
(c) Flask (d) Bag

Subjective Questions

Short Answer Questions (40-50 words) (3 M)

1. Describe how Custard the dragon fights with the Pirate. (CBSE, 2023)
2. Why did everyone laugh at the 'realio, trulio' dragon? (CBSE, 2022)
3. How does Custard save Belinda from danger?
4. How does Ogden Nash's The Tale of Custard the Dragon, challenge the notion that individuals should conform to societal expectations? (CBSE, SQP 2023)
5. How did Custard prove 'the cowardly dragon' tag to be untrue? (CBSE 2022, Term- II)
6. Bring out the central idea of the poem, 'The Tale of Custard the Dragon'. (CBSE 2024)
7. What makes custard, the dragon look fearsome? Explain. (CBSE 2024)

Long Answer Questions (100-120 words) (6 M)

8. How does the poet use irony in the poem, 'The Tale of the Custard Dragon'?
9. How was Belinda's behavior with the dragon? Why was the dragon called Percival by the other pets? (CBSE, 2022)

ANSWERS & EXPLANATIONS

Answer Key

Multiple Choice Questions

1. (b) 2. (a) 3. (d) 4. (d) 5. (c) 6. (d) 7. (d) 8. (a) 9. (c) 10. (a)
11. (a) 12. (b)

Explanations

Extract-Based Questions

I. 1. (d) Both (a) and (c).
2. (d) All of the above
3. (d) Both (b) and (c)
4. (c) Anaphora
5. (b) Repetition

II. 1. In the poem, Custard cried for a "nice safe cage."
2. (d) The correct answer is (a).
3. Based on the poem, the best description of Custard's character would be (b) Cowardly and Timid. This is because, despite his fierce appearance, Custard wants the security of a safe cage.
4. The use of similes in the poem adds a playful and imaginative way to describe the characters, exaggerating their traits for humorous effect. Comparing bravery to a barrel full of bears emphasizes the characters' courage in a way that's easy to visualize and adds to the light-hearted tone of the poem. It's a creative method to give personality to the characters and make them memorable to the reader.

III. 1. (a) The correct answer is (a).
2. The word "nasty" in the poem adds a sense of danger and menace. It creates a suspenseful and ominous atmosphere, contributing to the poem's overall mood of excitement and fear. The word intensifies the tone, highlighting the threat posed by the pirate and building tension.
3. (d) a house
4. The predominant literary device used in the poem to convey its central theme is personification. The animals in the poem, such as Mustard the dog and Ink the cat, are given human-like qualities and engage in adventurous actions, reflecting the theme of bravery and courage.

IV. 1. (c) He was shocked.
2. (c) Stare
3. (c) Consonance
4. (True)
5. (c) Flask

[6] **Intimidate:** scare
[7] **Laughing stock:** the one everyone makes fun of

Subjective Questions

Short Answer Questions

CBSE Marking Scheme: Content-1 M, Organisation of Ideas-1 M, Accuracy-1 M

1. Custard the Dragon's bravery in fight against the Pirate surprises everyone. Custard defeats the Pirate by using his wit.

   He produces a smokescreen with his burning breath, baffling the Pirate and launching successful counterattacks, demonstrating his creativity and determination.

2. Even though Custard looked ferocious on the outside, he was a cowardly dragon on the inside. He didn't intimidate[6] Belinda or her little pets, rather he had deep love for Belinda and his other animal friends.

   Because Custard always cried and wanted to rest in a 'nice safe cage' the other animals would tease him and call him a crybaby. His cowardice made him the laughing stock[7] of the house.

3. When the pirate enters Belinda's house through the window with two pistols in his hands and a cutlass in his mouth, neither Belinda nor her pets are brave enough to face him. Custard comes to Belinda's rescue by charging at the pirate with full force, fire coming out of his mouth and his tail thrashing.

   The pirate is surprised to see a dragon and shoots two times but misses. Custard eats up the pirate completely and saves Belinda and her pets.

4. Ogden Nash's "Tale of Custard the Dragon" can be interpreted as a subversion of societal expectations.
   - presents Belinda as a brave and independent female character (described as brave as a barrel full of bears, a trait that is stereotypically associated with masculinity), while the male characters (Ink, Blink, Mustard) are portrayed as weaker and less courageous
   - actions of Ink, Blink, Mustard seem motivated by fear of social judgment and ridicule - of being perceived as weak
   - while Custard is unafraid of crying for a nice safe cage
   - when faced with danger, Custard, the dragon, labelled a coward, is the one who steps up to defend Belinda and her household, while Ink, Blink, and Mustard flee or hide - finds the courage to protect those he cares about

   The poem promotes the idea that everyone has unique talents and abilities, and should be encouraged to pursue their passions and strengths, at their pace, rather than conforming to societal expectations or stereotypes.

5. Custard the dragon was labeled as cowardly by others due to their perception of him being passive and fearful.

   However, during a crisis, all of Custard's supposedly brave and energetic counterparts disappeared. It was Custard who bravely confronted the pirate, roaring and using his tail, ultimately saving his fellow mates.

6. The central idea of "The Tale of Custard the Dragon" is that true courage is not about how one appears, but how one acts in the face of danger. Custard the dragon seemed scared but was the one who saved everyone from a pirate. It shows that anyone can be brave when it really matters.

7. ***Topper's Explanation***

   Though Custard in the poem by 'Ogden Nash' was initially thought to be a coward dragon, but to the contrary custard had all the traits of a dragon that makes it look scary and fearsome. Custard has spikes on his back and scales underneath. He could bring out fire from his mouth. He was a huge dragon with ~~sharp~~ sharp teeth with which he ate the pirate. His sharp spikes, huge body, fire from the mouth, sharp claws which were compared to daggers and the smoke emitting out of his nose, all make him a fearsome and scary dragon.

Long Answer Questions

CBSE Marking Scheme: Expression-2 M, Accuracy-1 M

8. The poet Ogden Nash uses irony to add a comic flavour to the poem. At the very onset[8] in the poem, he describes the dragon Custard as cowardly.

   A big creature such as a dragon being cowardly is not the norm. This unexpected twist makes the reader laugh. **(1 M)**

   The poet then talks about the bravery of Belinda and all her little pets, such as the mouse, the cat and the dog, and then at the same time talks about Custard the dragon's lack of courage. This establishes the bravery of Belinda and her little pets and the cowardice of Custard as the expected standard. **(1 M)**

   When faced with danger, however, Belinda and her pets lose all their courage, and Custard saves everyone by eliminating[9] the danger. The readers are surprised to experience Custard in this way, and the twist brings irony at the end. **(1 M)**

9. Belinda was fond of Custard, the dragon. She would play with him, laugh and tickle him. Custard would also enjoy the games. She loved Custard but would join her pets in laughing and making fun of the cowardly dragon. **(1 M)**

   Percival was one of the most innocent but also brave knights in King Arthur's court. The other knights were envious of Percival's popularity with King Arthur. **(1 M)**

   The other pets call the dragon Percival because they feel that Belinda loves Custard the dragon more than them, and they are jealous of the love he gets from Belinda. **(1 M)**

❑❑❑

[8] **Onset:** start
[9] **Eliminate:** remove

10

FOR ANNE GREGORY

—William Butter Yeats

Poetic Sketch

1. The poem explores the idea that superficial attributes, such as hair colour, can attract attention and affection.
2. The speaker questions whether anyone can truly love her for who she is beyond her physical appearance.
3. She thinks of the possibility of changing her hair colour to test if someone would love her for herself alone.
4. The poem highlights the desire for genuine and unconditional love that goes beyond superficial qualities.
5. The speaker mentions about an old religious man who claims that only God can love her for herself alone.
6. The encounter with the religious man raises the question of the nature of love and its true source.
7. The poem is about wanting to feel valued for who you are and finding real relationships that are about more than just looks
8. It suggests that love based only on looks isn't deep and won't last.

BEFORE YOU READ

Central Idea

The central idea of the poem is the longing for authentic love and acceptance that go beyond superficial attributes. The poem delves into the question of whether one can be loved purely for their inner self rather than physical beauty. It engages with the idea that external attributes like hair color might wrongly influence affection. The poem raises questions about the nature of love, self-worth, and the search for connections based on inner qualities rather than superficial appearances.

STANZA-WISE ANALYSIS

Line 1

"Never shall a young man,
Thrown into despair[1]
By those great honey-coloured
Ramparts[2] *at your ear,*
Love you for yourself alone
And not your yellow hair."

Explanation

In the first stanza, the poem addresses Anne Gregory and tells her that her beautiful hair can make anyone fall in love with her. However, that love is not for Anne but for her external features. Her beautiful hair is just an object that stops a beholder to see her inner beauty. He says that this beauty can capture one's attention, but he may not be able to look beyond that into Anne's character. Thus, the poet concludes that no one can love Anne as she is. One can love her only for her physical beauty.

Line 2

"But I can get a hair-dye
And set such colour there,
Brown, or black, or carrot[3]*,*
That young men in despair
May love me for myself alone
And not my yellow hair"

Explanation

In the second stanza, Anne replies to the speaker that she can change the colour of her beautiful hair and dye it black, brown or carrot. She emphasizes that anyone falling in love with her must see the actual person behind her face. She adds that young men who falls in love with her must love her for who she is and not for her beautiful hair. She emphasizes that external beauty is artificial and can be arranged, while inner beauty is real.

Line 3

"I heard an old religious man
But yesternight declare
That he had found a text to prove
That only God, my dear,
Could love you for yourself alone
And not your yellow hair"

Rhyme Scheme

The rhyme scheme of Yeat's poem is ABCBDB.

[1] **Despair:** extreme sadness
[2] **Ramparts:** the high wall which stops one to see anything on other side
[3] **Carrot:** a bright orange colour

Literary Devices

Metaphor: Comparison between people or things without using the words 'like' or 'as'.

Examples from the poem: 'honey-coloured ramparts'.

The poet compares Anne Gregory's hair to the walls of a fort.

Alliteration: Repetition of a letter or sound at the start of closely packed words.

Examples from the poem: repeating the letter 'y' in "your yellow".

And 'h' in "he had".

Anaphora: Repetition of a word at the start of successive two or more lines.

Examples from the poem:

"That he had found a text to prove

That only God, my dear."

Enjambment: When the lines in a stanza ends or continues without any punctuation.

In the 2nd stanza, the 4th and the 5th lines

"That young men in despair

My love me for myself alone."

In the 3rd Stanza: 1st, 2nd and the 3rd lines.

"I heard an old religious man

But yesternight declare

That he had found a text to prove."

Explanation

In the last stanza, the poet tells Anne about the importance of love for internal beauty rather than external beauty. He adds that an old religious man announced that he had found a text with proof that only God is capable of looking beyond external beauty. He means to say that human beings are not capable of understanding and they don't have the insight to look into the real beauty of any individual. Thus, only God can love Anne for her real being and not for her beauty.

NCERT EXERCISE

Thinking about the Text

(NCERT, Page 141)

1. What does the young man mean by "great honey-coloured/Ramparts at your ear?" Why does he say that young men are "thrown into despair" by them?

Ans. The young man in the poem praises the great honey-coloured hair of Anne. Anne's hair has been called rampart which means 'a wall' because they act as a hindrance and they prevent young men from looking beyond those beautiful hair. Her hair is so attractive that young men are not able to look at anything else and fall in love with her.

2. What colour is the young woman's hair? What does she say she can change it to? Why would she want to do so?

Ans. The young woman's hair is honey-coloured. She claims she can make it black, brown, or carrot. She wishes to convey the message that outer beauty can be altered and is neither permanent nor genuine. She would do so because she wants young men to see her true self rather than what they see on the outside.

3. Objects have qualities which make them desirable to others. Can you think of some objects (a car, a phone, a dress...) and say what qualities make one object more desirable than another? Imagine you were trying to sell an object: what qualities would you emphasise?

Ans. Students should attempt on their own.

(Hint-try to write the things related to your own life experiences)

4. What about people? Do we love others because we like their qualities, whether physical or mental? Or is it possible to love someone "for themselves alone"? Are some people 'more lovable' than others? Discuss this question in pairs or in groups', considering points like the following.

(i) A parent or caregiver's love for a newborn baby, for a mentally or physically challenged child, for a clever child or a prodigy

(ii) The public's love for a film star, a sportsperson, a politician, or a social worker

(iii) Your love for a friend, brother or sister

(iv) Your love for a pet, and the pet's love for you.

Ans. (i) This love is very natural, regardless of any expectations or desire to make someone act the certain way they want.

(ii) This affection can be temporary or permanent based on one's choice or desire.

(iii) This is somehow fluctuating. We talk to them or befriend them when they do things as we want, but the moment they behave differently, we start hating them.

(iv) This is so genuine and unfailing. Because they both have unconditional affection for each other.

5. You have perhaps concluded that people are not objects to be valued for their qualities or riches rather than for themselves. But elsewhere Yeats asks the question: How can we separate the dancer from the dance? Is it possible to separate 'the person himself or herself' from how the person looks, sounds, walks and so on? Think of how you or a friend or member of your family has changed over the years. Has your relationship also changed? In what way?

Ans. Students should attempt on their own.

MISCELLANEOUS EXERCISE

Multiple Choice Questions

1. What is the central theme of the poem?
   (*a*) The power of religious texts.
   (*b*) The significance of hair color.
   (*c*) The search for true love and acceptance.
   (*d*) The influence of societal beauty standards.

2. The speaker contemplates changing her hair colour because she believes:
   (*a*) It will make her more attractive.
   (*b*) It will prove the religious man's point.
   (*c*) It will bring her closer to God.
   (*d*) It will test if someone can love her for herself alone.

3. According to the religious man, who can truly love the speaker?
   (*a*) Young men (*b*) God
   (*c*) People with yellow hair. (*d*) Those who dye their hair.

4. The speaker is concerned that young men are attracted to her:
   (*a*) Honey-colored ramparts.
   (*b*) Brown hair
   (*c*) Carrot hair
   (*d*) Yellow hair

5. The speaker suggests that changing her hair colour may make young men:
   (*a*) Love her more. (*b*) Fall into despair.
   (*c*) Appreciate her inner self. (*d*) Lose interest in her.

6. Name the literary device used in the line "honey-coloured ramparts at your ear".
   (*a*) Oxymoron (*b*) Metaphor
   (*c*) Assonance (*d*) None of these

7. The poem implies that superficial qualities like hair colour:
   (*a*) Are essential for love and acceptance.
   (*b*) Should be embraced and celebrated.
   (*c*) Can be changed to find true love.
   (*d*) Are unimportant in true love.

8. The speaker's encounter with the religious man suggests that:
   (*a*) Love cannot exist without religious beliefs.
   (*b*) Love should be based on external attributes.
   (*c*) Love is a divine and spiritual connection.
   (*d*) Love is determined by societal norms.

9. The poem raises questions about the influence of:
   (*a*) Religious teachings on love.
   (*b*) Society's beauty standards.
   (*c*) Hair dye on relationships.
   (*d*) Personal insecurities.

10. The overall tone of the poem can be described as:
   (*a*) Light-hearted and humorous.
   (*b*) Sad and melancholic.
   (*c*) Philosophical and introspective.
   (*d*) Romantic and passionate.

Extract-Based Questions

I. Read the following extract and answer the questions that follow: (5 M)

"Never shall a young man,
Thrown into despair[1]
By those great honey-coloured
Ramparts at your ear,
Love you for yourself alone
And not your yellow hair."

1. Fill the blank with one word.
When the speaker mentions 'thrown into despair', he is referring to the feeling of ________." **(1)**
2. What is the significance of the 'great honey-coloured ramparts at your ear' mentioned in the poem?" **(1)**
3. What does the speaker imply about love in the poem? **(1)**
(*a*) It is based solely on physical appearance.
(*b*) It is unconditional and everlasting.
(*c*) It is shallow and superficial.
(*d*) It is unpredictable and uncertain.
4. Comment on the poet's use of colour imagery in describing the young man's attraction. **(2)**

II. Read the following extract and answer the questions that follow: (5 M)

"I heard an old religious man
But yesternight declare
That he had found a text to prove
That only God, my dear,
Could love you for yourself alone
And not your yellow hair."

1. According to the religious man, who is capable of loving someone for themselves alone? **(1)**
(*a*) Young men in despair. (*b*) God
(*c*) People with yellow hair. (*d*) The speaker of the poem.
2. What is the religious man's view on love? **(1)**
(*a*) Love should be based on physical appearance.
(*b*) Love should be conditional.
(*c*) Only God is capable of true love.
(*d*) Love is irrelevant and superficial.
3. Select the option that applies the same rhyme scheme as the lines of the given extract: **(1)**
(*a*) I walked along the silent shore,
Beneath the sky so wide,
The waves were dancing in the night
As stars began to hide,
A whisper floated on the breeze
And drifted with the tide.
(*b*) The golden sun began to rise,
Spreading colors across the skies.
The birds awoke and sang with cheer,
A melody so bright and clear.
She walked along the garden way,
And felt the warmth of a new day.
(*c*) The autumn leaves fell from the tree,
Drifting down so wild and free.
The wind it whispered soft and low,
A tune that only dreamers know.
She stood beside the old oak tall,
And watched as nature changed it all.
(*d*) The storm arrived with thunder loud,
Lightning flashing through the cloud.
The raindrops fell on land so dry,
Bringing relief from summer sky.
She listened to the soothing sound,
As peace and calm came all around.
4. What role does the mention of the religious man and his belief about God's love play in the poem's exploration of true love and personal worth? **(2)**

Subjective Questions

Short Answer Questions (40-50 words) (3 M)

1. Why is the youth in despair in the poem "For Anne Gregory"?
2. How is the poet trying to convince Anne that only God can love you for yourself?
3. Explain, why the speaker mentions God in the poem "For Anne Gregory". **(CBSE, 2024)**

Long Answer Questions (100-120 words) (6 M)

4. How right or wrong is it to judge someone on the basis of their physical appearance? Answer in reference to the poem.
5. People should be valued for being themselves and not for what they look like as they are not objects. What lesson does the poet want to give the readers through this poem?
6. The poet in the poem, 'For Anne Gregory' conveys that we should give importance to the inner beauty and not to the physical appearance. Elaborate with reference to the poem. **(CBSE, 2019)**

ANSWERS & EXPLANATIONS

Answer Key

Multiple Choice Questions

1. (*c*) **2.** (*d*) **3.** (*b*) **4.** (*d*) **5.** (*a*) **6.** (*b*) **7.** (*d*) **8.** (*c*) **9.** (*b*) **10.** (*c*)

Explanations

Extract-Based Questions

I. 1. hopelessness

2. The "great honey-coloured ramparts at your ear" symbolize the physical attractiveness or charm of the person being addressed. It suggests that the young man may be attracted to the speaker primarily because of her physical appearance rather than her inner qualities.

3. (*a*) It is based solely on physical appearance.

4. The poet's use of colour imagery, specifically describing the young man's attraction to the "yellow hair," highlights the superficiality of love based on physical attributes. It implies that true love should be based on deeper qualities and not just external beauty.

II. 1. (*b*) God

2. (*c*) Only God is capable of true love.

3. (*a*) The correct answer is (*a*).

4. The mention of the religious man and his belief about God's love highlights the idea that true love should be unconditional and based on one's inner self, rather than superficial attributes like physical appearance. It raises questions about the nature of love and challenges societal standards of beauty and worth.

Subjective Questions

Short Answer Questions

CBSE Marking Scheme: Content-1 M, Organisation of Ideas-1 M, Accuracy-1 M

1. The young man loves Anne because of her fascinating yellow hair that falls behind her ears. He is drawn to her beauty, which is visible from the outside.

He is depressed because everyone wants her, which is impossible, so he is depressed.

2. The poet claims that he heard an old religious man say last night with proof that only God can love you for who you are alone, not for external appearance.

The poet emphasises that a young man is not capable of appreciating his true self.

3. ***Topper's Explanation***

The poem "For Anne Gregory" is a poem by 'William Butler Yeats' signifying that everyone except God love people for only the outer appearance but not their inner beauty. The speaker mentions God in the poem to give it a spiritual dimension. The speaker says that he met a man who said that only divine love, that is, the type of love shown by God is the only form of love that is free from the glamour and outer beauty. God love people for their inner beauty and not like people who are tempted towards the outer glamour, show and shine.

Long Answer Questions

CBSE Marking Scheme: Expression-2 M, Accuracy-1 M

4. Physical appearances are likely to change and never reveal a person's true identity because they can change over time depending on need and circumstance. **(1 M)**

Something that is not true or real should not be used to judge anyone. **(1 M)**

A person's true personality should only be judged based on his behaviour. Anne also mentions in her response to the first speaker that her attractive hair colour is something that can change with time, so men should not fall in love with her based on her hair colour. **(1 M)**

> **Nailing the Right Answer**
>
> When answering a question as above, students can focus on the idea that physical appearances are not a reliable indicator of a person's true identity.

5. People are not objects, and we should value them for who they are. Because what we see can deceive us. External appearances may fascinate anyone, but they are fleeting. **(1 M)**

Many people would adore Anne Gregory because of her beautiful honey-coloured hair.

However, it is difficult to find a true lover who would love only for herself. Anne is fascinated by the idea of being loved for her yellow hair because she can dye her hair however she wants. **(1 M)**

The irony is that this world is full of people who are tempted and dazzled by show off and outward appearances. The poet assures that only God can love a person for being himself/herself. **(1 M)**

6. In the poem 'For Anne Gregory,' the poet aims to convey the idea that inner beauty is true beauty, while physical appearance is changeable and of lesser importance. **(1 M)**

The initial speaker tells Anne that young men love her for her beautiful yellow hair, and they may never truly love her for who she is.

In response, Anne suggests that her hair colour can be changed, emphasizing that external beauty is superficial and should not be the basis for love. **(1 M)**

Through this exchange, the poet explicitly expresses a preference for inner beauty over physical appearance.

Physical appearance cannot provide a genuine understanding of a person since it can be altered through clothing, makeup, and other external means, whereas inner beauty is authentic and enduring. **(1 M)**

❑❑❑

A TRIUMPH OF SURGERY

1

—James Herriot

Narrative Sketch

1. Tricki, a small dog, is overly pampered by his mistress and gets overweight.
2. Tricki's owner, Mrs. Pumphrey, consults the narrator, a veterinary surgeon, due to Tricki's declining health.
3. The surgeon advises Mrs. Pumphrey to put Tricki on a strict diet and increase his exercise.
4. Mrs. Pumphrey finds it difficult to adhere to the new regimen and pampers Tricki with excessive treats and comforts.
5. The surgeon decides to hospitalize Tricki to monitor his progress and save him from further health complications.
6. Tricki was inactive and ate nothing for two days. However, on the third day, Tricki improved, became more active, and started socializing with other dogs and played with them.
7. Mrs. Pumphrey anxiously awaits updates on Tricki's recovery and sends fancy treats. The treats were happily consumed by the surgeon and his partners..
8. When she came to the hospital to pick up her pet, the dog joyfully greeted his mistress and jumped on her lap.
9. After two weeks, the narrator informs Mrs. Pumphrey that Tricki has fully recovered.
10. Tricki happily reunites with Mrs. Pumphrey and displays his newfound energy.
11. Mrs. Pumphrey expresses her gratitude towards Mr. Herriot and refers to Tricki's recovery as a triumph of surgery.

BEFORE YOU READ

Theme

"A Triumph of Surgery" is a story that revolves around a dog named Tricki. The subject of the story is indulgence of parents about their children's. Mrs. Pumphrey had no idea that her blind love for her dog could get him into trouble and become the reason for his illness. After reading the story, one can conclude that excess of anything can have extreme consequences.

Important Characters' Sketch

- **Tricki:** A small dog who is greedy for food (such as cakes and chocolates), which has caused him to become fat and rheumatic[1]. He became a victim of overindulgence and overfeeding. After cutting on sweets and consuming plenty of water, he transformed into a flexible and hard-muscled dog. He expresses his love for his mistress by jumping into her lap when she came to pick him up.
- **Mrs. Pumphrey:** She is a rich lady as she provided all the comforts to Tricki. She pampers Tricki like a spoiled child, as she thinks Tricki is malnourished, so she overfeeds and pampers him. She is impractical, but is extremely compassionate[2] and caring for Tricki. She is grateful to Dr. Herriot for saving Tricki's life.
- **Dr. James Herriot:** Herriot is a competent veterinary surgeon, as by just looking at Tricki, he gets to know about his condition. He is reasonable, practical, and pragmatic[3]. He is genuinely concerned about Tricki. He is tactful[4] and witty[5]. He cured Tricki's illness without any medical treatment and compassionately helps animals.

SYNOPSIS

Mrs. Pumphrey is a wealthy woman who loves her dog, Tricki, a lot. Tricki likes to eat treats such as ice cream and chocolates, which Mrs. Pumphrey gives him generously. However, Tricki becomes overweight because of this.

One day, while out for a walk, they meet Dr. Herriot, a vet surgeon. He notices that Tricki is too heavy and seems unhealthy, with symptoms like red and watery eyes. Mrs. Pumphrey thought Tricki was weak because he wasn't getting enough food, even though she gave him lots of treats and regular meals. Dr. Herriot explained that Tricki is actually sick because he is eating too much and not exercising enough. He warned her that Tricki needed to eat less and move more to avoid getting more sick. Unfortunately, Tricki's health worsened, which worried Mrs. Pumphrey. She called Dr. Herriot when Tricki stopped eating his favorite foods. Dr. Herriot decided that Tricki needed to stay at the vet clinic to control his diet and monitor his health.

In the clinic, Tricki was unwilling to eat and inactive for the first two days. But by the third day, he started interacting and playing with other dogs at the clinic, showing signs of improvement. During his stay, Mrs. Pumphrey wanted to make sure Tricki had everything he needed to get better, so she sent over some of his favorite things: brandy, wine, and eggs, thinking these would help him recover which were enjoyed by the staff. In two weeks, Tricki was much healthier and full of energy. Gradually, he was transformed into a hard-muscled dog. Mr. Herriot returns him to Mrs. Pumphrey, who is overjoyed and calls the recovery a "triumph of surgery," despite the fact that no surgery was performed. The story highlights the issues of overindulgence and the simplicity of effective dietary and exercise regimens in ensuring the health of pets.

Lessons to learn

- *Overindulgence and lack of exercise can lead to serious health issues.*
- *Clear communication and setting strict guidelines.*
- *Recovery requires discipline and commitment.*
- *A balanced approach to pampering.*

[1] **Rheumatic:** watery
[2] **Compassionate:** caring
[3] **Pragmatic:** practical
[4] **Tactful:** sensitive
[5] **Witty:** humorous

Tricki after being fed all day by day by Mrs. Pumphrey

Tricki after getting exercise for two weeks

NCERT EXERCISE

Read and Find Out

(NCERT Page 1)

1. Why is Mrs. Pumphrey worried about Tricki?

Ans. Mrs. Pumphrey was worried about Tricki because he was not eating anything, not even his favourite foods. Tricki was vomiting and lying on the carpet, panting. He didn't even want to go for walks.

2. What does she do to help him? Is she wise about it?

Ans. She called the doctor to examine Tricki because he hasn't been feeling well. Yes, this time she was wise. She was acting stupid when she overfed him. The doctor told her that Tricki must be hospitalized. She allowed the dog to go with the doctor, who successfully treated Tricki.

3. Who does "I" refer in this story?

Ans. "I" refers to the narrator, a veterinary surgeon, Mr. Herriot.

(NCERT Page 3)

1. Is the narrator as rich as Tricki's mistress?

Ans. According to the story, the narrator isn't as rich as Mrs. Pumphrey since Mr. Herriott can provide Tricki with a container bed, whereas at Mrs. Pumphrey's residence, he had his own bed, different bowls to eat from, and servants at his service. Mrs. Pumphrey used to send a dozen eggs, wine, and brandy for Tricki's fast recovery. At the end of the chapter, Tricki's mistress comes in a 30-foot-long, gleaming[11], luxurious car. So, it can be seen that Tricki's mistress used to live a high-priced existence in comparison to Dr. Herriot.

2. How does he treat the dog?

Ans. He treats the dog very well. He knows that Tricki does not need medicinal treatment; he just needs a change in his lifestyle. Mr. Herriot gave Tricki a healthy diet and made sure he got enough of exercise. He offered him plenty of water for two days, and then he observed that Tricki had started licking the empty meal bowls and was mixing up with other dogs.

Then he fed him, and Tricki started to recover quickly. After a few days, Tricki's health improved, and he returned home.

3. Why is he tempted to keep Tricki as a permanent guest?

Ans. He is tempted to keep Tricki as a permanent guest during his stay, Mrs. Pumphrey wanted to make sure Tricki had everything he needed to get better. So, she used to send a lot

[6] **Gleaming:** very clean or polished

of food, such as two dozen eggs, wine bottles, and brandy, every day.

Mr. Herriot knew that there was no need to give Tricki all that, so he used to eat those eggs and drink the wine together with his partners. With all that luxurious treatment, Mr. Herriot was tempted to have Tricki as a permanent guest.

4. Why does Mrs. Pumphrey think the dog's recovery is "a triumph of surgery"?

Ans. Tricki had recovered in two weeks. He turned into a hard-muscled animal. Upon seeing Mrs. Pumphrey, Tricki ran toward her, jumped on her lap, and started licking her face.

She was overwhelmed to see Tricki well so she said as a token of gratitude[12] that it turned into "a triumph of surgery."

Think about it

1. What do you think the narrator, the vet, or the person is like? Would you say he is tactful and full of common sense at the same time?

Ans. The narrator, a veterinarian, is a very compassionate and honest person. He goes out of his way to tell Mrs. Pumphrey that she should start strictly controlling Tricki's diet and exercise schedule.

He is tactful because he knows how to get Tricki to the hospital, and his sanity[13] can be seen in the simple fact that he just changed Tricki's diet and exercise plan, which helped him recover from his problems. He didn't medicate him unnecessarily.

2. Do you think Tricki was happy to go home? What do you think will happen now?

Ans. Yes, Tricki was just as happy to go home as he was to stay at the doctor's place. It was happy to stay at the doctor's place because he made many friends that he didn't have at home, but he was happy to be back home due to his love for his mistress.

His excitement to return home can be seen as soon as he sees his mistress. He jumps into the car and starts licking her face, flapping his ears, and waving his tail. I think he will be all right at home now, as earlier Mrs. Pumphrey did not take Mr. Herriot's advice seriously, which led to Tricki's hospitalization. If Mrs. Pumphrey limits the dog's food and takes good care of him, he will remain as healthy as it is at the end of the story. However, if Mrs. Pumphrey reverts to overfeeding and pampering, Tricki might face recurring health issues.

3. Do you think this is a real-life episode or just fiction? Or is it a mixture of both?

Ans. I feel, this story is a mixture of both, because it's nothing new that rich people overindulge their pets, For example, overfeeding, maintaining excess cabinets for their pets, pampering. This story showcase real veterinary issues—such as the consequences of overfeeding pets and the lack of exercise—wrapped in engaging, often humorous storytelling. This approach not only entertains but educates readers about animal care, reflecting common dilemmas faced by pet owners and veterinarians. Therefore, it's reasonable to say that the story is a mixture of both real-life experiences and fictional elements. Herriot masterfully combines his veterinary knowledge and encounters with animals and their owners with a touch of humor and warmth, creating stories that resonate with readers for their truthfulness to life's complexities and joys.

MISCELLANEOUS EXERCISE

Multiple Choice Questions

1. Who is the author of the story "A Triumph of Surgery"?

(*a*) James Herriot (*b*) Ruskin Bond

(*c*) Robert Arthur (*d*) Victor Canning

2. Who does "I" refer to in the story?

(*a*) Tricki (*b*) Mrs. Pumphrey

(*c*) Veterinary surgeon (*d*) None of the above.

3. What is the name of the veterinary surgeon?

(*a*) Tricki (*b*) Mrs. Pumphrey

(*c*) Hodgkin (*d*) Mr. Herriot

4. What problem does Mrs. Pumphrey think Tricki has?

(*a*) Diarrhea (*b*) Malnutrition

(*c*) Allergies (*d*) All of the above.

5. Did Mrs. Pumphrey cut down on sweets as was advised?

(*a*) Yes

(*b*) No

(*c*) Only for a while

(*d*) She has not advised anything like that.

6. Who is Hodgkin?

(*a*) Dog owner (*b*) Gardener

(*c*) Veterinary surgeon (*d*) Dog

[7] **Gratitude:** being thankful

[8] **Sanity:** reasonable and rational behaviour

7. What was the dog unable to play?

(*a*) Ring-throw (*b*) Walk

(*c*) Hide and seek (*d*) All of the above.

8. What did the doctor advise?

(*a*) Cut his food.

(*b*) Give him more exercise.

(*c*) Keep him on a very strict diet.

(*d*) All of the above.

9. Was the narrator waiting for a call from Mrs. Pumphrey?

(*a*) No (*b*) Yes

(*c*) Maybe (*d*) Maybe not

10. What is the meaning of 'distraught'?

(*a*) Bend (*b*) Worried

(*c*) Upset (*d*) Both (*b*) and (*c*)

Extract-Based Questions

I. Read the following extract and answer the questions/ complete the sentences that follow. (5 M)

"Out on the road, I glanced down at the pathetic little animal gasping on the seat by my side. I patted the head and Tricki made a brave effort to wag his tail. "Poor old lad," I said. "You haven't a kick in you but I think I know a cure for you."

1. What is the narrator's initial reaction to Tricki's condition? (1)

(*a*) He is angry at Tricki for being sick.

(*b*) He is sad and sympathetic towards Tricki.

(*c*) He is indifferent towards Tricki's condition.

(*d*) He is frustrated with Mrs. Pumphrey for not taking care of Tricki.

2. What does the phrase "haven't a kick in you" mean in this context? (1)

(*a*) To be energetic and lively.

(*b*) To be weak and unable to move.

(*c*) To be aggressive and violent.

(*d*) To be happy and content.

3. Based on the passage, what can be inferred about the speaker's attitude towards the sick animal? (1)

4. What does the speaker mean by saying, "You haven't a kick in you but I think I know a cure for you"? (2)

II. Read the following extract and answer the questions/ complete the sentences that follow. (5 M)

At the surgery, the household dogs surged round me. Tricki looked down at the noisy pack with dull eyes and, when put down, lay motionless on the carpet. The other dogs, after sniffing round him for a few seconds, decided he was an uninteresting object and ignored him.

1. What can be inferred about Tricki's behaviour in this scene? (1)

(*a*) He is energetic and playful.

(*b*) He is scared and timid.

(*c*) He is aggressive towards the other dogs.

(*d*) He is lethargic and unresponsive.

2. What can be inferred about the overall tone of this scene? (1)

(*a*) It is tense and dramatic.

(*b*) It is light-hearted and humorous.

(*c*) It is sad and emotional.

(*d*) It is romantic and sentimental.

3. What does this scene suggest about Tricki's social status among the other dogs? (1)

4. How does the behaviour of the household dogs towards Tricki reflect their perception of him? (2)

III. Read the following extract and answer the questions/ complete the sentences that follow. (5 M)

'And did you cut down on the sweet stuff as I told you to?'. Oh, I did for a bit, but he seemed to be so weak I had to relent. He does love cream cakes and chocolates. I can't bear to refuse him.'

1. Why does the speaker ask if the sweet things have been cut down? (1)

(*a*) As it was ruining Tricki's health.

(*b*) As it was ruining Tricki's teeth.

(*c*) As Tricki's mistress loved sweet things.

(*d*) None of the above.

2. What does the term "cut down" mean? (1)

3. These lines are written by _____. (1)

4. How does the speaker's reluctance to refuse the indulgence of sweet treats to the person being referred to reflect their approach towards their well-being? (2)

Subjective Questions

Short Answer Questions (40-50 words) (3 M)

1. How did Mrs. Pumphrey treat Tricki? **(CBSE, 2023)**

2. What excuses did Mrs. Pumphrey make about Mr. Herriot's advice? **(CBSE, 2023)**

3. The story, A Triumph of Surgery is a powerful example of the importance of saying "no". Explain. **(CBSE SQP, 2023)**

4. What does Mr. Herriot mean by "happy period" for himself and his partners? Explain. **(CBSE, 2024)**

5. Why was Mr. Herriot shocked at Tricki's appearance? **(CBSE, 2023)**

Long Answer Questions (100-120 words) (6 M)

6. Imagine that Mrs. Pumphrey from A Triumph of Surgery, reflects upon her behaviour, learns from her mistakes, and writes a diary entry about the consequences of overindulgence. Write this diary entry as Mrs. Pumphrey in about 120 words. **(CBSE APQ, 2023)**

7. Was Tricki also accused in multiple ways? How?

8. What would you do if you were:

(*a*) A member of staff in Mrs. Pumphrey's household?

(*b*) Neighbour? What would your life be like in general?

9. How do we know that Mrs. Pumphrey was extremely rich? Why do you think Mrs. Pumphrey pampered her dog Tricki so much?

ANSWERS & EXPLANATIONS

Answer Key

Multiple Choice Questions

1. (*a*) **2.** (*c*) **3.** (*d*) **4.** (*b*) **5.** (*c*) **6.** (*b*) **7.** (*a*) **8.** (*d*) **9.** (*b*) **10.** (*d*)

Explanations

Extract-Based Questions

I. 1. (*b*) He is sad and sympathetic towards Tricki.

2. (*b*) To be weak and unable to move.

3. The speaker displays empathy and concern for the sick animal, suggesting a compassionate and caring nature.

4. The speaker acknowledges the animal's weak and frail condition but expresses confidence in having a solution or treatment to help with alleviate its suffering. This statement implies that the speaker believes he can improve the animal's health.

II. 1. (*d*) He is lethargic and unresponsive.

2. (*b*) It is light-hearted and humorous.

3. He is considered an outsider by the other dogs.

4. The behaviour of the household dogs towards Tricki reflects their perception of him as an uninteresting object. They quickly lose interest in him after briefly sniffing around, indicating that they do not see him as a lively or engaging presence.

III. 1. (*a*) As it was ruining Tricki's health.

2. 'Cut down' means to reduce the amount.

3. James Harriot

4. The speaker's reluctance to refuse the person's cravings for cream cakes and chocolates suggests a prioritization of immediate pleasure over the long-term health and well-being of the individual.

Subjective Questions

Short Answer Questions

CBSE Marking Scheme: Content-1 M, Organisation of Ideas-1 M, Accuracy-1 M

1. Tricky was handled as if he were her son/child. She served him cream, pastries, chocolates, and cod-liver oil.

She spoiled him by providing him with a lavish lifestyle. She overfed him, which caused him to become ill.

2. Mrs. Pumphrey made several excuses about Mr. Herriot's advice by saying that Tricki was suffering from malnutrition and thus tried to build him up by supplementing his food with malt and cod-liver oil along with a bowl of Horlicks at night.

She further told him that she could not resist Tricki's pleading looks and always ended up feeding him cream cakes and chocolates.

3. The story - a powerful example of the importance of saying no when it comes to making decisions that affect the health and well-being of others, whether it be for pets or for people.

- Mrs. Pumphrey's love and indulgence for her dog, Tricki, leads to the dog becoming severely overweight and unhealthy.
- Despite Herriot's advice to put Tricki on a diet and exercise regimen, Mrs. Pumphrey is unable to say 'no' and abstain from overfeeding the dog — Tricki becomes seriously ill due to his weight and unhealthy habits.

- The story, thus, highlights the fact that sometimes, the best way to help someone is to say no and steer them towards a better path, even if it may be uncomfortable or unpopular in the moment.

4. Mr. Herriot refers to the "happy period" as a time when he and his partners enjoyed an unexpected luxury due to Mrs. Pumphrey's excessive but well-meaning efforts to 'help' her recovering dog, Tricki. This luxury came in the form of fresh eggs, fine wine, and brandy, which Mrs. Pumphrey sent over to the surgery to aid in Tricki's recovery, unaware that it was bringing more delight to the doctors than to Tricki himself. This 'happy period' was characterized by the enjoyment of these treats, reflecting a humorous side to Tricki's treatment and recovery phase.

5. ***Topper's Explanation***

When Dr. James Herriot saw Mrs. Pumphrey and her dog, Tricki, in the street, he pulled up his car as he was astonished at Tricki's appearance. Tricki had become fat, like a bloated sausage, with a leg at each corner. His eyes, bloodshot and rheumy stared straight ahead, while his tongue lolled from his jaws, highlighting the dog's listlessness, owing to his being fed with extras between meals (malt, cod liver oil and a bowl of Horlicks) apart from cream cakes and chocolates by his overindulgent mistress (who attributed his lack of energy to malnutrition rather than to Tricki being overweight).

Long Answer Questions

CBSE Marking Scheme: Expression-2 M, Accuracy-1 M

6. Today, I had a dreadful realisation. I love my dear Tricki, but I fear that love has caused me to excessively indulge and pamper my dear pet. I believed that showering him with treats and rich delicacies was a sign of care and would make him feel better. But instead, I was causing him more harm than good. **(1 M)**

Thank goodness for Mr Herriot. He aptly deduced that the reason for Tricki's decline in health was my lack of strict boundaries with Tricki. He advised me to cut down Tricki's food, make him exercise, and provide a strict diet. When he noticed that I was not following his advice, he took Tricki away from me to take care of him. **(1 M)**

During Tricki's absence, I began to reflect upon my actions. I was still deeply worried about Tricki though, so I sent indulgent gifts to Mr. Herriot.

Old habits die hard, but I will try my best to be a better caretaker for Tricki now that he is back home. It brought me great joy to see Tricki transform into a healthy and happy dog after his stay with Mr. Herriot. **(1 M)**

7. Tricki was Mrs. Pumphry's favourite. No doubt she loved him very much and pampered him. But then it was also Tricky's fault. He was a greedy dog who wanted to eat everything that was served to him. **(1 M)**

He never refused food and ate at any hour of the day or night. He became a glutton. He very easily changed his system according to the luxuries he got besides all that, he never believed in exercise walking. **(1 M)**

Rather, he tried to please his lady so that he would receive sweets, chocolates, and his favourite foods. So he was also to blame for his current state. **(1 M)**

Knowledge Hub

A glutton is someone who eats much more food than is necessary, often to the point of excess. For example, if someone eats a whole cake by themselves at once, you might jokingly refer to them as a "cake glutton." In the same way, someone who eagerly accepts a huge amount of work could be described as a "work glutton." However, it's important to note that this label is usually given in a negative light.

8. (*a*) If I were a member of staff in her household, I would not follow the lady Mrs. Pumphrey's order to blindly feed Tricki. I would feed him according to the vet's advice. I would also avoid sending useless things like toys, pillows, etc. to the hospital. My life would have been very busy, and I would have had to put up with taking care of chores and fulfilling Tricki's requests on time. **(1.5 M)**

(*b*) If I were Mrs. Pumphrey's neighbour, I would advise her to consult a veterinarian and monitor his care, keeping a strict watch over Tricki's deteriorating health. I would be supporting them during their difficult times when Tricki was hospitalized. My life as Mrs. Pumphrey's neighbour would be full of surprises and presents, for Mrs. Pumphrey was a loving lady. **(1.5 M)**

9. As seen in the story Tricki who is Mrs. Pumphrey's pet had a day bed, a night bed, some favourite cushions, toys. He also had his own wardrobe with different coats for different weather. To aid Tricki's recovery Mrs. Pumphrey also sent two dozen fresh eggs daily along with several bottles of wine. She also sent a bottle of brandy so that Tricki could recover, which was enjoyed by the doctor and his staff. **(1 M)**

The fact that Mrs. Pumphrey is able to spend so much money on her pet without a second thought shows how rich she is. **(1 M)**

At the end of the story, Mrs. Pumphrey arrives to take Tricki away in a thirty feet long luxurious car, which is also surely expensive.

It is possible that Mrs. Pumphrey pampered Tricki because she didn't have any close relations. She loved Tricki like her son which is probably because she didn't have any kids of her own. **(1 M)**

Nailing the Right Answer

When answering similar questions, it is essential to support your answers with evidence from the text and provide logical explanations for the characters' actions or circumstances.

THE THIEF'S STORY

—Ruskin Bond

2

Narrative Sketch

1. The protagonist, Hari Singh, an experienced thief, encounters Anil, a kind-hearted and trusting young writer.
2. Pretending to be someone else, Hari offers to work for Anil for free.
3. Anil takes the thief in, teaching him cooking and writing.
4. The thief thinks about stealing the money Anil made from selling a book.
5. Despite hesitation, the thief steals the money but misses the opportunity to escape on a train.
6. Regret sets in as the thief realizes the weight of his actions in the rain-soaked night.
7. The thief decides to return the stolen money, driven by the value of education and a chance for a better life.
8. Anil reveals he knew about the theft but shows no anger or disappointment.
9. Anil continues to teach the thief, promising regular payment and reinforcing trust.
10. The story highlights the importance of trust, the possibility of changing for the better, and the transformative power of education.

BEFORE YOU READ

Theme

One of the central themes of The Thief's Story is that of friendship and the trust that exists between two friends. Anil trusts the teenage boy with his friendship and becomes his guardian. The boy is not able to throw away the trust he has received from Anil for the sake of money. In the end, Anil realizes that the money has been taken and then returned. Even so, he continues to trust the young boy.

Another theme common in the story is that of kindness. In this story, from the young thief's words, we can understand that the world has not been kind to him. Anil treats the teenager with kindness, giving him food and a place to stay and teaching him how to read and write.

Important Characters' Sketch

- **Anil:** Anil is a simple, kind and easy-going young man. He is tall, lean and enjoys sports like wrestling. He was a twenty-five-year-old writer who made money by contributing to magazines and spending it luxuriously. Anil was generous[1] with money and didn't seem to care too much for it. He has the patience and goodness to teach Hari to cook and provide education to him. He knows that Hari has been stealing money from him, but he chooses to ignore this fact. Ultimately, his kindness changed the young boy's mind when the teenage thief decided to run away.
- **Hari Singh (Teenage thief):** The young boy was fifteen years old. Being a thief, he had many fake names. He introduced himself to Anil as Hari Singh. He took a job with Anil to rob him at the right moment. Anil taught the young boy how to cook and write his name. Even though he stole money from Anil, he brought it back because he didn't want to break Anil's trust.

SYNOPSIS

The story is told from the point of view of the fifteen-year-old thief. The readers never know his real name, but he introduces himself to Anil as Hari Singh. Hari thinks of himself as a skilled thief and hopes Anil will be an easy target. He flatters Anil and asks if he can work for him. Anil doesn't have enough money to pay the young boy, but he gives him food and shelter.

Anil teaches Hari how to cook and how to write his name. Hari knows he can achieve more things if he is educated, and he looks forward to learning addition and writing whole sentences. Hari would sleep on the balcony, make tea in the morning, and buy the things Anil needed for the day. Hari would make a profit of a rupee every day in this manner, and even though Anil knew, he did not mind.

Anil wrote for a magazine. He didn't have a regular paycheck but got some money sometimes. He would lend and borrow money. He would also spend money freely when he got his salary. Hari was surprised to see Anil bring home a small bundle of notes one evening.

Anil told Hari that the publisher had bought Anil's book. Hari had been working for Anil for about a month and had a key to his place. But seeing Anil was such a careless man, Hari questioned whether he should take the money. Hari made up his mind to steal the money and run away as Anil didn't even pay Hari a salary. While Anil slept, Hari took the money from under the mattress.

Lessons to learn

- The power of kindness and trust.
- Honesty and integrity are valuable traits.
- Education can open doors.
- Friendship and human connections matter.
- Second chance.

Hari then ran away, stopping only to count the notes. He had six hundred rupees in fifty-rupee notes, which was a lot of money. When he reached the station, the Express train to Lucknow was leaving. He rushed to catch it but hesitated[2] to get on the train. He missed the train, and he had nowhere to go. He didn't want anyone to be suspicious[3] of him, so he couldn't spend his stolen money.

Anil would not care about the loss of money. Hari knew that Anil would be saddened because Hari had broken his trust. Hari roamed in the bazaar and then tried to sleep on a bench. Soon it started to rain, and he took shelter under the clock tower. Hari imagined his life with Anil. Hari wouldn't cook for Anil anymore, and he wouldn't learn how to write complete sentences.

Hari had forgotten how he had wanted to be educated. He knew that stealing was simple and getting caught was even simpler. Having an education and a future seemed more important to Hari then. He decided to go back to Anil. He snuck into the room while Anil was still sleeping and quietly put the money under the mattress. Anil did not wake up, and Hari went to bed.

[1] **Generous:** unselfish; liberal

[2] **Hesitated:** pause; delay

[3] **Suspicious:** doubtful

Hari woke up late the next morning. When Anil gave Hari a fifty rupee note, he got scared because he thought Anil was firing him. But Anil simply told Hari that Anil would pay him regularly from that day. He would also teach Hari to write sentences. Hari felt the wetness of the fifty rupee note and realized that even though Anil knew what Hari might have done, Anil had given him a second chance. Hari was extremely happy.

NCERT EXERCISE

Read and Find Out

(NCERT, Page 8)

1. **Who does 'I' refer to in this story?**

Ans. I refers to Hari Singh, the narrator of the story who is a 15 year old thief.

2. **What is he "a fairly successful hand" at?**

Ans. He (Hari Singh) is a fairly successful hand at stealing. He is an experienced thief. He has been doing this kind of work without being caught by the police.

3. **What does he get from Anil in return for his work?**

Ans. In return for Hari Singh's work, Anil gives him food and a place to live. He also helped him read and write sentences.

(NCERT, Page 10)

1. **How does the thief think Anil will react to the theft?**

Ans. According to Hari, Anil would be sad to know that Hari has stolen money from him. He would be sad not because of the loss of money but because of the loss of trust he had in Hari.

2. **What does he say about the different reactions of people when they are robbed?**

Ans. Hari's experience at theft had made him aware of the reactions of different people when they are robbed. According to him, a greedy man shows fear, a rich man shows anger and a poor man shows acceptance.

3. **Does Anil realise that he has been robbed?**

Ans. Yes, Anil must have realized that he had been robbed. He knew this probably because all the notes were wet and damp from the previous night's rain. However, he did not say anything to Hari and behaved normally.

Think about it

(NCERT, Page 13)

1. What are Hari Singh's reactions to the prospect of receiving an education? Do they change over time? (Hint: Compare, for example, the thought: "I knew that once I could write like an educated man there would be no limit to what I could achieve" with these later thoughts: "Whole sentences, I knew, could one day bring me more than a few hundred rupees. It was a simple matter to steal — and sometimes just as simple to be caught. But to be a really big man, a clever and respected man, was something else.") What makes him return to Anil?

Ans. Hari Singh wanted to be educated. When Anil told him that he would help the teenage thief learn how to read and write, Hari was overjoyed because he believed it would make him an even better thief.

Moreover, he felt getting an education would make him a powerful man, and no one could stop him.

Once he succeeds in stealing the money from Anil, the young thief has a change of heart. Anil is a kind man, which makes it difficult for Hari to abandon him, but Anil also represents a new opportunity, a world of education.

As Hari had forgotten about education because he was thrilled about finally robbing someone, he understood that he had made the wrong choice.

Hari's time with Anil changes his point of view towards education. He feels that getting an education will help him get the life he wants. This is why Hari decides to return to Anil even after stealing from him and running away.

2. Why does Anil not hand the thief over to the police? Do you think most people would have done so? In what ways is Anil different from such employers?

Ans. Anil is a kind person. When Hari lies to him about cooking, he teaches him how to cook. He gives food and shelter to a stranger. Anil promises to teach Hari whole sentences and addition. Anil is also careless and generous in lending and borrowing money. He understands the difficulty of not having a regular source of income.

As Anil understands the hardships a person faces due to money, he does not hand over Hari to the police even though he knows that Hari had taken money from under the mattress. Anil may also have grown fond of Hari. Hari was ten years younger than Anil, and Anil may have felt protective of Hari.

It is unlikely that any employer would follow Anil's example and give their employee a second chance.

Anil is different from these employers because the relationship between Hari and Anil is not merely that of an employer and employee but also a teacher and a student. A teacher will always correct the students and help them overcome their mistakes. Anil is also trusting and carefree, so he does not hold grudges.

MISCELLANEOUS EXERCISE

Multiple Choice Questions

1. How old was the young thief?
(*a*) Eleven (*b*) Thirteen
(*c*) Fifteen (*d*) Seventeen

2. Where did the thief spot Anil?
(*a*) Cricket match (*b*) On the bus
(*c*) Wrestling match (*d*) In the market

3. Where was Anil's room?
(*a*) Opposite Ambala station.
(*b*) Above a sweet shop.
(*c*) Near the market.
(*d*) Above a library.

4. How did the boy get a key to Anil's room?
(*a*) Anil gave him the key.
(*b*) The boy stole the key.
(*c*) The boy found the key on the floor.
(*d*) The boy copied the original key.

5. Where did the boy want to run away?
(*a*) Mumbai (*b*) Lucknow
(*c*) Delhi (*d*) Patna

6. How did the boy hide the money?
(*a*) The money was tied to his waist.
(*b*) The money was in his inner pocket.
(*c*) The money was in a dirty bag under a tree.
(*d*) The boy could not hide the money.

7. Hari Singh was the boy's
(*a*) Name (*b*) False identity
(*c*) Brother (*d*) Father

8. How much money had the boy stolen?
(*a*) Four hundred rupees. (*b*) Five hundred rupees.
(*c*) Six hundred rupees. (*d*) Fifty rupees.

9. Another meaning of 'departure' is
(*a*) Coming (*b*) Leaving
(*c*) Hurry (*d*) Running

10. 'My heart sank' is an example of .
(*a*) Simile (*b*) Metaphor
(*c*) Alliteration (*d*) Personification

Extract-Based Questions

I. Read the following extract and answer the questions/ complete the sentences that follow: (5 M)

When the train had gone, I found myself standing alone on the deserted platform. I had no idea where to spend the night. I had no friends, believing that friends were more trouble than help. And I did not want to make anyone curious by staying at one of the small hotels near the station. The only person I knew really well was the man I had robbed. Leaving the station, I walked slowly through the bazaar.

1. What does the phrase "curious by staying at one of the small hotels near the station" imply? (1)
   (*a*) People would become inquisitive if the narrator stayed at a hotel.
   (*b*) The narrator would attract attention if seen at the hotels.
   (*c*) The narrator doesn't want to be bothered by curious hotel staff.
   (*d*) The hotels near the station are not comfortable for staying.
2. Which phrase best describes the narrator's view on friendships? (1)
   (*a*) Friends are essential for a fulfilling life.
   (*b*) Friends are often unreliable and troublesome.
   (*c*) Friends provide valuable assistance in difficult times.
   (*d*) Friends are unnecessary distractions.
3. Based on the passage, what can be inferred about the narrator's feelings towards the man he robbed? (1)
4. Analyze the narrator's decision to return the stolen money. What motivations or factors might have influenced this choice? (2)

II. Read the following extract and answer the questions/ complete the sentences that follow: (5 M)

My spirits rose. But when I took the note, I saw it was still wet from the night's rain. "Today we'll start writing sentences," he said. He knew. But neither his lips nor his eyes showed anything. I smiled at Anil in my most appealing way. And the smile came by itself, without any effort.

1. What does the phrase "My spirits rose" suggest about the narrator? (1)
   (*a*) The narrator felt a surge of happiness and optimism.
   (*b*) The narrator became fearful and anxious.
   (*c*) The narrator's mood remained unchanged.
   (*d*) The narrator felt a sense of guilt and regret.
2. What can be inferred from Anil's reaction to the wet note? (1)
   (*a*) Anil was disappointed but didn't want to show it.
   (*b*) Anil was aware of the theft and purposely gave the wet note as a signal.
   (*c*) Anil was oblivious to the wet note and its significance.
   (*d*) Anil was surprised by the wet note and questioned its origin.
3. Based on the passage, what can be inferred about the narrator's intentions behind smiling at Anil? (1)
4. Reflect on the significance of the wet note as a symbol in the story. How does it represent the consequences of the narrator's actions? (2)

III. Read the following extract and answer the questions/ complete the sentences that follow: (5 M)

Anil was asleep. A beam of moonlight stepped over the balcony and fell on the bed. I sat up on the floor, considering the situation. If I took the money, I could catch the 10.30 Express to Lucknow. Slipping out of the blanket, I crept up to the bed. Anil was sleeping peacefully. His face was clear and unlined; even I had more marks on my face, though mine were mostly scars.

1. What does the narrator's choice to sit up on the floor imply about the situation? (1)
   (*a*) The narrator is uncomfortable and uncertain about what to do.
   (*b*) The narrator is planning a surprise for Anil when he wakes up.
   (*c*) The narrator prefers sleeping on the floor rather than the bed.
   (*d*) The narrator is preparing to confront Anil about the stolen money.
2. Why does the narrator consider taking the money while Anil is asleep? (1)
   (*a*) The narrator wants to teach Anil a lesson for not paying him.
   (*b*) The narrator intends to use the money to buy food for both of them.
   (*c*) The narrator plans to escape and start a new life in Lucknow.
   (*d*) The narrator wants to prove that he can successfully steal without being noticed.
3. Based on the passage, what can be inferred about the narrator's past experiences? (1)
4. Analyze the internal conflict faced by the narrator when considering stealing the money. How does this conflict highlight the moral dilemma and the narrator's desire for a fresh start? (2)

IV. Read the following extract and answer the questions/ complete the sentences that follow: (5 M)

Found myself in the maidan and sat down on a bench. The night was chilly — it was early November — and a light drizzle added to my discomfort. Soon it was raining quite heavily. My shirt and pyjamas stuck to my skin, and a cold wind blew the rain across my face. I went back to the bazaar and sat down in the shelter of the clock tower. The clock showed midnight. I felt for the notes. They were damp from the rain.

1. Write a word from the passage for "slightly wet". (1)
2. What was the weather like when the narrator found themselves in the maidan? (1)
   (*a*) Sunny and warm (*b*) Cold and rainy
   (*c*) Windy and foggy (*d*) Humid and stormy

3. Based on the description of the narrator's discomfort, what can be inferred about his current situation? **(1)**
4. How does the adverse weather conditions and the discomfort experienced by the narrator contribute to the overall tone and atmosphere of the scene? **(2)**

V. Read the following extract and answer the questions/ complete the sentences that follow: (5 M)

I went back to the bazaar and sat down in the shelter of the clock tower. The clock showed midnight. I felt for the notes. They were damp from the rain.

Anil's Money. In the morning he would probably have given me two or three rupees to go to the cinema, but now I had it all.

I couldn't cook his meals, run to the bazaar, or learn to write whole sentences any more.

I had forgotten about them in the excitement of the theft. Whole sentences, I knew, could one day bring me more than a few hundred rupees. It was a simple matter to steal- and sometimes just as simple to be caught. **(CBSE, 2024)**

1. Which of the following is NOT a reason why Hari Singh thinks he would not be able to write whole sentences? **(1)**
   (*a*) Anil would not be there to teach him.
   (*b*) He had robbed Anil and left.
   (*c*) He would not go back to Anil to learn.
   (*d*) He had no money to take admission in school.
2. Why is it fair to say that Hari Singh's tone, when he says "I couldn't cook his meals, run to the bazaar or learn to write whole sentences any more," is filled with remorse and regret? Answer in about 40 words. **(2)**
3. What do you infer about Hari Singh from this statement? **(1)**
   "Whole sentences, I knew, could one day bring me more than a few hundred rupees."
4. State **True** or **False** with reference to the given extract. The reason Hari Singh was filled with a feeling of guilt was because Anil trusted him. **(1)**

Subjective Questions

Short Answer Questions (40-50 words) (3 M)

1. Why did Hari Singh smile in his most appealing way towards the end of the story? **(CBSE, 2023)**
2. Why does Hari say 'friends were more trouble than help'? How do you think he formed this opinion?
3. In which queer way did Anil make a living?
4. Why did the thief change his name every month ? How did he rob people?
5. What made Hari Singh come back to Anil? **(CBSE, 2020)**

Long Answer Questions (100-120 words) (6 M)

6. Trust and compassion can reform a person. Justify this statement in the light of the lesson 'The Thief's Story'. **(CBSE, 2023)**
7. Who was Anil? How did he treat Hari Singh and how did it influence Hari's life?
8. Why do people like Hari Singh win the confidence of others and make friends with them? Was Hari Singh able to do the same?
9. Hari Singh says – "He knew it but neither his lips nor his eyes showed anything."
   Anil successfully addressed the situation by not addressing it at all. Elaborate based on your reading of The Thief's Story. **(CBSE, 2024)**

ANSWERS & EXPLANATIONS

Answer Key

Multiple Choice Questions

1. (*c*) 2. (*c*) 3. (*b*) 4. (*a*) 5. (*b*) 6. (*a*) 7. (*b*) 8. (*c*) 9. (*b*) 10. (*b*)

Explanations

Extract-Based Questions

I. 1. (*b*) The narrator would attract attention if seen at the hotels.

2. (*b*) Friends are often unreliable and troublesome.

3. The narrator feels a sense of familiarity and connection with the man he robbed, considering him the only person he knows well.

4. A sense of guilt or remorse, realizing the value of trust and the desire for redemption, recognizing the potential for a better future through education, and the realization that stealing does not bring lasting satisfaction are the motivations that might have influenced.

II. 1. (*a*) The narrator felt a surge of happiness and optimism.

2. (*b*) Anil was aware of the theft and purposely gave the wet note as a signal.

3. The narrator tries to show he didn't do anything wrong by smiling, even though he had taken the money back.

4. The wet note shows the stolen money still affects the thief, reminding him of his wrong doing. It means he feels bad for what he did and knows he can't completely avoid the results of his actions.

III. 1. (*a*) The narrator is uncomfortable and uncertain about what to do.

2. (*c*) The narrator plans to escape and start a new life in Lucknow.

3. The narrator has faced hardships and encounters that have left visible marks on his face in the form of scars.

4. The narrator's internal conflict arises from the choice between stealing the money and starting a new life. This highlights the moral dilemma, as the narrator grapples with personal gain versus doing what is right. It also reflects the narrator's strong desire for a fresh start, free from their past actions.

IV. 1. Damp

2. (*b*) Cold and rainy

3. The narrator is facing a difficult and uncomfortable situation due to the heavy rain and cold wind.

4. The adverse weather condition and discomfort create a tone of hardship and despair, intensifying the atmosphere. They reflect the challenging circumstances and highlight the narrator's struggles, adding depth to the scene.

V. 1. (*d*) He had no money to take admission in School.

2. Hari Singh's tone reflects repentance as he understands how much Anil was helping him grow, not just with money but with knowledge too. He regrets losing the chance to learn and better his future, realizing that these lessons are more valuable than anything he could steal.

3. Hari Singh realizes that being good at writing can help him have a good future. He starts to see that learning and using his skills can give him a better life than just stealing. This shows he understands there are better ways to live his life.

4. True

Subjective Questions

Short Answer Questions

CBSE Marking Scheme: Content-1 M, Organisation of Ideas-1 M, Accuracy-1 M

1. Hari Singh's most 'appealing' smile, towards the close of the story is full of gratitude and there is no distonesty and selfishness in it. It is an effortless smile full of sincerity.

   It is Hari Singh's way of expressing thankfulness towards Anil's generosity for still keeping him as his domestic help even after knowing that he has made an attempt to rob him.

2. Hari had no friends and he kept no one around him because he was a thief. He felt he was skilled at his job and he operated alone. He could not trust anyone because he was not a trustworthy person himself. He felt a friend, or a partner would only betray him.

   From his words, we may say that Hari had been betrayed by people before. Hari was all alone in the world and he didn't find anyone to help him until he met Anil.

   Under Anil's good influence, Hari did become better in the end. So we can say that other people must have influenced Hari negatively, which is why he preferred to be alone.

3. Anil made a living by writing for magazines. He would make money by fits and starts, one week he would be borrowing and the next week lending.

   He kept worrying about his next cheque but celebrated as soon as it arrived.

4. The thief changed his name every month to avoid being caught by the police and his former employers.

   By using different identities, it became more difficult for people to track him down or recognize him based on his previous activities or reputation.

5. Anil had been teaching Hari Singh to read and write. He thought that without education, he would remain only a thief. But with education, he would become a big, clever and respected man. This made him come back to Anil.

Long Answer Questions

CBSE Marking Scheme: Expression-2 M, Accuracy-1 M

6. The lesson 'The Thief's Story' is a testament to the power of trust and compassion to reform a person. The protagonist, Hari Singh, is a thief who meets Anil, a kind and trusting man. **(1 M)**

Anil takes Hari in and teaches him to cook and write, despite the fact that Hari cannot pay him.Through Anil's trust and compassion, Hari is able to see a different way of life and is inspired to change his ways. **(1 M)**

Anil's kindness so moves him that he cannot bring himself to rob him, despite having the perfect opportunity. This shows that trust and compassion can be powerful tools in reforming a person and inspiring them to make positive changes in their life. **(1 M)**

7. Anil was 25 years old, a young, tall and lean man. He was easy going and kind. A 15 year old boy Hari Singh met Anil at a wrestling match. He tried to flatter Anil to win his confidence and later to rob him. The boy told him that he wanted to work for him. **(1 M)**

   Anil gave him a job as a cook but he cooked terrible food and was told by Anil to run away but later he taught him how to cook and how to learn reading and writing. Anil was very kind and trusted Hari Singh. **(1 M)**

   Hari Singh though broke his trust by stealing Anil's money but later his heart changed and he decided to put the money back. Anil discovered all this. But he was so large-hearted that he said nothing to the boy. Instead, he promised to pay him regularly. Hari Singh understood the importance of education and thought of a new beginning. **(1 M)**

8. Hari Singh was a thief. People like Hari Singh are mostly experienced thieves. They find their prey at different places by changing their names and personality and by flattering them they win their confidence. **(1 M)**

   Further, thieves try to become friends by talking about the topics of their prey's interest and innocent people start trusting them. They do it to rob people as robbery or stealing is their main profession. If people trust these thieves then it becomes easy for them to steal others. **(1 M)**

   Hari Singh was very clever and he knew that he could easily rob Anil because Anil was very easy going. Hari Singh won the confidence of Anil by his most appealing smile and started to stay with Anil. He almost became friends with Anil but because of Anil's kind behaviour his mind changed and even after stealing money he returned back and started a new life. Anil's kind heart was the motivation for Hari Singh and he changed a lot. **(1 M)**

9. ***Topper's Explanation***

'The Thief's Story' is an amazing story which shows us the importance of trust and values. Hari Singh was a thief. He started living at Anil's house to rob him. He befriended Anil and soon gained his trust. When Anil got a payment of six hundred rupees, he kept it under his mattress. At night while Anil was sleeping, Hari Singh slipped his hand under the ~~ra~~ mattress and stole the money. But he could not run far with the money. His conscience pricked him as he did not want to break Anil's trust. He felt guilty and came back home with the money which by then had been damp due to rain. He put the soggy notes back at the place from where he retrieved it. Anil, the next day, on knowing everything didn't react. Even on knowing about this incidence, he accepted Hari with open hands. This shows us the importance of values. Values can even change a bad person. Sympathy, education and good behaviour are capable of changing a criminal into a good person. Though circumstances made Hari a criminal, Anil ~~was~~ understood his position and decided to educate him. It was Anil's trust and good behaviour which brought Hari back on the good path. Thus the statement, 'Anil successfully addressed the situation by not addressing it at all'.

THE MIDNIGHT VISITOR

—Robert Arthur

3

Narrative Sketch

1. Ausable, who is described as fat and with an American accent, doesn't fit the typical image of a secret agent.
2. Ausable invites Fowler, a young writer, to his small and unromantic hotel room in France.
3. Ausable dismisses Fowler's disappointment and assures him that an important paper is expected to arrive, which may have an impact on history.
4. Upon entering the room, they discover Max, another secret agent, standing with a pistol in hand.
5. Ausable seems surprised by Max's presence and asks him why he is in his room.
6. Max expresses his desire to obtain the report concerning new missiles, believing it would be more secure with him
7. Ausable mentions that someone had previously entered his room through a balcony that belonged to the adjacent apartment.
8. Max learns about the balcony but says he used a passkey to enter.
9. Ausable explains that he asked the police to check on him for extra protection, causing Max to become nervous.
10. When there's knocking, Max thinks it's the police and threatens to escape via the balcony, but it turns out to be just a waiter with drinks.

Fowler is confused and mentions the police, but Ausable reveals there were no police, only the waiter.

11

Ausable reveals there is no balcony, showing he tricked Max into escaping through a non-existent exit.

12

BEFORE YOU READ

Theme

The most important theme in this story is intelligence versus violence. Ausable tricks Max and saves the missile report from falling into the wrong hands, without using any weapon. Another theme is appearance versus reality. Even though Ausable appears to be an average plump man to the common eye, in reality, he is a ruthless[1] detective who can calmly protect his mission in the face of danger.

Important Characters' Sketch

- **Detective Ausable**: Ausable is an American detective from Boston. He speaks German and French well but with a heavy accent[2]. He doesn't fit the public notion of a secret agent or a detective. When in danger and about to lose the precious object he was guarding, Ausable remained calm in that moment. He is able to lie calmly to survive his mission and at the same time he takes out his opposition permanently. This helps us understand that even though he may not look the part, Ausable is intelligent and has the ability to manipulate[4] the situation to his advantage.
- **Fowler:** Fowler is a young writer interviewing Ausable, as he wanted to delve into the world of secret agents and their thrills. Fowler also had a romantic notion of what that world was like. As Ausable points out, Fowler had imagined "mysterious figures in the night, the crack of pistols, drugs in the wine". The detective points out that Fowler must have imagined secret meetings to be scheduled with the help of notes from "dark-eyed beauties" but instead. It was only a boring phone call. Fowler is a contrast to Ausable; he is young, inexperienced, easily puzzled and innocent while the detective is mature, confident and ruthless. Fowler finds it difficult to process the fact that the person he spent all evening calmly chatting with, has the skills and lack of concern required to get the job done even at the cost of human life.
- **Max:** Max is a rival secret agent who wants to steal the important missile report that Ausable has in his care. Max and Ausable must have met earlier as Ausable recognised him. Fowler describes Max as slender with average height, and facial features resembling a fox. Max fails to snatch the report as Ausable tricks him into believing that the police is at the door. Ausable also lies to Max about a non-existent balcony outside his hotel room. When Max attempts to hide from the police by going over the ledge, he falls to his death.

SYNOPSIS

The Midnight Visitor, written by Robert Arthur follows an evening in the life of secret agent Ausable as he is accompanied by the writer Fowler. Set in France, the story starts with Fowler following Ausable to the his hotel room. Ausable doesn't fit into Fowler's romanticised[5] version of what a spy should look like. However, the detective assures Fowler that he has a very important piece of paper which will make the writer's evening worthwhile.

When Fowler and Ausable enter the detective's room, they find an intruder pointing a gun at them. Ausable identifies the new person as Max who happens to be a secret agent working for a rival group. Ausable is irritated as he remarks that it was the second time in a month that someone had broken into his hotel room using the adjacent balcony. Max replies that he was unaware of the balcony and had used a passkey to infiltrate[6] the hotel room.

[1] **Ruthless:** heartless
[2] **Accent:** way of pronouncing a language
[3] **Exemplifies:** illustrate
[4] **Manipulate:** footnote
[5] **Romanticised:** idealized; unrealistic
[6] **Infiltrate:** enter (an organization or place) secretly

Ausable goes on to explain to Fowler in detail how the room he was in at the time had been part of a larger unit which had been sectioned off to make different rooms. Max then gestures[7] at Fowler with the gun pointing at him and asks him to sit and wait for thirty minutes. Ausable corrects him and asks Max how he knew about the report. Max avoids answering and says that he would definitely get the crucial report back to his people by that night.

Suddenly there is a knock at the door. Max is frightened and asks who it is. Ausable coolly answers that he informed the police about the whole situation for extra protection. Max, in anger, makes his way to the balcony all the while pointing his gun towards Ausable and Fowler. He threatens to shoot them both, if Ausable doesn't send the police away. He goes out through the window-sill into the darkness while the knocking on the door intensifies.

As the door opens, Max drops from the window-sill to the balcony and a shrill scream is heard. Outside the room, Ausable and Fowler see a waiter with a tray, a bottle and two glasses. As the waiter enters with the drink that Ausable had previously ordered to be delivered to him once he had returned to his room, Fowler with a pale face asks about the police, and about Max. Answered that he had not informed the police and that there was no the story highlights Ausable's intelligence and ability to manipulate the situation to his advantage, using his knowledge of the hotel and his understanding of human behavior.

Despite his unassuming appearance, Ausable proves to be a competent and resourceful secret agent, showcasing that heroism and intelligence are not bound by physical characteristics.

Lessons to learn

- Appearances can be deceiving.
- Things are not always as they seem.
- Attention to detail is crucial.
- Trust can be misplaced.

Real life Secret Agent

Expectation

Ausable as a Secret Agent

Reality

NCERT EXERCISE

Read and Find Out

(NCERT Page 14)

1. How is Ausable different from other secret agents?

Ans. Ausable is different from other secret agents in a number of ways. He has a small room in a dingy French hotel's musty corridor. It was on the sixth and top floor, and it was hardly the setting of a romantic adventure. He was obese. Despite having lived in Paris for nearly two decades, he struggled to speak French and German and had an American accent. Instead of receiving messages from beautiful girls, he received just a normal phone call setting up an appointment. In these ways, he was different from the conventional notion of a secret agent.

[7] **Gestures:** signal

He dealt with Max by making up some stories and convincing Max to believe them in order for him to get what he wanted, which was to get rid of Max.

2. **Who is Fowler, and what is his first authentic thrill of the day?**

Ans. Fowler is a writer, and he had come to meet Ausable. His first authentic thrill of the day came when he saw a man in Ausable's room pointing a pistol towards them.

(NCERT Page 15)

1. **How has Max got in?**

Ans. Max had got into the room using a passkey or master key.

2. **How does Ausable say he got in?**

Ans. Ausable said that he thought Max had gotten into the room through the balcony. He said it was the second time in a month that somebody had gotten into his room this way.

Think about it

(NCERT Page 18)

1. **"Ausable did not fit any description of a secret agent Fowler had ever read." What do secret agents in books and films look like, in your opinion? Discuss in groups or in class some stories or movies featuring spies, detectives and secret agents, and compare their appearance with that of Ausable in this story. (You may mention characters from fiction in languages other than English. In English fiction, you may have come across Sherlock Holmes, Hercule Poirot, or Miss Marple. Have you watched any movies featuring James Bond?)**

Ans. In the text, Ausable is described as a middle-aged American who is quite fat. His physical description does not fit with the well-toned physique of various detectives such as James Bond, Jason Bourne or Gary Urwin from the Kingsman series. More often than not, these detectives are portrayed int the book and films by good looking actors with gym-trained bodies. Ausable himself remarks that his appearance as well the conditions under which he receives instructions are rather mundane[8], compared to the high-octane situations in which James Bond or Ethan Hunt from the Mission Impossible movies may find themselves. As a young writer in search of adventure, fowler is disillusioned[9] when he sees the boring ways in which real detectives work.

But the story becomes thrilling and similar to movies with the introduction of Max, a secret agent working to oppose Ausable's goals. Ausable's calm demeanor and use of intellect to defeat Max makes him akin[10] to Sherlock Holmes who solved crimes with minimal violence and maximum skill.

In this manner we can say that even though Ausable may seem mundane from the outside, the situations he finds himself in, are dangerous and worthy of being captured on the silver screen.

2. **How does Ausable manage to make Max believe that there is a balcony attached to his room? Look back at his detailed description of it. What makes it a convincing story?**

Ans. Ausable starts composing the story of a supposed break-in and the balcony, when he finds Max in his hotel room. He knew that the waiter would be coming up any time with his drink and he set his story in motion.

Ausable makes use of the mundane in his room to fabricate[11] this story. He explains the story offhandedly to Fowler, possibly making Max believe it should be true since the fact seems somewhat random. Ausable also gives a detailed description of the origin of the balcony; he says that the apartment in question had been broken up into various rooms which led to the balcony beside the living room being directly under the window in Ausable's room. Max believes he is in power just because he has a gun and Ausable is unarmed. Ausable is however armed, with intelligence, and he uses this to send Max to his death.

The story is convincing because it is said in an off-handed manner and includes details that otherwise seem unimportant. Coupled with the fact that Max had surprised Ausable and Ausable only had a small amount of time to cook up this lie, the story seemed real to Fowler and Max and the reader. Only Ausable knew about the waiter so it was easy to believe that it was the police, by all unknown parties.

3. **Looking back at the story, when do you think Ausable thought up his plan for getting rid of Max? Do you think he had worked out his plan in detail right from the beginning? Or did he make up a plan taking advantage of events as they happened?**

Ans. Ausable definitely thought up the plan on the fly. He had no idea that a rival agent would be waiting for him in his room. It is clear that Ausable knew Max so he may have figured out how he could fool Max and what his weaknesses might be. Ausable knew for certain that the waiter would come knocking at the door and he set the plan in motion by telling the story to Fowler while Max listened.

Even though Ausable could not have planned every detail of the plan from the very beginning he knew he had to use every opportunity to fool Max which was given to him when someone knocked at the door was uncertainty. Max might not have believed the 'balcony' story, the waiter may not have come at all, or they could have been interrupted by the people who were supposed to provide Ausable the secret report. But all the incidents worked in Ausable's favour and he could defeat Max.

---

[8] **Mundane:** dull; boring
[9] **Disillusioned:** disappointed; let down
[10] **Akin:** similar
[11] **Fabricate:** invent; create

MISCELLANEOUS EXERCISE

Multiple Choice Questions

1. Where does the story take place?
   (*a*) France (*b*) England
   (*c*) USA (*d*) Germany
2. Fowler is a ______.
   (*a*) Young agent (*b*) Young writer
   (*c*) Young cop (*d*) Rival agent
3. Fowler was surprised because
   (*a*) He found a huge rat in the room.
   (*b*) He found a pistol behind the couch.
   (*c*) He found a gunman in the room.
   (*d*) The room had no furniture.
4. The report contained information about ______.
   (*a*) Government secret (*b*) Interpol conspiracy
   (*c*) New missiles (*d*) Nuclear bombs
5. On which floor was Ausable staying?
   (*a*) Third floor (*b*) Fourth floor
   (*c*) Fifth floor (*d*) Sixth floor
6. How was Ausable notified about the report?
   (*a*) By a dark-eyed beauty.
   (*b*) By a letter.
   (*c*) By phone.
   (*d*) By a secret message hidden in the food.
7. How had Max entered Ausable's room?
   (*a*) A passkey (*b*) A duplicate key
   (*c*) Escape ladder (*d*) Balcony
8. Choose the word which best describes 'inflection'.
   (*a*) Voice (*b*) Sound
   (*c*) Intonation (*d*) Quality
9. What is the meaning of 'outwit'?
   (*a*) Beat with knowledge.
   (*b*) Beat with intelligence.
   (*c*) Beat with application.
   (*d*) Beat with skill.
10. Who was at the door of Ausable's hotel room?
    (*a*) Police (*b*) Waiter
    (*c*) Doorman (*d*) Security

Extract-Based Questions

I. Read the following extract and answer the questions/ complete the sentences that follow: (5 M)

Ausable did not fit any description of a secret agent Fowler had ever read. Following him down the musty corridor of the gloomy French hotel where Ausable had a room, Fowler felt let down. It was a small room, on the sixth and top floor, and scarcely a setting for a romantic adventure.

Ausable was, for one thing, fat. Very fat. And then there was his accent. Though he spoke French and German passably, he had never altogether lost the American accent he had brought to Paris from Boston twenty years ago. "You are disappointed," Ausable said wheezily over his shoulder. "You were told that I was a secret agent, a spy, dealing in espionage and danger. You wished to meet me because you are a writer, young and romantic. You envisioned mysterious figures in the night, the crack of pistols, drugs in the wine." **(CBSE APQ, 2023)**

1. Which of these describes how Fowler felt at the beginning of the extract? **(1)**
   (*a*) His heart sank.
   (*b*) He was shaken up.
   (*c*) His stomach was in knots.
   (*d*) He was at the end of his rope.
2. State one observation about Ausable based on the way he handled Fowler's disappointment with him. **(1)**
3. How did the atmosphere of the French hotel influence Fowler's mood? Answer in 40 words. **(2)**
4. Which of these means the same as 'romantic' in the line below? **(1)**
   It was a small room, on the sixth and top floor, and scarcely a setting for a romantic adventure.
   (*a*) great (*b*) exciting
   (*c*) idealistic (*d*) passionate

II. Read the extract given below and answer the questions that follow: (4 M)

And as the light came on. Fowler had his first authentic thrill of the day. For halfway across the room, a small automatic pistol in his hand, stood a man.

Ausable blinked a few times. **(CBSE, 2020)**

1. Who was standing in the room with a pistol in his hand? **(1)**
   (*a*) Ausable (*b*) Fowler
   (*c*) Max (*d*) A waiter

2. Ausable blinked because he: **(1)**

(*a*) was getting adjusted to the light

(*b*) got afraid of the man with a pistol

(*c*) was thrilled to have reached his room

(*d*) started thinking of how to get rid of the man

3. Fowler was thrilled because what he saw looked like a __________. **(1)**

4. Which word in the extract means the same as 'genuine/ real'? **(1)**

III. Read the following extract and answer the questions/ complete the sentences that follow: (5 M)

Ausable moved to an armchair and sat down heavily. "I'm going to raise the devil with the management this time, and you can bet on it," he said grimly. "This is the second time in a month that somebody has got into my room through that nuisance of a balcony!" Fowler's eyes went to the single window of the room. It was an ordinary window, against which now the night was pressing blackly.

"Balcony?" Max said, with a rising inflection. "No, a passkey. I did not know about the balcony. It might have saved me some trouble had I known."

1. What is Ausable planning to do regarding the management? **(1)**

(*a*) Compliment them on their service.

(*b*) Ignore the issue with the balcony.

(*c*) Raise a complaint or concern.

(*d*) Praise their security measures.

2. What reaction does Ausable show to Max's unexpected presence in his room? **(1)**

(*a*) He was amused. (*b*) He was indifferent.

(*c*) He acted surprised. (*d*) He was terrified.

3. Describe the significance of the "balcony" in Ausable's strategy against Max. Answer in 40 words. **(2)**

4. In the context of Ausable's complaint about someone entering his room, what does "raise the devil" most closely mean? (1)

(*a*) To leave quietly

(*b*) To cause a disturbance

(*c*) To summon supernatural forces

(*d*) To laugh it off

Subjective Questions

Short Answer Questions (40-50 words) (3 M)

1. How did Ausable get rid of Max without using a weapon. **(CBSE, 2023)**

2. Why does Ausable think Fowler is disappointed? Is he correct or incorrect? Illustrate with examples from the text.

3. 'Fowler had his first authentic thrill of the day.' In what situation did Fowler find himself? What does his reaction as reflected in the line prove?

4. The various elements of Robert Arthur's writing style work together to create a sense of tension, uncertainty, and suspense, well-suited to the mystery and suspense genre of the story, The Midnight Visitor. Comment, with reference to any one element. **(CBSE SQP, 2023)**

Long Answer Questions (100-120 words) (6 M)

5. Give a description of Max. How is he different from Ausable?

6. What realization does Fowler come to, at the end of passage, in regards to Ausable's character?

ANSWERS & EXPLANATIONS

Answer Key

Multiple Choice Questions

1. (*a*) **2.** (*b*) **3.** (*c*) **4.** (*c*) **5.** (*d*) **6.** (*c*) **7.** (*a*) **8.** (*c*) **9.** (*b*) **10.** (*b*)

Explanations

Extract-Based Questions

I. 1. (*a*) his heart sank

['His heart sank' implies that Fowler was 'disappointed' or 'let down'.]

2. We can infer that Ausable was confident. He didn't feel the need to apologise for disappointing Fowler. He accepted his disappointment without judgement.

3. The French hotel is described as 'gloomy', 'musty' and 'small'. This sombre atmosphere of the hotel added to Fowler's feeling of disappointment. He expected a grand atmosphere of mystery and danger, and was disappointed by the reality of the situation.

4. (*b*) exciting

II. 1. (*c*) Max

2. (*d*) started thinking of how to get rid of the man

3. dramatic scene

4. Authentic

III. 1. (*c*) Raise a complaint or concern.

2. (*c*) He acted surprised.

3. Ausable smartly tricks Max by talking about a "balcony" that doesn't exist. This shows how quickly Ausable thinks and how he can control the situation to his benefit. He turns a dangerous moment into a win for himself, all without actual confrontation or violence.

4. (*b*) To cause a disturbance

Subjective Questions

Short Answer Questions

CBSE Marking Scheme: Content-1 M, Organisation of Ideas-1 M, Accuracy-1 M

1. Ausable was the secret agent but he does not fit in the description of any secret agent. In general, secret agents are imagined to be tall and have dark eyebeauty, but Ausable was a fat and short man.

But Ausable has a very active mind and to get rid of his rival enemy Max he cooked up a false story of a balcony, that really does not exist he said that it is the second time that someone has entered his room through the balcony, the sudden knock on the door made Max to jump out of it and Ausable got rid of Max without using any weapon.

2. As a young writer. Fowler had a romantic notion about spies and their missions. According to Ausable, Fowler "envisioned[12] mysterious figures in the night, the crack of pistols, drugs in the wine."

But there are no beautiful women secretly conveying the mission to a well-toned handsome detective, only a "prosaic telephone call making an appointment in his (Ausable's) room." Ausable correctly determined that Fowler was disappointed in the lack of glamour in real-life spying.

3. When Ausable and Fowler entered Ausable's hotel room, they found a gunman pointing his pistol at them. Ausable identified the gunman as his rival Max.

Fowler was thrilled when he saw that a gunman was in the room. His reaction proves that he had no real life experience of how dangerous spy work could be, which is why he isn't fearful but thrilled.

4. Use of dialogue - The conversation between Ausable and Max is filled with half-truths and mystification, which creates a sense of ambiguity and heightens the story's sense of mystery. The reader is left wondering about Max's true motives and intentions, which adds to the sense of uncertainty and tension in the story.

Long Answer Questions

CBSE Marking Scheme: Expression-2 M, Accuracy-1 M

5. Max is portrayed as a slender, some what less than tall individual with a crafty, pointed appearance similar to a fox. He did not look dangerous, apart from the fact that he was pointing a gun at Fowler and Ausable. **(1 M)**

Max is a rival secret agent who is different from Ausable. The adjective used in the text for Max is 'evil' which by contrast makes Ausable good. **(1 M)**

This means that the author wants the reader to side with Ausable, marking the mature detective as the protagonist. Max being on the opposite side of Ausable becomes the antagonist. Max is therefore also expendable, and his death does not make the reader uncomfortable. **(1 M)**

6. Fowler was disillusioned from his romantic notions when he met Ausable and found out how boring real-life spy work was. Ausable was very fat and the spy-work he was involved in seemed mundane, unlike the detectives in Fowler's imagination. **(1 M)**

When Fowler encountered Max, a rival spy, things became rather thrilling for him. He did not process that this was a life and death situation. **(1 M)**

When at the end of the story Max fell to his death from the window sill, due to Asuable's fabrication of an imaginative balcony, Fowler was shocked. He realized even though Ausable looked ordinary he was a ruthless secret agent who would do anything to protect his mission objective. **(1 M)**

Nailing the Right Answer

Students should avoid adding personal opinions or unrelated information in their answers. Stick to the facts presented in the lesson and provide concise and accurate responses.

❑❑❑

[12] **Envision:** imagine as a possibility, visualize

A QUESTION OF TRUST

—Victor Canning

4

Narrative Sketch

1. Horace Danby, a seemingly respectable citizen, is revealed to be a skilled thief who steals rare books every year.

2. Horace meticulously plans his robberies and uses the stolen money to buy books through an agent.

3. He targets Shotover Grange, a house with valuable jewels worth thousands of pounds.

4. Horace enters the house, carefully avoiding leaving any fingerprints, but is interrupted by a young woman pretending to be the owner.

5. The woman engages in a conversation with Horace, revealing her knowledge of his intentions and offering a deal to spare him if he helps her retrieve her jewels from the safe.

6. Horace, desperate to avoid prison, agrees and successfully opens the safe, returning the jewels to the woman.

7. After two days, Horace is arrested for the jewel robbery, as his fingerprints are found at the crime scene.

8. Despite his claims of being manipulated by the woman, no one believes him, and he is sentenced to prison.

9. Horace becomes an assistant librarian in the prison, reflecting on the cunning young woman who deceived him and rejecting the notion of "honour among thieves."

BEFORE YOU READ

Theme

The story "A Question of Trust" explores themes of deception, mistaken identity, and irony. It shows how Horace Danby, a seemingly honest man with a secret life of crime, gets tricked by another thief pretending to be the house owner. Despite his careful planning, Horace learns a hard lesson about trust and honor among thieves. The story highlights that appearances can be deceiving and that sometimes, those who live by deceit can fall victim to their own games.

Important Characters' Sketch

- **Horace Danby:** Danby is the main character of the story. He was a fifty-year-old unmarried man who had the business of making locks and was considered a kind and honest citizen. Having great love for rare and expensive books, he used to rob once a year. But he got caught once when he compromised his own values of the profession, trusting another person who was also a thief.
- **The lady:** The lady in the story is a cunning and clever thief who skillfully deceives Horace Danby into believing she is the house owner. Dressed in red and appearing kind, she uses her intelligence and charm to manipulate[1] Horace. She was a masterful deceiver, who ultimately lead to Horace's arrest.

SYNOPSIS

"A Question of Trust" by Victor Canning is a story of two burglars who wanted to rob the same safe. Horace Danby was considered a good and respectful citizen. He had a business of making locks with two helpers. This story is about the day he sets out for the burglary with all his tools to steal the jewels worth fifteen thousand pounds. He imagined this was enough to buy the rare and expensive books for another year. As he was prepared with every information about the house that the family was in London, and the two servants had also gone to the movies. When he reached the big house, he met a lady who claimed to be the owner of the house. She also remarked on Danby's presence, saying she didn't expect that a burglar would be present when she came back before the expected time (1 month), as she had come there suddenly because she wanted to wear her jewels at the party in the night. (as she said this to Horace) She warns him that she will call the police if he tries to escape. Horace requested the lady to let him go. In return, the lady asked him to open the safe because she had forgotten the number. Since Horace thought that he would be forgiven and allowed to leave, he opened the safe without gloves. That lady then got the jewels, and Horace went away happily because he had escaped from being imprisoned. On the third day, he got arrested by a policeman for the jewel robbery, as his fingerprints were found at the rob site. He even confessed that he had opened the safe for the young lady, but he was shocked when he knew that the owner's wife was about 60 years old. That old lady said that this was not true, and no one believed Horace. Eventually, Horace ended up working as the assistant librarian in prison, and he often thought about that clever lady who tricked him and got angry whenever anyone talked about "honour among thieves".

Lessons to learn

- *Looks can be deceiving.*
- *Honesty is essential.*
- *Actions have consequences.*
- *Trust can be misplaced.*
- *The value of integrity.*

[1] **Manipulate:** influence unfairly (a person or situation)

Horace Danby

NCERT EXERCISE

Read and Find Out

(NCERT, Page 20)

1. **What does Horace Danby like to collect?**

Ans. Horace Danby likes to collect books. He loves rare and expensive books.

2. **Why does he steal every year?** **(CBSE, 2018)**

Ans. He steals to get money to satisfy his hobby of buying and collecting rare and expensive books which could last for one whole year so that he does not need to rob again and again.

(NCERT, Page 22)

1. **Who is speaking to Horace Danby?**

Ans. A lady in red is speaking to Mr Danby, who claims to be the mistress of the house.

2. **Who is the real culprit in the story?**

Ans. The real culprit is the lady thief. She tries to act as the landlady of the Grange. Danby entered the house to rob, but before him, that lady thief was already there.

Think about it

(NCERT, Page 25)

1. **Did you begin to suspect, before the end of the story, that the lady was not the person Horace Danby took her to be? If so, at what point did you realize this, and how?**

Ans. In the beginning, the lady was believable. I did not suspect her. But when she said, "I have always liked the wrong kind of people", I suspected[2] her. Then she said that if Horace did 'something' for her, she would let him go.

2. **What are the subtle ways in which the lady manages to deceive Horace Danby into thinking she is the lady of the house? Why doesn't Horace suspect that something is wrong?**

Ans. At first, the lady speaks with confidence to deceive Horace. She has firmness in her voice. She smiles at him while talking. There is sharpness also in her voice as she continues talking. She then threatens him with the idea of prison. In this way, she impresses him to be the landlady.

[2] **Suspected:** to not be sure that you can trust somebody or believe something

3. "Horace Danby was good and respectable — but not completely honest". Why do you think this description is apt for Horace? Why can't he be categorised as a typical thief?

Ans. Horace's habits were not typical of a thief. He was fond of books. He used to steal only once a year, so he never stole more than his needs. However, theft is still a crime, no matter how well a thief behaves, so this description is apt for Horace. He can't be categorised as a typical thief because he is not a regular offender like other thieves.

4. Horace Danby was a meticulous[3] planner but still he faltered. Where did he go wrong and why?

Ans. Horace Danby failed to get enough information about the real occupants of the house. He seems too occupied with collecting information about the house map, wiring and location of valuable items. Although he was smart enough to know the dog's actual name, he overlooked getting information about the house's occupants. When he landed in trouble with the young lady's appearance, his clever mind gave way to carelessness, leading him to open the safe without wearing gloves.

MISCELLANEOUS EXERCISE

Multiple Choice Questions

1. What was the main business Horace Danby used to do?
   (*a*) robbery (*b*) goldsmith
   (*c*) painting (*d*) making locks
2. How did Horace buy the books?
   (*a*) Through a shopkeeper. (*b*) From a local publication.
   (*c*) Through his relatives. (*d*) Through an agent.
3. What was the value of the jewel in the grange safe?
   (*a*) 15 thousand rupees. (*b*) 50 thousand pounds.
   (*c*) 15 thousand pounds. (*d*) 50 dollars.
4. What was Horace allergic to?
   (*a*) Dust (*b*) Flowers
   (*c*) Crowd (*d*) Dog
5. What was Horace suffering from?
   (*a*) Dengue (*b*) Cholera
   (*c*) Hay Fever[8] (*d*) Jaundice
6. What was the piece of evidence against Horace Danby?
   (*a*) His lighter (*b*) His gloves
   (*c*) His fingerprints (*d*) All of the above.
7. Sherry was the name of a
   (*a*) A servant (*b*) A dog
   (*c*) A thief (*d*) None of these.
8. What makes Horace angry at the end?
   (*a*) Talking about the woman.
   (*b*) Prison
   (*c*) Talking about the honour among thieves.
   (*d*) None of these.
9. What was Horace's first thought when she meets the lady?
   (*a*) To kill her (*b*) To shout
   (*c*) To run away (*d*) To blackmail her
10. Where had the servants gone?
   (*a*) To see a doctor (*b*) To movie
   (*c*) For shopping (*d*) To meet relatives

Extract-Based Questions

I. Read the following extract and answer the questions/complete the sentences that follow: (5 M)

How foolish people are when they own valuable things, Horace thought. A magazine article had described this house, giving a plan of all the rooms and a picture of this room. The writer had even mentioned that the painting hid a safe! But Horace found that the flowers were hindering him in his work. He buried his face in his handkerchief. Then he heard a voice say from the doorway, "What is it? A cold or hay fever?" Before he could think, Horace said, "Hay fever," and found himself sneezing again. The voice went on, "You can cure it with a special treatment, you know, if you find out just what plant gives you the disease. I think you'd better see a doctor, if you're serious about your work. I heard you from the top of the house just now." **(CBSE, QB)**

1. According to the extract, Horace was sneezing due to a **(1)**
   (*a*) sudden allergy (*b*) prior infection
   (*c*) long-standing disease (*d*) nasal pain

[3] **Meticulous:** careful

[4] **Hay fever:** summer ailment

2. Which magazine could have published the article mentioned in the given extract? **(1)**

(*a*) Paws & Claws (*b*) Outdoors & Landscaping

(*c*) Interiors (*d*) The Investor

3. Choose the image that correctly describes the location of the safe, based on the given extract **(1)**

(1)

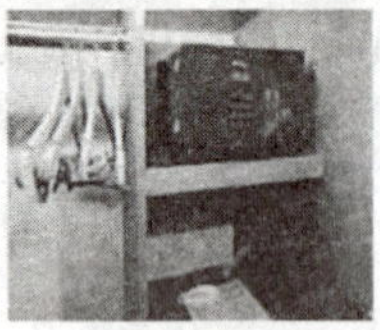

(2)

(3)

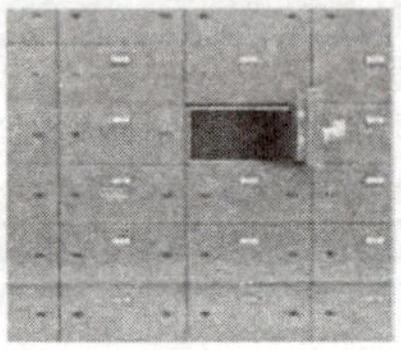

(4)

(*a*) Option (1) (*b*) Option (2)

(*c*) Option (3) (*d*) Option (4)

4. In the line – *Before he could think, Horace said, "Hay fever,"* —the response was **(1)**

(*a*) rehearsed. (*b*) spontaneous and natural.

(*c*) hesitant. (*d*) rapid and hostile.

5. The line from the extract that can be considered an example of sarcasm is **(1)**

(*a*) How foolish people are when they own valuable things.

(*b*) Horace found that the flowers were hindering him in his work.

(*c*) You can cure it with a special treatment.

(*d*) I think you'd better see a doctor, if you're serious about your work.

II. Read the following extract and answer the questions/ complete the sentences that follow: (5 M)

It was a quiet, kindly voice, but one with firmness in it. A woman was standing in the doorway, and Sherry was rubbing against her. She was young, quite pretty, and was dressed in red. She walked to the fireplace and straightened the ornaments there.

"Down, Sherry," she said. "Anyone would think I'd been away for a month!" She smiled at Horace, and went on, "However, I came back just in time, though I didn't expect to meet a burglar.

1. What was the woman's reaction to seeing Sherry? **(1)**

(*a*) She was angry. (*b*) She was sad.

(*c*) She was surprised. (*d*) She was scared.

2. What can we infer about the woman's relationship with Sherry? **(1)**

3. Write 'one word' for "A person who illegally enters buildings or houses with the intention of stealing". **(1)**

4. How does the woman's reaction to meeting a burglar contribute to the overall tone of the passage? **(2)**

III. Read the following extract and answer the questions/ complete the sentences that follow: (5 M)

His fingerprints, for he had opened the safe without gloves, were all over the room, and no one believed him when he said that the wife of the owner of the house had asked him to open the safe for her. The wife herself, a grey-haired, sharp-tongued woman of sixty, said that the story was nonsense.

1. What evidence was found in the room that indicated the person had opened the safe? **(1)**

(*a*) Fingerprints (*b*) Gloves

(*c*) Money (*d*) Jewellery

2. Why do you think the grey-haired woman denied the person's claim? **(1)**

3. "Sharp-tongued" means ________________. **(1)**

4. How does the use of the burglar's fingerprints in the passage contribute to the overall theme of the story? **(2)**

Subjective Questions

Short Answer Questions (40-50 words) (3 M)

1. How did Horace know all the details of the house?

2. What is Horace Danby's hobby? How did he manage to fulfill his hobby?

3. Why was it not difficult for Horace to open the safe?

4. What was Horace Danby suffering from? How did it affect him? **(CBSE, 2018)**

Long Answer Questions (100-120 words) (6 M)

5. How did Horace Danby enter the house?

6. Describe Horace Danby's encounter with the young lady.

7. Horace Danby represents people who take the wrong ways to fulfill their wishes. What values would you like such people to adopt to reform themselves?

8. What were Horace Danby's plans for his latest robbery? **(CBSE, 2020)**

ANSWERS & EXPLANATIONS

Answer Key

Multiple Choice Questions

1. (*d*) **2.** (*d*) **3.** (*c*) **4.** (*b*) **5.** (*c*) **6.** (*c*) **7.** (*b*) **8.** (*c*) **9.** (*c*) **10.** (*b*)

Explanations

Extract-Based Questions

I. 1. (*b*) prior infection

2. (*c*) Interiors

3. (*c*) Option (3)

4. (*b*) spontaneous and natural

5. (*d*) I think you'd better see a doctor, if you're serious about your work.

II. 1. (*c*) She was surprised.

2. We can infer that the woman is fond of Sherry as she calls her down and rubs against her.

3. burglar

4. Horace Danby intended to rob a large house called Shotover Grange. However, the presence of flowers in the house triggered his hay fever, causing him to sneeze. It was during one of these sneezing fits that he caught the attention of a gorgeous lady who happened to be in the house. She approached him and asked him to break open the safe for her. Unfortunately for Horace, this encounter led to his arrest.

Nailing the Right Answer

Students should pay attention to the context provided in the question or the accompanying passage. Understanding the context will help them recall the relevant information and provide an accurate answer.

III. 1. (*a*) Fingerprints

2. The grey-haired woman's denial may stem from her scepticism, distrust, or desire to protect her own interests, potentially implying that the person's story is fabricated or unreliable.

3. "Sharp-tongued" means harsh or bitter in speech or language.

4. The use of the burglar's fingerprints emphasises his carelessness and lack of attention to detail, ultimately leading to his capture and conviction. This highlights the consequences of his actions and reinforces the idea that crime doesn't pay.

Subjective Questions

Short Answer Questions

CBSE Marking Scheme: Content-1 M, Organisation of Ideas-1 M, Accuracy-1 M

1. For the past two weeks, Horace had been studying the house. Furthermore, a magazine article had described this house, including a floor plan and the picture of each room.

There were also safe details hidden behind the painting.

2. Reading expensive and rare books was Horaces' only hobby.

He used to rob a safe once a year to get money to fulfill his hobby. He used to buy these books from an agent.

3. Horace Danby had used locks and safes all his life, therefore, it was not difficult for him to unlock the safe.

The burglar alarm was badly constructed. He cut the wire without any trouble.

4. Horace Danby intended to rob a large house called Shotover Grange. However, the presence of flowers in the house triggered his hay fever, causing him to sneeze. It was during one of these sneezing fits that he caught the attention of a gorgeous lady who happened to be in the house. She approached him and asked him to break open the safe for her. Unfortunately for Horace, this encounter led to his arrest.

Long Answer Questions

CBSE Marking Scheme: Expression-2 M, Accuracy-1 M

5. Horace Danby kept an eye over the house for a long time, collecting each minute information about the activities. **(1 M)**

And one day, when the servants had gone for the movie, he saw them hanging the keys to the kitchen door. **(1 M)**

He then put on a pair of gloves, and thus he entered the house without any difficulty. **(1 M)**

6. As Horace was going to rob the house, he made all the preparations beforehand. He cut the wires of the alarm, but the flowers on the table made a tickle in his nose, and he started sneezing repeatedly. Just then, a lady in a red dress came in. **(1 M)**

   She spoke calmly, but her voice was confident. She claimed to be the owner's wife and had come there to take the jewels from the safe which she had to wear to a party at night. She told Horace that she had forgotten the number of the key and she would let him go if he opened the safe for her. **(1 M)**

   Danby now thought that it was better to escape helping her than anything. He opened the safe without gloves and gave all the jewels to that lady. She went away happy, and Danby got arrested for the jewel robbery and was sent to prison. **(1 M)**

7. Though Horace Danby was a successful businessman, he chose burglary to be one of the ways to fulfill his wishes. As he had immense love for rare and expensive books, he needed enough money to buy them without any problem. Therefore every year, he planned for a "burglary" carefully just to get what he wanted. Horace chose the wrong ways to fulfill his wishes and ultimately ended up in prison. **(1 M)**

   We can understand that he must have regret for choosing the wrong path.

   We can say that people should imbibe good values and stick to them irrespective of any hard times.

   They should understand that hard work is the only key to success and we should work hard honestly to fulfill our desires. **(1 M)**

   We can say that people should imbibe the qualities like honesty, perseverance, self-confidence and dedication towards our work to reform themselves. **(1 M)**

8. Horace was sure that the robbery he was planning for that year was going to be as successful as all the others so far. He had been observing and studying the house at Shotover Grange for two weeks. He had observed everything minutely. **(1 M)**

   That afternoon, when he planned to rob the house, he had seen the two servants, who remained in the Grange, going to the movies. He came out from behind the garden wall. **(1 M)**

   He had packed his tools carefully in a bag on his back. Horace knew that there were about fifteen thousand pounds worth of jewels in the Grange safe and if he sold them one by one, he was sure to get enough money to last him for another year. **(1 M)**

❑❑❑

FOOTPRINTS WITHOUT FEET

—H.G. Wells

5

Narrative Sketch

1. The story revolves around a scientist named Griffin who figures out how to make the human body invisible.
2. Two boys in London are shocked to see footprints appearing out of nowhere, which actually belong to Griffin.
3. They follow these mysterious footprints, which lead them through the streets.
4. Unfortunately, Griffin's invisibility leads to a lot of problems.
5. He becomes homeless and has to break into places to get food and shelter.
6. He steals some food and clothes but gets caught because he oversleeps in a restaurant.
7. To hide his invisibility, he stays at an inn and tries to keep a low profile, but his strange actions make the innkeeper, Mrs. Hall, very suspicious and scared.
8. Griffin can't control his temper and reveals his secret when he is confronted, causing fear and chaos.
9. Mr Jaffers, the constable tries to arrest him, but Griffin's invisibility creates a strange and confusing situation.
10. The story ends with Griffin escaping, leaving everyone puzzled and frightened.

BEFORE YOU READ

Theme

The story's protagonist[1] is a scientist named Griffin, who figured out how to become invisible. Everywhere he went, his reckless[2] and irrational[3] behaviour caused chaos. The lesson concerns how misusing science and technology can make people like Griffin into bad human beings. It draws attention to the tendency of people to abuse creativity, changing it from a source of social good into a danger.

Important Characters' Sketch

- **Griffin:** Griffin was a brilliant scientist as he invented the drug that makes the human body invisible and transparent. However, he exploited[4] his discovery for his gain, committing thefts, and beating and robbing innocent people. Though he was the protagonist of the story, all his deeds turn him into the antagonist[5]. He could have earned respect if he had used his great discovery for the welfare of mankind. Though his acts proved him lawless.
- **Mrs. Hall:** Mrs. Hall, the Landlord's wife, lives at the local inn in Iping village. Mrs. Hall was convinced that her guest was an eccentric[6] scientist. She was greedy or simply a good business-oriented lady as she ignored the strange habits and behaviour of Griffin because he had paid her in advance. When she noticed the strange behaviour of her furniture, she was convinced that the room was haunted by ghosts.

SYNOPSIS

A brilliant scientist, Griffin became invisible after taking a certain drug that he discovered. His landlord didn't like him because he was a lawless man, so he was thrown out of the premises. In revenge, Griffin set fire to his landlord's house. In order to escape, he had to remove his clothes to become invisible. Now, he became a homeless wanderer. To escape the cold, he entered the mall, but the shops were closed. He unpacked some clothes and made himself comfortable. After that, he had some meat and coffee from the restaurant's kitchen, followed by sweets and wine. Then he fell asleep under a blanket.

In the morning, he saw shop assistants coming towards him, he panicked and ran away. While running, he took off his clothes so as to become invisible. Again, he had to wander without clothes in the cold winters of London. He then decided to steal clothes from a theatrical company. To avoid being caught, he attacked the shopkeeper and looted him as well. He headed towards Iping Village in search of solitude.

Griffin initially stays at an Inn in Iping Village which is run by a landlady named Mrs. Hall. Mrs. Hall becomes increasingly suspicious of Griffin's behaviour, as he refuses to show himself or explain his strange actions. Griffin's invisibility causes Mrs. Hall to become increasingly afraid of him, as she cannot see or predict his movements. Mrs. Hall tries to confront Griffin about his behaviour but is met with hostility and aggression. When Griffin leaves the inn without paying his rent, Mrs. Hall becomes determined to track him down with the help of the community members.

After a few days, two strange events took place in the village. Someone stole the clergyman's money, and the landlord and innkeeper were attacked by a chair. These things made Griffin look suspicious.

Before the village constable, Jaffers, arrived, Griffin was confronted by Mrs. Hall. He got angry and took off his clothes one by one, thus becoming invisible. Jaffers tried to catch him, but he was knocked unconscious. In this way, Griffin managed to escape.

[1] **Protagonist:** leading character
[2] **Reckless:** careless
[3] **Irrational:** not logical
[4] **Exploited:** unfairly or meanly used for another's advantage
[5] **Antagonist:** opposing character
[6] **Eccentric:** uncommon

Constable (struggling to arrest the invisible man):
I guess, justice truly is blind!

Lessons to learn

- *The pursuit of power and knowledge can have dangerous consequences.*
- *Unchecked power can lead to isolation.*
- *Scientific experimentation should be conducted ethically.*
- *Fear can drive people to do terrible things.*

NCERT EXERCISE

Read and Find Out

(NCERT Page 26)

1. How did the invisible man first become visible?

Ans. Griffin was completely invisible until he accidentally stepped in the mud, which caused him to leave footprints while walking. Two boys noticed these tracks and followed him until the prints were visible. Griffin, after getting rid of them, went to a large London store and stole warm clothes. He got himself a coat, wide-brimmed hat and shoes. This made him visible to people who came to work at the store the next day.

2. Why did he wander the streets?

Ans. Griffin was a lawless man. His landlord didn't like him and tried to get rid of him. Out of revenge, Griffin set fire to his house. He had to take off his clothes to get away without being noticed. That is why he became a homeless wanderer—without clothes or money.

(NCERT Page 28)

1. Why does Mrs. Hall think the scientist is eccentric?

Ans. The arrival of a stranger at an inn in winter was in itself a special event. In addition, the stranger had an unusual appearance. Mrs. Hall tried to be friendly, but he responded coldly. He told her that he didn't have the desire to talk and wanted to live in solitude. He did not wish to be disturbed in his work. For all these strange reasons, she considered him an eccentric scientist.

2. What curious episode occurs in the study?

Ans. The clergyman and his wife were awakened by strange noises in the study room early in the morning. They crept downstairs and heard the jingle of where the money was coming from the clergyman's table. He and his wife looked under the table, behind the curtains, and into the chimney. There was no sign of anyone. Nevertheless, the table was opened, and there was no money in it.

3. What other extraordinary things happened in the inn?

Ans. The landlord and his wife were surprised to see the scientist's room door ajar. They thought it was a great chance to look around his room. Inside, they noticed the bed was already cold, hinting that the scientist must be up already. Suddenly, Mrs. Hall felt a sniff near her ear and, just then, the hat from the bedpost jumped up and hit her in the face. Right after, the bedroom chair leaped up, shoved them out of the room, and then forcefully closed the door, locking itself. Mrs. Hall nearly fell hysterically down the stairs. She was already convinced that the room was haunted by ghosts, and the stranger somehow caused these to enter the furniture.

Think about it

(NCERT Page 31)

1. **"Griffin was more of a lawless man." Comment.**

Ans. It is true in every sense to say that Griffin was a lawless man. A person who upholds law and order of the country cannot think of damaging anyone's property. But Griffin set on fire to his landlord's house and became a homeless wanderer. He robbed all the money from merchants he could find. He also stole money from the clergyman's desk. Griffin also attacked Mrs. Hall as she entered his room. All these activities and cases prove that he was not a law-abiding citizen.

2. **How would you rate Griffin as a scientist?**

Ans. After repeated experiments, Griffin discovered how to make the human body invisible. That was a great success. However, he used his discovery for personal gain and to harm others. So, although he can be described as a brilliant scientist, he was not a good man.

MISCELLANEOUS EXERCISE

Multiple Choice Questions

1. Where did Griffin go from the theatre store?
   (*a*) London (*b*) Iping
   (*c*) Snowland (*d*) None of these
2. Mrs. Halls thought that Griffin was _______
   (*a*) A necromancer (*b*) A tourist
   (*c*) An eccentric scientist (*d*) A traveller
3. The clergyman kept _______ on his desk.
   (*a*) Clothes (*b*) Money
   (*c*) Gold (*d*) Silver
4. Griffin was a _______ person.
   (*a*) Friendly (*b*) Lawless
   (*c*) Lawful (*d*) Helpful
5. _______ was the century of the theatre world.
   (*a*) Samson street (*b*) Drury street
   (*c*) Drury lane (*d*) Dubry lane
6. What do you understand about the word 'hysterics'?
   (*a*) An exaggerated reaction (*b*) Related to history
   (*c*) No reaction (*d*) None of the above
7. _______ was secretly called to the Inn.
   (*a*) A police (*b*) A clergyman
   (*c*) A landlord (*d*) A shopkeeper
8. At the end Mr. Jaffers ________
   (*a*) Became unconscious (*b*) Arrested Griffin
   (*c*) Ran away (*d*) None of the above
9. Who is the author of the story 'Footprints Without Feet'?
   (*a*) H.G. Wells (*b*) Robert frost
   (*c*) John Keats (*d*) Griffin
10. What did Griffin take from the theatrical shop?
    (*a*) Sleepers (*b*) Wine
    (*c*) Bandages (*d*) All of these

Extract-Based Questions

I. Read the following extract and answer the questions/ complete the sentences that follow: (5 M)

As she and her husband turned away in terror, the extraordinary chair pushed them both out of the room and then appeared to slam and lock the door after them.

Mrs. Hall almost fell down the stairs in hysterics. She was convinced that the room was haunted by spirits, and that the stranger had somehow caused these to enter into her furniture.

"My poor mother used to sit in that chair," she moaned! To think it should rise up against me now!

The feeling among the neighbours was that the trouble was caused by witchcraft." **(CBSE QB)**

1. Mrs Hall felt that the room was haunted by spirits because **(1)**
   (*a*) she could see evil spirits.
   (*b*) she heard strange noise.
   (*c*) uncanny things happened there.
   (*d*) the door slammed shut.
2. Pick the option that best describes how Mrs Hall must be feeling at the moment described in the extract. **(1)**
   (*a*) stunned and furious (*b*) shocked and outraged
   (*c*) outraged and nervous (*d*) stunned and agitated
3. Pick the sentence that brings out the meaning of 'hysterics' as used in the extract. **(1)**
   (*a*) My friend and I were in splits when we saw the clown's antics.
   (*b*) I don't know why I suddenly felt worried about flying home.
   (*c*) The sight of blood put the old man in a frenzy.
   (*d*) The people who had witnessed the accident were spellbound.

4. Pick the option that displays a cause ⇒ effect relationship. **(1)**

(*a*) pushed and locked out ⇒ hysterical[7]

(*b*) rising of the chair ⇒ moaning

(*c*) troubled neighbours ⇒ witchcraft

(*d*) stranger ⇒ haunted spirits

5. The neighbours thought it was 'witchcraft'. This tells us that neighbours were **(1)**

(*a*) suspicious (*b*) superstitious

(*c*) nervous wrecks (*d*) gossip-mongers

II. Read the following extract and answer the questions/ complete the sentences that follow: (5 M)

Brilliant scientist though he was, Griffin was rather a lawless person. His landlord disliked him and tried to eject him. In revenge Griffin set fire to the house. To get away without being seen he had to remove his clothes. Thus it was that he became a homeless wanderer, without clothes, without money, and quite invisible — until he happened to step in some mud, and left footprints as he walked!

1. What caused Griffin to become visible again? **(1)**

(*a*) A sudden gust of wind.

(*b*) Rainfall.

(*c*) Sunlight reflecting off a surface.

(*d*) Stepping in mud and leaving footprints.

2. What can be inferred about Griffin's character based on his actions? **(2)**

3. "Lawless" means ____________. **(1)**

4. (A) Griffin was stupid to remove his clothes to become invisible in December Chilly winds. **(1)**

(B) Griffin was a brilliant scientist.

(*a*) (A) is right (B) is wrong.

(*b*) (A) is wrong (B) is right.

(*c*) Both are right.

(*d*) Both are wrong.

III. Read the following extract and answer the questions/ complete the sentences that follow: (5 M)

The two boys started in surprise at the fresh muddy imprints of a pair of bare feet. What was a barefooted man doing on the steps of a house in the middle of London? And where was the man?

As they gazed, a remarkable sight met, their eyes. A fresh footmark appeared from nowhere!

Further footprints followed, one after another, descending the steps and progressing down the street. The boys followed, fascinated, until the muddy impressions became fainter and fainter and at last disappeared altogether. **(CBSE, 2023)**

1. The boys were surprised to see a barefooted man in London because ______. **(1)**

(*a*) everybody in London moved around in shoes.

(*b*) it was very cold in London to move around barefoot.

(*c*) the muddy footprints were fresh.

(*d*) only a homeless person would walk barefoot.

2. Select the option that correctly captures the usage of the word 'started' in the above extract. **(1)**

(*a*) When I reached the theatre the movie had already started.

(*b*) The fire started from the kitchen.

(*c*) On hearing the bell ring, the sleeping Raman started and jumped out of bed.

(*d*) Taking a deep breath, Ravi started down the stairs.

3. The boys reaction can best be described as **(1)**

(*a*) captivated, bored (*b*) repulsed, absorbed

(*c*) curious, unhappy (*d*) captivated, interested

4. Complete the analogy by selecting the suitable word from the text: **(1)**

Disappeared: Vanished:: Extraordinary: ____________

5. According to the extract the boys were _____ when they saw the footmark. **(1)**

i. terrified ii. nervous

iii. delighted iv. curious

v. puzzled

Select the correct option:

(*a*) i, ii and iv (*b*) Only i

(*c*) iv and v (*d*) ii and iii

IV. Read the following extract and answer the questions/ complete the sentences that follow: (5 M)

He broke open boxes and wrappers and fitted himself out with warm clothes. Soon, with shoes, an overcoat and a wide-brimmed hat, he became a fully dressed and visible person. In the kitchen of the restaurant he found cold meat and coffee, and he followed up the meal with sweets and wine taken from the grocery store. Finally he settled down to sleep on a pile of quilts.

1. How did the invisible man acquire warm clothes? **(1)**

(*a*) He broke open boxes and wrappers and fitted himself out with warm clothes.

(*b*) He found them in a store.

(*c*) He borrowed them from someone.

(*d*) He bought them from a shop.

2. The term "quilt" refers to ________________. **(1)**

3. What can be inferred about the invisible man's actions? **(2)**

4. Why does the author state "he became a fully dressed and a visible person"? **(1)**

[7] **hysterical:** in a state of uncontrolled excitement, anger, or panic

V. Read the following extract and answer the questions/ complete the sentences that follow: **(5 M)**

His landlord disliked him and tried to eject him. In revenge, Griffin set fire to the house. To get away without being seen he had to remove his clothes. Thus it was that he became a homeless wanderer, without clothes, without money and quite invisible until he -happened to step in some mud, and left footprints as he walked! **(CBSE, 2023)**

1. Griffin's landlord tried to eject him because **(1)**

(*a*) he was a lawless person.

(*b*) he had set his house on fire.

(*c*) he didn't like him.

(*d*) he was a drug addict.

2. Fill in the blank with one word only.

Griffin deliberately removed his clothes because he wanted to become __________. **(1)**

3. Select the option that correctly captures the application of the word 'fire' as used in this extract. **(1)**

(*a*) Griffin said that he would fire the manager.

(*b*) The soldiers opened fire at the enemy.

(*c*) His remarks provoked heavy fire from the political opponents.

(*d*) The Amar Palace was completely destroyed by the fire.

4. Griffin's presence was felt when **(1)**

(*a*) he jumped into the water with a splash.

(*b*) he wore clothes.

(*c*) he left muddy footprints.

(*d*) he stepped in mud.

5. Which of the following is not true with reference to the given extract? **(1)**

(*a*) Griffin had become penniless.

(*b*) Griffin promised to behave himself.

(*c*) Griffin revealed himself by his muddy footprints.

(*d*) No one could see Griffin when he took off his clothes.

Subjective Questions

Short Answer Questions (40-50 words) (3 M)

1. What did the Halls see in the scientist's room?

2. Describe the curious episode which took place in a clergyman's study. **(CBSE, 2020)**

3. How was Griffin received at the inn in Iping? **(CBSE, 2021)**

4. Scientists contribute to make the world a better place. Griffin is an antithesis to this statement. Justify. **(CBSE, 2024)**

Long Answer Questions (100-120 words) (6 M)

5. Did Griffin from Footprints without Feet follow the saying 'with great power comes great responsibility'? Justify your answer in 120 words. **(CBSE APQ, 2023)**

6. Describe Jaffer's fight with Griffin at the village of Iping.

7. A brilliant scientist though he was, Griffin misused his scientific discovery. Illustrate this point by giving any two examples from the story. **(CBSE, 2020)**

8. Discoveries of science can be used for the welfare of mankind as well as for its destruction. How is this applicable to Griffin's scientific discovery? Explain giving examples from the text. (100-120 words) **(CBSE, 2020)**

9. Imagine that Griffin's conscience pricks him and he decides to write a diary entry, about misusing science and endangering society, in the context of his own experience.

Write this diary entry, as Griffin, in about 120 words. **(CBSE, 2024)**

ANSWERS & EXPLANATIONS

Answer Key

Multiple Choice Questions

1. (*b*) **2.** (*c*) **3.** (*b*) **4.** (*b*) **5.** (*c*) **6.** (*a*) **7.** (*a*) **8.** (*a*) **9.** (*a*) **10.** (*c*)

Explanations

Extract-Based Questions

I. 1. (*c*) uncanny things happened there.

2. (*d*) stunned and agitated

3. (*c*) The sight of blood put the old man in a frenzy.

4. (*a*) pushed and locked out ⇒ hysterical

5. (*b*) superstitions

II. 1. (*d*) Stepping in mud and leaving footprints.

2. It can be inferred that Griffin possesses a vengeful and destructive nature. His decision to set fire to the house as revenge against his landlord demonstrates a disregard for the law and a willingness to resort to extreme measures to achieve his goals, suggesting a lack of moral restraint.

3. "Lawless" means someone who shows a disregard for the law, lacks restraint, and acts in a manner contrary to legal and societal norms.

4. (*c*) Both are right.

III. 1. (*b*) it was very cold in London to move around barefoot.

2. (*c*) On hearing the bell ring, the sleeping Raman started and jumped out of bed.

3. (*d*) captivated, interested

4. Remarkable

5. (*c*) iv and v

IV. 1. (*a*) He broke open boxes and wrappers and fitted himself out with warm clothes.

2. A quilt is a thick, padded bed covering made of two layers of fabric stitched together, often filled with down or other insulation material.

3. Based on his actions, it can be inferred that the invisible man resorts to theft and dishonesty to meet his needs. He demonstrates a lack of regard for others' property rights and a willingness to take advantage of his invisibility for personal gain.

4. The author states "he became a fully dressed and a visible person" as the protagonist was invisible.

V. ***Topper's Explanation***

i. c. He didn't like him.

ii. Griffin deliberately removed his clothes because he wanted to become invisible.

iii. d. The Omar Place was completely destroyed by the fire.

iv. c. He left muddy footprints.

v. b. Griffin promised to behave himself.

Subjective Questions

Short Answer Questions

CBSE Marking Scheme: Content-1 M, Organisation of Ideas-1 M, Accuracy-1 M

1. As the door of the room was opened and nobody was inside, Halls entered the scientist's room. Mrs. Hall saw that the bedclothes were cold, which implies that the scientist must have been up for a long time;

Still, the clothes and bandages that he always used to wear were lying there in the room only.

2. The strange incident in the clergyman's study was that, despite the missing money from the desk, no one was seen in the room. The robbery was peculiar because the thief was not visible, but the clergyman and his wife heard the sound of money being stolen, yet the room was empty.

3. Griffin arrived at an inn in the village of Iping in winter. It was quite unusual in that season and his unusual appearance set all tongues wagging in the village.

Mrs. Hall, the landlord's wife tried to be friendly with him but was snubbed. She excused Griffin's strange habits and irritable temper because he paid her in advance.

4. ***Topper's Explanation***

It is rightly said that 'scientists contribute to make the world a better place to live'. But Griffin, on the contrary, was an antithesis to this statement. Griffin discovered a rare drug that could make people invisible. He took that drug to become invisible. Griffin was a brilliant scientist but he was not a good person. He did not use his invention to help people, but to satisfy his own ego and do satanic deeds. He was a lawless person. His invention could be used to help his country as well as to bring fame for himself but he did not use it the right way. Patience would have been an asset for Griffin as would have common sense! Griffin was a scientist as well as a person prone to anger which proved to be a dangerous combination for him as well as the people around him.

Long Answer Questions

CBSE Marking Scheme: Expression-2 M, Accuracy-1 M

5. No, Griffin did not follow the saying 'with great power comes great responsibility'. The saying means that if one has the ability to do something, one should make sure to do it for the good of others. **(1 M)**

After he managed to make himself invisible, he did not use his powers of invisibility for doing good. Instead, one of the first things he did was to set fire to his landlord's house in an act of revenge. He did not think of helping anyone with his newfound powers, instead, he harmed other people for his own gain. **(1 M)**

He stole clothes and food for himself without feeling any remorse. He even attacked and robbed a shopkeeper. When his money ran low once more, he again resorted to stealing and robbed a clergyman. When Mrs. Hall entered his room, he attacked her with her own chair. Finally, when the police were about to catch him, instead of going quietly and accepting his arrest, he fought back and escaped the police. At no time did Griffin take any responsibility for his actions. **(1 M)**

6. Griffin sneaked into the clergyman's house with the intent to steal money. He opened the drawer of the table and stole the money. When the people learned about the larceny, they suspected the strange situation and called for the village constable. **(1 M)**

   When the scientist saw the constable, he became enraged and threw off his bandages, whiskers, spectacles, and false nose. Mr Jaffers was surprised that he had to arrest a headless man, but he tried to arrest the man who was becoming more and more invisible. **(1 M)**

   The constable was grappling[8] with someone he could not even see. Some people tried to support him but received punches. The constable was knocked down, and Griffin managed to escape from there. **(1 M)**

7. Griffin used his scientific breakthrough in the wrong way, which is clear from two events. The first time, when his landlord tried to kick him out, Griffin got back at him by setting the house on fire. He was able to do this because he had taken special drugs that turned him invisible, just like a clear piece of glass. **(1 M)**

   The second time happens after he is found sleeping in a store in London. To get warm and to put on clothes, he beats up the shopkeeper and steals money. After that, he checks into an inn and asks not to be bothered. That's when odd things start to happen. **(1 M)**

   The innkeeper and his wife sneak into the scientist's room while he's gone to look around. They find that his clothes and hat are scattered around. Out of nowhere, she hears a sniff right by her ear, and the hat hits her in the face. The bedroom chair seems to move on its own and knocks into her legs. Then, it forces Mr. and Mrs. Hall out of the room and locks the door behind them. These incidents show how the clever scientist abuses his own scientific invention. **(1 M)**

8. Griffin was a researcher. One day, while doing a scientific experiment, he found a liquid that has a capacity to render objects invisible. During his scientific experiment, he discovered this. Griffin, on the other hand, mishandled this liquid and used it to destroy humans, i.e. he used it to set fire to his landlord's mansion. **(1 M)**

   Yes, I agree with the statement. We may relate this statement to Griffin, a great scientist who found a liquid that can make things invisible. **(1 M)**

   However, Griffin was a lawless person who used his discovery for devastation, such as setting fire to landowner's house, carrying out theft, etc; and we can conclude that whether the found thing is useful or damaging is entirely dependent on the users. **(1 M)**

Nailing the Right Answer

Consider using transitional phrases to connect your ideas and create a logical flow in your response. These phrases can help guide the reader through your thought process and make your answer more coherent.

9. Today, a heavy heart bears down my conscience. I reflect on how my pursuit of science led to my own downfall and placed society at risk. Through my experiments, I achieved the power of invisibility, but at a great cost. **(1 M)**

   My early goals of progressing things turned chaotic and ended up causing more harm than good. I understand that when science is applied improperly, it can endanger the same foundation that it is meant to strengthen. **(1 M)**

   This diary is meant to serve as a reminder that responsibility and morality must always be balanced with ambition. I hope that this piece serves as a reminder of the delicate balance between discovery and humanity's safety. **(1 M)**

[8] **Grappling:** fighting

6

THE MAKING OF A SCIENTIST

—Richard Ebright

Narrative Sketch

1. Richard Ebright's journey into the world of science began with his childhood fascination with collecting butterflies, rocks, fossils, and coins.

2. His mother played a pivotal role in encouraging his love for learning and providing him with resources and opportunities to explore his interests.

3. The book "The Travels of Monarch X" opened his eyes to the wonders of butterfly migrations and sparked his scientific curiosity.

4. Ebright participated in butterfly tagging research, raising and tagging thousands of monarch butterflies in his basement.

5. Despite a setback at a science fair, he learned the importance of conducting real experiments and dedicated himself to more substantial projects.

6. His research on viral diseases in monarch caterpillars and the mimicry of viceroy butterflies earned him recognition and awards at science fairs.

7. Ebright's investigation into gold spots on monarch pupae led to significant discoveries in insect hormone research, indicating his maturity as a scientist.

8. His findings have implications for understanding cell life and could contribute to medical science, particularly in disease prevention.

9. Beyond his scientific achievements, Ebright was also well-rounded, excelling in academics, debate, public speaking, and other activities, demonstrating a balanced approach to personal development.

10. His journey underscores the importance of dedication, curiosity, and a competitive spirit in achieving success, serving as an inspiration to young scientists.

BEFORE YOU READ

Theme

The story's central theme is that brilliance is achieved through hard work and perseverance[1]. Richard Ebright is a successful scientist because he had unwavering[2] scientific curiosity since childhood and wanted to do the best job possible.

Important Characters' Sketch

- **Richard Ebright:** Richard Ebright is a passionate and driven scientist known for his curiosity and high achievements from a young age. As a child, he collected butterflies, which led to a lifelong interest in science. His mother supported his interests, providing tools like telescopes and microscopes. Ebright's dedication to his studies and natural curiosity led him to make significant contributions to understanding cell life and earn several prestigious awards in science.

SYNOPSIS

This story is a biographical[4] account of scientist Richard Ebright. He was an only child who was an introvert[5] and liked to collect things. Since kindergarten, he had collected butterflies, rocks, fossils and coins and enjoyed star-gazing.

Richard's mother took him on trips. She bought him telescopes, microscopes and cameras to encourage his interest in learning. She was a supportive mother and very close to her son. When Richard was in the third grade, his father passed away. Richard's mother would give learning tasks to her son to engage his mind. Richard enjoyed these activities. He received excellent grades in school.

Lessons to learn

- *Appearances can be deceiving.*
- *Things are not always as they seem.*
- *Attention to detail is crucial.*
- *Unexpected turn of events.*

Richard had loved butterflies from the very beginning. He had collected all twenty-five species of butterflies by the time he was in the second grade. His interest in butterflies grew when he discovered Dr Urquhart through the book 'The Travels of Monarch X'. He caught and tagged butterflies to help in Dr Urquhart's study regarding butterfly migrations. He also raised butterflies in his basement to help the study.

Richard got a real taste of science in the seventh grade. He entered the county science fair and presented slides of frog tissues. He lost because he had not done an actual experiment. He had only made a display. He took suggestions from Dr Urquhart regarding such experiments. Richard worked hard on his eighth-grade science fair entry. He tried to find the cause of a viral disease that killed almost all monarch butterflies every few years. He felt it could be due to a beetle, but he couldn't prove it. But he won because he had tried a real experiment.

Richard Ebright continued to work on several projects all through his school days. He tested the theory that viceroy butterflies copied monarch butterflies. Monarch butterflies are not tasty to birds, but viceroys are delicious. Richard wanted to see if a bird would eat a monarch, and he found that a starling ate all the monarch butterflies ignoring the bird's food. Then he tried to find the purpose of the twelve tiny gold spots on a monarch pupa. Richard and a fellow science student made a device that showed that these spots produced a hormone needed for the butterfly's full development. He won first place in the county science fair. The experiment got him a place at the International Science and Engineering Fair.

As an undergraduate at Harvard, Ebright discovered a new theory about cell life. He wanted to find out how a cell could read DNA. He and his college roommate James Wong wrote the paper together. When Ebright became a graduate student researcher at Harvard Medical

[1] **Perseverance:** determination; endurance

[2] **Unwavering:** steady; fixed

[3] **Biographical:** data dealing with a person's life

[4] **Introvert:** shy

School, he began experiments to test his theory. If the theory is correct, it could help us understand life processes. It could also prevent cancer and other diseases.

Ebright enjoys hobbies such as speech and debate, canoeing, and exploring nature. In addition, he is an expert photographer of nature and scientific exhibits. Even while doing his research, Ebright continued with his hobbies. Ebright was competitive, but winning a prize was not his goal. He wanted to do his best and win for that reason.

In the author's words, the ingredients required to make a great scientist are a brilliant mind, curiosity, and the will to do the right thing. Ebright has all these qualities. Ever since 'The Travels of Monarch X' opened the world of science to Richard, he has never lost his scientific curiosity.

NCERT EXERCISE

Read and Find Out

(NCERT Page 32)

1. How did a book become a turning point in Richard Ebright's life?

Ans. After collecting all 25 species of butterflies found in his surroundings, Richard thought his butterfly collection was over until his mother bought him a book called 'Travels of Monarch X,' which told him about how butterflies migrated to Central America. This book sparked his interest in learning more about what was to come, and he began researching monarch butterflies.

2. How did his mother help him?

Ans. His mother played a pivotal role in the scientist's life by purchasing telescopes, microscopes, cameras, mounting equipment, and trying to help him by getting him things to learn in the evenings when he was free. She also used to take him on field trips and purchased the book Travels of Monarch X. So we can say that his mother had a significant influence on who he became.

(NCERT Page 34)

3. What lesson does Ebright learn when he does not win anything at a science fair?

Ans. He learnt that simply displaying neat and clean simple slides will not win him anything, but that the actual experiment that he will perform will help him win the prize at any fair.

4. What experiments and projects does he then undertake?

Ans. He did an experiment to determine the cause of the viral disease that kills nearly all monarch butterflies after a few years, as well as a project to demonstrate that viceroy butterflies copy monarchs in order to survive by behaving similarly.

5. What are the qualities that go into the making of a scientist?

Ans. According to the chapter, there are three qualities that a scientist must possess. First, a first-rate mind, then curiosity, and finally, the desire to win for the right reasons.

Think about it

(NCERT Page 38)

1. How can one become a scientist, an economist, or a historian? Does it simply involve reading many books on the subject? Does it involve observing, thinking and doing experiments?

Ans. In order to become a scientist, an economist or an expert in any particular field, practical work is necessary. Reading lots of books for information and knowledge is not enough. We should develop our skills with experiments and projects to gain practical knowledge.

We need to think about the work we are doing, observe experiments and find results. We should work hard and never be depressed by failure. We should continuously try to improve our performance in any field and keep on experimenting.

2. You must have read about cells and DNA in your science books. Discuss Richard Ebright's work in light of what you have studied. If you get an opportunity to work like Richard Ebright on projects and experiments, which field would you like to work on and why?

Ans. DNA plays an important role in determining the genetics[6] of a human being. A person gets DNA from both parents, and inherits physical traits from them. Ebright's work on the theory of how a cell reads. DNA could tell us a lot about not only our traits but also prevent any future illnesses.

I would like to work on cancer and stem cell research if given the opportunity. It would be great if a cure for cancer was found.

NOTE: Please use this as a framework to write your own answer.

MISCELLANEOUS EXERCISE

Multiple Choice Questions

1. Ebright published a theory on ____________
   (*a*) How butterflies migrate
   (*b*) Natural camouflage[7] in butterflies
   (*c*) How butterflies mate
   (*d*) How cells identify DNA

2. How old was Ebright when he presented his new theory?
   (*a*) 22 (*b*) 23
   (*c*) 24 (*d*) 25

3. Which insect did Ebright research the most?
   (*a*) Ant (*b*) Moth
   (*c*) Butterfly (*d*) Silkworm

4. When did Richard Ebright's father pass away?
   (*a*) Kindergarten (*b*) First Grade
   (*c*) Second Grade (*d*) Third Grade

5. How many species of butterflies did Richard collect in his hometown?
   (*a*) Twenty (*b*) Twenty-five
   (*c*) Thirty (*d*) Thirty-five

6. Richard wanted to study
   (*a*) Monarch butterflies.
   (*b*) Peacock butterflies.
   (*c*) Red Admiral butterflies.
   (*d*) Small tortoise-shell butterflies.

7. Richard sent the tagged butterflies to
   (*a*) Frederick Urquhart (*b*) Robert W. Peterson
   (*c*) H.G. Wells (*d*) Sinclair Lewis

8. A synonym for 'tedious' is
   (*a*) Tired (*b*) Difficult
   (*c*) Boring (*d*) Lazy

9. "I found work for him – not physical works but learning things" This line is related to –
   (*a*) A triumph of Surgery.
   (*b*) The Thief's Story.
   (*c*) The Making of a Scientist.
   (*d*) Footprints without Feet.

10. Richard H. Ebright is
    (*a*) Dentist (*b*) Scientist
    (*c*) Astrologist (*d*) Astronaut

5 **Genetics:** the study of heredity and the variation of inherited characteristics
6 **Camouflage:** hide; disguise; conceal

Extract-Based Questions

I. Read the following extract and answer the questions/ complete the sentences that follow: (5 M)

And that is one of the ingredients in the making of a scientist. Start with a first-rate mind, add curiosity, and mix in the will to win for the right reasons. Ebright has these qualities.

From the time, the book, "The Travels of Monarch X" opened the world of science to him Richard H Ebright has never lost his scientific curiosity.

1. According to the passage, what role did "The Travels of Monarch X" play in Richard H Ebright's life? **(1)**
   (*a*) It sparked his scientific curiosity.
   (*b*) It helped him develop a first-rate mind.
   (*c*) It taught him the will to win for the right reasons.
   (*d*) It introduced him to the world of science.
2. What can be inferred about Richard H Ebright from the passage? **(1)**
3. Write the word from the passage which means Inquisitiveness or a strong desire to learn or understand something. **(1)**
4. How might Richard H Ebright's scientific curiosity have influenced his career? **(2)**

II. Read the following extract and answer the questions/ complete the sentences that follow: (5 M)

When he saw those photos, Ebright didn't shout, 'Eureka!' or even, 'I've got it!' But he believed that, along with his findings about insect hormones, the photos gave him the answer to one of biology's puzzles: how the cell can 'read' the blueprint of its DNA. DNA is the substance in the nucleus of a cell that controls heredity. It determines the form and function of the cell. Thus DNA is the blueprint for life.

1. What is DNA? **(1)**
   (*a*) The substance that controls heredity.
   (*b*) The substance that determines the form and function of a cell.
   (*c*) The blueprint for life.
   (*d*) All of the above.
2. Based on the passage, what can be inferred about Richard H Ebright's reaction to seeing the photos? **(1)**
3. "Blueprint" means ________________. **(1)**
4. How might Richard H Ebright's findings about insect hormones have contributed to his understanding of DNA's role in reading the blueprint of a cell? **(2)**

III. Read the following extract and answer the questions/ complete the sentences that follow: (5 M)

Richard Ebright has been interested in science since he first began collecting butterflies — but not so deeply that he hasn't time for other interests. Ebright also became a champion debater and public speaker and a good canoeist and all-around outdoors-person. He is also an expert photographer, particularly of nature and scientific exhibits.

1. What is one of Richard Ebright's hobbies besides science? **(1)**
   (*a*) Collecting butterflies (*b*) Playing chess
   (*c*) Writing poetry (*d*) Cooking gourmet meals
2. Based on the passage, what can be inferred about Richard Ebright's diverse skills and interests? **(1)**
3. Write 'one word' from the passage for 'a person who is skilled in canoeing'. **(1)**
4. How might Richard Ebright's diverse skills and interests outside of science contribute to his scientific endeavours? **(2)**

IV. Read the following extract and answer the questions/ complete the sentences that follow: (5 M)

The question he tried to answer was simple: What is the purpose of the twelve tiny gold spots on a monarch pupa?

"Everyone assumed the spots were just ornamental," Ebright said. "But Dr Urquhart didn't believe it."

To find the answer, Ebright and another excellent science student first had to build a device that showed that the spots were producing a hormone necessary for the butterfly's full development. This project won Ebright first place in the county fair and entry into the International Science and Engineering Fair. There he won third place for zoology. He also got a chance to work during the summer at the entomology laboratory of the Walter Reed Army Institute of Research.

(CBSE SQP, 2023)

1. State any one inference about Dr Urquhart from the given context: **(1)**
   Everyone assumed the spots were just ornamental," Ebright said, "But Dr Urquhart didn't believe it."
2. State TRUE or FALSE. **(1)**
   None of the terms (*a*) - (*d*) below, can be applied to the question - What is the purpose of the twelve tiny gold spots on a monarch pupa?
   (*a*) A hypothesis - a proposed explanation for a phenomenon
   (*b*) An assumption - something that is taken for granted or assumed to be true without proof
   (*c*) A premise - a proposition that forms the basis of an argument
   (*d*) A theory - a well-substantiated explanation for a natural phenomenon
3. Ebright's approach towards finding the purpose of the gold spots on a monarch pupa was highly effective. Elaborate in about 40 words, with reference to the extract. **(2)**
4. Which phrase would correctly substitute 'a chance', in the given sentence from the extract. **(1)**
   He also got a chance to work during the summer at the entomology laboratory of the Walter Reed Army Institute of Research.

Subjective Questions

Short Answer Questions (40-50 words) (3 M)

1. What lesson did Ebright learn when he did not win anything at a science fair? **(CBSE, 2023)**
2. Why did Richard Ebright raise a flock of butterflies? **(CBSE, 2023)**
3. What role did Ebright's mother play in his success? **(CBSE, 2022)**
4. How did Richard Ebright's mother help him? **(CBSE, 2020)**
5. How important is curiosity to scientific exploration and discovery? Justify your answer with examples from the text The Making of a Scientist. **(CBSE APQ, 2023)**
6. Justify how Ebright's mother played an important part in his becoming a scientist. **(CBSE, 2024)**

Long Answer Questions (100-120 words) (6 M)

7. Validate the importance of small, fun learning tasks which make successful careers, in the context of Richard Ebright in 'The making of a scientist.
8. Discuss the statement 'Failure is the pillar of success'. Use suitable examples from the story to support your argument.
9. Give a brief character sketch of Ebright's mother.
10. What can we learn about the importance of hobbies from Richard Ebright's story?

ANSWERS & EXPLANATIONS

Answer Key

Multiple Choice Questions

1. (*d*) **2.** (*a*) **3.** (*c*) **4.** (*d*) **5.** (*b*) **6.** (*a*) **7.** (*a*) **8.** (*c*) **9.** (*c*) **10.** (*b*)

Explanations

Extract-Based Questions

I. 1. (*a*) It sparked his scientific curiosity

2. Richard H Ebright possesses the qualities of a scientist, including a first-rate mind, curiosity, and the will to win for the right reasons.

3. Curiosity means 'inquisitiveness or a strong desire to learn or understand something'.

4. Richard H Ebright's scientific curiosity likely led him to ask challenging questions, seek out new research opportunities, and delve deeper into scientific investigations. It could have motivated him to pursue ground breaking research, contribute to scientific advancements, and make notable discoveries in his field.

II. 1. (*d*) All of the above.

2. Richard H Ebright's reaction to seeing the photos can be inferred as one of belief and recognition that they held the answer to a biology puzzle, rather than an immediate exclamation or claim of discovery.

3. Blueprint means a detailed plan or design that serves as a guide for creating or constructing something.

4. Richard H. Ebright's findings about insect hormones could have provided him with insights into the signaling pathways and molecular mechanisms involved in cellular communication. This knowledge could have helped him make connections between the behavior of hormones and the processes by which cells "read" the instructions encoded in DNA.

III. 1. (*a*) Collecting butterflies

2. Richard Ebright's diverse skills and interests imply a well-rounded and multifaceted personality, extending beyond his scientific pursuits.

3. Canoeist' is the appropriate word.

4. Richard Ebright's diverse skills and interests outside of science can contribute to his scientific endeavors by providing him with a broader perspective, effective communication skills, opportunities for interdisciplinary collaborations, and the ability to draw inspiration from various sources.

IV. 1. (Any one) We can infer that:

- Dr. Urquhart was a scientist who questioned assumptions
- He was willing to investigate alternative explanations for phenomena
- Dr. Urquhart was a curious/open-minded scientist
- He was not content to simply accept conventional wisdom

2. TRUE (It is simply a statement of the question that Ebright was trying to answer.)

3. Ebright's approach was highly effective in finding the purpose of the gold spots on a monarch pupa. By building a device that showed that the spots were producing a hormone necessary for the butterfly's full development, he was able to provide evidence that contradicted the prevailing assumption that the spots were purely ornamental. This earned him recognition in science fairs and provided him with opportunities to work at research laboratories.

4. an opportunity

Subjective Questions

Short Answer Questions

CBSE Marking Scheme: Content-1 M, Organisation of Ideas-1 M, Accuracy-1 M

1. Ebright learned an important lesson when he did not win anything at a science fair. He realised that science is not just about the display. It is about projects and experiments.

When Richard Ebright did not win, he realized that the winners had tried to conduct real experiments. He, on the other hand just displayed slides of frog tissues.

2. At the end of the book, "The travels of Monarch X", readers were invited to help study butterfly migrations. They were asked to tag butterflies for research by Dr Frederick A. Urquhart.

The butterfly collecting season around reading lasts six weeks in late summery. If Ebright went to chase them one by one, he could not catch very many. So he decided to raise a flock of butterflies.

3. Ebright's mother encouraged his learning by taking him on trips and providing him with telescopes, microscopes, and other equipment to explore his interests. She even gifted him a children's book called "The Travels of Monarch X," which introduced him to the fascinating world of monarch butterflies migrating to Central America, igniting his passion for science.

4. Richard Ebright's mother played a pivotal role in nurturing his curiosity and intellectual abilities, essential qualities for a scientist. She encouraged his thirst for knowledge by exposing him to the world around him through trips, purchasing books, and providing him with scientific equipment like telescopes, microscopes, cameras, and mounting materials. Her support facilitated Ebright's learning and development as a scientist.

5. Curiosity is extremely important to scientific exploration and discovery. It is curiosity that leads a person to question things around them, which in turn could help them stumble onto new discoveries.

- It was Ebright's curiosity that led him to collect items such as butterflies, fossils and coins. His desire to explore and constantly learn served as the foundation for his future scientific pursuits.
- It was curiosity that led Ebright to investigate different aspects of butterflies for his school projects. Since he was curious to understand the cause of the viral disease that killed monarch butterflies, that was what he studied.
- While in high school, Ebright was curious about the purpose of the twelve gold spots found on a monarch pupa. This drove him to conduct more research on the topic, which indirectly led to his new theory on the life of cells.

6. Ebright's mother played a pivotal role in the scientist's life by purchasing telescopes, microscopes, cameras, mounting equipment, and trying to help him by getting him things to learn in the evenings when he was free. She also used to take him on field trips and purchased the book, Travels of Monarch X. So we can say that his mother had a significant influence on who he became.

Long Answer Questions

CBSE Marking Scheme: Expression-2 M, Accuracy-1 M

7. If we do things that we enjoy, we put a lot of concentration into them, and they turn out wonderful. We see it in action in the context of Richard Ebright. He started collecting and breeding butterflies as a fun hobby. **(1 M)**

Richard Ebright was very curious. This scientific curiosity led him to discover a hormone chemical and figure out how DNA is read by the cell. **(1 M)**

Fun learning helped in Ebright's career as a renowned successful scientist. He determined the form and function of the cell. He found the hormone behind the full development of a butterfly's wings. His fun hobby led him to a career that he loved. **(1 M)**

8. Richard Ebright's life was filled with determination and hard work. Once when he didn't win the science fair with his presentation of frog slides, he became determined to win the next time through experiments. **(1 M)**

He later found the chemical hormone needed for wing development and how the cell reads DNA. He said that his first failure was the first ladder. He pointed out that we learn a lot of things from our failures. The important thing is to keep working on the things that we love. **(1 M)**

Failure is the stepping stone to success. It teaches us to take one step at a time and have patience. In the end, we will find the success that we worked hard for. **(1 M)**

9. Ebright received invaluable support from his mother who consistently encouraged his passion for learning and exploration. **(1 M)**

She not only took him on educational trips but also provided him with various tools such as a telescope, microscope, and other equipment that aided his scientific pursuits. As a vigilant parent, she attentively observed his interests and directed his energies in the right direction. **(1 M)**

By engaging him in constructive learning activities and providing him with books to fuel his curiosity, she played a significant role in shaping Ebright's journey as a scientist, making her an instrumental figure in 'The Making of a Scientist.' **(1 M)**

10. Richard Ebright's story shows how important hobbies can be in shaping someone's path. His hobbies, like collecting butterflies, debating, canoeing, and taking photos, show how hobbies are important. They make you curious, push you to explore, and make you want to learn more. **(1 M)**

These hobbies help you grow personally by building skills such as talking well, working with others, and being creative. Doing different things besides science keeps life balanced and gives new ideas. Hobbies can inspire you, give you a break from school stress, and help you think of new ideas. **(1 M)**

Richard Ebright's experiences tell us that hobbies are key in developing well-rounded people, boosting personal growth, and shaping one's scientific journey. They make life richer, add to your experiences, and keep the love for learning and discovering alive. **(1 M)**

Nailing the Right Answer

Mention Richard Ebright as an example to illustrate how hobbies can play a role in personal and professional development. Discuss the diverse range of hobbies that Richard Ebright engaged in, such as collecting butterflies, debating, canoeing, and photography.

❑❑❑

THE NECKLACE

—Guy de Maupassant

7

Narrative Sketch

1. Mme Loisel is unhappy because she believes she was born for a life of luxury and elegance, but she married a humble clerk and lives in poverty.
2. Mme Loisel's husband surprises her with an invitation to a grand party at the Minister's residence, but she is upset because she has no suitable dress or jewellery.
3. Mme Loisel borrows a beautiful diamond necklace from her friend Mme Forestier for the party.
4. At the party, Mme Loisel is a great success and enjoys the admiration of others, but she loses the necklace on the way home.
5. Mme Loisel and her husband search for the necklace but are unable to find it, so they decide to replace it without Mme Forestier's knowledge.
6. They purchase a new necklace, taking out loans and living a life of poverty for ten years to repay the debt.
7. Mme Loisel encounters Mme Forestier after many years and reveals the truth about the lost necklace and their struggles to replace it.
8. Mme Forestier confesses that the original necklace was a fake, worth only a fraction of the cost of the replacement.
9. Mme Loisel realizes that their years of hardship were unnecessary, and she feels a mix of contentment and pride for enduring the challenges.
10. The story highlights the theme of the deceptive nature of appearances and the consequences of excessive desire for material wealth.

BEFORE YOU READ

Theme

The theme of appearance versus reality can be found on two levels. The diamond necklace appears genuine but in reality it is a fake. Similarly, in the ball Matilda pretends to be wealthy when in reality she is not well off.

The loss of fortune tests Matilda and her husband. Matilda willingly gives up her comfort and faces the difficulties head-on. The theme of sacrifice in the story turns Matilda into a sympathetic[1] character because she suffers without complaint in a martyr[2]-like manner.

Matilda in the beginning of the story is not content[3] with her life situation. She wants more. But through the difficulties she faces, Matilda becomes a likable character, and at the end of the story she has accepted who she is and she is happy that way. That is why she can approach her friend Jeanne Forestier without shame or guilt.

Important Characters' Sketch

- **Matilda Loisel:** Matilda was born in a modest[4] household. Since she couldn't marry a rich person, she got married to a petty clerk. Matilda wanted a life of luxury and hated her current life. She considered it impoverished[5] and dull. Her life changed however, when she went to a party at the residence of the Minister of Public Instruction who was her husband's employer[6]. To appear rich at the party she borrowed a diamond necklace from her rich friend. After the party Matilda lost the diamond necklace and suffered for ten years, losing her comfortable life, money and looks to repay her debt. She changed her outlook[7] towards life, became modest and ordinary. In the end she gained the courage to tell the truth about the necklace.
- **Mr. Loisel:** Matilda's husband was a petty clerk at the Board of Education. He was content with his life and wanted to please his wife. He gave up his dream of going shooting for larks[8] with his new gun, so that his wife could have a new dress. He also advised her to borrow some jewels from her friend since she did not like flowers. When he was bored at the ball, he stayed there so that his wife could enjoy herself. Loisel took out high-interest loans and used his family inheritance[9] to pay for the replacement. He took on two other jobs apart from his office work, as an account keeper and also as a scribe[10] to repay the debt.
- **Mrs. Jeanne Forestier:** Jeanne Forestier was a friend of Matilda from school. She was really wealthy and had all the luxuries that Matilda wanted. Matilda would always compare her financial state with that of Mrs Forestier and would cry after her visit to the Forestier residence. Jeanne lent the diamond necklace to Matilda which Matilda wore to the ball.

SYNOPSIS

Guy de Maupassant's 'The Necklace' tells the story of the Loisels, and a simple error that changes their life completely. Published in 1884, this French tale follows the life of Matilda Loisel, wife to a clerk, who believes she was meant for the finer things in life. She fancies having delicious dishes, and expensive jewels. Whenever Matilda would visit her rich friend she would feel envious[11] and on returning home she would weep in despair and disappointment.

One day Matilda's husband gets an invitation to a fancy party at the Minister of Education's home. Loisel feels Matilda would be very happy at the news of the party but instead she gets irritated and tearful, and informs him that she doesn't have anything to wear to such a fancy event. Loisel uses the money he had set aside to buy a gun, to get Matilda a suitable costume for the party.

Matilda feels anxious, in the days leading up to the ball because even though her dress is ready she doesn't have any jewels to wear at the event. When her husband suggests natural flowers that are popular for the season[12]. Matilda feels it would be humiliating to wear something so inexpensive in front of wealthy women at the ball. Finally, she goes to her rich friend Mrs Forestier and borrows a superb diamond necklace to wear to the ball.

Matilda Loisel finds herself to be the centre of attention at the ball. She is noticed by all the people and admired as a great beauty. She dances eagerly with all who are introduced to her and enjoys the party thoroughly. At about four in the morning she makes her way

[1] **Sympathetic:** well-liked
[2] **Martyr:** self sacrificing person
[3] **Content:** happy with what they have
[4] **Modest:** simple
[5] **Impoverished:** poor
[6] **Employer:** boss
[7] **Outlook:** attitude
[8] **Lark:** type of bird
[9] **Inheritance:** family money
[10] **Scribe:** person who copies text for money
[11] **Envious:** wanting others' things
[12] **Season:** period of fashion

out of the gathering; her husband had been snoozing[13] in the parlour of the Minister's home with some others since midnight, whose wives were enjoying the revelry[14].

Matilda and her husband make their way out of the party. Matilda quickly wraps herself in her modest covering, avoiding the notice of the rich women at the party and hurries out of the party so that no one finds out she is not affluent[15]. Mister Loisel tries to hail[16] a cab but they are unable to find one and walk the streets of Paris, until they find a coachman with a carriage who drops them off at their door.

When Matilda removes her shoulder wrap she finds the necklace gone. Horror-struck she and her husband search for the necklace in vain[17] within the apartment. Mr Loisel goes all around town to all the places they had visited in order to retrieve the necklace but is unsuccessful. When he returns home in the morning he goes to the police and the cab company and offers a reward for the lost necklace but nothing turns up even in the evening.

Mr Loisel instructs his wife to write to Mrs Forestier and tell her that the clasp of the necklace is broken and they will return it once it is fixed. When the necklace doesn't turn up in a week, they lose all hope of finding it. They find a replacement, a diamond necklace worth forty thousand francs[18] and they take out loans and use their inheritance to buy the necklace for thirty-six thousand. When Mrs Loisel returns the replacement to the owner, her friend chides[19] her coolly for returning it so late. Matilda is terrified that her friend will find out about the substitution but Mrs Forestier doesn't open the jewel box.

Lessons to learn

- The danger of materialistic desires.
- The consequences of deceit.
- The significance of gratitude.
- The impact of choices and actions.
- The futility of living for appearances.

Matilda embraces a life of poverty with heroism. After dismissing the helper, and moving to a humble attic room with her husband, she works hard to maintain her house, washing dishes and soiled clothes, taking the garbage out, and bringing in water for household uses, all the way up to the attic. She dresses like a 'woman of the people' while going out to shop for food and other essentials, and haggles for every sou[20] of her money. Her husband spends evenings working on a merchant's accounts, and copying words for five sous a page. The Loisels endure[21] this life for ten years by the end of which they repay the debt owed for the diamond necklace.

After ten years of hard labour, Matilda is a changed woman. She resembles a strong, hard and crude housewife of a poor household. She doesn't fuss over her appearance and continues to wash the floors with her hardened hands with several pails[22] of water. When her husband is at work, Matilda remembers the good old days and the glamorous evening which changed her life forever.

One Sunday while Matilda is walking in the Champs-Elysees, she notices her friend Mrs Forestier, still young, pretty and attractive, walking with her child. Matilda isn't sure if she should approach her friend with the truth but since she has paid off the diamond necklace she doesn't worry. Matilda speaks to Jeanne Forestier and the latter[23] is shocked as she doesn't recognize Matilda. When Matilda tells her the truth Mrs Forestier is shocked. Matilda feels triumphant to have paid-off the substitute. Jeanne takes her friend's hands and informs her sadly that the diamond necklace Matilda had borrowed was a fake and not worth over five hundred francs.

[13] **Snoozing:** taking a nap
[14] **Revelry:** fun celebration
[15] **Affluent:** rich
[16] **Hail:** stop
[17] **In vain:** without success
[18] **Franc:** french currency
[19] **Chide:** scold
[20] **Sou:** french coin of low value
[21] **Endure:** suffer patiently
[22] **Pail:** bucket
[23] **Latter:** second mentioned of two people

NCERT EXERCISE

Read and Find Out

(NCERT, Page 39)

1. What kind of a person is Mme Loisel — why is she always unhappy?

Ans. Mme Loisel is a young, pretty, ordinary, but dissatisfied woman. She comes from a poor family but dreams of riches and comfort. She is proud of her beauty and wishes to be admired. Her meagre resources are insufficient to satisfy her expensive cravings, which make her angry all the time.

2. What kind of a person is her husband?

Ans. M Loisel, her husband, is an ordinary and average young man. He is a clerk by profession and is happy with his job. He is also a caring man because he is excited to show his wife the dinner invitation.

(NCERT, Page 41)

1. What fresh problem now disturbs Mme Loisel?

Ans. Mme Loisel is disappointed after spending a fortune on a beautiful gown. Another disaster has struck. She is concerned that she does not have a lovely jewel to match her gown. As a result, she requests that her husband forward the invitation to someone else.

2. How is the problem solved?

Ans. M. Loisel, Matilda Loisel's husband, comes to her rescue. First, he advises her to wear fresh flowers. Matilda simply mocked the idea. Then he advises her to borrow some jewels from her wealthy friend, Mme Forestier. Mme Forestier solves the problem by lending her a beautiful diamond necklace.

(NCERT, Page 42)

1. What do M. and Mme Loisel do next?

Ans. The Loisels leave no stone unturned. M. Loisel returns to look for the lost necklace. Then he goes to the police station and the cab company. They also put out an advertisement in the newspapers and offer a reward to anyone who finds the necklace. But all of their efforts are futile.

2. How do they replace the necklace?

Ans. After all other attempts have failed, Loisel decides to purchase a new identical necklace to replace the lost one. M. Loisel pooled his inheritance of eighteen thousand francs and borrowed the rest. The couple then managed to purchase the new necklace for 36,500 francs and return it to its rightful owner.

Think about it

(NCERT, Page 46)

1. The course of the Loisels' life changed due to the necklace. Comment.

Ans. Matilda Loisel was married to a simple clerk who worked in the Board of education. They had an average life but Matilda always dreamed of more. Mr. Loisel understood that his wife wished for the finer things of life and got an invitation to a ball at the Minister's residence in order to give her a taste of exclusivity[24]. Mr. Loisel gave in to his wife's demand for an expensive dress and asked her to borrow jewels from her friend to fulfill her fantasy.

Matilda was the belle[25] of the ball and enjoyed herself thoroughly. When she returned home after the party she had lost the necklace. Failing to find it, the Loisels used up their savings and inheritance and took out loans to pay for it. Their situation in life changed completely because of this loss of fortune. The Loisels had to work very hard and at the end of ten years and successfully repaying their debt, Matilda was a completely changed woman, who was decidedly different from the woman who had gone to the party; she was a hardened housewife from a poor household.

2. What was the cause of Matilda's ruin? How could she have avoided it?

Ans. Matilda's problems came from wanting too much. She dreamed of being part of the fancy, rich crowd. She wanted rich and famous people to like her and forgot she came from a poor family and her husband was just a regular office worker. She could have avoided all her troubles if she was happy with what she had and didn't try to act like the rich. Also, when she lost the necklace, she should have been careful with the borrowed item or simply told the truth to Mme Forestier.

3. What would have happened to Matilda if she had confessed to her friend that she had lost her necklace?

Ans. If Matilda had confessed to her friend Jeanne Forestier that she had lost the diamond necklace accidentally, Mrs Forestier though angry would have told her that it was a fake and not worth a huge amount. Knowing this, the Loisels could have looked for a cheaper copy to replace the fake, and they would not have lost their fortune in buying a real diamond necklace as a substitute.

---

[24] **Exclusivity:** special
[25] **Belle:** beauty

4. If you were caught in a situation like this, how would you have dealt with it?

Ans. In situations such as these, where a person has lost something that is precious and belongs to someone else, telling the truth is the best option. Since the truth came out at the end of the story anyway, the author is perhaps also telling us that it is best to be honest. If the Loisels had told the truth, instead of hiding it just to avoid embarrassment, they would have been able to maintain their life.

I would have told the truth, accepted the responsibility and faced the anger of the owner of the precious object and then I would have tried my best to make it up to them.

5. The characters in this story speak in English. Do you think this is their language? What clues are there in the story about the language its characters must be speaking in?

Ans. Even though the story is in English, the native[26] language of the characters is not English.

There are several clues in the story that tell us where the story takes place and the language the characters speak:

- **Names and salutations:** The names Loisel and Forestier are French. The couple in the story are called M. Loisel and Mme. Loisel which stands for 'Monsieur' and 'Madame' respectively. There is also a 'Madame George Ramponneau' who is also French.
- **Place:** The Loisels find the replacement jewel at Palais Royal. At the end of the story Matilda walks casually along the Champs-Elysees, which is an avenue in Paris.
- **Author:** The author Guy de Maupassant is definitely French, who writes French stories.

MISCELLANEOUS EXERCISE

Multiple Choice Questions

1. Matilda married a simple clerk because
(*a*) She came from a family of clerks.
(*b*) She had no dowry or money.
(*c*) She was deeply in love with him.
(*d*) She loved government service workers.

2. What did Mr Loisel think Matilda would wear to the party?
(*a*) Matilda's best dress for church.
(*b*) Matilda's best dress for theatre.
(*c*) Matilda's wedding dress.
(*d*) Matilda's new dress from the boutique.

3. Who lent Matilda the diamond necklace?
(*a*) Matilda's friend
(*b*) Matilda's sister Jeanne
(*c*) Matilda's mother
(*d*) Matilda's great-aunt

4. What did Mr Loisel want to buy?
(*a*) A gun (*b*) A pocket watch
(*c*) A gold chain (*d*) A smoking pipe

5. How long was Mr Loisel in the minister's salon dozing off?
(*a*) Two hours (*b*) Three hours
(*c*) Four hours (*d*) Five hours

6. Why did Matilda sneak out of the party?
(*a*) To avoid the rich men.
(*b*) To avoid the rich women.
(*c*) To avoid the Minister.
(*d*) To avoid the Minister's wife.

7. What kind of name is 'Loisel'?
(*a*) English (*b*) German
(*c*) French (*d*) Russian

8. How much do the Loisels pay for the necklace?
(*a*) Thirty-five thousand francs.
(*b*) Thirty-six thousand francs.
(*c*) Thirty-eight thousand francs.
(*d*) Forty thousand francs.

9. Where was Matilda walking on Sunday?
(*a*) Beside the Arc de Triomphe.
(*b*) Near the Notre dame cathedral.
(*c*) Along the Eiffel Tower.
(*d*) Along the Champ-Elysees.

10. Why was Jeanne shocked to see Matilda?
(*a*) She thought Matilda had died.
(*b*) Matilda was begging on the street.
(*c*) Matilda's appearance was hugely altered.
(*d*) Matilda was with a child.

[26] **Native:** placed by birth

Extract-Based Questions

I. Read the following extract and answer the questions / complete the sentences that follow: (5 M)

The next day she took herself to her friend's house and related her story of distress. Mme Forestier went to her closet, took out a large jewel-case, brought it, opened it, and said, "Choose, my dear." She saw at first some bracelets, then a collar of pearls, then a Venetian cross of gold and jewels of admirable workmanship. She tried the jewels before the glass, hesitated, but could neither decide to take them nor leave them. Then she asked, "Have you nothing more?"

1. The adjective 'Venetian' is from the noun______. (1)
   (*a*) Venus (*b*) Venice
   (*c*) Bellis (*d*) Belize
2. Which word best describes the workmanship of the jewels described in the passage? (1)
3. Based on Mme Forestier's actions, what can be inferred about her character? (1)
4. Explain the significance of Mme Loisel's hesitation in deciding whether to take the jewels or leave them. (2)

II. Read the following extract and answer the questions / complete the sentences that follow: (5 M)

He said, "Write to your friend that you have broken the clasp of the necklace and that you will have it repaired. That will give us time." She wrote as he dictated. At the end of a week, they had lost all hope. And Loisel, older by five years, declared, "We must replace this jewel." In a shop of the Palais-Royal, they found a chaplet of diamonds, which seemed to them exactly like the one they had lost. It was valued at forty thousand francs. They could get it for thirty-six thousand. Loisel possessed eighteen thousand francs, which his father had left him. He borrowed the rest. He made ruinous promises, took money from usurers and the whole race of lenders. Then he went to get the new necklace, depositing on the merchant's counter thirty-six thousand francs.

1. 'Loisel possessed eighteen thousand francs, which his father had left him.' What is the money left for someone called? (1)
   (*a*) Allowance (*b*) Fees
   (*c*) Inheritance (*d*) Expenses
2. What does the phrase 'older by five years' mean in this extract? (1)
   (*a*) Loisel was extremely nervous.
   (*b*) Loisel was getting old.
   (*c*) Loisel was five years of age.
   (*d*) Loisel was extremely angry.
3. Based on Loisel's actions, what can be inferred about his values and priorities? (1)
4. Explain the irony in the characters' attempts to replace the lost necklace. (2)

III. Read the following extract and answer the questions / complete the sentences that follow: (5 M)

She learned the odious work of a kitchen. She washed the dishes. She washed the soiled linen, their clothes and dishcloths, which she hung on the line to dry; she took down the refuse to the street each morning and brought up the water, stopping at each landing to catch her breath. And, clothed like a woman of the people, she went to the grocer's, the butcher's and the fruiterer's, with her basket on her arm, shopping, haggling to the last sou of her miserable money.

1. What does "haggling" mean in the given context? (1)
2. What can be inferred about the woman's financial situation? (1)
3. What does the woman's actions and sacrifices reveal about her character? (2)
4. How did the woman feel about her financial situation? (1)
   (*a*) Content and satisfied (*b*) Frustrated and resentful
   (*c*) Hopeful and optimistic (*d*) Indifferent and apathetic

IV. Read the following extract and answer the questions / complete the sentences that follow: (5 M)

She was not convinced. "No", she replied, "there is nothing more humiliating than to have a shabby air in the midst of rich women." Then her husband cried out, "How stupid we are! Go and find your friend Mme Forestier and ask her to lend you her jewels." She uttered a cry of joy. "It is true!" she said. "I had not thought of that."

1. What was the woman's initial reaction upon hearing her husband's suggestion? (1)
   (*a*) Indifference (*b*) Disgust
   (*c*) Joy (*d*) Confusion
2. What does the word "shabby" mean as used in the passage? (1)
   (*a*) Dirty or untidy in appearance.
   (*b*) Expensive and luxurious.
   (*c*) Exquisite or beautiful.
   (*d*) Refined and elegant.
3. What can be inferred about the woman's state of mind after her husband's suggestion? (1)
4. Analyze the significance of the woman's statement, "there is nothing more humiliating than to have a shabby air in the midst of rich women." How does it reflect her perception of social status? (2)

Subjective Questions

Short Answer Questions (40-50 words) (3 M)

1. How did the necklace change the life of Loisel? **(CBSE, 2022)**
2. Why was Matilda irritated after receiving the invitation to the party? How did Mr Loisel react to Matilda's behaviour?
3. How does The Necklace teach a moral lesson on the importance of contentment? **(CBSE APQ, 2023)**
4. Matilda wanted to live a life above her status. How did this desire of hers lead to her sufferings?

Long Answer Questions (100-120 words) (6 M)

5. Imagine that M. Loisel, from The Necklace by Guy de Maupassant, writes a diary entry, exploring the theme of class and social status, and the nature of social mobility, in the context of his own experience. Write this diary entry, as M. Loisel, in about 120 words. **(CBSE SQP, 2023)**
6. Was Madame Forestier a true friend of the Loisels? Use examples from the story to elaborate.
7. Matilda Loisel loved being the centre of attention. Do you agree? Discuss with examples from the text.
8. As a reader do you sympathise with Matilda? Give reasons from the text to support your answer.
9. Matilda was very proud of her beauty and charm and this led to her downfall. Elaborate. **(CBSE, 2023)**
10. A character arc is the transformation or development of a character throughout a story and refers to the changes a character undergoes as a result of their experiences, challenges, and interactions with other characters.

    In the light of the above information, trace the character arc of Matilda in Guy De Maupassants' 'The Necklace', in about 120 words. **(CBSE, 2024)**

ANSWERS & EXPLANATIONS

Answer Key

Multiple Choice Questions

1. (*b*) **2.** (*b*) **3.** (*a*) **4.** (*a*) **5.** (*c*) **6.** (*b*) **7.** (*c*) **8.** (*b*) **9.** (*d*) **10.** (*c*)

Explanations

Extract-Based Questions

I. 1. (*b*) Venice

2. The workmanship of the jewels is described as "admirable."
3. Mme Forestier's willingness to lend her friend a large jewel-case suggests that she is a wealthy and generous person.
4. Mme Loisel's hesitation reflects her internal conflict and foreshadows the moral dilemma she faces. On one hand, she is drawn to the beauty and allure of the jewels, representing the luxurious lifestyle she desires. On the other hand, she is aware that borrowing them comes with responsibility and potential consequences.

II. 1. (*c*) Inheritance

2. (*a*) Loisel was extremely nervous.
3. Loisel's actions suggest that his values and priorities prioritize external appearances and societal status over financial prudence and contentment.
4. The irony lies in the fact that the characters go through great lengths to replace the lost necklace, only to discover later that it was a worthless imitation. Their pursuit of materialistic desires leads them to further financial ruin, highlighting the futility of their efforts.

III. 1. Negotiating or bargaining over prices.

2. The woman's financial situation is extremely limited or impoverished.
3. The woman's willingness to take on arduous tasks, washing dishes, clothes, and endure physical strain demonstrates her resilience, adaptability, and determination to make ends meet in challenging circumstances.
4. (*b*) Frustrated and resentful.

IV. 1. (*c*) Joy

2. (*a*) Dirty or untidy in appearance.
3. The woman's state of mind after her husband's suggestion can be inferred as relieved and excited.
4. The woman's statement highlights her concern about social appearances and her desire to fit in with wealthier women, emphasizing the importance she places on external image and societal expectations.

Subjective Questions

Short Answer Questions

CBSE Marking Scheme: Content-1 M, Organisation of Ideas-1 M, Accuracy-1 M

1. Matilda Loisel was a charming young lady who always wanted a luxurious life. For attending a ball, she borrowed a necklace from her friend Mme Forestier but eventually lost it. In order to repay the debt for the replaced necklace, the Loisels had to live a life full of hardships and pain for ten years.
2. Matilda was irritated when she received the invitation to the party because she did not have the proper dress in which she could go to the party.

   Matilda was upset and crying and Mr Loisel was grieved when Matilda told him to pass on the invitation to someone richer. To bring peace, Mr. Loisel promised to buy Matilda suitable clothes for the party.
3. The Necklace teaches a powerful moral lesson on the importance of finding contentment in what one already has. Matilda's desire for social status and material possessions led to her own downfall and a decade of hardship. Had

Matilda simply been grateful and content with all that she had, she could have avoided a lot of pain. The twist at the end of the story, which revealed the true value of the necklace, emphasises the emptiness that lies in the pursuit of material wealth.

4. Matilda left the ball in a hurry because she did not want to be seen with the ordinary wrap that she carried , as its poverty contrasted with the elegance of the other ladies, who were wrapping themselves in rich furs.

   This shows that she only wants to keep up appearances just to flatter her pride without being in touch with the real truth of her life.

Long Answer Questions

CBSE Marking Scheme: Expression-2 M, Accuracy-1 M

5. It's been tough the past few years, for my wife, Matilda, and me. As I reflect on our experience, I can't help but think about the broader societal issues that have contributed to our predicament. **(1 M)**

   It's clear to me now that our society is structured in a way that makes upward mobility difficult, if not impossible. The rich get richer, while the rest of us struggle to make ends meet. We live in a world where social status is determined by the amount of wealth one possesses, rather than by one's character or virtues. This narrow view of success has led many people, including Matilda, to pursue material possessions at the expense of their own happiness. **(1 M)**

   The loss of the borrowed necklace was a painful lesson for both of us. It reminded us that the pursuit of social status and upward mobility can be a trap, leading people to sacrifice their happiness and well-being in the pursuit of an unattainable dream. **(1 M)**

6. Madame Forestier is one of the most important characters of the story upon whom the whole action of the narrative depends.

   When Matilda requires fancy jewels to wear to the party Jeanne Forestier pulls out her large jewel case without hesitation and asks Matilda to help herself to any ornament she might want. **(1 M)**

   When Matilda loses the diamond necklace she returns the substitute to her which she never checks if it is in the right condition or not. Later when she speaks to Matilda after ten years she feels saddened to hear of Matilda's misfortune vis-à-vis[27] the necklace. **(1 M)**

   Through all these instances we can see that Jeanne Forestier acts as a true friend to the Loisels in general and Matilda in particular. **(1 M)**

7. Initially Matilda is a vain character. She hates everything simple and wants to be associated with luxury. **(1 M)**

   She borrows a stunning diamond necklace from her rich friend to impress people who are unknown to her and whom she would never meet again after the party. She loves dancing, being introduced to the important people at the party and being a 'great success'. **(1 M)**

   She is the prettiest of all the women, and everyone feels she is elegant and gracious. When all the men at the party want to dance with her she feels overjoyed. She continues to party till early in the morning while her husband dozes off in the adjacent salon. So we may safely say that Matilda Loisel did love being the centre of attention, up until she lost the diamond necklace. **(1 M)**

8. Matilda is a woman with dreams and aspirations, but her lower social and economic status limits her opportunities. She longs for a luxurious life and feels dissatisfied with her current situation. **(1 M)**

   When she borrows an expensive necklace to fit in with the upper class at a party, she loses it, leading to significant hardship for her and her husband. **(1 M)**

   Despite the deception, Matilda's desperation to replace the lost necklace and her subsequent years of hard work to repay the debt evoke empathy from readers. However, sympathy should not overshadow the fact that her actions had consequences. **(1 M)**

9. Matilda, the protagonist in Guy de Maupassant's short story "The Necklace", was a woman who was unhappy with her mediocre life and longed for a more lavish existence. This desire led her to borrow an expensive necklace to wear to a party, where she wanted to look the most beautiful. Unfortunately, she lost the necklace and went into debt to replace it. **(1 M)**

   The heavy sum of money needed to repay the debt ruined her life and forced her into a life of poverty. Her pride and desire for material possessions led to her downfall and demonstrated the dangers of placing too much value on external appearances. **(1 M)**

   This highlights the importance of being content with what one has and not placing too much value on material possessions and external appearances. **(1 M)**

Nailing the Right Answer

- ❒ Discuss the concept of being humble and learning to appreciate what we have, whether it's living in a big house or adapting to a smaller one as per the demands of the time.
- ❒ Conclude by connecting Matilda's story to a broader lesson about the importance of being mindful, responsible, adaptable, and content in life.

10. Matilda Loisel undergoes a significant character arc in the chapter "The Necklace". At the beginning of the story, Matilda is dissatisfied with her lifestyle and dreams of wealth and luxury. Matilda, in "The Necklace," starts off unhappy with her simple life, wishing for glamour and riches. **(1 M)**

    Her life changes when she borrows a necklace for a party but loses it, leading to years of hard work to pay off the cost of a replacement. In the end, Matilda learns the original necklace was fake and not worth much, a harsh lesson about the truth and being content with what one has. **(1 M)**

    Her story shows how chasing false appearances can lead to a harder life and teaches us to value honesty and what we already own. The experience teaches her the importance of honesty, gratitude, and contentment. Mathilda's character arc highlights the theme of the deceptive nature of appearances and the ultimate value of inner qualities over external possessions. **(1 M)**

[27] **Vis-a-vis:** in regards to

❒❒❒

BHOLI

—K.A. Abbas

8

Narrative Sketch

1. Sulekha, known as Bholi, was the fourth daughter of Numberdar Ramlal and was considered a simpleton.
2. Bholi had facial disfigurement from smallpox and also suffered from a speech impediment, causing her to be teased and mocked by other children.
3. Ramlal had seven children, and Bholi was the youngest. The family was prosperous, except for Bholi who lacked good looks and intelligence.
4. A primary school for girls opened in their village, and the Tehsildar urged Ramlal to send his daughters to school as an example to others.
5. Bholi's mother was initially against sending the girls to school, fearing it would affect their chances of marriage. She suggested sending Bholi, believing the teachers could deal with her.
6. Bholi's first day at school is filled with fear and discomfort, but she finds solace in the kind and understanding teacher who encourages her.
7. The teacher helps Bholi overcome her stammering and instills in her a sense of hope and a desire for education.
8. Years pass, and Bholi's parents consider a marriage proposal from Bishamber Nath, a well-to-do grocer.
9. Bishamber demands a large dowry when he discovers Bholi's disfigured face, causing Bholi to refuse the marriage and speak up against his greed.
10. Bholi asserts herself, refusing to marry an old, greedy man, despite the shame and criticism from others.

Bholi's transformation from a neglected and voiceless girl to a confident and determined young woman showcases the power of education and self-belief.

12

Bholi decides to dedicate her life to serving her parents and becoming a teacher in the same school where she learned.

11

BEFORE YOU READ

Theme

This story is about an underestimated girl, Bholi. She is a little child who lacks self-confidence as a result of her parents' treatment. Her parents send her to school as they think that no-one will marry her. Her life turns when she joins a nearby school where her teacher encourages her and helps her to become a learned and confident person. She denies being married to an old aged man and decides to serve her parents in their old age.

Important Characters' Sketch

- **Bholi:** The story is about a little girl named Sulekha. She was the youngest child of Ramlal. She was called "Bholi" because of her simple nature. She was under-confident and an introverted[1] child. She was born fair but suffered from pox in her childhood which left some marks on her face. She started speaking late and stammered[2]. Other children used to make fun of her and even her family members treated her harshly. Her parents sent her to school as they thought no-one will marry her but as she got education and encouragement from her teacher, she became confident and well spoken. On the day of her wedding, she publicly refused to marry when she came to know that her father had to pay a huge amount of dowry and stood up for herself. She no longer stammered and surprised everyone. Despite being mistreated by her parents, she decided to serve them and teach in the school in which she had been taught.
- **Ramlal:** Bholi's father, Ramlal, was a Numberdar. He had three sons and four daughters, Bholi being the youngest. Ramlal was constantly worried about her as it seemed impossible to marry her since she was dull and not smart like the others. Ramlal was convinced to send Bholi to school when the Tehsildar pushed him, so the villagers were encouraged to send their children to school. In order to get Bholi married anyhow, Ramlal overlooked Bishamber, the groom's age and his disability. He was surprised to see Bholi speaking confidently at the wedding scene.
- **Bholi's Teacher:** Bholi's teacher in the school is a kind and loving human being. She encouraged Bholi a lot and helped her overcome her speech disorder and weaknesses. She trained her to speak without pause and made her believe in herself. She taught her that if she overcame her weaknesses, nobody would make fun of her anymore.

SYNOPSIS

This story has been written by K.A. Abbas, a very famous Indian film director, screenwriter, novelist and journalist who wrote his works in Hindi, Urdu and English. This particular story is about a girl, Bholi, whose real name was Sulekha, who had fallen off a cot and hit herself in the head.

This resulted in damage to some part of her brain and she remained a backward child. Due to her very simple nature, people started calling her Bholi. She stammered due to lack of confidence and also had pock-marks which occurred due to smallpox in her childhood.

[1] **Introverted:** shy
[2] **Stammered:** speak with pause, difficulty

She was made fun of for her low confidence. Ramlal had seven children-three sons and four daughters. Ramlal sent all his sons to school in the city. Bholi was the youngest of all. Rest of his children were healthy and happy except Bholi. Ramlal and his wife often worried about Bholi's marriage.

One day, the Tehsildar came to the opening ceremony of a primary school in the village. He asked Ramlal, who was a revenue official, to send his daughters to school in order to encourage others to send their children to the school. In the beginning Bholi's mother was not in support of sending her to school but later they concluded in favour. They thought it would be difficult for them to get her married because of look and lack of sense and they wanted the teachers take trouble for her.

Bholi was frightened of going to school initially, however, she started improving when she met a kind hearted teacher at the school who encouraged and helped her to overcome the problem of stammering.

Years passed and the village became a small town. One night at dinner, Ramlal and his wife decided to get Bholi married to a well-to-do man, Bishamber who had a shop, a big house and money in the bank.

They ignored Bishamber's elderliness as they thought he was unaware of Bholi's ugly face. They were overjoyed to see a grand opportunity coming for their fourth daughter.

Lessons to learn

- ❐ *The power of education.*
- ❐ *The importance of empathy and kindness.*
- ❐ *The consequences of societal judgment.*
- ❐ *Overcoming stereotypes and self-perception.*
- ❐ *Family support and acceptance.*

After this when Bishamber noticed the pock-marks on Bholi's face, he asked for five thousand rupees. Ramlal showed his inability at first but later he agreed to pay the amount.

Seeing all this, Bholi took a firm stand for herself and refused to marry a greedy man. She stated that she would instead serve her parents in their old age and expressed her wish of teaching in the same school where she learnt everything. Her teacher was seeing all this happening in a corner and felt very satisfied to experience the completion of her masterpiece under the effect of "education".

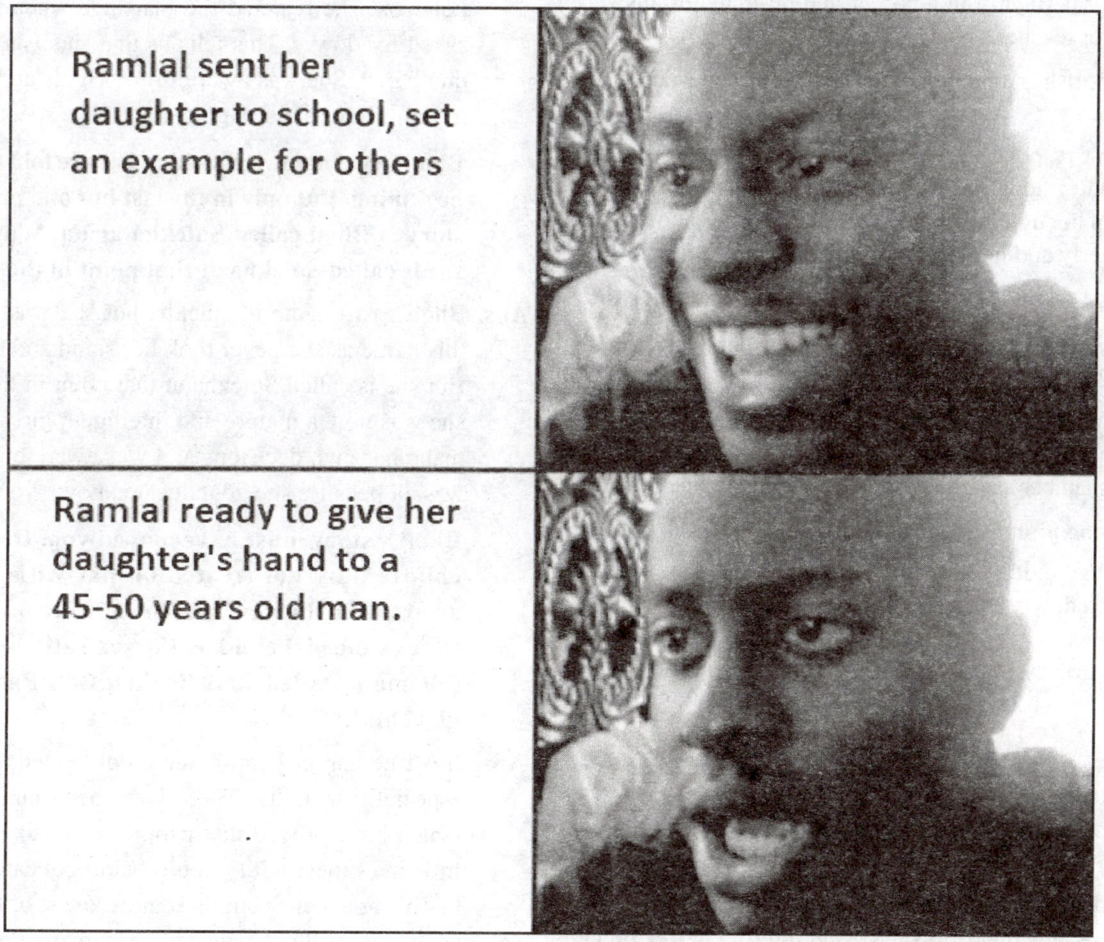

NCERT EXERCISE

Read and Find Out

(NCERT Page 54)

1. Why was Bholi's father worried about her?

Ans. Bholi was very ugly and lacked confident since her childhood. She started speaking late and used to stammer. Her father thought that it would be difficult to get her married. This worried him.

2. For what unusual reason was Bholi sent to school?

Ans. As Ramlal was a revenue official, the Tehsildar had demanded him to send his daughters to the new school in the village to encourage others. So, Ramlal and his wife decided that it would be good if they send Bholi to the school as they thought that there was little chance of her getting married.

3. Did Bholi enjoy her first day at school?

Ans. Bholi didn't know anything about school and she was afraid of it at first. She even cried when the teacher asked her name. She sat silently in a corner and hesitated to answer anything her teacher asked.

4. Did she find her teacher different from the people at home?

Ans. Bholi didn't respond to the teacher when she was asked a question but gradually she noticed that her teacher didn't make fun of her ugliness or her stammering. She encouraged Bholi tenderly and her affection touched Bholi's heart.

(NCERT Page 58)

1. Why did Bholi's parents accept Bishamber's marriage proposal?

Ans. Bholi's parents accepted Bishamber's marriage proposal because he was a well-to-do grocer and he didn't even ask for dowry. Bishamber also didn't know about her ugliness.

2. Why did the marriage not take place?

Ans. The marriage didn't take place because Bishamber started asking for a dowry of five thousand rupees, the moment he saw the pock marks on Bholi's face. But Bholi refused to marry the greedy man. This way the marriage didn't take place.

Think about it

(NCERT Page 62)

1. Bholi had many apprehensions about going to school. What made her feel that she was going to a better place than her home?

Ans. Bholi received rejection from her family members. She felt better when she met the school teacher who tried to understand Bholi and helped her awaken her inner strength and transformed her into a better person.

2. How did Bholi's teacher play an important role in changing the course of her life?

Ans. Bholi's teacher understood the weakness and the feeling of under-confidence that Bholi was experiencing and treated her kindly. She encouraged her to do her tasks confidently and not to be worried by anything. She taught her to read and write and made an independent girl who was aware of her rights. This way Bholi's teacher played an important role in changing the course of her life.

3. Why did Bholi at first agree to an unequal match? Why did she later reject the marriage? What does this tell about her?

Ans. At first, Bholi agreed to the match to fulfill her parents' wishes.

Later on, she rejected the marriage when the bridegroom asked for dowry. This tells us that she was not a timid and dumb girl. She was aware of her rights and she knew how to fight for her own dignity and self respect.

4. Bholi's real name is Sulekha. We are told this right at the beginning. But only in the last but one paragraph of the story is Bholi called Sulekha again. Why do you think she is called Sulekha at that point in the story?

Ans. Bholi's real name is Sulekha but she was never called by this name as she never took her stand and acted so simple. But she is called Sulekha at that point in the story because she was now a mature and intelligent girl who was able to make her own decisions and was aware of her rights. This was all because she got educated now.

5. Bholi's story must have moved you. Do you think girl children are not treated on par with boys? You are aware that the government has introduced a scheme to save the girl child as the sex ratio is declining. The scheme is called Beti Bachao Beti Padhao, Save the girl child.

Ans. It is true that girl children are not treated at par with boys, especially in India. There have been numerous incidents which have proved that people prefer to have male child. In some cities, with people being educated, the situation has become better but, in remote areas, or the towns where people are still not educated, the situation is still bad for the girl child.

MISCELLANEOUS EXERCISE

Multiple Choice Questions

1. Ramlal had __________ children.
   (*a*) Seven (*b*) Five
   (*c*) Eight (*d*) Three
2. Mangla was the __________ daughter of Ramlal.
   (*a*) Eldest (*b*) Youngest
   (*c*) Second (*d*) Third
3. __________ marriage had also been settled.
   (*a*) Sulekha's (*b*) Mangla's
   (*c*) Radha's (*d*) Champa's
4. __________ had come to open the girl's school for the village.
   (*a*) Tehsildar (*b*) D.M.
   (*c*) Panchayat Pradhan (*d*) Ramlal
5. What was the name of Bholi's cow?
   (*a*) Sunita (*b*) Sulekha
   (*c*) Lakshmi (*d*) Gauri
6. The real name of Bholi was:
   (*a*) Sulekha (*b*) Sumedha
   (*c*) Suricha (*d*) Samridhi
7. Bholi was the __________ daughter of Numberdar Ramlal.
   (*a*) Fifth (*b*) Third
   (*c*) Fourth (*d*) Second
8. Bholi had fallen from a narrow bed and got damaged some part of her brain, when she was:
   (*a*) 5 months old (*b*) 10 months old
   (*c*) 4 years old (*d*) 10 years old
9. At the age of two, Bholi got:
   (*a*) Malaria (*b*) Small pox
   (*c*) Yellow fever (*d*) Chicken pox
10. Little Sulekha could not __________ till she was five.
    (*a*) Listen (*b*) Walk
    (*c*) Speak (*d*) Sit

Extract-Based Questions

I. Read the following extract and answer the questions/ complete the sentences that follow: (5 M)

But Ramlal was worried about Bholi. She had neither good looks nor intelligence. Bholi was seven years old when Mangla was married. The same year a primary school for girls was opened in their village. The Tehsildar sahib came to perform its opening ceremony. He said to Ramlal, "As a revenue official you are the representative of the government in the village and so you must set an example to the villagers. You must send your daughters to school."

1. What does the word "Tehsildar" mean in the passage? **(1)**
   (*a*) Revenue official (*b*) School teacher
   (*c*) Village representative (*d*) Government officer
2. Based on the passage, what can be inferred about the importance of education in the village? **(1)**
3. Discuss the significance of Tehsildar Sahib's statement to Ramlal about sending his daughters to school in the context of the passage. **(2)**
4. Based on the passage, select the most appropriate statement that reflects the author's viewpoint. **(1)**
   (*a*) Education is the sole determinant of a person's worth.
   (*b*) Good looks and intelligence are the only qualities that matter in life.
   (*c*) The opening of a primary school for girls is a positive development in the village.
   (*d*) Ramlal's worry about Bholi's appearance and intelligence is justified.

II. Read the following extract and answer the questions/ complete the sentences that follow: (5 M)

The flames of the sacred fire slowly died down. Everyone was gone. Ramlal turned to Bholi and said, "But what about you, no one will ever marry you now. What shall we do with you?" And Sulekha said in a voice that was calm and steady, "Don't you worry, Pitaji! In your old age I will serve you and Mother and I will teach in the same school where I learnt so much. Isn't that right, Ma'am?" The teacher had all along stood in a corner, watching the drama. "Yes, Bholi, of course," she replied. And in her smiling eyes was the light of a deep satisfaction that an artist feels when contemplating the completion of her masterpiece.

1. What was Ramlal's initial concern about Bholi? **(1)**
   (*a*) Her lack of education.
   (*b*) Her disfigured appearance.
   (*c*) Her disobedience.
   (*d*) Her illness.
2. What does the word "satisfaction" mean in the context of the passage? **(1)**
3. What can be inferred about the teacher's feelings towards Bholi? **(1)**
4. Analyze the role of the teacher in Bholi's journey of self-discovery and empowerment. **(2)**

III. Read the following extract and answer the questions/ complete the sentences that follow: (5 M)

"What's the matter with you, you fool? Shouted Ramlal. "I am only taking you to school." Then he told his wife, "Let her wear some decent clothes today or else what will the teachers and the other schoolgirls think of us when they see her?

New clothes had never been made for Bholi. The old dresses of her sisters were passed on to her. No one cared to mend or wash her clothes. But today she was lucky to receive a clean dress which had shrunk after many washings and no longer fitted Champa. She was even bathed and oil was rubbed into her dry and matted hair. Only then did she believe that she was being taken to a place better than her home! When they reached the school, the children were already in their classrooms." **(CFPQ)**

1. Why did Ramlal call Bholi a fool? This was because ________. **(1)**
   (*a*) Bholi had become hysterical and was screaming.
   (*b*) Bholi shouted in fear and pulled her hand away.
   (*c*) Bholi was behaving foolishly and was running away.
   (*d*) Bholi had been behaving very strangely with her father
2. Pick the sentence that brings out the meaning of 'decent' as used in the extract. **(1)**
   (*a*) He gets a decent amount of salary.
   (*b*) One must be decent when having a conversation with strangers.
   (*c*) She was dressed in a decent manner for the interview.
   (*d*) It was very decent of him to lend me some money
3. Pick the option that best describes how Bholi felt at the end of her first day in school. **(1)**
   (*a*) lost and scared (*b*) calm and peaceful
   (*c*) elated and peaceful (*d*) hopeful and elated
4. Why was Bholi's hair matted? **(1)**
   (*a*) It was entangled and oiled.
   (*b*) It was never oiled or combed.
   (*c*) It was not combed regularly.
   (*d*) It was unkempt and oiled.
5. What fear did Bholi have when she was told about being taken to school? **(1)**
   (*a*) She thought she was going to be neglected by her parents.
   (*b*) She thought her parents were going to get rid of her.
   (*c*) She felt that she would be thrown out of the house and sold.
   (*d*) She thought her parents were thinking of ways to throw her out.

IV. Read the following extract and answer the questions/ complete the sentences that follow: (5 M)

Bishamber Nath was a well-to-do grocer. He came with a big party of friends and relations with him for the wedding. A brass-band playing a popular tune from an Indian film headed the procession, with the bridegroom riding a decorated horse. Ramlal was overjoyed to see such pomp and splendour. He had never dreamt that his fourth daughter would have such a grand wedding. Bholi's elder sisters who had come for the occasion were envious of her luck.

1. What led to the envy of Bholi's elder sisters? **(1)**
   (*a*) Bholi's grand wedding.
   (*b*) Bishamber Nath's popularity.
   (*c*) The presence of a brass band.
   (*d*) The decorated horse in the procession.
2. Write a word from the passage for "Great excitement or showiness". **(1)**
3. Based on the passage, what can be inferred about Bholi's family? **(1)**
   (*a*) They were wealthy and influential.
   (*b*) They were supportive and loving towards Bholi.
   (*c*) They had never expected Bholi to have a grand wedding.
   (*d*) They were envious of Bishamber Nath's success.
4. Discuss the significance of the brass band and the decorated horse in the wedding procession. Answer in about 50 words. **(2)**

Subjective Questions

Short Answer Questions (40-50 words) (3 M)

1. Bholi's heart was overflowing with a 'new hope and a new life'. What does the phrase 'the new hope and the new life' means? **(CBSE SQP, 2018)**
2. Why was Bholi scared of going to school?
3. What were the reasons for Bholi to get comfortable in the school?
4. Why did Bholi not marry Bishamber? **(CBSE, 2020)**
5. How does education play a transformative role in Bholi's life? **(CBSE SQP, 2023)**

Long Answer Questions (100-120 words) (6 M)

6. School education turned Bholi from a dumb cow to a bold girl. How did she save her father from a huge expense and become his support in his old age?
7. Love and encouragement make the impossible possible. Explain this statement on the basis of the story.
8. Education provides the required stimulus to overcome one's personal barriers and explain the role of education in shaping the life of a child with respect to the lesson 'Bholi'?
9. Destiny had been cruel to Bholi yet she made a place for herself in a conservative society. Discuss. **(CBSE, 2023)**
10. Bholi was believed to be a 'dumb cow'. What turned her into a fearless, bold and confident girl? **(CBSE, 2023)**
11. Why did Bholi's teacher feel like an artist admiring her masterpiece? **(CBSE, 2024)**

ANSWERS & EXPLANATIONS

Answer Key

Multiple Choice Questions

1. (*a*) **2.** (*c*) **3.** (*b*) **4.** (*a*) **5.** (*c*) **6.** (*a*) **7.** (*c*) **8.** (*b*) **9.** (*b*) **10.** (*c*)

Explanations

Extract-Based Questions

I. 1. (*a*) Revenue official

2. Education is considered valuable and necessary in the village, as indicated by the opening of a primary school for girls and the Tehsildar sahib's insistence on sending daughters to school.

3. The Tehsildar sahib's statement holds significance as it emphasizes the role of Ramlal, as a representative of the government, to set an example by educating his daughters. It highlights the importance of education in the village and the need for individuals in positions of influence to promote it.

4. (*c*) The opening of a primary school for girls is a positive development in the village.

II. 1. (*b*) Her disfigured appearance.

2. Contentment or fulfillment.

3. The teacher feels a deep sense of satisfaction and accomplishment in witnessing Bholi's transformation and success.

4. The teacher serves as a guiding figure who instills hope, helps Bholi overcome her challenges, and empowers her to embrace her potential. Through her supportive and nurturing approach, the teacher becomes instrumental in Bholi's personal growth and transformation.

III. 1. (*b*) Bholi shouted in fear and pulled her hand away.

2. (*c*) She was dressed in a decent manner for the interview.

3. (*d*) hopeful and elated

4. (*b*) It was never oiled or combed.

5. (*c*) She felt that she would be thrown out of the house and sold.

IV. 1. (*a*) Bholi's grand wedding.

2. Pomp

3. (*c*) They had never expected Bholi to have a grand wedding.

4. The brass band and the decorated horse symbolize the grandeur and extravagance of the wedding. They add a touch of celebration and festivity, highlighting Bishamber Nath's status and making the event memorable for Ramlal. They also create envy among Bholi's elder sisters, emphasizing the contrast between their lives and Bholi's unexpected fortune.

Subjective Questions

Short Answer Questions

CBSE Marking Scheme: Content-1 M, Organisation of Ideas-1 M, Accuracy-1 M

1. The phrase 'new hope and a new life' means Bholi's heart was overflowing with new hope and a new life when she promised herself to serve her parents in their old age and to teach the students in the same school where she had learnt. Her teacher made her 'Sulekha' from 'Bholi'. The education she received made her a confident person.

2. Bholi was scared to go to school as she had never been to school. She didn't know anything about school and thought of the time when the cow was sold.

She was thinking of getting rejected by other children in the school as she was neglected by her family members.

3. Bholi started feeling comfortable when the teacher didn't scold or humiliate her for her low confidence.

Her teacher accepted her and encouraged her to stop getting afraid of anything.

4. Bholi was devoted to her parents and for their sake, respect and pleasure she agreed to marry Bishamber.

When Bishamber demanded 5,000 rupees as dowry because she had marks on her face and insulted her father, she refused to marry him in order to safeguard Ramlal's dignity.

5. Education plays a transformative role in Bholi's life. It helps her gain confidence and self-esteem, enabling her to stand up for herself and challenge societal norms. It empowers her to break free from the chains of patriarchy and choose her own path. It also enables her to recognize and resist oppression and inequality, making her an agent of change in her community. Through education, Bholi becomes an embodiment of the transformative power of knowledge and its ability to challenge and change societal norms.

Long Answer Questions

CBSE Marking Scheme: Expression-2 M, Accuracy-1 M

6. It's ironic that Bholi was sent to school as her mother thought she was a burden and wanted the teachers to worry for her. But when she reached the school her teacher encouraged her to speak confidently like others. **(1 M)**

After so many years of hard work Bholi was changed into a bold and confident young lady.

At the time of her marriage, Bishamber demanded five thousand rupees in order to marry Bholi who had pock marks on her face. **(1 M)**

Bholi saw how her father was humiliated for a stupid reason. She refused to marry him and assured her father that she would serve him and her mother in their old age. **(1 M)**

7. Bholi was sent to school as her mother thought that she was a burden to them. She was neglected by her parents because she was not beautiful and lacked intelligence.

When the teacher asked her name, Bholi stammered and started to cry as she thought that here also she will be humiliated for her simpleton nature. **(1 M)**

The teacher understood her situation and showed affection and acceptance to Bholi. She encouraged her to be friendly and put all her fear aside. Bholi somehow uttered her name. Gradually she noticed some growth in herself. **(1 M)**

The teacher asked her to come to school regularly. Love and encouragement shown by the teacher brought out a drastic change in her personality. Within a few years she became so confident that she took her own stand and refused to marry a greedy man. **(1 M)**

Nailing the Right Answer

Students can mention the scene where Bholi's teacher encourages her and helps her overcome her stammering, or the moment when Bholi stands up against societal expectations and refuses to marry a man who demands a dowry. These specific examples will provide more depth and context to the answer.

8. Bholi initially lacks confidence because of her disabilities. She was quiet, fearful, and mentally weak. Her ugly appearance and stammer issues were posing a hindrance to her moving forward and growing as an individual. She was not even confident enough to talk with others, as people around her were mocking and making fun of her. **(1 M)**

The school environment completely transformed her life. It gave her new hopes for the world. Her teacher was compassionate and loving towards Bholi. She was able to believe in herself because of her teacher's love and encouragement. She has learned and developed into a confident young lady. She was aware of her rights and actively exercised them. **(1 M)**

She declined to wed a man who demanded dowry. Education has subsequently transformed Bholi's outlook on life. In light of the aforementioned situations, we can say the solution to all social evils is education. Ignorance and illiteracy only result in disappointment, suffering, and poverty. **(1 M)**

Nailing the Right Answer

- ❒ Discuss how education helped Bholi overcome personal barriers and gain confidence.
- ❒ Emphasize the role of the school environment: Explain how the supportive teacher and positive school atmosphere influenced Bholi's development.

9. Bholi's destiny was cruel to her due to her disability and not-so pretty appearance, which made her the target of ridicule and discrimination. However, she was determined to make a place for herself in a conservative society. **(1 M)**

Despite the negative treatment she received, Bholi didn't let the opinions of others define her self-worth. **(1 M)**

By attending school and pursuing education, she defied societal expectations and norms, showcasing her determination to rise above her challenges. She even denied to wed an older man who asked for a dowry from her father. **(1 M)**

10. ***Topper's Explanation***

Bholi's (Sulekha's) life was not a bed of roses. Her early years were fraught with difficulties - falling from her cot on her head when she was ten months old and damaging a part of her brain, resulting in her remaining a backward child, an attack of smallpox at the age of two, rendering her face disfigured with deep black pockmarks and learning to speak only at five years (~~and that too~~, with a stammer). As she was neither as healthy nor as good-looking as her siblings, she was neglected by her parents and subjected to ridicule by the other children. Hence, unsurprisingly, the 'dumb cow' kept to herself. However, her life changed, when, unable to disregard the suggestion of a higher official (the Tehsildar), her father, Ramlal enrolled her in the newly-established village primary school for girls.

At the school, Bholi found in the teacher, a friend, philosopher and guide. With the teacher's constant encouragement, love, empathy and compassion, Bholi soon overcame her stutter. Education kindled in her the hope of a new life and transformed the timid, reclusive Bholi into a confident and self-assured young lady who could not only fight her battles courageously when she opposed the societal evil of dowry and refused to marry the greedy, devious Bishamber Nath but also support her parents in their old age and teach at the very same school where she learnt to stand on her own feet.

Undoubtedly, education is the movement from darkness to light and the passport to freedom for education breeds ~~has~~ confidence and confidence breeds hope.

11. ***Topper's Explanation***

'Bholi's teacher felt like an artist admiring her masterpiece'. This statement holds true according to the story of Bholi. Bholi was like a dumb cow. She used to stammer and was ugly with pock marks on her face. Luckily, she was sent to school on the demand of the Tehsildar. At school, it was Bholi's teacher who helped her gain confidence. When Bholi was being married off to an old man, she did not say anything. But when the old man demanded dowry, she was against it and spoke against it infront of everyone. Everyone was shocked to hear Bholi speaking without stammering. Her teacher played a crucial role in transforming her. Her teacher was proud that Bholi chose to live a dignified life rather than surrendering ~~herslef~~ herself to a greedy man. It was Bholi's teacher who helped her transform from a dumb cow to a confident woman, that is, from Bholi - the simpleton to 'Sulekha'.

❒❒❒

THE BOOK THAT SAVED THE EARTH

9

—Claire Boiko

Narrative Sketch

1. The twentieth century was known as the 'Era of the Book' due to the abundance and significance of books during that time.
2. In the twenty-first century, Earth faced a potential invasion from Martians in the year 2040.
3. A single book played a crucial role in preventing the Martian invasion.
4. Think-Tank, the powerful Martian commander-in-chief, attempts to invade Earth with the help of Lieutenant Iota, Sergeant Oop, and Captain Omega.
5. Think-Tank consults his mirror, considering himself the most intellectually gifted being in the universe.
6. The Martian crew arrives on Earth and is puzzled by the presence of books in a public library, mistaking them for hats or a storage barn.
7. Think-Tank identifies the books as communication sandwiches and orders the crew to listen to them.
8. The crew realizes the books are meant for visual communication, not auditory, and attempt to decipher the code within them.
9. By taking intelligence-boosting vitamins, the crew successfully decodes a nursery rhyme, discovering Earth's ability to combine agriculture and mining.
10. Think-Tank recognizes the significance of the discovery, as Earthlings can grow rare metals like silver and even cultivate resources like cockle shells.

The story sets the stage for an exciting adventure where a book becomes the key to saving Earth from an impending Martian invasion.

11

The chapter highlights the importance of books and their potential to hold valuable knowledge and information.

12

BEFORE YOU READ

Theme

This imaginary play is science fiction set in the 25th century. It depicts a significant historical event of 2040 in which an old book of rhymes, "Mother Goose", saved the world from Martian[1] invasion. This play highlights that little knowledge is always dangerous.

Important Characters' Sketch

- **Think Tank (Commander-in-chief):** He is the ruler of Mars and likes to be called the "The great and the mighty". He thinks books are sandwiches. He leads a team with Captain Omega, Lieutenant Iota, Sergeant Oop and Apprentice Noodle. Think Tank tries to show his intelligence and tells his crew that the book is a sandwich. As upstarts reach the book of nursery rhymes to Think Tank he feels troubled. He leaves the idea of invading[2] the earthlings. He orders his crew to leave the earth at once and he himself runs to safety.
- **Noodle:** Noodle is the apprentice of Think-Tank. He is a smart and intelligent individual. Despite being in charge of making the right decisions, he makes sure that his boss receives all the credit. This shows his humility[3] and modesty.[4]

SYNOPSIS

A comical and fictional play called "The Book That Saved The Earth" is set four centuries in the future. The different characters are the Martian living beings. The play recounts in great detail how the book successfully saved the planet from the Martian invasion. Think-Tank, who is clever and the most brilliant among all the Martians, is the commander-in-chief. He gave the go-ahead to send a spacecraft to Earth to look into the planet's mysteries. The invaders were rude and arrogant and thought themselves vastly superior to humans whom they called 'Earthlings'.

The probe team consisted of Captain Omega, Sergeant Oop and Lieutenant Iota. Centerville public library was the first location they went into. Think Tank assumed that it was a place that sold food due to the building structure and its content. He assumed the books were like sandwiches. Trying to ascertain one Martian even bit off a piece from one book. Then Noodle made the joke that these were hearing aids for communication. He then corrected himself and said they were visual communication devices because they didn't emit[5] any sounds. The group chose to take some intelligence-boosting pills and attempt to decode one of the books' texts. They opened a book of nursery rhymes with Mother Goose on the cover. Iota read one rhyme and believed humans had taught their animals the magic of music. At the same time, Omega recited the nursery rhyme and

Lessons to learn

- Books are important for knowledge and entertainment.
- Be respectful while correcting mistakes.
- Books still hold an important place in our lives.
- Simple books can have unexpected value.

[1] **Martian:** relating to the planet Mars
[2] **Invading:** occupy; conquer
[3] **Humility:** quality of not thinking yourself as better
[4] **Modesty:** quality of not being too proud
[5] **Emit:** to send out something

suggested that humans knew both farming and mining. Oop finally opened the rhyme "Humpty Dumpty" and began to read it. The picture of Humpty Dumpty resembles the appearance of Think Tank, the Martian leader.

Furthermore, the story had Humpty Dumpty had a great fall which Think Tank believed as a direct danger to his Martian throne. Frightened by the prospect of a human invasion, the Think Tank ordered the probe to return instantly and left the planet without any sign. The historian further tells the audience that the human race contacted their Martian neighbours again a few centuries later and entered a peaceful arrangement of co-existence and friendship.

Martians had a new leader by then, an enlightened and compassionate Noodle. Humans also developed impressive and grand libraries on Mars to foster[6] the habit of reading in Martians. However, they could never get their hands on one particular book, the book with 'Mother Goose' on the cover.

NCERT EXERCISE

Read and Find Out

(NCERT Page 63)

1. **Why was the twentieth century called the 'Era of the book'?**

Ans. The twentieth century was referred to as the "Era of the Book" because there were books on everything from anteaters to Zulus, and they also taught people what to do, how to do it, when to do and why to do it. They explained, educated, directed and decorated.

2. **Who tried to invade the Earth in the twenty-first century?**

Ans. Martians tried to invade the Earth in the twenty-first century.

[6] **Foster:** to help or encourage the development of something

(*NCERT Page 65*)

1. **What guesses are made by Think-Tank about the books found on Earth?**

Ans. They are initially assumed to be sandwiches by Think-Tank. Then he calls them communication devices after Noodle concludes. After that, he considers them to be some kind of eye communication device.

Think about it

(*NCERT Page 74*)

1. **Noodle avoids offending Think-Tank, but at the same time, he corrects his mistakes. How does he manage to do that?**

Ans. Noodle avoided offending Think-tank but at the same time corrected his mistakes. Noodle never gives a sense of inferiority to Think- tank whenever he corrects anything. He always provides the correct information, but he makes it clear that it comes from the so-called 'highly clever boss'.

2. **If you were in Noodle's place, how would you handle Think-Tank's mistakes?**

Ans. If I were in Noodle's place, I would follow in Noodle's footsteps. No matter how annoying the boss is, it's never appropriate to irritate them. I would have corrected Think-Tank's mistakes as politely as Noodle did.

3. **Do you think electronic media are replacing books? Can we do away with books altogether?**

Ans. To a considerable extent, electronic media are replacing books. Instead of searching for information in a book, the majority of children utilize the internet. However, one can read a book at their pace. It can run without electricity as well. But given how quickly technology is developing, books might soon be a thing of the past.

4. **Why are books referred to as a man's best companion? Which is your favourite book and why? Write a paragraph about that book.**

Ans. A book is a man's best companion because it is always there with us whenever we need it, and it never leaves us alone. It is there with us even when there is no one with us. Books are always true to us, no matter what, and they lead, counsel, instruct, amuse, inform, inspire, and make us laugh.

MISCELLANEOUS EXERCISE

Multiple Choice Questions

1. The story 'The Book That Saved the Earth' is set in:
   (*a*) Seventeenth century (*b*) Twenty-first century
   (*c*) Twenty-fourth century (*d*) Twenty-fifth century

2. Who was the 'Commander-in-Chief' of the Mars Space Control?
   (*a*) Omega (*b*) Iota
   (*c*) Think-Tank (*d*) Noodle

3. Which book saved the earth from invasion?
   (*a*) A book of science.
   (*b*) A world encyclopedia.
   (*c*) A book of military techniques.
   (*d*) A book of nursery rhymes.

4. Who was the deputy of the Think-Tank?
   (*a*) Omega (*b*) Iota
   (*c*) Noodle (*d*) Oop

5. Who included the crew of the Martian Space Craft ?
   (*a*) Omega (*b*) Iota
   (*c*) Oop (*d*) All of the above.

6. Who was the lieutenant of the spacecraft crew?
   (*a*) Think-Tank (*b*) Omega
   (*c*) Iota (*d*) Oop

7. Who was Great and Mighty?
   (*a*) Think-Tank (*b*) Noodle
   (*c*) Oop (*d*) Omega

8. With what name is the twentieth century called?
   (*a*) The era of the Book. (*b*) Era of the Science.
   (*c*) Era of the Mars. (*d*) Era of the Invasion.

9. Who tried to invade the earth in the twenty-first century?
   (*a*) Martians (*b*) Earthlings
   (*c*) Anteaters (*d*) Zulus

10. In which year was the Martian invasion on the earth planned?
    (*a*) 2041 (*b*) 2040
    (*c*) 2140 (*d*) 2060

Extract-Based Questions

I. **Read the following extract and answer the questions/ complete the sentences that follow: (5 M)**

THINK-TANK: Mirror, mirror, in my hand. Who is the most fantastically intellectually gifted being in the land?

OFFSTAGE VOICE: (after a pause) You, sir.

THINK-TANK: (smacking mirror) Quicker. Answer quicker next time. I hate a slow mirror. (He admires himself in the mirror.) Ah, there I am. Are we Martians not a handsome race? So much more attractive than those ugly Earthlings with their tiny heads. Noodle, you keep on exercising your mind, and someday you'll have a balloon brain just like mine.

NOODLE: Oh, I hope so, Mighty Think-Tank. I hope so.

THINK-TANK: Now, contact the space probe. I want to invade that primitive ball of mud called Earth before lunch.

NOODLE: It shall be done, sir. (He adjusts levers on the switchboard. Electronic buzzes and beeps are heard as the curtains open. **(CFPQ)**

1. Choose the option that lists the most appropriate meaning of think-tank from those given below.
   (*a*) A tank that helps you think deeper than an average person, if you use its contents regularly.
   (*b*) Non-stop flow of ideas from a fixed source about one particular issue.
   (*c*) A pool of ideas and solutions to various problems via an individual, group or organization.
   (*d*) A method by way of which people think collectively to identify stray thoughts among them.
2. "Mirror, mirror, in my hand. Who is the most fantastically intellectually gifted being in the land?"
   Choose the option that lists the genre having the original reference to the above lines.
   (*a*) Biography (*b*) Science-fiction
   (*c*) Mystery (*d*) Fairy tale
3. Choose the option that correctly categorizes the phrase "(after a pause)" based on the dialogue given above.
   (*a*) aside (*b*) stage direction
   (*c*) narration (*d*) setting
4. Choose the option that fits the example of an irony from the ones given below.
   (*a*) "Who is the most fantastically intellectually gifted being in the land?"
   (*b*) "I hate a slow mirror."
   (*c*) "Noodle, you keep on exercising your mind, and someday you'll have a balloon brain just like mine.
   (*d*) "I want to invade that primitive ball of mud called Earth before lunch."
5. Choose the option that includes the display of 'smacking' as used in the extract.

(1) (2) (3) (4)

(*a*) Option (1) (*b*) Option (2)
(*c*) Option (3) (*d*) Option (4)

II. Read the following extract and answer the questions/ complete the sentences that follow: **(5 marks)**

OOP : I haven't a clue. I've been to seven galaxies, but I've never seen anything like this. Maybe they're hats. (He opens a book and puts it on his head.) Say, maybe this is a haberdashery!

OMEGA : (bowing low) Perhaps the Great and Mighty Think-Tank will give us the benefit of his thought on the matter.

THINK-TANK : Elementary, my dear Omega. Hold one of the items up so that I may view it closely. (Omega holds a book on the palm of her hand.) Yes, yes, I understand now. Since Earth creatures are always eating, the place in which you find yourselves is undoubtedly a crude refreshment stand.

OMEGA : (to Iota and Oop) He says we're in a refreshment stand.

OOP : Well, the Earthlings certainly have a strange diet.

1. Who does Omega suggest seeking assistance from? **(1)**
   (*a*) Iota (*b*) Think-Tank
   (*c*) Earthlings (*d*) Oop
2. Write a word from the passage for "a shop or store that sells men's clothing, hats, and accessories." **(1)**
3. Based on the excerpt, what can be inferred about the Martian crew's understanding of Earth and its culture? **(1)**
4. Discuss the comedic effect created by the crew's misunderstanding of the Earthlings' "strange diet." **(2)**

III. Read the following extract and answer the questions/ complete the sentences that follow: **(5 marks)**

HISTORIAN: (chuckling) And that's how one dusty old book of nursery rhymes saved the world from a Martian invasion. As you all know, in the twenty-fifth century, five hundred years after all this happened, we Earthlings resumed contact with Mars, and we even became very friendly with the Martians. By that time,

Great and Mighty Think: Tank had been replaced by a very clever Martian – the wise and wonderful Noodle!

1. Who succeeded Great and Mighty Think-Tank in Martian leadership according to the historian? **(1)**
   (*a*) A book of military strategies.
   (*b*) A manual on diplomacy.
   (*c*) A book of nursery rhymes.
   (*d*) A collection of Martian laws.
2. What is the significance of the "twenty-fifth century" in the context of Earth-Martian relations? **(1)**
3. From the historian's chuckle, what can we infer about the perception of nursery rhymes in saving the world? **(1)**

4. Discuss the transition in Martian leadership from Great and Mighty Think-Tank to Noodle and its implications for understanding leadership qualities. **(1)**

5. A satire is when a person, idea, or institution is criticised by highlighting their faults and weaknesses using humour. Describe how The Book That Saved the Earth can be considered a satire with supporting examples from the text. **(CBSE, ASQP 2023)**

6. A well known book of nursery rhymes saved the world from a Martian invasion. Comment with reference to **(CBSE, 2024)**

Subjective Questions

Short Answer Questions (40-50 words) (3 M)

1. Think-Tank thinks that Earthlings are after him. What is the reason?
2. How did Think-Tank interpret the poem 'The Cat and the Fiddle'?
3. Who are Earthlings? What does Think-Tank say about them?
4. Write two points from the play "The book that saved the Earth", where Think-Tank showed his little knowledge.

Long Answer Questions (100-120 words) (6 M)

7. Compare and contrast the characters of Noodle and Think-Tank.
8. What guesses are made by Think-Tank about the books found on the Earth?
9. How did the people on the earth help the Martian people? How did this effort help the people on both the planets? **(CBSE, 2020)**

ANSWERS & EXPLANATIONS

Answer Key

Multiple Choice Questions

1. (*d*) **2.** (*c*) **3.** (*d*) **4.** (*c*) **5.** (*d*) **6.** (*c*) **7.** (*a*) **8.** (*a*) **9.** (*a*) **10.** (*b*)

Explanations

Extract-Based Questions

I. 1. (*c*) A pool of ideas and solutions to various problems via an individual, group or organization.

2. (*d*) Fairy tale

3. (*b*) stage direction

4. (*c*) "Noodle, you keep on exercising your mind, and someday you'll have a balloon brain just like mine.

5. (*d*) Option (4)

II. 1. (*b*) Think-Tank

2. Haberdashery

Knowledge Hub

In the story "The Book that Saved the Earth," the word "haberdashery" refers to a small retail store that sells items related to men's clothing, accessories or needles, thread, button etc. In this tale, aliens from Mars find a book about haberdashery and get confused, thinking it's very important for Earth's people. They don't understand Earth's things well, which leads to funny mix-ups.

3. The Martian crew has a limited understanding of Earth's culture and is often confused by Earthly objects and their purposes.

4. The crew's confusion about the Earthlings' diet adds humour to the situation. Their misinterpretation of books as refreshments highlights their lack of familiarity with Earth's culture and their tendency to make assumptions based on their own experiences.

III. 1. (*c*) A book of nursery rhymes.

2. It marks the period when Earthlings and Martians resumed contact and established a friendly relationship, 500 years after the events described.

3. The chuckle suggests a sense of amusement or disbelief at the unconventional and unexpected role that nursery rhymes played in saving the world, highlighting the story's ironic and humorous tone.

4. The transition from Great and Mighty Think-Tank to the wise and wonderful Noodle signifies a shift towards valuing wisdom and cleverness in leadership, rather than just strength or might. This change suggests an evolution in Martian society's values, emphasizing the importance of intellectual and diplomatic qualities in leaders.

Subjective Questions

Short Answer Questions

CBSE Marking Scheme: Content-1 M, Organisation of Ideas-1 M, Accuracy-1 M

1. The crew of Think-Tank read the poem about Humpty-Dumpty's fall and showed the picture to Think-Tank.

   The head of the Think-Tank resembled Humpty- Dumpty's. Think-Tank becomes convinced that humans are preparing to invade Mars and capture them.

2. The cow jumped over the moon in the second poem about the cat and the fiddle. The dog chuckled when he heard it; the dish fled with the spoon.

   Think-Tank misinterpreted it. He believed humans had imparted musical culture and space techniques to their domestic animals. They could be attacking billions of cows from another planet!

3. Earthlings are creatures of planet Earth. Think-Tank is a commander-in-chief of planet Mars. He has a huge, egg-shaped head and wears a long robe decorated with stars and circles.

   He says to Noodle that Martians are handsome and much more attractive than Earthlings. Earthlings are ugly and have tiny heads.

4. Think-Tank from Mars came to Earth to invade it but due to little knowledge he made blunders such as:

   (1) First of all he mistook the library for a refreshment stand and books as sandwiches.

   (2) He ordered his commanders to evacuate Mars and settle at Alpha Centauri, which was a hundred million miles away.

5. The Book That Saved the Earth can be considered as satire because it uses humour and exaggeration to criticise and mock the Martians' intelligence.

   - The Martians misinterpret Earth's books, especially the nursery rhymes. This creates a satirical commentary on cultural misunderstandings and the dangers of jumping to conclusions.
   - In the end, it was a simple book of nursery rhymes that became the key to saving the Earth from the invasion by an alien military force, creating an ironic and satirical twist to the story.
   - Think-Tank's intelligence is described in exaggerated terms as the 'most powerful and intelligent creature in the whole universe'. He is even described as having a large 'balloon brain'. This is an example of satire and mockery as Think-Tank is shown to be more pompous than intelligent. Satire is a form of expression that uses humor, irony, or exaggeration to criticize or mock various aspects of society, politics, or human behavior. It often aims to provoke thought, challenge norms, and highlight absurdities.

6. In the play "The Book That Saved the Earth," the Martians mistake a book of nursery rhymes, "Mother Goose," as a guide to Earth's culture and technology. They believe the rhymes are coded messages about advanced Earth practices and potential threats, like agriculture of precious metals and advanced animal training. Their misunderstandings lead them to perceive Earthlings as highly advanced, causing them to abort their invasion plans. Ultimately, the playful innocence of nursery rhymes in the book misguides the Martians, safeguarding Earth.

Long Answer Questions

CBSE Marking Scheme: Expression-2 M, Accuracy-1 M

7. The personalities of Noodle and Think-Tank are different. Think-Tank likes to refer to itself as "Great and Mighty." He issues orders and exercises authority. Although he is Mars's ruler, he is not intelligent. **(1 M)**

   Books are like sandwiches to him. He is mistaken in every single way. He commands the crew to follow him. He enjoys using other people's ideas as his own. He is a coward who just exaggerates his strength. **(1 M)**

   Noodle is his knowledgeable apprentice. He gently corrects the ruler's (Think-Tank) errors. He never takes credit for his ideas, but tenderly presents them to the ruler. Think-Tank claims ownership of them. **(1 M)**

8. Think-Tank makes guesses that the books are a kind of crude refreshment and refers to them as sandwiches or a communication satellite. **(1 M)**

   On the suggestion of Noodle, chemical vitamins enable Omega to decipher the code of nursery rhymes such as 'Mistress Mary', 'Humpty Dumpty' and 'The cat and the Fiddle'. **(1 M)**

   All the poems make Think-Tank conclude that Earthlings have a high level of civilization and that they have targeted them, so they decide to escape from Mars. **(1 M)**

9. After the departure of Think-Tank from the Mars, the wise and intelligent Noodle was elected as the ruler of the Mars. **(1 M)**

   The earthlings resumed contact with the Martians, became friends with them and taught the Martians how to read.

   It helped people on both the planets as they became friendly and did not consider invasion as an option. **(1 M)**

   The people on both the planets exchanged their views and values. They established a model library in the capital city of Marsopolis. **(1 M)**

SELECTED LAQs

As per the latest pattern observed in CBSE Board Exam 2024 for Q. 10 & Q.11

CBSE Marking Scheme: Content-3 M, Expression-2 M, Accuracy-1 M

1. Evaluate the impact of friendship and companionship in both "Mijbil the Otter" and "From the Diary of Anne Frank."

Compare and contrast the significance of friendship in the lives of the main characters, highlighting the role it plays in their emotional well-being, support system, and overall survival. Write this presentation draft, including your insights, in about 120 words.

You may begin this way:

One acknowledges that both "Mijbil the Otter" and "From the Diary of Anne Frank" emphasize the importance of friendship and companionship in the lives of their main characters.

Ans. Good morning! Today, I want to discuss the importance of friendship in both the stories: "From the Diary of Anne Frank" and "Mijbil the Otter." In "Mijbil the Otter," a man and an otter named Mijbil share a special friendship that provides comfort and delight, particularly during difficult times. This special friendship demonstrates the value of friends in providing companionship and a sense of happiness. In "From the Diary of Anne Frank," Anne considers Kitty, her diary, to be her closest companion. She expresses in Kitty her deepest feelings, which helps her get through difficult times. These stories demonstrate the value and strength of friendship by providing us with consolation, courage, and a sense of understanding. Thank you.

2. In the chapter 'Bholi,' explore the theme of self-acceptance and the power of inner strength. Discuss how Bholi's journey from insecurity to self-confidence highlights the transformative nature of self-acceptance. Support your answer with relevant examples from the chapter, emphasizing key moments that showcase Bholi's growth and the impact of her inner strength on her life. Write your response in about 120 words.

Ans. Bholi's journey from insecurity to self-confidence in the chapter "Bholi" exemplifies the transformative nature of self-acceptance. Initially, Bholi is burdened by her physical appearance and speech impairment, leading to low self-esteem. However, her encounter with the compassionate teacher, at her school becomes a reason for change. Her understanding and support enabled Bholi to believe in herself and express her thoughts. Bholi's newfound confidence is further reinforced when she confronts her elders who were ready to marry her to a man asking for dowry from her father. Additionally, her decision to reject the marriage proposal from the rich but greedy man-Bishamber showcases her self-worth and determination to prioritize her own happiness. Through these key moments, Bholi's growth highlights the power of self-acceptance in transforming one's life.

3. You have been asked to present an evaluation of the theme of "faith" in both "A Letter to God" and "The Ball Poem." Write this presentation draft including your insights, in about 120 words, comparing the theme of faith in both.

You may begin this way: *One acknowledges that both "A Letter to God" and "The Ball Poem" portray characters who face challenging situations that test their faith; however, ...*

(Reference - "A Letter to God" and "The Ball Poem")

Ans. Good morning! Today, I want to share how the stories "A Letter to God" and "The Ball Poem" explore the idea of faith during tough times. In "A Letter to God," Lencho, a farmer, believes strongly in God. After a storm ruins his crops, he asks God for money, showing his complete trust in God's help. Meanwhile, "The Ball Poem" tells us about a boy who loses his ball and feels very sad. This loss teaches him an important lesson about life's ups and downs and the importance of believing in oneself. Lencho's story shows faith in God, and the boy's story teaches us to have faith in ourselves and appreciate the happy moments. Both stories highlight the power of faith in overcoming challenges.

4. You have been asked to present an evaluation of the character of Nelson Mandela and the theme of "resilience" in both "Nelson Mandela" and "Trees." Write this presentation draft including your insights, in about 120 words, comparing the character of Mandela and the theme of resilience in both.

You may begin this way: *One acknowledges that both texts "Nelson Mandela" and "Trees" exhibit remarkable resilience in the face of adversity; however, ...*

(Reference - "Nelson Mandela" and "The Trees")

Ans. Good morning! Today, I'd like to discuss the powerful theme of resilience in "Nelson Mandela: Long Walk to Freedom" and the poem "The Trees." Nelson Mandela is a hero who bravely fought against unfair laws in South Africa, showing incredible strength and never giving up, even when things got really tough. In "The Trees," the poet talks about how trees stand strong through storms and tough weather, showing us how to keep going no matter what. Mandela's story is about fighting for what's right, while the trees remind us of our inner strength. Both stories teach us about being resilient, which means not giving up, even when facing hard times. Mandela's fight and the enduring trees both inspire us to stay strong. Thank you.

5. Imagine that Mrs. Pumphrey, from 'A Triumph of Surgery,' writes a diary entry reflecting on her own misconceptions about care and affection toward pets, especially in the context of her experience with Tricki. Write this diary entry, as Mrs. Pumphrey, in about 120 words.

Ans. Dear Diary,

Today made me think a lot. I always thought giving Tricki lots of food and treats was the way to show love. But I was so wrong! After sending him to the vet, I've learned that too much of anything is bad. Mr. Herriot helped Tricki get healthier and happier with just the basics: good food in right amounts and plenty of exercise. It wasn't fancy creams or luxury beds that Tricki needed. It was simple care and attention. I've learned that love isn't about giving things, but about providing what's really needed.

Mrs. Pumphrey

6. Present an evaluation of the character development in both "His First Flight" and "Amanda." Compare and contrast the growth and transformation of the main characters in both stories, focusing on their aspirations, challenges faced, and the impact of their experiences on their personal development. Write this presentation draft, including your insights, in about 120 words.

You may begin this way:

One acknowledges that both "His First Flight" and "Amanda" showcase the journey of their main characters, highlighting their aspirations and the obstacles encountered along the way.

Ans. Good morning, everyone. Today, I'd like to discuss the development and transformation of the two major characters in the stories, "His First Flight" and "Amanda." A baby bird that is first afraid of flying is shown in "His First Flight". But when he finally tries, he loves the freedom and learns to be brave. We encounter a girl in "Amanda" who feels frustrated by her mother's constant criticism. For freedom and happiness, she longs to be someone else. The stories demonstrate how these characters overcome obstacles, pursue their dreams, and grow as a result of their experiences. They convey us important lessons about bravery, achieving independence, and having the inner strength to face hardship. Thank you.

7. A character arc is the transformation or development of a character throughout a story and refers to the changes a character undergoes as a result of their experiences, challenges, and interactions with other characters. In the light of the above information, trace the character arc of Bholi in "Bholi," in about 120 words.

Ans. In "Bholi," we see an amazing story of a girl named Bholi who starts off feeling shy and unsure of herself because she looks different and has trouble speaking clearly. She often gets picked on, which makes her feel even worse. But everything begins to change when she meets a caring teacher who believes in her and encourages her to go to school. This kind act helps Bholi find hope and courage. As she learns more at school, Bholi becomes confident and strong, ready to stand up for herself and challenge what people expect from her. Her story is about learning to accept herself, realizing how powerful education can be, and daring to be different from what others might want her to be.

8. You have been asked to present an evaluation of the approaches of "Gautama Buddha" and "Nelson Mandela" towards alleviating suffering and bringing about change. Write this presentation draft including your insights, in about 120 words, comparing the approaches of both influential figures.

(Reference- The Sermon at Benaras and Nelson Mandela - Long Walk to Freedom)

Ans. Gautama Buddha and Nelson Mandela took different but impactful routes to alleviate suffering and induce change. Buddha, witnessing the inevitable sufferings of life—birth, aging, illness, and death—sought enlightenment and shared his wisdom in the Sermon at Benaras. His approach was spiritual and aimed at individual enlightenment for collective well-being. Mandela, on the other hand, took a more political route. Imprisoned for 27 years, his fight was against the concrete social injustice of apartheid. He aimed for legislative change and social equality. While Buddha provides a philosophical solution to life's sufferings, Mandela gives a practical, social one. Both are different but essential ways to address the human condition.

9. A character arc is the transformation or development of a character throughout a story and refers to the changes a character undergoes as a result of their experiences, challenges, and interactions with other characters. In the light of the above information, trace the character arc of Mathilda Loisel in the chapter 'The Necklace' from 'Footprints without Feet,' in about 120 words.

Ans. In "The Necklace" from "Footprints without Feet," Mathilda Loisel isn't happy with her simple life and dreams of being rich. Her life changes when she borrows a necklace for a fancy party from her friend, Madame Forestier, but loses it. Instead of telling the truth, she buys a new one, leading to huge debt. Mathilda works hard for years to pay it off, learning about hard work and humility. When she finally tells Madame Forestier the truth, she learns the necklace was fake and not worth much. This shocks Mathilda and makes her understand that chasing after wealth and status was a mistake. She learns to value honesty, thankfulness, and being happy with what you have. Mathilda's story shows us that things aren't always what they seem and that true value comes from who we are, not what we own.

10. You are invited to speak at a community event about the theme of independence and personal growth as seen through the eyes of children and nature. Prepare a speech draft in not more than 120 words, discussing the common themes of freedom and growth in 'Madam Rides the Bus' and 'The Trees' by Adrienne Rich.

Ans. Hello everyone! Today, I want to talk about the idea of freedom and growth. In 'Madam Rides the Bus,' Valli shows us that you don't have to be big or old to want independence. Her bus ride is a big step toward growing up and feeling free. Similarly, in 'The Trees' by Adrienne Rich, the trees break free from the ground to find their own space and light. Both stories teach us that the desire for freedom is natural, whether you're a young girl or a tree. It's a part of growing up and becoming who you are.

Thank you.

11. You've been selected to address students from local schools about overcoming fears and the significance of support systems in that process. Prepare a speech draft in not more than 120 words, discussing the common themes in "The Ball Poem" and "His First Flight."

Ans. Good morning, everyone. Today, I'd like to talk about "The Ball Poem" and "His First Flight," that teach us valuable lessons about overcoming fears. In "The Ball Poem," a young boy faces the fear of loss and learns to move on, signaling the difficult yet inevitable journey towards maturity. In "His First Flight," a seagull overcomes his fear of flying, thanks to the encouragement and tough love from his mother. Both stories tell us that fears and obstacles are a part of life, but with courage and a good support system, we can conquer them. To conclude, I'd like to say that challenges make us stronger and help us grow, so face your fears and spread your wings. Thank you.

12. Imagine Robert Frost from A Dust of Snow met with Lencho from A Letter to God and discussed the various ways nature can influence a person's mood.

Create this conversation in not more than 120 words. 6

(CBSE APQ 2023)

You may begin this way:

Lencho: As a farmer, my livelihood depends on nature and sometimes nature can be cruel.

Ans. Lencho: As a farmer, my livelihood depends on nature, and sometimes nature can be cruel. I've seen my entire crop destroyed by hail, and only my faith in God kept hope alive.

Frost: I understand, Lencho. Nature's unpredictability affects us deeply. Once, a simple act by a crow, shaking snow off a tree, changed my entire outlook on a day I thought was ruined.

Lencho: It's that power of nature, isn't it? Whether it's bringing despair through a storm or a moment of joy with a dust of snow, it deeply influences our emotions and state of mind.

Frost: Precisely. It's all about perspective. The same nature that brings us to despair can also be the source of profound happiness and change. It's fascinating how it molds our feelings and perceptions.

Lencho: True, Frost. I learned to keep my faith through the worst, hoping for a sign from above. Nature's harshness taught me resilience.

Frost: And for me, nature's simple, unexpected moments teach us to find hope and joy in the smallest things, changing a dreaded day into a moment of gratitude.

13. Imagine that Anil, from "The Thief's Story" by Ruskin Bond, writes a diary entry reflecting on his choice to trust people and the transformative power of trust and kindness, using his experience with the thief as context. Write this diary entry as Anil, in about 120 words.

Ans. Dear Diary,

Today was a revealing day. The young thief I took in tried to rob me. But what he doesn't know is that I was somewhat aware of his intentions from the start. So why did I let him stay? Because I believe that trust can transform people, it gives them a chance to rethink their actions. When he returned the money, I felt a strange mix of relief and hope. Hope that my trust was not misplaced and that he, maybe for the first time, experienced a sense of guilt and responsibility. This event reassures me that trusting people, even those deemed untrustworthy, has the power to change them for the better.

Anil

14. You have been asked to present an evaluation of the characters of both Anne Frank from and Custard, the dragon towards facing challenges. Write this presentation draft including your insights, in about 120 words, comparing the characters of both.

You may begin this way: One acknowledges that both Anne Frank and Custard both face challenges in their respective stories; however, ...

(Reference - "From the Diary of Anne Frank" & "The Tale of Custard the Dragon")

Ans. Anne Frank and Custard the Dragon show us different ways of dealing with hard times. Anne, a unique and brave girl, often felt alone and turned to her diary, "Kitty," to share her deepest thoughts. She always tried to see the bright side, even when things were tough. Custard, on the other hand, was known as a scared dragon, but when his friends needed him, he found bravery within himself and became a hero. Anne's story teaches us the power of hope and finding a friend in ourselves, while Custard's adventure shows that courage can surprise us in challenging moments. Both stories remind us that difficulties can help us discover strengths we never knew we had.

15. Imagine that Mrs Pumphrey from A *Triumph* of Surgery, reflects upon her behaviour, learns from her mistakes, and writes a diary entry about the consequences of overindulgence. Write this diary entry as Mrs Pumphrey in about 120 words. (6) (CBSE APQ, 2023)

Ans. Today I realized my love for Tricki made me spoil him with too much food, making him sick. Seeing him unhealthy made me very sad. I thought treats were a way to show love, but it was hurting him. Mr. Herriot noticed my mistake and said Tricki needed less food and more exercise. He even took Tricki to help him get better because I struggled to follow his advice. I missed Tricki and sent gifts to Mr. Herriot, still trying to pamper Tricki. I've learned my lesson and will take better care of him now. Seeing Tricki healthy and energetic again after returning from Mr. Herriot's care made me incredibly (extremely) happy. I'm determined to be a good caretaker and keep Tricki happy and healthy.

16. You are asked to write an essay comparing the struggles faced by the tiger in "A Tiger in the Zoo" and the young seagull in "His First Flight" in their respective environments. Discuss how the two characters yearn for freedom, but are trapped by their circumstances or fears. Write your essay in 120 words.

You may begin this way: ***Both the tiger in 'A Tiger in the Zoo' and the young seagull in 'His First Flight' exemplify the intrinsic desire for freedom in living beings, yet are…***

Ans. Both the tiger in "A Tiger in the Zoo" and the young seagull in "His First Flight" show us how important freedom is to all living beings. The tiger is caged and separated from his natural habitat, longing to prowl freely in the forest. His eyes at night show his unfulfilled desires. The young seagull is also trapped, but by his own fear of flying. He longs to fly high and join his family, searching for food. Both characters show that freedom isn't just physical; it's also mental and emotional. The seagull overcomes his fear and finally tastes freedom, unlike the tiger who remains physically confined. The stories teach us that while some barriers can be broken, others remain insurmountable.

17. You have been asked to present an evaluation of the themes of both "Madam Rides the Bus" and "For Anne Gregory" towards the concept of identity and self-expression. Write this presentation draft including your insights, in about 120 words, comparing the themes of both.

You may begin this way: ***One acknowledges that both "Madam Rides the Bus" and "For Anne Gregory" explore the concept of identity and self-expression; however, ...***

(Reference - "Madam Rides the Bus" & "For Anne Gregory")

Ans. Good morning! Today, let's explore how "Madam Rides the Bus" and "For Anne Gregory" talk about being true to ourselves and expressing who we are. In "Madam Rides the Bus," Valli, a young girl, takes a big step by going on a bus adventure alone, showing her bravery and willingness to explore beyond what's expected of her. In "For Anne Gregory," we meet a young girl who proudly accepts her looks, proving that being true to ourselves is what really matters. While the first story shows us how Valli challenges what society expects from her, the second celebrates loving ourselves as we are. Both stories teach us the importance of following our own path and valuing our uniqueness. Thank you.

18. You have been chosen to address a student gathering from the neighbourhood schools, to speak on the resilience of human spirit required to transcend discrimination. Prepare the speech draft in not more than 120 words, with reference to the commonality of themes in Nelson Mandela: Long Walk to Freedom and The Trees by Adrienne Rich. **(CBSE SQP, 2023)**

You may begin this way:

Good morning, everyone. Today, I'd like to discuss two pieces of literature that offer a powerful insight into the resilience of the human spirit required to transcend discrimination.

You may end this way.

To conclude, I'd like to say that ...

Thank you

Ans. Good morning, everyone! Today, I'd like to discuss two pieces of literature that offer a powerful insight into the resilience of the human spirit required to overcome discrimination. "Nelson Mandela: Long Walk to Freedom" tells the story of Mandela's fight against apartheid, a system that denied basic human rights based on race, showcasing immense resilience against oppression. Similarly, "The Trees" by Adrienne Rich metaphorically describes trees breaking free from confinement, symbolizing the natural urge for freedom and resistance against constraints. Both texts emphasize the inherent desire for freedom and dignity, despite the challenges posed by unjust systems or situations. To conclude, I'd like to say that these stories inspire us to fight for justice and equality, proving that the human spirit can overcome even the most difficult challenges. Thank you.

19. Using the concept of a character arc, trace the development of Dr. Herriot's character in the chapter 'A Triumph of Surgery'. How does his transformation throughout the chapter reflect the impact of his experiences and interactions with others?

Ans. In "A Triumph of Surgery," Dr. Herriot starts as a skilled vet but changes a lot because of Tricki, a dog he treats. Tricki's surgery and recovery, along with dealing with Tricki's owner, Mrs. Pumphrey, who gives Tricki too many treats and not enough exercise, teach Dr. Herriot new lessons. He learns that being a great vet isn't just about being good at surgery; it's also ab out caring for animals' feelings, having patience, and teaching pet owners how to look after their pets better. His time with Tricki and Mrs. Pumphrey makes him a kinder vet who understands the connection between how pets are treated by their owners and their health. Dr. Herriot becomes more thoughtful and caring, showing how his experiences make him better at helping animals and their owners.

20. Imagine that Ausable, from "The Midnight Visitor" by Robert Arthur, writes a diary entry reflecting on the themes of deception, intelligence, and the unexpected facets of spy craft in the context of his recent experience with Fowler and Max. Write this diary entry, as Ausable, in about 120 words.

Ans. Dear Diary,

Wow, what a night! Fowler, the young journalist, always thought spying was all about exciting fights and chases. However, tonight was different. It was all about being smart and thinking fast.

He tricked Max, the enemy spy, with a story about a balcony and a fake police setup. Surprisingly, the plan worked, and Max jumped out the window! This shows that in spying, being clever is just as important as being brave.

This experience taught me to always be ready for surprises. Life can be unpredictable, but if you're clever, you can turn any situation to your advantage. Being a spy means always being prepared for the unexpected and knowing how to use it.

Goodnight, diary!

21. You have been invited to give a talk about the themes of independence and self-realization in young individuals. Create your speech draft in not more than 120 words, comparing Valli's journey in "Madam Rides the Bus" and the message conveyed in the poem "For Anne Gregory."

Ans. Good morning, everyone. Today, I'd like to explore the themes of independence and self-realization as illustrated in "Madam Rides the Bus" and "For Anne Gregory." Valli, an eight-year-old girl, takes a bold step by riding the bus alone to experience freedom and satisfy her curiosity. On the other hand, "For Anne Gregory" teaches us that true worth comes from our inner self, not from external appearances. Both stories remind us that age and looks are not barriers when it comes to discovering ourselves. It's the courage to take action and the wisdom to understand oneself that really counts. So, let's not be bound by society's norms and dare to take our own paths. Thank you.

22. You have been asked to evaluate the contrasting roles of guidance and intuition in "Black Aeroplane" and "Fog," specifically focusing on the pilot in "Black Aeroplane" and the metaphorical fog in Carl Sandburg's "Fog." How do these elements help or hinder the characters' journey? Write this evaluation draft, including your insights, in about 120 words. **6**

Ans. In the story "Black Aeroplane," a pilot finds his way out of a dangerous storm thanks to a mysterious second plane that appears and leads him to safety. This help seems almost magical and prevents a possible disaster. On the other hand, the poem "Fog" by Carl Sandburg talks about how fog represents confusion and uncertainty. The poem describes the fog as something that quietly comes and goes, suggesting that sometimes we have to wait patiently for things to become clear. While the pilot receives clear help, the fog indicates that there are times we must trust our intuitions (own feelings) and be patient to get through tough situations. Both pieces show that navigating life involves a mix of getting help from others and listening to our inner voice.

23. You have been asked to present an evaluation of the approaches of the mothers of both, the baby seagull and Amanda, towards helping their children. Write this presentation draft including your insights, in about 120 words, comparing the approaches of both parents.

(CBSE SQP, 2023)

You may begin this way:

One acknowledges that both parents, Amanda's mother and the baby seagull's mother both....however, ...

(Reference - Amanda! & His First Flight)

Ans. One acknowledges that both parents, Amanda's mother and the baby seagull's mother, aim to teach their children important life lessons. However, their methods vastly differ. Amanda's mother uses constant reminders and criticism, focusing on Amanda's behavior and tasks she hasn't completed, which seems to restrict Amanda's imagination and freedom. In contrast, the baby seagull's mother employs a tough love approach, pushing her child out of his comfort zone to discover his ability to fly, thereby instilling confidence through direct experience. While Amanda's mother's approach is more verbal and possibly overbearing, the seagull's mother uses action and silence to encourage independence and growth. These contrasting parenting styles highlight the balance between guidance and freedom in nurturing growth and self-discovery in children.

24. You have been asked to present an evaluation of the role that nature plays in positively impacting the lives of individuals in the chapters "Coorg" and "Dust of Snow." Write this presentation draft including your insights, in about 120 words, comparing how nature serves as a source of inspiration or transformation in both chapters.

Ans. In "Coorg," the chapter describes nature as a peaceful, lovely place full of life, offering a spot for people to feel at ease and happy. The vivid details about Coorg's landscape show that spending time in nature is a wonderful way to unwind and boost your spirits. The poem "Dust of Snow" illustrates how even a small, natural event, such as snow falling from a tree because of a crow, can instantly make someone's day better. "Coorg" gives a wider perspective on how nature brings joy, whereas "Dust of Snow" suggests that even short moments with nature can lift your mood. Both stories together emphasize that nature has the power to make us feel good and spread positivity.

25. Trace the character arc of Nelson Mandela in "Nelson Mandela: Long Walk to Freedom," focusing on how he evolves as a leader committed to equality and justice. Discuss the changes he experiences and the lessons he learns, in about 120 words.

Ans. In "Nelson Mandela: Long Walk to Freedom," we follow Mandela as he grows from understanding unfair social rules to fighting for everyone's equal rights. He realizes true freedom requires giving up a lot, including his own freedom and time with his family. Spending 27 years in jail doesn't make him angry or wanting revenge. Instead, he becomes a wise and patient leader who prefers making peace over getting even.

Mandela's story shows how he changes, proving his strong will and dedication to fairness. As South Africa's President, he shows that being a leader means bringing people together and promoting peace. Starting as a young fighter for justice, Mandela became a thoughtful leader, showing us it's crucial to stick to our values, even when times are really tough.

26. You have been invited to speak at a community gathering about the themes of loss and acceptance depicted in "The Sermon at Benares" and "The Ball Poem." Prepare your speech draft in not more than 120 words, elaborating on how both works offer insights into dealing with loss and moving forward in life.

Ans. Good morning, everyone. Today, we're looking at "The Sermon at Benares" and "The Ball Poem," both stories about dealing with loss and learning to accept it. In "The Sermon at Benares," Buddha talks about how suffering and death are part of life, and accepting them is important for peace. "The Ball Poem" shows us how losing a ball teaches a boy about loss and moving on, showing that we can't hold onto everything. Both stories teach us that we all face losses, but it's how we handle these moments that helps us grow stronger. To conclude, both stories encourage us to accept and overcome challenges, teaching us valuable lessons about resilience. Thank you.

27. You have been chosen to address a students gathering about the characters Natalya and Lomov who lose their temper on trivial issues. It shows their poor skills at anger management. Suggest some ways that help you in maintaining cordial relationships with people around you. (The Proposal)

Ans. In the play "The Proposal" by Anton Chekhov, Natalya and Lomov show us exactly how not to handle minor disagreements. Their inability to manage their anger leads to a series of absurd and comical arguments over trivial matters, such as the ownership of a piece of land or the merits of their dogs. This highlights the importance of good communication and patience in maintaining healthy relationships. To avoid such situations, it's helpful to take a deep breath before responding in anger, listen actively to understand the other person's perspective, and remember that being right is not always as important as being kind. Practicing empathy and considering the other person's feelings can turn potential conflicts into opportunities for strengthening bonds. Remember, it's not about winning an argument, but about valuing your relationships.

28. If you had to summarize the evolution of the character of Think-Tank, the Great and Mighty, in "The Book that Saved the Earth," how would you do it? Discuss his change in perception about Earth and its literature in 120 words.

Ans. In the beginning, Think-Tank is extremely dismissive of Earth, considering it a primitive planet. He ridicules the idea that books could be a form of 'sandwich' showcasing his ignorance. However, as he attempts to understand the contents of a nursery rhyme book, he becomes more and more puzzled. By the end, he reverses his opinion, declaring that Earth people are far too advanced. He orders an immediate retreat, fearing the intellectual capabilities of Earthlings. His character arc is one of humbling realization, showing how initial arrogance can lead to ultimate respect.

Mistakes 101 : What not to do!

Summarizing the Plot instead of focusing on the Character Arc.

29. Did Griffin from Footprints without Feet follow the saying 'with great power comes great responsibility' ? Justify your answer in 120 words. (CBSE APQ , 2023)

Ans. No, Griffin didn't follow the idea that having great power means you should do good things for others. After becoming invisible, instead of helping people, he started doing bad things for his own benefit. He burned down his landlord's house for revenge and stole food and clothes because he wanted them for himself. He didn't feel bad about taking things from others, even hurting people if they got in his way. For example, he attacked a shopkeeper and stole from a clergyman. When someone tried to catch him, he didn't surrender; he fought and ran away. Griffin never thought about the consequences of his actions or about helping anyone but himself.

30. "The life of mortals in this world is troubled and brief and combined with pain". In the light of the above statement, write your views in the context in about 120 words. *(The Sermon at Benaras)*

Ans. "The Sermon at Benares" teaches us about the transient nature of life, emphasizing that everyone experiences suffering and death. This wisdom, shared by Buddha, shows us that life's brief moments are often filled with challenges and pain. However, understanding and accepting this truth can lead to enlightenment and inner peace. Buddha's teachings encourage us to see beyond our personal grief and recognize that suffering is a universal experience, not something that isolates us. Instead of being consumed by sorrow, we should strive to find meaning and joy in the impermanence of life, helping us to appreciate the precious moments we have and to live more compassionately towards others. This perspective shifts our focus from despair to a deeper understanding of life's cycle, guiding us towards peace.

31. In light of the concept of a character arc, which represents the transformation or development of a character through the story, describe the changes Bholi's parents undergo as a result of their experiences, challenges, and interactions with other characters in the chapter "Bholi".

Ans. In the beginning, Bholi's parents are not very hopeful for her future due to her speech defect and scars. They are more inclined to marry her off to an older man, disregarding her feelings. However, as the story progresses, their perception changes. Bholi's brave refusal to marry the older man surprises them. It's a wake-up call. They begin to realize the potential and courage in their daughter. By the end of the story, they no longer see her as a burden but as a strong individual capable of making her own decisions. This change in their viewpoint is subtle but significant, highlighting how parents can learn from their children too.

32. Compare the approach of the people in Coorg towards their environment with the approach of Custard towards facing challenges in his life. Write your insights in about 120 words.

Ans. The people of Coorg have a deep connection with their environment, living amidst lush coffee plantations and rainforests, showing respect and harmony with nature. Their lifestyle integrates with the natural world, appreciating its bounty and preserving its beauty. In contrast, Custard the Dragon from "The Tale of Custard the Dragon" faces challenges with a mix of fear and bravery. Initially seen as cowardly for desiring a safe cage, Custard ultimately confronts a pirate, proving his courage. While the Coorg people live in harmony with nature daily, Custard's bravery emerges when faced with immediate danger. Both scenarios teach the value of understanding one's environment or situation, whether it's the steady courage of living with nature in Coorg or Custard's sudden act of bravery amidst fear.

33. You've been invited to speak to a group of students about overcoming fears and breaking free from restrictions, drawing parallels between the themes in "His First Flight" and "A Tiger in the Zoo." Prepare your speech draft in not more than 120 words.

Ans. Facing fears and breaking free from restrictions are vital lessons in life, much like the young seagull in "His First Flight" and the tiger in "A Tiger in the Zoo." The young seagull, initially terrified to fly, eventually conquers his fear by taking a leap into the unknown, learning that bravery is about facing your fears head-on. Similarly, "A Tiger in the Zoo" depicts a tiger trapped in an environment that restricts its natural instincts and freedom. This contrast between confinement and the wild's openness reflects the limitations we sometimes face and how they hinder our true potential. Drawing parallels, both narratives encourage us to break free from the metaphorical cages that hold us back, urging us to embrace the freedom and growth that come from facing our fears and challenging our limitations.

34. You have been chosen to give a presentation discussing the themes of faith and providence as presented in "A Letter to God" and "The Black Aeroplane." Prepare your presentation draft in no more than 120 words.

You may begin this way: ***Good afternoon, I am honored to discuss two stories today that delve into the themes of faith and providence, namely 'A Letter to God' and 'The Black Aeroplane'...***

Ans. Good afternoon. Today, let's talk about the fascinating themes of faith and providence as shown in "A Letter to God" and "The Black Aeroplane." In "A Letter to God," Lencho has immense faith in God to help him through tough times. Despite losing his crops, he believes God will save him and writes a letter asking for help. His faith is so strong that he even believes the money sent by the postmaster is from God. Similarly, in "The Black Aeroplane," the pilot puts his faith in a mysterious black aeroplane that guides him safely through the storm. In both stories, the characters are saved through what they believe is divine intervention, highlighting the power of faith and the mysterious ways in which help can arrive.

35. Compare the role of the baker in the Goan community from "A Baker from Goa" with the metaphorical fog in Carl Sandburg's "Fog" in shaping their respective environments. Discuss how each contributes to the atmosphere and mood of their settings. Write your answer in about 120 words.

Ans. The baker from "A Baker from Goa" deeply touches his community's life, spreading joy and warmth as he goes about his daily bread delivery, reminding folks of cherished traditions. This baker's presence strengthens bonds among neighbors, keeping their shared history alive. In contrast, Carl Sandburg's "Fog" silently transforms its landscape into a serene and slightly mysterious world, offering a brief pause to admire nature's quiet grace. While the baker nurtures community ties and celebrates enduring customs, the fog invites a moment of quiet reflection, showcasing the beauty of fleeting moments. Despite their differences, both play vital roles in their settings: the baker enriches community life with human warmth, whereas the fog gently highlights the natural world's ephemeral (momentary) beauty. Each, in its way, adds a unique layer to the atmosphere of its environment.

36. A character arc is the transformation or development of a character throughout a story and refers to the changes a character undergoes as a result of their experiences, challenges, and interactions with other characters.

In the light of the above information, trace the character arc of the thief in Ruskin Bond's The Thief's Story, in about 120 words. (CBSE SQP, 2023)

Ans. In the story, we follow a thief who starts off living a life of crime, always trying to outsmart the law. He meets Anil and thinks he can easily deceive him. However, as they spend time together, Anil teaches the thief to cook, read, and write, sparking a change in him. This change peaks when the thief decides not to steal money from Anil, showing he's beginning to think about right and wrong. Initially, he only cared about himself, but now, he's hesitant to continue his life of crime. The story suggests the thief starts to see that crime doesn't lead to happiness and is considering a new, honest path for a better future.

37. Explain with reference to the lesson "Nelson Mandela - Long Walk to Freedom", the following statement, "Hunger for freedom" is the greatest virtue which one enjoys. How did Mandela fight for freedom?
(Nelson Mandela - Long Walk to Freedom)

Ans. In the lesson "Nelson Mandela: Long Walk to Freedom," the phrase "hunger for freedom" highlights the intense desire and determination for liberation, which Mandela viewed as the most admirable quality. Mandela fought for freedom by joining the African National Congress, becoming actively involved in the anti-apartheid movement. Despite facing immense challenges, including 27 years in prison, Mandela's dedication never wavered. His struggle was not just for his own freedom but for the liberation of all South Africans from racial discrimination and inequality. Mandela's leadership was pivotal in ending apartheid and establishing a democratic South Africa, where he became the first black president. His journey from a freedom-hungry young man to a wise leader shows the power of resilience and the importance of fighting for justice and equality for all.

38. You have been selected to talk to a group of young students about the paradox of courage and vulnerability in facing life's challenges. Create a speech draft in not more than 120 words, drawing parallels between the characters in "The Proposal" and "The Tale of Custard the Dragon".

Ans. In "The Proposal" and "The Tale of Custard the Dragon," we see how courage and vulnerability play out in unexpected ways. In "The Proposal," characters quarrel over land and dogs, showing boldness but also revealing their insecurities during the conflict. Similarly, in "The Tale of Custard the Dragon," Custard is seen as timid, yet he's the one who bravely defeats the pirate when danger arises. Both stories teach us that courage isn't about never being scared. It's about facing fears and sometimes, about showing vulnerability. Just like Lomov shows courage to propose amidst quarrels and Custard fights the pirate despite his fears, we learn that bravery and vulnerability are two sides of the same coin in life's challenges.

39. Imagine that M. Loisel, from The Necklace by Guy de Maupassant, writes a diary entry, exploring the theme of class and social status, and the nature of social mobility, in the context of his own experience.
Write this diary entry, as M. Loisel, in about 120 words.
(CBSE SQP, 2023)

Ans. It's been a tough the past few years, for my wife, Matilda, and me. As I reflect on our experience, I can't help but think about the broader societal issues that have contributed to our predicament. It's clear to me now that our society is structured in a way that makes upward mobility difficult, if not impossible. The rich get richer, while the rest of us struggle to make ends meet. We live in a world where social status is determined by the amount of wealth one possesses, rather than by one's character or virtues. This narrow view of success has led many people, including Matilda, to pursue material possessions at the expense of their own happiness. The loss of the borrowed necklace was a painful lesson for both of us. It reminded us that the pursuit of social status and upward mobility can be a trap, leading people to sacrifice their happiness and well-being in the pursuit of an unattainable dream.

40. You have been asked to present an evaluation of the contrasting lifestyles in 'Glimpses of India' and the humor in 'How to Tell Wild Animals'. Write this presentation draft, including your insights, in about 120-130 words, comparing these two very different pieces.

Ans. "Glimpses of India" captures the essence of traditional lifestyles across various Indian landscapes, highlighting the deep-rooted cultural practices in Goa, Coorg, and Assam. It paints vivid images of the Goan baker, the serene beauty of Coorg's coffee plantations, and the rich tea gardens of Assam, each narrative rich with the local flavor and traditions. Contrarily, "How to Tell Wild Animals" employs humor to navigate the wild, offering whimsical (playful) advice on identifying dangerous animals, blending wit with wildlife knowledge. While "Glimpses of India" offers a sincere portrayal of India's diverse cultures and their harmony with nature, the poem humorously challenges our understanding of the wild, showcasing the amusing side of human interaction with nature. Together, they provide a multifaceted view of life's seriousness and humor.

41. You have been invited to speak at a community gathering about the universal lessons that can be learned from "The Sermon at Benares" and "The Trees". Prepare a speech draft in not more than 120 words, highlighting the shared themes of change and acceptance in these two pieces.

Ans. In "The Sermon at Benares" and "The Trees," we learn about change and acceptance. Buddha's sermon teaches us to accept death as part of life, showing us that grief and loss are universal experiences that everyone must face. Similarly, "The Trees" speaks of change, depicting trees breaking free from confinement, symbolizing growth and liberation. Both pieces encourage us to embrace change as a natural part of existence, urging us to find peace in acceptance. They remind us that though life involves suffering and loss, understanding and accepting these truths can lead to enlightenment and freedom. These universal lessons highlight the importance of embracing life's inevitable changes with grace and understanding.

42. You have been invited to talk to a group of students about the power of hope and dealing with loss, drawing on themes from "A Letter to God" and "The Ball Poem." Prepare your speech draft in not more than 120 words.

Ans. In "A Letter to God" and "The Ball Poem," we explore hope and dealing with loss. Lencho, despite losing his crops to hail, never loses hope. His unwavering faith in God shows us that hope can guide us through tough times. Similarly, the boy in "The Ball Poem" faces the loss of his ball, symbolizing his first encounter with loss and growing up. This poem teaches us that letting go and facing the pain of loss is part of growing up. Both stories remind us that hope and acceptance are powerful tools in facing life's challenges. While Lencho's hope lies in divine intervention, the boy's loss teaches him the harsh realities of life, underlining that hope and resilience are crucial in overcoming adversities.

43. You have been chosen to present your evaluation on "Sometimes we learn many things from the act of punishment. Write this presentation draft including your insights, in about 120 words in reference to the lesson 'From the diary of Anne Frank'.

Ans. In "From the Diary of Anne Frank," Anne's experiences with punishment, notably from her teacher Mr. Keesing, illustrate that discipline can lead to unexpected growth and learning. When Anne is punished for talking too much in class, rather than becoming resentful, she engages in the task by writing essays. This not only showcases her creativity but also changes Mr. Keesing's view of her, eventually leading him to enjoy her lively nature. This situation highlights how punishment, when approached with the right attitude, can transform into a learning opportunity, encouraging personal development and mutual understanding. Anne's story teaches us that facing consequences can lead to positive outcomes, including improved relationships and self-expression.

44. You have been asked to give a speech on the topic 'The journey is more important than the destination'. Prepare a draft for the speech, in not more than 120 words, with reference to the texts Madam Rides the Bus and The Black Aeroplane. (CBSE APQ, 2023) 6

You may begin this way:

Good morning, everyone. Today, I would like to talk to you about how the journeys that we experience in life are often more important than their destinations.

You may end this way:

To conclude, I would like to say that... Thank you.

Ans. Good morning, everyone. Today, I would like to talk to you about how the journeys that we experience in life are often more important than their destinations. In the story "Madam Rides the Bus," Valli's bus journey is not just a physical trip but a journey of discovery, filled with new experiences, joys, and the harsh realities of life, much more enriching than merely reaching the town. Similarly, "The Black Aeroplane" tells of a pilot's mysterious flight, where the journey's unexpected turns and the unknown helper make the flight memorable, not just the safe landing. Both stories highlight that it's the experiences, lessons, and memories we gather along our journeys that truly shape us, not just the endpoint. To conclude, I would like to say that the essence of our lives lies in the paths we take and the experiences we gather, not just the goals we achieve. Thank you.

45. You are asked to compare the approach of Pranjol's father, who is a tea-estate manager in Assam, in educating Pranjol about tea cultivation with the manner in which Amanda's mother deals with Amanda's behavior and dreams. Write a brief evaluation discussing the differences and similarities in their approaches.
Reference: "Tea from Assam" and "Amanda!"

Ans. Pranjol's father, managing a tea estate in Assam, gently educates about tea cultivation, sharing knowledge and fostering curiosity, encouraging learning through direct experience and storytelling. Contrastingly, Amanda's mother, in her approach to Amanda's behavior and dreams, uses a series of commands and reprimands, focusing on discipline and conformity rather than exploration. While Pranjol is encouraged to embrace his heritage and learn, Amanda is urged to conform to expectations, stifling her imaginative world. Both parents aim to guide their children, but their methods diverge: one through engagement and education, the other through control and correction. This highlights the difference in nurturing curiosity versus enforcing discipline, though both seek to prepare their children for the world.

46. A desire is more personal whereas a vision has broader connotations. You have been asked to present an analysis of Valli's desire and Mandela's vision and how they are respectively fulfilled. Write this presentation draft including your insights, in about 120 words, comparing the approaches of both Valli and Mandela.

You may begin like this:

One acknowledges that both, Valli and Mandela _______ however,

(Reference - Nelson Mandela - A Long Walk to Freedom & Madam Rides a Bus)

Ans. Valli's desire to ride the bus represents a child's simple, personal wish to experience something new, reflecting innocence and a small-scale desire. In contrast, Mandela's vision symbolizes a deep, collective longing for equality and freedom, impacting an entire nation's future.

Valli, through her calculated planning and savings, achieves her goal independently, illustrating determination at a personal level. Mandela, however, through years of struggle and determination, realized his vision of ending apartheid, showcasing the power of resilience and leadership in bringing about significant societal changes.

Both journeys inspire one to pursue both personal dreams and larger societal visions with courage and determination.

47. You have been chosen to address the student gathering from the nearby schools, to speak on "How to Deal with Loss - Personal or Material". Prepare the speech draft in not more than 120 words, with reference to the commonality of themes in John Berryman's. 'The Ball Poem' and 'A Sermon at Benaras'.

You may begin this way.

Good Morning everyone. Today, Id like to discuss two pieces of literature that offer a powerful insight into how we can learn to deal with loss.

You may end in this way -

To conclude, I'd like to say that -

Thank you.

Ans. Good Morning everyone. Today, I'd like to discuss two pieces of literature that offer a powerful insight into how we can learn to deal with loss. "The Ball Poem" by John Berryman captures the poignant moment of a boy losing his ball, symbolizing the loss of innocence and the first step toward maturity.

He learns that possessions are impermanent, and through loss, we learn to move on. Similarly, "A Sermon at Benares" by Gautama Buddha discusses overcoming grief. After the death of her son, Kisa Gotami learns that death is a natural and universal process.

Both texts teach us to accept loss as an inevitable part of life and that through loss, we gain strength and understanding. To conclude, I'd like to say that these narratives are vital in teaching us the resilience(strength) necessary to face the personal and material losses we encounter.

Thank you.

❑❑❑

MOCK TEST PAPERS

Scan Me for Detailed Mock Test Explanations

MOCK TEST PAPER-1

Time allowed : 3 hours | **Maximum Marks : 80**

GENERAL INSTRUCTIONS:

*(i) This question paper comprises **11** questions. **All** questions are compulsory.*

*(ii) The question paper contains **THREE** sections- Reading Skills, Writing Skills and Grammar, Literature Textbook.*

(iii) Attempt questions based on specific instructions for each part.

SECTION - A

READING SKILLS **(20 marks)**

1. Read the following text. **(10 m)**

1. My childhood had always been a sheltered one. My parents, along with my teachers, tried to instill good ethics in me. But sharing was one moral value which I was never comfortable with. "Why should I give?" It was my question. During one vacation to my hometown, I was at the railway station with my parents. As we were waiting for a train, something caught my attention. Two small children, perhaps siblings, were seeking alms nearby. Though they appeared at ease, I was shocked by their overall untidiness. When they approached us, my father promptly gave the older one some money.

2. Those were the days when I was constantly reminded of the virtues of —sharing" things with others. So, when my mother nudged me, I knew why and the look my mother gave me, confirmed. I had a pack of my favourite chocolates in my pocket and, even though I pretended to have forgotten about it, she remembered them. I was devastated. With a heavy heart I fished out one and placed reluctantly on the outstretched hand of the girl. She flashed a smile and the duo moved on. But my gaze never left them as I wanted to know about the fate of my chocolate. After a while I saw her unwrap it. She then did something which moved me. Without a moment's hesitation, she put the chocolate in her brother's mouth and watched his face brighten up as he savoured it. Her action puzzled me. Why did she not eat it herself? Regret and shame overcame me when I realised that I had deliberately given only one chocolate. I quickly decided to give her one more chocolate voluntarily. Strangely, my actions made me feel better than I had thought. As our train approached the station, the girl rushed to give me something. It was a small paper doll which she had made with the wrapper of the chocolates. I was speechless. Was she trying to convey a —Thank you? That little girl taught me the joy of sharing and also answered one big question of —Why should I give? I now ask "Why not?", as sharing is all about loving. Happiness abounds when shared.

3. Years have rolled by and I still cherish that valuable lesson I learnt during that vacation. Sometimes life teaches us things we fail to learn from classrooms. I still think of that girl and her brother and wonder where they would be now. Those sparkling eyes and beautiful smile.

Answer the following questions, based on the passage above.

(*i*) What emotion does the author express through the phrase "I was devastated" in the passage? (paragraph 2) **1**

(*ii*) How does the author's inner conflict about sharing reflect a broader theme in "Life is Beautiful"? Provide an explanation in 40 words of how this internal struggle contributes to the overall message of the passage. **2**

(*iii*) Complete the following with the correct option from the two given. (paragraph 2) **1**

The author's memory of the little girl and her brother impacts them because ________.

(*a*) They still think about their smile and wonder where they might be now.

(*b*) They regret not giving more chocolates to the children.

(*iv*) State whether the following statement is True or False. (paragraph 2) 1

The author gave both children chocolates willingly and without hesitation when his mother reminded him about sharing.

(*v*) Select the option that best reflects the concept of 'sharing' in the context of the given passage. (paragraph 2) 1

(*a*) Sharing only because someone else insists.

(*b*) Sharing willingly and experiencing joy from the act.

(*vi*) How does the author's initial discomfort with sharing contrast with the lesson they learn from the little girl's actions? Explain in your own words. (Word limit: 40). 2

(*vii*) Fill in the blank with the correct option from those given. (paragraph 2) 1

The emotional shift in the author's tone as the passage progresses is evident when it changes from ________ to ________.

(*a*) joyful; melancholic (*b*) frustrated; satisfied

(*c*) sombre; indifferent (*d*) curious; indifferent

(*viii*) How did the author feel after giving the girl another chocolate? 1

(*a*) Angry and frustrated. (*b*) Indifferent and uncaring.

(*c*) Better than expected. (*d*) Regretful and sad.

2. Read the following text. **(10 m)**

SPEEDING UP INDIA'S JOURNEY BY BULLET TRAINS

By: Vijay Kumar Dutt

1. Indian Railways High speed in Indian Railways is at present limited to 150 KMPH. However, in many other countries the speed of Railways is of the order of 200 KM per hour (KMPH). In France, Japan, Germany, China, Spain and South Korea high speed traction above 280 KMPH has been introduced. India and Japan have signed a memorandum of understanding (MoU) on 12th December, 2015 on cooperation and assistance in the Mumbai–Ahmedabad High Speed Rail (HSR) Project referred to by many as the Bullet Train Project. Japan has offered an assistance of over Rs. 79,000 crore for the project. The loan is for a period of 50 years with a moratorium of 15 years, at an interest rate of 0.1 per cent.
2. The project is a 508-kilometre Railway line costing a total of Rs. 97,636 crore, to be implemented in a period of seven years. It has been agreed for the Mumbai – Ahmedabad HSR Project. Japan's Shinkansen Technology, known for its speed, reliability and safety, will be adopted. Transfer of technology and "Make in India" will be an essential part of this assistance package. Japan will also assist India in training personnel for HSR. The two countries have also entered into two comprehensive technological cooperation agreements on 11th December 2015, for modernization and up gradation of Indian railways.
3. These agreements have been signed during the official visit to India of His Excellency Mr. Shinzo Abe, the Prime Minister of Japan, during December 11-13, 2015.

Answer the following questions, based on the passage above.

(*i*) Complete the sentence appropriately. 1

The Mumbai-Ahmedabad High-Speed Rail Project aims to adopt Japan's Shinkansen Technology, ______________ .

(*ii*) Complete the following with a suitable reason, with reference to the passage provided above: 1

The introduction of the Mumbai–Ahmedabad High-Speed Rail Project, facilitated by a memorandum of understanding (MoU) between India and Japan, can be considered a fact because __________.

(*iii*) How does the Mumbai-Ahmedabad High-Speed Rail Project, with assistance from Japan, aim to significantly enhance India's railway infrastructure and modernization efforts? Answer in about 40 words. 2

(*iv*) What key aspect of India's railway modernization does Japan's Shinkansen technology contribute to in the Mumbai- Ahmedabad High-Speed Rail Project? 1

(*v*) What is one inference that can be drawn from the passage regarding the collaboration between India and Japan on the Mumbai-Ahmedabad High-Speed Rail Project? 1

(*vi*) Identify the word that indicates the financial support provided by Japan for the Mumbai–Ahmedabad High-Speed Rail Project. 1

(*a*) Loan (*b*) Moratorium

(*c*) Assistance (*d*) Agreement

(*vii*) Read the given prompt and select the correct option in the brackets to fill in the blank. 1

The Mumbai–Ahmedabad High-Speed Rail Project involves a loan with a 50-year repayment period and a 15-year moratorium at a 0.1% interest rate. Japan is providing technological assistance through its Shinkansen Technology.

The loan structure for the Mumbai–Ahmedabad High-Speed Rail Project benefits India by providing ____________.

(increased repayment burden / longer repayment time / higher project costs).

(*viii*) How does the loan terms for the Mumbai–Ahmedabad High-Speed Rail Project, with a 50-year duration and 15-year moratorium, influence the financial feasibility of the project? **1**

(*a*) It increases the burden of repayment in the initial years.

(*b*) It provides a longer period for repayment, easing financial stress.

(*c*) It discourages India from accepting international assistance.

(*d*) It ensures a high-interest rate, impacting overall project costs.

(*ix*) Select the option that is true for the assertion and reason given below. **1**

Assertion: The Mumbai–Ahmedabad High-Speed Rail Project will be implemented using Japan's Shinkansen Technology.

Reason: Shinkansen Technology has been selected because it is cost-effective for India.

(*a*) Both the assertion and reason are true, and the reason is the correct explanation of the assertion.

(*b*) Both the assertion and reason are true, but the reason is not the correct explanation of the assertion.

(*c*) The assertion is true, but the reason is false.

(*d*) The assertion is false, but the reason is true.

SECTION - B

WRITING SKILLS & GRAMMAR (20 marks)

GRAMMAR 10

3. Attempt ANY TEN of twelve of the following questions. (10 × 1 = 10)

(*i*) Fill in the blank by using the correct form of the word in the bracket, for the given portion of an article:

The research findings ________ (strong) the need for stricter environmental regulations in industrial zones.

(*ii*) Read the given sentence from a travel blog. Identify the error and supply the correction in the sentence.

The beautiful beach view was really breath-taking and reminds me of my childhood summer vacations.

Use the given format for your response.

Error	Correction

(*iii*) Rohan and Sarah had a conversation about the destination of summer vacation. Report Rohan's question.

Have you decided your summer vacation destination yet?

(*iv*) Read the dialogue between Aakash and Neetu.

Aakash: Why did you decide to take up gardening as a hobby?

Neetu: Well, I find it incredibly relaxing and healing.

Select the correct option to complete the reporting of the above dialogue.

Aakash asked Neetu ________________ as a hobby. Neetu replied that she found it incredibly relaxing and healing.

(*a*) why did she decide to take up gardening

(*b*) why she had decided to take up gardening

(*c*) why do you decide to take up gardening

(*d*) why you decided to take up gardening

(*v*) Fill the blank by choosing the correct option, to complete the following.

In the email to all staff members, please make sure to attach the revised guidelines and __________ (those/then/these) should be reviewed before our meeting on Friday.

(*vi*) Identify the error and supply the correction for the following sentence from the travel agency's promotional campaign.

Our agency ensures the best accommodations in all the exotic destinations.

Use the given format for your response.

Error	Correction

(*vii*) Select the option that identifies the error and supplies the correction for the following sentence from a research paper.

The study examines the relationship amongst diet and heart health.

Option	Error	Correction
(*a*)	**examines**	**examine**
(*b*)	**amongst**	**between**
(*c*)	**and**	**or**
(*d*)	**relationship**	**relation**

(*viii*) Complete the sentence by filling in the blank with the correct option:

Her recent success at the competition made her ____________ proud of her hard work and dedication.

(*a*) feeling (*b*) having felt (*c*) feel (*d*) feels

(*ix*) Report the conversation between the teacher and the student by completing the sentence:

Teacher: How have you been finding the new maths lessons?

Student: Honestly, a bit challenging at first, but I'm starting to understand better now.

The teacher inquired about the student's experience with the new maths lessons, and the student responded by admitting that __________ .

(*x*) Fill the blank by choosing the correct option to complete the announcement during a school assembly.

The science fair results are in! We are proud to announce that our robotics team ____________ the top honours.

(*a*) had been awarded (*b*) will be awarding (*c*) was awarded (*d*) has been awarded

(*xi*) Complete the line from a motivational speech by choosing the correct option:

If doubts cloud your mind, know that you ____________ the clarity to see through them.

(*a*) will have (*b*) have (*c*) had (*d*) having

(*xii*) Identify the error and supply the correction for the following sentence in a user manual for a smartphone:

To unlock your phone, swipe down from the top of the screen, than enter your PIN.

Use the given format for your response.

Error	Correction

WRITING 10

Note: All details presented in the questions are imaginary and created for assessment purpose.

4. Attempt ANY ONE from A and B given below: **5**

(A) Write a letter in 100-120 words to the Editor of The Times of India, Delhi, expressing your concerns about the urgent need to save our rivers. Suggest some ways to improve the situation. Sign yourself as Renuka Sinha.

OR

(B) Virtual World in the present scenario seems to have completely taken the people in its grip. Particularly the young generation finds it much more appealing than the physical and practical one. As the Head Girl/Head Boy, write a letter to your school's Principal, expressing your concern over its pros and cons. You are Alakh/Arya, a resident of 235, Krishna Niwas, Indra Colony, New Delhi. (150–200 words)

5. Attempt ANY ONE from A and B given below: **5**

(A) Read the product details on a label for a pair of running shoes:

HIGH-PERFORMANCE RUNNING SHOES

1. Lightweight and breathable mesh fabric
2. Cushioned sole for shock absorption
3. Anti-slip rubber outsole for traction
4. Arch support for comfort during long runs
5. Available in various sizes and colors
6. Water-resistant material for use in all weather conditions

Now, assess why these running shoes would be a smart investment. Write an analytical paragraph in 120 words, considering factors such as comfort, performance, durability, and design.

OR

(B) Read the given details of a community library planned for your neighborhood:

1. A dedicated children's section with colorful seating, storytime areas, and educational toys
2. A quiet study area for adults with comfortable chairs and individual reading lights
3. Digital resources including e-books and tablets for easy access to information
4. A cafe section with snacks and drinks, overlooking an outdoor reading garden
5. Regular book clubs and reading events for different age groups
6. Free Wi-Fi and printing services

Analyse the details and write an analytical paragraph in about 120 words about the suitability of this library.

Focus on factors such as accessibility, resource variety, atmosphere, suitability for different age groups, and overall community benefit.

SECTION - C

LITERATURE TEXTBOOK (40 marks)

6. Read the given extracts and answer the questions for ANY ONE of the two, given. **5**

(A) **CHUBUKOV:** What a weight off my shoulders, ouf!

NATALYA: But, still, you will admit now that Guess is worse than Squeezer.

LOMOV: Better! NATALYA: Worse!

CHUBUKOV: Well, that's a way to start your family bliss! Have some champagne!

LOMOV: He's better! NATALYA: Worse! Worse! Worse!

CHUBUKOV: [trying to shout her down] Champagne! Champagne!

(*The Proposal*)

(*i*) From the line "What a weight off my shoulders, ouf!", what can be inferred about Chubukov's feelings? **1**

(*ii*) What can be inferred from Chubukov's exclamation "What a weight off my shoulders, ouf!" in the extract? **1**

(*a*) He is angry.

(*b*) He feels a sense of relief.

(*c*) He is feeling nervous.

(*d*) He is frustrated.

(*iii*) With reference to the extract, explain the disagreement between Natalya and Lomov regarding the comparison of "Guess" and "Squeezer" in about 40 words. **2**

(*iv*) Fill in the blank with the correct word from the bracket. **1**

From the line "What a weight off my shoulders, ouf!", it can be inferred that Chubukov feels _________. (relieved / confused)

OR

(B) The Buddha answered, "I want a handful of mustard seed." And when the girl in her joy promised to procure it, the Buddha added, "The mustard seed must be taken from a house where no one has lost a child, husband, parent or friend." Poor Kisa Gotami now went from house to house, and the people pitied her and said, "Here is a mustard seed; take it!" But when she asked, "Did a son or daughter, a father or mother, die in your family?" they answered her, "Alas! The living are few, but the dead are many. Do not remind us of our deepest grief." And there was no house but some beloved one had died in it.

(*The Sermon at the Benares*)

(*i*) Which of the following is NOT a reason why Kisa Gotami is unable to find the mustard seed? **1**

(*a*) She was not looking for it properly.

(*b*) She cannot find a house where no one has lost a loved one.

(*c*) The people do not want to be reminded of their grief.

(*d*) She is unable to locate the specific type of mustard seed.

(*ii*) Describe the emotions that Kisa Gotami experiences as she goes from house to house in search of the mustard seed. (Word limit: 40 words) **2** (*iii*) Fill in the blanks with the correct word from the bracket. 1

The Buddha asked Kisa Gotami to bring mustard seeds from a house where ________. (no one had experienced a loss / everyone had lost a loved one)

(*iv*) Why did the Buddha ask Kisa Gotami to find mustard seeds from a house where no one had lost a loved one? 1

7. Read the given extracts and answer the questions for ANY ONE of the two, given. **5**

(A) The way a crow
Shook down on me
The dust of snow
From a hemlock tree
(*Dust of Snow*)

(*i*) Fill the blank with ONE word. 1

The significance of the 'dust of snow' falling from the hemlock tree is ________.

(*ii*) What is the significance of the 'dust of snow' falling from the hemlock tree? 1

(*iii*) Choose the option that applies the same rhyme scheme as the lines of the extract. 1

(*a*) **The wind so cold,**
Blew on the shore,
The night grew old,
And darkness poured more.

(*b*) **The moonlight shines so bright,**
Casting shadows on the trees,
The stars dance in the sky,
As whispers float upon the breeze.

(*c*) **The leaves so green,**
Fell on the ground,
With a crackling sound,
As they danced unseen.

(*d*) **The cat that walks by night,**
Leaps with all its might,
Catching every mouse,
Before heading back to the house.

(*iv*) Comment on the use of imagery in these lines. 2

OR

(B) Some say the world will end in fire
Some say in ice.
From what I've tasted of desire
I hold with those who favour fire.
(*Fire and Ice*)

(*i*) How does the language in the poem deviate from conventional poetic expressions? 1

(*ii*) What is the significance of the word "desire" in the poem, and how does it shape the poem's overall mood and tone? Answer in about 40 words. 2

(*iii*) Based on the content of the poem, what do the contrasting elements of fire and ice symbolise? 1

(*a*) Passion and desire
(*b*) Hatred and destruction
(*c*) Urban and rural
(*d*) Warmth and coldness

(*iv*) Complete the following suitably. 1

The word "fire" in the poem implies ________.

8. Answer ANY FOUR of the following five questions, in about 40-50 words. **(4 × 3 = 12)**

(*i*) Justify the opinion that the relationship between humans and animals is portrayed as significant in the chapter "Mijbil the Otter."

(*ii*) How does the poet use vivid imagery and metaphorical language in the chapter "Fog" to effectively depict the feeling of uncertainty and confusion?

(*iii*) Explain how the description of the storm intensifies the sense of danger and urgency in the chapter "Black Aeroplane" from "The First Flight".

Refer to the given lines from the text, "The clouds were coming towards me, black and angry. I knew I couldn't fly up and over them, and I didn't have enough fuel to fly around them."

(*iv*) Describe the role of Kisa Gotami in "The Sermon at Benares."

(*v*) How does the chapter "For Anne Gregory" challenge the notion that physical beauty is the most important aspect of a person?

9. Answer ANY TWO of the following three questions, in about 40-50 words. **(2 × 3 = 6)**

(*i*) Justify the opinion that the chapter "The Book That Saved the Earth" highlights the importance of literature and storytelling in preserving knowledge and culture.

(*ii*) In the lesson 'The Thief's Story', what role does Anil's innocence play in Hari's life?

(*iii*) In the lesson "The Triumph of Surgery", explain the relationships between the characters in the story. Comment with reference to the context.

10. Answer ANY ONE of the following two questions, in about 100-120 words. **6**

(A) You have been asked to present an evaluation of the theme of "faith" in both "A Letter to God" and "The Ball Poem." Write this presentation draft including your insights, in about 120 words, comparing the theme of faith in both.

You may begin this way: *One acknowledges that both "A Letter to God" and "The Ball Poem" portray characters who face challenging situations that test their faith; however, ...*

(Reference - "A Letter to God" and "The Ball Poem")

OR

(B) You have been asked to present an evaluation of the character of Nelson Mandela and the theme of "resilience" in both "Nelson Mandela" and "Trees." Write this presentation draft including your insights, in about 120 words, comparing the character of Mandela and the theme of resilience in both.

You may begin this way: *One acknowledges that both texts "Nelson Mandela" and "Trees" exhibit remarkable resilience in the face of adversity; however, ...*

(Reference - "Nelson Mandela" and "The Trees")

11. Answer ANY ONE of the following two questions, in about 100-120 words. **6**

(A) In the passage provided, we learn about the journey of Richard Ebright, a young and determined scientist. Imagine you are Richard Ebright and you are writing a diary entry reflecting on your scientific journey and the key moments that led to your breakthroughs. Describe your early fascination with collecting butterflies and your evolving interest in science. Reflect on the challenges you faced, the experiments you undertook, and the qualities that contributed to your success. In about 120 words, capture the essence of how your curiosity and determination paved the way for your achievements in the field of science.

OR

(B) A character arc is the transformation or development of a character throughout a story and refers to the changes a character undergoes as a result of their experiences, challenges, and interactions with other characters. In the light of the above information, trace the character arc of Bholi in "Bholi," in about 120 words.

MOCK TEST PAPER-2

Time allowed : 3 hours **Maximum Marks : 80**

GENERAL INSTRUCTIONS:

*(i) This question paper comprises **11** questions. **All** questions are compulsory.*

*(ii) The question paper contains **THREE** sections- Reading Skills, Writing Skills and Grammar, Literature Textbook.*

(iii) Attempt questions based on specific instructions for each part.

SECTION - A

READING SKILLS

(20 marks)

1. Read the following text. **(10 m)**

1. In the realm of Fantasy Adventure, heroes are often faced with daunting challenges that test their strength, courage, and determination. These challenges come in various forms, from treacherous quests to battles against formidable foes. Just like in our own lives, these challenges serve as opportunities for growth and self-discovery. They push the boundaries of what is possible and reveal the true potential within us.

2. Imagine a young hero, thrust into a world of magic and danger, tasked with a seemingly impossible mission. At first, they may feel overwhelmed, doubting their abilities and questioning whether they are capable of triumphing over the obstacles that lie ahead. But as they embark on their quest, they begin to realize that the greatest challenges often hide the greatest rewards. Through perseverance and unwavering determination, they learn to navigate treacherous terrains, outsmart cunning adversaries, and unlock their hidden strengths. It is through these challenges that they discover their true potential and become the heroes they were destined to be.

3. Along their journey, our hero encounters a diverse cast of characters, each with their own unique challenges to overcome. They form unlikely alliances and learn the value of teamwork and friendship. Together, they face insurmountable odds, supporting and uplifting one another when the going gets tough. They remind us that we don't have to face our challenges alone. By leaning on the strengths of others and offering our own support, we can conquer even the most formidable obstacles.

4. In Fantasy Adventure, challenges often come in the form of mythical creatures and mystical realms. These fantastical elements serve as metaphors for the challenges we face in our own lives. Just as our hero battles dragons and navigates enchanted forests, we too must confront our fears and venture into the unknown. The journey may be perilous, but it is through these challenges that we discover our true selves and unlock our inner magic.

5. As our hero reaches the climax of their adventure, they are faced with the ultimate challenge, a test of their character and resolve. It is in this moment that they realize that the greatest challenge they must overcome is not external, but internal. They must confront their own doubts, fears, and insecurities. It is through this introspection and self-reflection that they find the strength to overcome the impossible and emerge victorious.

6. In conclusion, Fantasy Adventure offers us a captivating world filled with challenges that mirror the ones we face in our own lives. Through the journey of our hero, we learn that challenges are not meant to break us, but to shape us into the heroes we are meant to be. They teach us the importance of perseverance, teamwork, and self-belief. So, the next time you find yourself facing a daunting challenge, remember the lessons learned from the world of Fantasy Adventure and embrace the opportunity to overcome and grow.

Answer the following questions, based on the passage above.

(*i*) Which of the following best describes the author's attitude towards challenges in the realm of Fantasy Adventure? **1**

(*a*) Challenges in Fantasy Adventure are insurmountable and impossible to overcome.

(*b*) Challenges in Fantasy Adventure are opportunities for growth and self-discovery.

(*c*) Challenges in Fantasy Adventure are trivial and insignificant.

(*d*) Challenges in Fantasy Adventure are meant to break the heroes.

(*ii*) What is the tone of the writer in the given lines from the paragraph? Rationalize your response in about 40 words: **2**

Through perseverance and unwavering determination, they learn to navigate treacherous terrains, outsmart cunning adversaries, and unlock their hidden strengths.

(*iii*) Complete the sentence appropriately:

The author's main argument in the paragraph is that ______. **1**

(*iv*) From the sets below, identify the set of synonyms based on the paragraph: **1**

(*a*) Overwhelming - Easy (*b*) Treacherous - Safe
(*c*) Formidable - Weak (*d*) Exhilarating - Thrilling

(*v*) Complete the sentence appropriately.

Based on the reading of the paragraph, it can be inferred that the author's perspective on challenges in Fantasy Adventure is ______. **1**

(*vi*) Based on the reading of the paragraph, compare the author's viewpoint on challenges in Fantasy Adventure to facing challenges in real life. Explain in about 40 words. **2**

(*vii*) What message is conveyed by the hero's encounter with diverse characters in the paragraph? **1**

(*a*) The hero should avoid forming alliances with others.

(*b*) The hero should rely solely on their own strengths to overcome challenges.

(*c*) The hero learns the value of teamwork and friendship in overcoming challenges.

(*d*) The hero realizes that others are not trustworthy and should be avoided.

(*viii*) Classify the following lines from the paragraph as lessons learned from Fantasy Adventure/characteristics of the hero/challenges faced by the hero: **1**

They form unlikely alliances and learn the value of teamwork and friendship. Together, they face insurmountable odds, supporting and uplifting one another when the going gets tough.

2. Read the following text. **(10 m)**

1. Ayurveda, or the science of life, is an ancient system of Indian medicine that is 4000 years old. According to Ayurveda, health depends on the normal balance of three elements of the body-vata (air), pitho (bile), and kapha (phlegm).

2. Information about the system with proof is contained in two important medical treatises in Sanskrit language - the Charaka Samhita and the Sushruta Samhita, considered as belonging to the physician Charaka, and Sushruta who were surgeons. These are compilations of up-to-date medical knowledge made in the 1st century AD and later in the 7th century AD. Another work widely followed in recent times is Vaghabhatta's 'Ashtangahridoyam'.

3. Sushruta identified as many as 1200 diseases, including tuberculosis and small pox. Ayurvedic treatment is largely dietetic (food prescribed) and medicinal. All drugs used are obtained from indigenous plants. Charaka lists 500 medicinal plants, and Sushruta mentions 760. In the older days, physicians used to collect the plants and prepare the drugs themselves. Many of these have finally appeared in Western pharmacopoeias (books describing drugs). Ancient Ayurveda included advanced surgical practices. Details of instruments for different operations are given in the classical texts. Even plastic surgery was done, particularly for the restoration of an amputated (cut off) nose, by transplanting tissue from the cheek. Modern surgeons have adopted this technique.

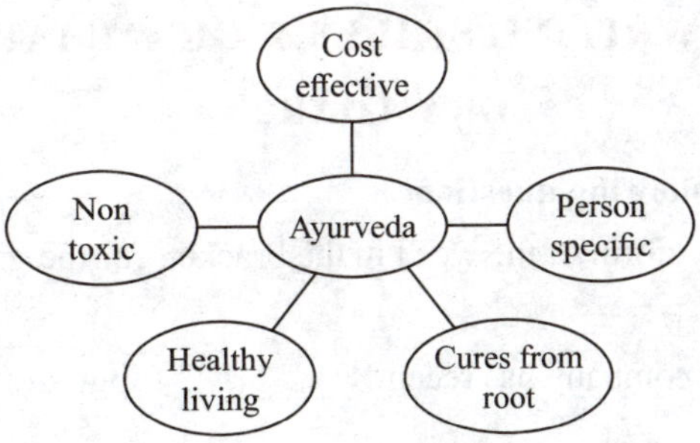

4. Sushruta describes 20 sharp and 101 blunt surgical instruments including knives of various patterns. During the British rule, large sections of the population, especially in the rural areas, continued to rely on Ayurveda. But Allopathic (Western system of medicine) was officially encouraged by the British. Since independence, however, Ayurveda has received official recognition. Ayurvedic universities and colleges have been started and integrated courses are set up, combining the study of ancient remedies and modern medicine. Many research institutions are now documenting ancient health practices and herbal remedies.

Answer the following questions, based on the passage above.

(*i*) What happened to Ayurveda after India gained independence? **1**

(*a*) It lost official recognition.

(*b*) It was integrated with the Western system of medicine.

(*c*) It continued to be practiced primarily in rural areas.

(*d*) Ayurvedic universities and colleges were closed down.

(*ii*) What are some of the recent developments in the field of Ayurveda, as mentioned in the passage? **1**

(*a*) The revival of ancient health practices and herbal remedies.

(*b*) The closure of Ayurvedic universities and colleges.

(*c*) The promotion of Allopathy over Ayurveda.

(*d*) The discontinuation of integrated courses combining ancient remedies and modern medicine.

(*iii*) Based on the information provided in the passage, what can be inferred about the recognition and development of Ayurveda in India? **2**

(*iv*) Supply one point to justify the following: **2**

The establishment of Ayurvedic universities and colleges in India after independence demonstrates the official recognition and support given to Ayurveda.

(*v*) Complete the sentence appropriately: **1**

The transplantation of tissue from the cheek for the restoration of an amputated nose, as described in Ayurvedic texts, indicates the utilization of advanced surgical techniques, including ________.

(*vi*) Which option below provides the closest meaning to the phrase "indigenous plants"? **1**

(*a*) Plants that are commonly used in Ayurvedic treatments.

(*b*) Plants that are exclusively found in tropical regions.

(*c*) Plants that are artificially cultivated in botanical gardens.

(*d*) Plants that naturally grow in a particular region without human involvement.

(*vii*) Complete the analogy based on the information in the passage: **1**

Ancient Ayurveda : Traditional Healing Practices :: Ayurvedic Universities and Colleges : ________

(*a*) Modern Education System

(*b*) Research Institutions

(*c*) Allopathic Medicine

(*d*) Western Pharmacopoeias

(*viii*) Complete the line: **1**

In the field of Ayurveda, the ancient Indian system of medicine, the balance of vata (air), pitho (bile), and kapha (phlegm) is crucial for maintaining ________.

SECTION - B

WRITING SKILLS & GRAMMAR **(20 marks)**

GRAMMAR **10**

3. Attempt ANY TEN of twelve of the following questions. **(10 × 1 = 10)**

(*i*) Fill in the blank by using the correct form of the word in the bracket, for the given portion of a letter:

Dear Sir/Madam,

I am writing to inform you that our company has recently ________ (upgrade) its production facilities to improve efficiency and productivity.

(*ii*) Read the given sentence from a recipe review article. Identify the error and supply the correction in the sentence.
To achieve the perfect texture, the batter needs to be beaten for a few minutes until it get smooth.

Use the given format for your response.

Error	Correction

(*iii*) Akansha and Raman were having a conversation about a project. Report Akansha's question.
Did you manage to get the necessary financial backing for your new startup?

(*iv*) Report the dialogue between Riya and Shekhar regarding their plan for summer break.
Riya: Are you planning to travel during the summer break?
Shekhar: Yes, I'm thinking of going to Bir Billing.
Select the correct option to complete the reporting of the above dialogue.
Riya asked Shekhar ______________ during the summer break. Shekhar mentioned that he was thinking of going to Bir Billing.

(*a*) if he was planning to travel
(*b*) that he was planning to travel
(*c*) when he decided to travel
(*d*) where he intended to travel

(*v*) Fill the blank by choosing the correct option.
A teacher is giving instructions to a group of students for a group project.
Please choose ________ (any/some/many) topic for your group project.

(*vi*) Identify the error and supply correction for the given sentence:
My current employer and coworker feels that I am an asset to the team.

Use the given format for your response.

Error	Correction

(*vii*) Select the option that identifies the error and supplies the correction for the sentence from a cookbook.
"Add the tomatoes, onions, and garlics into the pot."

Option	Error	Correction
(*a*)	and	or
(*b*)	into	to
(*c*)	garlics	garlic
(*d*)	the	a

(*viii*) Complete the given narrative, by filling the blank with the correct option.
The detective carefully examined the crime scene, ____________ *searching for any clues that could lead to the identity of the culprit.*

(*a*) carefully
(*b*) while
(*c*) also
(*d*) by

(*ix*) Report the dialogue between two friends.
Arun: I am surprised to see you here in London. When did you come ?
Varun: I came here yesterday. I have been offered a job here.
Arun told Varun that (*a*) ________________ and asked when he had come. Varun replied that he had come the previous day and added that (*b*) ________

(*x*) Fill in the blank by choosing the correct option to complete the live feed on a sports news channel.
The team captain __________ the trophy to the winning team.

(*a*) will present
(*b*) presented
(*c*) presents
(*d*) has presented

(*xi*) Complete the line from a song, by filling the blank with the correct option:

In laughter and silence,
through highs and through lows,
You're the steady companion,
the one that life ______.
Through challenges faced and memories made,
Forever grateful for the bond that won't fade.

(*a*) will know
(*b*) knowing
(*c*) had known
(*d*) knows

(*xii*) Identify the error and supply correction for the following note in a user manual.

Note: Users must not turn off the device while it is updating.

Use the given format for your response.

Error	Correction

WRITING **10**

Note: All details presented in the questions are imaginary and created for assessment purpose.

4. Attempt ANY ONE from A and B given below: **5**

(A) You are a parent concerned about the lack of playground facilities in your community. Write a letter, in about 120 words, to the local council expressing your concerns and requesting the establishment of a new playground for children.

OR

(B) You are a concerned citizen who wants to address the issue of increasing plastic waste in your community. Write a letter to the editor of a local newspaper in about 120 words, expressing your concerns and suggesting measures to reduce plastic usage and promote recycling. Provide suggestions, the feasibility of implementing these measures, the benefits of reducing plastic waste, activities that can be undertaken to raise awareness etc.

5. Attempt ANY ONE from A and B given below: **5**

(A) Read the given details of a student-friendly laptop designed for school use:

1. Lightweight and compact design, easy to carry in a backpack.
2. Long battery life, lasting up to 12 hours on a single charge.
3. Pre-installed educational software and tools for learning and assignments.
4. High-resolution screen to reduce eye strain during extended use.
5. Built-in camera and microphone for online classes and video calls.
6. Durable body with spill-resistant keyboard for added protection.

Analyse the details and write an analytical paragraph in about 120 words about the suitability of this laptop.

OR

(B) Read the given details of a cafeteria intended for your school:

1. A variety of healthy food options, including salads, sandwiches, and fresh fruit juices.
2. An outdoor seating area with shade and comfortable benches for students to relax.
3. Eco-friendly utensils and packaging to reduce waste.
4. A special section for vegetarian and gluten-free meals.
5. Bright, colorful décor that creates a welcoming atmosphere.
6. Water refill stations to encourage students to stay hydrated.

Analyse the details and write an analytical paragraph in about 120 words about the suitability of this cafeteria. Focus on factors such as health, sustainability, inclusivity of dietary needs, comfort, and overall student experience.

SECTION - C

LITERATURE TEXTBOOK **(40 marks)**

6. Read the given extracts and answer the questions for ANY ONE of the two, given. **5**

(A) Lencho was a man of strong faith. For him, God was not an abstract belief but a concrete, physical presence. He went about his work and his life with the assurance of one who knows that God is always watching over him.

(*A Letter to God*)

(*i*) What is the main theme of this story? **1**

(*a*) The power of faith and prayer.

(*b*) The importance of hard work and perseverance.

(*c*) The dangers of relying on others for help.

(*d*) The consequences of greed and dishonesty.

(*ii*) What can be inferred about Lencho's perception of God based on the given extract? **1** (*iii*) Fill in the blank with the correct word from the bracket: **1**

The phrase "God is always watching over him" indicates that Lencho had faith in God's presence as being ______ (abstract / real).

(*iv*) What does the author imply about the nature of Lencho's relationship with God through the statement that God is a "concrete, physical presence"? **2**

OR

(B) I can make you a present of them myself because they're mine! Your behaviour, Ivan Vassilevitch, is strange, to say the least! Up to this, we have always thought of you as a good neighbour, a friend; last year we lent you our threshing machine, although on that account we had to put off our own threshing till November, you behave to us as if we were gypsies. Giving me my own land, indeed! No, really, that's not at all neighbourly! In my opinion, it's even impudent, if you want to know.

(*The Proposal)*

(*i*) From the phrase 'Your behaviour, Ivan Vassilevitch, is strange, to say the least!', what can be inferred about the speaker's feelings towards Ivan Vassilevitch? **1**

(*ii*) Read the following descriptions (*a*)-(*c*) and identify which one correctly corresponds to the extract. **1**

(*a*) The speaker is thanking Ivan Vassilevitch for his generosity and kindness.

(*b*) The speaker is expressing his frustration and disappointment at Ivan Vassilevitch's behaviour, feeling disrespected by his offer.

(*c*) The speaker is asking Ivan Vassilevitch for a favour, hoping to borrow his threshing machine.

(*iii*) Why is it fair to say that the speaker's tone when he says "Giving me my own land, indeed! No, really, that's not at all neighbourly!", is annoyed and sarcastic? Answer in about 40 words. **2**

(*iv*) Fill in the blank with the correct word from the bracket: **1**

The word "impudent" in the line "In my opinion, it's even impudent, if you want to know" indicates that Natalya found Ivan's behavior to be __________ (disrespectful / considerate).

7. Read the given extracts and answer the questions for ANY ONE of the two, given. **5**

(A) The fog comes
on little cat feet.
It sits looking
over harbour and city
on silent haunches
and then moves on

(*Fog*)

(*i*) Fill the blank with ONE word: **1**

The fog, like a quiet observer, __________ over the harbour and city before moving on silently.

(*ii*) What does the poet mean when he says the fog sits 'on silent haunches'? Which figure of speech has been used here? Elaborate. **2**

(*iii*) What does the fog symbolize in the poem? **1**

(*a*) Mystery (*b*) Danger (*c*) Peace (*d*) Joy

(*iv*) Comment on the poet's use of metaphor in the given lines. **1**

OR

(B) And no one buys a ball back. Money is external.
He is learning, well behind his desperate eyes,
The epistemology of loss, how to stand up
Knowing what every man must one day know
And most know many days, how to stand up.

(*The Ball Poem*)

(*i*) Complete the following suitably. **1**

Knowing what every man must one day _______, how to stand up.

(*ii*) Explain what the boy in the poem is learning about loss and how it is a significant life lesson for him. Answer in about 40 words. **2**

(*iii*) How would you describe the tone of the poet in the poem "The Ball Poem"? **1**

(*iv*) 'Desperate eyes' is an example of _____ . **1**

(*a*) Assonance (*b*) Metaphor (*c*) Imagery (*d*) Personification

8. Answer ANY FOUR of the following five questions, in about 40-50 words. **(4 × 3 = 12)**

(*i*) Justify the opinion that the chapter "Black Aeroplane" from "The First Flight" exemplifies the themes of faith, mystery, and the unexpected assistance one can encounter in difficult situations.

(*ii*) How does "The Trees" confront the societal norm of deforestation and its impact on the environment?

(*iii*) Discuss the significance of Anne's diary in her life. *(From the Diary of Anne Frank)*

(*iv*) Describe the value of freedom for human beings and how it is important for the growth of civilisation and humanism as described in the lesson 'Nelson Mandela: Long Walk to Freedom'.

(*v*) Pranjol buried his head in his detective book while Rajvir was eager to look at the beautiful scenery during the train journey. Compare and contrast both their attitudes? *(Glimpses of India: Tea from Assam)*

9. Answer ANY TWO of the following three questions, in about 40-50 words. **(2 × 3 = 6)**

(*i*) The story is a powerful example of how technology and scientific advancement can have ethical and moral implications. Discuss how the invention of invisibility in the story serves both as a boon and a curse. *(Footprints without Feet)*

(*ii*) How does Ausable's unassuming appearance and demeanor serve as an advantage in his line of work as a spy? *(The Midnight Visitor)*

(*iii*) What does the story reveal about the human tendency to manipulate systems for personal gain? *(A Question of Trust)*

10. Answer ANY ONE of the following two questions, in about 100-120 words. **6**

(A) You have been asked to present an evaluation of the approaches of "Gautama Buddha" and "Nelson Mandela" towards alleviating suffering and bringing about change. Write this presentation draft including your insights, in about 120 words, comparing the approaches of both influential figures.

(Reference- The Sermon at Benaras and Nelson Mandela - Long Walk to Freedom)

OR

(B) You are invited to speak at a community event about the theme of independence and personal growth as seen through the eyes of children and nature. Prepare a speech draft in not more than 120 words, discussing the common themes of freedom and growth in 'Madam Rides the Bus' and 'The Trees' by Adrienne Rich.

11. Answer ANY ONE of the following two questions, in about 100-120 words. **6**

(A) Imagine that Mrs. Pumphrey, from 'A Triumph of Surgery,' writes a diary entry reflecting on her own misconceptions about care and affection toward pets, especially in the context of her experience with Tricki. Write this diary entry, as Mrs. Pumphrey, in about 120 words.

OR

(B) Considering the concept of a character arc, describe how Bholi transforms over the course of the story due to her experiences and interactions. Trace her development in about 120 words.